ENTERPRISE ACT 2002

Related titles by Law Society Publishing

The New Law of Insolvency

Insolvency Act 1986 to Enterprise Act 2002

Vernon Dennis and Alexander Fox
1–85328–812–8

Titles from Law Society Publishing can be ordered from all good legal bookshops or direct from our distributors, Marston Book Services (telephone 01235 465656 or e-mail **law.society@marston.co.uk**). For further information or a catalogue call our editorial and marketing office on 020 7320 5878.

ENTERPRISE ACT 2002

The new law of mergers, monopolies and cartels

Tim Frazer
Solicitor
Partner, Arnold & Porter
former Professor of Law, Newcastle University

Susan Hinchliffe
Solicitor
Senior Associate, Arnold & Porter

and

Kyla George
Solicitor
Associate, Arnold & Porter

The Law Society

ISBN 1–85328–896–9

Published in 2003 by the Law Society
113 Chancery Lane, London WC2A 1PL

Typeset by J&L Composition, Filey, North Yorkshire
Printed by TJ International Ltd, Padstow, Cornwall

CONTENTS

11   Enforcement undertakings and orders   177

12   Transitional provisions   189

APPENDIX

PREFACE

Competition laws are a bit like buses. You wait over 20 years for one to come along and, no sooner is it round the corner, when another one arrives. Hot on the heels of the Competition Act 1998 comes the Enterprise Act 2002, to complete the cycle of reform that has so thoroughly transformed the competition law regime in the United Kingdom.

The 1998 Act left in place the merger and monopoly provisions of the Fair Trading Act 1973, making for a somewhat unhappy blend of legal styles and objectives. These important areas of the law are now reformed and refocused, so that competition becomes the driving principle over the whole area of agreements, dominant firm practices, mergers and market enquiries. These reforms are supported by a raft of new remedies and means of redress and are marked by a greater accessibility to, and transparency of, the law. The draconian cartel offence, which perhaps grabbed the most lurid headlines, is only one small piece of the comprehensive new enforcement environment.

This book concerns only the competition aspects of the Act. Consumer provisions, and the new law on insolvency, are not included.

This was a team effort. The authors would like to thank Silvia Valverde and Alison Boyle for their valuable research work, and Samantha Power for her Herculean efforts in typing and organising the manuscript (assisted by Jayne Sinclair, Rebekka Davie, Denise Hall and Bernadette Saliba). We also salute the forbearance of our spouses, partners and families. Thanks also to Stephen Honey, of the Law Society, for keeping the faith that a manuscript even existed, let alone that it would be delivered two weeks after Royal Assent.

The text attempts to take account of developments up to 31 December 2002.

Tim Frazer
Susan Hinchliffe
Kyla George
Arnold & Porter, 31 December 2002, London

TABLE OF CASES

TABLE OF STATUTES

TABLE OF STATUTORY INSTRUMENTS

References are to paragraph numbers.

TABLE OF EC MATERIALS

References are to paragraph numbers.

ABBREVIATIONS

The Act	The Enterprise Act 2002
1973 Act	The Fair Trading Act 1973
1980 Act	The Competition Act 1980
1998 Act	The Competition Act 1998
Commission	The Competition Commission
DGFT	Director General of Fair Trading
ECMR	European Community Merger Regulation
EC Treaty	Treaty of Rome 1957, as amended
ECSC Treaty	The European Coal and Steel Community Treaty 1951
OFT	Office of Fair Trading
Secretary of State	The Secretary of State for Trade and Industry
SLC	Substantial lessening of competition

GLOSSARY

abuse of dominance   There are a wide range of activities which, when carried on by a dominant undertaking, are contrary to Chapter II of the Competition Act 1998. Examples of such conduct are set out in s.18 of the 1998 Act.

adverse effect on competition   In the context of a **market investigation reference**, where any **feature** or features of a relevant market prevent, restrict or distort competition in connection with the supply or acquisition of any goods or services in the UK or part of the UK.

adverse public interest finding   A finding made by the **Secretary of State** in relation to a **relevant merger situation** following a report by the Competition Commission on a **public interest reference**. The detailed nature of the finding differs according to the nature of the reference made to the Competition Commission. The different kinds of adverse public interest findings are described in s.54(3).

agreement   Any agreement or arrangement, in whatever way and whatever form it is made, and whether it is, or is intended to be, legally enforceable or not. See s.129(1).

anti-competitive outcome   A substantial lessening of competition within any UK market for goods or services, where such an outcome is or may be expected to be the result of the creation of a **relevant merger situation**. See s.35(2).

appropriate minister   In the context of a market investigation reference, the Secretary of State acting alone or the Secretary of State acting in conjunction with another minister or ministers of the Crown.

Article 81   Article 81 EC Treaty, prohibiting anti-competitive agreements which may affect trade between EU Member States. Previously referred to as Article 85.

Article 82   Article 82 EC Treaty, prohibiting the abuse of dominance insofar as it may affect trade between EU Member States. Previously referred to as Article 86.

associated persons   Are defined in s.127(4) as (i) an individual and his or her spouse or partner and any **relative**, or spouse or partner of a **relative** of that individual or of that individual's spouse or partner; (ii) any person in his capacity as trustee of a settlement and the settlor or grantor, and any person associated with them; (iii) persons carrying on business in partnership and the spouse or partner and relatives of any of them; and (iv) two or more persons acting together to secure or exercise control of a body of persons corporate or unincorporate or to secure control of any enterprise or assets.

business (and carrying on business)   A professional practice, any other **undertaking** carried on for gain or reward, or any undertaking in the course of which goods or services are supplied (otherwise than free of charge). See s.129(1) and (3). It is relevant to the definition of an **enterprise** for the purposes of Part 3 of the Act (Mergers).

cartel   Arrangements between at least two **undertakings** which, if operating as the parties intended, would directly or indirectly fix the price that each of them charges third parties for the supply of a product or service in the UK, or limits or prevents the parties from supplying a product or service, or producing a product, in the UK, or shares customers between them for the supply of products or services in the UK, or amounts to bid-rigging arrangements. A cartel is more fully defined in s.188.

Chapter I prohibition   The prohibition of anti-competitive practices contained in s.2 Competition Act 1998.

Chapter II prohibition   The prohibition of abuse of dominance contained in s.18 Competition Act 1998.

Commission   The Competition Commission.

Community law   All the rights, powers, liabilities, obligations, restrictions and all the remedies and procedures from time to time created or arising by or under the Community Treaties (s.129(1)).

Competition Appeal Tribunal   A body created under s.12 and Scheds. 2 and 3

conglomerate merger   A merger between firms in different markets. Conglomerate mergers will rarely lessen competition substantially. However, a conglomerate merger may reduce competition through **portfolio power**.

consumer   Any person to whom goods or services are or are sought to be supplied (whether by way of sale or otherwise) in the course of a business carried on by the person supplying or seeking to supply them (who does not receive or seek to receive the goods or services in the course of a business carried on by them) (s.129(1)).

consumer claim   A claim for damages or money brought on behalf of two or more **consumers** by a **specified body** before the **Competition Appeal Tribunal** under s.47B Competition Act 1998.

customer   A customer who is not a consumer (s.128(1)).

designated body   A body designated by the **Secretary of State** to make **super-complaints** under s.11 of the Act.

detrimental effect on customers   A detrimental effect on customers or future customers in the form of higher prices, lower quality or less choice of goods or services in any market in the UK (whether or not the market to which the feature or features concerned relate) or less innovation in relation to such goods or services.

ECMR   The European Community Merger Regulation – Council Regulation (EEC) No.4064/89 of 21 December 1989 on the control of concentrations between undertakings, as amended by Council Regulation (EC) No.1310/97 of 30 June 1997.

enforcement undertaking   An undertaking under s.71 (initial undertakings, completed mergers), s.73 (undertakings in lieu of references under s.22 or s.33), s.80 (interim undertakings) or s.81 (final undertakings) or under Sched. 7, paras 1 (pre-emptive undertakings), 3 (undertakings in lieu of reference under s.45 or s.62) or 9 (final undertakings).

enterprise   The activities, or part of the activities, of a business.

enterprises ceasing to be distinct   Any two enterprises cease to be distinct enterprises if they are brought under common ownership or common control (whether or not the business to which either of them formerly belonged continues to be carried on under the same or different ownership or control).

European intervention notice   A notice provided to the **OFT** by the **Secretary of State** if he believes that the merger is, or may be, a concentration with a Community dimension (within the meaning of the ECMR), or a part of such concentration. The Secretary of State can give a European intervention notice if he suspects that it is or may be the case that a **European relevant merger situation** has arisen (s.67).

European relevant merger situation   A merger situation which is, or is expected to be, a concentration with a Community dimension (as defined in the **ECMR**), or part of a concentration with a Community dimension (s.68).

feature of a market   A reference to the structure of the market concerned or any aspect of that structure, any conduct (whether or not in the market concerned) of one or more than one person who supplies or acquires goods or services in the market concerned, or any conduct relating to the market concerned of customers of any person who supplies or acquires goods or services.

goods   Includes buildings and other structures, and ships, aircraft and hovercraft (s.129(1)).

horizontal merger   A merger between parties that operate at the same level on the economic market. Competitive pressure can be reduced on the merging firms to the extent they could unilaterally impose a profitable post-merger price increase or otherwise behave anti-competitively. A horizontal merger may also increase the likelihood of either express or tacit coordination.

interconnected bodies corporate (and a group of interconnected bodies corporate)   Two bodies corporate are interconnected if one of them is a body corporate of which the other is a subsidiary, or both of them are subsidiaries of one and the same body corporate. A group of interconnected bodies corporate is a group consisting of two or more bodies corporate all of whom are interconnected with each other.

intervention notice   Notice given to the **OFT** by the **Secretary of State** that he believes that it is (or may be) the case that one or more than one **public interest consideration** is relevant to a consideration of the **relevant merger situation** concerned or a relevant **market investigation**. The most significant effect of an intervention notice is to give the **Secretary of State** the power to determine remedies in relation to the market investigation reference.

legitimate interests   Under Article 21(3) **ECMR**, legitimate interests are defined as public security, plurality of the media and prudential rules. The Article provides that Member States may take appropriate measures to protect legitimate interests other than these. However, these additional legitimate interests must be communicated to the European Commission by the Member State, for assessment of their compatibility with the general principles and other provisions of Community law, before any action may be taken.

market in the UK   Any market which operates either only in the UK (or a part of the UK) or also there and in another country or territory (or in a part of another country or territory).

market investigation   This refers to the investigation into a market carried out by the **Commission** in response to a **market investigation reference** by either the **OFT** or the **appropriate minister**. The primary question considered by the Commission is whether there is an **adverse effect on competition** arising from any **feature** or combination of features, of each relevant market which prevents, restricts or distorts competition in connection with the supply or acquisition of any goods or services in the UK or part of the UK.

market investigation reference   A reference by the **OFT** under s.131 or a reference by the **appropriate minister** under s.132, made where the OFT (or as the case may be) the appropriate minister has reasonable grounds for suspecting that any **feature** or features of a market in the UK for goods or services, prevent, restrict or distort competition in the supply or acquisition of any goods or services in the UK or a part of the UK.

market investigation enforcement order   Any enforcement order made under ss.158, 160 or 161 of the Act.

market investigation enforcement undertaking   Any enforcement undertaking accepted under ss.154, 157 or 159 of the Act.

Merger Control Regulation   *See* **ECMR**.

merger investigation   The investigation by the relevant competition authority (either the **OFT**, the **Commission** or the **Secretary of State**) of the **relevant merger situation**. Both the OFT and the Commission's Guidelines explain the review process and indicate the salient features and characteristics of the merger (and the market in which it operates) which are taken into consideration during an investigation.

merger notice   A notice given to the **OFT**, in the prescribed form, of proposed arrangements which might result in the creation of a **relevant merger situation**. This is a voluntary pre-notification of a merger transaction under the provisions of Part 3, Chapter 5 of the Act

OFT   The Office of Fair Trading.

person   a corporation or an individual.

portfolio power   When the market power deriving from a portfolio of brands exceeds the sum of its parts, a firm is said to have 'portfolio power'. This may enable a firm to exercise market power in individual markets more effectively, with the result that competition is substantially lessened. Portfolio effects may have an effect on the structure of the market, increase the feasibility of entry deterrence strategies and/or eliminate the competitive constraint imposed by firms in neighbouring markets.

price   Any charge or fee (however described) (s.129(1)).

public interest consideration   In the context of **a market investigation**, a public interest consideration is defined as national security or any other consideration that is specified in accordance with the provisions of s.153 of the Act. It is the same in the context of a merger enquiry. A consideration, which, at the time of the giving of the **intervention notice** (or the **European intervention notice**) concerned is specified in s.58 (see ss.41(3) and 67(9)).

relative   A brother, sister, uncle, aunt, nephew, niece, lineal ancestor or descendant (for such purposes the stepchild of any person, or anyone adopted by a person whether legally or otherwise as his child, is regarded as a relative or taken into account to trace a relationship in the same way as that person's child). References to a spouse or partner include a former spouse or former partner (s.127(6)).

relevant customer benefit   A benefit to customers or future customers in the form of lower prices, higher quality or greater choice of goods or services in any market in the UK, or greater innovation in relation to such goods or services. A feature that may be taken into account by the Commission for the purposes of a market investigation.

relevant government contractor   Either: (i) a government contractor who has been notified by or on behalf of the **Secretary of State** of information, documents or other articles relating to defence and of a confidential nature, which the government contractor or an employee of his may hold or receive in connection with being such a contractor (and whose notification has not been revoked by the **Secretary of State**); or (ii) a former government contractor who was so notified when he was a government contractor and whose notification has not been revoked by or on behalf of the **Secretary of State**. Government contractor has the same meaning as under the Official Secrets Act 1989 and includes any sub-contractor of a government contractor, any sub-contractor of that sub-contractor and any other sub-contractor in a chain of sub-contractors which begins with the sub-contractor of the government contractor.

relevant merger situation   A relevant merger situation is created if two or more enterprises have ceased to be distinct enterprises at a time or in circumstances falling within s.24 (time-limits and prior notice) and *either*: (i) the value of the UK turnover of the enterprise being taken over exceeds £70 million; or (ii) the enterprises have a share of the market of 25 per cent or more.

Secretary of State   Secretary of State for Trade and Industry.

special intervention notice   The **Secretary of State** may give a special intervention notice to the **OFT** if he believes that it is or may be the case that one or more than one **public interest** consideration specified in s.58 is relevant to a consideration of the **special merger situation** concerned (s.59(2)).

special merger situation   Special public interest cases are provided for by s.59. The Secretary of State's right to intervene arises where he has 'reasonable grounds for suspecting' that a 'special merger situation' has been created or is in progress or contemplation (s.59(1)). In such circumstances, the intervention is commenced by the delivery of a 'special intervention notice'. However, a special intervention notice is given only where the Secretary of State believes that one, or more, of the public interest considerations specified in s.58 (see para. 6.6 to 6.8) is relevant to a consideration of the special merger situation.

specified body   A body entitled to bring **consumer claims** for damages or money on behalf of consumers, under s.47B Competition Act 1998.

specified considerations   The list of public interest considerations set out in s.58. Mergers which contain a public interest consideration are dealt with under Chapter 2 of the Act, and are significant because the **Secretary of State** retains the power to intervene.

starting date   The date on which the Act or any part of it comes into force. Some sections are expected to come into force during summer 2003.

subsidiary   A subsidiary within the meaning of s.736 Companies Act 1985 (c.6).

substantial lessening of competition   This has no definition in the Act. However, the OFT considers that a merger may be expected to lead to a substantial lessening of competition when it is expected to weaken rivalry between firms to such an extent that the competitive process would no longer deliver a similar level of customer benefits as it would without the merger, in terms of product choice, prices, output, quality or innovation.

super-complaint   A complaint brought to the **OFT** by a **designated body** in relation to any **feature of a market** in the UK that is, or appears to be, significantly harming the interests of **consumers**.

supply (in relation to the supply of goods)   Includes supply by way of sale, lease, hire or hire-purchase (s.129(1)).

the 1973 Act   The Fair Trading Act 1973.

the 1998 Act   The Competition Act 1998.

period for considering a merger notice   The period of 20 days beginning with the first day after the notice has been received by the OFT; and any fee payable in respect of the notice have been paid.

supply of services (and a market for services)   Includes: performing for gain or reward any activity other than the supply of goods; rendering services to order; and the provision of services by making them available to potential users. The supply of services does not include the provision of services under a contract of service or of apprenticeship whether it is express or implied and (if it is express) whether it is oral or in writing (s.128).

vertical merger   A merger between parties operating at different levels of the supply chain of an industry, for example, supplier and wholesaler or distributor and retailer. In some circumstances, such a merger may be anti-competitive by foreclosing a substantial part of the market to competition or increasing the likelihood of post-merger collusion. However, this is only likely where one of the parties has market power or where there is significant vertical integration/restraints in the market.

1 OVERVIEW OF THE ACT

BACKGROUND AND MAJOR REFORMS

1.1 Following a joint statement by the Treasury and the Department of Trade and Industry (DTI) in June 2001, the two government departments issued a discussion document, *Productivity in the UK: Enterprise and the Productivity Challenge.*[1] That document announced, inter alia, the Government's plans for 'major reforms to the competition regime including full independence for better resourced competition authorities, a new duty to promote competition across the economy, reform of the complex monopoly regime, and a proposal of criminal penalties for those involved in cartels' (para. 1.13). Although many of the reforms proposed in *Productivity in the UK* had been the subject of debate for some time, the scale of the reform proposals was very ambitious, particularly since the radical reforms of the Competition Act 1998 had so recently been put into place. *Productivity in the UK* was quickly followed by a White Paper, *A World Class Competition Regime.*[2]

1.2 The philosophy of *Productivity in the UK* and the White Paper was orthodox: vigorous competition will lead to increases in innovation, efficiency and productivity; a reduction in barriers to entry enables new entrants to challenge incumbent enterprises; competition promotes an entrepreneur friendly environment; and competition favours consumers through reductions in price and increases in the quality and availability of products. Some of the elements of the Government's strengthened competition policy had already been put into place: the Competition Act 1998 (the 1998 Act) was a massive project to reform the laws relating to agreements and undertakings having dominant market power; and the Financial Services and Markets Act 2000 extended the powers of the competition authorities in the financial services sector. The Office of Fair Trading (OFT) had been granted a greatly enhanced budget, and had put in place an advisory panel to advise the Director General.

Commencement

1.3 The various provisions of the Act will enter into force on different dates in accordance with a series of commencement orders. At the time of writing the DTI had not published the draft statutory instruments. However, it is envisaged that the institutional provisions will be brought into effect first, both to provide for an easier transition to the new procedural provisions and to facilitate an easier means of closing out the accounts of the current institutions. The DTI's current implementation schedule (**www.dti.gov.uk/enterpriseact/implementation.htm**) anticipates that the new OFT will be instituted early in the financial year, and that the other competition provisions of the Act will come into effect as from Summer 2003.

The six principles of reform

1.4   In *Productivity in the UK*, the Government identified the six principles underlying its recent and proposed reforms. These principles are intended to be the basis for the Act. They are:

- competition decisions should be taken by strong, proactive and independent competition authorities;
- the regime should root out all forms of anti-competitive behaviour;
- there should be a strong deterrent effect;
- harmed parties should be able to get real redress;
- Government and competition authorities should work for greater international consistency and cooperation; and
- competition policy should have a high profile.

1.5   The Act is intended to achieve these principles in the following ways.

Strong, proactive and independent competition authorities

- reducing the role of the Secretary of State in the merger and market investigation regimes; and
- establishing the OFT as a body corporate having the status of a non-Ministerial Government Department, with a chairman, a chief executive (at a later stage) and a Board.

Rooting out anti-competitive behaviour

- the enhanced role of the OFT in scrutinising new laws and regulations; and
- the strengthened investigatory powers of the OFT.

Strong deterrence

- the criminal sanctions now available for the cartel offence; and
- the disqualification of directors of companies that engage in anti-competitive conduct.

Availability of redress

- the enhanced role of the Competition Appeal Tribunal in awarding damages; and
- the role of super-complaints by designated consumer bodies.

Greater international consistency and cooperation

- the new criterion for assessing mergers: 'substantial lessening of competition'; and
- the provisions enabling cooperation with overseas competition authorities.

High profile

- the provisions requiring the publication of guidelines and guidances; and
- the proactive nature of the OFT.

1.6   The government has also adopted a 'mission statement' in relation to competition policy (White Paper, para. 3.7), which broadly respects the independence of competition authorities. This mission statement has no statutory status and is of political interest only. Of greater significance is a new role given to the OFT, the Competition Commission (the Commission) and to the sectoral competition regulators to advise the government on the potential competitive effect of existing or proposed laws and regulations. The government has undertaken to consider any such reports from the competition authorities and to respond publicly within 90 days. Such response may include an intention to amend legislation, under the delegated powers of the Regulatory Reform Act 2001.

MAJOR CHANGES TO THE COMPETITION ACT 1998

1.7   The Act has made some significant changes to the regime established by the Competition Act 1998, and a very large number of relatively minor and consequential changes under Scheds. 24 and 25. The more important of the changes are set out below. Some of these changes are dealt with in detail elsewhere in this book. They are:

- the establishment of the OFT as a corporate body to take over the functions of the Director General of Fair Trading;
- the establishment of the Competition Appeal Tribunal in place of the Competition Commission Appeal Tribunals;
- a new right for persons to claim damages or other monetary awards for breach of competition law;
- a new right for designated bodies to bring claims on behalf of consumers in respect of breaches of competition law;
- a new right for third parties to bring appeals to the Competition Appeal Tribunal;
- the introduction of criminal penalties for certain cartel activity; and
- the ability for civil courts to transfer matters for determination by the Competition Appeal Tribunal.

Modifications to the 1998 Act for the modernisation of EC law

1.8   Section 209 provides for the future modification of the 1998 Act in order to remove any differences that might arise as a result of the modernisation of EC competition law. This will be achieved through regulations made by the Secretary of State. The changes to EC law arising as a result of the modernisation instruments to be made under Article 83 EC Treaty will take effect on 1 May 2004; s.209 makes forward provision for those changes. These regulations will also enable the Secretary of State to make changes to, or repeal, other Acts that exclude matters from the Chapter I or Chapter II prohibition (s.209(3)).

REFORM OF THE MERGER CONTROL REGIME

1.9 Part 3 of the Act introduces a number of significant changes to the merger control regime in the UK. The key reforms to the UK merger regime contained in the Act are intended to make merger scrutiny more transparent by removing the participation of the Secretary of State, and adopting a system of scrutiny based on a substantial lessening of competition within markets in the UK for goods or services.

1.10 As in the Fair Trading Act 1973, the concept of a merger (referred to in the legislation as a 'merger situation') is very wide and covers a variety of transactions and arrangements – including full mergers, acquisitions of all or a majority share interest, joint ventures and also the acquisition of a minority interest (perhaps as low as 15 per cent if the acquiring company has the ability materially to influence the policy of the target enterprise). Again, as before, the Act's provisions apply to mergers that have already taken place (completed mergers) and to those that are proposed or in contemplation (anticipated mergers).

Jurisdiction

The 1973 Act

1.11 The Competition Commission (Commission) had the jurisdiction to review a merger if it led to a combined market share of 25 per cent or more, or if the worldwide value of the assets acquired was at least £70 million.

The new regime

1.12 There will no longer be an assets value test. The 25 per cent market share test will remain, and mergers will also be reviewable where the total UK turnover of the target enterprise exceeds £70 million (s.23).

Criteria for assessing mergers

The 1973 Act

1.13 The Commission's role under the 1973 Act was to determine whether a merger situation operated, or might be expected to operate, against the 'public interest'. The public interest test was mainly concerned with issues of competition.

The new regime

1.14   Mergers will now be assessed on the basis of a 'substantial lessening of competition' test, applied to markets in the UK (ss.22 and 33). This will bring UK law more into line with analysis applied in the USA under the Horizontal Merger Guidelines of the Department of Justice and Federal Trade Commission. Even the European Commission was at one stage considering whether to use this test in the analysis of mergers under EU law (see para. 8.6), though that currently seems to be unlikely.

Process

The 1973 Act

1.15   Under the 1973 Act, if a merger was considered to raise significant public interest issues (in practice, mainly competition issues), the OFT recommended to the Secretary of State that the merger be referred to the Commission. There was no obligation on the Secretary of State to accept such recommendation. Where the OFT made such a recommendation, and a specific public interest issue had been identified, the parties could offer to make disposals or other solutions in order to avoid a reference being made. If a merger was referred, the Commission investigated and reported on whether the merger operated, or might be expected to operate, against the public interest. If so, it would recommend that the merger be disallowed, or suggest other remedies to alleviate or remove the adverse effects that had been identified. The Commission submitted its report to the Secretary of State. Only the Secretary of State had the authority to act on the recommendations. Where disposals or other remedies were required, this was normally achieved through negotiations between the OFT and the parties, without the Secretary of State making an order.

The new regime

1.16   There will be less governmental involvement in the merger control process: the OFT will decide on whether to make a reference to the Commission (and not merely recommend). The Commission will conclude on the merits of the merger and will decide what remedial action should be taken (rather than merely recommend). Ministerial involvement will be limited to those special mergers which are referred to the Commission on specific public interest grounds, such as national security (see para. 6.1).

1.17   The decision to remove ministers from the decision-making process was met with a mixed reaction from the House of Commons, but was eventually supported. It is part of the move towards the creation of independent decision-making competition and regulatory authorities. The removal of ministers from the process was carried to a further stage in April 2002, when the Secretary of State announced that ministers would be withdrawing from the competition aspects of EC merger cases.[3] From 3 September 2002, the OFT took sole charge of rendering UK competition advice to the European Commission in relation to mergers falling under the jurisdiction of the ECMR. Ministers will devolve responsibility for making requests under Article 9 ECMR for mergers to be referred back to the UK. The OFT will also decide on whether to refer a merger (other than one automatically qualifying under the ECMR) to the European Commission under Article 22 ECMR.

The decision to refer

The 1973 Act

1.18   The decision to refer a merger to the Commission was that of the Secretary of State, who had a very wide discretion. The process was frequently thought to have a strong 'political' element. Approximately 10 to 15 mergers were referred to the Commission each year under the 1973 Act.

The new regime

1.19   The decision to refer will be that of the OFT, and will be made on the basis of the 'substantial lessening of competition' test. Under the Act, the OFT may decide not to make a reference if it believes that it is or may be the case that:

- the market concerned is not of sufficient importance to justify the making of a reference to the Commission;
- any relevant consumer benefits (such as lower prices, higher quality, greater choice or greater innovation) in relation to the creation of the merger, outweigh any concerns relating to the substantial lessening of competition; or
- in the case of anticipated mergers, the arrangements concerned are not sufficiently far advanced, or are not sufficiently likely to proceed, to justify the making of a reference to the Commission (ss.22(2) and 33(2)).

1.20   There are special rules relating to mergers in the water industries (s.70). The rules under the 1973 Act, relating to newspapers, will remain (s.69), though this is currently under review.

1.21   Figure 1.1 summarises the merger control procedure under the Act and shows how a notification or an investigation in relation to a merger that raises no public interest considerations will progress through the various stages.

Notification of a merger to the OFT

1.22   Notification of mergers in the UK will remain voluntary. Where it is clear that there are no reasons to believe that the transaction will lead to a substantial lessening of competition, it may be reasonable to proceed with the transaction without notifying it to the OFT, even where the market share or turnover thresholds are exceeded. If the parties elect to notify the transaction to the OFT, they can do so formally or informally, as at present.

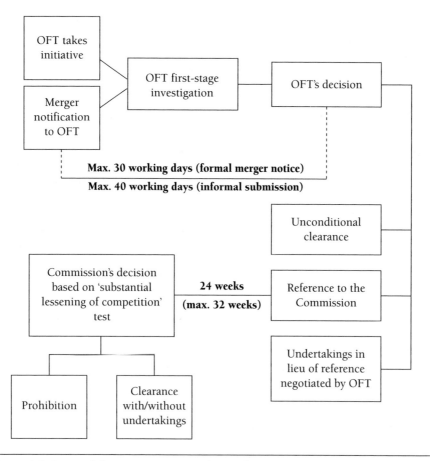

Figure 1.1 Stages of the new merger control procedure

Assessment by the Competition Commission

1.23 Under the 1973 Act, the Secretary of State determined how long the Commission had in which to produce a report, typically three months. The Act introduces a statutory timetable, under which the Commission will normally have 24 weeks from the date of reference in which to publish its merger report. This period may be extended by up to eight weeks if the Commission considers that there are special reasons why the report cannot be prepared and published in that time (s.39). The period may be further extended where the Commission considers that a person has failed to comply with a request for information made by the Commission.

1.24 The Act introduces the possibility for penalties for failure to comply with a notice to give evidence or documents. The maximum penalty must be established by the Secretary of State in secondary legislation, but will not exceed a fixed fine of up to £30,000 or a daily penalty of £15,000, or both (s.111).

1.25 As under the 1973 Act, it will also be an offence for anyone knowingly or recklessly to provide materially misleading or false information to the OFT, the Commission or the Secretary of State. This is punishable by a fine or a prison sentence of up to two years, or to both (s.117).

Public interest cases and special public interest cases

1.26 Where the Secretary of State considers that a particular transaction raises 'public interest considerations' he may request the OFT to investigate the merger and advise him as to whether a reference should be made to the Commission. The only public interest consideration identified in the Act is national security (s.58). However, the Secretary of State has the power to expand the list of public interest grounds. Once in receipt of the OFT advice, the Secretary of State will decide whether to make a reference to the Commission. The Commission will then report to the Secretary of State, who retains the final decision as to whether to prohibit the merger, or to impose remedies.

1.27 Special public interest cases are mergers which do not qualify as 'merger situations' under the Act (either because the UK turnover of the enterprise being taken over does not exceed £70 million or because the 25 per cent market share test is not met) but where nevertheless the Secretary of State believes that a public interest consideration is relevant to the creation of the merger. In relation to public interest cases and special public interest cases, the review process is much more similar to that which existed under the 1973 Act.

THE APPLICATION OF THE ACT TO PROFESSIONAL RULES

1.28 Sched. 4 to the 1998 Act provided for the exclusion from that Act of professional rules, such as those regulating solicitors. The basis for such exclusion was always rather tenuous, and the fact that the 1998 Act continued these exclusions after the demise of the Restrictive Trade Practices Act 1976 was a surprising concession. The 2002 Act now remedies that lapse. Section 207 repeals s.3(1)(d) of, and Sched. 4 to, the 1998 Act. In future, professional rules of any kind will fall within the regime of the 1998 Act and may be measured against the normal criteria for anti-competitive agreements and/or decisions of associations of undertakings.

---

1   HM Treasury and Department of Trade and Industry, *Productivity in the UK: Enterprise and the Productivity Challenge*, June 2001 (hereafter *Productivity in the UK*).
2   Published 31 July 2001 (hereafter the White Paper).
3   See DTI Press Release P/2002/532, 27 August 2002. *www.nds.coi.gov.uk*

2 INSTITUTIONAL REFORMS

THE OFFICE OF FAIR TRADING

> The new OFT will be independent, encompass a broad mix of interests and skills in the decision-making process, will be fully accountable through working arrangements that are open and clear, and will be able to act swiftly and effectively.
> (Melanie Johnson, MP, Standing Committee debates, House of Commons, 16 April 2002, col. 12)

2.1 Section 1 of the Act establishes the OFT as a body corporate, and s.2 abolishes the office of Director General of Fair Trading. Apart from certain transitional arrangements, all references to such an office in any Act or statutory instrument must now be read as if a reference to the Director was a reference to the OFT. The OFT, having existed for so long as a virtual institution, is now made flesh. The OFT will be headed by a chairman and will have at least four other members. Schedule 1, para. 5 provides for a further office, namely the Chief Executive of the OFT. This appointment was the subject of a bitter controversy between the Commons (who preferred to have only a chairman) and the Lords, who wished to have both chairman and chief executive from the beginning. At the last moment, the Bill was saved from running out of parliamentary time through the compromise in Sched. 1, para. 5. This provides that, in addition to the chairman, a person (who may be one of the members of the OFT) shall be appointed as chief executive. However, these roles may be combined for the first two years of the operation of the OFT. The intention is that no such separate appointment will be made until the retirement from the chairmanship of the first chairman, John Vickers. The chairman, the chief executive and the members will all be appointed by the Secretary of State for renewable terms of up to five years. An agreement existed with the current Director (John Vickers) that he would become the first chairman of the OFT for the remainder of his term.

2.2 The Lords wanted the OFT to be managed in accordance with principles of good corporate governance. Since it would be difficult to apply such principles to what is essentially an enforcing agency, the provisions of s.1 were toned down. This was, again, a last-minute compromise. The provision now requires that the OFT shall have regard to such generally accepted principles as it is reasonable to regard as applicable to the OFT.

2.3   Schedule 1 to the Act provides for the OFT's structure and powers. It is broad in its scope – providing the OFT with the power 'to do anything which is calculated to facilitate, or is conducive or incidental to, the performance of its functions' (Sched. 1, para. 13).

2.4   It is the intention of the Government for the OFT to have between five and seven members. These members are intended to constitute the body known informally as the 'Board'. The term is not used in the Act, since – as the Government stated during parliamentary debates – the OFT and the Board are one and the same entity. The Act does not therefore provide for the manner in which the Board will operate. As indicated in Sched. 1, para. 8, the OFT is to regulate its own procedures. It has a duty to consult the Secretary of State only in relation to the adoption of procedures dealing with conflicts of interest.

2.5   The motivation for the replacement of the Director by the OFT was a desire to remove the Director's individual responsibility for the exercise of competition law functions, in favour of a more collective, institutional approach. The breadth of the competition law regime and the potency of the Act's provisions make an institutional approach far more appropriate. The Act has carefully avoided the problems that exist in some other antitrust authorities, where the technique for de-personalising the competition law of the relevant institution's functions has taken the form of a college approach. In such an approach, the requirement for majority voting has often given rise to stagnation and voting compromises. The Act, by contrast, has established a Board to assist and advise the chairman, without limiting his ability to act effectively on his own on day-to-day matters. Although the Act does not set out any separate powers or functions for the Board and the chairman respectively, the expectations of the government are that the Board will play a strategic role rather than an operational one – including 'high-level decisions, market studies and cases of strategic significance . . . approving the annual plan, the annual report, financial statements, the budget, negotiating strategy, matters such as the service delivery agreement and major or unusual capital projects . . . considering the OFT's communications strategy and approving the OFT pay and human resources issues, all at a high strategic level' (Melanie Johnson MP, Standing Committee Debates, Hansard, 16 April 2002, col. 27).

2.6   The informal advisory panel that had been appointed by the Director General prior to the Act is not a model for the Board, but is merely its precursor. It will cease to exist when the new OFT comes into being.

2.7   The Board is intended to broaden the transparency and accountability of the OFT, in keeping with the basic principles espoused by the government prior to the introduction of the Bill. As a further measure of transparency, the OFT is obliged to produce an annual plan (s.3) and an annual report (s.4). The first annual plan is to be published within three months of the establishment of the OFT (Sched. 24, para. 4).

2.8   In the annual plan, it is intended that the OFT will publish its main objectives and priorities for the year in question. It is a planning document with no legal effect; it will be used only to determine the extent to which the OFT has achieved its objectives. In other words, this is a political document, which may come into play when, for example, the OFT seeks to maintain or increase its funding during Treasury budget rounds. In compiling its plan, the OFT must consult by publishing consultation documents at least two months prior to publishing the annual plan (s.3(2)); the plan and the consultation documents must be laid before Parliament (s.3(3)).

2.9 Of far more practical interest are the annual reports that must also be published by the OFT and laid before Parliament. The Director General has for many years published such a report setting out his activities and providing useful detail on the manner in which the law has been applied. The model for such annual reports is that adopted by the European Commission. Its reports are detailed and lengthy; they provide a useful description of individual cases and initiatives, policy statements, trends and enforcement statistics.

2.10 The annual report concerns the OFT's 'activities and performance' (s.4(1)); s.4(2) lays down that it shall include at least a general survey of developments concerning matters relating to the OFT's functions, and an assessment of the extent to which the OFT has met its 'main objectives and priorities' (as set out in the statutory annual plan). The Commission is subject to a similar obligation under s.186.[1] The OFT is also given the power to publish reports on any matter relating to its functions (s.4(4)).

Functions of the OFT

2.11 Section 5 provides the OFT with a number of general 'functions' in relation to the acquisition and use of information. Such functions are intended principally to ensure that: (i) its decisions are adequately informed; and (ii) its other 'functions' are carried out effectively. It is to be noted that the OFT is not under a 'duty' to obtain, compile and review such information. In this respect, the Act differs from the provisions of the Fair Trading Act 1973 (the 1973 Act), which imposed a duty on the Director General to keep himself informed of, for example, commercial activities in the UK. In the debates in the House of Commons, the government provided assurances that no such difference was intended, insisting that 'function' includes both power and duty. Since a power and a duty are obviously so different, the use of this confusing language is rather bizarre.

2.12 In keeping with its practice over recent years, the OFT remains free to obtain, compile and review information through the commissioning of outside research projects.

Educating the public

2.13 A feature of recent competition legislation has been a requirement for the Director General to take a proactive role in displaying the advantages of competition and the features of the legislation. Section 6 of the Act provides the OFT with the 'function' of raising public awareness of the benefits – to consumers and to the economy – of 'competition'. The OFT also has the function of informing and advising the public in relation to any of its functions.

2.14   The OFT may carry out such activities itself or support such activities being carried out by others.

Championing competition

2.15   A new and potentially very important function is provided to the OFT under s.7. The OFT's functions include interfacing with all government departments and any other public authority on matters relating to any of the OFT's functions, that is in relation to any matter concerning competition or consumer protection. Indeed, here is a rare glimpse of an express general duty being imposed on the OFT: if a Minister requests the OFT to make a proposal or to give information or advice, then the OFT 'shall, so far as is reasonably practicable and consistent with its other functions' comply with the request. Where there is no such request, the OFT still has the function of making such proposals or giving such information or advice. The section specifies a particularly apt occasion for such functions to be carried out – in relation to any aspect of the law or a proposed change in the law. The OFT may therefore function[2] as a champion of competition by reviewing the conformity of new legislation with the competitive ideals and principles enshrined in the Act and the 1998 Act. It can also root out existing legislation and regulations which fall short of these ideals.

2.16   Section 7 provides a real opportunity to the OFT to crusade for competition, to assist other public authorities and the whole of government (and not just the Department of Trade and Industry) in developing a legal system that provides a more propitious environment for competition.

2.17   Similarly, s.8 gives the OFT the function of promoting good consumer practice, particularly through the approval or otherwise of codes of practice intended to safeguard or promote the interests of consumers.

THE COMPETITION APPEAL TRIBUNAL

2.18   Section 12 establishes a new tribunal, the Competition Appeal Tribunal. This takes over from the Competition Commission Appeal Tribunals, established under the 1998 Act. In keeping with the pattern established by the 1998 Act, there will be a president, a panel of chairmen and ordinary members. Under the Act, the president and the chairmen are appointed by the Lord Chancellor (the corresponding office holders under the 1998 Act having been appointed by the Secretary of State). The first president of the Tribunal is to be the president of the outgoing Competition Commission Appeal Tribunals. Similar arrangements are made for the appointment of the first registrar (see below). Ordinary members of the Competition Commission Appeal Tribunals (i.e. those who are not members of the panel of chairmen) become members of the Tribunal. Those who were in the panel of chairmen become chairmen of the Tribunal. These transitional rules are provided in Sched. 24, paras. 7 to 11.

2.19 The qualifications required for appointment to the Office of president or chairmen are the same as those established under the 1998 Act (Sched. 2). The Secretary of State will also appoint a registrar. The qualifications required for appointment as registrar, and the functions of the registrar, are set out in the Competition Appeal Tribunal Rules 2002 (draft of September 2002). Section 12(4) provides that the expenses of the Tribunal shall be paid for by the newly established Competition Service. Similarly, Sched. 2, para. 7 provides that the staff, office accommodation and equipment required for the Tribunal shall be provided by the Competition Service. The Tribunal's features and functions are described in paras. 2.50 to 2.109 in the section dealing with appeals.

2.20 At a very late stage in the passage of the Act through Parliament, a new section was added (following a government defeat in the Lords) providing additional powers to the Competition Appeal Tribunal. Section 16 provides for a species of preliminary reference to the Tribunal, along the lines of the system of preliminary references which may be made by courts to the European Court of Justice under the EC Treaty. In the system provided for by s.16, the Lord Chancellor can make regulations empowering the High Court or a county court, the Court of Session or a sheriff court to transfer to the Tribunal an 'infringement issue' for determination arising in any civil proceedings before the court.

2.21 The purpose behind the provision is to enable civil courts to rely on the expertise of the Tribunal in the determination of whether an infringement (of Chapter I or II of the 1998 Act, or of Articles 81 or 82 EC Treaty) has taken place. Although the determination of that question will be preliminary only to the issues before the court (such as questions of causation and quantum or the exercise of the court's discretion in providing remedies or interim measures), the transfer of the issue will relieve the court of the requirement to examine the complex issues of law and economics arising under the competition provisions. As Lord Borrie (a former Director General of Fair Trading) said in the Lords' debates, the Tribunal

> will have the benefit of economists and others as members of the tribunal, not merely as expert witnesses in particular cases. They will help determine . . . mixed questions of law, economics and fact and involve determining whether, for example, there is a substantial lessening of competition in a merger case. It is unlikely that a High Court judge, who may deal with a competition law case only once in a blue moon, can match the Competition Appeal Tribunal on that score.
>
> (Lords' Debates, 28 October 2002, col. 14.)

On the other hand, it will tend to diminish the courts' own ability to build up sufficient expertise and jurisprudence to determine these issues for themselves. As the government responded in the Lords, Lord Borrie's 'blue moon' point could be met by the nomination of judges as specialists in competition law.

2.22 The transferring court will be able to give effect to the determination of the issue by the Tribunal. Unlike the Lords' version of this provision in the

Bill, the determination by the Tribunal will not be treated as a determination by the transferring court.

THE COMPETITION SERVICE

2.23   The Competition Service is an entirely new institution, established by s.13 as a body corporate. Its purpose is to fund and to provide staff, accommodation and other support services to the Competition Appeal Tribunal. The Competition Service, unlike the OFT, does not carry out its activities on behalf of the Crown. Rather, it acts as an intermediary between the Secretary of State, who funds it, and the Competition Appeal Tribunal, whom it funds.

2.24   The Competition Service comprises the president and the registrar of the Competition Appeal Tribunal, together with one or more members appointed by the Secretary of State (after consulting the president). The Secretary of State shall designate who will be the first chairman of the Competition Service; subsequent chairmen will be selected by the members of the service (Sched. 3, para. 2).

2.25   As indicated above, the Service has rather limited functions, restricted to the funding of the Competition Appeal Tribunal. However, Sched. 3 provides it with the power to do anything which is calculated to facilitate, or is conducive or incidental to, the performance of its functions (Sched. 3, para. 10).

THE COMPETITION COMMISSION

2.26   The changes to the way in which merger situations are referred to the Competition Commission, and to the manner in which it is financed, has required a number of changes to its organisation and structure. These are provided in Sched. 11 to the Act. It is to be noted that Sched. 11 also changes the maximum term of office of Commission members. This is extended from a renewable period of five years to a renewable period of eight (Sched. 11, para. 5).

2.27   Changes have also been made to the Commission's procedures, through the insertion of a new schedule to the 1998 Act, Sched. 7A. This is set out in Sched. 12 to the Act. Sched. 7A provides for rules to be made by the chairman of the Competition Commission for the Commission's procedures in relation to merger reference groups, market reference groups and special reference groups (defined in the new Sched. 7, para. 19A to the 1998 Act, inserted by s.187(3) of the Act; these references are mainly in relation to regulated sectors under sector-specific legislation).

Rules of Procedure

2.28   Rules under the new Sched. 7A have been published in draft by the Competition Commission (Competition Commission Rules of Procedure, draft of

September 2002, hereafter the 'Rules of Procedure'). Although the Rules of Procedure preserve in many respects the pre-existing procedures, they are described in full below for convenience. The Rules of Procedure apply to all references made to the Commission under general and sector-specific legislation.[3] Anything not provided for in the Rules of Procedure or legislation may be determined by the reference group, subject to it first consulting the Chairman of the Commission.

Groups

2.29   Following a reference to the Commission, the chairman must appoint a group of at least three people, one of whom will be the chairman of the group. The chairman will have a casting vote. The chairman of the Commission may take part in the proceedings of a group in order to offer it advice in the exercise of its functions; but he may not vote or have a note of his dissent recorded (rr.4.6 and 4.8). Where a member of a group cannot continue to act, the chairman of the Commission will appoint a replacement. Groups are constituted as 'market reference groups' for an investigation under Part 4 of the Act (Market Investigations), as 'merger investigation groups' in connection with references under s.59 of the 1973 Act (newspaper mergers) or under Part 3 of the 2002 Act (Mergers), or as 'special reference groups' for references under s.11 of the 1980 Act[4] or under sector-specific legislation). Appointments to the groups must take account of the ethical matters set out in the Commission's Code of Practice (*http://www.competition-commission.org.uk/about/annexa.htm*) and its guidance on conflicts of interest (*http://www.competition-commission.org.uk/inquiries/guidecoi.htm*).

Timetable

2.30   Each group must draw up an administrative timetable in order to enable it to comply with the statutory timetable relevant to its enquiry. The administrative timetable will make provision for the following major stages:

- gathering information;
- issuing questionnaires;
- hearing witnesses;
- verifying information;
- providing a statement of issues;
- considering responses to that statement;
- notifying and publishing provisional findings;
- considering remedies;
- considering exclusions from disclosure; and
- publishing reports.

The timetable is published on the Commission's website. For an example, see the timetable for the inquiry 'Extended Warranties for Domestic Electrical Goods', due to report in June 2003: (*http://www.competition-commission.org.uk/inquiries/*

timetablewarranty.htm). The timetable is intended to be respected also by the main parties to the enquiry. Further, where the group sets a date by which an individual or body is to provide information, the group is not obliged to take account of that information if it is delivered late (r.8.3).

Hearing

2.31   It is for the group itself to determine whether any of its hearings shall be held in public. Rule 6.2 provides a list of factors that the group must take into account in making this determination. These relate to items such as the views of the main parties, the likelihood of confidential information becoming known, the effect a public hearing may have on the willingness of witnesses to give information, the efficient conduct of the investigation, and resource implications. In some cases, public hearings have been 'webcast' (i.e. audio-streamed over the Internet) to enable a greater number to attend without having to travel to the hearing. Those participating by webcast are also able to interact electronically. It is also for the group to decide who shall be heard, be entitled to cross-examine witnesses or otherwise take part in hearings.

Investigation and penalties

2.32   The group has powers of investigation under the Act, by virtue of ss.109 to 117 (mergers investigations) and s.176 (market investigations). These powers are described in paras. 2.35 to 2.41. The group may also impose penalties for non-compliance with its powers of investigation. These penalties are described in paras. 2.42 to 2.49. Before imposing a penalty, the group must have regard to the Commission's Statement of Policy on Penalties (see paragraph 2.43).

Findings

2.33   The group must give a notice to the main parties of its provisional findings (redacted to take account of confidential information and other information covered by s.244), copied to the Commission's website.[5] Those parties must be given no fewer than 21 days in which to provide reasons as to why the provisional findings should not become final, or as to why they should be varied. Responses received after the due date do not need to be taken into account by the group. The notice will also normally indicate what procedure the group will follow upon receipt of the parties' responses above. This does not have to include an oral hearing. The group will also normally send a notice detailing, on a hypothetical basis, what remedies may be appropriate, should the Commission determine that such remedies are necessary to remedy, mitigate or prevent adverse competitive effects. The remedies notice will therefore be published prior to the final findings of the group. Where the group makes an adverse finding, it is to consider what remedial actions it should take. It will consult individuals and undertakings likely to be affected by such actions, and will consider whether to accept an undertaking under ss.82 and 159 or to make an order under ss.84 and 161. Undertakings and orders are considered in paras. 7.1 to 7.92.

Reports

2.34   Reports are published as official documents; copies appear on the Commission's website (*http://www.competition-commission.org.uk/reports/report1. htm*).[6] Where the final decision of the group is taken by majority, then the report may contain dissenting reports by members of the minority. The group must consider what information to exclude from its reports, on the basis of s.244. This section provides that a public authority must have regard to certain matters before disclosing information acquired by it (in this case by the Commission) in connection with its functions under the Act or under a range of other statutes specified in Sched. 14.[7] Those matters are: (a) the need to exclude from disclosure information the disclosure of which the authority thinks is contrary to the public interest (s.244(2)); (b) the need to exclude commercial information the disclosure of which the authority thinks might significantly harm the legitimate business interests of the undertaking to which it relates (s.244(3)(a)); (c) the need to exclude information relating to the private affairs of an individual the disclosure of which the authority thinks might significantly harm the individual's interests (s.244(3)(b)); and (d) the extent to which disclosure of the information specified in (b) and (c) above is necessary for the purposes for which the authority is permitted to make the disclosure (s.244(4)).

Information and investigation powers

2.35   The Commission has stressed the importance: (a) to the Commission of having access to detailed information regarding companies and markets in order to enable it to make soundly based decisions on the competition and remedies questions; and (b) to those affected or potentially affected by the Commission's decisions to have the opportunity to put their views to the Commission. To that end, the Commission invites evidence from all parties likely to have an interest in its merger and market investigation inquiries. These include: the main parties to the inquiries (the merging companies in merger inquiries, or companies that form a part of the market under investigation in market inquiries); third parties that might be affected (for example, competitors, customers, suppliers, and trade or consumer organisations); and other interested bodies, such as government departments and expert bodies.

2.36   The Commission is under a duty to have regard to the information which has been made available to it by the OFT at the outset of a reference (s.104 for merger investigations and s.169 for market investigations). The Commission then collects further information in a variety of ways, which will include: (a) letters and questionnaires to the main parties and other interested parties; (b) press notices, advertisements in relevant publications and entries on the Commission website (*www.competition-commission.org.uk/*); (c) mining publicly available data; (d) commissioning surveys or expert advice; (e) visits to the main parties; (f) hearings.

2.37   The Commission is aware of how time consuming it can be for the parties to provide evidence, and it will attempt to restrict its requests to the minimum consistent with carrying out its duties. The Commission will also maintain regular contact with representatives of the main parties, to obtain and check information, and to inform them of progress.

2.38   The Commission staff review the information collected. Some documents received are considered in their entirety by the group, others form the basis of papers written by the Commission's staff, which summarise or analyse the information. The members of the group meet regularly with Commission staff to discuss and analyse the evidence and findings in these papers. This enables the group to gain an understanding of the market and companies in question, and therefore puts them in the best position to make informed decisions on the competition and remedies questions.

2.39   Some of the evidence gathered may be included in an issues letter sent to the main parties, setting out the main lines of inquiry the group intend to pursue, and as a basis for the hearings with the main parties.

2.40   The Commission has certain powers of investigation to assist it in its merger and market investigation functions (s.109 for mergers and s.176 for market investigations). These include the power to: require a person to appear to give evidence and/or to produce documents; or to supply estimates, forecasts, returns or other information. Both of these powers must be exercised through the giving of a notice to the person concerned. Neither extend to documents or information that is legally privileged. The Commission can also take evidence under oath.

2.41   Although the Commission has long had similar powers, the Act introduces a new sanction for non-compliance with such notices. As mentioned elsewhere, in place of the 1973 Act's power to institute contempt proceedings, the Commission can now impose penalties, as indicated below. The Commission is also free to ignore any information that it receives after the date specified for its receipt.

Penalties for obstructing the Commission's work

2.42   The Commission may impose penalties for failure to comply with a notice. Such penalties may take the form of fixed or daily penalties, or both, at an amount that the Commission considers appropriate (s.111(1) and (2)). A penalty (fixed only) may also be imposed where a person intentionally delays or obstructs another person in carrying out their obligations to comply with such a notice (s.110(3)). Neither such penalty may be imposed more than four weeks after the publication of the relevant Commission report, except in the circumstances outlined in s.110(4). A person may, alternatively, be prosecuted for intentionally altering, suppressing or destroying any document which the Commission has required be produced under s.109 (s.110(5)). Conviction for such an offence carries a penalty of a fine at the statutory maximum (on summary conviction), or to a term of two years' imprisonment, or a fine or both (on indictment). Section 111(5) contains detailed rules in relation to the imposition of daily penalties.

2.43 The Commission has articulated its policy objectives in relation to the imposition of penalties under the Act, as it is obliged to do under s.116. Its policy document, in draft form, was published as *Statement of Policy on Penalties* (draft of September 2002). The adverse consequences identified as arising from a failure to comply with the Commission's investigatory powers, contain no surprises:

- increasing the costs of investigation;
- delaying the investigation;
- adversely affecting the accuracy and quality of Commission reports; and
- possibly causing the Commission to arrive at the wrong conclusion.

2.44 The Commission has a discretion as to whether to impose a penalty. In its policy statement, it identified the following factors as those that make it more likely that a penalty will be imposed:

- the wrongdoing adversely affected the efficiency in the way in which the Commission carried out its functions;
- the wrongdoing adversely affected other persons in relation to the Commission's functions;
- the penalty is likely to provide an incentive and a deterrent;
- the degree of culpability is relatively high; and
- the wrongdoer sought or obtained an advantage through the wrongdoing.

2.45 The Commission has also set out its policy on the criteria for determining the amount of a penalty to be imposed in any case. This is subject to a maximum to be specified by the Secretary of State under s.111 (a maximum that may not be set above £30,000 for a fixed penalty, or £15,000 for daily penalties (s.111(7)). The Commission's criteria are divided into aggravating and mitigating factors.

Aggravating factors include:

- repeat wrongdoing;
- continuation of the contravention after the person became aware of it, or aware of the Commission's concern that a contravention may have occurred;
- the involvement of officers or senior managers;
- lack of compliance procedures; and
- attempts to conceal the wrongdoing.

Mitigating factors include:

- adequate steps taken to secure compliance; and
- previous good conduct in the same inquiry.

2.46 The Commission must send a notice of penalty to the person to be penalised, in a form compliant with s.112.

2.47 Appeals from penalty decisions may be brought before the Competition Appeal Tribunal within 28 days of receipt of the notice of penalty (see paras. 2.50

to 2.85), in relation to the imposition or the nature of the penalty, its amount or the date by which it must be paid. An appeal has a suspensory effect (s.114(7)). The Tribunal may quash the penalty, substitute a lower one or change the dates on or by which it must be paid (s.114(5)).

2.48   In addition to the penalties provided for above, a person will be guilty of a criminal offence under s.117 (mergers) or s.180 (market investigations) where he supplies to the OFT, the Commission or the Secretary of State, information that is false or misleading, and he knows that it is, or is reckless as to whether it is. It is also an offence for a person knowingly or recklessly to supply false or materially misleading information to another person, knowing that it will be used to supply information to the competition authorities. Conviction for either offence carries a maximum penalty, on summary conviction, of a fine at the statutory maximum and, on indictment, to two years' imprisonment or to a fine or both.

2.49   Where an offence is committed by a body corporate, and it is proved to have been committed with the consent or connivance of, or to be attributable to any neglect by, a director, secretary or other similar officer (or someone purporting to act in such a capacity), that individual will also be liable to be proceeded against and punished. This also applies to members of a corporation where they are entitled to manage the affairs of the corporation (s.125(2)), and to partners in a Scottish partnership (s.125(3)).

APPEAL PROCEDURES: THE NEW LAW

Appeals to the Competition Appeal Tribunal

Tribunal proceedings

2.50   The Tribunal sits in panels comprising a chairman (who may be the president or a member of the panel of chairmen) and two other members (who may be selected from either the panel of chairmen or from the ordinary membership). Decisions of the panel may be taken by majority if unanimity is unavailable. Where the decision is taken by majority, the decision must state so. Rule 52 of the Competition Appeal Tribunal Rules 2002 (draft of 10 September 2002 – the 'Rules') provides that if the chairman of the panel is unable to continue after the commencement of a hearing, the president of the Tribunal may appoint either of the other two members to act as chairman, and the Tribunal shall consist of the remaining two members for the rest of the proceedings. If the person appointed as chairman is not a member of the panel of chairmen, the president may appoint himself or a member of the panel of chairmen to attend proceedings and advise the remaining members on any questions of law. If a member other than the chairman is unable to continue, the president may decide that the Tribunal shall consist of the remaining two members for the rest of the proceedings. Clearly, when a Tribunal consists of two members, decisions must be unanimous.

2.51   In the course of its proceedings, the Tribunal has a duty to refrain from publishing certain information, where:

- the disclosure would be contrary to the public interest;
- it is commercial information, and its disclosure would or might significantly harm the legitimate business interests of an undertaking; or
- it is information concerning the private affairs of an individual, and its disclosure would or might significantly harm his interests.

However, the need to protect these interests must be balanced against the Tribunal's duty to 'have regard to the extent to which any disclosure [of such information] is necessary for the purpose of explaining the reasons for the decision' (Sched. 4, para. 1(3)).

Enforcement of decisions

2.52 Decisions of the Tribunal are enforceable in England and Wales if they are registered by the registrar or a party to the proceedings, under applicable court rules. In those circumstances, awards of damages, costs and expenses and any direction given by the Tribunal, are enforceable by the High Court as if the award or direction had been made by the High Court (Sched. 4, para. 2). In this context, 'damages' includes any award of money (other than for costs or expenses) under the new s.47A Competition Act 1998 (Monetary claims before Tribunal) or s.47B (claims brought on behalf of consumers). In Scotland, such awards and directions are recordable by the registrar or a party, for execution in the Books of Council and Session, and enforceable accordingly (Sched. 4, para. 3). In Northern Ireland, decisions of the Tribunal are enforceable with the leave of the High Court (Sched. 4, para. 5).

2.53 There are special rules relating to the enforcement of 'consumer claims' brought under the new s.47B Competition Act 1998. Awards made to an individual in respect of a consumer claim made on his behalf cannot be enforced by that individual without the permission of the High Court or the Court of Session (Sched. 4, para. 6(a)). Under para. 6(b), this also applies to the award of costs or expenses to an individual in respect of a claim made by him under the new s.47A Competition Act 1998 for the period prior to the proceedings being continued on his behalf as a consumer claim under s.47B. An award of costs or expenses made against a specified body in the course of a consumer claim proceedings cannot be enforced against an individual on whose behalf the proceedings were either commenced or continued (Sched. 4, para. 7).

Location of the Tribunal

2.54 The address for service of documents on the Tribunal is: the Registrar of the Competition Appeal Tribunal, New Court, 48 Carey Street, London WC2A 2JT. Its web address is *www.competition-tribunal.org.uk*. The website is used for the publication of matters relating to appeals, such as information concerning lodged notices of appeal, the withdrawal of notices of appeal, notices concerning consent order impact statements, decisions of the Tribunal, etc. See also para. 2.71 on the forum for hearings.

Rules of the Tribunal

2.55   Section 15 of the Act provides for the Secretary of State to make rules for the Tribunal. Part 2 of Sched. 3 makes further provisions for such Rules. The Rules were published in draft on 10 September 2002 prior to the insertion into the text of s.16 (providing additional powers to the Tribunal). The Rules as finally adopted may differ from those described below insofar as they take account of s.16 and the regulation made under it.

2.56   The Rules relating to appeal proceedings, described below, are modified in certain respects in relation to appeals against penalties imposed during merger investigations (s.114) or market investigations (s.176(1)(f)). They are also modified in relation to applications to the Tribunal for the judicial review of certain decisions, decisions to refer a relevant merger situation or a special merger situation to the Competition Commission (s.120), and decisions to make a reference to the Competition Commission under the market investigation powers of Part 4 of the Act (s.179). These modifications are noted below. In the case of applications for review, references in the Rules to 'appeals' are to be read as references to 'reviews'.

2.57   Proceedings that are commenced prior to the coming into force of the rules continue to be governed by the Competition Commission Appeal Tribunal Rules 2000 (SI 2000/261).

Time for appeal

2.58   Appeal proceedings must be commenced within two months[8] of the earlier of the date on which the appellant was notified of the decision, or its date of publication. An application for the review of a decision in connection with the reference or possible reference of a merger situation, special merger situation or market investigation must be made within three months, rather than two (rr.26 and 27).[9] Appeals against penalties imposed during merger or market investigations (for failure to comply with a notice under ss.109 and 176(1)(a) to attend and give evidence and produce documents, or for obstruction or delay) must be made within 28 days.

2.59   The period for appeal may be extended by the Tribunal only where the Tribunal is satisfied that the circumstances are exceptional.

Notice of appeal

2.60   Proceedings are commenced by sending a notice of appeal or, in the case of an application for the review of decisions concerning references to the Competition Commission, a notice of application (r.28) to the registrar at the address mentioned above. The original notice must be accompanied by seven certified copies.

2.61   The notice of appeal must contain the following information and annexes:

- the name and address of the appellant ('applicant' in the case of applications for the review of decisions to refer) and of the appellant's legal representative;
- an address for service in the UK;
- the name and address of the respondent to the proceedings;
- a concise statement of the facts;
- a summary of the grounds for contesting (or reviewing) the decision, including: the statutory provision under which the appeal is brought; the extent to which the claim is based on an alleged error of fact or law; and the extent to which the appeal concerns the respondent's exercise of discretion in making the decision;
- a succinct presentation of the arguments supporting each ground of appeal;
- the relief and the directions sought;
- a schedule of documents annexed to the notice;
- a copy of the disputed decision; and
- as far as practicable, a copy of every document on which the appellant relies (including statements by expert witnesses or witnesses of fact). Note that r.51(3) provides that, unless the Tribunal otherwise directs, no witness of fact or expert shall be heard at the substantive hearing unless the witness statement or expert report was submitted in advance and in accordance with any directions.

2.62   Requests for the confidential treatment of any document, or part of a document, filed in proceedings must be made in writing at the latest within 14 days after the filing. The application must be reasoned, and must indicate the relevant words, figures or passages claimed to be confidential. The registrar may direct the person making the request to supply a non-confidential version of the document (r.53). Requests made in disregard of this rule will be permitted only in exceptional circumstances.

2.63   The notice of appeal may also contain 'observations' on the question of where in the UK the Tribunal proceedings shall be treated as taking place. This is important to the nature of appeals from Tribunal decisions. The actual forum of the hearings may differ from the deemed location of proceedings.

2.64   Notices of appeal may be returned as defective if they do not comply with the above rules, or are otherwise incomplete. They may also be rejected if they are 'unduly prolix or lacking in clarity', an incentive to render appeal arguments in an accessible and fully worked form. Defective notices of appeal may not be served on the respondent until the defects have been remedied in accordance with directions given by the Tribunal.

2.65   Other than in these circumstances, a notice of appeal may be amended by the appellant only with the Tribunal's consent (which may be subject to terms and directions of the Tribunal). No amendment will be permitted if it adds a new ground for contesting the decision, unless: the relevant facts or law came to light since the appeal was made; or it was 'not practicable' to include such ground in the notice of appeal; or the circumstances are exceptional (r.11).

2.66   Once served, notices of appeal may not be withdrawn without the consent of the Tribunal (or of the president, if the case has not yet proceeded to a hearing). Consent to withdrawal may be subject to terms, and notice of the withdrawal may be published by the Tribunal (r.12). Interim orders (other than costs orders) cease to have effect on withdrawal of the notice of appeal. No fresh appeal may be brought by the appellant withdrawing the notice in relation to the disputed decision.

2.67   Under r.10, appeals may be partly or wholly rejected at any stage in the proceedings if:

- the notice of appeal does not disclose a valid ground of appeal;
- the appellant does not have a sufficient interest in the disputed decision (or, in the case of applications to review a decision, where the applicant is not a person aggrieved by the decision) or represents those having an insufficient interest;
- the appellant is deemed to be a vexatious litigant; or
- the appellant fails to comply with any rule, direction, practice direction or order of the Tribunal.

Defence

2.68   A defence must be served on the Tribunal by the respondent within six weeks[10] of the receipt by the respondent of the notice of appeal (r.14). The Tribunal will send a copy to the appellant (see r.63 for provisions relating to the service of documents). The defence must contain a succinct presentation of the arguments of fact and law upon which the respondent intends to rely, together with a description of the relief and any case management directions sought, and a schedule of documents annexed. Such documents are of the same type as those annexed to the notice of appeal. The defence may also contain observations on the location in the UK at which the proceedings are to be deemed to take place. The rules applicable to notices of appeal concerning defects, rejection, withdrawal and amendment apply also to the defence, except that the respondent is taken to have sufficient interest in the matter, and is not subject to the provisions concerning vexatious litigation (r.14(7)).

Intervention

2.69   A person with 'sufficient interest' may apply to the Tribunal for permission to intervene in the proceedings, except in relation to appeals against penalties imposed during merger or market investigations. The form of the application is laid down in r.16(4) and (5). Such an application must be made within one month[11] of the publication of the notice of the appeal on the Tribunal's website. The application is sent to all the parties, who may make observations on it within a period laid down by the registrar. If the Tribunal consents to the application, it may make directions to take account of the lodging of documents, and so on. The rules relating to the requirement to protect certain confidential information, in

Sched. 4, para. 1(2) of the Act, also apply to these directions. In particular, the Tribunal may require the submission of a notice of intervention and of a response by the principal parties. A notice of intervention must contain a succinct presentation of the facts and arguments supporting the intervention, together with a description of the relief sought and a schedule of documents annexed (which shall be of the same type as are required to be annexed to the notice of appeal and the defence). The rules applicable to notices of appeal concerning defects, rejection, withdrawal and amendment apply also to the notice of intervention except that the intervener's interest in the matter is determined at the stage of his application to intervene (r.16(10)).

Consolidation

2.70   Under r.17, the Tribunal may consolidate proceedings that concern the same decision or that involve the same or similar issues. Consolidation may be on the Tribunal's initiative or at the request of the parties.

Forum

2.71   The Tribunal will determine whether proceedings are to be *treated* as taking place in England and Wales, Scotland or Northern Ireland (for the purposes of appeals from the Tribunal's decisions and for other matters connected with the proceedings). Rule 18(3) directs the Tribunal to take account of the following factors in reaching a decision on this matter:

- where the appellant, applicant, claimant or defendant is habitually resident or have their head office or principal place of business;
- where the majority of the parties are habitually resident or have their head offices or principal places of business;
- where any agreement, decision or concerted practice (to which the proceedings relate) was made or implemented, or intended to be implemented; and
- where any conduct (to which the proceedings relate) took place.

2.72   Rule 18(4) provides further considerations in relation to claims for damages under the new ss.47A and 47B Competition Act 1998.

2.73   The actual location of the hearings will not necessarily be the place at which hearings are to be treated as taking place. Rule 18(2) permits the Tribunal to hold meetings, case management conferences, pre-hearing reviews or hearings, or to give directions, 'in such place . . . as it thinks fit having regard to the just, expeditious and economical conduct of the proceedings'.

Case management directions

2.74   Such just, expeditious and economical conduct of the proceedings is also to be achieved through the giving of directions by the Tribunal, either on its own initiative or at the request of the parties. A request by a party for directions should be made in writing and served by the registrar on any other party who might be affected by them. Those parties may make observations on the application.

2.75   Directions may be given at any time, but are clearly relevant to case management conferences and pre-hearing reviews. Rule 19(2) provides for a number of such directions:

(a) the manner in which the proceedings are to be conducted, including time limits for the oral hearing;
(b) the filing of pleadings, including reply, rejoinder or other additional pleadings and particulars;
(c) the preparation and exchange of skeleton arguments;
(d) the requirement for persons to attend and give evidence or to produce documents;
(e) the evidence which may be required or admitted, and the extent to which it shall be oral or written;
(f) the advance submission of witness statements or expert reports;
(g) the examination or cross-examination of witnesses;
(h) time limits to be applied to any aspect of the proceedings;
(i) the abridgement or extension of time limits;
(j) to enable a disputed decision to be referred back (in whole or in part) to the person by whom it was taken;
(k) disclosure and production of documents;
(l) the appointment and instruction of experts (by the Tribunal or the parties) and the manner in which expert evidence is to be given;
(m) the award of costs or expenses, and for attendance allowances; and
(n) for hearing a person who is not a party to the proceedings (where there is a proposal to make an order or give a direction in relation to that person).

2.76   In conducting its case management functions, the Tribunal may do any of the following, under r.19(3):

■   put questions to the parties;
■   invite the parties to make written or oral submissions;
■   ask the parties or third parties for information or particulars;
■   ask for the production of document or papers relating to the case;
■   summon the representatives of the parties to attend meetings in person.

Case management conference

2.77   A case management conference or pre-hearing review may be held at the request of a party or on the Tribunal's initiative (r.20(4)). The purpose of this is to:

(a) ensure the efficient conduct of proceedings;
(b) determine the points on which the parties must present further argument, or which call for further evidence to be produced;

(c) clarify the forms of order sought by the parties, arguments of fact and law and the points of issue between them;

(d) ensure that all agreements that can be reached between the parties as to the matters in issue and the conduct of the proceedings are made and recorded; and

(e) to facilitate settlement.

2.78   The conference or review is normally to be held as soon as practicable after an appeal has been filed, even before the expiry of the period for the service of a defence. The conference or review is held in private unless the Tribunal otherwise directs.

Oral hearing timetable

2.79   The Tribunal will set a timetable as soon as practicable, outlining the steps to be taken by the parties in preparation for the oral hearing. The date of the hearing will also be fixed, and notified to the parties. The Tribunal may also send the parties a report for the hearing, which summarises the factual context and the principal submissions of the parties (r.21(1)(d)).

Evidence

2.80   The Tribunal can admit or exclude evidence, whether or not it was available to the respondent when the disputed decision was taken. It may also control evidence by giving directions as to the issues on which it requires evidence to be given, the nature of that evidence and the way in which it is to be placed before the Tribunal. Witnesses may be required to give evidence under oath, under affirmation or by way of written affidavit. The Tribunal may dispense with the need to call a witness to give oral evidence where a witness statement has been submitted (r.22(5)). Under r.23, the Tribunal has the power to summon witnesses (or to cite them, in Scotland) to attend and answer questions or produce documents. Any such summons shall give the witness at least seven days' notice of the hearing; the witness is also entitled to an attendance allowance. Evidence may be permitted to be given through a video link or by other means.

The hearing

2.81   Hearings are held in public, except where the Tribunal is satisfied that it will be considering information the disclosure of which would be contrary to the public interest; or is information that is commercial the disclosure of which would or might harm the legitimate business interests of the undertaking to which it relates; or is information relating to the private affairs of an individual the disclosure of which would or might significantly harm his interests.

2.82   The Tribunal is directed to avoid formality in the proceedings.

The decision

2.83   Rule 54 provides for the manner in which the decision is to be delivered and published. Where the decision of the Tribunal imposes, confirms or varies a penalty under Part 1 of the Competition Act 1998, it may also order that interest is to be payable (r.56).

Consent orders

2.84   The parties can request the Tribunal to make a consent order under r.57. The procedure includes the delivery of a 'consent order impact statement', which provides, inter alia, an explanation of the anticipated effects on competition of the relief to be obtained. Where the Tribunal considers that such an effect might be significant, the registrar will publish a notice on the Tribunal website, stating the particulars of the relief sought, and indicating where the draft consent order may be inspected. The copy of the consent order which is open for inspection will exclude confidential information. Anyone can send in written comments within one month of the publication of such notice. The parties will receive copies of such comments and have 14 days in which to send a response to the registrar. Claims for damages cannot be settled by way of a consent order.

Interim orders and measures

2.85   An application may be made to the Tribunal under r.61 for an interim order: suspending the effect (in whole or part) of the effect of a disputed decision; varying conditions or obligations attached to an exemption granted under the Competition Act 1998; or granting any remedy which the Tribunal has the power to grant in a final decision. An application may be granted on familiar grounds – i.e. either to prevent 'serious, irreparable damage to a particular person or category of persons' or to protect the public interest. In making its decision, the Tribunal considers the urgency of the matter, the effect on the applicant if the application is refused, and the effect on competition if the application is granted (r.61(3)). Interim orders are not available in claims for damages (r.61(12)).

Claims for damages

2.86   Claims to the Tribunal for damages under the new ss.47A and 47B Competition Act 1998 are dealt with in Part IV of the Rules. The substantive rights themselves are discussed in paras. 3.21 to 3.28. The rules applicable to these claims differ from the rules relating to appeals, except for those rules relating to consolidation, forum and case management. Rules contained in Part V of the Rules (dealing with the hearing, confidentiality, decision of the Tribunal, appeals from the Tribunal, references to the European Court of Justice, interim orders and measures, supplementary rules and transitional arrangements) also apply to claims for damages.

Time for claim

2.87   A claim for damages must be made within a period of two years beginning with the 'relevant date', which is the later of the following:

(a) the end of the relevant period for appeal against the decision on the basis of which the claim is made (these periods are specified in s.47A(7) and (8) of the Competition Act 1998); and

(b) the date on which the cause of action accrued.

Under r.31, the Tribunal may give permission for a claim to be made before the period set out in (a) if all the parties agree. Note also that if a claim for damages could not have been brought before a court because of the expiry of a limitation period, then no claim can be brought under s.47A where that period expired before the commencement of s.47A.

Claim form

2.88   A claim for damages under s.47A Competition Act 1998 is commenced by sending a claim form to the registrar. The claim form must contain the following information (r.32):

■ the name and address of the claimant, and of the claimant's legal representative;

■ an address for service in the UK;

■ the name and address of the defendant to the proceedings;

■ a concise statement of the relevant facts, identifying the findings in the decision on the basis of which the claim for damages is made;

■ a summary of the contentions of law which are relied upon;

■ a statement of the amount claimed, supported by evidence of losses incurred and of any calculations which have been made to arrive at the claimed amount; and

■ any other matter specified in practice directions.

2.89   A claim for damages brought under s.47A may be continued by a 'specified body' under s.47B, subject to any directions given by the Tribunal (r.33(2)). A claim form in respect of a claim for damages under s.47B Competition Act 1998 ('consumer claims'), must contain the following additional information.

■ the name and address of the specified body, and a concise statement of its aims and objectives;

■ the names and addresses of the persons it seeks to represent;

■ an indication as to whether each individual so listed is a 'consumer' for the purposes of s.47B.

It must also be accompanied by a document or documents by which each of the individuals so listed give consent to the specified body to act on his behalf.

2.90   The contents of the claim form must be verified by a statement of truth, signed and dated by or on behalf of the claimant.

2.91   A copy of the relevant decision should be annexed to the claim form, together with (as far as practicable) a copy of all essential documents on which the claimant relies. The original claim form must be accompanied by seven certified copies.

2.92   A claim form cannot be amended except with the written consent of all the parties or with permission of the Tribunal. The Tribunal may give consent for one or more parties to be joined in addition to or in substitution to the existing parties.

2.93   The registrar will acknowledge the receipt of the claim form and send a copy to the defendant.

Defence

2.94   The defendant must send an acknowledgement of service to the registrar within seven days. Within 28 days of the receipt of the claim form, the defendant must send to the registrar a defence (r.37). The defence must be sufficiently detailed, and specify which of the facts and contentions of law in the claim form it admits or denies, and the grounds, facts and contentions of law upon which it relies. The contents of the defence must be verified by a statement of truth signed and dated by or on behalf of the defendant.

2.95   The defendant may make a counterclaim against the claimant, or a claim against any other person. If the counterclaim or claim is included in the defence, no consent is required. If it is not so included, the Tribunal must consent to it being made. The rules relating to the timing and form of claims apply also to counterclaims and claims made by the defendant. The rules relating to the obligations of the defendant, and the form of defences, apply also to the response to such claims by the claimant. Other than as mentioned above, no further pleadings may be filed without the consent of the Tribunal.

2.96   A claimant can withdraw his claim only with the consent of the defendant, or with the consent of the Tribunal (or of the president, if the case has not yet proceeded to a hearing). The Tribunal may make a consequential order where a claim is withdrawn; and no further claim may be brought by the claimant in respect of the same subject matter (r.42(2)).

Summary rejection of a claim

2.97   The Tribunal can reject a claim in whole or in part at any stage, either upon application by a party or on its own initiative (r.40). It must first give the parties an opportunity to be heard. Such a disposal can take place where:

(a) the Tribunal considers that there are no reasonable grounds for making the claim;

(b) the Tribunal considers that the body bringing a claim under s.47B Competition Act 1998 is not entitled to do so, or that an individual on whose behalf the claim is made is not a consumer for the purposes of that section;

(c) the Tribunal is satisfied that the claimant is a vexatious litigant; or

(d) the claimant fails to comply with any rule, direction, practice direction or order of the Tribunal.

Summary judgment on a claim

2.98   The Tribunal can give summary judgment on a claim or reject a claim or defence in a claim in whole or in part, at any stage, either upon application by a party or on its own initiative (r.41). It must first give the parties an opportunity to be heard. Such a summary judgment can be made where the Tribunal considers that the claimant has no real prospect of succeeding on the claim or issue, or that the defendant has no reasonable grounds for defending the claim or issue. In each such case there must be no other compelling reason why the case or issue should be disposed of at a substantive hearing. A summary judgment will not be made until the defence has been filed.

Payments to settle

2.99   Under r.43, once a claim for damages has been commenced, the defendant may make a payment into the Tribunal, by way of an offer to settle the whole or part of a claim. Notification of such a payment must be sent to the registrar and to the party to whom the offer is made. The notification must be precise in relation to the basis on which the payment has been calculated. The fact that a payment to settle has been made is not communicated to the members of the Tribunal who are hearing the case until all questions of liability and quantum have been agreed or settled. Payments to settle are treated as being made 'without prejudice' save as to costs. They can be reduced or withdrawn only with the consent of the registrar. Once made, such an offer may be accepted at any time up to 14 days prior to the substantive hearing of the claim.

2.100   A claimant who accepts the offer is entitled to costs relating to the part of the proceedings to which the offer related, up to the date of serving notice of acceptance (r.43(6)). Where, following a substantive hearing, a claimant fails to better a payment to settle, he will be ordered to pay any costs incurred by the defendant after the last date upon which the offer could have been accepted, unless the Tribunal considers this unjust.[12] As a means of encouraging claimants to accept reasonable offers to settle, the Tribunal may order such costs to carry interest and to be paid on an indemnity basis (r.43(7)).

2.101   Rule 43(10) makes it clear that the payment to settle procedure is not the only means by which the parties can make offers of settlement. If, following a substantive hearing, a claimant fails to recover an amount equal to an offer made by the defendant (outside the payment to settle procedure), the Tribunal is entitled to take that into account in determining the award of costs. Under r.57(10), claims for damages cannot be settled by way of a consent order.

Case management

2.102   Case management powers (including the rules described above relating to consolidation, forum, directions, case management conferences, timetable for oral hearings, evidence, witnesses and failure to comply with directions) must be exercised actively by the Tribunal with a view to dealing with the case justly. Under r.44(2), this includes:

(a) ensuring that the parties are on an equal footing;
(b) saving expense;
(c) dealing with the case in ways which are proportionate:
    (i)   to the amount of money involved;
    (ii) to the importance of the case;
    (iii) to the complexity of the issues; and
    (iv) to the financial position of each party;
(d) ensuring that the case is dealt with expeditiously and fairly; and
(e) allotting to it an appropriate level of resource.

2.103   Rule 44(3) provides that the Tribunal may: encourage and facilitate alternative dispute resolution procedures where appropriate, dispense with the need for parties to attend hearings, and use technology actively to manage cases.

2.104   The Tribunal may (on request by a party or on its own initiative) transfer a claim for damages to the High Court or a county court or, in Scotland, to the Court of Session or a sheriff court (r.48). Conversely, a claim which may be made under s.47A Competition Act 1998 may be transferred *to* the Tribunal from any court.

Interim payments

2.105   The Tribunal can make an interim order for payment on account of damages, under r.46. No request for such payment can be made prior to the filing of the defence, but the claimant can make multiple requests. Such an interim payment will be ordered only where the defendant has admitted liability to pay damages, or the Tribunal is satisfied that, on a substantive hearing, the claimant would obtain judgment for a 'substantial amount' of damages against the defendant. Even then, the Tribunal may not award more than a reasonable proportion of the final award.

Appeals from the Competition Appeal Tribunal

2.106   Section 49 Competition Act 1998 is amended by Sched. 5, para. 4. The new s.49 provides for appeals to be made from the Tribunal to the Court of Appeal or the Court of Session (s.49(1) and (3) Competition Act 1998). Such appeals may be brought by a party to the proceedings or by a person having sufficient interest in the matter. In either case, the appeal requires the permission of the Tribunal (under rr.58 and 59) or the court to which the appeal would be made (s.49(2) of the 1998 Act).

2.107   Appeal lies in relation to the following decisions of the Tribunal:

- as to the amount of a penalty under s.36 of the 1998 Act (penalty for infringing Parts I or II of the 1998 Act);
- as to the award of, or the amount of, damages or other sum in respect of a claim under s.47A (claims for damages) or 47B (consumer claims) of the 1998 Act, other than a decision on costs or expenses;
- any other decision of the Tribunal on an appeal under s.46 Competition Act 1998 (appealable decisions of the director) or s.47 of the 1998 Act (third-party appeals). In this case, the appeal may only be on a point of law.

2.108   In all cases, the appeal may be brought only by a party to the proceedings or by a person who has sufficient interest in the matter. The appeal may only be made with the consent of the Tribunal or the appropriate court.

2.109   Part III of Sched. 7 to the 1998 Act, which established the organisation of the Appeal Tribunals, is repealed. Also repealed are Sched. 8, paras. 4 to 14 which provided for the appeal process.

THE BINDING NATURE OF OFT AND TRIBUNAL RULINGS

2.110   Section 20 of the Act adds a new s.58A into the 1998 Act. It will be recalled that s.58 of the 1998 Act provides that, unless the court directed otherwise, findings of fact by the Director General of Fair Trading are binding on parties to court proceedings relating to an alleged infringement of the Chapter I or Chapter II prohibitions. Section 58A relates to proceedings brought before a court for damages or other money claim in respect of an infringement of either Chapter I or Chapter II, or of Article 81(1) or 82 EC Treaty. In these proceedings, the court is bound by any decision of the OFT or of the Tribunal, made *after* the commencement of s.20 of the Act, that any such provision has been infringed. Such decisions do not become binding until after all relevant periods of appeal have expired and, where an appeal has been made, until after the determination of the appeal.

---

1   The Competition Commission currently publishes an annual review and accounts for the period April to March. The highly illustrated review for 2001/2002, having all the appearance of a brash corporate publication (but very informative nonetheless), was published in July 2002.
2   It is easy to slip into the usage.
3   Under the following Acts and Orders: Fair Trading Act 1973, Competition Act 1980, Telecommunications Act 1984, Airports Act 1986, Gas Act 1986, Electricity Act 1989, Broadcasting Act 1990, Water Industry Act 1991, Electricity (Northern Ireland) Order 1992, Railways Act 1993, Airports (Northern Ireland) Order 1994, Gas (Northern Ireland) Order 1996, Postal Services Act 2000, Transport Act 2000, Financial Services and Markets Act 2000, and Enterprise Act 2002. Note that these Acts and Orders, and others, are amended and supplemented under Sched. 25 to the 2002 Act.
4   Note that s.11 is amended and supplemented under the 2002 Act, Sched. 25, para. 10.
5   Rule 9 of the Rules of Procedure (provisional findings) does not apply to special reference groups (other than those considering a reference under s.32 Water Industry Act 1991).

6   Rule 11 of the Rules of Procedure (final findings) does not apply to special reference groups (other than those considering a reference under s.32 Water Industry Act 1991).

7   Fair Trading Act 1973, Parts 2, 3, 4, 5, 6, 7, 8 and 11; Trade Descriptions Act 1968; Prices Act 1974; Consumer Credit Act 1974; Estate Agents Act 1979; Competition Act 1980; Consumer Protection Act 1987; Property Misdescriptions Act 1991; Timeshare Act 1992; Competition Act 1998; and Financial Services and Markets Act 2000, Part 10, Chapter 3, Part 18, Chapter 2, and an order under s.96.

8   At the time of writing, the period had not been finally settled.

9   At the time of writing, neither of these periods had been finally settled

10 At the time of writing, the period had not been finally settled.

11 At the time of writing, the period had not been finally settled.

12 Note that r.45 makes provisions for applications by a defendant for security for costs. Rule 55 makes provisions for costs generally.

3 NEW RIGHTS OF REDRESS

SUPER-COMPLAINTS

The purpose of super-complaints

> The arrival of the super complaint must have seemed like the arrival of gunpowder and cannons to the proprietor of a medieval castle – alarming and impressive at the same time.
>
> (Nigel Watson MP, Standing Committee Debates)

3.1 A much-heralded feature of the Act is the introduction of a scheme of super-complaints under which certain designated organisations are able to submit complaints to the OFT. The OFT is under an obligation to respond within 90 days, a period that may be changed by the Secretary of State by way of an order under s.11(4).

3.2 So keen was the OFT to introduce the super-complaint procedure that it put it in place prior to the Bill being passed. Shortly after the Bill received Royal Assent, it also accepted a super-complaint from the National Association of Consumers' Advice Bureaux on doorstep selling (November 2002). Although formally accepted under s.2 of the 1973 Act, this was treated in all practical respects as a super-complaint under the Act.

3.3 The super-complaint must be sufficiently detailed and reasoned to enable the OFT to review it within the statutory period. For that reason, the OFT is under an obligation to issue guidance on the manner of presentation of a super-complaint (see para. 3.7). It may also issue other appropriate guidance (s.11(7)).

3.4 It is not incumbent on the OFT to take any action within the 90-day period. Its only obligation is to declare whether it has decided to take action (and, if so, what), or to take no action. In either case, it must give reasons for the decision. Although the intention is that the OFT shall have made such decision within such period, the strict wording of the Act enables it to respond to the super-complainant that neither such decision has yet been taken – in which case it is under no further obligation as to the speed of its substantive response.

Super-complainants

3.5 Only those bodies which represent consumers' interests and which have been designated by the Secretary of State for such purpose may make a super-complaint. Obvious examples include the Consumers' Association, which has over many years had an active dialogue with the competition authorities in the UK and the EU, and the National Association of Consumers' Advice Bureaux. Also likely to be designated are sector-specific consumer bodies such as those existing in the various utility sectors.

The scope of super-complaints: market failure

3.6 The subject of a super-complaint may be 'any feature, or combination of features, of a market in the United Kingdom for goods or services [that] is or appears to be significantly harming the interests of consumers' (s.11(1)). This goes beyond the ability to complain about alleged anti-competitive agreements or abuses of dominance; it extends to any market failure. A feature of a market, defined in s.131(2), includes: (a) the structure of a market (or any aspect of that structure); (b) any conduct (whether or not in the market concerned) of any person who supplies or acquires goods or services in the market concerned; and (c) any conduct of the customers of such persons. In this context 'conduct' includes unintentional conduct, as well as an intentional or unintentional failure to act. The meaning of market features is more fully discussed in Chapter 9, dealing with market investigation references.

3.7 The OFT has alerted potential super-complainants to the type of feature that may indicate market failure. These are set out as examples in Annex B to the OFT's (draft) guidance on super-complaints. Such features are divided into primary indicators of a market that is not functioning effectively, and secondary features. Primary features include:

- low productivity;
- high profitability, or substantial price dispersion or prices that do not reflect costs;
- poor quality or poor variety; and
- poor levels of innovation.

3.8 Since such primary features are unreliable in indicating market failure on their own, the OFT will also examine secondary features, which include, *inter alia*:

- few firms;
- high entry barriers; and
- low buyer power.

3.9 The OFT guidance indicates that these features may be of particular concern when combined with features that facilitate collusion:

- product homogeneity;

- transparency of market information relating to prices, outputs and market shares;
- similarity of market shares, cost structures and planning periods as between undertakings on the market;
- stability of demand and of costs;
- excess capacity; and
- high multi-market contact.

3.10   The OFT also provides examples of certain market behaviour that might indicate that competition is restricted. Such behaviour includes:

- predation;
- price discrimination;
- discounts;
- refusal to supply;
- vertical restraints; and
- bundling.

The OFT also mentions switching costs, high search costs, quality of products not easily observable, and regulatory problems.

3.11   The effect of this very broad remit is that super-complainants will have an enhanced standing to bring to the attention of the OFT any issue which has, or may have, an adverse impact on consumers, whether as a result of structure, conduct or performance in the market concerned. Of course, any other person may also bring such issues to the attention of the OFT; a super-complainant merely has the expectation that the OFT will respond in substance more expeditiously. As a means of acquiring detailed and well-presented information and analysis, the super-complaint system will clearly be of some use to the OFT. In its draft guidance on super-complaints, the OFT describes the process as 'an efficient way of bringing genuine concerns about market failure to the attention of regulatory bodies'.[1] It will also be a useful focus for those consumers' organisations that have engaged with the OFT (and the European Commission) at a more informal level. Whether it will really change the nature of the competition control process, or significantly enhance the protection of consumer interest, remains to be seen.

The process for making a super-complaint

3.12   Super complaints should be made to the Markets and Policy Initiatives Division of the OFT at its usual address, or e-mailed to *supercomplaints@oft. gsi.gov.uk*. The complainant should include a short paper stating, with reasons, why the terms of s.11(1) are satisfied – i. e. why the market in question contains a feature or combination of features that is, or appears to be, significantly harming the interests of consumers. This paper should be supported by facts and evidence. It is clear from the OFT's draft guidance on super-complaints that the paper to be submitted does not have to be a fully worked economic or legal case, nor even a fully reasoned basis on which a decision to investigate may be made. What is required is assistance 'to help the OFT to undertake a further appraisal of whether there are factors indicating market failure that may warrant launching [a] market investigation or whether [another] outcome . . . may be appropriate' (OFT draft guidance, para. 2.7). Complaints that do not provide such assistance, because insufficiently evidenced or because they are frivolous or vexatious, will either not progress or will be rejected.

Evidence to be provided by a super-complainant

3.13   The OFT has provided guidance on the type and level of evidence that should be submitted in support of a super-complaint. This is set out in Annex A of the draft guidance as a non-exhaustive list of information. In addition to basic and obvious features such as the nature of the complaint and the way in which consumers' interests are harmed, the OFT recommends that super-complainants consider submitting the following:

- the extent of the problem (the market as a whole or only certain suppliers or certain parts of the market?);
- the extent of the harm (all or only certain consumers?);
- whether vulnerable groups of consumers feature disproportionately;
- information on market shares (value and volume) and the manner in which they have changed in recent years;
- evidence of barriers to entry;
- information relating to buyer power and whether any benefits arising from such power is passed to consumers;
- information on prices: discounts, discrimination, dispersion, trends and timing of price changes;
- information on profitability of suppliers in the sector;
- evidence of harmful practices by suppliers (i.e. those which may restrict or distort competition or which could have a detrimental effect on consumers);
- evidence of complex contractual terms or bundling;
- switching costs incurred by consumers;
- information on general quality levels;
- information on the extent to which consumers are well informed;
- whether 'complex aspects of the goods or service', the way in which it is supplied, or difficulties in assessing quality, present particular problems for consumers;
- means of redress available to consumers; and
- details of relevant codes of practice.

OFT procedures

3.14   The OFT will acknowledge receipt of a super-complaint and assign a team within five working days. Where the matter concerns one of the regulated sectors, the OFT will liaise with the appropriate regulator to determine which body will deal with the complaint under the concurrency arrangements developed under the 1998 Act. Section 205 of the 2002 Act enables the Secretary of State to make regulations providing for super-complaints to be made directly to specified regulators (i.e. those in the concurrency arrangements).

3.15 The first stage of the process will comprise an assessment by the OFT of the sufficiency of the evidence put forward by the super-complainant. Following that, the OFT will carry out wider enquiries to obtain information and to list the evidence already submitted. At the end of the process, within 90 days of receiving the super-complaint, the OFT will publish its response to the super-complainant. This response will be reasoned and will state what action (if any) the OFT intends to take. There are several different possible responses, including a dismissal or rejection of the super-complaint, or its transfer to a sector regulator for action under the Competition Act 1998 or under sector-specific legislation. If the OFT wishes itself to take the matter further, it may do so in a number of ways. If the matter raises possible infringements of the Competition Act 1998, it can be referred to the appropriate division of the OFT. Similarly, if consumer legislation appears to have been breached, that division can then pursue enforcement action under the appropriate legislation. Alternatively, the matter can be referred to the Competition Commission as a market investigation reference under the 2002 Act. Finally, the Markets and Policy Initiatives Division of the OFT may launch its own market investigation with a view to making broader recommendations concerning the operation of relevant laws and regulations.

3.16 The provisions relating to super-complaints provide a platform for consumers whose interests might not otherwise have been represented. There are other provisions of the Act that further the interests of consumers in relation to competition infringements – principally s.18, which provides for 'consumer claims' for damages to be brought before the Competition Appeal Tribunal (see paras. 3.26 to 3.28).

THIRD-PARTY APPEALS

3.17 Under the Competition Act 1998, parties to an agreement in respect of which the Director had made a decision, and persons in respect of whose conduct the Director had made a decision, had a right of appeal to the Competition Commission Appeal Tribunals. Third parties – those falling outside the two groups described above – did not have direct rights of appeal. If they had sufficient interest in the relevant decision they had the right, under s.47 of the Competition Act 1998, to make an application to the Director to withdraw or vary a decision. Those third parties could then bring an appeal in relation to the rejection of such an application or the refusal of the Director to withdraw or vary the decision. Such appeal was heard by the Competition Commission Appeal Tribunals.

3.18 The 2002 Act now provides a more direct right of appeal for third parties. This is achieved through the replacement of the old s.47 of the 1998 Act with a new one set out in s.17 of the 2002 Act. Third parties may now appeal to the Competition Appeal Tribunal 'with respect to a decision falling within paragraphs

(a) to (f) of s.46(3) or such other decision of the OFT under this Part as may be prescribed' (new s.47(1) of the 1998 Act). The appealable decisions are:

(a) as to whether the Chapter I prohibition (anti-competitive agreements) has been infringed;
(b) as to whether the Chapter II prohibition (abuse of dominance) has been infringed;
(c) as to whether to grant an individual exemption to an agreement;
(d) in respect of an individual exemption –

   (i) as to whether to impose any condition or obligation under s.4(3)(a)[2] or s.5(1)(c) of the 1998 Act;[3]
   (ii) where such a condition or obligation has been imposed, as to the condition or obligation;
   (iii) as to the period fixed under s.4(3)(b) of the 1998 Act;[4] or
   (iv) as to the date fixed under s.4(5) of the 1998 Act;[5]

(e) as to –

   (i) whether to extend the period for which an individual exemption has effect, or
   (ii) the period of any such extension; or

(f) cancelling an exemption.

3.19   As before, third-party appellants will only be permitted to make an appeal if they (or the persons they represent) have a sufficient interest in the decision.

3.20   A third-party appeal does not suspend the effect of the disputed decision.

CLAIMS FOR DAMAGES TO THE COMPETITION APPEAL TRIBUNAL

Introduction

3.21   The government envisaged that the effectiveness of the new approach enshrined in the Competition Act 1998 would lay in the ability of those harmed by anti-competitive agreements or conduct to recover damages for their injury. Sections 18 and 19 of the 2002 Act place two new sections in the 1998 Act, immediately following the revised section on third-party appeals: ss.47A (monetary claims before Tribunal) and 47B (claims brought on behalf of consumers). Such private actions were intended both to underscore the OFT's activities, and enable alternative means of enforcement. In the heyday of private antitrust enforcement in the USA, private actions for damages and other relief amounted to some 90 per cent of enforcement activities. The Act has provided a new forum for bringing actions for damages, while leaving in place the ability of claimants to bring actions for damages and other civil remedies in the ordinary courts. In this regard, the new s.47A(10) Competition Act 1998 provides that the right to make a claim under that section 'does not affect the right to bring any other proceedings in respect of the claim'.

3.22   The new s.47A of the 1998 Act[6] preserves one advantage of seeking remedies for competition-related issues in the civil courts rather than the European Commission: the ability to combine claims under UK and EU laws. The section achieves this through the definition of 'relevant prohibition' in subsection (2), discussed below. In addition, the Tribunal's ability to order interim payments on account of damages, and the expert nature of the Tribunal panels, add to the attractiveness of using the Tribunal as a forum for damages claims. However, claimants still face the same difficulties in bringing a successful claim that they encounter in the courts: namely the need to prove causation and the requirement to demonstrate evidence of quantum – the twin pillars of a successful defence.

Scope of claim: infringement of a relevant prohibition

3.23   Section 47A covers claims for damages and claims for any other sum of money, in either case in respect of loss or damage suffered by the claimant as a result of the infringement by the defendant of a 'relevant prohibition'. Any such claim that may be brought in civil proceedings in the UK, may now be brought before the Tribunal (s.47A(1) and (4)). For the purpose of identifying claims that may have been so brought, the rules of limitation are to be ignored (s.47A(3)). However, although s.18(2) of the 2002 Act confirms that the new s.47A will apply also to claims arising before the commencement of the section, r.31 of the (draft) Competition Appeal Tribunal Rules 2002 provides that if a claim for damages could not have been brought before a court because of the expiry of a limitation period, then no claim can be brought under s.47A where that period expired before the commencement of s.47A.

3.24   Relevant prohibitions are defined in s.47(2); they are those arising in UK or EU competition law. The existence of the infringement of the prohibition must have already been established by a decision of the appropriate authority (s.47A(5)(a) and (b)), a decision which the Tribunal is not entitled to reopen or question (s.47A(6)). It is important to note that the claims covered by s.47A are for monetary amounts, and not to establish that a prohibition has occurred. No claim may therefore be brought until a prohibition has been definitively established in other proceedings.

3.25   The claim may not be brought, except with the permission of the Tribunal, until the end of the periods noted below in Table 3.1. Where an appeal is brought within the relevant period, then the period before which a monetary claim may be brought before the Tribunal is extended until the appeal has been determined.

Table 3.1 Claims for infringement of a relevant prohibition

Relevant prohibition	Pre-existing decision establishing that prohibition has been infringed	Period that must expire before claim is brought
The Chapter I prohibition of the 1998 Act (anti-competitive agreements) (s.47A(2)(a))	A decision of the OFT that the prohibition has been infringed (s.47A(6)(a))	The period during which an appeal may be made to the Tribunal under ss.46 or 47 or under the EC Competition Law (Articles 84 and 85) Enforcement Regulations 2001 (two months after the date upon which the applicant was notified of the disputed decision) (r.8)
	Or a decision of the Tribunal (on appeal from the OFT) that the prohibition has been infringed (s.47A(6)(c))	The period during which a further appeal may be made under the above provisions (one month) (r.58). If a further appeal is made, the period during which an appeal to the House of Lords from a decision of the Court of Appeal (one month)
The Chapter II prohibition of the 1998 Act (abuse of dominant position) (s.47(2)(b))	A decision of the OFT that the prohibition has been infringed (s.47A(6)(a))	as above
	Or a decision of the Tribunal (on appeal from the OFT) that the prohibition has been infringed (s.47A(6)(c))	as above
The prohibition in Article 81(1) of the EC Treaty (anti-competitive agreements which may affect trade between Member States) (s.47A(2)(c))	A decision of the European Commission that the prohibition has been infringed (s.47A(6)(d))	The period during which proceedings against the decision may be instituted in the European Court of Justice (two months of the publication of the decision, or of its notification to the claimant, or, in the absence thereof, of the day on which it came to his knowledge) (Article 230 EC Treaty (ex Article 173))
The prohibition in Article 82 EC Treaty (abuse of dominant position in so far as it may affect trade between Member States) (s.47A(2)(d))	A decision of the European Commission that the prohibition has been infringed (s.47A(6)(d))	as above

Relevant prohibition	Pre-existing decision establishing that prohibition has been infringed	Period that must expire before claim is brought
The prohibition in Article 65(1) European Coal and Steel Community Treaty (anti-competitive agreements within the scope of the ECSC Treaty. Note that Treaty expired on 23 July 2002) (s.47A(2)(e))	A decision of the European Commission that the prohibition has been infringed (s.47A(6)(e))	as above
The prohibition in Article 66(7) European Coal and Steel Community Treaty (pre-notification of mergers within the scope of the ECSC Treaty. Note that Treaty expired on 23 July 2002) (s.47A(2)(f))	A finding made by the European Commission under Article 66(7) (s.47A(6)(e))	as above

Consumer claims

3.26   Section 19 of the 2002 Act inserts a new s.47B into the Competition Act 1998, providing for claims for monetary amounts to be brought before the Tribunal on behalf of consumers. Many of the provisions of s.47A apply to these proceedings; there are also provisions for proceedings that are commenced under s.47A to be continued on behalf of the claimant under s.47B. It is important to note that s.47B does not provide for a 'class action'; it enables certain specified bodies to bring (or to continue) actions on behalf of at least two individuals. All individuals so represented must be named and must have given their consent to such representation (see paras. 2.86 to 2.105, on the Tribunal Rules concerning claims made under s.47B). The claims included in the proceedings must all relate to the same infringement (s.47B(4)).

3.27   Bodies may apply to be specified by the Secretary of State as bodies which may bring proceedings under s.47B (s.47B(10)). The Secretary of State will so specify, by order, in accordance with criteria to be published by him under s.47B(9). The proceedings available to a specified body are certain of those which could have been brought (or were properly brought) by the represented individuals under s.47A. Where any of the represented individuals did bring a claim under s.47A, it may be continued by the specified body as a claim under s.47B, with the consent of the individual.

3.28   However, consumer claims under s.47B may only be brought where the individuals are represented *as consumers*. Rule 40 of the Competition Appeal Tribunal Rules 2002 provides that the Tribunal can summarily reject a claim brought under s.47A where the represented individual is not a consumer for these purposes. The characterisation of the individual as a consumer is made by limiting claims under s.47B to those in respect of infringements affecting, directly or indirectly, certain goods or services. The relevant goods or services are specified in subsection (7); they must fulfil two criteria – one expressed in the negative and relating to the purpose of their receipt, the other expressed in the positive and relating to the purpose of their supply. Thus, they must be goods or services:

(a) which the individual either received or sought to receive otherwise than in the course of a business carried on by him; this criterion is fulfilled even if the individual received or sought to receive the goods with a view to carrying on a business (s.47B(7)(a)); and
(b) were supplied, or would have been supplied to the individual in the course of a business carried on by the supplier or would-be supplier.

For the purposes of both criteria, 'business' is defined to encompass a professional practice, any undertaking carried on for gain or reward, and any undertaking in the course of which goods or services are supplied otherwise than free of charge (s.47B(8)).

JUDICIAL REVIEWS

3.29   The Act contains its own internal judicial review provisions in connection with a reference or possible reference to the Commission of a relevant merger situation or a special merger situation (s.120) or of a market investigation reference (s.179). Any person aggrieved by a decision of the OFT, the Competition Commission or the Secretary of State may apply for it to be reviewed by the Competition Appeal Tribunal. Reviewable decisions include decisions to refer or not to refer those matters to the Commission, and the failure to make a decision on a reference that the reviewed body was entitled to make.

3.30   When hearing such an application, the Tribunal is required to apply the same principles as would be applied by a court hearing an application for judicial review. The Tribunal may quash the decision and may refer it back to the original decision-maker to reconsider the matter. A further appeal is available on a point of law, to the Court of Appeal or Court of Session, with the consent of either the Tribunal or that court.

3.31   The procedure relating to applications for review have been noted (paras. 2.58 to 2.105); the procedure for appeal applies to such applications, except for the differences noted in those paragraphs.

REFERENCES TO THE EUROPEAN COURT OF JUSTICE

3.32   Rule 60 provides for the Tribunal to exercise its discretion in requesting a preliminary ruling from the European Court of Justice under Article 234 (previously Article 177) EC Treaty. Article 234 provides that:

The Court of Justice shall have jurisdiction to give preliminary rulings concerning:
(a) the interpretation of this Treaty;
(b) the validity and interpretation of acts of the institutions of the Community and of the European Central Bank;
(c) the interpretation of the statutes of bodies established by an act of the Council, where those statutes so provide.

Where such a question is raised before any court or tribunal of a Member State, that court or tribunal may, if it considers that a decision on the question is necessary to enable it to give judgment, request the Court of Justice to give a ruling thereon.

Where any such question is raised in a case pending before a court or tribunal of a Member State against whose decisions there is no judicial remedy under national law, that court or tribunal shall bring the matter before the Court of Justice.

---

1   OFT, *Super-complaints: Guidance for Designated Consumer Bodies*, a consultation paper, August 2002, para. 2.2.
2   Section 4 of the 1998 Act provides: '(1) The Director may grant an exemption from the Chapter I prohibition with respect to a particular agreement . . . (3) The exemption (a) may be granted subject to such conditions or obligations as the Director considers it appropriate to impose.'
3   Section 5 of the 1998 Act provides: '(1) If the Director has reasonable grounds for believing that there has been a material change of circumstance since he granted an individual exemption, he may by notice in writing . . . (c) impose one or more additional conditions or obligations.'
4   'The exemption . . . (b) has effect for such period as the Director considers appropriate.'
5   'An individual exemption may be granted so as to have effect from a date earlier than that on which it is granted.'
6   References below to 's.47A' or 's.47B' should be taken to be references to those sections in the Competition Act 1998.

4 NEW MEANS OF ENFORCEMENT: THE CARTEL OFFENCE AND DISQUALIFICATION OF DIRECTORS

THE NEW OFFENCE

4.1 One of the most radical innovations of the Act is the criminalisation of competition law, through the introduction of the new 'cartel offence' in Part 6 of the Act (ss.188–202). This offence, applicable only to individuals, arises where the defendant 'dishonestly agrees with one or more other persons to make or implement, or to cause to be made or implemented, arrangements [of the kind described in subsection (2)] relating to at least two undertakings (A and B)' (s.188(1)).

4.2 The government deliberately targeted individuals rather than companies involved in anti-competitive agreements. If companies were to be targeted, through increased fines set at an optimal level to disincentivise cartel behaviour, many would go into liquidation, with all the consequent economic and social disadvantages. By targeting individuals, the government was convinced that it would catch the right people: '[t]he Government wishes to ensure that the law targets those who set up and maintain the cartel, as well as any senior executives or directors who know about the arrangement and condone or encourage it'.[1]

4.3 The scope of the offence is limited to acts taking place within the UK or which affect the UK market. The essential features of the offence are therefore:

- dishonesty on the part of an individual;
- an agreement with one or more other persons to:
  - make;
  - implement;
  - cause to be made; or
  - cause to be implemented;
- arrangements of the kind described in subsection 2;
- relating to at least two undertakings.

DISHONESTY

4.4 In designing the offence, the government had identified two alternative approaches: the first would make it unlawful for a person to participate in 'an agreement whose purpose is one or more . . . hard-core cartel activities . . . where the agreement also involves a breach of either Article 81 EC Treaty or the equivalent prohibition of the Competition Act 1998 (Chapter I)'.[2] The disadvantage of such an approach would have been that, unless there was a pre-existing decision that such an infringement had occurred, it would be necessary for the court hearing the cartel offence case to determine that an infringement had taken place, as a precondition for examining the liability of the defendant. As the government pointed out, this could 'require a lay jury with no competition expertise to consider potentially complex economic arguments'.[3] The second approach, and the one adopted in the Act, is to establish an offence based on 'the dishonest participation in an agreement which has, as a purpose, one or more of the specified hard-core cartel activities. A jury would need to determine whether a defendant had acted dishonestly. A defendant could use as his defence the claim that he honestly believed he was acting in accordance with Article 81 or Chapter I'.[4]

4.5   In adopting the 'dishonesty' approach, the government stated that it had recognised 'the need to define carefully the criminal offence so as to make it clear that only individuals actively involved in agreements which could never be exempt would be caught. The government has no desire to criminalise involvement in benign agreements which would not be unlawful under existing competition law'.[5] A paper prepared for the OFT also recommended that the definition of the offence should, so far as possible, exclude those activities which could arguably attract exemption under UK or EC law.[6] The cartel offence is much broader than the classic price-fixing cartel, incorporating a broad range of anticompetitive arrangements such as limiting supply or production, market-sharing, customer sharing and bid-rigging arrangements. Some of these activities are regarded as hard core or per se anti-competitive in other jurisdictions. For example, horizontal price-fixing and bid-rigging arrangements are universally excoriated as being contrary to the requirements of free and competitive markets.

4.6   There are, however, occasions on which customer-sharing and market-sharing arrangements are either not significantly anti-competitive or even may be efficiency enhancing. The requirement on the prosecution to show that the defendant was dishonest means that it is insufficient merely to demonstrate that the defendant agreed to make the arrangements, except perhaps in the hardest of the hard-core activities (horizontal price-fixing and bid-rigging) where it would be difficult for an individual to maintain a successful defence of honesty. The breadth of the offence will therefore afford a defence that the parties did not realise what they were doing was dishonest and contrary to the law.[7]

4.7   The test for dishonesty in England and Wales is that adopted by the Court of Appeal in *R v. Ghosh*,[8] i.e. whether what was done by the individual was dishonest by the ordinary standards of reasonable and honest people and, if so, whether the defendant realised that his actions were dishonest according to those standards. Dishonesty only arises where the jury is certain of both of these matters, beyond reasonable doubt.[9]

AGREEMENT

4.8   It is clear that the agreement to which the defendant is a party need not be a formal transaction. The government chose not to use the word 'conspiracy' in this context, preferring the ordinary meaning of 'agree'. Being a criminal offence, conspiracy is available to the prosecution authorities, as are the offences of aiding and abetting, and so on. It is for the jury to determine whether the circumstances can be said to amount to an agreement.

ARRANGEMENTS WITHIN THE SCOPE OF THE OFFENCE

4.9   The arrangements agreed upon by the individual defendant must be of the kind set out in s.188(2) and (3). Although the term is not used in the section, the arrangements are horizontal in nature. This is a result of the terms used in s.188(2)(d), (e) and (f), and as a result of the combination of paras. (a), (b) and (c) of that subsection with the three paragraphs of subsection (3) and with s.189. Section 188(2) and (3) describes the arrangements in terms of the required minimum participation of two undertakings, referred to in the section as A and B, and describes them in terms of the effects the arrangements would achieve if operating as the parties to the agreement intend. There is therefore no requirement for the intended effects to have occurred, so long as there is evidence that the defendant *and* the other parties intended those effects to have been achieved. It is therefore not open to the defendant to plead that the agreement was unsuccessful in its objects. The arrangements include those described in the following paragraphs.

Horizontal price fixing

4.10   Under s.188(2)(a), the arrangements must amount to directly or indirectly fixing a price for the supply by A in the UK of a product or service, otherwise than to B (i.e. to a third party), *and* for the supply by B in the UK of a product or service, otherwise than to A (s.188(2)(a) and (3)(a)). The prosecution must also show that the products or services are, or would be, supplied by A and B at the same level in the supply chain (i.e. that the arrangements would be horizontal). This latter requirement arises as a result of a combination of ss.188(4) and 189(1) and (5).

Limiting or preventing supply

4.11   Under s.188(2)(b), the arrangements must amount to the limiting or prevention of supply by A *and* by B in the UK of a product or service (s.188(2)(b) and (3)(b)). The prosecution must also show that A and B supply, or would have supplied, the products or services at the same level in the supply chain (ss.188(4), 189(2) and (6)).

Limiting or preventing production

4.12   Under s.188(2)(c), the arrangements must amount to the limiting or pre-vention by A *and* by B in the UK of a product (s.188(2)(c) and (3)(c)). The prosecution must also show that A and B supply, or would have supplied, the products or services at the same level in the supply chain (ss.188(4), 189(3) and (7)). There is no need to demonstrate that the product would have been supplied in the UK. Since this offence is deliberately not linked to the concept of the Chapter I prohibition, an effect on trade within the UK, or an effect on the UK market, is not required. See also the discussion on territorial jurisdiction in paras. 4.17 to 4.18.

Market-sharing

4.13   Under s.188(2)(d), the arrangements must amount to dividing between A and B the supply in the UK of a product or service to a customer or customers, where A and B supply the product or service at the same level in the supply chain (ss.188(4), 189(3) and (7)); or dividing between A and B customers for the supply in the UK of a product or service (s.188(2)(e)).

Bid-rigging arrangements

4.14   Under s.188(2)(f), the arrangements must amount to bid-rigging, i.e. where the response to a request for bids for the supply of products or services within the UK, or for the production of a product in the UK, takes one of the following forms: A but not B may make a bid; or A and B may each make a bid but in relation to either or both of them, the bid is one arrived at in accordance with the arrangements (s.188(2)(f) and (5)). These cover the classic bid-rigging scenarios, where there is an agreement that only one member of the ring will enter a bid, or where the members of the ring agree who will make the winning bid. Arrangements do not count as bid-rigging if the person requesting the bid is told of them before or at the time the bid is made. Although this may take the individuals concerned outside the arena of the cartel offence, presumably because the requesting person is not defrauded, the arrangements may be an infringement by the participating undertakings of Part I of the 1998 Act. It may also amount to the exercise by the undertakings of joint dominance under Part II of that Act.

Penalty

4.15   In considering the level of penalty, the government had regard to offences which have similar characteristics, such as insider dealing and obtaining property by deception. It also had regard to offences similar to the cartel offence in other jurisdictions, such as Canada and Japan, where there are penalties of five years' imprisonment for engaging in cartels, and in the USA, where the maximum sentence is three years' imprisonment. The government was in no doubt that the offence should be regarded as a serious one: '[h]ard-core cartels are serious conspiracies which defraud business customers and consumers and have wide economic impacts . . . they jeopardise the interests of shareholders, creditors and employees. Their costs to the global economy runs [sic] into billions of dollars. The offence merits a strong sentence'.[10] The White Paper indicated that the Act should not provide for fines as an alternative to custody, in order to avoid the possibility of the fines being paid by employers (who are the main beneficiaries of the cartel). However, the Act does so provide.

4.16   Under s.190, the offence is triable either way, i.e. on indictment or by summary conviction. On indictment, the maximum sentence is five years' imprisonment or an unlimited fine or both. On summary conviction, the maximum sentence is six months' imprisonment or a fine at the statutory maximum, or both. There is no possibility for private prosecutions for the cartel offence (for example by or on behalf of consumers who may have suffered as a result of a price-fixing arrangement). Indeed, prosecutions cannot even be instigated in the normal way by the Crown Prosecution Service. Under s.190(2), proceedings for the cartel offence may only be instituted by the Director of the Serious Fraud Office, or by (or with the consent of) the OFT.

Territorial jurisdiction

4.17   The UK has traditionally had disdain for claims to extraterritoriality of competition law, especially those based on the 'effects doctrine' under which jurisdiction is claimed in respect of acts committed anywhere if they have an effect on the market of the state claiming jurisdiction. Section 190 therefore limits the territorial scope of the cartel offence, in a manner in keeping with the approach adopted by the European Court of Justice in the *Woodpulp* case ([1985] 3 CMLR 474). Under s.190(3), no proceedings can be brought for agreements concluded outside the UK 'unless it has been implemented in whole or in part in the United Kingdom'. Thus, merely because the parties have concluded the agreement offshore does not mean that it cannot form the basis for a prosecution – where it has been put into effect in the UK. The expression 'implemented' has been taken from the European Court of Justice judgment in *A Ahlstrom and others v. Commission (Woodpulp)* [1993] ECR I-01307 which held that a price-fixing agreement concluded outside the EU could be regulated under Article 85 (now Article 81) EC Treaty where it was implemented in the EU.

4.18   By requiring an agreement concluded overseas to have 'been implemented' in the UK, the extraterritorial scope is narrower than is provided for in the definition of the cartel offence itself in s.188. In that section, an offence is committed where the arrangements have the specified anti-competitive characteristics, had they been operating as the parties to the agreement intend. In other words, if the arrangements do not in fact operate in that way, or do not operate at all, it is still enough that the parties agreed to make (etc.) those arrangements. In the case of prosecutions brought in respect of agreements made abroad, it appears that no prosecution may be brought unless the arrangements *have been implemented* in the UK (whether or not they had the intended effects).

'NO-ACTION' LETTERS FROM THE OFT

4.19   Section 190(4) enables the OFT to give a person notice that no action will be taken against him. Where such a letter is sent, no proceedings may be brought under s.188 for an offence described in that notice, except in the circumstances specified in the notice. This immunity from prosecution does not apply to proceedings in Scotland, where no guarantee can be given. However, the OFT has indicated that cooperation by an individual will be reported to the Lord Advocate who can take this into account in deciding whether or not to prosecute the individual.

4.20   Section 190(4) and the 'no-action' letters are part of a wider scheme under which leniency and immunity from penalties has been successfully used by competition authorities to encourage early and full reporting of cartel behaviour. The recently revised leniency programme of the European Commission[11] and the scheme adopted by the OFT under the Competition Act 1998[12] were devised in the light of the leniency policy schemes established in the USA. The existing EU and UK leniency schemes concern only the civil liability of undertakings; the scheme of s.190 extends this to immunity from prosecution. The draft guidelines published by the OFT provide for immunity from prosecution to be sought as part of an approach by an undertaking for immunity from fines or leniency under either the UK or the EU leniency programmes. These sanctuary provisions are extraordinary. The OFT has explained the reasons behind the government's approach:

> [I]t is the secret nature of cartels and their damaging effects that justify such a policy. The interests of customers and end-consumers in ensuring that such practices are detected and brought to an end outweigh the policy objectives of imposing penalties on those individuals who have committed an offence but who co-operate with the OFT and, where appropriate, any other competition authorities.[13]

4.21   The OFT envisages that a no-action letter will not be required by most employees of a company that is party to the specified anti-competitive arrangements. It is only those employees who have been dishonest within the meaning of s.188 who will require such immunity. In the OFT's view, most employees will not fall within the definition of 'dishonest' under the *Ghosh* test described above. Those who were not involved in making the arrangements, and who are unaware of its existence, are clearly not dishonest. Those who were not involved in making the arrangements but become aware of its existence fall into two types, according to the OFT.[14] Managers or directors fall into the first category. Such employees and office holders who, on discovering the existence of a cartel and then take steps to end it *and* to report its existence to the OFT 'cannot be said to have behaved dishonestly'. It is, of course, for the jury, and not the OFT, to determine the dishonesty or otherwise of a defendant. It is quite possible, therefore, that a manager or director who does less than indicated above – for example ends the arrangements immediately on their discovery but does not report them to the OFT – may also be regarded as not being dishonest. The OFT's second category includes employees other than managers or directors. Such employees who become aware of the existence of a cartel, are not involved in its operations, and do nothing to end it, are not guilty of a criminal offence according to the OFT. Although, as stated above, it is not for the OFT to determine the guilt or otherwise of an individual, these statements give clear guidance as to the OFT's prosecutorial intentions.

4.22   The OFT also divides into three types those employees who have engaged in cartel activity.[15] The first type comprises employees who knowingly engaged in cartel activity but whose involvement is 'peripheral'. The OFT will exercise its prosecutorial discretion not to prosecute these individuals. The second type comprises those who are 'more closely involved' but who come forward and co-operate at an early stage. This group is 'unlikely to face prosecution'. Both such categories may, of course, include individuals who are dishonest or not dishonest. The OFT's statement relates only to the likelihood of these individuals being prosecuted. Although its view is that neither category of individuals will need a no-action letter, any such individual who wishes to secure freedom from doubt will most probably earnestly seek a letter. The third category comprise those who, 'although not ring leaders or instigators have participated fully in the activities of the cartel, sometimes over an extended period'. These individuals will require a no-action letter in order to avoid the possibility of prosecution. This leaves those employees who were ring leaders or instigators; they are not entitled to no-action letters.

4.23   The OFT has issued draft guidelines on the conditions and procedures for the issuance of no-action letters.[16] Under these guidelines, the individual seeking immunity from prosecution must:

(a) admit participation in the criminal offence;
(b) provide the OFT with *all* the information, documents and other evidence available to him regarding the existence and activities of the cartel;
(c) maintain continuous and complete cooperation throughout the investigation until the conclusion of the criminal proceedings;
(d) not have acted as the instigator or played the leading role in the cartel;[17] and
(e) refrain from participating further after the time they disclose the cartel, except as directed by the investigating authority.

4.24   The caveat to the last condition indicates that the OFT or other investigating authority may use the individual to set up a 'sting', or act as an insider, until they have acquired sufficient evidence to prosecute other guilty individuals and/or bring infringement proceedings under Part I of the 1998 Act.

4.25   Even when all the conditions are satisfied, the OFT will not issue a no-action letter if it already had sufficient information to bring a successful prosecution. There is no express opportunity under the guidelines for an individual to make a 'hypothetical' approach to the OFT, as is the case under the European Commission's leniency programme under Article 81. However, an approach may be made by a lawyer representing the individual, and it remains to be seen whether the OFT will accept such an approach on behalf of an unnamed individual.

4.26 The OFT's draft procedure may be used either as a means of acquiring a no-action letter or for an early determination as to whether they are liable to be prosecuted in Scotland. In both cases, the approach should be to the OFT's Director of Cartel Investigations. This approach may be made by any of the following:

- the individual himself;
- a lawyer representing the individual;
- an undertaking seeking leniency under the OFT's leniency programme relating to the 1998 Act, or under the European Commission's leniency programme. In this case, the approach must be on behalf of named employees.

4.27 Following the approach, the Director of Cartel Investigations will give an 'early indication' of the likelihood of the OFT issuing a no-action letter. Where the approach has been made in combination with an application by the relevant undertaking for leniency under the OFT or European Commission scheme, a grant of leniency to the undertaking will 'normally' be accompanied by a grant of a no-action letter to the named individuals requiring them.

4.28 If the OFT is open to issue a no-action letter, it will first require the individual to attend an interview or a series of interviews, at which the individual will be required to provide information to the OFT. Even where no immunity is granted following such interviews, the information provided by the individual will not be used against him in criminal proceedings. As an exception to this, if the individual knowingly or recklessly provides false or misleading information during this interview, the OFT may rely on any information given by him during the interview in a prosecution against him for the cartel offence. Moreover, any immunity that has been granted will be retrospectively withdrawn on the discovery that the individual had acted in the way described above.

4.29 Following the interview, the individual is entitled to discuss the question of immunity. At this stage, the OFT will issue a no-action letter (though not necessarily at that time), so long as there is otherwise a likelihood of prosecution and the individual fulfils all the conditions described in para. 4.23.[18]

4.30 No-action letters, once issued, may be withdrawn if the individual fails to fulfil any of the conditions. It may also be withdrawn if there were 'material inaccuracies in the information given to the OFT'.[19] This is in addition to the threat of withdrawal for the knowing or reckless provision of false or misleading information during the interview. It is therefore possible that if the individual honestly provides materially inaccurate information, his immunity may be withdrawn. The no-action letter may also be withdrawn if documents or other information have been withheld by the individual.

4.31 Approaches for immunity from prosecution may be made by individuals without the knowledge or consent of their employers, or (in most cases) of the other parties to the anti-competitive arrangements. Individuals will often, therefore, have a significant interest in maintaining their anonymity. For this reason, the OFT intends to withhold from the public domain any information which might identify individuals who have received no-action letters. This is subject only to obligations to disclose such identity in criminal proceedings or 'when there is an overriding public interest in doing so'.[20]

4.32   The OFT has issued a draft no-action letter as part of its consultation exercise. The letter articulates the conditions and other matters discussed above, and is annexed to the OFT's consultation document.[21]

EXTRADITION

4.33   Under s.191, extradition arrangements under s.2 Extradition Act 1870 apply to the cartel offence, conspiracy to commit the cartel offence, and an attempt to commit the cartel offence.

CARTEL OFFENCE: OFT POWERS OF INVESTIGATION

4.34   The OFT has extremely wide powers of investigation to determine whether a cartel offence has occurred. The threshold for triggering such powers are the same as those which give rise to the, more modest, investigatory powers under s.25 of the 1998 Act, i.e. where there are 'reasonable grounds for suspecting' that the cartel offence has been committed (s.192(1)). Section 192(2) is somewhat otiose in that it directs the OFT to exercise those powers only where it appears to it that there is good reason to do so.

4.35   The powers available to the OFT include:

- requiring persons to answer questions or to produce documents;
- entering premises under warrant; and
- undertaking 'intrusive surveillance' operations.

Powers of interrogation

4.36   Under s.193, the OFT may *require* persons to answer questions, provide information and/or produce specified documents or documents of a specified description. A document includes information recorded in any form (s.202). This power extends not only to the person under investigation but also to any other person who the OFT has reason to believe has relevant information. These powers are draconian; under s.201, conviction on indictment for failure to comply with the request may lead to a prison term of up to two years, or to a fine, or both (on summary conviction the maximum penalties are six months imprisonment or a fine at the statutory maximum, or both). In consequence, there are certain procedural safeguards. First, the OFT must send a written notice to the person subject to these powers (unless entry to premises is authorised under s.194). Under s.193(5), the notice must indicate the subject matter and the purpose of the investigation, and state that it is an offence to fail to comply with the notice.

4.37   The second procedural safeguard is that the evidence gathered under the powers described above may only be used in evidence against the person giving it in very limited circumstances. Such statements cannot be used in the prosecution of the individual for the cartel offence, since there would otherwise be an egregious departure from the requirements of the Human Rights Act 1998. Section 197 provides that a statement made by a person in response to an interrogation under s.193 may *only* be used against him:

(a) for an offence under s.201(2) (deliberately or recklessly making a false or misleading statement);
(b) in a prosecution for *another* offence where in giving evidence he makes a statement inconsistent with the statement made under s.193.

The 1998 Act is also amended by the inclusion of a new s.30A, so that any statement made to the OFT under the powers of ss.26 to 28 (provision of information and documents, entry of premises without warrant, and entry of premises with warrant) cannot be used against the person making it in a prosecution against him for a cartel offence, unless the statement made in the cartel offence proceedings are inconsistent with those made in response to the Competition Act proceedings *and* evidence relating to his statement is adduced or he asks a question relating to it (s.198).

4.38   The OFT may take copies of or extracts from any documents produced by a person under these powers, and it may require the person producing them to provide explanations of them.

Entry under warrant

4.39   As in the exercise of its powers under the 1998 Act, the OFT may make an application to the court under the 2002 Act for a warrant to enter premises. The application procedure is similar to that under the 1998 Act, except that in Scotland the application is made by the procurator-fiscal to the sheriff. The application must demonstrate that there are reasonable grounds for believing that there are documents on the relevant premises the production of which the OFT could have ordered under s.193, *and* either it is not practical to serve a notice under s.193, or the service of a notice 'might seriously prejudice the investigation' (s.194(1)(b)). A warrant issued under s.194 entitles the named OFT officer (or another person authorised by the OFT to carry out these activities) to enter using reasonably necessary force; he may search the premises and either take possession of documents appearing to be relevant, or take other steps to prevent interference with them. The OFT officer can also require any person for an explanation of any such document or to state where a document may be found. In other words, there is a duty of active assistance during the course of a search under warrant.

4.40   This extends to information stored in any electronic form that is accessible from the premises. The OFT officer can require such information to be produced in transportable, visible and legible form.

4.41   The search procedures also benefit from the wide powers of seizure available by virtue of s.50 Criminal Justice and Police Act 2001. That section enables a person lawfully conducting a search to remove property that may turn out to be non-seizable if it is not reasonably practicable to determine that at the time. That section also entitles such a person to take non-seizable material if it is not reasonably practicable to separate it from seizable material (s.194(5)).

4.42   The right to seize documents does not extend to legally privileged documents, or to documents which are confidential by virtue of the fact that the person concerned carries on a banking business. However, this last protection is removed if the person to whom the confidential information relates has consented, or if 'the OFT has authorised the making of the requirement' (s.196(2)(b)).

Other provisions concerning powers of entry

4.43   Section 203 amends certain of the provisions of the Competition Act 1998 in relation to powers of entry. Section 28 of the 1998 Act is amended by the insertion of subsection (3A), enabling a search warrant issued under that section to authorise named persons to accompany the OFT officer. Sections 62 and 63 of the 1998 Act are amended by the insertion of subsection (5A) into each, making similar provisions in relation to a search carried out as part of European Commission investigations or OFT special investigations respectively.

Intrusive surveillance

4.44   Section 199 of the Act amends the Regulation of Investigatory Powers Act 2000 (the 2000 Act), in a manner which gives the chairman of the OFT the power to authorise intrusive surveillance. For these purposes, 'intrusive surveillance' is a type of 'covert surveillance', which in turn is a type of 'surveillance'. All these terms are defined by the 2000 Act. Surveillance includes: (a) monitoring, observing or listening to persons, their movements, their conversations or their other activities or communications; (b) recording anything monitored, observed or listened to in the course of surveillance; and (c) surveillance by or with the assistance of a surveillance device (s.48(2), 2000 Act). Surveillance also includes the interception of a postal communication or a telecommunication if, and only if, the communication is one sent by or intended for a person who has consented to the interception of communications sent by or to him, and there is no interception warrant authorising the interception. Covert surveillance is surveillance that is 'carried out in a manner that is calculated to ensure that persons who are subject to the surveillance are unaware that it is or may be taking place' (s.26(9)(a), 2000 Act). Intrusive surveillance is covert surveillance that: (a) is carried out in relation to anything taking place on any residential premises or in any private vehicle; and (b) involves the presence of an individual on the premises or in the vehicle or is carried out by means of a surveillance device (other than one designed or adapted principally for the purpose of providing information about the location of a vehicle) (s.26(3) and (4), 2000 Act). Covert surveillance carried out by means of a surveillance device that is outside the relevant premises or vehicle is intrusive only if the device is such 'that it consistently provides information of the same quality and detail as might be expected to be obtained from a device actually present on the premises or in the vehicle' (s.26(4), 2000 Act). Covert surveillance comprising the kind of communications interception described above is not intrusive.

4.45 Under s.32(3A) of the 2000 Act, inserted by s.199(2) of the 2002 Act, the chairman of the OFT, acting on an application by an OFT officer, can authorise intrusive surveillance. In order to do so, he has to satisfy two criteria. First, the intrusive surveillance must be necessary for the purpose of preventing or detecting a cartel offence, *and* that surveillance must be proportionate to what is sought to be achieved by carrying it out.

4.46 The OFT is also granted the extensive powers to interfere with property provided under the Police Act 1997, through suitable amendments made under s.200 of the 2002 Act.

OTHER ACTION AGAINST INDIVIDUALS: COMPETITION DISQUALIFICATION ORDERS

4.47 In addition to the power to prosecute individuals for the cartel offence described in ss.188 to 190, the Act also provides for the disqualification (for up to 15 years) of a director where the company of which he is a director commits a breach of competition law, and his conduct in that regard is culpable.

4.48 Section 204 amends the Company Directors Disqualification Act 1986 (the 1986 Act) by inserting a new s.9A into that Act ('Disqualification for competition infringements'). Under the new s.9A, the High Court or the Court of Session must make a disqualification order against a director where the company of which he was the director commits a breach of competition law *and* the court considers that his conduct as a director 'makes him unfit to be concerned in the management of a company' (s.9A(1)(2) and (3), 1986 Act).

4.49 The Order is made on the application of the OFT or of a 'specified regulator', i.e. those for telecommunications, gas and electricity, water services, rail and civil aviation. The 1986 Act also now contains (in new s.9D) arrangements for the coordination of the concurrent powers of the OFT and specified regulators.

4.50 The breaches of competition law envisaged in these provisions are infringements of the Chapter I or Chapter II prohibitions of the Competition Act 1998 (interpreted consistently with EC competition law) or of Articles 81 or 82 EC Treaty. Where it is not clear if the breach has occurred, but the OFT or a specified regulator has reasonable grounds for suspecting that it has, then the OFT or the regulator has the same powers of investigation as are available for investigations by the OFT under s.25 Competition Act 1998 (new s.9C(2) of the 1986 Act).

4.51   As to the director's conduct (which may take the form of an omission), there are certain things that the court must, may and must not have regard to in determining whether the director is unfit.

The court *must* have regard to whether:

■   the director's conduct contributed to the breach of competition law (whether or not he knew that the conduct constituted a breach of competition law);
■   where it did not so contribute, but he had reasonable grounds to suspect that the company's conduct was in breach and he did nothing to prevent it; or
■   he did not know, but ought to have known, that the company's conduct was in breach.

The court *may* have regard to the conduct of the director in connection with any other breach of competition law.

The court *must not* have regard to the matters mentioned in Sched. 1 to the 1986 Act, i.e. the director's fiduciary duty to act honestly and for the benefit of the company; his duty to act with that degree of skill as may reasonably be expected of a person with the director's knowledge and experience; his duty to comply with other statutory obligations, under companies legislation; and the extent to which the unfit conduct affects his ability to manage the company.

4.52   As an alternative to making a competition disqualification order, the OFT or a specified regulator can accept a competition undertaking from the director concerned, under which he undertakes not to do the things that he would have been prohibited from doing had the order been made (new s.9B of the 1986 Act).

---

1   *A World Class Competition Policy*, Department of Trade and Industry, July 2001, Cm. 5233 (hereafter, White Paper), para. 7.27.
2   White Paper, para. 7.29.
3   Ibid., para. 7.30.
4   Ibid., para. 7.31.
5   Ibid., para. 7.26.
6   Sir Anthony Hammond and Roy Penrose, *Proposed Criminalisation of Cartels in the UK*, OFT 365, Office of Fair Trading, November 2001 (hereafter *Proposed Criminalisation*).
7   *Proposed Criminalisation* sought a regime that would not afford such a defence: see para. 2.5.
8   *R* v. *Ghosh* [1982] QB 1053, CA.
9   See also the OFT's views on dishonesty, and its likely prosecutorial policy, in the discussions in paras. 4.21 to 4.22.
10   White Paper, para. 7.35.
11   *Commission Notice on Immunity from Fines or Reduction of Fines in Cartel Cases*, 2002 OJ C45/3.
12   *Director General of Fair Trading's Guidance as to the Appropriate Amount of Penalty*.
13   OFT, *The Cartel Offence: No-action Letters for Individuals*, a consultation document, July 2002 (hereafter, OFT *No-action Letters*), para. 1.1.
14   See OFT, *No-action Letters*, paras. 1.6 and 1.7.
15   *Ibid.*, paras 1.8 and 1.9.
16   *Ibid.*, paras 3.1 to 3.8.
17   The alternative words suggested by the OFT in its consultation document are that the individual did not compel others to take part in the cartel.

18 For individuals who may be prosecuted in Scotland, the OFT will report the co-operation to the Lord Advocate with a request for an early decision on the individual's liability to prosecution.
19 OFT consultation document, para. 3.7.
20 *Ibid.*, Annex A
21 *Ibid.*, Annex A.

5 MERGER CONTROL UNDER THE ACT

TRANSACTIONS TO WHICH THE ACT APPLIES

5.1   Under the 1973 Act, a merger situation qualified for investigation if it satisfied the 'share of supply test', or the 'assets test'. The assets test was satisfied if the total assets of the acquired enterprise amounted to more than £70 million. The assets test has been removed. Under the Act, the critical financial threshold is whether the UK turnover of the target enterprise exceeds £70 million.

5.2   The Act applies to transactions which are considered to give rise to 'a relevant merger situation'. Under ss.23 and 24 of the Act a 'relevant merger situation' has been created if two or more enterprises ceased to be distinct enterprises during the period mentioned below (see para. 5.16); and either:

 (i) the value of the turnover in the UK of the enterprise being taken over exceeds £70 million ('the turnover test') (s.23(1)); or
(ii) as a result, at least one quarter of goods or services of any description which are supplied in the UK are supplied by, or to, one and the same person, or by, or to, the persons carrying on the enterprises ('the share of supply test') (s.23(3) and (4)). Where the enterprises already held a 25% share of supply, the test is satisfied if the transaction increases that share. For example, a combination of 30% and 1% satisfies the test, but a combination of 80% and 0% does not.

5.3   An enterprise is defined as the activities, or part of the activities, of a business (s.129(1)).

5.4   Services are defined in s.128.[1]

5.5   It is to be noted that there is no requirement for any of the enterprises to be carried on in the UK or by or under the control of a body corporate incorporated in the UK. Sections 23 and 24 of the Act no longer contain this requirement (which was a feature of the 1973 Act). Now the link with the UK is the value of UK turnover of the enterprise being taken over, or the share of the supply of the UK market.

ENTERPRISES CEASING TO BE DISTINCT ENTERPRISES

5.6   Section 26 of the Act provides that enterprises cease to be distinct if they are brought under common ownership or common control. This is regardless of whether a business to which either of them formerly belonged continues to be carried on under the same or different ownership or control.

5.7   The additional test provided in s.65(1) of the 1973 Act (where enterprises were also considered to cease to be distinct if either them ceases to be carried on in the UK as a consequence of an arrangement or transaction between the enterprises to prevent competition) is not included in the Act.

Control

5.8   Section 26(2) identifies a number of situations in which enterprises will be considered as being 'under common control'. These situations are where they are:

(a) enterprises of interconnected bodies corporate;
(b) enterprises carried on by two or more bodies corporate of which one and the same person or group of persons has control; or
(c) an enterprise is carried on by a body corporate and another enterprise is carried on by a person or group of persons having control of that body corporate.

5.9   Section 26(3) defines 'control' as the ability of a person or group of persons: (a) directly or indirectly to control; or (b) materially to influence the policy of an enterprise, or the person carrying on that enterprise (but without actually having a controlling interest). These provisions are the same as the corresponding provisions of s.65 of the 1973 Act. The OFT's guidelines on mergers (draft of October 2002, hereafter 'OFT draft guidelines') explain that control is not limited to the acquisition of outright voting control, but includes situations falling short of outright control.

5.10   Enterprises are also brought under common control where there is a change in the nature of control, i.e.:

(a) where a person or group of persons who are already able to control or materially influence the policy of the person carrying on the enterprise, acquires a controlling interest in the enterprise or a controlling interest in a body corporate; or
(b) where a person or group of persons who are already able materially to influence the policy of the person carrying on the enterprise, becomes able to control that policy (s.26(4)).

5.11   Whether a shareholder can materially influence the policy of the company concerned is not only determined by the size of his shareholding. Other key factors include: the distribution of the remaining shares; whether the shareholder has representation on the board; any agreements with the company which allow the shareholder to have influence; and special provisions allowing for voting rights (for example, weighted or veto rights).

5.12   The OFT will regard a shareholding of 25 per cent (which enables the holder to block special resolutions) as likely to confer the ability materially to influence policy. This is the case even if the remaining shareholding is held by one person. A shareholding of as little as 15 per cent may confer the ability materially to influence the policy of an enterprise. In exceptional circumstances, a shareholding of less than 15 per cent may do so if, for example, the shareholder has board representation or control rights.

Associated persons

5.13   Section 127 states that 'associated persons' and any bodies corporate which they or any of them control (within the broad meaning of 'control') shall be treated as one person for the purposes of deciding whether any two enterprises have been brought under common ownership or common control and for the purpose of determining what activities or business activities are carried on by any one person (in the event that an order is to be made to acquire or divide a business under Sched. 8, para. 13(2)).

5.14   Associated persons are defined in s.127(4) as including the following groupings:

(a)   an individual and his or her spouse or partner and any 'relative',[2] or spouse or partner of a relative, of that individual or of that individual's spouse or partner;

(b)   any person in his capacity as trustee of a settlement and the settlor or grantor and any person associated with them;

(c)   persons carrying on business in partnership and the spouse or partner and relatives of any of them; and

(d)   two or more persons acting together to secure or exercise control of a body of persons corporate or unincorporate or to secure control of any enterprise or assets.

Joint control

5.15   It is possible that two or more major shareholders may 'control' a company. This will be the case, for example, where one company has a controlling interest and another has an ability materially to influence the policy of the target. Control may be exercised by a person or a group of persons. Such control is regarded as common under s.26(2), 'in particular' where the group comprises interconnected bodies corporate or those under the control or ownership of common shareholders. However, circumstances may arise where it is necessary to consider whether two unrelated shareholders may be aggregated, so that together they can be said to exercise common control. No guidance has been issued on this aspect; however, the European Commission has issued guidelines for the purposes of defining when undertakings are under 'joint control' of two or more others (Commission Notice on the Concept of Concentration, 1998 OJ C66). In the European Commission's view, shareholders may be aggregated for these purposes either where there is an agreement between them to vote together, or where common voting is established on a de facto basis. The latter is described as 'very exceptional' and exists where there are strong common interests between the minority shareholders concerned so that they would not act against each other in exercising their voting rights. However, where there are changing coalitions between minority shareholders, it is unlikely that they should be aggregated.

Time limits

5.16   A transaction is a relevant merger situation only if it has taken place in the period and/or circumstances set out in ss.24 and 34. These provide that, for completed and anticipated mergers, the transaction must have taken place prior to the reference to the Commission, but not more than four months prior to that date. Alternatively, no such limitation period applies to merger transactions that have not been made public. Transactions will not count as having been made public unless the material facts (such as the identity of the parties and the subject matter of the transaction) were either given to the OFT or made public (through, for example, a press release) before the transaction took place or more than four months prior to the reference. The four-month period starts only once the transaction is the subject of such notice or publicity. The notice to the OFT does not have to be formal, or even in writing.

5.17   Section 25 of the Act provides that the four-month period may be extended by no more than 20 days, by agreement between the OFT and the persons carrying on the merged or merging enterprises.

5.18   The four-month period may also be extended by the OFT on giving notice to the persons carrying on the merged or merging enterprises, if it considers that those persons have failed to provide any relevant information within the period stated, or in the manner authorised or required in that notice (s.25(2)). An extension in this case begins with the end of the period within which the information is to be provided and ends with the provision of the information to the satisfaction of the OFT or, if earlier, the cancellation by the OFT of the extension.

5.19   The OFT may also extend the four-month period if it is seeking undertakings in lieu of a reference. An extension in this case begins with the receipt of the notice from the OFT extending the four-month period and ends with the earliest of: the giving of the undertaking concerned; the expiry of 10 days from the time the person from whom undertakings are being sought has stated that he does not intend to give undertakings; or a cancellation by the OFT of the extension.

5.20   The OFT may also extend the four-month period by notice, if the European Commission is considering (but is not yet proceeding with) a request made by the UK under Article 22(3) ECMR. The OFT is under a duty to inform the persons carrying on the merged or merging enterprises of the completion by the European Commission of its consideration under Article 22. An extension under this provision begins with the receipt of the notice that the four-month period is being extended, and ends with the receipt of the notice stating that the European Commission has completed its consideration.

5.21　Not more than one extension of the four-month period is possible.

5.22　In determining any time period described above, Saturdays, Sundays, Good Friday, Christmas Day, and other bank holidays in England and Wales are not taken into account.

5.23　Section 103 of the Act places an obligation on the OFT to act expeditiously in deciding whether to make a merger reference to the Commission, 'with a view to the prevention or removal of uncertainty'. Under s.103(2), the Secretary of State is placed under the same obligation in relation to decisions to refer public interest or special public interest cases to the Commission. Although this overall duty is a welcome addition, it would be extremely difficult for anyone affected by a delay to show that the duty had been broken, if the statutory periods are otherwise observed. Nevertheless, it enables a person to put the OFT or Secretary of State on notice that a person is minded to claim a breach of the duty, by way of a 'wake up call'.

5.24　Section 104 provides a general duty on the OFT, the Secretary of State and the Commission to consult persons whose interests are likely to be adversely affected by a proposed decision (e.g. to refer a matter to the Commission, to vary a reference, whether a relevant merger situation has arisen, or is in progress, whether it has resulted in a substantial lessening of competition, or is adverse to the public interest, whether remedial action is necessary, or to accept an undertaking in lieu of a reference.

THE TURNOVER TEST

5.25　The Act introduces, for the first time, the concept of a turnover test into the UK's merger control regime.

5.26　Section 28 explains how the turnover figure of £70 million is to be calculated. To calculate UK turnover, it is necessary to add the total value of the turnover in the UK of all the enterprises which cease to be distinct and then deduct the turnover in the UK of any enterprise which continues to be carried on under the same ownership and control. Where none of the enterprises remains under the same ownership and control, the value of the turnover is calculated by taking the sum of the turnovers of the enterprises ceasing to be distinct and then deducting the turnover of the highest value.

5.27　The Secretary of State may specify what constitutes the 'turnover' of an enterprise. The order may include the amounts which are and are not to be considered relevant in determining an enterprise's turnover; the date or dates by reference to which an enterprise's turnover is to be determined; and the connection with the UK by virtue of which an enterprise's turnover is 'turnover in the UK'.

5.28　At the time of writing, the Secretary of State has not yet published any orders in relation to turnover requirements. It is expected that these will be in force before or at the same time as the Act comes into force. It is expected that account will be taken of the approach of the ECMR, which bases turnover on the amounts derived by the relevant undertakings, in the preceding financial year, from the sale of products and the provision of services falling within 'the undertakings' ordinary activities' (Article 5 ECMR). From this sum are deducted sales rebates, value-added tax and other taxes directly related to turnover. Intra-enterprise turnover is not counted for these purposes. Special rules exist for calculating the turnover of credit and financial institutions (income from interest, securities and commissions, net profit on financial operations and other operating income) and for insurance undertakings (value of gross premiums written). The most recently published accounts are normally used for the purposes of calculating turnover, unless these are not a reliable guide (e.g. because of more recent acquisitions or disposals, or because only part of an undertaking is acquired).[3]

5.29   The £70 million value used for the turnover test gave rise to great controversy and debate during the passage of the Bill through the House of Commons and the House of Lords. The turnover threshold was set at £45 million until the third reading of the Bill in the House of Lords. It was the government's intention that it should be capable of catching roughly the same number of merger cases as did the assets test under the 1973 Act. The government stated that it did not intend to change the figure, but provision was made in the Act (s.28(6)) to change the figure if necessary.

5.30   The House of Lords amended the figure to £100 million, on the basis that, since turnover should be expected to exceed gross assets, the new turnover figure should exceed the old £70 million gross assets figure. The government was further criticised for failing to take into account inflation, as the last threshold was set in 1994. If inflation had been considered, the old figure of £70 million would be equivalent in real terms to £85 million; this should have been the benchmark figure from which to calculate the turnover test.

5.31   On the government's figures, only 7,000 companies would have been caught by the £45 million threshold. If it was raised to £100 million, that figure would be cut in half. This would bring the number of companies which may be open to review in line with the number of companies that qualified under the assets test of the 1973 Act.

5.32   Although the House of Commons accepted the Lords' proposal to amend the turnover figure, they did not agree to it being raised to as much as £100 million, preferring the figure of £70 million that was finally agreed on. This was because amending the threshold to £100 million 'runs a serious risk of allowing anti-competitive mergers to proceed without any form of scrutiny by the competition authorities' (Commons Debates, 30 October 2002, col. 928). The OFT estimated that approximately 50 per cent of the mergers that can be currently scrutinised would no longer be eligible for any form of investigation: 'far greater reliance would have to be placed on the share of supply test . . . [and this] goes against the grain of international notification regimes, which are invariably based on turnover thresholds' (Melanie Johnson, Commons Debates, 30 October 2002, col. 928). By having such a high turnover threshold, the government felt that there would be a risk that mergers involving small but potentially significant companies with low market shares would not be caught.

5.33   It was finally agreed to set the turnover threshold initially at £70 million, with the intention of keeping this figure under review to ensure that the threshold is maintained at an appropriate level (see s.28(5) and (6)).

Turnover in the UK

5.34   In keeping with the European Commission's approach to geographical allocation of turnover, the turnover test applies to the turnover of the acquired enterprise that was generated by customers within the UK at the time of completion of the merger or, if it has not yet taken place, at the time of reference to the Commission. The OFT will be publishing guidelines specifically on the application of the turnover test, before the Act comes into force.

SHARE OF SUPPLY TEST

5.35   The share of supply test, under s.23(3) and (4), is described in para. 5.2.

5.36   The share of supply test is not to be confused with the evaluation of the share of the relevant market, used in the assessment of mergers by the OFT or the Commission. The description of the goods or services used as a basis for determining whether a relevant merger situation has been created need not amount to a 'relevant market' (for a description of which see para. 5.94).

5.37   The OFT draft guidelines state that when considering what the relevant description of the goods or services should be, the OFT will generally have regard to the 'narrowest reasonable description' to determine whether the share of supply test is met. This practice is intended to provide predictability and certainty for companies and their advisers to determine whether the Act applies to a particular merger situation.

5.38   The share of supply test can be applied in relation to the UK as a whole or to a 'substantial part of it'. The Act, as with the 1973 Act, does not define 'a substantial part'. The UK courts have ruled that, for the purposes of merger control, while there can be no fixed definition, the area or areas to be considered must be of such size, character and importance to make it worth considering (*R. v. MMC and another, ex p. South Yorkshire Transport Ltd* [1993] 1 WLR 23). Factors that have been considered previously by the OFT, under the 1973 Act, include the size, population, social, political, economic, financial and geographic significance of the area affected by the proposed transaction.

5.39   In determining the share of supply, the OFT and the Commission have a very wide discretion in applying such criteria, or combination of criteria, as they consider appropriate. Share of supply can therefore be measured by reference to value, cost, price, quantity, capacity or number of workers employed, or by reference to any other measure.

5.40   The Commission draft guidelines on merger references (draft of September 2002, hereafter 'Commission Guidelines'), explain that when applying the share of supply test, the Commission will generally have regard to the value of the goods, taking into account any rebates or discounts offered.

5.41   The OFT and the Commission may have to consider whether to aggregate goods or services of a particular description, where they are made available by different forms of supply, i.e. where the supply transactions are materially different in terms of the nature of the transactions, the parties involved, the terms of supply or the circumstances surrounding them. In dealing with any such situation, the OFT and the Commission are given the freedom to describe the goods or services as being described by reference to the different forms of supply taken together, taken separately, or taken in groups (s.23(6) and (7)).

TIME WHEN ENTERPRISES CEASE TO BE DISTINCT

5.42   Section 27 provides for the application of merger control to cases where ownership or control of an enterprise is obtained over a period of time. Mergers are treated as having been completed at the moment when the parties become bound to such extent as will result in the enterprises ceasing to be distinct enterprises. The section makes clear that, in determining the time at which any two enterprises cease to be distinct, no account is to be taken of options that have not been exercised or conditional rights where the conditions have not been satisfied. In deciding whether it is appropriate to treat different arrangements or transactions as arrangements or transactions between the same interests, the decision-making authority shall, in particular, have regard to the persons 'substantially concerned' in the arrangements or transactions concerned.

ACQUIRING CONTROL BY STAGES (s.29)

5.43   Creeping mergers – those made by way of a series of transactions – sometimes present difficulties, since it is often hard to pinpoint the time at which undertakings ceased to be distinct. In order to plug this particular loophole, in cases where ownership or control has been acquired in the course of two or more transactions ('a series of transactions') the transactions may be treated, for the purposes of a reference, as all having occurred on the date of the last transaction – subject to a two-year cut-off period. The authorities do not therefore need to decide which of many individual transactions resulted in a change of control – provided the overall effect is such as to constitute a change of control.

5.44   This aggregation of transactions concerns those which lead to direct or indirect control of policy or to the ability materially to influence policy. It also concerns any transactions which enable such control or influence to be exercised to a greater degree than before. Additionally, where the transaction does not lead to such control or influence, but is a step towards it, it will also be subject to aggregation under s.29. Finally, a transaction which leads to the acquisition of a controlling interest will also be included in s.29. In sum, any series of transactions of the kind described above may be treated as having all occurred on the date of the last one. However, no account may be taken of any transaction that occurs after the acquisition of control of the target enterprise (s.29(3)). In addition, where the series of transactions takes place over a period of more than two years, the aggregation cannot include any transaction taking place more than two years prior to the most recent transaction included (s.29(4)).

DUTY TO MAKE A REFERENCE: COMPLETED AND ANTICIPATED MERGERS

5.45   A new and potentially very important function is provided for the OFT under ss.22 and 33 of the Act. Under the 1973 Act, the Director General's role was to advise whether a merger should be referred to the Commission for further investigation, and subsequently, if there was a reference, on what action to take after the Commission had reported. In cases where a merger was still being contemplated, he could, after consulting with the Secretary of State, provide confidential guidance to the parties involved and (where so requested by the Secretary of State), negotiate undertakings in lieu of a reference to the Commission.

5.46   Under s.22 of the Act, the OFT is now under a duty to make a reference to the Commission on a completed merger if it believes that it is (or may be) the case that:

  (i) a 'relevant merger situation' has been created; and
 (ii) the creation of that situation has resulted, or may be expected to result, in a 'substantial lessening of competition' within any market or markets in the UK for goods or services.

5.47   Under s.33 of the Act, the OFT is under a duty to make a reference to the Commission on an anticipated merger if it believes that it is (or may be) the case that:

  (i) arrangements are in progress or in contemplation which, if carried into effect, will result in the creation of a relevant merger situation; and
 (ii) the creation of that situation may be expected to result in a substantial lessening of competition within any market or markets in the UK for goods or services.

5.48   Section 22 gave rise to lengthy debate in the House of Commons. The issue concerned the perceived 'obligation' of the OFT to refer a merger as opposed to a discretion as to whether to do so. It was claimed that this shift would lead, in effect, to obligatory pre-clearance for mergers, resulting in extra burdens on industry and companies and on the OFT. The government stated that 'leaving Ministers out simply reflects that the OFT is expert on this', and maintained that the legislation would not have any effect on the amount of mergers taking place. The obligation to refer was defended in the following terms:

> Broad discretion on whether to refer is appropriate under the Fair Trading Act 1973, under which decisions are taken against a broad public-interest test and lie in the hands of Ministers, who are accountable to Parliament for their actions. However, if there is a more focused test, such as the . . . substantial lessening of competition, and the decision lies in the hands of an independent body, there should be less discretion.
> (Melanie Johnson, Commons Debates Standing Committee B, 25 April 2002, col. 258)

5.49   With respect to the minister, this is not quite right; there are very significant discretions available to the OFT. These are described in the next section.

EXCEPTIONS TO THE DUTY TO REFER

5.50   There are three circumstances, under ss.22 and 33, in which the OFT may exercise a discretion not to refer a merger to the Commission. These are where:

(i) the merger in progress or in contemplation is not likely to proceed or is insufficiently advanced to warrant a reference being made (s.33(2)(a));

(ii) the market or markets in question are 'not of sufficient importance' to warrant the making of a reference (s.22(2)(a) and s.33(2)(a)); or

(iii) there are countervailing customer benefits which would outweigh the adverse effects (s.22(2)(b) and s.33(2)(c)).

Merger is insufficiently advanced

5.51 The OFT states that, in practice it would take a view early in an investigation that no real competition analysis is required because of the early stage of proceedings, to prevent the expense of an unnecessary investigation where the parties are still not sure whether they will proceed. In such a situation, the parties are recommended to seek informal advice or confidential guidance from the OFT.

5.52   The OFT will regard a merger to be 'sufficiently advanced' if:

(i) the parties to the transaction have publicly announced a completed merger or their intention to merge (in whole or in part); or

(ii) one of the parties to a proposed transaction has announced an intention to make an offer for the other party (regardless of whether this may be subject to conditions or be a hostile bid).

Markets of insufficient importance

5.53   This exception is included to enable the OFT to refrain from making references where the costs involved would be disproportionate to the size of the markets concerned. The OFT's draft guidelines state that this exception is likely to apply only very rarely.

5.54 The OFT does not rule out the possibility of referring a merger taking place in such a market where:

- the product concerned is an important input into a larger market;
- the market is developing quickly, so the size of the market at the time of the merger is not an indicator of the potential size or importance of the market;
- the goods or services concerned are considered to be essential to vulnerable consumers;
- the market is one of many smaller or local markets that, when considered together, are of considerable importance; or
- the outcome of the case in question is likely to be of relevance to other cases or markets.

Customer benefits

5.55 The OFT has the discretion to determine the nature of possible customer benefits as a factor in its assessment of whether to refer a relevant merger situation. During the House of Commons debates the government provided an insight into how the customer benefits criteria developed:

> In developing the new merger regime we have sought to retain a tight definition of customer benefits to maintain the primary focus on competition while providing flexibility to deal appropriately with the rare circumstances where a merger may produce customer benefits notwithstanding a substantial lessening of competition. Expanding the definition, and expanding the factors that can in certain circumstances be weighed against a loss of competition, risks undermining the competition focus of the regime, undermining its uncertainty, and complicating the assessment task of the competition authorities.
> (Melanie Johnson MP, Commons Debates, 25 April 2002, col. 307)

5.56 The Act defines a customer broadly: s.30(4) provides that a 'relevant customer' means a customer of any person carrying on an enterprise which will cease to be or has already ceased to be a distinct enterprise because of the merger. The definition includes customers of such customers, and any other customers in a chain of customers beginning with the customers of the enterprise concerned. Future customers are also included.

5.57 Section 30 of the Act provides an exhaustive list of what types of customer benefits can be considered by the OFT in its consideration of whether to refer a merger. These are limited to:

- *lower prices in any UK market*: economies of scale may give rise to cost savings, large enough 'in rare cases' to lead to lower prices passed through to consumers;
- *higher quality or greater choice in any UK market*: for example through increasing the size of a network and making incompatible products more compatible post-merger – this would increase value to customers; and

- *greater innovation*: a merger might facilitate innovation through research and development that could only be achieved through a certain critical mass, especially where large fixed and sunk costs are involved; only in exceptional situations, however, will the resulting benefits to consumers outweigh a substantial lessening of competition.

5.58   The OFT acknowledges the importance of ensuring that consumer benefits are directly attributable to the transaction itself; the burden is on the merging parties to provide evidence that any claimed benefit does in fact fall within the meaning of a relevant customer benefit.

VOLUNTARY NOTIFICATION: MERGER NOTICES

5.59   Section 96 provides for the voluntary notification of mergers, through the merger notice procedure. This voluntary system was available under the 1973 Act, but was not extensively used because the statutory form of the notice was not very helpful to an advocacy approach: practitioners preferred to present the relevant arguments in a persuasive manner that did not sit easily with the notice. Nevertheless, the advantage conferred by the merger notice procedure is that it provides a finite period within which a merger situation has to be referred to the Commission. Where unconditional closing by a certain date is an important consideration, this process is helpful and unavoidable.

5.60   Section 96(3) provides that no reference may be made to the Commission after the expiry of the merger notice period. The period begins the day after the notice and the notice fees have been received by the OFT. The period expires in 20 days, unless extended by the OFT for a further 10 days (s.97(1) and (2)). There are special rules for extensions in the presence of intervention notices (see para. 6.33).

5.61   A reference may be made to the Commission even where a merger notice has been delivered in due form, in the circumstances set out in s.100. These are:

- Where the OFT rejects the merger notice within the due period. Section 99(5) provides for such rejection if:

(a) the OFT suspects that any information (whether in the notice or not) given by the person who gave the notice or any connected person[4] is in any material respect false or misleading;
(b) the OFT suspects that it is not proposed to carry the notified arrangements into effect;
(c) the merger notice is incomplete, because it fails to give any prescribed information; or alternatively if any information requested by the OFT is not provided the OFT may extend the notice period in these circumstances (see para. 5.67); or
(d) the OFT considers that the arrangements fall within the jurisdiction of the European Commission under the ECMR.

■   Where the merger notice is rejected for other reasons, namely:

(a) the merger transaction takes place during the merger notice period;
(b) the merger notice was incomplete, because any material information which
     is, or ought to be, known to the person who gave the notice (or a connected
     person), is not disclosed to the OFT before the end of the period;
(c) where the notified merger transaction has not taken place, but one or more
     of the enterprises cease to be distinct from any *other* enterprise;
(d) the notified merger does not take place within six months of the end of the
     merger notice period;
(e) the merger notice is withdrawn by the parties;
(f) the merger notice is flawed, because any information given in respect of the
     notified arrangements by the notifying party or a connected person (in the
     merger notice or otherwise) is materially false or misleading;
(g) where a number of different transactions may be treated under the Act as hav-
     ing all occurred on the same date (see s.27) and there is no merger notice
     under s.96(3) in relation to the last of those transactions, then a reference
     may be made in relation to any transaction that occurred within six months
     prior to that date, or within the six months prior to the actual occurrence of
     any of the transactions so grouped together.

MERGER FEES

5.62   As provided for under the 1973 Act, s.12 of the Act makes provision for
fees to be paid on certain merger-related events. Details of the fees payable and
the event to which they relate will be provided by an Order of the Secretary of
State.

5.63   In determining the amount of the fees to be prescribed in any such Order,
the Secretary of State may take into account all costs incurred by him and the
OFT in respect of the exercise of their functions. Fees paid are not hypothecated
to the OFT, the Commission or the Department of Trade and Industry.

5.64   The events in relation to which fees will be payable are:

■   the delivery of a merger notice;
■   the application for the consent of the Secretary of State to the transfer of a
     newspaper or of newspaper assets;
■   the decision of the OFT (in relation to a possible reference of an anticipated
     or a completed merger) that it is, or may be, the case that a relevant merger
     situation has been created, or that arrangements are in progress or contem-
     plation which, if carried into effect, will result in the creation of a relevant
     merger situation;
■   the decision of the Secretary of State (in relation to a possible reference of a
     relevant merger situation under a public interest consideration) that it is, or
     may be, the case that a relevant merger situation has been created, or that

arrangements are in progress or contemplation which, if carried into effect, will result in the creation of a relevant merger situation;

- the decision of the Secretary of State (in relation to a possible reference under the special merger procedure) that: (i) a special merger situation has been created, or that arrangements are in progress or contemplation which, if carried into effect will result in the creation of a special merger situation; and (ii) one or more public interest considerations are relevant to a consideration of the special merger situation; and

- the decision of the OFT in relation to a possible reference under s.32 Water Industry Act 1991 that it is, or may be, the case that arrangements are in progress which if carried into effect, will result in a merger of two or more water enterprises, or that such a merger has already taken place other than as approved pursuant to a reference under that Act.

Merger notices and intervention notices

5.65 Special rules exist for the extension of merger notice periods where the Secretary of State has made an intervention notice (see para. 6.33). Where an intervention notice is in force, but no 10-day extension to the merger notice period has been made by the OFT, then the period may be extended once by 20 days (s.97(3)). Where there has been a 10-day extension, the OFT may extend the merger notice period by a further number of days, amounting to 20 days in all. In either case, the merger notice period cannot be extended beyond a 40-day period.

5.66 The Secretary of State may extend the merger notice period if he delays a decision as to whether to accept an undertaking or make a reference to the Commission, because he believes a public interest test mentioned in the intervention notice has a 'realistic prospect' of being finalised (i.e. added to the list specified in s.58) within a period of 24 weeks, beginning with the giving of the intervention notice concerned. Such an extension will be for the period of the delay (s.97(9) and (10)).

Other extensions to the merger notice period

5.67 The OFT may extend the merger notice period under s.97(5) where it has requested the notifying party to provide additional information (by notice under s.99(2)); such an extension will be for as long as it takes the person to provide the information to the satisfaction of the OFT or, if earlier, the cancellation of the extension by the OFT (s.97(6)).

5.68 The OFT may also extend the merger notice period if it, or the Secretary of State, is seeking undertakings in lieu of a reference (under s.73 or under Sched. 7, para. 3). Such an extension will end with the earliest of the following events:

(a) the giving of the undertakings concerned;

(b) 10 days after the day on which the party informs the OFT that he does not intend to give undertakings; or

(c) the cancellation by the OFT of the extension (s.97(8)).

5.69 The OFT may also extend the period for consideration if the European Commission is considering or proceeding with a request made by the UK under Article 22(3) ECMR. Such an extension ends by way of a notice from the OFT to the person who made the merger notice, stating that the European Commission has completed its considerations under Article 22(3).

5.70 Section 98 provides further details on the calculation of extension periods. For example, in relation to any extension, no account is taken of a Saturday, Sunday, or Good Friday, Christmas Day or any other bank holiday in England and Wales.

The processing of merger notices

5.71 On receipt of a merger notice, the OFT is obliged, so far as practicable, to take appropriate steps to notify all those it considers would be affected by the notified arrangements. The purpose is to notify such persons of: the existence of the proposal; the fact that the merger notice has been given; and the date on which the merger notice will expire (though such expiry date will be subject to any extensions – see paras. 5.67 to 5.70) (s.99(1)). This means that the merger notice procedure is suitable only for those transactions or proposals the existence of which is in the public domain.

5.72 The OFT may also request further information from the person who notified the merger. Such a request is made by a notice under s.99(2), stating the information required, the period within which it is to be provided, and the possible consequences of not providing the information as requested (s.99(3)). The notice must be given to the person before the end of the end of the merger notice period.

ASSESSMENT OF COMPLETED MERGERS AND ANTICIPATED MERGERS

5.73 When considering whether a completed or anticipated merger does, or may lead to a substantial lessening of competition, the Commission must answer the following question: has a relevant merger situation been created (or is it in the process of being created), and if so, has the creation of that situation resulted, or may be expected to result, in a substantial lessening of competition within any market or markets in the UK for goods or services? In determining the first question, the Commission may be relieved of the need to examine both the share of supply test and the turnover test; it will usually be sufficient if they find either. Alternatively, the Commission can be directed to examine only one of the tests (s.35(6)).

5.74   In relation to mergers that are in progress or in contemplation, the Commission will address itself to the same question, based on the premise that the anticipated merger is carried into effect.

5.75   A merger which results in or may be expected to result in a substantial lessening of competition is said to have an 'anti-competitive outcome' (s.35(2)(a)).

5.76   Once the Commission has decided that a merger has, or may have, an anti-competitive outcome, it must then consider whether it should take action to remedy, mitigate or prevent the substantial lessening of competition or any adverse effect that has or may be expected to result. Such action may take the form of:

- accepting undertakings from the parties;
- making an enforcement order; or
- recommending the taking of action by others.

In determining these matters, if action should be taken, the Commission should identify what this should be and what is to be remedied, mitigated or prevented. The Commission should also have regard to the need to achieve as comprehensive a solution as is reasonable and practicable to the substantial lessening of competition and any adverse effects which result, or may result, from it (s.34(4)). It may also consider the effect of any action on any relevant customer benefits resulting from the merger (s.35(5)).

5.77   Figure 5.1 shows the typical shape of a merger enquiry. It is taken from the Commission's Draft General Advice and Information.

SUBSTANTIAL LESSENING OF COMPETITION

5.78   The new substantial lessening of competition (SLC) test is considered by the government to be one of the cornerstones of the proposed new merger regime. It is a purely competition-based test, and remains undefined in the Act. The change from a public interest test to one based on competition has given rise to a great deal of controversy and debate. In the House of Commons Standing Committee debates, the test was referred to as entering 'murky waters'. On the other hand, in debates in the Commons,[5] the SLC test was regarded as 'sounding a bit like a sandwich'. The debate broadly focused on two issues, namely why the UK should adopt a competition-based test to assess mergers while the European Commission uses a dominance test, and the exclusion of broader, social issues such as unemployment and the geographical allocation of industry.

Changes from the 1973 Act

5.79   Under the 1973 Act, mergers were referred to the Commission in order to determine whether or not they 'operated, or may be expected to operate, against the public interest'. This test was capable of taking account of many issues, such as the effect on employment and the allocation of industry. The 1973 Act required the Commission to take into account 'all matters which appear to them in the

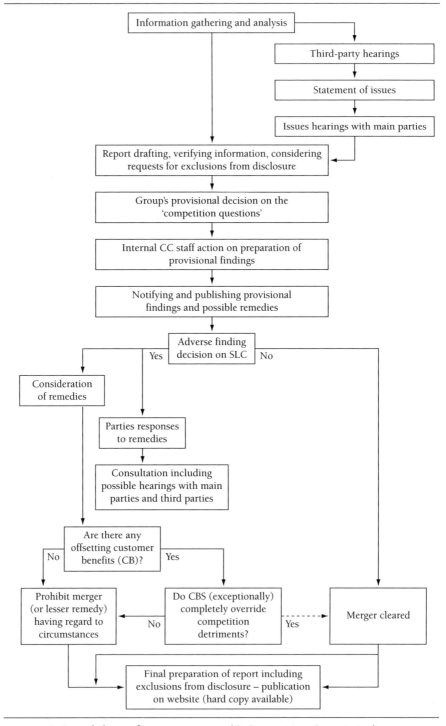

Figure 5.1 Typical shape of a merger inquiry (© Competition Commission)
Source: Competition Commission, *General Advice and Information* (draft consultation document),
September 2002 (see **www.competition-commission.org.uk/inquiries/enterprisebill.htm** for latest
version)

particular circumstances to be relevant' in determining whether a merger operates or may be expected to operate against the public interest. In particular, s.84 of the 1973 Act stressed the desirability of taking account of the following when considering the public interest issue:

(i) maintaining and promoting effective competition;
(ii) promoting the interests of consumers, purchasers and other users of goods and services in the UK with regard to the prices, quality and variety of the goods and services supplied;
(iii) promoting through competition the reduction of costs and the development and use of new techniques and new products, and facilitating the entry of new competitors into existing markets;
(iv) maintaining and promoting the balanced distribution of industry and employment in the UK; and
(v) maintaining and promoting competitive activity in overseas markets on the part of UK producers and suppliers.

5.80   In practice, the Commission took account, almost exclusively, of competition issues only. Nevertheless, it was empowered to take other considerations into account.

5.81   The public interest test as initially envisaged in the 1973 Act is much broader in scope than the SLC test. However, in practice a merger which substantially reduced competition was the most common example of a merger which was regarded as not being in the public interest. Indeed, as discussed above (para. 1.13), latterly the government has limited the application of the public interest test to circumstances in which competition issues arise.

5.82   There has been criticism levied at the introduction of the SLC test insofar as the policy on mergers will now be governed solely by the effect of a particular transaction on competition, rather than its impact on wider public interest issues, such as the social implications of mergers. However, set against this reduction in scope is the increased certainty and predictability of a test formally restricted to competition. It is also unclear whether a statute designed principally to protect the competitive process is appropriate to be used as a mechanism for the protection of employment, the allocation of industry, the protection of UK industry or any of the other issues that might be involved under a broad public interest test. It was for that reason that the 1973 Act was eventually restricted in practice to the examination of competition issues only.

5.83   There are a number of jurisdictions worldwide which have an SLC test for determining whether a merger should be cleared, prohibited or modified; for example, the USA, Canada, Australia and South Africa.

5.84   Concerns were raised that the SLC test will move the UK's merger control away from that of the ECMR, which currently assesses mergers on whether they 'create or strengthen a dominant position as a result of which effective competition would be significantly impeded . . .'. Many Member States of the European

Union have followed the substantive test of dominance as adopted by the ECMR, as have a number of accession countries.

5.85   During the House of Commons debates, this issue was one of the most controversial. The government stated that the move to the SLC test was supported by 'the large majority' of lawyers, as it had the key advantage of being more flexible, and allowed the authorities to concentrate on the overall effect of a merger on competition, rather than on structures. The government argued that there was uncertainty about the ability of a 'dominance' test to deal with the creation of non-collusive oligopolistic markets. The European Commission and the European Court of Justice developed the concept of 'collective dominance' to bridge the gap, but the application of that concept remains uncertain in some situations. The government argued that the SLC test will allow the authorities to act when there is an increase of sole, joint or collective market power resulting from a merger, while making the outcome more certain and predictable. Moreover, since mergers are already assessed on whether they result in a substantial lessening of competition, there will be little difference to the assessment in practice. If this is the case, as the OFT claims, then existing case law will provide useful precedent and there will be no need for an overarching change in approach.

The interpretation of the SLC test

5.86   Both the OFT and the Commission have issued draft guidelines on merger analysis, setting out how each body will address its tasks under the Act. These detailed guidelines are to be welcomed as part of the enhanced transparency of the merger control regime. The general approach and philosophy of the two guidelines are so similar in most respects that it is to be hoped that they will in due course be combined into one document – similar to the equivalent guidelines of the US Department of Justice and Federal Trade Commission – forming a detailed and public guide to merger analysis.

5.87   The OFT will make a merger reference if it has a 'reasonably held belief that, on the basis of the evidence available to it, there is at least a significant prospect that a merger may be expected to lessen competition substantially' ('Mergers: substantive assessment: a consultation paper'; draft of October 2002, OFT 506, p.9, hereafter 'Draft Guidelines on Mergers'), applying the same standard of proof as was applied to references made under the 1973 Act.

5.88   The OFT views competition as 'a process of rivalry between firms seeking to win customers' business.' (Draft Guidelines on Mergers, p.9). When this process of rivalry is effective, it impels firms to deliver benefits to customers in terms of prices, quality and choice. When rivalry is reduced, the effectiveness of the process may diminish and this will likely have a knock-on effect on customers. The OFT acknowledges in its Draft Guidelines on Mergers that many mergers may be pro-competitive or neutral, having no effect on the competitive situation on the market. Other mergers may reduce competition, but not significantly, where other market features protect the competitive process, and discipline the conduct of the merged enterprise. A merger may be expected to lead to a substantial lessening of competition when it is 'expected to weaken rivalry to such an extent that the competitive process would no longer deliver a similar level of customer benefits as it would without the merger', where such post-merger effects are expected to be sustained for more than a short period of time.

5.89   The following paragraphs set out the issues that will be examined during the merger review process – commencing with the consideration by the OFT of the question whether to refer a relevant merger situation to the Commission and then continuing with the Commission's review of whether a relevant merger situation has been created or is in contemplation and, if so, whether the result is, or may be, a substantial lessening of competition and, if so, whether any action should be taken or recommended.

5.90   The issues are as follows:

- Market definition:
  - relevant product market; and
  - relevant geographical market;
- identifying the correct counterfactual;
- measuring the extent of loss of competition;
- consideration of exceptions to the duty to refer;
- consideration of accepting undertakings in lieu of a reference; and
- considering appropriate remedies.

These issues are considered or referred to below.

5.91   Paras. 5.102 to 5.131 describe how the OFT assesses a merger, depending on the nature and structure of the relationship between the merging parties. As the OFT's Draft Guidelines on Mergers (p.10) state, there are three basic merger situations that affect competition in different ways:

- *Horizontal mergers.* Mergers between parties that operate in the same relevant market and at the same level of operation may lead to coordinated anti-competitive conduct between the merged parties which would enable them to act as if they were monopolists. The increased concentration of a market enables such monopoly-like conduct as well as facilitating collusion between the remaining undertakings.
- *Vertical mergers.* Mergers between parties that operate in the same relevant market but at different levels of the supply chain are generally considered to be less problematic in so far as they tend to be pro-competitive. Any anti-competitive effects that may arise will be a result of existing market power at one level of the supply chain, or where there is considerable vertical integration.
- *Conglomerate merger.* Mergers between firms in different markets will rarely lessen competition substantially – by definition, there is no overlap on the relevant market. However, competition may in some circumstances be reduced through the exercise of portfolio power.

5.92   The guidelines published by the Commission provide some guidance as to how it will interpret and apply the SLC test. The Commission's Consultation Document on Merger References (draft of September 2002, hereafter, Commission Draft Merger Guidelines),[6] states that a substantial lessening of competition must be more than merely possible. The merger must have already resulted in a substantial lessening of competition, or the Commission must expect such a result will occur, i.e. where such a result is considered to be more likely than not.

5.93   Part 2 of the Commission's Draft Merger Guidelines provides a comprehensive analysis of how the Commission will assess competition and how it will define the market. Competition may be substantially lessened where rivalry between firms is 'dampened' and where existing and future needs of customers are not met as effectively and efficiently as possible. The Commission will evaluate the merger in the light of the situation that would have been expected to prevail in the absence of the merger, in the same manner as the OFT. The Commission's focus is the same as the analysis under the OFT guidelines and focuses on the effects that the merger has on competition:

> The degree of rivalry between firms or other producers for customer business and the threat of entry faced by incumbents are the main competitive constraints on firms, although other constraints such as buyer power may also, in some cases, be significant.

> (p.10)

MARKET DEFINITION

5.94   The essential nature of a proper market definition is a truism in competition law. Although not critical to determining whether the 'share of supply' test is satisfied, it is indispensable to determining whether there has been a substantial lessening of competition. Because the OFT has already issued comprehensive guidelines under the 1998 Act on the definition of the relevant market, the new guidelines under the 2002 Act are relatively brief.

5.95   The Commission and the OFT both refer to the fact that market definition is not an end in itself, but rather a framework within which to analyse the effects of a merger on competition. The Commission devotes considerably more space to the definition in its merger guidelines. However, it is important to note that the question of market definition is not an exact science, however persuasive econometric models appear to be. The approaches adopted by the OFT and the Commission, although seductively scientific in their demeanour, should not be regarded as more than useful tools – a fact noted by the Commission. Having said that, the Commission intends to adopt the SSNIP (small but significant and non-transitory increase in price) test wherever it is feasible to do so.

5.96   Since the SSNIP test is now a settled and orthodox approach to market definition, it is not proposed to examine it *de novo* here. However, the basic approach of the test is discussed in paras. 9.76 to 9.81 in the context of market investigations. In the case of a merger, the Commission (and the OFT) will consider whether a hypothetical monopolist of a set of products (the narrowest group of overlapping products produced by each of the parties to the merger) would be able profitably to impose an SSNIP. If such a price rise is unprofitable, then the closest substitute products are added to the set and the SSNIP is again hypothesised. This process continues until the hypothetical monopolist could profitably sustain an SSNIP.

5.97   Since the authorities are unlikely to have precise information on the extent to which customers will switch to other products in response to a price increase, estimates will be used instead. But such estimates must be thoroughly worked in order to be persuasive. As the Commission states in its merger guidelines, econometric estimates can provide information on demand elasticities 'but their value depends on the robustness of the economic models used and the quality of the underlying data' (para. 2.19). The full data set must therefore be submitted, together with the manner of calculation.

5.98   Where such estimates are not available in merger cases, market surveys are often used instead. If these take the form of questionnaires, evidence submitted must include the complete survey results and a description of the methodology.

5.99   The SSNIP test is relevant also to the definition of the relevant geographical market. Where an SSNIP cannot be profitably sustained because consumers switch to products offered in adjacent areas, those areas will be added to the set, until the SSNIP is profitable. This test is, of course, quite different from the question of whether the merger gives rise to a 25 per cent share of supply in a 'substantial part' of the UK.

5.100   The OFT Draft Guidelines on Mergers state that it will have regard to previous decisions of the OFT, Commission and European Commission (and other competition authorities where appropriate) that provide guidance on market definition within an industry sector, but it will not consider itself bound by those precedents, particularly because markets may change over time.

IDENTIFICATION OF THE CORRECT COUNTERFACTUAL

5.101   Following the definition of the market, the OFT will identify what it refers to as the correct counterfactual. As the OFT states, the core concept of the SLC test is a comparison of prospects for competition with and without the merger. The counterfactual is the competitive situation without the merger. The obvious counterfactual is the prevailing conditions of competition, but this might not be the case where that would change in any event, even in the absence of the merger, for example where imminent entry or exit is likely. Similarly, forthcoming changes to the regulatory structure of the market will affect the counterfactual. Although the Commission does not refer explicitly to the counterfactual in its guidelines, it deploys the same approach – an evaluation of the competitive constraints on firms compared to the situation that would have been expected to prevail without the merger (para. 2.3).

ASSESSMENT OF HORIZONTAL MERGERS

5.102   Horizontal mergers remove an independent competitor from the market; they are normally considered to be potentially more anti-competitive than either a vertical merger or a conglomerate merger. This is because competition may be affected in a number of ways:

- there is a loss of an actual or potential competitor, and market concentration will usually increase as a result;
- the merger can change the 'competitive incentives' of the merging parties, their competitors and their customers, leading to changes in the intensity of competition;
- a merger can also affect entry barriers and buyer power;
- the merging parties may however make efficiency gains and in some situations this could increase competition in the industry.

5.103   The basic concern of the OFT and of the Commission is whether, as a result of the merger, there will be such a loss in competitive pressure that the merged entity will be able profitably to raise prices, reduce output, or restrict choice and innovation.

5.104   The focus of both the OFT and the Commission is on the unilateral and coordinated effects of merger.

Unilateral effects of mergers

5.105   Unilateral effects arise where the merger permits the merged firm to exploit market power on its own. The OFT has identified the following characteristics of markets that may (either alone or in combination) give rise to unilateral effects and which may therefore lead to a substantial lessening of competition:

- there are few suppliers of the relevant product(s) or service(s);
- the merger creates or increases a high combined market share and the increment in that share is significant (it is in this context that calculations made on the basis of Herfindahl-Hirschman Index (HHI) will be particularly relevant – see para. 9.83);
- the merging parties are close competitors producing highly substitutable products;
- customers have little real choice of alternative suppliers;
- rivals are unable to react to price changes or changes in output or quality;
- remaining competitors on the market have little spare capacity, so are unable to expand to supply customers as a response to the merged entity reducing output;
- there is no strong competitive fringe;

- the merger removes a maverick firm from the market;
- there are barriers to entry, or the merger increases barriers to entry;
- the merger removes a recent new entrant or a strong potential new entrant;
- there is limited countervailing buyer power or where the merger actually reduces buyer power.

5.106   The Commission also assesses whether the merger would create market power for the merging firms in the relevant product market. The Commission is clear that a small increment to an already large market share may bring about enough of a change to the structure of the market for the merger to lead to a substantial lessening of competition. This is consistent with the Commission's approach to mergers under the 1973 Act. However, the Commission does point out that there is no particular market share threshold that will denote the likelihood of the Commission deciding that the merger has resulted in, or is expected to result in, a substantial lessening of competition. A combined market share of 25 per cent or more would be sufficient to raise potential concerns regarding the effect of the merger on competition. If the combined market share is less than 25 per cent, it is less likely to raise potential concerns; although the possibility cannot be ruled out.

Coordinated effects of a merger

5.107   Coordinated effects occur where a group of firms acquire power through the merger. This increases the probability that the surviving firms will coordinate their behaviour with adverse effects on prices, quality and output. This coordination may take place in the absence of agreement (in other words, it is tacit collusion). This is a similar approach to that relating to 'joint dominance' under the ECMR. The OFT considers that coordinated effects will arise only where:

- the participants have an ability to align their behaviour in the market; in the absence of express agreement (which might be difficult or costly), market transparency and stability are the basic elements necessary to give rise to an ability to align conduct;
- they have incentives to maintain coordinated behaviour through an ability to detect and to punish departures from it (for example through retaliatory price wars); deviation is more likely to be detected where products are homogeneous or where there are few product types or where deviations are observable within a short period; punishment threats must be credible – for example, firms must be free to enter into a price war or to introduce new products or advertise/market in order to expand output; and
- the coordinated behaviour is sustainable; this might be difficult if, for example, a maverick firm is able to disrupt the collusion, through innovation or other competition.

Barriers to entry and expansion

5.108   The entry by new competitors or the expansion by existing competitors may be sufficient to counteract a substantial lessening in competition by removing from the merging parties or their competitors the ability to exploit increased market power and reduced levels of rivalry. Where new entry is a likely response to an increase in prices (or other adverse competitive outcome), it will act as a deterrent to the merging parties from increasing their prices, reducing their output or reducing customer choice. Even the credible threat of entry or expansion may be a sufficient deterrent.

5.109   The possibility for entry cannot simply be claimed by the parties as a feature likely to avoid or offset a substantial lessening of competition. There must be sufficient evidence. The factors taken into account by the Commission are set out in para. 9.86 (in the context of market investigation reports). The OFT will also need to be convinced that entry is possible and likely. To do this, it will take account of: the experience of any firms that have entered or withdrawn from the relevant market(s) in recent years; evidence of planned entry by third parties; the 'sunk' cost of entry; and the minimum efficient scale needed for entry. The OFT Draft Guidelines on Mergers define entry barriers broadly: 'any feature of a market that gives incumbent firms an advantage over the potential entrants or control of the assets, such that incumbents can persistently raise their prices above (or reduce quality below) competitive levels without new firms entering the market' (para. 4.21).

5.110   In the context of mergers, the relevant barriers are those that give rise to absolute advantages and those that provide strategic advantages. Absolute advantages arise where entry is limited or prevented by government regulations (such as licensing), preferential access to essential facilities, intellectual property rights or the control of essential assets. Strategic advantages arise as a result of the fact that the incumbents are already in the market. These may arise through the possession of, say, economies of scale or through a deliberate strategy of responding to new entry through maintaining excess capacity.

5.111   The Commission refers to barriers as being of three types: natural or intrinsic, where they comprise inevitable start-up costs (of these, the Commission is particularly interested in 'sunk costs' – those that cannot be recovered on exit from the market); regulatory barriers of the type described in the previous paragraph; and strategic barriers, as described above.

5.112   Where entry is feasible, it should also be shown to be large enough to counteract the enhanced market power of the merged enterprises. Moreover, the entry must be rapid and sustained in order to have such an effect.

5.113   The parties should be careful to submit sufficient evidence to convince the authorities of the likely effect of entry. This may be of a historical nature (such as the effect of past entry on competition in the market). Additionally, evidence showing high growth in demand, a high level of product innovation, forthcoming (or 'pipeline') products, short product life cycles and the absence of constraints on advertising, will assist in demonstrating that any apparent barriers to entry will not facilitate a substantial lessening of competition.

Buyer power

5.114 Buyer power may act as an effective counterweight to the ability of the merged entity to raise prices. In these cases, a substantial lessening of competition may be avoided. The OFT has identified a number of different ways in which buyer power can be exploited. These comprise: switching to another supplier (or a credible threat to do so); imposing costs on the supplier; punishing the supplier by dealing less favourably with its products at retail outlets (for example, displaying products in non-premium locations); or by entering the market themselves (vertical integration upwards) or subsidising or supporting entry by others.

5.115 As the Commission points out in its guidelines, buyer power does not arise simply because buyers are large relative to suppliers. Buyers will only be able to wield power if they are able to deploy any of the strategies outlined above.

Failing firm defence

5.116 Where one of the parties to a merger is failing, the merger may not have the same effects on competition as it would have had the firm represented an effective continuing competitor. This might persuade the Commission or the OFT that the effects of the merger should not be measured against the pre-merger situation.

5.117 For such a 'defence' to work, it must be clear that the firm is genuinely failing. The Commission considers this to be the case where it is unable to meet its financial obligations in the near future and it is unable to restructure itself successfully. The OFT adopts a similar approach. However, the mere fact that the firm is failing is not sufficient for a successful defence. The OFT and the Commission will also consider whether another person might have acquired the firm with less restrictive outcomes. Also relevant would be the consequences of the firm exiting the market; if its assets would, but for the merger, have been distributed widely in the market, that would be a different – and possibly less damaging – competitive outcome.

5.118 Parties wishing to exploit the 'failing firm' defence will need to produce evidence to the OFT and the Commission of the type detailed in the OFT's guidelines. This looks for evidence of imminent failure, of the efforts made to secure refinancing, of the absence of credible alternative purchasers, and of the use to be made of the firm's assets after the merger.

Efficiencies

5.119 Efficiency gains are often claimed for mergers. The Act allows the OFT to take efficiency gains into account at two separate points in the analytical framework: where they increase rivalry in the market so that no substantial lessening of competition would result from a merger: and where they do not avert a substantial lessening of competition, but will nonetheless be passed on after the merger in the form of customer benefits. A discussion on efficiencies as part of a consideration of customer benefits is examined in paras. 5.123 to 5.126. The following paragraphs examine efficiencies as part of the consideration of whether a substantial lessening of competition has occurred.

5.120 Where efficiencies are claimed for the purpose of demonstrating that a merger will not substantially lessen competition, they can be of a much broader type than is allowed for by s.30 in relation to customer benefits. The OFT has identified a range of efficiencies that may be used, including savings in fixed or variable costs, more intensive use of capacity, economies of scale or scope, increased network size and product quality. In addition, positive changes in the merged firm's incentives (e.g. to invest in innovation) could also be considered. However, the standard of proof is high. Parties must demonstrate that the efficiencies are demonstrable, merger specific and likely to be passed on to consumers.

5.121 Efficiencies are merger specific where they are a direct consequence of the merger. The OFT draft guidelines explain that 'this does not imply that the merger needs to be the only conceivable way of capturing those efficiencies, but rather, because it is an incremental analysis, efficiencies must be judged relative to what would have happened without the merger'. The OFT must be satisfied that not only will the post-merger position be such that the parties still have an incentive to pursue the claimed cost savings, but also that consumers will obtain a reasonable share of the benefits.

5.122 The Commission adopts a similar approach to efficiency claims. In its draft guidelines the Commission stated:

> If such efficiencies have arisen or will arise as a direct result of the merger, they will have a positive effect on rivalry in the market, such that there may be no reduction in rivalry despite the combination of erstwhile competitors. However, such efficiency gains are easily claimed and the onus will be on the parties to demonstrate that the gains genuinely make rivalry stronger than it would be without the merger.
> (para. 2.19)

Efficiencies as a form of customer benefit

5.123 In order to be taken into consideration, efficiencies must be clear and quantifiable, materialise within a reasonable period of time and be contingent on the merger. The efficiencies that can be claimed are limited to those set out in s.30 (lower prices, higher quality, greater choice and greater innovation). To avert a reference, such efficiencies must not only be passed on to consumers, they must also be of sufficient intensity to outweigh the adverse impact on competition.

5.124 The OFT will need to be convinced with compelling evidence that cost savings arising, for example increased economies of scale, will be passed through to consumers 'in good part', so that they lead to lower prices. Innovation sufficient to avert a reference is described by the OFT as likely to occur 'in rare cases'. Only 'exceptionally' will the OFT expect to see these advantages outweighing a substantial lessening of competition.

5.125 The level of proof required is best summed up by the following statement from the OFT's draft guidelines in merger assessment:

> to count as customer benefits, by definition, customers need to be better off with the merger, despite the fact that the OFT believes that the merger might lessen competition substantially. These will be rare cases since, ordinarily, we would expect competition to deliver lower prices, higher quality and greater customer choice. The OFT does not expect to be sufficiently confident of customer benefits to clear mergers that it believes may or may be expected to result in a substantial lessening of competition except on rare occasions.

5.126 Where the benefits are claimed to accrue to customers in a different market to that in which the substantial lessening of competition arises, there will be an even higher burden of proof.

Merger efficiencies and the EU

5.127 The ECMR does not specifically contain any reference to the European Commission having to consider prevailing efficiencies or other customer benefits. However, in a speech given by Philip Lowe to the American Antitrust Institute in Washington, DC on 1 July 2002, the newly appointed EU Competition Director General, commented that:

> Some commentators – even eminent US ones – have criticised the [European] Commission's incapacity or unwillingness to offset efficiencies of a merger against its restrictive effects on competition . . . few on our side of the Atlantic are in favour of giving an advantage to the merging parties where the post-merger competitive conditions make it extremely unlikely that consumers can benefit from the efficiencies . . . I can conclude . . . by confirming quite categorically that there is no 'efficiencies defence' in [the EU's] merger policy.

5.128 The European Commission's Green Paper on merger review has invited views as to the proper role and scope of efficiency considerations in the field of EU merger control. Perhaps this indicates the beginning of a shift in policy by the European Commission through broadening the scope of efficiency issues.

ASSESSMENT OF VERTICAL MERGERS

5.129 Vertical mergers are often efficiency enhancing, but can have anti-competitive outcomes. This is likely to be the case only where market power exists somewhere along the vertical axis. The Commission has identified the following possible circumstances that might cause it concern:

- the use of market power in one market to enhance market power in a vertically related market; this will occur where a competitor in that other market is foreclosed from the supply of an input previously available in the open market;
- the acquisition of a new entrant in a downstream market in a manner that has the effect of dampening the growth of competition in that market (for example the retail market);
- vertical mergers that increase the likelihood of coordinated effects; and
- vertical mergers that raise entry barriers by reserving inputs or distribution facilities.

ASSESSMENT OF CONGLOMERATE MERGERS

5.130   These rarely lead to a substantial lessening of competition. The OFT believes that such an effect may arise where there is 'portfolio power'.

5.131   The OFT Draft Guidelines on Mergers define 'portfolio power' as when the market power deriving from a portfolio of brands exceeds the sum of its parts (para. 6.2). This is likely to be the case only where customers derive some advantage in buying packages of products from a single source rather than from multiple sources. The bundling of products (requiring or incentivising the purchase of a range of products) will be a concern only if other enterprises are unable to match the practice.

LIMITATIONS ON THE OFT'S RIGHT TO REFER MERGERS

5.132   In addition to the ability of the OFT to exercise discretion in selecting the mergers to be referred to the Commission, the Act removes its ability to refer relevant merger situations in the following circumstances (s.33(3)):

- it is a newspaper merger (under s.69);
- the merger is a concentration having a Community dimension under the ECMR;
- the OFT has accepted an undertaking in lieu of a reference (under s.74);
- the Secretary of State has accepted an undertaking in lieu of a reference (under Sched. 7, para. 3);
- the period for considering a merger notice has expired without a reference being made;
- the transaction is already subject to another reference under ss.22 or 33;
- the case is the subject of an intervention notice (in which case the Secretary of State will make the reference to the Commission under s.45); or
- the European Commission is considering a request made by the UK (whether alone or with other Member States) under Article 22(3) ECMR, is proceeding with the matter, or has dealt with the matter in pursuance of such a request (s.33(3)(e)).[7]

CANCELLATION AND VARIATION OF REFERENCES FOR COMPLETED AND ANTICIPATED MERGERS

5.133   The Commission will cancel a reference for an anticipated merger if it considers the proposals have been abandoned (s.37(1)). This is a change from the 1973 Act, where the Secretary of State had power to cancel a reference in relation to an anticipated merger but not in relation to a completed merger (see *NTL Communications Corp./Newcastle United plc*, July 1999).

5.134   Section 37 also provides that the Commission may, if it considers that doing so is justified by the facts (including events occurring on or after the making of the reference concerned), treat a reference made under s.22 (anticipated mergers) as if it is a reference made under s.33 (completed mergers), and vice versa. Also, ss.77–81 (interim restrictions and powers of enforcement) apply as if a reference under s.33 had been made under s.22 or vice versa

5.135   The OFT may vary a reference at any time, but it must consult the Commission before doing so. The OFT cannot vary the time period of 24 weeks within which the Commission has to prepare and publish its report on the reference. However, the Commission has indicated that, in practice, it estimates the period is more likely to be 16–17 weeks.

INVESTIGATIONS AND REPORTS ON REFERENCES FOR COMPLETED OR ANTICIPATED MERGERS (ss.37–40)

5.136   The Commission is under a duty to publish a report on a reference within 24 weeks, beginning with the date of the reference concerned (s.39(1)).

5.137   Where Article 9(6) ECMR applies (publication by the authorities of a Member State of findings on a concentration remitted to it for examination), the Commission shall prepare its report within the period of 24 weeks beginning with the date of the reference, or, if a shorter period is prescribed under Article 9(6), within such period as is necessary to ensure compliance with that Article. Where the ECMR applies, any extension period beyond 24 weeks shall not exceed the time required to ensure compliance with Article 9(6) ECMR. In the latter case, no extension of the time period is possible.

5.138   If there are special reasons why the Commission cannot prepare its report within the 24 weeks, it may extend it, but only once and by no more than eight weeks. The Commission may also extend the period in which to prepare its report if a 'relevant person' has failed to comply with any requirement of a notice to attend as a witness or produce any necessary documents regardless of whether that person had a reasonable excuse. For these purposes, a 'relevant person' means any person carrying on any of the enterprises concerned, any person who (alone or as a member of a group) owns or has control of any such person, or any officer, employee or agent of any person connected to these. A person or group of persons able, directly or indirectly, to control or materially influence the policy of a body of persons corporate or unincorporate, but without having a controlling interest in that body of persons, may be treated as having control of it. Section 40(5) implies that a number of extensions are possible.

5.139   The fact that an extension has been made is to be published in accordance with s.107 and shall continue into force until the person concerned provides the information or documents to the satisfaction of the Commission (or appears as a witness in accordance with the requirements of the Commission); or until the Commission publishes its decision to cancel the extension (s.39(8)).

5.140   The Secretary of State has the power to make an order reducing the 24- and eight-week time periods (or amending any other time period used in substitution for these periods so long as periods do not exceed 24 and eight weeks respectively). However, the Commission and any other person that the Secretary of State considers appropriate, must be consulted before such an order is made. If the Commission is already considering a reference under existing time periods, any order by the Secretary of State will not affect the time period under which the Commission is obliged to produce its report. The Secretary of State is also empowered to make regulations under this section in relation to the time limits for investigations and reports.

THE REPORT

5.141   The report contains the Commission's decisions in relation to the issues set out in para. 5.73 above. The decisions must be reasoned, thereby placing a duty on the Commission to obtain as much information as it considers appropriate to facilitate an understanding of the issues considered. In order to achieve this, the Commission has been given wide information-seeking powers, so it now has the power to carry out 'such investigations as it considers necessary'. The Act has also introduced financial penalties for failure to provide the information requested, or providing false or misleading information.

5.142   The Commission must provide a copy of the report to the OFT on publication.

MINORITY REPORTS OF THE COMMISSION

5.143   Under s.119, if a member of the Commission who has reviewed the reference disagrees with any of the Commission's decisions contained in the Commission's report, he may include a statement of his disagreement and his reasons for disagreeing (there is a corresponding provision in relation to minority reports of the Commission in relation to market investigations: s.178).

PUBLICATION OF PROVISIONAL FINDINGS

5.144 Although the Commission previously published statements and issues, the Act now requires the Commission to consult parties whose interests are likely to be adversely affected by a merger decision (s.104). The Commission will publish provisional findings, and parties may respond within 21 days (Rules of Procedure, r.9.5). The Commission may then decide to amend the provisional findings. The publication of provisional findings is in addition to the publication of statements of issues. The new procedures, incorporating a welcome degree of transparency, will assist in avoiding the difficulties encountered in the *Interbrew* case: in that case the decision of the Commission was overturned on judicial review, because the Commission had acted unfairly in failing to give Interbrew sufficient opportunity to comment on proposed remedies.

DISCLOSURE AND CONFIDENTIALITY OF INFORMATION

5.145 Under the Act, the Commission will often need to publish some of the information provided to it, principally in the final report. The Act provides that the Commission must exclude from disclosure as far as possible: any information the disclosure of which the Commission thinks is against the public interest; commercial information whose disclosure the Commission thinks might significantly harm legitimate business interests of the business concerned; and information relating to the private affairs of an individual the disclosure of which the Commission thinks may substantially harm the individual's interests.

DEFAMATION IN REPORTS AND OTHER DOCUMENTS

5.146 Section 108 provides that, for the purposes of defamation, absolute privilege attaches to any advice, guidance, notice or direction given, or decision or report made by the OFT, the Commission or the Secretary of State in the exercise of any of their functions under Part 3 of the Act (mergers). Similar protection exists for the purposes of Part 4 (market investigations) under s.173.

DUTY TO REMEDY EFFECTS OF COMPLETED OR ANTICIPATED MERGERS

5.147 Where the Commission has published its report and decides that the merger has an anti-competitive outcome, it is under a duty to take such action in relation to undertakings or enforcement orders as it considers reasonable and practicable to remedy, mitigate or prevent the substantial lessening of competition and to remedy any consequential effects which have arisen or may arise as a result. It may also consider the effect that any action will have on any relevant customer benefits.

5.148   The decision of the Commission must be consistent with that contained in its report, unless there has been a 'material change of circumstances' since the report was prepared or the Commission has a 'special reason' for deciding differently (s.41).

---

1   According to s.127, the supply of services does not include the provision of services under an express or implied contract of service or of apprenticeship. The supply of services includes: rendering services to order; the provision of services by making them available to potential users; making arrangements for the use of computer software or for granting access to data stored in any form which is not readily accessible; making arrangements for sharing the use of telecommunications apparatus under a 'relevant agreement' under s.190(2) of the Broadcasting Act 1990; and permitting or making arrangements to permit the use of land in circumstances to be specified by the Secretary of State.

2   Under s.127(6) a 'relative' is a brother, sister, uncle, aunt, nephew, niece, lineal ancestor or descendant (for such purposes the stepchild of any person, or anyone adopted by a person, whether legally or otherwise as his child, is regarded as a relative or taken into account to trace a relationship in the same way as that person's child); references to a spouse or partner include a former spouse or partner.

3   European Commission's Notice on calculation of turnover under the ECMR (98/C 66/04).

4   'Connected person' means any person who is associated with the person giving the merger notice; or any subsidiary of the person who gave the merger notice or of any person associated with him.

5   Parliamentary debates Wednesday 10th April, 2002. Volume 383/No. 125.

6   Available on *www.competition-commission.org.uk*.

7   Article 22(3) ECMR (Council Regulation (EEC) No. 4064/89) states: 'If the Commission finds, at the request of a Member State, that a concentration [. . .] has no Community dimension [i.e. it does not meet the turnover thresholds required], or strengthens a dominant position as a result of which effective competition would be significantly impeded within the territory of the Member State concerned it may, in so far as the concentration affects trade between Member States, adopt the decisions provided for in Article 8(2), second subparagraph, (3) and (4)' (i.e. if the merger has significant impact on the competitive situation in a Member State and it will affect trade between Member States, it can refer a merger back to that Member State for review under national merger legislation, and declare that it is either incompatible with the common market; decide that a concentration that has already been implemented must be demerged; or attach conditions and obligations intended to ensure that the parties' commitments are adhered to with a view to modifying the original concentration).

6 MERGER CONTROL: PUBLIC INTEREST CASES AND OTHER SPECIAL CASES

INTRODUCTION

6.1 As an exception to the general removal of the Secretary of State from the merger process, the Act provides for two situations in which the Secretary of State retains a right to intervene. These situations arise where certain non-competition public interest considerations arise that could not otherwise be taken into account by the OFT or Commission (public interest considerations, s.42) or where the merger concerns a government contractor and would not otherwise be referable to the Commission because neither the share of supply test nor the UK turnover test are satisfied (special merger situations, s.59).

6.2 However, the Secretary of State cannot intervene if:

(i) a reference has already been made under ss.22 or 33 in relation to a completed or anticipated merger;
(ii) a decision has already been made not to make a reference;
(iii) the operation of the ECMR prevents a reference being made;
(iv) the merger relates to newspapers;
(v) a merger notice has already been submitted to the OFT; or
(vi) the OFT or Secretary of State has accepted an undertaking or group of undertakings in lieu of a reference.

6.3 For the purposes of a merger containing a public interest consideration, the question whether a relevant merger has been created is determined as at:

(a) the time when an intervention notice is given;
(b) the time of making of the OFT's report in relation to the case which is the subject of an intervention notice; or
(c) the time that the Commission may determine in relation to a reference made by the Secretary of State.

INTERVENTION NOTICES

6.4 Unless prevented by the considerations outlined above in para. 6.2, the Secretary of State may intervene in the merger process by issuing an 'intervention notice' to the OFT. An intervention notice may only be given where the Secretary of State: (a) has reasonable grounds for suspecting that a relevant merger situation is completed or is in progress or contemplation; and (b) believes that one or more 'public interest considerations' is relevant to a consideration of the merger (s.42(2)).

6.5   Public interest considerations are those specified in s.58. Although s.58 contains provisions for the list of specified considerations to be amended, s.4(2) provides that a public interest consideration may either be specified in s.58 at the time the intervention notice is given or, if not specified, in the opinion of the Secretary of State, ought to be so specified. This gives the Secretary of State a degree of freedom to respond to public interest concerns that had not been anticipated, without the need to wait for amendments to be made to the list specified in s.58. In these cases, the Secretary of State is obliged to ensure that the new consideration is included in the specified list as soon as practicable. This obligation arises under s.42(7) and (8).

6.6   Currently only one public interest consideration is specified in s.58, namely national security. This includes public security and is defined to have the same meaning as that attributed to it under Article 22(3) ECMR (which permits Member States to apply certain non-competition considerations to mergers, even though the transactions fall within the jurisdiction of the European Commission for competition purposes).

6.7   Provision is made in s.58(3) for the Secretary of State to amend the list of public interest considerations. The OFT and Commission can make representations to the Secretary of State in relation to the exercise of his powers to make an order to add, remove or amend any consideration. The government stated during debates on the Bill that there was no intention to define such public interest considerations other than for national and public security concerns. The power to add other specified considerations provides a 'safety valve' for the new regime, ensuring that exceptional cases can be dealt with appropriately.

6.8   The OFT is under an obligation to bring to the Secretary of State's attention, cases where public interest issues (as currently defined in the Act) arise, in order to determine whether to intervene in the case (unless it considers the Secretary of State would consider it immaterial).

6.9   Under s.43, an intervention notice must contain the following information:

- the relevant merger situation;
- the public interest consideration(s) which is, or may be, relevant in assessing the relevant merger situation; where two or more public interest considerations are relevant to a consideration of the relevant merger situation concerned, the Secretary of State may decide not to mention any of those considerations that he considers appropriate; and
- where any public interest consideration is not finalised (that is, not included in the list specified in s.58), the proposed timetable for finalising it.

6.10   When the OFT receives an intervention notice, it is under a duty to pub-licise this fact and to invite representations on the public interest issue(s) from interested parties. The intervention notice comes into force when it is given, and ceases to be in force when the matter to which it relates is 'finally determined'. This is on one of the following events (s.43(4)):

(a) the expiry of the time within which the OFT is to report to the Secretary of State following its investigation (see para. 6.11) and no report has been made;
(b) the Secretary of State decides to accept an undertaking or group of under-takings in lieu of a reference to the Commission;
(c) the Secretary of State decides not to make a reference;
(d) the Commission cancels the Secretary of State's reference; the Commission may do this either where it considers that the proposed merger has been abandoned (s.48(1) or under the following cumulative provisions of s.53(1):

  (i) the intervention notice mentions a public interest consideration which was not finalised on the giving of that notice or public interest con-siderations which, at that time, were not finalised;
  (ii) no other public interest consideration is mentioned in the notice;
  (iii) at least 24 weeks has elapsed since the giving of the notice; and
  (iv) the public interest consideration(s) mentioned in the notice has/have not been finalised within that period of 24 weeks;

(e) the expiry of the time in which the Commission is to report to the Secretary of State following its investigation (see para. 6.34), and no report has been made;
(f) the time at which the Secretary of State is to make and publish his decision on the public interest case has expired, and no such decision has been made or published;
(g) the Secretary of State decides to make no finding at all in the matter;
(h) the Secretary of State decides not to make an adverse public interest finding;
(i) the Secretary of State decides to make an adverse public interest finding but decides neither to accept final undertakings nor to make an enforcement order; or
(j) the Secretary of State decides to make an adverse public interest finding and accepts a final undertaking or makes an enforcement order.

INVESTIGATION AND REPORT BY THE OFT

6.11   The OFT must produce a report on the public interest case, within such period as the Secretary of State requires. The purpose of the OFT report is to pro-vide advice on the competition aspects and other issues arising and which are also relevant to a consideration by the Secretary of State as to whether to make a reference on the basis of the public interest considerations.

6.12   Under s.44(4), the report of the OFT will include decisions as to whether the OFT believes that:

- a relevant merger situation has been created or arrangements are in progress or in contemplation which, if carried into effect, will result in the creation of a relevant merger situation;
- the merger situation has resulted, or may be expected to result, in a substantial lessening of competition;
- the market or markets concerned are too small to justify the making of a reference;
- in the case of arrangements which are in progress or in contemplation, it is unlikely that the arrangements will proceed or are not sufficiently far advanced to justify the making of a reference;
- any relevant customer benefits outweigh the substantial lessening of competition and any adverse effects of the substantial lessening of competition; or
- other than in relation to the public interest considerations mentioned in the intervention notice concerned, it would be appropriate to deal with the matter by way of undertakings (in which case the report shall contain descriptions of the undertakings which the OFT believes are, or may be, appropriate).

6.13   The OFT's report will provide its relevant advice to the Secretary of State to assist him in making his decision on making a reference to the Commission. The report also summarises any representations about the case which have been received by the OFT, are relevant, and which relate to the public interest consideration(s). However, the OFT's report will usually not contain any recommendations on the public interest issue because it does not consider itself competent to provide expertise on such matters.

6.14   In summary, the report may include advice and recommendations on any public interest consideration mentioned in the intervention notice, and which may be relevant to the Secretary of State's decision as to whether to make a reference to the Commission. The OFT has the power to carry out such investigations as it considers appropriate for the purposes of producing a report to the Secretary of State, under s.44.

POWER OF THE SECRETARY OF STATE TO REFER THE MATTER TO THE COMMISSION

6.15   The Secretary of State, in deciding whether to make a reference, must accept the decisions of the OFT on the matters listed in s.44(4) (see para. 6.12), and any descriptions of undertakings included in the OFT's report. However, his decision to refer does not have to follow the OFT's recommendation. If the Secretary of State considers that public interest considerations are not material to the case, he will refer the case back to the OFT for a review under normal merger procedures. This may result in clearance, undertakings or a reference, all on competition grounds.

6.16 There are several different circumstances in which the Secretary of State may decide whether or not the merger should be referred to the Commission on the basis of public interest considerations (s.45). The common elements are that the Secretary of State believes that it is or may be the case that:

(a) a relevant merger situation has been created (or arrangements are in progress or in contemplation which, if carried into effect, will result in the creation of a relevant merger situation); and

(b) one or more public interest consideration mentioned in the intervention notice is relevant to the consideration of the relevant merger situation.

6.17 Where those elements are present, s.45 provides for the Secretary of State to make a reference to the Commission in the following alternative circumstances:

■ the creation of the relevant merger situation has resulted (or may be expected to result) in a substantial lessening of competition in any UK market, and – taking account of that and of the public interest consideration(s) concerned – the creation of the relevant merger situation operates or may be expected to operate against the public interest (s.45(2));

■ as above, but where arrangements are in progress or contemplation which, if carried into effect, will result in the creation of a relevant merger situation (s.45(4));

■ the creation of the relevant merger situation has not resulted (and may not be expected to result) in a substantial lessening of competition in any UK market, and – taking account only of the public interest consideration(s) – the creation of the relevant merger situation operates or may be expected to operate against the public interest (s.45(3)); or

■ as immediately above, but where arrangements are in progress or contemplation which, if carried into effect, will result in the creation of a relevant merger situation (s.45(5)).

6.18 Under s.49, the Commission may treat a reference under s.45(2) or (3) as if it was a reference under s.45(4) or (5) (and vice versa). Section 49 makes further provisions for these variations. In other words, a reference may be made on grounds of substantial lessening of competition and grounds of public interest consideration, or on grounds of the public interest consideration alone. The Secretary of State may therefore make a reference even if there is no actual or potential substantial lessening of competition.

6.19 The Secretary of State may not make a reference in the circumstances set out in para. 6.2 (i.e. where an intervention notice may not be made) or where the European Commission is considering a request from the UK under Article 22(3) ECMR (or where the European Commission is or has dealt with the matter in pursuance of such a request).

6.20 The Secretary of State may decide not to make a reference if he believes that there is no relevant public interest consideration. In this case, he shall by notice require the OFT to deal with the matter (s.56). The OFT will then go through the normal procedure of deciding whether to make a reference in relation to the merger.

6.21   Where the Secretary of State decides there is no adverse public interest finding in relation to a reference under s.45, he will proceed to review the reference as if it had been made under the normal procedure from the OFT.

6.22   Section 56(3) states that where the Commission cancels a reference where the public interest consideration is not finalised, but the report of the OFT contains the decision that it is or may be the case that there is an anti-competitive outcome from the merger, the Commission will proceed as if a 'normal' reference had been made to it by the OFT under ss.22 or 33.

6.23   Where the Secretary of State's decision to make a reference to the Commission is made more than 24 weeks after the intervention notice was given, he must make that decision without regard to any public interest consideration which has not been finalised (i.e. which has not been included in the list specified in s.58). This is also the case if the effect of the non-finalised public interest consideration would be to prevent, or to help to prevent, an anti-competitive outcome from being adverse to the public interest (s.46(4)). However, if the Secretary of State believes there is a realistic prospect of this public interest consideration being finalised within the period of 24 weeks beginning with the giving of the intervention notice concerned, he may delay deciding whether to make the reference concerned until the public interest consideration is finalised or, if earlier, the period expires (s.46(5)).

The Secretary of State's reference

6.24   The Secretary of State's reference specifies the section of the Act under which it is made, the date on which it is made, and the public interest consideration(s) which he believes may be relevant to a consideration of the relevant merger situation concerned. Section 48 of the Act states that a reference by the Secretary of State may be framed so that the Commission does not have to consider both the share-of-supply test and the UK turnover test.

Variation of references (s.49)

6.25   The Secretary of State may vary a reference which is referred to the Commission at any time, but must first consult with the Commission (unless it is the Commission which has requested the variation). No variation can alter the public interest consideration(s) specified in the reference, or the time limits within which the Commission's report is to be prepared and given to the Secretary of State.

Cancellation of reference

6.26   Where the Commission cancels a reference made by the Secretary of State under s.53(1) (see para. 6.22), but the OFT's report contains a decision that it is or may be the case that there is an anti-competitive outcome in relation to the relevant merger situation, the Commission must proceed with its analysis as if a normal reference had been made by the OFT in relation to an anticipated or completed merger.

6.27   If the Commission is to prepare and publish a report as under a normal merger reference, it proceeds as if the merger reference had been made at the same time as the reference made by the Secretary of State. The timetable for preparing and giving its report, is the same for the now 'normal' relevant merger situation as it was for the Secretary of State's reference (including any remaining powers of extension and as extended by an additional period of 20 days) (s.56(4)).

QUESTIONS TO BE DECIDED ON REFERENCES BY THE SECRETARY OF STATE

6.28   The Commission's review broadly follows the same process as is prescribed for normal relevant merger situations.

6.29   When a reference is made by the Secretary of State to the Commission, it first decides whether a relevant merger situation has been created, or whether arrangements are in progress or contemplation which, if carried into effect, will result in the creation of a relevant merger situation. If the Commission decides it has (or will), and the Secretary of State's reference was made on the grounds of both substantial lessening of competition and public interest considerations (under s.45(2) or (4)), the Commission then decides whether the merger has resulted, or may be expected to result, in a substantial lessening of competition in any UK market(s), and (taking account only of the substantial lessening of competition and the public interest consideration(s) concerned), whether the creation of that situation operates or may be expected to operate against the public interest (s.47(2) and (5)). When a reference is made on public interest considerations only, the Commission must make its assessment on the basis of those considerations only (s.47(3) and (6)).

6.30   Where the Commission decides that there is, or will be, a substantial lessening of competition within any UK market(s), it must also decide whether it or any other person should take any action under s.41 to remedy, mitigate or prevent the substantial lessening of competition concerned or any adverse effect which has resulted from, or may be expected to result from it (s.47(8)).

6.31   If the Commission decides that the creation of the relevant merger situation operates, or may be expected to operate, against the public interest, it must then decide whether enforcement action or any other action should be taken by the Secretary of State or any other person (other than the Commission) for the purpose of remedying, mitigating or preventing any of the effects adverse to the public interest. The Commission also decides what type of action should be taken and what is to be remedied, mitigated or prevented (s.47(7)).

6.32   In making the decision as to what action, if any, need be taken, the Commission is obliged to have regard to the need to achieve as comprehensive a solution as is reasonable and practicable to the adverse effects to the public interest or (as the case may be) the substantial lessening of competition and any adverse effects resulting from it (s.47(9)). Where the Commission has decided that there will be a substantial lessening of competition, it may also have regard to the effect of any action on any relevant customer benefits in relation to the creation of the relevant merger situation concerned (s.47(10)). This is reiterated in the Commission's Draft Merger Guidelines (para. 5.5), which also state that, to the extent that it is appropriate in the case to do so, the Commission will have regard to these same considerations when determining the appropriate remedy.

TIME LIMITS FOR INVESTIGATIONS AND REPORTS

6.33   The extension of time limits applicable under normal merger situations applies to public interest mergers. However, in addition, the Secretary of State may by notice to the parties extend the four-month time period if he decides to delay a decision as to whether to make a reference to the Commission. The powers to extend the time limits or request information are not exercisable before the giving of the intervention notice. Up until the time the intervention notice is given, the existing time limits in relation to references under ss.22 and 33 apply for the purposes of giving the intervention notice. After the intervention notice has been given, the existing time limits remain applicable, and any extensions made are to be in accordance with the Secretary of State's notice of extension. All of these provisions arise under s.42(6).

6.34   Under s.51, the Commission's report must be with the Secretary of State within 24 weeks, beginning with the date of the reference concerned.

6.35   Where Article 9(6) ECMR[1] applies to the reference, the Commission may have to prepare its report in a shorter period, if necessary in order to comply with Article 9.

6.36   The Commission may extend the period within which the report must be prepared and given to the Secretary of State in two circumstances:

- if there are 'special reasons' why the report cannot be prepared within the original period (s.51(3)), in which case one extension of up to eight weeks may be made; or
- if the Commission considers that a relevant person has failed to comply with the Commission during a request by the Commission to produce information or documents, or to appear as a witness under a notice given under s.109. In such a case, an extension comes into force when the Commission publishes a notice of its intention to extend the time period (in accordance with s.107) and remains in force until the person complies with the original requirement to the satisfaction of the Commission; or until the Commission publishes its decision to cancel the extension.

6.37   For these purposes, a 'relevant person' means any person carrying on any of the enterprises concerned, any person who (alone or as a member of a group) owns or has control of any such person, or any officer, employee or agent of any person connected to these. A person or group of persons able, directly or indirectly, to control or materially influence the policy of a body of persons corporate or unincorporated, but without having a controlling interest in that body of persons, may be treated as having control of it for these purposes. The extension may be made whether or not the relevant person had a reasonable excuse for the failure to comply with the requirement.

6.38   Under s.52(8), the Secretary of State has the power to make an order reducing the 24- and 8-week time periods (or amending any other time period used in substitution for these periods), so long as the Secretary of State does not exceed the 24- and 8-week periods respectively). However, the Commission and any other person the Secretary of State considers appropriate, must be consulted before such an order is made. If the Commission is already considering a reference under existing time periods, any order by the Secretary of State shall not affect the time period under which the Commission is obliged to produce its report (s.52(10)). The Secretary of State is also empowered, by virtue of s.52(12), to make regulations under this section in relation to the time limits for investigations and reports.

DECISIONS OF THE SECRETARY OF STATE IN PUBLIC INTEREST CASES

6.39   Where the Secretary of State receives a report from the Commission, he must decide whether to make an adverse public interest finding in relation to the relevant merger situation or whether to make no finding at all in the matter (s.54). In deciding whether to make a finding, the Secretary of State must accept: the Commission's decision as to whether there is an anti-competitive outcome, or whether a relevant merger situation has been created or is in progress or contemplation; and the decision of the OFT as to the absence of a substantial lessening of competition (s.54(7)).

6.40   An adverse public interest finding is made if he decides that:

(i) a relevant merger situation has been created (or arrangements are in progress or in contemplation which, if carried into effect, will result in the creation of a relevant merger situation);

(ii) the creation of that situation has resulted, or may be expected to result, in a substantial lessening of competition within any UK market(s);

(iii) one or more public interest consideration(s) mentioned in the intervention notice is relevant to the consideration of the relevant merger situation; and

(iv) taking account only of the substantial lessening of competition and/or the relevant public interest consideration(s) (depending on the nature of the reference – see para. 6.29), the creation of that situation operates or may be expected to operate against the public interest.

6.41   The Secretary of State may make no finding only if he decides that there is no public interest consideration relevant to the consideration of the relevant merger situation (s.54(4)). Otherwise, the Secretary of State must publish his decision within 30 days of receiving the report from the Commission (s.54(5)).

ENFORCEMENT ACTION BY THE SECRETARY OF STATE

6.42   Where the Secretary of State decides to make an adverse public interest finding, and has published his decision within the 30-day period, he may take such action permitted by Sched. 7, paras. 9 or 11 as he considers to be reasonable and practicable to remedy, mitigate or prevent any of the effects adverse to the public interest. This includes obtaining final undertakings and orders (including those available in Sched. 8). He must consider the Commission's report in this regard. He must also consider the effect of any enforcement action on relevant customer benefits, if the relevant merger situation has been found to lead to a substantial lessening of competition.

SPECIAL PUBLIC INTEREST CASES

6.43   The Act also provides for an exceptional category of mergers which do not qualify for scrutiny under the general merger regime, and which can only be referred on certain public interest grounds.

6.44   Special public interest cases are provided for by s.59. The Secretary of State's right to intervene arises where he has 'reasonable grounds for suspecting' that a 'special merger situation' has been created or is in progress or contemplation (s.59(1)). In such circumstances, the intervention is commenced by the delivery of a 'special intervention notice'. However, a special intervention notice is given only where the Secretary of State believes that one, or more, of the public interest considerations specified in s.58 (see paras. 6.5 to 6.8) is relevant to a consideration of the special merger situation.

6.45   A specified merger situation arises under s.59 where:

 (i) no relevant merger situation exists (because neither the share of supply nor the UK turnover tests are satisfied); and
 (ii) the transaction would have been a relevant merger situation had those criteria been ignored (in other words, two or more enterprises have ceased to be distinct, etc.); and
 (iii) at least one of the enterprises ceasing to be distinct was carried on in the UK (or by or under the control of a company incorporated in the UK); and
 (iv) a person carrying on one or more of the enterprises was a 'relevant government contractor'.

6.46   As indicated above, special merger situations involve the presence of a relevant governmental contractor. This is a person who has been notified (by or on behalf of the Secretary of State) of information, documents or articles, relating to defence of a confidential nature and held by him in connection with his role as a contractor, and where his notification has not been revoked. Former government contractors holding extant notifications are also relevant governmental contractors for these purposes. Sub-contractors are also covered.

6.47   Where a special merger situation is referred, similar procedures to those in public interest cases apply (see paras. 6.1 to 6.42). However, in a special merger situation, the question of whether the merger will result in a substantial lessening of competition is not an issue that can be considered. The procedures for instigating and reporting on a special public interest merger are otherwise the same.

EUROPEAN INTERVENTION NOTICE

6.48   The section introducing a European intervention notice was added as a late amendment by the House of Lords. This process allows the Secretary of State to intervene in mergers that would otherwise have been dealt with by the European Commission under the exclusive jurisdiction provided under the ECMR. That exclusive jurisdiction is relaxed in Article 21(3) to enable Member States to protect certain non-competition interests affecting that State. The amended s.67 provides that the Secretary of State may give a European intervention notice to the OFT where he has reasonable grounds for suspecting that a European relevant merger situation has arisen. A 'European relevant merger situation' is defined as:

(i) a relevant merger situation has been created (or arrangements are in progress or in contemplation which, if carried into effect, will result in the creation of a relevant merger situation); and
(ii) a concentration with a Community dimension (as defined in the ECMR), or a part of a concentration, has thereby arisen or will thereby arise; and
(iii) a reference which would have otherwise been possible under ss.22 or 33 is prevented from being made under that section by virtue of EC law; and
(iv) the Secretary of State is considering whether to take measures to protect legitimate interests of the UK under Article 21(3) ECMR.

6.49   Article 21(3) ECMR describes legitimate interests as including public security, plurality of the media and prudential rules. However, other legitimate interests may be claimed by Member States, and may be agreed to by the European Commission (if otherwise compatible with EC law) within one month of the Member State's request.

6.50   A European intervention notice will include details of:

(i) the relevant merger situation;
(ii) the public interest consideration(s) which are or may be relevant to a consideration of the relevant merger situation concerned; and
(iii) where any public interest consideration is not finalised, the proposed timetable for finalising it.

6.51   As with notices relating to public interest and special public interest cases, where the Secretary of State believes that there is, or may be, two or more relevant public interest considerations, he may decide not to mention in the intervention notice any of those considerations as he considers appropriate.

6.52   Only one European intervention notice can be given in relation to the same relevant merger situation.

6.53   Where a European intervention notice has been given, the Secretary of State has the power to make orders providing for the taking of action to remedy, mitigate or prevent adverse effects to the public interest which have resulted from, or may be expected to result from, the creation of a European relevant merger situation. Provision may also be made to ensure that provisions which are not public interest considerations may not be taken into account in determining whether anything operates, or may be expected to operate, against the public interest.

NEWSPAPER MERGERS

6.54   Newspapers are one industry which has been partially excluded from the application of the Act. The analysis and approval of newspaper mergers will remain the responsibility of the Secretary of State under the 1973 Act. However, this area is currently under review. The Communications White Paper (*A New Future for Communications*)[2] indicates that newspaper mergers will eventually fall under the remit of the OFT. Broader public interest considerations, such as plurality of the media, will continue to be reviewed by the DTI with input from Ofcom. It is expected that these kinds of public interest issues will be considered in parallel to the provisions made for public interest considerations under Chapter 2 of the Enterprise Act.

6.55   Except in certain limited circumstances, the Secretary of State cannot give consent to the transfer of ownership of the newspaper until the Commission has investigated and reported on the proposed merger. This means that, in most cases, there is an automatic reference to the Commission in newspaper cases. Under the 1973 Act, it is a criminal offence to proceed with a newspaper merger without consent, or to breach any conditions attached to the consent.

6.56   Section 69(2) provides that, unless the newspaper merger falls within the special provisions for newspapers under the 1973 Act, the OFT will be involved in the analysis of newspaper mergers in the same way as provided for under the general requirements of the mergers provisions of the Act. In the House of Commons debates, the government stated its intention to ensure that the new merger regime applies to mergers that involve the transfer of newspaper or newspaper assets, which meet the general merger thresholds, and which the Secretary of State does not refer under the 1973 Act. The policy behind this is the government's belief that the newspaper regime should be retained to address plurality concerns, but that it should be better targeted. This, according to the government, justifies the split between the Enterprise Act and the 1973 Act, and also justifies the continuing involvement of ministers where the newspaper merger issues fall under the 1973 Act.

6.57 The OFT Draft Guidelines on Mergers (para. 9.4) provide useful additional clarification: where a newspaper merger is linked to a merger of a non-newspaper business, the Secretary of State may make parallel references of both mergers. However, where only the newspaper element of such a dual merger is referred, the Commission will not normally consider any non-newspaper aspects of the transaction unless they had a direct bearing on the newspaper merger.

WATER AND SEWERAGE MERGERS

6.58 Water and sewerage mergers are now dealt with under the 2002 Act, and not the Water Industry Act 1991. Section 70 of the 2002 Act substitutes ss.32–5 of the 1991 Act. Schedule 6 of the 2002 Act also provides for the application of provisions of the Enterprise Act 2002, to mergers of water enterprises.

6.59 It is now the duty of the OFT to make a merger reference to the Commission if it believes that it is (or may be) the case that arrangements are in progress which, if carried into effect, will result in a merger of any two or more water enterprises; or that such a merger has otherwise taken place

6.60 A 'water enterprise' is defined as an enterprise carried out by a water or sewerage undertaker appointed under s.6 Water Industry Act 1991.

6.61 Under s.33 of the 1991 Act, the OFT is relieved from its obligation to make a merger reference in respect of any actual or prospective water merger if the value of the turnover of the water enterprise being acquired does not exceed £10 million (or would not, in the case of prospective mergers), or that the value of turnover of the water enterprises already belonging to the acquirer does not (or would not) exceed £10 million. For this purpose, every water enterprise ceasing to be distinct, and whose turnover is deducted as below, shall be treated as a water enterprise belonging to the person making the takeover.

6.62 The value of the turnover of the water enterprise being acquired is determined by taking the total value of the turnover of all the water enterprises ceasing to be distinct enterprises, and deducting the turnover of any water enterprise continuing to be carried on under the same ownership or control. If there is no water enterprise continuing to be carried on under the same ownership and control, the turnover having the highest value is deducted (s.33(2) of the 1991 Act.)

6.63 The Secretary of State may make regulations to alter the sum of £10 million (or whatever sum is substituted for it); or otherwise to modify the conditions set out in s.33(1) of the 1991 Act.

6.64 Where the OFT is not required to make a reference under the new s.32 of the 1991 Act, nothing in subsections 32–4 of that Act prevents the OFT or the Secretary of State from making a reference under Part 3 (mergers) of the 2002 Act, in respect of any actual or prospective merger of two or more water enterprises. Where a situation arises where two or more enterprises have merged, or will merge, which involves the merger of two or more water enterprises, Part 3 of the Act applies in relation to the non-water enterprises. References can therefore be made as normal in relation to the non-water parts of the transaction. Part 3 of the Act shall not apply where the OFT is required to make a reference on a water or sewerage undertaker under s.32 of the Water Industry Act 1991.[3] However, the OFT will consult the Director General of Water Services (the Director) and the parties before making such a reference, taking account of whether, in the case of an anticipated merger, the arrangements are sufficiently far advanced to warrant reference, or are sufficiently likely to succeed.

6.65   Schedule 6 of the Act inserts a new Sched. 4ZA into the 1991 Act. It is this schedule that provides for the issues which must be decided by the Commission on a reference:

(i) whether a water merger has taken place or whether arrangements are in progress which, if carried into effect, will result in a water merger; and

(ii) if so, whether the merger may be expected to prejudice the ability of the Director, in carrying out his functions under the Act, to make comparisons between different water enterprises (such comparisons are required to enable the Director to set price controls and service level targets and to promote economy and efficiency on the part of the water enterprises).

6.66   Questions (i) and (ii) require at least a two-thirds majority if remedies are to be considered.

Enforcement action in relation to water mergers

6.67   In deciding whether to take action for the purpose of remedying, mitigating or preventing the prejudice to the Director of any adverse effect which has resulted from, or may be expected to result from, that prejudice, the Commission may have regard to the effect of any such action on any relevant customer benefits provided that:

(i) a consideration of those benefits would not prevent a solution to the prejudice concerned; or

(ii) the benefits which may be expected to accrue are substantially more important than the prejudice concerned.[4]

6.68   No enforcement action shall be taken on a merger reference under s.32(b) Water Industry Act 1991 in respect of a completed merger if the reference was made more than four months from the date of the reference, unless it took place without being made public and without it coming to the attention of the OFT. If the Commission is satisfied that the reference was not made within the period of four months, it shall state that fact in its report on the reference.

Relevant customer benefits and water mergers.

6.69 Paragraph 7 of Sched. 4ZA of the Water Industry Act (as set down in Sched. 6 of the 2002 Act) provides that a benefit is a relevant customer benefit if:

(a) it is a benefit to relevant customers in the form of:

  (i) lower prices, higher quality or greater choice of goods or services in any market in the UK; or
  (ii) greater innovation in relation to such goods or services; and

(b) the Commission believes;

  (i) in the case of a merger reference under s.32(a) of the Water Industry Act, the benefit may be expected to accrue within a reasonable period as a result of the merger concerned and is unlikely to accrue without the merger concerned or a similar prejudice to the Director;
  (ii) in the case of a merger reference under s.32(b) of the Water Industry Act, the benefit has accrued as a result of the merger concerned or may be expected to accrue within a reasonable period as a result of the merger concerned; and the benefit was or is unlikely to accrue without the merger concerned or a similar prejudice to the Director.

6.70 Apart from these changes, the 1991 Act now provides (Sched. 4ZA, para. 1) that the normal merger regime set out in Part 3 of the 2002 Act will apply to water enterprises, and be the responsibility of the Commission.

REGULATED UTILITIES

6.71 There are no special provisions under UK merger legislation for regulated utilities such as electricity, gas, telecommunications or rail. Therefore, in principle, mergers in regulated industries will be subject to the Act in the same way as any other merger. However, a merger in a regulated industry may well require the modification of an operating licence, or there may be regulator or sector-specific requirements which must be complied with.[5]

Assessment of mergers in regulated industries by the Commission

6.72 The Commission investigates references relating to issues in some regulated industries under the relevant sectoral statutes. The regulated industry sectors are airports, air traffic services, electricity, gas, postal services, railways, telecommunications and water. The types of references investigated by the Commission in relation to these industries are:

 (i) licence modification references;
 (ii) water and other price determination references;
 (iii) water merger references;

(iv) airport references; and

(v) references under the Financial Services and Markets Act 2000.

6.73   Schedules 9 and 25 to the Act provide lengthy amendments to the various sections of the regulated industries' legislation. However, Table 6.1 provides a quick-reference guide for various types of enquiries in various regulated industries. The table also indicates which piece of legislation is relevant to the particular merger, and who is the relevant referring organisation. Readers should note that this information is under review and is likely to change in the near future. The Competition Commission website (**www.competition-commission. org.uk/inquiries/enterprisebill.htm**) should be consulted for the latest version.

Table 6.1 Enquiries in the regulated industries

Type of Enquiry	Statute	Referring organisation
Newspaper merger	Fair Trading Act 1973	Secretary of State
Water merger	Water Industry Act 1991 s.32	Office of Fair Trading
Water licence modification or price determination	Water Industry Act 1991 ss.12 or 14	Director General of Water Services
Airports price regulation (quinquennial reviews)	Airports Act 1986 s.43 or Airports (Northern Ireland) Order 1994 art.34	Civil Aviation Authority
Gas licence modification	Gas Act 1986 s.24 or 41E, or Gas (Northern Ireland) Order 1994 art.15	GEMA [Director General of Gas Supply] (or counterpart in Northern Ireland)
Electricity licence modification	Electricity Act 1989 ss.12 or 56c, or Electricity (Northern Ireland) Order 1996 art. 15	GEMA [Director General of Electricity Supply] (or counterpart for Northern Ireland)
Railways licence modification	Railways Act 1993, s.13 or Sched. 4A	Office of the Rail Regulator
National Air Traffic System	Transport Act 2000, s.12	Civil Aviation Authority
Telecommunications licence modification	Telecommunications Act, 1984, s.13	Director General of Telecommunications
Postal Services licence modification	Postal Services Act 2000, s.15	Postal Services Commission
Broadcasting licences – networking arrangements	Broadcasting Act 1990, Sched. 4	ITC and holders of regional Channel 3 licences
Regulatory provisions or practices	Financial Services and Markets Act 2000, ss.162 or 306	Office of Fair Trading
Public bodies – efficiency and costs	Competition Act 1980, s.11	Secretary of State

1 Article 9 sets out the process of referral to the competent authorities of the Member States – Council Regulation 4064/89 (corrected version published in OJ L257, 21.9.1990).
2 *www.communicationswhitepaper.gov.uk/* and specifically *www.communicationsbill.gov.uk/pdf/newspaper_regime_memorandum.pdf*
3 Except as applied by Sched. 6 of the Enterprise Act which replaces Sched. 4ZA of the Water Industry Act 1991.
4 However, this is without prejudice to the ability of the Secretary of State to make regulations stating what other matters may be considered by the Commission, including matters which are to take priority over the effect of action on relevant customer benefits.
5 The OFT Draft Guidelines on Mergers state that the OFT and the sectoral regulators work closely together on mergers in regulated industries. The OFT draft merger guidelines stress that neither the OFT nor the Secretary of State (in public interest cases) will be bound by the regulator's views but they will pay close attention to them since the regulator may comment on matters that fall outside the OFT's area of expertise.

7 ENFORCEMENT MEASURES RELATING TO MERGER SITUATIONS

INTRODUCTION

7.1   Enforcement measures may be taken at three separate stages in the merger reference procedure. First, prior to a reference on a completed merger being made, steps may be taken to prevent action being taken that might prejudice the reference. Alternatively, undertakings in lieu of a reference may be accepted in simple cases where it is possible to identify at an early stage both the causes of the substantial lessening of competition and suitable remedies. Second, certain enforcement measures may be taken while a merger reference is under consideration by the Commission. These powers supplement the restrictions on conduct that automatically apply during that period. Finally, enforcement measures may be taken at the end of the Commission's review.

7.2   There are a number of common themes that run through the Act in relation to enforcement undertakings and orders applicable to merger references. In general, there is more freedom in relation to the content of undertakings than in relation to the content of orders. Thus the body accepting them is free to include in undertakings any matter it considers appropriate (ss.71(2), 73(2), 80 and 82 and, in relation to public interest and special public interest cases, Sched. 7, paras. 1, 3 and 9)). In contrast to initial and interim orders, measures are restricted to matters required to ensure that no pre-emptive action is taken (ss.72(2), 76(4) and 81(2) and, in relation to public interest and special public interest cases Sched. 7, paras. 2 and 6. Final orders and orders made when undertakings are not being fulfilled may include any provision set out in Sched. 8 of the Act (ss.75(4), 83(4) and 84(2) and, in relation to public interest and special public interest cases, Sched. 7, paras. 5, 10 and 11).

7.3   As far as procedure is concerned, the general rule is that initial and interim undertakings or orders will cease to be in effect once other enforcement measures are taken. Additionally, most undertakings or orders may be varied or revoked by the body that accepts them; that body is generally required, as soon as reasonably practicable, to consider representations received by it in relation to a variation or revocation. In paras. 7.4 to 7.62 we focus on enforcement measures in relation to mergers generally. Public interest and special public interest cases are dealt with subsequently in paras. 7.63 to 7.83.

INITIAL UNDERTAKINGS: COMPLETED MERGERS

7.4   When the OFT is considering whether to make a reference in relation to a completed merger under s.22, and has reasonable grounds for suspecting that it is, or may be, the case that a relevant merger situation has been created, it may take steps by way of an initial undertaking (s.71) to prevent the taking of any action by the parties to the merger which might pre-empt a possible reference to, and assessment by, the Commission. In s.71(8) pre-emptive action is defined as 'action which might prejudice the reference concerned or impede the taking of any action under Part 3 of the Act which may be justified by the Commission's decision on the reference'.

7.5   The OFT has not provided any specific guidance as to the circumstances in which it would consider using these enforcement powers. However, the powers are broad and could be used to prevent further steps being taken to progress the merger. The types of measures that might be considered include provisions restricting the parties from completing any outstanding matters in connection with the merger or transferring ownership or control of any enterprise to which the reference might relate. These are the types of restrictions that are automatically imposed on parties once a reference is made.

INITIAL ENFORCEMENT ORDERS: COMPLETED MERGERS

7.6 Instead of an undertaking, the OFT may make an order (s.72) for the purposes of preventing pre-emptive action being taken, before making a reference in relation to a completed merger. Section 72(2) sets out the matters that can be dealt with by way of initial order. In particular, the order may:

(a) prohibit or restrict the doing of things which the OFT considers would constitute pre-emptive action;
(b) impose on any person concerned obligations as to the carrying on of any activities or the safeguarding of any assets;
(c) provide for the carrying on of any activities or the safeguarding of any assets either by the appointment of a person to conduct and supervise the conduct of any activities (on such terms and with such powers as may be specified or described in the order) or in any other manner; or
(d) require any person to supply information to the OFT (or any other 'relevant authority' as defined in Sched. 8, para. 24), and to provide for the publication of that information.

7.7   An initial order may only be made where the OFT has reasonable grounds for suspecting that pre-emptive action is in progress or in contemplation.

Circumstances in which initial undertakings and orders cease to be in force

Initial undertaking

7.8   Unless – once a reference is made – the initial undertaking is adopted as an interim undertaking by the Commission or (in a public interest or special public interest) adopted as an undertaking by the Secretary of State (Sched. 7, para. 1), it will cease to be in force on the first of the following events:

(a) an initial order being made by the OFT under s.72;
(b) an interim order being made by the Commission under s.81 (see para. 7.30);
(c) the expiry of a period of seven days after a decision by the OFT to refer the merger situation to the Commission under s.22;
(d) the acceptance by the OFT of undertakings in lieu of a reference under s.73 (see para. 7.10); or
(e) a decision by the OFT not to make a reference.

In addition, in public interest and special public interest cases, the following events will cause the initial undertaking to lapse:

(f) an order by the Secretary of State to prevent pre-emptive action (Sched. 7, para. 2; see para. 7.69);
(g) the expiry of seven days from the date the intervention notice was made.

Initial orders

7.9   Unless – once a reference is made – the initial order is adopted by the Commission as an interim order under s.81 or by the Secretary of State (in the context of a public interest or special public interest case) as an order under Sched. 7, para. 2, it will cease to be in force on the first of the events mentioned in para. 7.8(c), (d), (e) and (g), or when:

(a) an initial undertaking or interim undertaking comes into force under either ss.71 or 80; or
(b) the Secretary of State accepts an undertaking under Sched. 7, para. 1 in relation to a public interest or special public interest case.

UNDERTAKINGS IN LIEU OF A REFERENCE UNDER ss.22 OR 33

7.10   Under the Act, the OFT can accept undertakings in lieu of a reference in relation to both completed and anticipated mergers. It has said in its Guidance that these powers are likely to be used only in cases where the competition concerns raised, and the remedies proposed to address them, are clear-cut. It recognises the fact that, in the past, such undertakings have tended to be used in cases where a substantial lessening of competition arises from an overlap in an area that is relatively small in the context of the merger as a whole. In such cases, divestment is relatively easy. However, although the OFT expresses a preference for structural remedies, it is nevertheless clear that undertakings in lieu of a reference may also include behavioural undertakings.

7.11   In accepting any undertakings, the OFT shall have regard to the need to achieve as comprehensive a solution to the substantial lessening of competition and any adverse effects resulting from it as is reasonable and practicable (s.73(3)). The OFT may have regard to the effect of any action on any relevant customer benefits in relation to the creation of the merger situation concerned (s.73(4)).

Restriction on the making of a reference once undertakings in lieu have been accepted

7.12   Once an undertaking in lieu of a reference has been accepted by the OFT under s.73 there can be no reference either by the OFT under ss.22 or 33, or by the Secretary of State under s.45 in relation to the creation of the relevant merger situation. Nevertheless, a reference may still be made if material facts about relevant arrangements, the transaction or the proposals were not notified (whether in writing or otherwise) to the OFT or made public before the undertaking concerned was accepted.

7.13   In this respect, s.74(4) provides that 'made public' means 'so publicised as to be generally known or readily ascertainable'.

ORDERS WHERE UNDERTAKINGS IN LIEU OF A REFERENCE ARE NOT FULFILLED OR WHERE MISLEADING INFORMATION WAS PROVIDED TO THE OFT

7.14   The OFT has powers to make an enforcement order instead of an undertaking in lieu of a reference where it considers that the undertaking is not being, or is unlikely to be, fulfilled (s.75). This also applies where the OFT considers that it has been provided with materially false or misleading information by the parties giving the undertaking. Such enforcement order may go beyond what is required in the undertaking it replaces, and it may be preceded by an interim order to prevent any action which might prejudice the making of the enforcement order.

7.15 In making the order under s.75, the OFT must have regard to the need to achieve as comprehensive a solution as is reasonable and practicable and may take into account relevant customer benefits (s.75(3)).

7.16   There is no requirement that the order should be in the same terms as the undertaking it replaces and it is therefore the case that an order under s.75 may contain provisions which are different from the provisions contained in the undertaking it replaces.

SUPPLEMENTARY INTERIM ORDER-MAKING POWERS OF THE OFT

7.17   Pursuant to s.76, where the OFT has the power to make an order under s.75 in respect of undertakings in lieu of a reference, and intends to make such an order, the OFT may for the purpose of preventing any action which might prejudice the making of that order, make an interim order under s.76.

7.18   The powers under this s.76 may only be used if the OFT has reasonable grounds for suspecting that it is, or may be, the case that action that might prejudice the making of an order under s.75 is in progress or in contemplation.

7.19   An order under s.76 may:

(a) prohibit or restrict the doing of things which the OFT considers would prejudice the making of the order under s.75;
(b) impose on any person concerned obligations as to the carrying on of any activities or the safeguarding of any assets;
(c) provide for the carrying on of any activities or the safeguarding of any assets either by the appointment of a person to conduct or supervise the conduct of any activities (on such terms and with such powers as may be specified or described in the order) or in any other manner;
(d) require the provision of information to the OFT (or other relevant authority as defined in Sched. 8, para. 24) and make provision for its publication.

INTERIM RESTRICTIONS APPLICABLE ONCE A REFERENCE IS MADE

7.20   Once a reference is made by the OFT, under either ss.22 or 33, certain restrictions automatically apply absent any specific initial (in the case of completed mergers) or interim undertakings or orders having been made. Essentially, in the case of completed mergers, s.77 operates so as to ensure that no further steps can be taken to progress the merger. In relation to anticipated mergers s.78 applies to ensure that no shares in the target enterprise can be acquired. Both provisions are described more fully below.

Restriction on certain dealings: completed mergers

7.21   In the case of completed mergers where a reference has been made under s.22 but not finally determined, and where no initial or interim undertakings or orders are in force in relation to the merger situation, s.77 provides that no further action may be taken to progress the merger. In particular, s.77(2) provides that no relevant person shall without the consent of the Commission:

(a) complete any outstanding matters in connection with any arrangements which have resulted in the enterprises concerned ceasing to be distinct;

(b) make any further arrangements in consequence of that result (other than arrangements which reverse that result);

(c) transfer the ownership or control of any enterprises to which the references relate; or

(d) assist in any of the activities mentioned in (a)–(c) above.

7.22 A 'relevant person' is 'any person who carries on any enterprise to which the reference relates or who has control of any such enterprise, any subsidiary of any person falling within the aforementioned description or any person associated with any person falling within that description or any subsidiary of any person so associated' (s.77(8)). The restrictions in s.77 extend to a person's conduct outside the UK only if he is a UK national, a body incorporated under the laws of the UK (or any part of the UK), or a person carrying on business in the UK.

7.23 In order to do any of the activities referred to in para. 7.21, the consent of the Commission is required. The consent of the Commission may be general or special and is subject to revocation by the Commission. Such consent must be published in such a manner as the Commission considers appropriate for the purpose of bringing it to the attention of any person entitled to benefit from it. However, publication is not required if the Commission does not consider it necessary.

Restrictions on certain share dealings: anticipated mergers

7.24 Section 78 of the Act provides that, in the case of a reference concerning an anticipated merger under s.33, in respect of which no interim undertakings under s.80 or interim orders under s.81 are in force: 'no relevant person shall without the consent of the Commission, directly or indirectly acquire, during the "relevant period" an interest in shares [or stock] in a company if any enterprise to which the reference relates is carried on by or under the control of that company'. Acquiring an interest in shares will occur where the person enters into a contract to acquire them, acquires the right to exercise (or control the exercise) of right attaching to them, or acquires a 'call' right (s.79). However, s.78 limits the concept of the acquisition of an interest in shares in circumstances such as a person accepting appointment to act as a proxy at a shareholders' meeting.

7.25 The 'relevant period' is the period beginning with the making of the reference and ending when the reference is finally determined.

7.26 The Commission's consent may be given and revoked in the same way as described in para. 7.23, and is subject to the same publication requirements.

7.27 These restrictions apply to a person's conduct outside the UK, as described in para. 7.22.

INTERIM UNDERTAKINGS: COMPLETED AND ANTICIPATED MERGERS

7.28   Where a merger reference has been made in relation to either a completed or anticipated merger, the Commission may for the purpose of preventing pre-emptive action, accept from the parties (or some of them) undertakings to take such action as it considers appropriate (s.80). In this respect, pre-emptive action is defined in the same way as in para. 7.65.

7.29   If the OFT has already accepted undertakings under s.71 in relation to a completed merger, the Commission may adopt that undertaking (s.80(3)). Any undertaking so adopted will continue in force in accordance with its terms (s.80(4)).

INTERIM ORDERS: ANTICIPATED AND COMPLETED MERGERS

7.30   Where a reference has been made in relation to either a completed or anticipated merger, but the reference is not finally determined, the Commission may make an order for the purpose of preventing pre-emptive action. Any such order may deal with any of the issues referred to in para. 7.69.

7.31   As with interim undertakings, the Commission may simply adopt any initial orders already made by the OFT (s.81(3)).

FINAL ENFORCEMENT POWERS

7.32   Once the Commission's report on the merger reference is published, the Commission may take steps to remedy any substantial lessening of competition or detriments arising therefrom, by way of final undertakings or orders. Similar to the procedure in relation to undertakings in lieu of a reference, if a final undertaking is not being, or may not be, fulfilled, or if misleading information was provided to the Commission, then the Commission may make an order in place of that undertaking. If appropriate, this may be preceded by an interim order.

FINAL UNDERTAKINGS

7.33   Section 82 provides that the Commission may, in accordance with s.41, accept from such persons as it considers appropriate undertakings to take actions specified or described in the undertakings.

7.34   The undertaking will cease to be in force if an enforcement order is made in respect of the undertakings under s.83 where they are not being fulfilled or if an interim enforcement order is made under s.76(1)(b) in respect of these undertakings.

Restriction on the acceptance of final undertakings

7.35   Section 82(4) provides that final undertakings cannot be accepted once an order has been made in relation to the reference either under s.83 (where final undertakings are not fulfilled), s.76(1)(b) (where an interim order is made where final undertakings are not fulfilled) or under s.84 (a final order).

ORDER-MAKING POWERS WHERE FINAL UNDERTAKINGS ARE NOT FULFILLED

7.36   Under s.83, if the Commission considers that an undertaking accepted by it under s.82 has not been, is not being, or will not be, fulfilled, or that it was provided with false or misleading information by the person giving the undertaking, the Commission may make an order under s.83 to remedy, mitigate or prevent the substantial lessening of competition concerned and any adverse effects which have resulted from, or which may be expected to result from it (s.41(2)). This provision mirrors s.75.

SUPPLEMENTARY ORDER-MAKING POWERS

7.37   The provisions of s.76 also apply where the Commission intends to make an enforcement order under s.83.

7.38   The powers under s.76 are set out in paras. 7.17 to 7.19 and may only be used in relation to final undertakings where the Commission has reasonable grounds for suspecting that it is or may be the case that action which might prejudice the making of an order under s.83 is in progress or contemplation.

FINAL ORDERS

7.39   The Commission may in accordance with s.41 make an order under s.84 containing anything permitted in Sched. 8 and such supplementary, consequential or incidental provisions as the Commission considers appropriate.

CONTENTS OF ENFORCEMENT ORDERS

7.40   The Act contains certain restrictions on the scope of enforcement orders. In particular, enforcement orders may extend to a person's conduct outside the UK only if he is a UK national, a body incorporated under the laws of the UK (or of any part of the UK), or a person carrying on business in the UK (s.86).

7.41   An enforcement order cannot impact on conditions in licences granted under UK or European patents or in respect of registered designs or require licences of right in relation to such patents or design rights (s.86). An enforcement order can include any of the provisions referred to in Sched. 8 and can include modification of licence conditions related to regulated markets under Part 1 of Sched. 9 (s.86). The swingeing nature of orders is demonstrated by the fact that an enforcement order may prohibit the performance of an agreement already in existence when the order is made.

7.42   Additionally, the Act states in s.87 that an enforcement order may authorise the person making the order to give directions to any person specified in those directions, or to the holder for the time being of an office (specified in the order) in any body of persons corporate or unincorporate. Such directions may include a requirement to take such action as is specified or described in the directions for the purpose of carrying out or ensuring compliance with the enforcement order concerned; or to do or refrain from doing any thing so specified or described which the person might be required by that order to do or refrain from doing.

7.43   The High Court or the Court of Session may order any person who has failed to comply with directions to comply with them or remedy his failure to comply with them, within such time as may be specified in the order. This procedure is set out in s.87 of the Act.

REMEDIES: PROVISIONS OF SCHED. 8

7.44   The remedial provisions referred to in Sched. 8 are divided into two broad categories: structural remedies and behavioural remedies. These are described in detail below.

Structural remedies

7.45   In terms of structural remedies an order may:

(a) prohibit an acquisition or any other act that would result in two or more bodies corporate becoming interconnected, or ceasing to be distinct;
(b) where such acquisition has already been completed, or where the bodies are already interconnected, or have ceased to be distinct, impose prohibitions or restrictions on the relevant persons;
(c) provide for the division or divestment of a business or of any group of interconnected bodies corporate (e.g. by sale of any part of the undertaking, or of assets) or the division.

7.46   Structural remedies may require a number of ancillary provisions. The Act provides for these to be included in the order – in particular, provisions as to:

(a) the transfer or creation of property, rights, liabilities or obligations;
(b) the number of persons to whom the property, rights, liabilities or obligations are to be transferred or in whom they are to be vested;
(c) the time within which the property, rights, liabilities or obligations are to be transferred or vested;

(d) the adjustment of contracts (whether by discharge or reduction of any liability or obligation or otherwise);

(e) the creation, allotment, surrender or cancellation of any shares, stock or securities;

(f) the formation or winding up of any company or other body of persons corporate or unincorporate;

(g) the amendment of the memorandum and articles or other instruments regulating any such company or other body of persons;

(h) the extent to which, and the circumstances in which, provisions of the order affecting a company or other body of persons corporate or unincorporate in its share capital, constitution or other matters, may be altered by the company or other body of persons concerned;

(i) the registration of the order under any enactment by a company or other body of persons corporate or unincorporate which is affected by it, as mentioned in para. (h);

(j) the continuation, with any necessary change of parties, of any legal proceedings;

(k) the approval by the relevant authority, or another person, of anything required by virtue of the order to be done or of any person to whom anything is to be transferred, or in whom anything is to be vested, by virtue of the order; or

(l) the appointment of trustees or other persons to do anything on behalf of another person which is required of that person by virtue of the order, or to monitor the doing by that person of any such thing.

7.47   Schedule 8 para. 15 provides that an order may also impose requirements to publicise or notify certain items, such as price lists. An order may also prohibit the publication or notification of information, for example, recommended price lists.

7.48   Other items of which an order may require publication include:

(a) accounting information concerning the supply of goods or services (including information as to the costs of supply, such as fixed costs and overheads); the manner in which fixed costs and overheads are calculated and apportioned; and the income attributable to the supply;

(b) information in relation to the quantities of goods or services supplied; and

(c) information in relation to the geographical area in which goods or services are supplied.

7.49   Sched. 8, para. 19 provides that an order may include a requirement that information be supplied to the relevant authority, or to the OFT, and provide for publication by it.

7.50   An order may also include any provisions that the person making the order deems appropriate. Such provisions may include both positive and negative obligations in the interests of national security as defined by s.58(1) of the Act concerning market investigation references.

Behavioural remedies

7.51   The behavioural remedies permitted under Sched. 8 are wide ranging. Paragraph 2 lists the general restrictions on behaviour that can be required by order. These include a prohibition on the making or performance of an agreement, or a requirement that an agreement be terminated. Note, however, that such order cannot be made in respect of an agreement relating to terms and conditions of employment or the physical conditions in which workers are required to work. Orders may also prohibit any threat or refusal to supply goods or services, or any procurement of a threat or refusal to supply. Orders may also concern requirements in relation to the supply of goods or services, including, for example, a requirement which concerns bundling (making the supply of goods or services conditional upon the buying of any goods or the payment for services other than the goods or services supplied).

7.52   An order may be used to prohibit: discriminatory practices (or the procurement of discriminatory practices); practices through which preferences in relation to the supply of goods or services are given; or practices whereby prices are charged that differ from those that are published. Where the Commission's report requires remedial action in relation to the prices charged for the goods or services, the order may amount to a price regulation for the goods or services concerned. Finally, an order may include terms prohibiting the exercise of any right to vote exercisable by virtue of the holding of any shares, stocks or securities.

THE COMMISSION'S APPROACH TO REMEDIES

7.53   In the Commission's guidelines on merger references, it has set out its views on remedial action. It points out that where it finds that a merger results or is expected to result in a substantial lessening of competition, it is likely to conclude that no action is appropriate only in exceptional circumstances. These might arise where the cost of any practicable remedy are disproportionate in light of the size or expected decline of the relevant market, or where the only appropriate remedial action would fall outside the UK's jurisdiction (i.e. it relates to behaviour outside the UK by non-UK nationals, or by bodies incorporated outside the UK, or by a person not carrying on business in the UK). Even in these circumstances, the Commission might recommend that action be taken by others, for example by the OFT, to keep the future conduct of the merged entity under review. Remedies will be decided on a case-by-case basis; however, the Commission has said that it will have regard to aspects such as costs, proportionality and effectiveness.

The costs of remedies

7.54   The Commission will consider the cost of any action in deciding on the reasonableness of remedies. However, in relation to completed mergers, the Commission will not consider the cost to the parties of divestment. The rationale for this is that the parties would have had the opportunity to seek clearance of the merger before it took place, so the cost was avoidable. The cost to companies of foregone economies will generally be considered in the context of relevant customer benefits. Further, the Commission has said that it will not consider environmental costs or the social costs of unemployment, unless it is required to do so by the Secretary of State through a public interest consideration. However, the Commission will have regard to the cost to the OFT in monitoring compliance of any remedies that the Commission may put in place.

Proportionality

7.55   In its guidelines, the Commission states that it will abide by the principle of proportionality in determining appropriate remedies. In other words, when deciding between two possible remedies it will choose the remedy that imposes the least costs or is the least restrictive.

Effectiveness of remedies

7.56   The Commission makes three general points in relation to effectiveness. First, it points to the fact that the effectiveness of any remedy will be influenced by its clarity both for the persons to whom it is directed and to other interested parties (for example the OFT, or competitors who would be interested in ensuring compliance). Second, there must be consideration of the prospects of remedial action being implemented and complied with. The effectiveness of any remedy is reduced if the parties are unwilling to implement it. In general, one-off remedies to change the structure of the market are likely to be preferable to remedies that depend upon the behaviour or conduct of firms. Finally, the Commission will tend to favour a remedy that can be expected to show results in a relatively short period of time.

Structural remedies

7.57   In its Guidelines, the Commission discusses how it might choose between different types of remedies. In particular, it discusses the merits of structural remedies, behavioural remedies and regulatory remedies.

Prohibition and divestment

7.58   The Commission takes the view that the most effective remedy for an anticipated merger will likely be a prohibition. For completed mergers, this remedy will take the form of divestment. The aim is to ensure that divestment takes place within a specified and reasonable time after the Commission has published its decision, so as to minimise the possible reduction in the commercial value of the business to be divested. Until divestment is complete, measures intended to safeguard the commercial value of the business including possibly the appointment of a trustee or other person to monitor the process may be implemented. The Commission will usually require the subsequent purchase to be approved by the OFT.

Partial prohibition and divestment

7.59 This may be the most appropriate remedy where the merged firms also carry out activities in markets other than those to which the merger is expected to bring about a substantial lessening of competition. As long as those areas can be clearly identified, a partial divestment or a partial prohibition may be appropriate. The Commission highlights two key questions that will determine whether partial divestment can be an effective remedy:

(a) where the assets to be divided provide the basis of a viable business that can operate independently of the merged firm and in a reasonably short time (say within one year) can be expected to provide effective and sustained competition to the other firms in the market; and

(b) where a purchaser of the assets will be capable of operating the assets and running a viable, competitive business, and to have the incentive to compete with the merged firm.

Other structural remedies

7.60 These might include licensing or assignment of know-how or intellectual property rights or the removal of restrictions in contracts that tie customers to the merged firm.

Behavioural remedies

7.61 Behavioural remedies may prevent or limit the anti-competitive effects of a merger, while allowing the gain from the merger to be realised. The Commission considers that there are several shortcomings to such remedies. They can involve detailed prescriptive behaviour and may not be fully effective for dealing with a merger in a market where coordinated behaviour is a concern. Further, they will usually require continual monitoring by the OFT. It can be difficult to keep them in tune with current market conditions and therefore they can introduce their own distortions to competition. Derek Morris said in an article published in the *Financial Times* on 18 November 1998 that the Commission would tend to prefer structural remedies and tend to 'fall back' on behavioural measures and price controls if other remedies are likely to be disproportionate or not effective.

Regulatory remedies

7.62 The Commission will always consider whether to recommend action be taken by others. Such action could be aimed at encouraging competition in the affected market. For example, it might recommend action by ministers to change legislation or regulations. Of course, third parties are not bound by these recommendations, but the government has given a commitment to consider any recommendations within 90 days of publication of the Commission's report.

ENFORCEMENT REGIME FOR PUBLIC INTEREST AND SPECIAL PUBLIC INTEREST CASES: SCHED. 7 TO THE ACT

7.63   The enforcement regime for public interest and special public interest cases is set out in Sched. 7 to the Act. It is broadly the same as the regime prescribed for other merger situations. There is a system for pre-emptive undertakings and orders to be made prior to a reference in the case of completed mergers similar to the system of initial undertakings and orders in other completed merger cases. The Secretary of State can accept undertakings in lieu of a reference in relation to public interest cases and special public interest cases in the same way as the OFT can in relation to other merger situations. There is also the power to make an enforcement order, preceded if necessary by an interim enforcement order where such undertakings are not, or may not be, fulfilled.

7.64   Again, the ability to take pre-emptive measures applies to all mergers once a reference is made, and the Schedule sets out the procedures for final undertakings and orders to be accepted or made by the Secretary of State.

PRE-EMPTIVE UNDERTAKINGS: COMPLETED MERGERS

7.65   Where an intervention notice or special intervention notice is in force in relation to a completed merger, the Secretary of State may (for the purposes of preventing pre-emptive action), accept undertakings from such of the parties concerned as he considers appropriate. The undertakings may relate to the taking of any action he considers appropriate. In this context, pre-emptive action is defined as action which might prejudice the reference or possible reference under s.45 or (as the case may be) s.62, or impede the taking of any action which might be justified by the Secretary of State's decision on the reference (Sched. 7, para. 1(12)).

7.66   Alternatively, rather than accepting new undertakings, the Secretary of State may, for the purposes of preventing pre-emptive action, simply adopt an initial undertaking in relation to a completed merger (under s.71) which has been accepted by the OFT, provided that undertaking is still in force.

7.67   A pre-emptive undertaking in relation to a reference of a public interest case or a special public interest case ceases to be in force if a pre-emptive order under Sched. 7, para. 2 or an undertaking in lieu of a reference under Sched. 7, para. 3 comes into force in relation to that reference. A pre-emptive order in relation to a reference of a public interest case or a special public interest case ceases to be in force if an undertaking under Sched. 7, paras. 1 or 3 comes into force in relation to that reference. Further, a pre-emptive undertaking or order shall (if it has not already done so) cease to be in force when the intervention or special intervention notice (as the case may be) ceases to be in force.

PRE-EMPTIVE UNDERTAKINGS: ANTICIPATED MERGERS

7.68 Pursuant to Sched. 7, para. 1 the Secretary of State may accept pre-emptive undertakings in relation to anticipated mergers in the same way as in relation to completed mergers (described in paras. 7.65 to 7.67) except that the Secretary of State cannot accept such pre-emptive undertakings unless a reference has been made under ss.45 or 61.

PRE-EMPTIVE ORDERS: COMPLETED MERGERS

7.69 Schedule 7, para. 2 provides that where an intervention notice or special intervention notice is in force, the Secretary of State or the OFT may, for the purposes of preventing pre-emptive action, by order:

(i) prohibit or restrict the doing of things which the Secretary of State or (as the case may be) OFT considers would constitute pre-emptive action;

(ii) impose on any person concerned, obligations as to the carrying on of any activities or the safeguarding of any assets;

(iii) provide for the carrying on of any activities or the safeguarding of any assets, either by appointing someone to conduct or supervise the conduct of any activities or in any other manner;

(iv) require that information is provided to the OFT (or other relevant authority defined in Sched. 8, para. 24) and make provision for its publication.

Alternatively, where an initial order had been made by the OFT in relation to the order in respect of which the public interest intervention notice is made, the Secretary of State can simply adopt that pre-emptive order.

PRE-EMPTIVE ORDERS: ANTICIPATED MERGERS

7.70 Schedule 7, para. 2 applies in the same way to anticipated mergers as to completed mergers except that no pre-emptive order can be made by the Secretary of State until a reference has been made under ss.44 or 60.

Undertakings in lieu of a reference in relation to public interest or special public interest cases

7.71 If the Secretary of State has power to make a reference to the Commission in relation to a public interest or special public interest case, and intends to make such a reference, Sched. 7, para. 3 provides an alternative. Instead of making a reference, the Secretary of State may accept undertakings from any of the parties to take appropriate action. This will be for the purpose of remedying, mitigating or preventing any of the adverse effects which have, or may have resulted, or may be expected to result from the creation of the relevant merger or special relevant merger situation concerned.

7.72   In this event, the Secretary of State shall, in particular, accept the OFT's decisions (relating to whether undertakings would be sufficient) which are contained in its report on the merger situation concerned. In this regard, the Secretary of State may consider the effect of any action on any relevant customer benefits arising from the creation of the relevant merger situation.[1]

7.73   An undertaking in lieu of a public interest or special public interest reference shall come into force when it is accepted; it may be varied or superseded by another undertaking, or may be released by the Secretary of State. An undertaking which is in force in relation to a relevant merger situation or special merger situation, ceases to be in force if an order comes into force in relation to that undertaking.

Effect of undertakings in lieu of a reference

7.74   The relevant authority[2] shall not make a reference under ss.22, 33, 45 or 62 if the Secretary of State has accepted an undertaking or group of undertakings in lieu of a reference of a public interest or special public interest case. The same is true if the relevant merger situation or special merger situation is the same situation by reference to which the undertaking or group of undertakings was accepted. However, this does not prevent the making of a reference if 'material facts' about relevant arrangements or transactions, or proposed arrangements or transactions were not notified to the Secretary of State or the OFT (either by a merger notice or otherwise) or made public[3] before any undertaking concerned was accepted.

ORDERS WHERE THE UNDERTAKINGS IN LIEU OF A REFERENCE ARE NOT FULFILLED OR WHERE MISLEADING INFORMATION WAS PROVIDED

7.75   The Secretary of State may make an order where he considers that an undertaking accepted by him in lieu of a public interest or special public interest reference has not been, is not being, or will not be, fulfilled. He may also make an order where he considers that information which was false or misleading in a material respect was given to him or to the OFT by the person giving the undertaking (before the Secretary of State decided to accept it). The Secretary of State shall have regard to the OFT's report and the effect of any action on relevant customer benefits; as referred to in paras. 7.72 and 7.73.

Supplementary interim order making powers

7.76   The Secretary of State may, for the purpose of preventing any action which might prejudice the making of an order, make a supplementary order. However, no such order shall be made unless the Secretary of State has reasonable grounds for suspecting that it is, or might be, the case that action which might prejudice the making of an order under Sched. 7, para. 5, is in progress or in contemplation.

7.77   Such an order may:

(i) prohibit or restrict the doing of things which the Secretary of State considers would prejudice the making of the order under Sched. 7, paras. 5 or 10;

(ii) impose on any person concerned, obligations as to the carrying on of any activities or the safeguarding of assets;

(iii) provide for the carrying on of any activities or the safeguarding of assets either by the appointment of a person to conduct or supervise the conduct of the activities, or in any other manner;

(iv) do anything which may require a person to provide information to the relevant authority.

STATUTORY RESTRICTIONS FOLLOWING A REFERENCE IN RELATION TO A PUBLIC INTEREST CASE OR SPECIAL PUBLIC INTEREST CASE

7.78   Paragraphs 7 and 8 of Sched. 7 reiterate the provisions of ss.77 and 78 in relation to other merger cases except that consent should be sought from the Secretary of State, rather than the Commission, to do anything that is prohibited by those paras.

FINAL UNDERTAKINGS AND ORDERS

7.79   The Secretary of State may, in accordance with s.55 (enforcement action by the Secretary of State in public interest cases) and s.66(5) to (7) (enforcement action by the Secretary of State in special public interest cases), accept undertakings from such persons he considers appropriate. The undertakings themselves will specify or describe the action to be taken.

7.80   If an undertaking is already in force in relation to a public interest or special public interest reference, it ceases to be in force if an order under Sched. 7, paras. 6(1)(b) or 10 comes into force in relation to the subject matter of the undertaking.

7.81   Further, no final undertaking shall be accepted in relation to a public interest or special public interest case reference if an order has been made under Sched. 7, paras. 6(1)(b) or 10 in relation to the subject matter of the undertaking, or para. 11 in relation to that reference.

MAKING OF SUPPLEMENTARY ORDERS BY THE SECRETARY OF STATE

7.82   Where the Secretary of State considers that a final undertaking accepted by him has not been, is not being, or will not be, fulfilled, or that materially false or misleading information was provided to him or to the OFT before the decision was made to accept the undertakings; he may make an order. The creation of the order will be for the purpose of s.55(2) or, as the case may be, s.66(6), which provides the Secretary of State with power to take such action as he considers to be reasonable and practicable to remedy, mitigate or prevent any of the adverse effects which have resulted from, or may be expected to result from, the creation of the relevant merger situation or special merger situation.

7.83   An order under para. 10 may contain anything permitted in Sched. 8, and such supplementary, consequential or incidental provisions as the Secretary of State considers appropriate. The Secretary of State also has power to make such an order, in accordance with s.55 generally or s.66(5) to (7) as the case may be. An order under para. 11 may contain the same provisions as an order under para. 10, with the one difference being that no order shall be made under para. 11 in relation to a reference of a public interest case or a special public interest case if a final undertaking has already been accepted in relation to that reference.

ENFORCEMENT FUNCTIONS OF THE OFT

7.84   Under s.91, the OFT has a duty to compile and maintain a comprehensive register of undertakings and orders including details of all enforcement undertakings or orders and any subsequent variation or revocation, and the details of any consents given by the Commission or the Secretary of State lifting the statutory restrictions on parties that otherwise come into effect when a reference is made. The register shall be kept in whatever form the OFT considers to be appropriate, but must be publicly available.

7.85   The OFT must also keep the effectiveness of enforcement undertakings and orders under review. The OFT is required to prepare reports of its findings on the effectiveness of enforcement undertakings and orders, and to publish such reports.

7.86   The OFT must monitor undertakings and orders and consider:

(a) whether an enforcement undertaking or order has been complied with;
(b) whether, by reason of any change of circumstances, an enforcement undertaking is no longer appropriate and one or more parties needs to be released from it or it needs to be varied or to be superseded by a new enforcement undertaking; and
(c) whether circumstances have changed to the extent an enforcement order is no longer appropriate and needs to be varied or revoked (s.92(2)).

7.87   The OFT will give the Commission or (as the case may be) the Secretary of State such advice as it considers appropriate in relation the following:

(a) any possible variation or release by the Commission or the Secretary of State of an enforcement undertaking accepted by it or him;
(b) any possible new enforcement undertaking to be accepted by the Commission or the Secretary of State so as to supersede another enforcement undertaking given to it or him;
(c) any possible variation or revocation by the Commission or the Secretary of State of an enforcement order made by it or him;
(d) any possible enforcement undertaking to be accepted by the Commission or the Secretary of State instead of an enforcement order or, any possible enforcement order to be made by the Commission or the Secretary of State instead of an enforcement undertaking;
(e) the enforcement of any enforcement undertaking or order by way of civil proceedings; or
(f) the enforcement of the restrictions set out in paras. 7.21 and 7.27 (s.92(3)).

7.88   Additionally, the OFT is under an obligation to take such action as it considers appropriate in relation to the variations or release by it of any enforcement undertaking or order that it has accepted or made, any new enforcement measures or the possibility of enforcing undertakings or orders by way of civil proceedings (s.92).

The role of the OFT in relation to the negotiation of undertakings

7.89   The Commission or (as the case may be) the Secretary of State, may require the OFT to consult with such persons as they consider appropriate[4] with a view to discovering whether they will offer undertakings which the Commission or Secretary of State would be prepared to accept.

Rights to enforce undertakings and orders

7.90   Any person to whom an enforcement undertaking or order relates, has a duty to comply with it (s.94(2)). Compliance with enforcement undertakings or enforcement orders is enforceable by civil proceedings brought by the OFT for an injunction, interdict or other appropriate relief or remedy (s.94(6)). Compliance with undertakings accepted by it or orders made by it may also be enforced by the Commission and compliance with enforcement undertakings or orders in relation to public interest cases is also enforceable by civil proceedings brought by the Secretary of State.

Rights to enforce statutory restrictions

7.91   A breach of the restriction on certain dealings in relation to both completed mergers and public interest and special public interest mergers (s.77(2) or

(3) to the Act and Sched. 7, para. 7(2) or (3) respectively) or share dealing in s.78(2) to the Act (Sched. 7, para. 8(2)) is actionable by any person who sustains loss or damage as a result.

7.92   Additionally, compliance with those provisions shall be enforceable by civil proceedings brought by the OFT, Commission or Secretary of State (as appropriate) for an injunction or for interdict or for any other appropriate relief or remedy.

---

1   No undertaking shall be accepted by the Secretary of State in lieu of a reference of a public interest case if a public interest consideration mentioned in the intervention notice concerned has not been finalised, and the period of 24 weeks beginning with the giving of that notice has not expired. However, if he considers there is a 'real prospect' of that consideration being finalised within the period, the Secretary of State may delay making the decision as to whether to accept any undertaking (and any related decision as to whether to make a reference). Such a delay will not extend beyond the time when the public interest consideration is finalised, or if earlier, the expiry of the 24 weeks.
2   In relation to a reference under ss.22 or 33, this is the OFT, and in relation to a reference under ss.45 or 62, the Secretary of State.
3   'Made public' means so publicised as to be readily ascertainable (para. 4(5)).
4   This is without prejudice to the power of the relevant authority to consult the persons concerned itself.

8 EUROPEAN MERGER CONTROL: REVIEW OF THE ECMR

INTRODUCTION

8.1   On 11 December 2002 the European Commission adopted a comprehensive reform of its merger control regime. On 11 December 2001, the European Commission published a Green Paper on the Review of the EC Merger Regulation (ECMR)[1] The aim of the paper was to identify possible improvements, based on experience gathered since the introduction of the ECMR in 1991. The underlying objective of the review was to meet the challenges posed by global mergers, monetary union, market integration, enlargement of the EU and the need to co-operate with other jurisdictions.

8.2   The European Commission's press release announcing the adoption of the December 2002 reforms described them as 'a comprehensive merger control reform package, which is intended to deliver a world class regulatory system for firms seeking approval for their mergers and acquisitions in the 380 million, soon to be 450 million, consumer-strong European Union'. The proposals were first revealed by Mario Monti, the European Commissioner for Competition Policy, in a speech to the IBA conference in Brussels on 7 November 2002 (**www.europa.et.int/rapid. Speech/02/545**). Following the adoption by the Commission of the reform package, Monti stated that the new merger control system would be 'a model to be emulated worldwide'.

8.3   The package of reforms consists of: (a) a proposal for a revision of the ECMR; (b) draft guidelines on the appraisal of horizontal mergers; and (c) a series of non-legislative measures intended to improve the decision-making process (some of which are contained in best-practice guidelines). The explanatory memorandum to the proposal for the new ECMR deals with the various categories of reform: jurisdictional issues; substantive issues; procedural issues; and other proposed amendments. It is expected that the EU Council will discuss the proposed revisions to the ECMR, with a view to it coming into force on 1 May 2004. The following paragraphs look at the proposed reforms.

REFERRAL OF MERGERS TO AND FROM THE MEMBER STATES

8.4   The jurisdictional changes affect both the allocation of responsibilities between the European Commission and the Member States, and the concept of a concentration.

8.5   The European Commission was concerned that the jurisdictional thresholds contained in Article 1(3) ECMR had not solved the problem of the need to make multiple national filings in a large number of transactions, problems which such criteria were designed to tackle. In 2000, only one in five cases known to be subject to the requirement to notify in three or more Member States were over the thresholds in Article 1(3). Of particular concern to the European Commission was the trend indicating an increase in multiple filings (i.e. to three or more Member States), and the fact that enlargement of the European Commission is likely to exacerbate this trend. This causes significant unnecessary expense and inconvenience to the parties. The Green Paper had suggested the introduction of an automatic Community competence over cases that would otherwise have been subject to multiple filing requirements in three or more Member States.

8.6   The responses to the Green Paper showed that the respondents believed that an alteration to the criteria in Article 1(3) was unlikely to impact significantly on the multiple filings problem. In addition, there would be a risk that such automatic competence would have the undesired effect of conferring Commission jurisdiction over a number of cases that are not subject to such multiple filings.

8.7   There was broad support for an alternative suggestion for simplifying the tests used in the referrals to the Member States under Article 9 and from the Member States under Article 22. However, there is still some concern that the reliance on the discretion of Member States to determine the question of Community jurisdiction on a case-by-case basis may prove inconsistent. However, Monti discussed this issue in his Brussels speech in November 2002. He stated that one of the objectives of the review of the ECMR is to optimise the allocation of merger cases between the European Commission and national competition authorities in light of the principle of subsidiarity, while at the same time tackling the 'persistent phenomenon' of multiple filings.

8.8   The amended ECMR provides for enhanced recourse to the referral mechanisms under Articles 9 and 22, including their use at a pre-notification stage. The Commission's explanatory memorandum sets out the main elements of the proposed system as follows:

(a)   the simplification of the referral criteria to and from the Member States under Articles 9 and 22, including a closer 'mirroring' of the criteria for referral in both directions (i.e. increasing the utilisation of Articles 9 and 22);

(b)   the possibility for referral applications to be made at the pre-notification stage. The notifying parties would make a reasoned request for a pre-notification referral in either direction, subject to the agreement of the European

Commission and the national competition authorities; the request would be deemed to be accepted if not expressly opposed within 10 days of the relevant Member State(s) receiving a copy of the submission for a referral;

(c) the creation of exclusive competence for the Community where at least three relevant Member States agree to a case being referred to the European Commission; and

(d) the ability of the European Commission to invite Member States to make referrals, or to request the Commission to refer cases to them.

DEFINITION OF A CONCENTRATION

8.9   Article 3 of the amended ECMR makes it clear that a concentration will arise only where there is a change of control on a lasting basis. The underlying definitions of the transactions themselves – mergers and acquisitions – are unchanged, except that the concept of a merger in Article 3(1)(a) now expressly covers mergers of parts of undertakings. The application of the ECMR to joint ventures is not changed.

MULTIPLE TRANSACTIONS

8.10   The new Article 3(4) provides that two or more transactions which are conditional on one another or are so closely connected that their economic rationale justifies their treatment as a single transaction, shall be deemed to constitute a single concentration arising on the date of the latest transaction. This provision will more explicitly deal with related transactions, where the jurisdictional thresholds are crossed only where the transactions are viewed in the aggregate.

THE SUBSTANTIVE TEST

8.11   The Green Paper launched a debate on the merits of the substantive test enshrined in Article 2 ECMR, under which mergers are assessed on the basis of whether they create or strengthen a dominant position as a result of which effective competition would be significantly impeded in the common market or in a substantial part of it. The Green Paper discusses the merits of moving to a 'substantial lessening of competition' (SLC) test (as has been adopted under the Enterprise Act in the UK). Although inviting observations from interested parties, the Green Paper states that 'experience in applying the dominance test does not reveal major loopholes in the scope of this test. Nor has it frequently led to different results from SLC-test approaches in other jurisdictions'. However, there is an argument that the SLC test allows greater flexibility, especially in relation to collective dominance. The principal arguments for a change to the SLC test is that such a test would be inherently better suited to dealing with 'the full range and complexity of competition problems that mergers can give rise to, and in particular there may be a gap or gaps in the scope of [the dominance test]'.[2]

8.12 However, Professor Monti stated in his speech that the arguments against retention of the dominance test were overstated. The dominance test has produced outcomes broadly in line with the SLC test (as used in the USA) and, according to Prof. Monti, is capable of being adapted to a wide variety of situations. He claimed that the additional advantage of maintaining the dominance test was the preservation of the jurisprudence that the European Courts have developed in interpreting its meaning. This case law helps to maintain a high degree of legal certainty for parties and their advisers. The amended ECMR has therefore retained the dominance test.

8.13 However, Monti signalled in his speech that the amended Regulation would adopt its own definition of dominance different to that adopted under Article 82. Recital 20 of the amended ECMR provides that dominance should be defined 'in such a way as to reflect a considerable level of economic power held by one or more undertakings'. Recital 21, dealing with oligopoly market power, adds that

> the notion of dominance within the meaning of this Regulation should . . . encompass situations in which, because of the oligopolistic structure of the relevant market and the resulting interdependence of the various undertakings active on that market, one or more undertakings would hold the economic power to influence appreciably and sustainably the parameters of competition, in particular, prices, production, quality of output, distribution or innovation, even without coordination by the members of the oligopoly.

8.14 This is reflected in Article 2.2, which will provide that, for the purpose of the Regulation:

> one or more undertakings shall be deemed to be in a dominant position if, with or without coordinating, they hold the economic power to influence appreciably and sustainably the parameters of competition, in particular, prices, production, quality of output, distribution or innovation, or appreciably to foreclose competition.

8.15 Notwithstanding the arguments put forward by the Commission justifying it, the adoption of a dominance test for the purposes of the ECMR that is different from that adopted under Article 82 has clear disadvantages for the development of a sound EU jurisprudence.

EFFICIENCIES

8.16 The Commission's Green Paper sought comments on how and the extent to which efficiencies should be taken into account in EU merger control. Criticism had been levied at the European Commission for not allowing parties to rely on an efficiency defence. Most respondents to the Green Paper considered that the Commission should take efficiencies into account. Mario Monti, in his speech to the IBA Conference, agreed that an explicit recognition of merger-specific efficiencies is possible without having to change the wording of the substantive test in the ECMR. In this regard, Article 2(1)(b) ECMR provides a clear legal basis for a discussion of efficiencies in a merger, by stating that the Commission shall take account of, *inter alia*, 'the development of technical and economic progress, provided it is to the consumers' advantage and does not form an obstacle to competition'. Monti confirmed that the majority of the respondents to the Green Paper favoured the publication of comprehensive guidelines indicating: (a) what the Commission will be prepared to consider as an efficiency claim in the overall assessment of the merger; and (b) in what circumstances it may ultimately decide that efficiencies will constitute a defence.

8.17 Recital 24 of the amended ECMR provides for the Commission to publish guidelines on the treatment of efficiencies. Monti's view is that efficiency claims should only be accepted when the Commission is in a position to conclude with sufficient confidence that the efficiencies generated by the merger will enhance the incentive of the merged entity to act pro-competitively for the benefit of consumers. He stated that the efficiencies will have to be:

(a) of direct benefit to consumers;
(b) merger specific;
(c) substantial;
(d) timely; and
(e) verifiable.

8.18 Monti also stated that the burden of proof will rest on the parties claiming the efficiencies, including the burden of demonstrating that the efficiencies 'are of such a magnitude' as to outweigh the negative effects of the merger on competition. This is in line with the responses to the Green Paper.

PROCEDURAL ISSUES

8.19 The Green Paper opened a debate on the processes for notification process, decision making and consultation, many of which are picked up in the amended ECMR.

8.20 A proposal to introduce more flexibility into the notification process elicited almost unanimous support from respondents. Although Monti was 'firmly opposed to general erosion of the tight timetable inherent in the current regime under the Merger Regulation', he considered it important to introduce a degree of flexibility, in particular in complex Phase II cases. The amended ECMR proposes a number of significant changes.

Time limits

8.21 The Regulation will drop the requirement that mergers be notified within one week of their conclusion. Concentrations must still be notified prior to implementation (subject to the derogations discussed in para. 8.23). Having removed the obligation to notify before a certain date, the amended ECMR also provides for the earliest date on which a transaction can be notified. Article 4(1) now provides that, although the general rule is that notification shall be made following the conclusion of the agreement, the announcement of the public bid, or the acquisition of a controlling interest, notification may also be made:

> where the undertakings concerned demonstrate to the Commission a good faith intention to conclude an agreement or, in the case of a public bid, where they have publicly announced an intention to make such a bid, provided that the intended agreement or bid would result in a concentration with a Community dimension.

8.22   The periods set out in the Regulation for the assessment of mergers will be expressed in terms of working days. Phase I will be 25 working days, with an automatic extension to 35 working days where remedies are offered. Phase II will be 90 working days, extended to 105 working days where remedies are offered, so long as they have been offered at least 55 working days after the initiation of proceedings. Phase II may also be extended at any time with the consent, or at the request, of the notifying parties. The parties may make one such request only; it must be made not later than 15 working days after the initiation of proceedings. The total duration of any such voluntary extension or extensions may not exceed 20 working days.

Suspension of concentrations

8.23   There will be an automatic derogation from the requirement to suspend the implementation of a concentration in the case of all stock market acquisitions from multiple vendors – i.e. 'a series of transactions in securities including those convertible into other securities admitted to trading on a market such as a stock exchange, by which control within the meaning of Article 3 is acquired from various sellers'. In order to take advantage of this derogation, the concentration must be notified to the Commission without delay, and the acquirer must not exercise the voting rights attached to the securities in question except to maintain the full value of its investments, and then only on a derogation granted by the Commission. The Regulation will also provide the Commission with the power to issue block derogations to categories of concentrations which, in general, do not lead to a combination of market positions giving rise to competition concerns. The intended categories will likely correspond to the ones set out in the Commission Notice on a simplified procedure for the treatment of certain concentrations under the ECMR (OJ C217, 29/7/2000, page 32).

Investigative and enforcement powers

8.24   The size of possible level of fines and periodic penalty payments are to be increased from its current 50,000 to 1 per cent of the turnover of the undertaking or association of undertakings concerned. The maximum daily amount of periodic penalty payments, currently €25,000, will instead be set at 5 per cent of the aggregate average daily turnover of the undertaking or association of undertakings concerned. The same will apply to periodic penalty payments related to the enforcement of remedy decisions or decisions ordering a de-merger.

8.25   The Commission will also be empowered to conduct interviews with individuals. These oral submissions can be introduced as evidence in proceedings where the interviewee consents. There will be the power to impose penalties where interviewees provide false or misleading information. The Commission points out that it is not taking the power to conduct sector inquiries or to search private homes in the context of merger control.

Commission powers

8.26   Article 8(4) makes more explicit the powers of the Commission to order restoration of the arrangements existing prior to the implementation of a merger that is subsequently blocked. The provision will now enable the Commission to require the undertakings concerned:

> to dissolve the concentration, in particular through the dissolution of the merger or the disposal of all the shares or assets acquired, so as to restore the situation prevailing prior to the implementation of the concentration. In circumstances where restoration of the situation prevailing prior to the implementation of the concentration is not possible through dissolution of the concentration, the Commission may take any other measure appropriate to achieve such restoration as far as possible.

8.27   The new Article 8(5) will provide that where a concentration has been implemented, in contravention of either Article 7 or of a condition attached to a Commission decision, the Commission may take:

> any measure appropriate to restore or maintain conditions of effective competition, including interim measures. A decision requiring the undertakings concerned to dissolve the concentration or imposing any other measures, with the exception of interim measures, may only be taken [where the concentration is incompatible with the common market under Article 2(4), and in the case of joint ventures with co-ordinative effects] where the criteria laid down in Article 81 (3) of the Treaty are not fulfilled.

Procedure following annulment by the European Courts

8.28   A new Article 10(5) has been added to the ECMR to provide for the consequences of a judgment of the CFI or ECJ annulling in whole or in part a Commission decision under the ECMR. If the decision was subject to a time limit under Article 10 (deadlines for Phase I and Phase II decisions), the transaction will have to be re-examined by the Commission – in the light of current market conditions – in order to adopt a new decision under Article 6(1). Where the original notification is incomplete as a result of changes in market conditions, or in the information provided, subsequent to the original notification, then the notification must be supplemented by the parties.

Decision-making process

8.29   Monti has laid out a general approach to reform which would provide for greater transparency, flexibility, accountability and legal certainty. Several of his proposals detail internal processes within the European Commission which do not require a change to the ECMR. These are broadly:

(a) the enhancement of DG Comp's economic capability in order to deal with the increasing complexity and global scale of merger cases; this will involve the creation of a new position of Chief Competition Economist, with the staff necessary 'to provide an independent economic viewpoint to decision makers at all levels, as well as guidance throughout the investigative process';

(b) a panel review in Phase II merger cases; this panel will be independent from the Merger Task Force, and be composed of experienced officials; it will have the task of scrutinising the investigating team's conclusions with a fresh pair of eyes at key points of enquiry.

Enhancing the parties' ability to defend their points of view

8.30   Monti recognises the criticism of the Commission that it is 'too prone to capture' by the merging parties' competitors who are said to have an 'excessive influence' in the investigation. Although stating that this problem may be exaggerated, Monti's intention is to allow ample opportunity for the merging parties to defend their points of view during the investigation, and to confront the concerns of third parties at the earliest stage possible. Monti proposes that the merging parties should have access to the Commission's file shortly after the opening of a Phase II investigation. Further, the merging parties would continue to have access throughout the investigation to the submissions of third parties, challenging the merger. Monti also envisages an opportunity for the merging parties and their challengers to meet before the statement of objections is sent out. This will allow for some of the arguments to be 'thrashed out' informally before a statement of objections is issued. More transparency and discipline will come in the form of 'state of play' meetings with the Commission at decisive points in the procedure. This will keep the merging parties constantly updated on progress and provide them with the opportunity to discuss the case with senior Commission officials.

Strengthening the Hearing Officer's role

8.31   Monti intends to strengthen the role of Hearing Officers, as a means of guaranteeing the protection of merging parties' rights of defence and ensuring the appropriate conduct of the Commission's procedures. The Commission press release announced that the Hearing Officers will have additional support staff.

Improving case management and investigation

8.32   The Commission press release announced the creation of a new post, Deputy Director General for Mergers, to oversee practical management of the

Commission's investigations. Philip Lowe, the new Director General of DG Comp will assume this responsibility in the interim.

Judicial review

8.33   No doubt conscious of the three recent cases in which the CFI overturned the Commission's merger decision[3] Monti praised the Court's fast-track procedure as a means of 'keeping the deal alive' (somewhat realistic, even with fast-track), but stated that there is also room for improvement within the Commission in terms of reviewing cases with more speed. Monti suggested introducing improvements in the field of interim measures. He noted that the EC Treaty already allows for interim relief, but suggested that this procedure could perhaps be adapted to 'better serve the needs of merger proceedings'. He also suggested the creation of 'judicial panels' as a way of speeding up the judicial review process. These panels would be able to deal with certain categories of cases at first instance (e.g. staff cases) or could lead to the creation of a specialised merger chamber within the CFI. This would free up resources within the CFI itself, which could then deal specifically with competition cases. However, this would only be a realistic proposal if and when the CFI obtains new resources. The Commission press release was circumspect in its proposals.

CONCLUSIONS

8.34   The Green Paper, the responses to the Green Paper, and Monti's speech to the IBA Conference all advocate the need for radical reform of the ECMR, which has not undergone serious review or reform since its introduction. The Commission has now presented this package of reforms to the EU Council.

8.35   Interestingly, there are several aspects which reflect the overhaul of the UK's competition reform under the Enterprise Act 2002. These include the desirability for a system which is transparent, disciplined, accountable and predictable. Another common theme is the possible availability of efficiencies as a merger defence. Monti's concluding comment applies as much to the UK's competition reform as it does the EU's: 'By reforming the present merger control system as radically as needed, I am determined to ensure that it remains a key instrument to foster . . . economic success in the years ahead'.

1   COM(2001)745/6 final.
2   Mario Monti's speech of 7 November 2002.
3   *Airtours plc* v. *Commission* (Case T-342/99, 6 June 2002); *Schneider Electric SA* v. *Commission* (Case T-310/01, 22 October 2002); *Tetra Laval BV* v. *Commission* (Case T-5/02, 25 October 2002).

9 MARKET INVESTIGATION REFERENCES

INTRODUCTION

9.1 Part 4 of the Act sets out the rules relating to market investigations. These rules are intended to replace the provisions of the Fair Trading Act 1973 (the 1973 Act) dealing with monopoly investigations, and to supplement those provisions of Competition Act 1998 (the 1998 Act) which provide for the control of monopoly power through the Chapter II prohibition on the abuse of dominance. The provisions of Part 4 of the Act retain the basic structure of the monopoly reference procedure of the 1973 Act. However, there are some significant changes. In particular, the market investigation process has been depoliticised, and the role of the various participants in the reference process has been clarified. With regard to the reference process, the role of the Secretary of State is very limited, with the majority of reference decisions now being made by the OFT. The grounds for making a reference have been modified. The 25 per cent market share test, prescribed by the 1973 Act for the identification of monopoly situations has been replaced by a broad competition-based approach. Finally, in the majority of cases, the Commission will have the final decision on remedies, rather than deferring that decision to the Secretary of State. The Secretary of State will retain a significant role only in relation to 'public interest cases' under s.139.

POWER OF THE OFT TO MAKE A REFERENCE

9.2 Under the Act, the primary power to refer a market to the Commission for investigation rests with the OFT. The Secretary of State will retain a reserve power to make a reference in exceptional circumstances (more fully described in para. 9.58 below).

9.3 Section 131 sets out the criteria for market investigation references by the OFT. It provides that the OFT may refer a market for investigation if it has reasonable grounds for suspecting that:

> any feature, or combination of features, of a market in the United Kingdom for goods or services prevents, restricts or distorts competition in connection with the supply or acquisition of any goods or services in the United Kingdom or a part of the United Kingdom.

9.4   Under ss.50 and 51 of the 1973 Act, a reference could only be made where it appeared that a monopoly situation existed or may have existed in relation to the supply of goods or services or the export of goods from the UK. The 1973 Act distinguished between two types of monopoly situation:

(a) a 'scale' monopoly situation; and
(b) a 'complex' monopoly situation.

9.5   A scale monopoly situation was one in which at least one-quarter of all the goods and services of a certain description were supplied by or to one and the same person or group of interconnected bodies corporate, or, in the case of exports, where at least one-quarter of the specified goods produced in the UK were produced by one and the same person or group of interconnected bodies corporate.

9.6   A complex monopoly situation arose where at least one-quarter of all the goods or services of a certain description were supplied by, or to, members of one and the same group, where that group comprised two or more unrelated persons aggregated by reason of the conduct of their affairs. Therefore, while a reference could be made in relation to either structural or behavioural issues, the Director General of Fair Trading (DGFT) and the Secretary of State were constrained by the need to demonstrate that at least 25 per cent of the market was in the hands of a person or a group.

The meaning of 'reasonable grounds for suspecting'

9.7   Under the 1973 Act, a reference decision could be made either by the DGFT or the Secretary of State (or other appropriate minister) where 'it appeared to him' that a monopoly situation existed. This was generally considered to confer a very broad discretion on the authorities, making it difficult to challenge a reference decision by way of judicial review. The Act now requires that the OFT has 'reasonable grounds for suspecting' that any of the features referred to prevents, restricts or distorts competition. This test was preferred by the government in *Productivity and Enterprise – A World Class Competition Regime*, December 2001 (para. 30). As part of the consultation process two options were considered to form the basis of a threshold sufficient to trigger the OFT's power to refer: (a) 'reasonable suspicion'; or (b) 'belief'. The government preferred 'reasonable suspicion', which it viewed as a lower standard than belief. It remains to be seen whether 'reasonable grounds for suspecting' is in practice a significantly different test than under the 1973 Act, and whether it is more – or less – likely that a reference decision could be successfully challenged by way of judicial review for want of 'reasonable grounds'.

The meaning of 'features of the market'

9.8   Features of the market are defined in s.131(2) as being:

(a) the structure of the market concerned or any aspects of that structure;
(b) any conduct (whether or not in the market concerned) of one or more than one person who supplies or acquires goods or services in the market concerned; or

(c) any conduct relating to the market concerned of customers of any person who supplies or acquires goods or services.

9.9   Conduct is defined in s.131(3) to include any failure to act (whether or not intentional) and any other unintentional conduct. According to the OFT, conduct includes decisions that firms take, how they make them and the resulting action or lack of it.

9.10   Relevant features of the market may include structural features of that market, conduct of any person, including customers on that market, as well as conduct in other markets which has an impact on the reference market. Although structural and behavioural issues are referred to separately in the Act, there is no requirement to identify in the reference whether the particular features of the market that is the subject of a reference are to be considered structural features or some aspect of conduct.

'Market in the United Kingdom'

9.11   This is defined in s.131(6) to include:

> so far as it operates in the United Kingdom or a part of the United Kingdom, any market which operates and in another country or territory or in a part of another country or territory; and

> any market which operates only in a part of the United Kingdom.

Thus, the OFT will not be limited to making a reference in relation to a market which is purely national; it can make a reference in relation to a broader geographical market, so long as the UK is included in that wider market. It appears from this provision that the reference can be made in relation to the market as a whole, which may be broader than just the UK. This appears to be confirmed by virtue of the fact that under s.86 of the Act, which applies to market investigation remedies as well as merger remedies, remedial action may be required in relation to conduct outside the UK in certain circumstances (see para. 9.111 for remedial action).

LIMITATION ON THE ABILITY OF THE OFT TO MAKE A REFERENCE

9.12   The OFT is prevented under s.131(4) of the Act from making a reference in relation to a particular feature or combination of features of a market where either:

(a) undertakings in lieu of a reference have been accepted by the OFT from one or more firms under s.154 of the Act in relation to the same goods or services to which that feature or combination of features relates within the previous twelve months; or

(b) if the Secretary of State (acting alone or jointly with another minister) has stepped in and made a reference in relation to the same matter under s.132, and that reference has not been finally determined. The power of ministers to step in to make a market investigation reference is described in paras. 9.58 to 9.60. For the purposes of s.131(4), the meaning of 'finally determined' is provided in s.183(3) to (6).

THE OFT'S DISCRETION TO MAKE A REFERENCE

Introduction to the OFT's Guidance

9.13   Section 171 of the Act requires that, as soon as reasonably practicable after the passing of the Act, the OFT shall prepare and publish general advice and information about the making of references by it under s.131. The OFT has published draft guidelines on its reference policy under s.131 (public consultation on guidance for market investigation references, July 2002, hereafter 'the Guidance'). The Guidance sets out the OFT's views on a number of key issues. The main aspects of them are summarised in the following paragraphs. The Guidance is not binding on the OFT, but is nevertheless an extremely useful guide to the grounds on which the OFT may decide that a market investigation reference is justified.

9.14   By way of introduction, in para. 2.1 of the Guidance, the OFT states that it will exercise its discretion to make a reference to the Commission where the reference criteria set out in s.131 are met and where the following criteria are also met:

(a) it would not be more appropriate to deal with the relevant competition issues under the 1998 Act or by using any other powers available to the OFT, or where appropriate, to the sectoral regulators;
(b) it would not be more appropriate to address the problem identified by means of undertakings in lieu of a reference;
(c) the scale of the suspected problem, in terms of its detrimental effect on customers, is such that a reference would be an appropriate response to it; and
(d) there is a reasonable chance that appropriate remedies will be available.

Relationship with the 1998 Act

9.15   During the House of Commons Select Committee hearings, the government stated that it would expect the OFT to use the 1998 Act in cases where it suspected that the 1998 Act's prohibition on anti-competitive agreements or abuse of dominance was being infringed. A market investigation reference would generally be used in cases where the 1998 Act was not applicable. However, the government gave the assurance that the OFT would have absolute discretion in that respect.

9.16   In the Guidance, the OFT expresses the view that market investigations are concerned with something different from particular anti-competitive agreements or the abuse of dominance. Their purpose is to determine whether the process of competition is working effectively in a market as a whole by analysing and, where appropriate, remedying industry-wide or market-wide competition problems in circumstances where there is no legal basis for addressing them under the 1998 Act, or where action under the 1998 Act has been, or is likely to be, ineffective in dealing with the adverse effects on competition that are identified.

9.17   In the Guidance, the OFT gives some examples of situations in which the 1998 Act would not apply, and where market investigation references are more likely to be made. These include competition problems arising from uncoordinated parallel conduct by a number of firms, or industry-wide features of the market where the OFT does not have reasonable grounds to suspect the existence of anti-competitive agreements or dominance.

9.18   As a general point, the OFT suggests that single firm conduct will, where necessary and possible, be dealt with under the 1998 Act. Nevertheless, the OFT does not exclude the possibility of making a market investigation reference concerning single-firm activity, and cites two examples in the Guidance of when such a reference might be considered:

(a) where a firm has sufficient market power to prevent, restrict or distort competition but falls short of meeting the test for dominance; and
(b) where the only effective remedies are likely to be structural ones.

In relation to networks of vertical agreements, the OFT recognises that it could deal with this issue through the withdrawal of the benefit of the 1998 Act exclusion[1] in relation to a particular agreement. However, the OFT envisages that such course may not always be the best way of dealing with the consequences of a network of parallel agreements, and that a market investigation might offer a better solution.

Undertakings in lieu of a reference

9.19   Under s.154 of the Act, the OFT has the power to accept undertakings in lieu of a reference. In its Guidance, the OFT considers that undertakings in lieu of a reference are likely to be rare. The circumstances in which the OFT would consider using this power as an alternative to a reference are described in para. 11.14.

Scale of the adverse effects on competition

9.20   Where it seems likely that the detrimental effect on customers is not significant, the OFT may take the view that the burden on business, particularly in terms of management time, and the public expenditure costs of an investigation by the Commission, are likely to be disproportionate to any benefits that may be obtained from remedying the adverse effects. In the Guidance, the OFT does not make any definitive statements about the circumstances in which detrimental effects on customers will be viewed as not significant. However, it lists a number of factors that will be taken into account in assessing that significance, including:

(a) the size of the market: in general, the cost of investigating a very small market would not be justified but the OFT does not indicate what size of market it would consider to be too small;

(b) the proportion of the market affected by the feature giving rise to adverse effects on competition; if the proportion of the market affected by the feature is small, a reference would be unlikely; again, the OFT does not specify the proportion below which a reference would not be made; and

(c) the persistence of the feature giving rise to the adverse effects; if the features are short-term, a reference is unlikely; there is no indication as to what 'short-term' would be for these purposes.

9.21   The OFT's Guidance recognises that, in some cases, those market features which have an adverse effect on competition may also produce offsetting customer benefits. Where it is clear that such benefits exceed the likely detriment from the adverse effect on competition, the OFT will not make a reference. In cases of uncertainty, it will refer and leave it to the Commission to weigh the benefits and detriments to customers.

Availability of remedies

9.22   According to the Guidance, the OFT will only make a market investigation reference where it considers that appropriate remedies are likely to be available. By way of example, the OFT explains that, if the market is global and a remedy imposed in the UK would be unlikely to have a significant effect on the way the market operates (even within the UK), it may not be appropriate to make a reference. Further, where the adverse effects on competition arise primarily from legislative regulations or the actions of regulators, so that the Commission would be unable to remedy such adverse effects, a reference is unlikely to be made.

APPLICATION BY THE OFT OF THE REFERENCE CRITERIA IN s.131(1)

Prevention, restriction or distortion of competition

9.23   These terms are not defined in the Act. However, in its Guidance, the OFT describes competition as:

> a process by which firms strive in various ways to win customers from rivals. Competition will be effective and markets will work well when firms engaged in the market are subject to competitive constraints from other firms already in the market and/or from firms that could readily enter it, and from their customers.

9.24   The OFT intends to interpret the phrase 'prevention, restriction or distortion of competition' broadly, to encompass any reduction or dampening of actual or potential competition. It considers this to be consistent with EC case law under Article 81(1) EC Treaty as well as the past practice of the Commission.

9.25   The OFT states in its Guidance that there may not be a clear divide between structural features and those relating to conduct. By way of example, it refers to exclusionary conduct by firms in the market; this conduct will affect structure to the extent that it raises entry barriers. In most cases, the OFT's assessment of the need for a reference would be likely to be based on a combination of features, and will include evidence about both structure and conduct.

Market definition

9.26   In its Guidance, the OFT has stated that its approach to market definition in relation to possible market investigation references will be the same as in relation to other competition cases. The market definition will usually comprise both a product market definition and a geographic market definition. The product market will comprise those products (or services) that are close enough substitutes for each other so that their price is constrained by the price of the other products within the market. Products are close substitutes if a significant number of customers are able, and prepared, to switch their purchasing from one to another on a small but significant change in their relative prices. This is referred to as demand-side substitutability. The OFT will also have regard to supply-side substitutability, i.e. the ability of firms that do not currently supply a particular product to quickly, and at minimal cost, switch to the production of products within the market. For details of the manner in which the Commission approaches market definition, see paras. 9.74 to 9.81.

Structural features of a market

9.27   In its Guidance, the OFT identifies the following structural features of the market as being relevant when considering a possible market investigation reference:

(a) concentration levels in the market;
(b) the extent of vertical integration;
(c) conditions of entry, exit and expansion;
(d) government regulations;
(e) information asymmetries;
(f) switching costs; and
(g) countervailing buyer power.

Concentration in the market

9.28   Market concentration refers to the number and size of firms in the market. High market shares usually indicate some level of market power. The OFT refers to the fact that often, although certainly not always, markets in which firms have high market shares are markets with high barriers to entry. The OFT considers that firms that have less than 40 per cent market share may nevertheless have market power which might be subject to investigation by way of a market investigation reference. Additionally, the OFT points to the fact that oligopolistic markets may provide an opportunity for firms to coordinate their behaviour for mutual advantage, or can simply reduce the incentive to compete. The OFT does recognise that not all oligopolistic market structures produce these results. Factors such as the symmetry of market shares, the homogeneity of products, the stability of market conditions, and the transparency of the market are more likely to produce a situation in which an understanding on price can be reached and maintained.

Vertical integration

9.29   Markets in which there is a significant amount of vertical integration may have increased barriers to entry if a potential competitor would have to enter at all levels of the market in order to compete effectively. Similarly, if vertically integrated firms refuse to deal with new entrants or discriminate against them, this will raise barriers to entry. This is only likely to be the case where vertically integrated firms have a sizeable share of any of the vertically linked markets. A market investigation reference might be appropriate if a number of firms in the market are vertically integrated and if they engage in some common form of anticompetitive conduct, for example discrimination against any non-integrated competitor.

Conditions of entry, exit and expansion in the market

9.30   In the Guidance, the OFT states that the markets in which the OFT is interested will likely have significant barriers to entry for potential entrants. It defines 'entry barriers' as being any feature of the market that gives incumbent suppliers a cost or other advantage over efficient potential entrants. The OFT distinguishes between three types of entry barriers:

(a) absolute advantages, such as access to scarce inputs, intellectual property rights or regulatory barriers that limit the number of market participants;
(b) strategic or first mover advantages of incumbents; and
(c) exclusionary behaviour by incumbents, such as predatory price cuts or restrictive distribution agreements which raise new entrants' distribution costs.

9.31   In the Guidance, the OFT indicates that barriers caused by the behaviour of firms might well be addressed under the 1998 Act, rather than by way of market investigation, particularly where they involve a dominant undertaking or an agreement between several firms.

Government regulations

9.32   Government regulations are most likely to have a direct effect on competition when they limit the number of firms that can operate in the market.

However, regulations may also affect the conduct of undertakings. This might arise when the regulations raise those costs which may bear more heavily on smaller undertakings and new entrants rather than a larger competitor.

Information asymmetries

9.33   In markets where customers have inadequate access to information or are unwilling or unable to search for the best deals, firms may be able to exercise a degree of market power even if there are many firms supplying the market. Where product quality is difficult for customers to assess, either because of their complexity or the infrequency with which they are purchased, the lack of transparency can have a significant adverse effect on the level of competition in the market.

Switching costs

9.34   Where customers face difficulties in switching between suppliers either because of financial costs, administrative hurdles or the inconvenience of doing so, competition may be adversely affected.

Countervailing power of purchasers

9.35   The effectiveness of buyer power in constraining suppliers will depend on a number of factors identified by the OFT, including the relative dependence of sellers and buyer and the credibility of any threat by the buyer to switch sourcing.

The conduct of firms

9.36   The OFT interprets conduct to include the decisions that firms take, how they make them and the resulting action or lack of it. It anticipates that, although conduct on the part of an individual firm may occasionally be the basis of a reference, most market investigation references are likely to involve markets where the conduct of a number of firms (whether sellers or buyers) appears to have the effect of preventing, restricting or distorting competition. The OFT gives a number of examples of the kind of conduct which may be relevant, although stresses that the list should not be regarded as exhaustive.

9.37   The type of conduct listed includes the conduct of oligopolistic firms where those firms are aware of the mutual interdependence of their actions, resulting in parallel behaviour. The question will therefore be whether the oligopolists' conduct reflects the restriction of effective competition and would be an appropriate ground for an OFT investigation. Where firms in an oligopolist market reach a tacit understanding to pursue their joint interests by coordinating their behaviour, the adverse effects on competition are likely to be severe. To support a reference, the OFT will need to establish that the market features that make collusion a feasible strategy are present and will need to have a reasonable sus-picion that the oligopolists are not competing effectively with consequences that are likely to be detrimental to their customers.

9.38   In assessing this, the OFT will examine evidence such as:

(a) the pattern of price changes over time;
(b) price inertia;
(c) any evidence that, notwithstanding evidence of parallelism in, for example, published prices, the oligopolists compete in discounts or other concessions from the published price; and
(d) the oligopolists' rates of return, compared to returns in comparable markets or to the costs of capital.

9.39   The OFT takes the view that, even if the conditions necessary for tacit col-lusion are not met, other market features – such as switching costs and informa-tion inadequacies – may limit competition in oligopolist markets.

Facilitating practices

9.40   The OFT identifies facilitating practices as being those practices that make it easier for oligopolists to arrive tacitly at a collusive outcome. The OFT gives a number of examples of facilitating practices, including arranging price increases well in advance of implementation, most favoured customer clauses in contracts, uniform systems for reflecting transport charges in prices, and information exchanges on such issues as costs.

Custom and practice

9.41   The OFT envisages using its powers under the Act to initiate market inves-tigations into industry customs or practices that are adopted by an industry gen-erally, without any agreement or understanding. Such practices would include the practice of manufacturers in recommending retail prices.

Networks of vertical agreements

9.42   The OFT anticipates using the Act to investigate networks of vertical agreements in the same way as it has under the 'complex monopoly' provisions of the 1973 Act.

Conduct of customers

9.43   Section 131(2)(c) identifies conduct by customers as a market feature that could give rise to an adverse effect on competition and, as such, may be the subject of a market investigation reference.

9.44   In the Guidance the OFT has highlighted the search process as being one feature of consumers' conduct that can affect competition. Where customers have high search costs, competition may be restricted. In particular, the extent to which customers do not engage in search practices may impact on competition in a market. Where search costs are combined with high switching costs, the effect on competition may be compounded.

INVESTIGATIVE POWERS OF THE OFT

9.45   Section 174 of the Act sets out the powers of investigation available to the OFT for the purpose of assisting it in deciding whether to make a reference under s.131, or whether to accept undertakings in lieu of a reference under s.154.

9.46   The use of investigative powers under s.174 are limited to circumstances in which the OFT already considers that it has the power to make a reference, i.e. when it has reasonable grounds for suspecting that any feature of a market prevents, restricts or distorts competition. Thus the OFT cannot go on a 'fishing exercise' with these powers.

9.47   The OFT has said that, because the threshold for using its powers of investigation is the same as for making a reference; it will not always be necessary to have recourse to these powers in order to determine whether a reference should be made. Section 174 gives the OFT three broad investigatory powers:

(a) it may require the attendance of any person to give evidence at a time and place specified by the OFT in the notice;

(b) it may require the production by any person of specified documents, or of documents that fall in a specified category; those documents or categories of documents may also be identified by description; the OFT may copy any such documents; and

(c) it may require any person who carries on any business to produce such estimates, forecasts or returns or other information as may be specified or described in the notice.

9.48   The OFT takes the view that, in practice, it is unlikely to summon people to give evidence in normal circumstances, and the Act specifies that no person shall be required to travel more than 10 miles from his place of residence unless his necessary travel expenses are paid or offered to him (s.174(9)).

9.49   The powers exercisable under s.174 must be exercised by way of notice. The Act does not specify the form of the notice but does require, pursuant to s.174(6) of the Act, that any notice requiring a person to attend or supply documents or information must include information about the consequences of non-compliance.

Rule against self-incrimination

9.50   Section 174(8) specifies that no person shall be required to give evidence, produce documents or provide information, that he could not be compelled to give, produce or provide in civil proceedings before the High Court or the Court of Session.

Failure to comply with a notice under s.174

9.51   A person who, intentionally and without reasonable excuse, fails to attend to give evidence, produce documents or provide information to the OFT as required to do so by a notice under s.174 commits an offence by virtue of s.175(1). Further, s.175(2) provides that an offence is committed by any person who intentionally, and without reasonable excuse, alters, suppresses or destroys any document that he has been required to produce by notice under s.174. Both offences are punishable on summary conviction, by a fine not exceeding the statutory maximum, or on conviction on indictment, to imprisonment for up to two years, or to a fine, or to both.

9.52   It is also an offence, under s.175(4) to intentionally obstruct or delay: (a) the OFT in the exercise of its powers under s.174; or (b) any person to whom documents are produced under a s.174 notice. Penalties for such actions are limited, on summary conviction, to a fine not exceeding the statutory maximum, and, on indictment, to a fine.

CONSULTATION, INFORMATION AND PUBLICITY

9.53   Section 169 of the Act provides that, whenever the OFT decides to make a market investigation reference under s.131 or a decision to vary such reference under s.135, or whenever the OFT is considering accepting undertakings under s.154 in lieu of a reference, and the OFT thinks that the decision is likely to have a substantial impact on the interests of any person, it should consult such person, so far as is practicable. In considering what is practicable for the purposes of this section, the relevant authority is required in particular to have regard to any restrictions imposed by any timetable for making the decision and any need to keep what is proposed, or the reasons for it, confidential.

9.54   The OFT has indicated in the Guidance that any statement of reasons for its decision included in the consultation would normally be expected to cover the following points:
(a) a description of the goods or services concerned;
(b) the identity of the main parties affected by the reference, whether as suppliers or as customers;
(c) a view as to the possible definition of the market (or markets) affected; and
(d) the evidence that has led the OFT to have a reasonable suspicion that competition has been prevented, restricted, or distorted (including the possible market feature that may be relevant).

9.55 The OFT has stated that the length of the formal consultation period, following the issue by the OFT of a statement of its reasons for a proposed reference, will depend on the complexity of the issues and the extent to which discussion has already taken place with the affected parties. In general, the OFT considers a period of two weeks is likely to be appropriate.

9.56 The above obligations of consultation under s.169 apply also to the Commission (in relation to decisions relating to market investigation references under ss.134 or 141) and the Secretary of State or other minister (in relation to decisions on the making or varying of a reference under ss.132 and 135 respectively).

9.57 Pursuant to s.172, the OFT is required to publish *inter alia*, any market investigation reference made by it under s.131. The Commission, Secretary of State and any other appropriate minister are also under similar publication obligations under s.172.

Reserve ministerial power to make references

9.58 Section 132 of the Act provides that the appropriate minister (being either the Secretary of State acting alone or jointly with one or more other ministers) may make a reference to the Commission on the same grounds as the OFT in certain limited circumstances:

(a) where the appropriate minister is not satisfied with a decision of the OFT not to make a reference under s.131 of the Act; or

(b) where the appropriate minister has brought information to the attention of the OFT which he (or they) consider to be relevant to the question of whether the OFT should make a reference under s.131, but is not satisfied that the OFT will decide, within a reasonable period, whether to make such a reference.

9.59 During parliamentary debates, the government made it clear that it intends the primary responsibility for making a reference to be with the OFT, with the powers set out in s.132 being reserve powers to be used in very rare circumstances. Although it did not specify what those circumstances might be, the Secretary of State's (or appropriate ministers') powers to make a reference are significantly more constrained than under the 1973 Act, being limited to the two situations described above. Under the 1973 Act, the Secretary of State had a broad discretion to refer whenever it appeared to him that a monopoly situation existed. The Secretary of State also had the power to veto a reference decision by the DGFT, a power which is no longer available to him. Nevertheless, the practice under the 1973 Act was that most references were made by the DGFT. The government cited that fact in the support of its assertion that s.132 would be rarely used.

9.60 Section 132(4) of the Act provides that the appropriate minister cannot exercise the powers referred to above where a matter has previously been subject to a reference, and an undertaking or group of undertakings have been given in the last twelve months.

Publicity requirements

9.61   When a market investigation reference is made by the Secretary of State (acting alone or with another minister) under s.132, the reference and any variation of a reference by the appropriate minister, must be published pursuant to s.172.

Contents of a market investigation reference

9.62   Section 133 of the Act requires that any market investigation reference shall, in particular, specify:

(a) the enactment under which it is made;
(b) the date on which it is made; and
(c) the description of goods or services to which the feature or combination of features concerned relates.

9.63   The reference may be framed so as to require the Commission to confine its investigation into the effects of features of markets in the UK for goods or services of a description specified in the reference.

Variation of market investigation references

9.64   Section 135 provides that, at any time, the OFT, or (as the case may be), the appropriate minister, may vary a market investigation reference which it or he made but must first consult the Commission. There is no obligation to consult if the Commission has, itself, requested the variation.

9.65   Such variation might be appropriate where the Commission discovers that the description of goods or services in the original reference is inadequate. This might be the case if it discovers that the anti-competitive effects persist in markets beyond that for the goods or services under investigation – perhaps related goods or services. The OFT has indicated that it will respond positively to any such request.

9.66   No such variation will effect the period permitted within which the Commission is to prepare and publish its report in relation to normal market investigation references, or market investigation references which contain a public interest concern (s.135(4)).

QUESTIONS TO BE DECIDED BY THE COMMISSION ON A MARKET INVESTIGATION REFERENCE

Introduction

9.67   Section 134 of the Act sets out the questions to be decided by the Commission following a reference. The Commission first has to decide whether there is an adverse effect on competition – that is, whether any feature, or combination of features of the market concerned, prevents, restricts or distorts competition in connection with the supply or acquisition of any goods or services in the UK or part of it.

9.68   Where the Commission finds that there is an adverse effect on competition, it must consider what measures to take, or to recommend that the Secretary of State takes, in order to mitigate or prevent the adverse effect on competition or any consequential detrimental effect on customers.

'Adverse effect on competition'

9.69   During the consultation procedure, consideration was given to whether the substantive test under s.134 of the Act should be, 'a substantial lessening of competition' rather than an 'adverse effect on competition'. However, in its response to consultation, the government preferred the latter. The government thought that this test would be more flexible. Although the new merger regime applies a 'substantial lessening of competition' test, the fact that a merger inquiry is linked to a definite event means that it is easier to state that competition in a market will be substantially lessened if companies merge. It is more difficult to say that competition is substantially less than it would be if the market structure or the behaviour of players in the market was different in some way.

CONTENTS OF THE COMMISSION'S REPORT

9.70   Section 136 of the Act provides that the Commission must prepare and publish a report on the market investigation within the period specified in s.137.[2] In its report, the Commission must set out a reasoned decision as to whether any feature or combination of features of the market in question, is likely to lead to an adverse effect on competition, in accordance with the criteria set out in s.131 of the Act. The report will also contain details of the action that should be taken, or is recommended by the Commission to be taken, to remedy that adverse effect on competition or any resulting detrimental effect on customers. Further, the report should contain all the information that the Commission considers appropriate to allow a proper understanding of the reasons for its decision.

9.71   If a member of the Commission disagrees with any decisions contained in the report of the Commission, s.178 provides that he or she may include in the report a statement of his or her disagreement and of his or her reasons for disagreeing.

THE COMMISSION'S GUIDELINES ON MARKET INVESTIGATION REFERENCES

9.72   Section 171 of the Act requires the Commission, as soon as reasonably practicable after the passing of the Act, to publish general advice and information about the consideration by it of market investigation references. The Commission has published draft guidelines setting out its approach to market investigation references (Market Investigation References: Competition Commission Guidelines, Consultation Document, September 2002; hereafter, the Commission Guidelines). The Commission Guidelines explain how the Commission intends to address the question of whether there is an 'adverse affect on competition' within the meaning of s.134. The Commission Guidelines contain quite detailed information as to methodology and analysis that it will apply. However, the Commission Guidelines are non-binding, and the Commission reserves to itself the right to take a different approach on a case-by-case basis.

9.73   In its Guidelines, the Commission states that its approach to market investigation references will be in two stages. First, the Commission will identify the relevant market (or markets). It specifies that this may not coincide with the markets identified by the OFT, particularly if the OFT does not have to reach a conclusive view on market boundaries. The second stage will involve a competition assessment.

Market definition

9.74   In defining both the product dimension and the geographical dimension of the relevant product market, the Commission has stated that it will adopt the SSNIP test. This mirrors the approach used at the EU level by the European Commission in analysing the application of European rules to mergers, competitive agreements and abuses of dominance. It also closely follows in most respects the practice of the Commission and the OFT in defining markets for the purposes of Part 3 of the Act (merger control), as discussed in paras. 5.94 to 5.100.

9.75   The Commission has identified a number of other factors that would be taken into account in defining the relevant market. These include issues such as where markets are subject to rapid changes as a result of new technology, bidding markets or markets where the chain of substitution is an important factor. The Commission acknowledges that the SSNIP test may not be sufficient when looking at these types of markets and that it would take these factors into account when necessary.

The SSNIP test

Demand-side analysis

9.76   In defining the relevant product market, the Commission will consider whether a hypothetical monopolist of a certain set of products, which might constitute a market, could profitably impose a small but significant and non-transitory increase in price (SSNIP). The Commission has said that its practice will be to hypothesise an increase of around 5 per cent. There will be an assumption that all other prices will remain unchanged and that the price increase will last for at least a year. If the price rise will be unprofitable then the group of products within the possible market definition will be expanded to include substitute products to which customers would switch in response to the initial price rise. This question is repeated until a group of products for which such price rise would be profitable is identified. That group of products is the relevant market.

9.77   The Commission has identified some difficulties in applying the SSNIP test where the existing price is significantly above or below the price level that would arise in a competitive market. Because it may be difficult at the outset of an inquiry to judge whether existing price levels are competitive, the Commission has indicated that it will most likely use existing prices in its initial consideration of market definition. However, this may be adjusted as the investigation continues.

9.78   The Commission recognises that it is usually impossible to apply the SSNIP test other than in an hypothetical way, and lists the types of other information that could be useful in assessing the degree of demand-side substitutability. These include:

(a) product characteristics, such as physical properties and intended use;
(b) responses from customers, competitors and interested and informed third parties to questions raised by the Commission about customer behaviour and the application of the SSNIP test;
(c) information enabling the Commission to estimate switching costs that customers might incur in changing from the products of one supplier to those of another; the Commission notes that these may be financial and non-financial, and might include factors such as timing, effort and uncertainties;
(d) information from the main parties and third parties that was used, or could have been used, to make past and future business decisions; this might include documents such as marketing studies, consumer surveys, market analysis prepared for investors and internal business analysis (such as business plans and strategy documents); the Commission states that it might also consider similar types of studies prepared for the purpose of the enquiry;
(e) any available information on the extent to which variations and price differentials through time have occurred, and on their impact on trends in sales; and
(f) estimates of own-price and cross-price elasticities of demand, including econometric studies and sales data.

9.79   The Commission also identifies that in some cases it may be useful to look at two other types of calculation:

(a) estimates of the sales that must be lost before a given price increase would be unprofitable (referred to as critical loss); or

(b) estimates of maximum own price elasticity of demand that would make an increase in price profitable (referred to as critical elasticity).

Supply-side analysis

9.80   The Commission will also take into account supply-side substitution in relation to market definition. This refers to the situation in which a price rise would prompt other firms to start supplying, in the short term, an effective substitute for the product in question. In order to be considered to have an impact on the definition of the relevant market, any supply-side substitution will need to occur within a year of the hypothetical price rise and should not involve significant investments in plant, equipment, skills or training. The Commission has listed the type of information to which it is likely to have regard when analysing the effect of supply side substitution on the definition of the relevant market:

(a) information on past supply-side substitution;
(b) information on the willingness of customers to switch to new suppliers following a SSNIP;
(c) information on the size of adjustment costs for potential suppliers (adjustment costs are defined as those costs incurred in adjusting to the supply of a new product);
(d) the business plans of potential suppliers and the assessment of their competitive threat by firms in the market;
(e) any assessment by independent technical consultants and interested third parties of the likelihood and feasibility of supply-side substitution; and
(f) information on supply-side substitution in similar markets and in other countries.

Geographical market

9.81   The SSNIP test will also be used to establish the geographical scope of the market. Instead of looking at whether customers would turn to substitutable products in response to a 5 per cent price rise, the Commission will instead look at whether they would switch to products sourced from a different region. Factors that the Commission will likely take into account when looking at the geographical scope of the market would include: the cost to customers of switching to products supplied in other geographical areas; the cost of supplying in those areas; product characteristics; information on differences in prices and sales by area; and information on sale of goods between regions or into the UK. The Commission acknowledges that in some cases the application of the SSNIP test will result in a market definition that is wider than the UK.

Assessment of competition

9.82   The starting point for the Commission's analysis will be market shares and concentration. In calculating market shares, the Commission may rely on information from a number of sources including the main parties, other competitors, customers, buyers, suppliers trade associations and market research reports. Market shares may be measured in terms of revenues, volumes, production capacities or inputs depending on the markets concerned and the information available to the Commission. The Commission will measure the level of concentration in the market by reference to two measures of market concentration: the concentration ratio; and the Herfindahl-Hirschman Index (HHI).

9.83   The concentration ratio measures the combined market share of the largest firms in the market. By way of example, the Commission refers to the measurement of the 'five firm' concentration ratio. Interestingly, in the context of merger references, the OFT has stated that it will look at the concentration ratio of the three or four largest firms. The HHI takes account of all firms in the industry and their relative size. It is defined as the sum of the squares of all the market shares in the market. The Commission acknowledges that, in some cases, one of the measures may be more appropriate than the other, and either may be used by the Commission as it thinks appropriate.

9.84   In assessing the relevance of market shares, the Commission will look at changes in market shares over time and will have regard to other factors which could limit the ability of firms with high market shares from adversely affecting competition, such as low switching costs, barriers to entry and countervailing buyer power.

Non-price factors in competition

9.85   The Commission will take account of non-price competition in a market, including product development, product range and quality, marketing, servicing and R&D. The Commission points to the assumption that an emphasis on non-price competition may reflect a desire to raise barriers to entry or to avoid price competition; although it does recognise that strong non-price competition may lead to product differentiation, thereby reducing the risk of coordination. Nevertheless, the Commission accepts that product differentiation may also segment the market and facilitate price discrimination schemes that may be detrimental to the consumer.

Barriers to entry, expansion and exit

9.86   In considering the extent to which potential and completely new entry may act as a competitive constraint in a market, the Commission will have regard to the following factors:

- the history of past entry or evidence of planned entry or expansion by third parties;
- the extent to which past entrants have successfully gained market share, as well as the cost of gaining significant shares of the relevant market;

- direct observations or statistical information on barriers to entry, expansion and exit;
- the costs involved in entry or expansion, and in operating at the minimum efficient scale necessary to achieve a reasonably competitive level of costs;
- the likelihood of entry within such a timescale that it bears on the incentives and decisions of the existing firms in the market;
- the costs of exiting the market – if this is high it may deter new entry by raising the costs of failure for new firms;
- the potential effect of technological change and innovation on barriers to entry; and
- the likely response to entry by incumbent firms.

9.87   The Commission distinguishes between 'natural' or 'intrinsic' barriers to entry, 'regulatory' barriers and 'strategic' barriers. Intrinsic barriers include the costs of putting a production process in place, the acquisition of relevant intellectual property rights and sunk costs. Natural barriers to entry also include the network effects allowing incumbents with an existing customer base to have an automatic advantage over new entrants. Regulatory barriers include rules designed to provide safety or other types of consumer protection that may make it difficult for new firms to develop products. These barriers would include licensing systems and tax systems. Quality environmental and health and safety standards may also restrict entry. Strategic barriers are described as being the result of existing firms in the market acting with the specific intention of deterring entry. These barriers include, for example, strategies involving investment in excess capacity or predatory conduct targeted at entrants. Efforts made to increase the switching costs of customers (such as fidelity discounts and other actions, such as advertising), will also raise barriers to entry.

Countervailing buyer power

9.88   The Commission will look at the extent to which buyers may have sufficient bargaining power to prevent the exercise of suppliers' market power. The Commission states that while buyer power can offset the market power of suppliers, the benefits in lowering suppliers' prices do not necessarily get passed on to customers. The Commission also refers to 'supplier power'; that is, the presence of strong firms in the upstream markets.

Vertical integration

9.89   The Commission will also take into account the extent of vertical integration in the market, and the extent to which this may have an anti-competitive effect. The Commission cites the possibility of vertically integrated firms refusing to supply their rivals operating in the downstream markets.

Switching costs

9.90   The Commission refers to the costs that customers may face by switching suppliers. As referred to earlier, these may include inconvenience, monetary costs, administrative hurdles and lack of information about the products of alternative suppliers. The presence of switching costs may intensify competition but may also result in customers that are effectively trapped by suppliers.

9.91   Evidence that customers rarely switch suppliers, together with evidence that significant switching costs exist, may indicate a lack of effective competition. If there is a low level of information in the market about the availability or cost of alternative products, this lack of knowledge may be exploited and may thereby result in less competition on price or quality.

Information asymmetries

9.92   The Commission will have regard to the level of information available to customers in the market. Where information is limited, this may reduce the possibility for switching. Firms may therefore have less incentive to compete on either price or quality, as regardless of these issues, customers will be unlikely to switch.

Conduct

9.93   The Commission points out that it is unlikely to be interested in the conduct of a single firm on the market. Such conduct would most likely be dealt with by the OFT under Part II of the 1998 Act, as an abuse of dominant position. Nevertheless, the Commission will have regard to any conduct of firms in the market that could, in the circumstances of the particular market, have an adverse effect on competition.

9.94   Market investigations will usually be concerned with the conduct of several firms. In its Guidelines, the Commission focuses in particular on the conduct of firms in oligopolistic markets. The Commission's approach to this issue is outlined in the following paragraphs.

Conduct of oligopolist

9.95   In concentrated markets, firms may behave in an interdependent manner. A number of conditions are necessary for such oligopolistic behaviour to occur and to be sustainable. First, the market must be sufficiently concentrated for firms to be aware of the behaviour of their competitors, and for any significant deviation from the prevailing behaviour by a firm to be observed by the other firms in the market. This is most likely to be the case when prices are transparent. Second, there must be a cost in deviating from the prevailing market behaviour. The frequency with which prices may be adjusted would be likely to influence the ability of firms to depart from the general market behaviour. Finally, the Commission points out that oligopolistic behaviour can only be sustained in markets where there are relatively weak competitive restraints. Thus, barriers to entry must be high. The presence of fringe firms and their ability to attract volumes away from the core oligopolists will be a factor in the assessment.

9.96 The Commission emphasises that it is not necessary for there to be any collusion between oligopolists, nor even any contact between them. Moreover, the behaviour does not have to be 'conscious' in the form of an explicit or documented analysis of interdependent pricing strategies. The Commission explains that reduced competition can emerge purely from the independent recognition of the interdependent conduct and the gains from anticipating the rational but independent response of competitors.

9.97 In its Guidelines, the Commission lists the characteristics of the market that may facilitate coordination, including:

- a high level of concentration in the market;
- the existence and significance of entry barriers;
- evidence of a long-term commitment to the market by firms;
- a high degree of homogeneity of firms' products;
- a high degree of homogeneity of firms;
- a high degree of market transparency;
- the existence of institutions that may aid coordination (such as information-sharing agreements and trade associations);
- the existence of switching costs;
- excess capacity in the market;
- stable demand and costs;
- limited short term financial pressure on firms;
- the inability of small fringe firms (for example those producing specialist niche products) to embark on large-scale and more developed production;
- a lack of strategic intervention by interested third parties (e.g. buyers and suppliers);
- limited scope for, or pressure on, firms to bring new products to the market; and
- limited buyer power.

9.98 Similar prices do not always indicate tacit collusion. The Commission recognises that similar or identical prices can result from intense competition. In distinguishing between the two types of behaviour, it will have regard to the level of profitability generated by the price level established. If they are excessive, it is more likely to be an indicator of oligopoly pricing. A further indicator might be that, in competitive conditions, prices tend to exhibit significant volatility as they respond to changing supply and demand conditions. The Commission also refers to the fact that other marketing practices (other than price) that are adopted by custom or practice in a particular market may adversely affect competition.

Other market-wide horizontal conduct

9.99   The Commission identifies other market-wide practices that are adopted as custom and practice in a particular market without agreement, communication or contact between competitors, and which might be the subject of market investigation references even if they are the result of adherence to recommendations of a trade or professional body, or government regulations.

9.100   Rebating and discount practices may also be subject to review by the Commission, although it recognises that discounts are likely to be detrimental only when offered by a firm possessing market power.

Vertical agreements

9.101   The Commission recognises that vertical agreements, such as exclusive dealing arrangements or selective distribution arrangements, may have positive effects on competition. Nevertheless, where they result in foreclosure of the market, this may be the subject of review by the Commission.

Prices and profits

9.102   Finally, the Commission explains that it will not often be able to arrive at a conclusion as to whether there are adverse effects on competition (or whether there are detrimental effects on customers) from the investigation of structural and conduct features of the market alone. It will have regard to the outcome of the competitive process, and in particular prices, and the pattern of price changes over time. The Commission considers that, in competitive conditions, although prices may tend to be at the same level, over time they are likely to exhibit significant volatility as they respond to changing supply and demand conditions. Profit levels are also an indicator of the level of competition in the market. High profit levels may indicate lack of competition. However, the Commission acknowledges that even low profits may conceal ineffective competition if it simply means that companies are able to operate with higher costs. Therefore, in assessing the levels of profitability, the Commission will have regard to costs of capital, and may make comparisons with businesses operating in similar markets.

9.103   The Commission may also have regard to international price comparisons, taking into account factors which may affect such comparisons (such as the different products sold in each country, different quantities, quality differences, popularity and the extent to which prices in certain countries benefit from economies of scale).

COMMISSION DECISIONS FOLLOWING A FINDING THAT THERE IS AN ADVERSE EFFECT ON COMPETITION

9.104   Pursuant to s.134, if the Commission decides that there is an adverse effect on competition, it must decide:

(a) whether action should be taken by it (under s.138) to remedy, mitigate or prevent the adverse effect concerned or any detrimental effect on customers so far as it has resulted from or may be expected to result from, the adverse effect on competition identified;

(b) whether it should recommend any action to be taken by others; and

(c) in either case, what action – if any – should be taken.

Detrimental effect on customers

9.105   Section 134(5) provides that detrimental effect on customers, or future customers, takes the form of:

(a) higher prices, lower quality or less choice of goods or services in any market in the United Kingdom (whether or not the market to which the feature or features concerned relate); or

(b) less innovation in relation to such goods or services.

9.106   In deciding on the above issues, the Commission must have regard to the need to achieve as comprehensive a solution as is reasonable and practicable to the adverse effects on competition and any resulting detrimental effects on customers. Additionally, the Commission may have regard to the effect of any remedial action on any relevant customer benefits of the feature or features of the market concerned.

'Relevant customer benefit'

9.107   Section 134(8) provides that a relevant customer benefit takes the form of a benefit to customers, or future customers, in the form of:

(a) lower prices, higher quality, a greater choice of goods or services in any market in the United Kingdom (whether or not the market to which the feature or features concerned relate); or

(b) greater innovation in relation to such goods or services.

The customer benefit is relevant where the Commission, the Secretary of State or, as the case may be, the OFT believes that the benefit has accrued as a result (either wholly or partly) of the feature or features concerned. Likewise, the benefit is relevant if it may be expected to accrue within a reasonable period as a result of those features, and is otherwise unlikely to accrue.

9.108   The Act imposes a duty on the Commission to remedy any adverse effect on competition and any detrimental effect on customers that it identifies in its report. In deciding what action to take, the Commission must have regard to the need to achieve a comprehensive solution, and it may have regard to relevant customer benefits.

Limitations on the ability of the Commission to act

9.109   The Commission cannot take remedial action in relation to any detrimental effect on customers which has not yet occurred, if action is not also being taken to remedy the adverse effect on competition identified in the Commission's report (s.138(6)).

9.110   The Commission's decision on what remedies to impose – either through undertakings or by order – must be consistent with the decisions included in its report, unless there has been a material change of circumstances since the preparation of the report, or the Commission otherwise has a special reason for deciding differently (s.138(3)). For these purposes a change of circumstances is defined in the Act as also including any discovery that information has been supplied which is false or misleading in a material respect (s.183(1)). There is no definition of 'special reasons' and this provision therefore appears to allow the Commission a broad discretion in relation to remedies.

Remedial action by the Commission

9.111   In its Guidelines, the Commission has considered the matters that it is likely to take into account when determining the appropriateness of remedies, including the effectiveness of different types of remedies, costs and proportionality. The Commission also describes how it will take account of relevant customer benefits when deciding on appropriate remedial action. It should be noted that remedial action can be directed at the adverse effect of a market feature on competition, or at the detrimental effect on customers of the adverse effect on competition. It can therefore address the source of the problem or its consequences. In practice, the Commission states that it will seek remedies that will both ameliorate the competition problem and mitigate its effect on customers.

Consideration of appropriate remedies

9.112   In most cases, where it determines that there is an adverse effect on competition, the Commission anticipates that some type of remedial action will be required. The limited circumstances in which it may nevertheless decide that no remedial action is necessary, may include the situation where the costs of any practicable remedy are disproportionate in light of the size of the market, or in view of its expected decline, or where the only appropriate remedial action would fall outside the UK's jurisdiction (if, for example, it required action to be taken outside the UK by a non-UK national not incorporated in the UK or carrying on business there). Nevertheless, even in those circumstances it may recommend action be taken by others, for example by requesting the OFT to keep a particular market under surveillance. Also, the consideration of countervailing customer benefits may lead to a decision that no action should be taken.

9.113   In deciding what remedies are appropriate, the Commission will have regard to costs, proportionality and effectiveness. Relevant costs include the cost of implementing the remedy, and the cost of compliance. The Commission will also have regard to the costs to society of the failure in effectiveness of a particular market, and these costs might be taken to outweigh the costs of remedies to the firms in the relevant markets. The Commission has stated that it will endeavour to minimise ongoing compliance costs, and that it will have regard to the costs to the OFT of monitoring compliance with any remedies that it puts in place. The Commission states that it will abide by the principle of proportionality in considering the relative merits of different remedies.

Effectiveness of remedies

9.114   In the Guidelines, the Commission categorises the types of remedies that can be imposed, as follows:

- remedies designed to make a significant and direct change to the structure of the market, by a requirement to divest the business or assets to a newcomer or to an existing, but smaller, competitor;
- remedies designed to change the structure of the market less directly, by reducing any barriers to entry or by lowering switching costs (for example, by requiring the licensing of necessary intellectual property rights, or by extending the compatibility of products through industry-wide technical standards);
- recommendations for changes to regulations found to have adverse effects on competition, or detrimental effects on customers (such as those that limit entry to a market);
- remedies directing firms (whether sellers or buyers) to discontinue certain behaviour; an example of such behaviour is the giving of advance notice of price changes; alternatively the Commission may direct firms to adopt certain behaviour, such as more prominently displaying prices and other terms and conditions of sale;
- remedies designed to restrain the way in which firms would otherwise behave, for example the imposition of a price check; and
- monitoring remedies – for example, a requirement to provide the OFT with information on prices or profits.

9.115   The Commission will consider whether it should take remedial action itself, or require action be taken by other persons or bodies, such as sector regulators or other public bodies. Such methods could include changes to regulation, or remedies designed to increase market transparencies. In relation to regulated industries, this could include a modification to licence conditions or the inclusion of new licence conditions. Where the Commission recommends that the government or other persons should act, there is no obligation on them to do so.

However, the government has given a commitment to consider any Commission recommendation, and to give a public response within 90 days of the publication of the Commission's report.

Choice of remedies

9.116   The Commission will first have regard to any remedies designed to deal with the adverse effects on competition and then to remedies that relate to the detrimental effects on consumers. The Commission will have regard to the time period within which the remedies will likely improve competition in the market. It is likely to favour a remedy which will have more expeditious results. It is likely to consider behavioural remedies, where the adverse and detrimental effects are caused by the conduct of firms. The problem from a regulatory perspective is that they require detailed monitoring by the OFT or sector regulators. Although behavioural remedies are flexible, they need to adapt to developing market conditions. Remedial action on behaviour may have a direct impact in the form of price restraints but may not provide a long-term solution to the underlying problems; they are therefore likely to be less preferable.

Countervailing customer benefits

9.117   In considering the issue of remedies, the Commission will consider beneficial effects of the features on customers. It has shied away from giving detailed guidance on the kind of benefits that it may consider to be relevant customer benefits in market investigations. However, it has given some examples. Highly concentrated markets may enable economies of scale to be obtained that would not be available in an unconcentrated market. If this is passed on in the form of price reductions, customers will benefit. High concentration may also result in increased innovation, though this is a controversial proposition. Prices may be higher than they would be in a more competitive market but nevertheless customer benefits may pertain. Some barriers to entry may benefit customers through the exclusion of those who are not properly qualified. Vertically integrated firms may provide advantages to customers to the extent that they can save transactional and inventory costs. If the Commission is satisfied that there are relevant customer benefits deriving from a market feature that also has adverse effects on competition, it will consider whether to modify the remedy which it might otherwise have imposed or recommended.

9.118   Where the Commission chooses to act itself, it may seek undertakings from the firms that are the subject of the investigation. Alternatively, it may make an order. Undertakings are more flexible than orders, but it may be difficult to obtain them from all the firms in the market. This can involve complex negotiations. When the particular circumstances of the case point to the need for action to be taken speedily, the Commission may choose to impose an order to avoid delay.

INVESTIGATIVE POWERS OF THE COMMISSION

9.119   Section 176 provides that in all material respects, the investigative powers of the Commission in relation to market investigations are the same as it has in relation to merger investigations (see paras. 2.35 to 2.41).

CIRCULATION AND PUBLICATION OF THE REPORT

9.120   At the same time as the Commission's report is published, a copy must be given by the Commission to the OFT (s.136(4)) and, where a reference has been initiated by the appropriate minister, to the appropriate minister. Further, if the reference is one that might have been made by a relevant sector regulator, a copy of the report shall at the same time be given that regulator. If the reference was made under s.131, using the concurrent powers of a sector regulator, then a copy must at the same time be given to the OFT (s.136(6)).

TIMETABLE FOR REPORT

9.121   Section 136 provides that the Commission has two years from the date of the reference in which to prepare and publish its report under s.136 of the Act. This period is extended by 20 days where a public interest intervention notice had been made in respect of the references but was subsequently revoked, or where the Commission has terminated its investigation as far as the public interest consideration is concerned under s.145(1) of the Act.

9.122   However, by virtue of s.137(3), the Secretary of State may reduce the two-year period. Such order will not affect the timetable of any market investigation that is ongoing at the time the order is made.

9.123   During the parliamentary debate on the proposed timetable for the Commission's investigation, the government stated that the two years should be viewed very much as a long-stop date; it indicated that it did not anticipate that the Commission's investigation would take much longer than the 13 months which was the average period of investigation for monopoly references under the 1973 Act.

OBLIGATIONS OF THE OFT TO PROVIDE INFORMATION TO THE COMMISSION

9.124   Section 170 of the Act provides that the OFT shall give the Commission all such information as the Commission may require to enable it to carry out its functions, and any other assistance which it is within the power of the OFT to give. Under subsection (2), the OFT is required to give the Commission not just information that the Commission has specifically requested, but any information which, in the opinion of the OFT, it would be appropriate to convey.

9.125   Both the OFT and the Commission are required to give the Secretary of State or, as the case may be, the appropriate minister, such information in their possession and such other assistance as may be required to enable the Secretary of State or the appropriate minister to carry out his functions in relation to market investigation references.

9.126   This obligation extends not only to information which has specifically been requested of the OFT, but any other information which in the opinion of the OFT would be appropriate to convey for the purposes of assisting the Secretary of State or the appropriate minister, in carrying out his functions in relation to the market investigation reference. Section 170(5) requires the Commission and the Secretary of State or, as the case may be, the appropriate minister, to 'have regard to' any information given to him.

SUMMARY OF PROCESS

Figure 9.1 overleaf, published by the Competition Commission in its Draft General Advice and Information, summarises the stages in a typical market investigation.

---

1   Competition Act 1998 (Land and Vertical Agreements Exclusion) Order 2000, SI 2000/310.
2   That is, two years from the date of the market investigation reference concerned. However, the Secretary of State has the power to reduce this period (unless the Commission is already preparing a report in relation to a reference when the order is made).

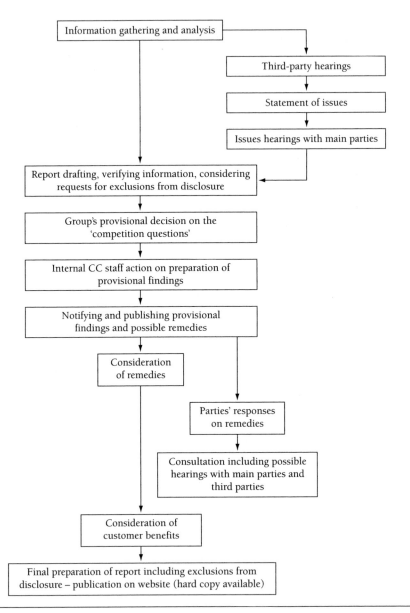

Figure 9.1 Typical shape of a market investigation (© Competition Commission)
Source: Competition Commission, *General Advice and Information*, September 2002
(see **www.competition-commission.org.uk/inquiries/enterprisebill.htm** for latest version)

10 MARKET INVESTIGATION: PUBLIC INTEREST CASES

INTRODUCTION

10.1 Under the regime for market investigations introduced by the Act, the Secretary of State will retain the authority to make decisions concerning market investigation references where 'public interest considerations' are involved.

10.2 Sections 139 to 153 of the Act set out the procedure by which the Secretary of State may intervene in the market investigation process where he believes that a public interest consideration may be relevant to the investigation, and describes how such intervention will affect the consideration of the market investigation reference by the Commission.

'Public interest consideration'

10.3 The only public interest consideration specified in the Act (s.153(1)) is 'the interests of national security'. Section 153(2) defines 'national security' to include public security, which is to have the same meaning as in the EC Merger Control Regulation.

10.4 Section 153(3) provides that the Secretary of State may add to the list of public interest considerations by order (or may remove or amend any addition). Under s.153(4), the Secretary of State can make such order at any stage in the market investigation process – including when a case is already under consideration by the OFT, the Secretary of State (whether acting alone or formally with another minister) or the Commission.

10.5 The provisions for 'the finalisation' of new public interest considerations is similar to that provided in Part 3 for merger references made by the Secretary of State (see paras. 6.22 and 6.23). Pursuant to s.139(7) of the Act, a public interest consideration is 'finalised' when: (a) it is specified in s.153 otherwise than by an order under s.153(3); or (b) has been specified under such an order, and the order for it to be so specified has been laid before, and approved by, Parliament in accordance with s.181(6).

10.6 The government made it clear in the parliamentary debates that the Secretary of State's power to intervene in 'public interest' cases is a reserve power, which it does not expect to be used save in exceptional circumstances. The government was unable to give any examples, and relied on that inability to support its assertion that it would be used only very rarely.

10.7   There are essentially two stages during the course of a market investigation at which the Secretary of State may intervene. He will do so by issuing an intervention notice under s.139. These stages are:

(a) at any time within four months of a market investigation reference being made, provided it has not been determined by the Commission within that period (s.139(1)); or
(b) where the OFT is considering accepting an undertaking in lieu of a reference under s.154, or accepting an undertaking varying or superseding any such undertaking which has already been made, and has published a notice indicating its intention to accept such undertaking under s.155(1) or (4).

10.8   In either case, s.139 provides that an intervention notice may only be made where the Secretary of State believes that it is, or may be the case, that one (or more than one) public interest consideration is relevant to the case.

10.9   The Secretary of State is limited to one intervention notice in relation to the same market investigation reference and in relation to the same or similar proposed undertakings (s.139(4)).

10.10   As referred to above, the Secretary of State may make an intervention notice in relation to a public interest consideration which is not, at the time, specified under s.153. When he does so, he must, as soon as practicable, take such action within his power, to ensure that it is finalised in accordance with s.139(7), as referred to in para. 10.5.

INTERVENTION NOTICE IN THE CONTEXT OF AN ONGOING MARKET INVESTIGATION BY THE COMMISSION

10.11   Section 140 provides that an intervention notice issued in respect of an existing market investigation reference must identify the reference concerned, and its reference date. It should also identify the public interest consideration or considerations which are or which may be relevant to the case. Where the public interest consideration identified in the intervention notice is not yet finalised, the notice must contain a proposed timetable for finalising it.

10.12   Where the Secretary of State believes that two or more public interest considerations are relevant to the case, he may decide not to mention one or more of them in the intervention notice.

10.13   The Secretary of State may revoke an intervention notice under s.139(1) at any time while it remains in force. An intervention notice under s.139(1) ceases to be in force when it is finally determined in accordance with s.140(5). This replicates the provisions of s.183(3)–(6) as they apply to market investigation references, described in paras. 11.20 and 11.21.

QUESTIONS TO BE DECIDED BY THE COMMISSION ON RECEIPT OF AN INTERVENTION NOTICE

10.14   Where the Commission is in receipt of an intervention notice, it is required under s.141 to consider the same substantive issues in relation to whether there is an adverse effect on competition as it would consider under s.134, had no intervention notice been made. The Commission must consider whether any feature or features of each relevant market prevents, restricts or distorts competition in connection with the supply or acquisition of any goods or services in the UK or a part of the UK.

10.15   However, in accordance with s.141(3), when considering what remedial action should be taken, it must first decide:

(a)   what action should be taken by the Secretary of State under s.147 for the purpose of remedying, mitigating or preventing the adverse effect on competition or any resulting detrimental effect on customers;

(b)   whether to recommend the taking of other action by the Secretary of State, or persons other than itself, to remedy, mitigate or prevent such adverse effects on competition or the resulting detrimental effects on customers.

10.16   As a second step, s.141(4) provides that, in anticipation of matters reverting to the Commission under s.148, it should consider whether action should be taken by itself under s.138 or whether it should recommend action be taken by any other person to remedy, mitigate or prevent the adverse effect on competition or any resulting detrimental effect on customers.

10.17   In deciding what remedial action to recommend, or to take, under s.141(3) and (4), the Commission must have regard to the need to achieve as comprehensive a solution as is reasonable and practicable. Additionally, it may have regard to the effect of any proposed remedial action on any relevant customer benefits arising from the relevant feature or features of the market. The concept of 'relevant customer benefit' is the same as in general market investigation references and is defined in para. 9.107.

10.18   Interestingly, in s.141 there is no reference to any additional factors that the Commission should consider in relation to the public interest considerations that are the subject of the intervention notice. In previous drafts of the legislation, the Commission was required specifically to consider public interest issues but this was removed from the final version of the Bill. Instead, there is a reference (s.145(3)) to the fact that where a public interest consideration has not been finalised by the time the report is given, the Commission shall disregard any public interest considerations. Further, s.145(5) refers to the power of the Commission to carry out investigations in relation to any public interest consideration to which it may have regard in its report.

10.19   Section 142 provides that the Commission must prepare a report on the reference in the same way as where there is no public interest consideration. The report will contain the decision of the Commission on questions which it is required to answer by virtue of s.141 (including a decision as to whether there is an adverse effect on competition), the reason for its decision, and such information as the Commission considers appropriate to facilitate the understanding of those questions and the reasons for its decisions (s.142(2)).

10.20   In accordance with s.143, where the Commission concludes that there is no adverse effect on competition, or that there is one or more adverse effects on competition but that no remedial action should be taken by the Commission under s.141(4)(a), the Commission shall publish a report to that effect. At the same time, a copy of the report is given to the OFT (and where relevant the appropriate sectoral regulator) (s.143(2)), and – where the reference was made to the Commission under s.132 – to the appropriate minister.

10.21   Where the Commission identifies one or more adverse effects on competition in its report, and finds that remedial action should be taken, the Commission shall give the report to the Secretary of State pursuant to s.143(3). However, if the intervention notice referred to a public interest consideration that was not finalised on the giving of the notice, s.145(2) provides that the Commission must not give its report to the Secretary of State until either 24 weeks have passed or the public interest consideration has been finalised.

INTERVENTION NOTICES WHERE THE OFT IS CONSIDERING UNDERTAKINGS IN LIEU OF A REFERENCE

10.22   Section 139(2) provides that the Secretary of State may give a public interest intervention notice to the OFT in circumstances where the OFT is considering accepting an undertaking in lieu of a reference or varying or superseding any such reference once the OFT has published a notice to that effect under s.155(1) or (4).

10.23   Section 149 provides that, in those circumstances, the intervention notice must identify the proposed undertaking which the OFT is considering accepting, and the notice to that effect which has been published by the OFT. The intervention notice must also identify the public interest consideration(s) which the Secretary of State considers are, or may be, relevant to the case. Additionally, where any public interest consideration has not been finalised, the notice should identify the timetable for finalising it. However, by virtue of s.149(2), where the Secretary of State believes that two or more public interest considerations may be relevant, he may decide not to mention in the intervention notice such of those considerations as he considers appropriate.

10.24   An intervention notice under s.139(2) may be revoked by the Secretary of State at any time. Other than where it has been revoked, an intervention notice described in s.149 will cease to be any of the following events:

(a) the OFT, with the consent of the Secretary of State, accepts an undertaking which is the same (or which does not differ in any material respect from), the undertaking that was proposed by the OFT as referred to in the intervention notice;

(b) the OFT decides not to accept the undertaking mentioned in the intervention notice under s.149 or any materially similar undertaking; or

(c) the Secretary of State makes a decision to revoke the intervention notice

10.25   Where an intervention notice under s.139(2) is in force, the OFT shall not, without the consent of the Secretary of State, accept the proposed undertaking concerned or materially similar undertaking (s.150). The details of the veto power vested in the Secretary of State in these circumstances is described more fully in para. 11.7.

10.26   Finally, should the OFT decide not to proceed with the undertakings as a result of the intervention notice, such a decision must be published (s.172).

TIMING OF THE COMMISSION'S REPORT

10.27   Section 144 sets out the time limits for a report by the Commission where an intervention notice is in force. As with other market investigation references, the Commission must publish its report or, as the case may be, give it to the Secretary of State within two years from the date of the reference.

10.28   This period may be shortened by order of the Secretary of State. Before making such order, the Secretary of State must consult with the Commission and such persons as he considers appropriate pursuant to s.144(5). However, if such order is made, existing references will continue to be considered within the original two-year period.

The consequences of a public interest not being finalised within 24 weeks of the notice being given

10.29   As referred to in para. 10.22, the Secretary of State may give an intervention notice in relation to a public interest consideration which is not yet specified in the Act. The public interest consideration must subsequently be incorporated into the Act in accordance with s.139(7). The public interest consideration is then referred to as having been 'finalised'.

10.30   Pursuant to s.145 of the Act, if none of the public interest considerations referred to in the intervention notice are finalised within 24 weeks of the notice, the Commission terminates its investigation under s.145. Section 151, then provides that the Commission should proceed with the market investigation as if no intervention notice had been given, but extends the timetable for the Commission's report by 20 days.

10.31   Pursuant to s.145(3) and (4), the Commission must disregard any public interest consideration that has not been finalised by the time of the report, either before the giving of the report or within 24 weeks of the giving of the intervention notice.

DECISION OF THE SECRETARY OF STATE UPON RECEIPT OF THE COMMISSION'S REPORT

10.32   Assuming that the Commission has identified one or more adverse effects on competition, and has found that remedial action should be taken, it will have given its report to the Secretary of State in accordance with s.143(3). Section 146 provides that, upon receipt of the Commission's report, the Secretary of State must decide whether any eligible public interest consideration or considerations, is, or are, relevant to any remedial action recommended in the Commission's report as being action which should be taken by the Commission. He must make a report setting out his decision on this question within 90 days of receipt of the Commission's report.

'Eligible public interest consideration'

10.33   This is defined in s.146(4) as a public interest consideration which was mentioned in the intervention notice concerned, and not required to be disregarded in the Commission's report. A public interest consideration is required to be disregarded where it has not been finalised within 24 weeks of the intervention notice being given.

10.34   The Secretary of State is required to publish the Commission's report no later than the date on which he publishes his decision on whether an 'eligible public interest consideration' is relevant to the case under s.146(2). At the same time as the report is published by the Secretary of State, a copy must be given to the OFT and, where the reference was made to the Commission under s.132, to the appropriate minister.

10.35   However, in accordance with s.177, the Secretary of State may exclude a matter from the Commission's report if he considers that its publication would be inappropriate. In deciding whether a matter is inappropriate, the Secretary of State shall have regard to the need to avoid disclosure of any information if such disclosure is considered to be contrary to the public interest. Additionally, under s.244, he is required to have regard to the need to exclude from disclosure (so far as practicable) any of the following:

(a) commercial information the disclosure of which the Secretary of State thinks might significantly harm the legitimate business interests of the undertaking to which it relates; or

(b) information relating to the private affairs of an individual the disclosure of which the authority thinks might significantly harm the individual's interests.

10.36   The Commission advises the Secretary of State as to the matters, if any, it considers should be excluded by him.

REMEDIAL ACTION BY THE SECRETARY OF STATE

10.37 Section 147 provides that where the Secretary of State decides that an eligible public interest consideration is relevant and has published his decision to that effect in accordance with s.146(3), he may take such action under ss.159 and 161 as he considers both reasonable and appropriate, that is:

(a) reasonable and practicable to remedy the adverse effects on competition identified and/or any resulting detrimental effects on customers in so far as they result from, or which may expect to result from, the adverse effect on competition; and

(b) appropriate in view of the eligible public interest consideration(s) concerned.

10.38 As with all decisions on remedies in relation to market investigations, the Secretary of State must have regard to the need to produce as comprehensive a solution as is reasonable and practicable, and to the Commission's report. He may take into account the effect of any action on relevant customer benefits.

Limitations on action by the Secretary of State

10.39 The Secretary of State may not take any action to remedy, mitigate or prevent any detrimental effect that may be expected to result from the adverse effect on competition if no anticipated detrimental effect has actually occurred and the adverse effect on competition is not itself being remedied, mitigated or prevented. In deciding on appropriate remedial action, the Secretary of State may not challenge the findings of the Commission in relation to any adverse effects on competition.

REVERSION OF THE MATTER TO THE COMMISSION

10.40 If the Secretary of State decides that no eligible public interest consideration is relevant, or if he fails to publish his decision taken under s.146, the decision on remedial action reverts to the Commission (s.148(1)).

10.41 In deciding what action should be taken, the Commission must proceed as if it had reported under s.137 – in other words, as if no public interest consideration(s) had been raised. If, when the matter reverts to the Commission, the Secretary of State had not yet published the Commission's report in accordance with s.143, then the Commission shall publish its report, giving a copy to the OFT, and to the appropriate minister (other than the Secretary of State) as if a reference had been made under s.132.

10.42 Where the Commission intends to proceed in a way that is not consistent with the decision included in its report under s.141(4) (action on remedies) it requires the consent of the Secretary of State. The Secretary of State shall not withhold his consent unless he considers that the proposed alternative way of proceeding will operate against the public interest.

SPECIFIED DUTIES OF THE OFT AND THE COMMISSION IN RELATION TO PUBLIC INTEREST CASES

10.43   Section 152 of the Act requires the OFT, when it is considering whether to make a market investigation reference, to bring to the attention of the Secretary of State any case which it believes raises a potential material public interest consideration. Section 152 also imposes an obligation on the Commission to bring any case which it believes raises a material public interest consideration to the attention of the Secretary of State within four months of the date of a reference.

10.44   Finally, both the OFT and the Commission are required to bring to the attention of the Secretary of State any representations which have been made to the OFT, or (as the case may be) the Commission concerning the exercise of his powers to specify further public interest considerations by way of order under s.153(3).

10.45   Figure 10.1 sets out the outline of the procedure once a public interest intervention notice is made in respect of an investigation.

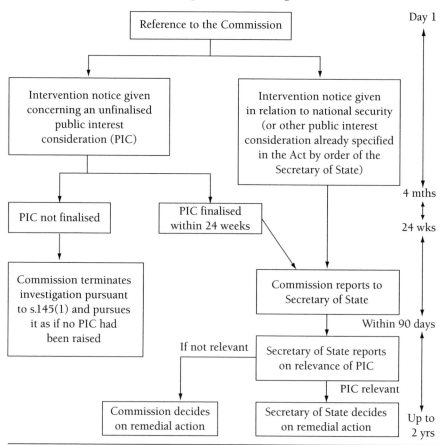

Figure 10.1 Outline of the procedure once a public interest intervention notice is made in respect of a market investigation reference under s.140(1).

11

ENFORCEMENT UNDERTAKINGS AND ORDERS

INTRODUCTION

11.1 The Act provides for various measures to be taken by the OFT, the Commission or the Secretary of State to remedy, mitigate or prevent any adverse effects on competition and the detrimental effects on customers, identified in the context of a market investigation. These may take the form of orders or undertakings negotiated with participants in the market and can include both structural and behavioural remedies (see paras. 7.57 to 7.61).

11.2 As with merger references, undertakings may be negotiated with firms in the market for a number of reasons: in order to avoid a market investigation reference being made; as an interim measure to avoid pre-emptive action being taken which might prejudice a market investigation reference; or following an investigation, in order to remedy the adverse effects on competition identified by the Commission. Orders may be used either as an interim measure or following an investigation.

11.3 Table 11.1 identifies the various different orders and undertakings that can be made or given and, in each case, identifies who has the authority to make such orders or to negotiate such undertakings. The enforcement provisions of the Act in relation to market investigation references are extensive and confer on the authorities concerned a broad discretion as to the type of remedial action to be taken, and its form. This does not represent a substantial departure from the 1973 Act or indeed the practices of the Commission (and its predecessor, the Monopolies and Mergers Commission) under the provisions of the Competition Act 1980. Under that legislation, the Commission was able to recommend a wide range of remedies broadly in line with the behavioural and structural remedies listed in Sched. 8 of the Act.

Undertakings in lieu of a market investigation reference

11.4 Under s.154(2) of the Act, the OFT has the power to accept undertakings in lieu of a reference to the Commission for the purpose of remedying, mitigating or preventing: (a) any adverse effect on competition concerned; or (b) any

Table 11.1 Enforcement provisions of the Act – market investigation references

Enforcement measure	OFT	Secretary of State	Commission
Undertakings in lieu of a reference	Power to negotiate	Power of veto where a public interest intervention notice is in force	
Interim undertakings	Negotiated by the OFT at the request of the Commission or Secretary of State	Accepted by the Secretary of State in public interest cases	Accepted by the Commission in other cases
Interim orders		Made by the Secretary of State in public interest cases	Made by the Commission in other cases
Final undertaking	Negotiated by the OFT at the request of the Commission or the Secretary of State	Accepted by the Secretary of State in public interest cases	Accepted by the Commission in other cases
Final orders		Made by the Secretary of State in public interest cases	Made by the Commission in other cases

detrimental effect on customers in so far as it has resulted from, or may be expected to result from, those adverse effects on competition. The OFT may negotiate undertakings with all such persons as it considers appropriate, and the undertakings may require any such action as the OFT considers appropriate. Thus, the OFT is given a broad discretion in the negotiation of undertakings in lieu of a reference.

11.5   When considering appropriate undertakings, the OFT must take into account similar factors to those that the Commission must consider it is contemplating what action to take following a market investigation. Thus, s.154(3) and (4) provide that the OFT must have regard to the need to achieve as comprehensive a solution as is reasonable and practicable, and that it may have regard to the effect of any action on any relevant customer benefits arising from the feature or features of the markets in question.

Limitations on the ability of the OFT to accept undertakings

11.6   Section 154(5) provides that the OFT may not negotiate undertakings in lieu of a reference where no detrimental effects on customers have yet resulted from the adverse effects on competition, unless it also addresses the underlying adverse effect on competition that will give rise to that detrimental effect.

Right of veto by Secretary of State where an intervention notice is in force

11.7   Section 150 provides that the OFT may not accept undertakings where a public interest intervention notice is in force, without first obtaining the consent of the Secretary of State. Section 146(2) directs the Secretary of State to withhold his consent if he believes that it is, or may be, the case that the proposed undertaking will, if accepted, operate against the public interest. This will only be the case where the public interest consideration or considerations referred to in the intervention notice have been finalised in accordance with s.153 and they outweigh the considerations which have led the OFT to propose accepting undertakings. The veto right is clearly limited to public interest considerations, and the Secretary of State is expressly prevented by s.150(6) from considering any other matter. When the relevant public interest consideration has not yet been finalised in accordance with s.153, the Secretary of State must wait 24 weeks from the date of the intervention notice before deciding whether to grant the consents referred to above (or, if earlier, until the date on which the public consideration in question has been finalised).

PROCEDURAL REQUIREMENTS IN RELATION TO UNDERTAKINGS IN LIEU OF A REFERENCE

11.8   The procedural requirements applicable to the acceptance of undertakings by the OFT are set out in s.155 of the Act. Before accepting any undertakings under s.154, the OFT must publish a notice of the proposed undertakings and consider any representations made in accordance with the notice. The notice must describe the purpose and effect of the proposed undertakings and the situation which they are seeking to address. In addition, the OFT should set out any of the facts which it considers justify the acceptance of the undertakings. The notice must detail how interested third parties can access an accurate version of the proposed undertakings at all reasonable times and must set out a time limit for third-party representations, being not less than 15 days from the date of publication of the notice setting out the proposed undertakings. In particular, s.154(3) provides that the notice must set out the terms of any reference which the OFT would otherwise make to the Commission, absent the undertakings, and describe the adverse effects on competition, and any detrimental effects on customers resulting from those adverse effects on competition, which the OFT has identified.

11.9   Once the OFT has decided to accept undertakings, it is required to serve a copy of those undertakings on any person who is giving them, and to publish details of the undertakings that have been accepted. If, instead, the OFT decides not to accept the undertakings concerned, then it must publish notice of that decision pursuant to s.155(6).

Modification of the proposed undertakings

11.10   If the OFT decides to modify the proposed undertakings (as published), either as a result of the third-party comments received during the consultation process or otherwise, it must publish a notice of such modifications and consider any further representations made in accordance with s.154(4). In any subsequent notice containing details of the proposed modifications, the OFT must describe the reason for the modifications and identify a period (of not less than seven days from the date of publication of the notice) within which third-party representations may be made. The requirement to publish a notice of the modifications only applies where those modifications are material, either in relation to the original undertakings or subsequent modifications that have been made.

Termination of undertakings

11.11   Section 154(6)(c) gives the OFT the power to release firms from undertakings. Paragraphs 6 to 8 of Sched. 10 to the Act sets out the procedural steps that must be taken by the OFT when undertakings are released. In particular, pursuant to para. 6 of Sched. 10, the OFT must publish a notice to the effect that it intends to release the undertakings in question and serve a copy on the person who gave the undertaking, and it must consider any representations made in connection with the notice.

11.12   Such notice must set out the reasons why the OFT intends to release the undertakings, and must specify a period (of not less than 15 days) in which third parties may make representations to the OFT concerning the proposed release. If, after consultation with third parties, the OFT decides to release the undertakings, the OFT must serve a copy of the release on the person who gave the undertaking, and publish a copy. Similarly, if the OFT decides not to release the undertaking, that decision must be notified to the person who gave the undertaking and it must be published.

EFFECT OF UNDERTAKINGS IN LIEU OF A REFERENCE

11.13   Section 156 of the Act provides that no market investigation reference may be made within 12 months of the OFT accepting undertakings. This suspension of the right to make a reference relates to goods or services of the same description as those which the relevant market feature(s) relate. Such a suspension is removed if: (a) the OFT considers that the undertaking has been breached and a notice of that fact has been given to the person responsible for giving the undertaking; or (b) if the person who gave the undertaking gave materially false or misleading information to the OFT.

THE PRACTICE OF THE OFT IN RELATION TO UNDERTAKINGS IN LIEU OF A REFERENCE

11.14   In its Guidance on market investigation references, the OFT has said that undertakings in lieu of a reference are unlikely to be common. In most cases, the OFT will not have had sufficient opportunity to carry out a detailed investigation of the competition issues which would allow it to determine whether undertakings in lieu of a reference would be appropriate. Where the market features in question involve a number of firms or industry-wide practices, the logistics of negotiating undertakings in lieu of a reference with a number of different firms may make this option unavailable to the OFT.

11.15   It is worth noting that the powers under the 1973 Act to accept undertakings in lieu of a monopoly reference have never been used, although on a few occasions informal assurances (rather than statutory undertakings) have been accepted. In view of this, it is reasonable to assume – and this assumption is made by the OFT in its draft Guidance – that these similar powers under the Act will rarely be used.

INTERIM UNDERTAKINGS

11.16   Section 157 of the Act sets out the circumstances in which interim undertakings may be accepted by either the Commission or the Secretary of State. Interim undertakings may be accepted once the Commission has published its report under s.137 of the Act. In a public interest case, they may be accepted where a report has been prepared by the Commission under s.142, given to the Secretary of State and published in accordance with s.143(3), but where the market investigation has not yet been finally determined. The circumstances in which a market investigation is finally determined is set out in para. 11.20.

11.17   In most cases it is for the Commission to accept interim undertakings although, in public interest cases, it will be the Secretary of State. In both cases, the OFT may be asked to negotiate the undertakings on behalf of the other body.

'Pre-emptive action'

11.18   Section 157(2) provides that interim undertakings may be negotiated where it is necessary to prevent pre-emptive action. Pre-emptive action is defined in s.157(6) to mean 'action which might prejudice the market investigation reference concerned or impede the taking of any action under s.138(2) or (as the case may be), s.147(2) in relation to the reference'.

Procedural requirements

11.19   The Act does not set out any specific procedural requirements in relation to the acceptance of interim undertakings. Instead, s.157(3) provides that such undertaking shall come into force when accepted; that they may be varied or superseded by another undertaking, and may be released by the Commission or (as the case may be) the Secretary of State. In any event, the undertaking ceases to be in force when the market investigation reference is finally determined. Finally, the Commission or (as the case may be) the Secretary of State must consider any representations made concerning the variation and, or release, of the undertakings. Section 172 provides that the Commission or (as the case may be) the Secretary of State shall publish any interim undertaking accepted under s.157 and any variation, release or revocation of such undertaking.

Meaning of finally determined

11.20   This phrase is defined differently according to whether or not there has been an intervention notice. Where no intervention notice has been given under s.139(1), an investigation is finally determined on the following events:

(a) expiry of the two-year period permitted by s.137 for the preparation and publication of the Commission's report on the market investigation reference, the Commission not having published such report;

(b) publication of a Commission report in which the Commission has decided that there is no adverse effect on competition;

(c) a decision by the Commission under s.138(2) to take no remedial action by way of either undertakings under s.159 nor an order under s.161; or

(d) the acceptance by the Commission of an undertaking under s.159 or the making of an order under s.161.

11.21   Where a public interest intervention notice has been given by the Secretary of State under s.139(1) in relation to a particular market investigation reference, that reference will be 'finally determined' upon:

(a) expiry of the two-year period permitted by s.144 for the preparation of the report of the Commission under s.142 and for action to be taken in relation to it under s.143(1) or (3) while the intervention notice is still in force and no such report has been so prepared or no such action has been taken;

(b) the termination of the Commission's investigation under s.145(1) and the reference being finally determined under s.183(3)(a) (disregarding the fact that the notice was given);

(c) the publication of the Commission's report on the investigation under s.143(1) stating that there is no adverse effect on competition or that no adverse effects on competition require action;

(d) the revocation of the intervention notice and final determination of the reference under s.183(3)(a) (disregarding the fact that the notice was given);

(e) the failure of the Secretary of State to make and publish a decision stating whether there are any relevant eligible public interest considerations and the final determination of the reference under s.183(3)(a) (disregarding the fact that the notice was given);

(f) the decision of the Secretary of State under s.146(2) that no eligible public interest consideration is relevant and the final determination of the reference under s.183(3)(a) (disregarding the fact that the notice was given);

(g) the decision of the Secretary of State under s.146(2) that a public interest consideration is relevant but that, pursuant to s.147(2) no undertakings under s.159 nor orders under s.161 are required; or

(h) the decision of the Secretary of State under s.146(2) that a public interest consideration is relevant and the acceptance of an undertaking under s.159 or the making of an order under s.161.

INTERIM ORDERS

11.22 As an alternative to interim undertakings, s.158(2) gives the Commission or (as the case may be) the Secretary of State (collectively, the relevant authority), the power to make an order, for the purposes of preventing pre-emptive action, which:

(a) prohibits or restricts the doing of things which the relevant authority considers would constitute pre-emptive action;

(b) imposes on any person concerned, obligations as to the carrying on of any activities or the safeguarding of any assets;

(c) provides for the carrying on of any activities or the safeguarding of any assets either by the appointment of a person to conduct or supervise the conduct of any activities (on such terms and with such powers as may be specified or described in the order) or in any other manner; or

(d) provides that specified information should be provided to either the Commission, the Secretary of State or the OFT and as well as for publication of that information as appropriate (by virtue of Sched. 8, para. 19).

11.23 The order will specify when it is to come into force; and that it may be varied or revoked by another order. The relevant authority must, as soon as reasonably practicable, consider any representations received by the relevant authority in relation to the revocation or variation of an order under this section. By virtue of s.158(4), if it has not previously ceased to be in force, it will cease to be in force when the market investigation reference is finally determined.

11.24 Pursuant to s.172, the Commission must publish any interim orders made under s.158.

FINAL UNDERTAKINGS

11.25 Once the market investigation reference has been determined, the Commission may, in accordance with s.138 of the Act, accept from such persons as it considers appropriate undertakings to address the identified adverse effects on competition and/or the detriment to customers arising therefrom. In a public interest case it is the Secretary of State who is empowered to accept such undertakings (s.147).

11.26   Section 159 sets out the rules on final undertakings, and provides that a final undertaking accepted either by the Commission or the Secretary of State under s.159 comes into effect as soon as it is accepted. Final undertakings accepted under s.159 may be varied or superseded by another undertaking under that section, and may be released by the body that accepted it (either the Commission or the Secretary of State). Under s.159 the Commission or (as the case may be) the Secretary of State must, as soon as practicable, consider any representations received in relation the variation or release of an undertaking under this section.

Role of OFT in negotiating interim undertakings

11.27   Under s.163 the Commission or the Secretary of State will be assisted by the OFT in relation to the negotiation of either interim or final undertakings. Pursuant to s.163(2) the OFT may be required to consult with such persons as the relevant authority considers appropriate to discover whether they would consider offering undertakings which the authority would be prepared to accept. The OFT may be required to report back to the relevant authority in relation to the outcome of those discussions. When reporting back to the relevant authority, the OFT will advise the Commission, or the Secretary of State, as to whether the undertakings offered should be accepted. Note however that pursuant to s.163(5) the Secretary of State and/or the Commission retains the right to consult on those undertakings directly, if they wish to do so.

POWER TO MAKE ORDERS WHERE UNDERTAKINGS ARE NOT FULFILLED

11.28   Instead of undertakings, the relevant authority (being either the Commission or, if it is a public interest case, the Secretary of State) may make an order under s.160 where it, or he, considers that a final undertaking is not being or will not be fulfilled, or where the person who gave the undertaking, provided information which was false or misleading in a material respect, before the relevant authority decided to accept the undertaking.

11.29   In deciding what action should be required in the order, the Commission is required to have regard to the provisions of s.138(3) to (6) of the Act. By virtue of s.138(3), the Commission must be consistent with the decisions included in its report, unless there has been a material change of circumstances since preparation of the report, or the Commission otherwise has a special reason for deciding differently.

11.30   Further, s.138 (4) requires the Commission to have regard to the need to achieve as comprehensive a solution as is reasonable and practicable, to the adverse effects on competition and any resultant detrimental effects on customers. The Commission may have regard to the effect of any action on any relevant customer benefits of the feature or features of the market concerned. No action may be taken in relation to an anticipated detriment to customers where no detriment has yet occurred, and action is not being taken to remedy the adverse effect on competition that has been identified. The same factors have to be taken into account by the Secretary of State in public interest cases.

11.31   By virtue of s.160(4), an order under s.160 may include anything that is permitted to be included in remedial orders under Sched. 8 of the Act as well as any supplementary, consequential or incidental provisions as the relevant authority considers appropriate.

11.32   An order under s.160 shall come into force at such time as is determined by or under the order, and may contain provision which is different from the provision contained in the undertaking concerned. Such order may not be varied or revoked unless the OFT advises that such variation or revocation is appropriate by reason of a change in circumstances (s.160(6)).

FINAL ORDERS

11.33   Section 161 of the Act provides the Commission and the Secretary of State with the authority to remedy any adverse effects on competition identified as a result of the market investigation reference (s.138 for Commission, s.147 for Secretary of State). The order may provide for anything permitted by Sched. 8 or such supplementary, consequential or incidental provisions as are considered appropriate. Again, a final order may not be varied or revoked unless the OFT advises that such variation or revocation is appropriate by reason of a change in circumstances.

REMEDIES THAT MAY BE IMPOSED BY WAY OF AN ENFORCEMENT ORDER: MARKET INVESTIGATION ORDERS

11.34   Schedule 8 of the Act specifies the type of remedies that may be imposed by way of an order under ss.158, 160 and 161.

11.35   Schedule 8 provides that orders may include both structural and behavioural remedies. The structural remedies consist of various provisions concerning acquisitions and divestment. Behavioural remedies are wide ranging and include: general restrictions on conduct, general obligations to be performed; and requirements in relation to the supply and publication of information. A full explanation of the provisions of Sched. 8 is contained in paras. 7.44 to 7.52.

ENFORCEMENT FUNCTIONS OF THE OFT

11.36   The OFT has a number of enforcement functions concerning market investigation references that are expressly set out in the Act. In particular, it is required to keep a register of all undertakings and orders given in relation to market investigation references. Further, it has a duty to monitor compliance with undertakings and orders and to advise the Commission or the Secretary of State on any necessary enforcement action.

Duty of OFT to monitor undertakings and orders

11.37   Under s.162 of the Act, the OFT is required to monitor compliance with enforcement undertakings or orders. This will involve consideration of whether:

(a) an enforcement order or undertaking has been, or is being, complied with; or
(b) by reason of any change of circumstances, an enforcement undertaking is no longer appropriate and the parties need to be released from it or it needs to be varied or superseded by a new enforcement undertaking; or an order needs to be varied or revoked.

11.38   By virtue of s.162(3), the OFT is required to give advice to the Commission or, as appropriate, the Secretary of State, in relation to:

(a) any possible variation or release by the Commission or (as the case may be) the Secretary of State of an enforcement undertaking;
(b) any possible new enforcement undertakings to be accepted;
(c) any possible variation or revocation by the relevant authorities of an enforcement order; and
(d) any possible enforcement undertakings to be taken instead of an enforcement order or any possible enforcement order to be made instead of an undertaking or any enforcement action under s.163(6) or (8) to be taken in relation to any undertaking or order.

11.39   Additionally, the OFT shall take any action as it considers appropriate in relation to any undertakings in lieu of a reference accepted by it under s.154 of the Act and any possible new undertakings to be accepted under that section, superseding existing undertakings in lieu of a reference. It shall also take any action it considers appropriate in relation to enforcement undertakings or orders under s.167(6).

11.40   Under s.162(5), the OFT will review the effectiveness of enforcement undertakings or orders in relation to market investigation references and, whenever requested to do so by the Secretary of State, and in any event on a regular basis, publish a report on its findings pursuant to s.162(7).

11.41   Finally, it should be noted that s.163(6) provides that whenever it is asked to do so, the OFT will give such advice as it considers appropriate in relation to any enforcement action (not just undertakings).

Public register

11.42   Section 166 sets out the requirements for the OFT to compile and maintain a public register which should include details of:

(a) the provisions of any enforcement undertakings accepted in relation to market investigation references (whether by the OFT, the Commission, or the Secretary of State);
(b) the provisions of any enforcement order made in relation to a market investigation reference; and
(c) the details of any variation, release or revocation of such an undertaking or order.

11.43   The onus is on the Commission, or as the case may be, the Secretary of State, to inform the OFT of matters to be included in the register. Additionally, where a sectoral regulator has been involved in the negotiation of undertakings under his concurrent powers, he must inform the OFT of matters to be included in the register.

DIRECT ENFORCEMENT OF UNDERTAKINGS AND ORDERS IN THE UK COURTS

11.44   Pursuant to s.167, both enforcement undertakings and enforcement orders, accepted or adopted as a result of a market investigation reference, may be subject to direct enforcement in the UK courts by a third party who suffers loss or damage as a result of a failure to comply with an undertaking or, as the case may be, an order. In such action, it is a defence for the person to whom an enforcement undertaking or order relates to show that he took all reasonable steps and exercised all due diligence to avoid contravening the undertaking or order.

11.45   Further, pursuant to s.167(6), compliance with enforcement undertakings or orders are enforceable by civil proceeding brought by the OFT for an injunction or for interdict or any other appropriate relief or remedy.

11.46   Under s.167(7) both the Commission and the Secretary of State may bring civil proceedings for an injunction, and so on in relation to any enforcement undertaking or order in relation to any undertaking or order that the Commission (or as the case may be) the Secretary of State has accepted or ordered.

REGULATED MARKETS

11.47   The market investigation functions of the OFT (with the exception of the duty to maintain a register of undertakings and orders) may be exercised concurrently by sectoral regulators. Section 136(5) and (7) of the Act contains a list of all relevant sectoral legislation and the provisions of that legislation that confer concurrent powers on the regulators.

11.48   The sectoral regulators with concurrent powers are the Director General of Telecommunications, the Gas and Electricity Markets Authority, the Director General of Water Services, the Director General of Electricity Supply for Northern Ireland, the Director General of Gas for Northern Ireland, the Rail Regulator and the Civil Aviation Authority. These regulators have the power to make references in relation to the supply of some or all of the goods or services that fall within their regulated sectors.

11.49   When either the sectoral regulator or the OFT is considering making a reference of such goods or services, they must consult one another. The OFT has said that where a matter involves goods or services that are unambiguously part of a regulated industry, in practice references will be dealt with by the sectoral regulators. Where there is some ambiguity, the reference will be made by the authority best placed to do so.

11.50   Section 168 of the Act provides that where the Commission or the Secretary of State is considering what 'relevant action' is appropriate to remedy, mitigate or prevent the adverse effects on competition (or the detrimental effect on consumers), they shall, in deciding what is reasonable and practicable, have regard to the relevant statutory functions of the sectoral regulators concerned. That section lists what is meant by 'relevant action' in the context of the regulated industries. These include the granting and modification of any licences.

12 TRANSITIONAL PROVISIONS

12.1 The provisions of Sched. 24 do not make for light reading. In attempting to anticipate every circumstance in which transitional arrangements might be necessary, the Act has planted a pretty impenetrable thicket of transitional provisions. Where there is unfinished business under the 1973 Act, or transactions or procedures which fall within both regimes, there is no alternative but to consider the application of each of the following series of prolix provisions.

12.2 All the transitional rules below are themselves subject to the rules set out in Sched. 24, paras. 15 to 18, which relate to enforcement undertakings and orders. Each of the following paragraphs should therefore be read in that light.

12.3 Schedule 24, para. 13(1) provides that the 1973 Act shall continue to apply where:

(a) two or more enterprises have ceased to be distinct enterprises under the 1973 Act;

and

(b) they have ceased to be distinct enterprises before the appointed day (i.e., the date on which the Act comes into force).

12.4 The general rule under Sched. 24, para. 13(2) is that, the 1973 Act shall continue to apply in relation to any relevant arrangements which were in progress or in contemplation before the appointed day and remain so on that day, where, before the appointed day:

(a) a merger notice was given and was neither rejected under s.75B(7) of the 1973 Act nor withdrawn;
(b) no merger notice was given, but: (i) a reference was made under s.75 of the 1973 Act (anticipated merger); or (ii) undertakings were accepted by the Secretary of State under s.75G of the 1973 Act; or (iii) the Secretary of State decided neither to make a reference nor to accept undertakings; or
(c) a merger notice was given, was either rejected or withdrawn, and the situation described in (a) above does not apply in relation to a different merger notice given in relation to the arrangements and, in relation to the arrangements, any of the circumstances described in paragraph (b) above applies.

12.5   This general rule, which is complex enough in itself, is subject to the special rules described in paras. 12.6 to 12.10 below.

12.6   Subject to the special rules in Sched. 24, para. 13(8) in relation to (concentrations with a Community dimension notified before the appointed day), the Act shall (in a case of the kind mentioned in (a) in para. 12.4 above, apply in relation to any relevant arrangements and to the actual results of those arrangements if, on or after the appointed day, a merger notice is rejected under the old law or was withdrawn (Sched. 24, para. 13(3)).

12.7   Subject again to the special rules set out in Sched. 24, para. 13(8), under the provisions of Sched. 24, para. 13(4) the Act shall apply in a case where the circumstances described in para. 12.4(a) above obtain, in relation to any relevant arrangements and the actual results of those arrangements if:

(a)   the making of a reference of a completed or anticipated merger under the 1973 Act in relation to those arrangements (and the actual results of those arrangements) was not prevented immediately before the appointed day by virtue of s.75C(1)(c), (e) or (g) of the 1973 Act;[1]

(b)   the period for considering the merger notice has expired (whether before on or after the appointed day); and

(c)   no reference has been made in relation to a completed or anticipated merger under the 1973 Act and no undertakings have been accepted under s.75(G) of that Act.

12.8   Subject again to the rules of Sched. 24, para. 13(8), the Act shall (under Sched. 24, para. 13(5)) apply, in a case of a kind described above in para. 12.3(a) in relation to any relevant arrangements and the actual results of those arrangements if:

(a)   the making of a reference relating to a completed or anticipated merger under the 1973 Act in relation to those arrangements and the actual results of those arrangements was not prevented on or after the appointed day by virtue of s.75C(1)(b), (c), (d), (e) or (g) of the 1973 Act;[2]

(b)   the merger notice period has expired (whether before, on, or after the appointed day); and

(c)   no reference has been made in relation to a completed or anticipated merger under the 1973 Act and no undertakings have been accepted under s.75(G) of that Act.

12.9   Subject, as usual, to the rules in Sched. 24, para. 13(8), the provisions of Sched. 24, para. 13(6) are that the Act will apply in relation to any relevant arrangements (and the actual results of those arrangements) if:

(a)   the arrangements were in progress or in contemplation before the appointed day and are in progress or in contemplation on that day;

(b)   before the appointed day, and in relation to the arrangements, no reference was made in relation to an anticipated merger; no undertakings were accepted and the Secretary of State had not made a decision neither to make a reference nor to accept undertakings; and

(c) no merger notice was given to the Director or the OFT before that date in relation to the arrangements.

12.10   Subject, as always to Sched. 24, para. 13(8), under Sched. 24, para. 13(7), the Act shall apply in a case described in para. 12.3(c) above (except that there is no need to show that the concentrations described in (d) of that paragraph apply). Schedule 24, para. 13(8) – to which the other transactional merger rules are subject – provides that the 1973 Act shall continue to apply in relation to concentrations with a Community dimension under the ECMR which were notified to the European Commission before the appointed day.

MARKET INVESTIGATION REFERENCES: TRANSITIONAL PROVISIONS

12.11   The transitional provisions in Sched. 21 in relation to the new rules on market investigation references, are, in contrast with the rules in relation to merger references, refreshingly simple.

12.12   Schedule 24, para. 14 provides that, with the exception of the rules relating to enforcement of orders and undertakings set out in paras. 15–18, the 1973 Act shall continue to apply to any monopoly reference made before the appointed day.

12.13   However, after the appointed day, any person who is in receipt of an information request from the DGFT under s.44 of the 1973 Act will no longer be required to comply with that request.

---

1   The power to make a reference is not prevented under those provisions if: any material information that is or ought to be known by the person who gave the merger notice or any connected person, is not disclosed to the Secretary of State or the Director before the end of the merger notice period; or where six months have elapsed since the merger notice expired without the enterprises to which it relates ceasing to be distinct from each other; or where any information given in respect of the notified arrangements is materially false or misleading.

2   In addition to the provisions described in the footnote above, s.75C1(b) and (d) provide that the power to make a reference is not prevented if, before the end of the merger notice period, any of the enterprises cease to be distinct from each other, or where after the merger notice has been given and before the notified merger has taken place, any of these enterprises cease to be distinct from any *other* enterprise.

Appendix
ENTERPRISE ACT 2002 (c. 40)

Establish and provide for the functions of the Office of Fair Trading, the Competition Appeal Tribunal and the Competition Service; to make provision about mergers and market structures and conduct; to amend the constitution and functions of the Competition Commission; to create an offence for those entering into certain anti-competitive agreements; to provide for the disqualification of directors of companies engaging in certain anti-competitive practices; to make other provision about competition law; to amend the law relating to the protection of the collective interests of consumers; to make further provision about the disclosure of information obtained under competition and consumer legislation; to amend the Insolvency Act 1986 and make other provision about insolvency; and for connected purposes.

[7th November 2002]

Be it enacted by the Queen's most Excellent Majesty, by and with the advice and consent of the Lords Spiritual and Temporal, and Commons, in this present Parliament assembled, and by the authority of the same, as follows:–

PART 1   THE OFFICE OF FAIR TRADING

Establishment of OFT

1 The Office of Fair Trading

(1) There shall be a body corporate to be known as the Office of Fair Trading (in this Act referred to as 'the OFT').

(2) The functions of the OFT are carried out on behalf of the Crown.

(3) Schedule 1 (which makes further provision about the OFT) has effect.

(4) In managing its affairs the OFT shall have regard, in addition to any relevant general guidance as to the governance of public bodies, to such generally accepted principles of good corporate governance as it is reasonable to regard as applicable to the OFT.

2 The Director General of Fair Trading

(1) The functions of the Director General of Fair Trading (in this Act referred to as 'the Director'), and his property, rights and liabilities, are transferred to the OFT.

(2) The office of the Director is abolished.

(3) Any enactment, instrument or other document passed or made before the commencement of subsection (1) which refers to the Director shall have effect, so far as necessary for the purposes of or in consequence of anything being transferred, as if any reference to the Director were a reference to the OFT.

3 Annual plan

(1) The OFT shall, before each financial year, publish a document (the 'annual plan') containing a statement of its main objectives and priorities for the year.

(2) The OFT shall for the purposes of public consultation publish a document containing proposals for its annual plan at least two months before publishing the annual plan for any year.

(3) The OFT shall lay before Parliament a copy of each document published under subsection (2) and each annual plan.

4 Annual and other reports

(1) The OFT shall, as soon as practicable after the end of each financial year, make to the Secretary of State a report (the 'annual report') on its activities and performance during that year.

(2) The annual report for each year shall include –

(a) a general survey of developments in respect of matters relating to the OFT's functions;

(b) an assessment of the extent to which the OFT's main objectives and priorities for the year (as set out in the annual plan) have been met;

(c) a summary of the significant decisions, investigations or other activities made or carried out by the OFT during the year;

(d) a summary of the allocation of the OFT's financial resources to its various activities during the year; and

(e) an assessment of the OFT's performance and practices in relation to its enforcement functions.

(3) The OFT shall lay a copy of each annual report before Parliament and arrange for the report to be published.

(4) The OFT may –

(a) prepare other reports in respect of matters relating to any of its functions; and

(b) arrange for any such report to be published.

General functions of OFT

5 Acquisition of information etc.

(1) The OFT has the function of obtaining, compiling and keeping under review information about matters relating to the carrying out of its functions.

(2) That function is to be carried out with a view to (among other things) ensuring that the OFT has sufficient information to take informed decisions and to carry out its other functions effectively.

(3) In carrying out that function the OFT may carry out, commission or support (financially or otherwise) research.

6 Provision of information etc. to the public

(1) The OFT has the function of –

(a) making the public aware of the ways in which competition may benefit consumers in, and the economy of, the United Kingdom; and

(b) giving information or advice in respect of matters relating to any of its functions to the public.

(2) In carrying out those functions the OFT may –

(a) publish educational materials or carry out other educational activities; or

(b) support (financially or otherwise) the carrying out by others of such activities or the provision by others of information or advice.

7 Provision of information and advice to Ministers etc.

(1) The OFT has the function of –

    (a) making proposals, or

    (b) giving other information or advice,

on matters relating to any of its functions to any Minister of the Crown or other public authority (including proposals, information or advice as to any aspect of the law or a proposed change in the law).

(2) A Minister of the Crown may request the OFT to make proposals or give other information or advice on any matter relating to any of its functions; and the OFT shall, so far as is reasonably practicable and consistent with its other functions, comply with the request.

8 Promoting good consumer practice

(1) The OFT has the function of promoting good practice in the carrying out of activities which may affect the economic interests of consumers in the United Kingdom.

(2) In carrying out that function the OFT may (without prejudice to the generality of subsection (1)) make arrangements for approving consumer codes and may, in accordance with the arrangements, give its approval to or withdraw its approval from any consumer code.

(3) Any such arrangements must specify the criteria to be applied by the OFT in determining whether to give approval to or withdraw approval from a consumer code.

(4) Any such arrangements may in particular –

    (a) specify descriptions of consumer code which may be the subject of an application to the OFT for approval (and any such description may be framed by reference to any feature of a consumer code, including the persons who are, or are to be, subject to the code, the manner in which it is, or is to be, operated and the persons responsible for its operation); and

    (b) provide for the use in accordance with the arrangements of an official symbol intended to signify that a consumer code is approved by the OFT.

(5) The OFT shall publish any arrangements under subsection (2) in such manner it considers appropriate.

(6) In this section 'consumer code' means a code of practice or other document (however described) intended, with a view to safeguarding or promoting the interests of consumers, to regulate by any means the conduct of persons engaged in the supply of goods or services to consumers (or the conduct of their employees or representatives).

Miscellaneous

9 Repeal of certain powers of direction

Section 12 of the Fair Trading Act 1973 (c. 41) (in this Act referred to as 'the 1973 Act') and section 13 of the Competition Act 1980 (c. 21) (powers of Secretary of State to give directions) shall cease to have effect.

10 Part 2 of the 1973 Act

(1) The following provisions of the 1973 Act shall cease to have effect –

    (a) section 3 and Schedule 2 (which establish, and make provision with respect to, the Consumer Protection Advisory Committee);

    (b) sections 13 to 21 (which relate to references made to, and reports of, that Committee); and

    (c) section 22 (power of Secretary of State to make orders in pursuance of a report of that Committee).

(2) But subsection (1)(c) does not affect –

    (a) any order under section 22 of the 1973 Act which is in force immediately before the commencement of this section;

    (b) the continued operation of that section so far as applying to the revocation of any such order.

(3) If the orders saved by subsection (2)(a) have been revoked, the Secretary of State may by order –

    (a) repeal any unrepealed provision of Part 2 of the 1973 Act and subsection (2) above; and

    (b) make such other consequential modifications of any Act or subordinate legislation (whenever passed or made) as he thinks fit.

(4) An order under subsection (3) –

    (a) may make transitional or saving provision in connection with any modification made by the order; and

    (b) shall be made by statutory instrument subject to annulment in pursuance of a resolution of either House of Parliament.

11 Super-complaints to OFT

(1) This section applies where a designated consumer body makes a complaint to the OFT that any feature, or combination of features, of a market in the United Kingdom for goods or services is or appears to be significantly harming the interests of consumers.

(2) The OFT must, within 90 days after the day on which it receives the complaint, publish a response stating how it proposes to deal with the complaint, and in particular –

    (a) whether it has decided to take any action, or to take no action, in response to the complaint, and

    (b) if it has decided to take action, what action it proposes to take.

(3) The response must state the OFT's reasons for its proposals.

(4) The Secretary of State may by order amend subsection (2) by substituting any period for the period for the time being specified there.

(5) 'Designated consumer body' means a body designated by the Secretary of State by order.

(6) The Secretary of State –

    (a) may designate a body only if it appears to him to represent the interests of consumers of any description, and

    (b) must publish (and may from time to time vary) other criteria to be applied by him in determining whether to make or revoke a designation.

(7) The OFT –

    (a) must issue guidance as to the presentation by the complainant of a reasoned case for the complaint, and

    (b) may issue such other guidance as appears to it to be appropriate for the purposes of this section.

(8) An order under this section –

    (a) shall be made by statutory instrument, and

    (b) shall be subject to annulment in pursuance of a resolution of either House of Parliament.

(9) In this section –

    (a) references to a feature of a market in the United Kingdom for goods or services have the same meaning as if contained in Part 4, and

    (b) 'consumer' means an individual who is a consumer within the meaning of that Part.

PART 2   THE COMPETITION APPEAL TRIBUNAL

The Competition Appeal Tribunal

12 The Competition Appeal Tribunal

(1) There shall be a tribunal, to be called the Competition Appeal Tribunal (in this Part referred to as 'the Tribunal').

(2) The Tribunal shall consist of –

    (a) a person appointed by the Lord Chancellor to preside over the Tribunal (in this Part referred to as 'the President');

    (b) members appointed by the Lord Chancellor to form a panel of chairmen; and

    (c) members appointed by the Secretary of State to form a panel of ordinary members.

(3) The Tribunal shall have a Registrar appointed by the Secretary of State.

(4) The expenses of the Tribunal shall be paid by the Competition Service.

(5) Schedule 2 (which makes further provision about the Tribunal) has effect.

13 The Competition Service

(1) There shall be a body corporate called the Competition Service (in this Part referred to as 'the Service').

(2) The purpose of the Service is to fund, and provide support services to, the Competition Appeal Tribunal.

(3) In subsection (2) 'support services' includes the provision of staff, accommodation and equipment and any other services which facilitate the carrying out by the Tribunal of its functions.

(4) The activities of the Service are not carried out on behalf of the Crown (and its property is not to be regarded as held on behalf of the Crown).

(5) The Secretary of State shall pay to the Service such sums as he considers appropriate to enable it to fund the activities of the Tribunal and to carry out its other activities.

(6) Schedule 3 (which makes further provision about the Service) has effect.

14 Constitution of Tribunal for particular proceedings and its decisions

(1) For the purposes of any proceedings before it the Tribunal shall consist of a chairman and two other members.

(2) The chairman must be the President or a member of the panel of chairmen.

(3) The other members may be chosen from either the panel of chairmen or the panel of ordinary members.

(4) If the members of the Tribunal as constituted in accordance with this section are unable to agree on any decision, the decision is to be taken by majority vote.

(5) This section has effect subject to paragraph 18 of Schedule 4 (consequences of a member of the Tribunal being unable to continue after the proceedings have begun to be heard).

(6) Part 1 of Schedule 4 (which makes further provision about the decisions of the Tribunal and their enforcement) has effect.

15 Tribunal rules

(1) The Secretary of State may, after consulting the President and such other persons as he considers appropriate, make rules (in this Part referred to as 'Tribunal rules') with respect to proceedings before the Tribunal.

(2) Tribunal rules may make provision with respect to matters incidental to or consequential upon appeals provided for by or under any Act to the Court of Appeal or the Court of Session in relation to a decision of the Tribunal.

(3) Tribunal rules may –

  (a) specify qualifications for appointment as Registrar;

  (b) confer functions on the President or the Registrar in relation to proceedings before the Tribunal; and

  (c) contain incidental, supplemental, consequential or transitional provision.

(4) The power to make Tribunal rules is exercisable by statutory instrument subject to annulment in pursuance of a resolution of either House of Parliament.

(5) Part 2 of Schedule 4 (which makes further provision about the rules) has effect, but without prejudice to the generality of subsection (1).

16 Transfers of certain proceedings to and from Tribunal

(1) The Lord Chancellor may by regulations –

  (a) make provision enabling the court –

    (i) to transfer to the Tribunal for its determination so much of any proceedings before the court as relates to an infringement issue; and

    (ii) to give effect to the determination of that issue by the Tribunal; and

  (b) make such incidental, supplementary, consequential, transitional or saving provision as the Lord Chancellor may consider appropriate.

(2) The power to make regulations under subsection (1) is exercisable by statutory instrument subject to annulment in pursuance of a resolution of either House of Parliament.

(3) Rules of court may prescribe the procedure to be followed in connection with a transfer mentioned in subsection (1).

(4) The court may transfer to the Tribunal, in accordance with rules of court, so much of any proceedings before it as relates to a claim to which section 47A of the 1998 Act applies.

(5) Rules of court may make provision in connection with the transfer from the Tribunal to the High Court or the Court of Session of a claim made in proceedings under section 47A of the 1998 Act.

(6) In this section –

  'the court' means –

  (a) the High Court or a county court; or

  (b) the Court of Session or a sheriff court; and

  'infringement issue' means any question relating to whether or not an infringement of –

  (a) the Chapter I prohibition or the Chapter II prohibition; or

  (b) Article 81 or 82 of the Treaty,

  has been or is being committed;

  but otherwise any terms used in this section and Part 1 of the 1998 Act have the same meaning as they have in that Part.

Proceedings under Part 1 of 1998 Act

17 Third party appeals

For section 47 of the 1998 Act (third party appeals) there is substituted –

'47 Third party appeals

(1) A person who does not fall within section 46(1) or (2) may appeal to the Tribunal with respect to a decision falling within paragraphs (a) to (f) of section 46(3) or such other decision of the OFT under this Part as may be prescribed.

(2)   A person may make an appeal under subsection (1) only if the Tribunal considers that he has a sufficient interest in the decision with respect to which the appeal is made, or that he represents persons who have such an interest.

(3)   The making of an appeal under this section does not suspend the effect of the decision to which the appeal relates.'

18 Monetary claims

(1)   After section 47 of the 1998 Act there is inserted –

'47A Monetary claims before Tribunal

(1)   This section applies to –

    (a)   any claim for damages, or

    (b)   any other claim for a sum of money,

which a person who has suffered loss or damage as a result of the infringement of a relevant prohibition may make in civil proceedings brought in any part of the United Kingdom.

(2)   In this section "relevant prohibition" means any of the following –

    (a)   the Chapter I prohibition;

    (b)   the Chapter II prohibition;

    (c)   the prohibition in Article 81(1) of the Treaty;

    (d)   the prohibition in Article 82 of the Treaty;

    (e)   the prohibition in Article 65(1) of the Treaty establishing the European Coal and Steel Community;

    (f)   the prohibition in Article 66(7) of that Treaty.

(3)   For the purpose of identifying claims which may be made in civil proceedings, any limitation rules that would apply in such proceedings are to be disregarded.

(4)   A claim to which this section applies may (subject to the provisions of this Act and Tribunal rules) be made in proceedings brought before the Tribunal.

(5)   But no claim may be made in such proceedings –

    (a)   until a decision mentioned in subsection (6) has established that the relevant prohibition in question has been infringed; and

    (b)   otherwise than with the permission of the Tribunal, during any period specified in subsection (7) or (8) which relates to that decision.

(6)   The decisions which may be relied on for the purposes of proceedings under this section are –

    (a)   a decision of the OFT that the Chapter I prohibition or the Chapter II prohibition has been infringed;

    (b)   a decision of the OFT that the prohibition in Article 81(1) or Article 82 of the Treaty has been infringed;

    (c)   a decision of the Tribunal (on an appeal from a decision of the OFT) that the Chapter I prohibition, the Chapter II prohibition or the prohibition in Article 81(1) or Article 82 of the Treaty has been infringed;

    (d)   a decision of the European Commission that the prohibition in Article 81(1) or Article 82 of the Treaty has been infringed; or

    (e)   a decision of the European Commission that the prohibition in Article 65(1) of the Treaty establishing the European Coal and Steel Community has been infringed, or a finding made by the European Commission under Article 66(7) of that Treaty.

(7)   The periods during which proceedings in respect of a claim made in reliance on a decision mentioned in subsection (6)(a), (b) or (c) may not be brought without permission are –

    (a)   in the case of a decision of the OFT, the period during which an appeal may be made to the Tribunal under section 46, section 47 or the EC Competition Law (Articles 84 and 85) Enforcement Regulations 2001 (S.I. 2001/2916);

    (b)   in the case of a decision of the OFT which is the subject of an appeal mentioned in paragraph (a), the period following the decision of the Tribunal on the appeal during which a further appeal may be made under section 49 or under those Regulations;

    (c)   in the case of a decision of the Tribunal mentioned in subsection (6)(c), the period during which a further appeal may be made under section 49 or under those Regulations;

    (d)   in the case of any decision which is the subject of a further appeal, the period during which an appeal may be made to the House of Lords from a decision on the further appeal;

and, where any appeal mentioned in paragraph (a), (b), (c) or (d) is made, the period specified in that paragraph includes the period before the appeal is determined.

(8) The periods during which proceedings in respect of a claim made in reliance on a decision or finding of the European Commission may not be brought without permission are –

    (a)   the period during which proceedings against the decision or finding may be instituted in the European Court; and

    (b)   if any such proceedings are instituted, the period before those proceedings are determined.

(9) In determining a claim to which this section applies the Tribunal is bound by any decision mentioned in subsection (6) which establishes that the prohibition in question has been infringed.

(10) The right to make a claim to which this section applies in proceedings before the Tribunal does not affect the right to bring any other proceedings in respect of the claim.'

(2) Section 47A applies to claims arising before the commencement of this section as it applies to claims arising after that time.

19 Claims on behalf of consumers

After section 47A of the 1998 Act (which is inserted by section 18), there is inserted –

'47B Claims brought on behalf of consumers

(1) A specified body may (subject to the provisions of this Act and Tribunal rules) bring proceedings before the Tribunal which comprise consumer claims made or continued on behalf of at least two individuals.

(2) In this section "consumer claim" means a claim to which section 47A applies which an individual has in respect of an infringement affecting (directly or indirectly) goods or services to which subsection (7) applies.

(3) A consumer claim may be included in proceedings under this section if it is –

    (a)   a claim made in the proceedings on behalf of the individual concerned by the specified body; or

    (b)   a claim made by the individual concerned under section 47A which is continued in the proceedings on his behalf by the specified body;

and such a claim may only be made or continued in the proceedings with the consent of the individual concerned.

(4) The consumer claims included in proceedings under this section must all relate to the same infringement.

(5) The provisions of section 47A(5) to (10) apply to a consumer claim included in

proceedings under this section as they apply to a claim made in proceedings under that section.

(6) Any damages or other sum (not being costs or expenses) awarded in respect of a consumer claim included in proceedings under this section must be awarded to the individual concerned; but the Tribunal may, with the consent of the specified body and the individual, order that the sum awarded must be paid to the specified body (acting on behalf of the individual).

(7) This subsection applies to goods or services which –

    (a)   the individual received, or sought to receive, otherwise than in the course of a business carried on by him (notwithstanding that he received or sought to receive them with a view to carrying on a business); and

    (b)   were, or would have been, supplied to the individual (in the case of goods whether by way of sale or otherwise) in the course of a business carried on by the person who supplied or would have supplied them.

(8) A business includes –

    (a)   a professional practice;

    (b)   any other undertaking carried on for gain or reward;

    (c)   any undertaking in the course of which goods or services are supplied otherwise than free of charge.

(9) "Specified" means specified in an order made by the Secretary of State, in accordance with criteria to be published by the Secretary of State for the purposes of this section.

(10) An application by a body to be specified in an order under this section is to be made in a form approved by the Secretary of State for the purpose.'

Other amendments of 1998 Act

20 Findings of infringements

(1)   After section 58 of the 1998 Act there is inserted –

'Findings of infringements

58A Findings of infringements

(1)   This section applies to proceedings before the court in which damages or any other sum of money is claimed in respect of an infringement of –

    (a)   the Chapter I prohibition;

    (b)   the Chapter II prohibition;

    (c)   the prohibition in Article 81(1) of the Treaty;

    (d)   the prohibition in Article 82 of the Treaty.

(2)   In such proceedings, the court is bound by a decision mentioned in subsection (3) once any period specified in subsection (4) which relates to the decision has elapsed.

(3)   The decisions are –

    (a)   a decision of the OFT that the Chapter I prohibition or the Chapter II prohibition has been infringed;

    (b)   a decision of the OFT that the prohibition in Article 81(1) or Article 82 of the Treaty has been infringed;

    (c)   a decision of the Tribunal (on an appeal from a decision of the OFT) that the Chapter I prohibition or the Chapter II prohibition has been infringed, or that the prohibition in Article 81(1) or Article 82 of the Treaty has been infringed.

(4)   The periods mentioned in subsection (2) are –

(a)   in the case of a decision of the OFT, the period during which an appeal may be made to the Tribunal under section 46 or 47 or the EC Competition Law (Articles 84 and 85) Enforcement Regulations 2001 (S.I. 2001/2916);

(b)   in the case of a decision of the Tribunal mentioned in subsection (3)(c), the period during which a further appeal may be made under section 49 or under those Regulations;

(c)   in the case of any decision which is the subject of a further appeal, the period during which an appeal may be made to the House of Lords from a decision on the further appeal;

and, where any appeal mentioned in paragraph (a), (b) or (c) is made, the period specified in that paragraph includes the period before the appeal is determined.'

(2)   Section 58A does not apply in relation to decisions made before the commencement of this section.

(3)   In section 59(1) of that Act (interpretation), in the definition of 'the court', after '58' there is inserted ', 58A'.

21 Amendment of 1998 Act relating to the Tribunal

Schedule 5 (which contains amendments of the 1998 Act relating to, and to the proceedings of, the Tribunal) has effect.

PART 3   MERGERS

CHAPTER 1   DUTY TO MAKE REFERENCES

Duty to make references: completed mergers

22 Duty to make references in relation to completed mergers

(1)   The OFT shall, subject to subsections (2) and (3), make a reference to the Commission if the OFT believes that it is or may be the case that –

(a)   a relevant merger situation has been created; and

(b)   the creation of that situation has resulted, or may be expected to result, in a substantial lessening of competition within any market or markets in the United Kingdom for goods or services.

(2)   The OFT may decide not to make a reference under this section if it believes that –

(a)   the market concerned is not, or the markets concerned are not, of sufficient importance to justify the making of a reference to the Commission; or

(b)   any relevant customer benefits in relation to the creation of the relevant merger situation concerned outweigh the substantial lessening of competition concerned and any adverse effects of the substantial lessening of competition concerned.

(3)   No reference shall be made under this section if –

(a)   the making of the reference is prevented by section 69(1), 74(1) or 96(3) or paragraph 4 of Schedule 7;

(b)   the OFT is considering whether to accept undertakings under section 73 instead of making such a reference;

(c)   the relevant merger situation concerned is being, or has been, dealt with in connection with a reference made under section 33;

(d)   a notice under section 42(2) is in force in relation to the matter or the matter to which such a notice relates has been finally determined under Chapter 2 otherwise than in circumstances in which a notice is then given to the OFT under section 56(1); or

(e)   the European Commission is considering a request made, in relation to the matter concerned, by the United Kingdom (whether alone or with others) under article 22(3) of the European Merger Regulations, is proceeding with the matter in pursuance of such a request or has dealt with the matter in pursuance of such a request.

(4)   A reference under this section shall, in particular, specify –

(a)   the enactment under which it is made; and
(b)   the date on which it is made.

(5)   The references in this section to the creation of a relevant merger situation shall be construed in accordance with section 23, the reference in subsection (2) of this section to relevant customer benefits shall be construed in accordance with section 30 and the reference in subsection (3) of this section to a matter to which a notice under section 42(2) relates being finally determined under Chapter 2 shall be construed in accordance with section 43(4) and (5).

(6)   In this Part 'market in the United Kingdom' includes –

(a)   so far as it operates in the United Kingdom or a part of the United Kingdom, any market which operates there and in another country or territory or in a part of another country or territory; and
(b)   any market which operates only in a part of the United Kingdom;

and references to a market for goods or services include references to a market for goods and services.

(7)   In this Part 'the decision-making authority' means –

(a)   in the case of a reference or possible reference under this section or section 33, the OFT or (as the case may be) the Commission; and
(b)   in the case of a notice or possible notice under section 42(2) or 59(2) or a reference or possible reference under section 45 or 62, the OFT, the Commission or (as the case may be) the Secretary of State.

23 Relevant merger situations

(1)   For the purposes of this Part, a relevant merger situation has been created if –

(a)   two or more enterprises have ceased to be distinct enterprises at a time or in circumstances falling within section 24; and
(b)   the value of the turnover in the United Kingdom of the enterprise being taken over exceeds £70 million.

(2)   For the purposes of this Part, a relevant merger situation has also been created if –

(a)   two or more enterprises have ceased to be distinct enterprises at a time or in circumstances falling within section 24; and
(b)   as a result, one or both of the conditions mentioned in subsections (3) and (4) below prevails or prevails to a greater extent.

(3)   The condition mentioned in this subsection is that, in relation to the supply of goods of any description, at least one-quarter of all the goods of that description which are supplied in the United Kingdom, or in a substantial part of the United Kingdom –

(a)   are supplied by one and the same person or are supplied to one and the same person; or
(b)   are supplied by the persons by whom the enterprises concerned are carried on, or are supplied to those persons.

(4)   The condition mentioned in this subsection is that, in relation to the supply of services of any description, the supply of services of that description in the United Kingdom, or in a substantial part of the United Kingdom, is to the extent of at least one-quarter –

(a)   supply by one and the same person, or supply for one and the same person; or

(b) supply by the persons by whom the enterprises concerned are carried on, or supply for those persons.

(5) For the purpose of deciding whether the proportion of one-quarter mentioned in subsection (3) or (4) is fulfilled with respect to goods or (as the case may be) services of any description, the decision-making authority shall apply such criterion (whether value, cost, price, quantity, capacity, number of workers employed or some other criterion, of whatever nature), or such combination of criteria, as the decision-making authority considers appropriate.

(6) References in subsections (3) and (4) to the supply of goods or (as the case may be) services shall, in relation to goods or services of any description which are the subject of different forms of supply, be construed in whichever of the following ways the decision-making authority considers appropriate –

(a) as references to any of those forms of supply taken separately;
(b) as references to all those forms of supply taken together; or
(c) as references to any of those forms of supply taken in groups.

(7) For the purposes of subsection (6) the decision-making authority may treat goods or services as being the subject of different forms of supply whenever –

(a) the transactions concerned differ as to their nature, their parties, their terms or their surrounding circumstances; and
(b) the difference is one which, in the opinion of the decision-making authority, ought for the purposes of that subsection to be treated as a material difference.

(8) The criteria for deciding when goods or services can be treated, for the purposes of this section, as goods or services of a separate description shall be such as in any particular case the decision-making authority considers appropriate in the circumstances of that case.

(9) For the purposes of this Chapter, the question whether a relevant merger situation has been created shall be determined as at –

(a) in the case of a reference which is treated as having been made under section 22 by virtue of section 37(2), such time as the Commission may determine; and
(b) in any other case, immediately before the time when the reference has been, or is to be, made.

24 Time-limits and prior notice

(1) For the purposes of section 23 two or more enterprises have ceased to be distinct enterprises at a time or in circumstances falling within this section if –

(a) the two or more enterprises ceased to be distinct enterprises before the day on which the reference relating to them is to be made and did so not more than four months before that day; or
(b) notice of material facts about the arrangements or transactions under or in consequence of which the enterprises have ceased to be distinct enterprises has not been given in accordance with subsection (2).

(2) Notice of material facts is given in accordance with this subsection if –

(a) it is given to the OFT prior to the entering into of the arrangements or transactions concerned or the facts are made public prior to the entering into of those arrangements or transactions; or
(b) it is given to the OFT, or the facts are made public, more than four months before the day on which the reference is to be made.

(3) In this section –

'made public' means so publicised as to be generally known or readily ascertainable; and

'notice' includes notice which is not in writing.

25 Extension of time-limits

(1) The OFT and the persons carrying on the enterprises which have or may have ceased to be distinct enterprises may agree to extend by no more than 20 days the four month period mentioned in section 24(1)(a) or (2)(b).

(2) The OFT may by notice to the persons carrying on the enterprises which have or may have ceased to be distinct enterprises extend the four month period mentioned in section 24(1)(a) or (2)(b) if it considers that any of those persons has failed to provide, within the period stated in a notice under section 31 and in the manner authorised or required, information requested of him in that notice.

(3) An extension under subsection (2) shall be for the period beginning with the end of the period within which the information is to be provided and which is stated in the notice under section 31 and ending with –

  (a) the provision of the information to the satisfaction of the OFT; or
  (b) if earlier, the cancellation by the OFT of the extension.

(4) The OFT may by notice to the persons carrying on the enterprises which have or may have ceased to be distinct enterprises extend the four month period mentioned in section 24(1)(a) or (2)(b) if it is seeking undertakings from any of those persons under section 73.

(5) An extension under subsection (4) shall be for the period beginning with the receipt of the notice under that subsection and ending with the earliest of the following events –

  (a) the giving of the undertakings concerned;
  (b) the expiry of the period of 10 days beginning with the first day after the receipt by the OFT of a notice from the person who has been given a notice under subsection (4) and from whom the undertakings are being sought stating that he does not intend to give the undertakings; or
  (c) the cancellation by the OFT of the extension.

(6) The OFT may by notice to the persons carrying on the enterprises which have or may have ceased to be distinct enterprises extend the four month period mentioned in section 24(1)(a) or (2)(b) if the European Commission is considering a request made, in relation to the matter concerned, by the United Kingdom (whether alone or with others) under article 22(3) of the European Merger Regulations (but is not yet proceeding with the matter in pursuance of such a request).

(7) An extension under subsection (6) shall be for the period beginning with the receipt of the notice under that subsection and ending with the receipt of a notice under subsection (8).

(8) The OFT shall, in connection with any notice given by it under subsection (6), by notice inform the persons carrying on the enterprises which have or may have ceased to be distinct enterprises of the completion by the European Commission of its consideration of the request of the United Kingdom.

(9) Subject to subsections (10) and (11), where the four month period mentioned in section 24(1)(a) or (2)(b) is extended or further extended by virtue of this section in relation to a particular case, any reference to that period in section 24 or the preceding provisions of this section shall have effect in relation to that case as if it were a reference to a period equivalent to the aggregate of the period being extended and the period of the extension (whether or not those periods overlap in time).

(10) Subsection (11) applies where –

  (a) the four month period mentioned in section 24(1)(a) or (2)(b) is further extended;
  (b) the further extension and at least one previous extension is made under one or more of subsections (2), (4) and (6); and
  (c) the same days or fractions of days are included in or comprise the further extension and are included in or comprise at least one such previous extension.

(11) In calculating the period of the further extension, any days or fractions of days of the kind mentioned in subsection (10)(c) shall be disregarded.

(12) No more than one extension is possible under subsection (1).

26 Enterprises ceasing to be distinct enterprises

(1) For the purposes of this Part any two enterprises cease to be distinct enterprises if they are brought under common ownership or common control (whether or not the business to which either of them formerly belonged continues to be carried on under the same or different ownership or control).

(2) Enterprises shall, in particular, be treated as being under common control if they are –

    (a) enterprises of interconnected bodies corporate;

    (b) enterprises carried on by two or more bodies corporate of which one and the same person or group of persons has control; or

    (c) an enterprise carried on by a body corporate and an enterprise carried on by a person or group of persons having control of that body corporate.

(3) A person or group of persons able, directly or indirectly, to control or materially to influence the policy of a body corporate, or the policy of any person in carrying on an enterprise but without having a controlling interest in that body corporate or in that enterprise, may, for the purposes of subsections (1) and (2), be treated as having control of it.

(4) For the purposes of subsection (1), in so far as it relates to bringing two or more enterprises under common control, a person or group of persons may be treated as bringing an enterprise under his or their control if –

    (a) being already able to control or materially to influence the policy of the person carrying on the enterprise, that person or group of persons acquires a controlling interest in the enterprise or, in the case of an enterprise carried on by a body corporate, acquires a controlling interest in that body corporate; or

    (b) being already able materially to influence the policy of the person carrying on the enterprise, that person or group of persons becomes able to control that policy.

27 Time when enterprises cease to be distinct

(1) Subsection (2) applies in relation to any arrangements or transaction –

    (a) not having immediate effect or having immediate effect only in part; but

    (b) under or in consequence of which any two enterprises cease to be distinct enterprises.

(2) The time when the parties to any such arrangements or transaction become bound to such extent as will result, on effect being given to their obligations, in the enterprises ceasing to be distinct enterprises shall be taken to be the time at which the two enterprises cease to be distinct enterprises.

(3) In accordance with subsections (1) and (2) (but without prejudice to the generality of those subsections) for the purpose of determining the time at which any two enterprises cease to be distinct enterprises no account shall be taken of any option or other conditional right until the option is exercised or the condition is satisfied.

(4) Subsections (1) to (3) are subject to subsections (5) to (8) and section 29.

(5) The decision-making authority may, for the purposes of a reference, treat successive events to which this subsection applies as having occurred simultaneously on the date on which the latest of them occurred.

(6) subsection (5) applies to successive events –

    (a) which occur within a period of two years under or in consequence of the same arrangements or transaction, or successive arrangements or transactions between the same parties or interests; and

(b) by virtue of each of which, under or in consequence of the arrangements or the transaction or transactions concerned, any enterprises cease as between themselves to be distinct enterprises.

(7) The decision-making authority may, for the purposes of subsections (5) and (6), treat such arrangements or transactions as the decision-making authority considers appropriate as arrangements or transactions between the same interests.

(8) In deciding whether it is appropriate to treat arrangements or transactions as arrangements or transactions between the same interests the decision-making authority shall, in particular, have regard to the persons substantially concerned in the arrangements or transactions concerned.

28 Turnover test

(1) For the purposes of section 23 the value of the turnover in the United Kingdom of the enterprise being taken over shall be determined by taking the total value of the turnover in the United Kingdom of the enterprises which cease to be distinct enterprises and deducting –

(a) the turnover in the United Kingdom of any enterprise which continues to be carried on under the same ownership and control; or

(b) if no enterprise continues to be carried on under the same ownership and control, the turnover in the United Kingdom which, of all the turnovers concerned, is the turnover of the highest value.

(2) For the purposes of this Part (other than section 121(4)(c)(ii)) the turnover in the United Kingdom of an enterprise shall be determined in accordance with such provisions as may be specified in an order made by the Secretary of State.

(3) An order under subsection (2) may, in particular, make provision as to –

(a) the amounts which are, or which are not, to be treated as comprising an enterprise's turnover;

(b) the date or dates by reference to which an enterprise's turnover is to be determined;

(c) the connection with the United Kingdom by virtue of which an enterprise's turnover is turnover in the United Kingdom.

(4) An order under subsection (2) may, in particular, make provision enabling the decision-making authority to determine matters of a description specified in the order (including any of the matters mentioned in paragraphs (a) to (c) of subsection (3)).

(5) The OFT shall –

(a) keep under review the sum for the time being mentioned in section 23(1)(b); and

(b) from time to time advise the Secretary of State as to whether the sum is still appropriate.

(6) The Secretary of State may by order amend section 23(1)(b) so as to alter the sum for the time being mentioned there.

29 Obtaining control by stages

(1) Where an enterprise is brought under the control of a person or group of persons in the course of two or more transactions (in this section a 'series of transactions') to which subsection (2) applies, those transactions may, if the decision-making authority considers it appropriate, be treated for the purposes of a reference as having occurred simultaneously on the date on which the latest of them occurred.

(2) This subsection applies to –

(a) any transaction which –

(i) enables that person or group of persons directly or indirectly to control or materially to influence the policy of any person carrying on the enterprise;

(ii) enables that person or group of persons to do so to a greater degree; or

(iii) is a step (whether direct or indirect) towards enabling that person or group of persons to do so; and

(b) any transaction by virtue of which that person or group of persons acquires a controlling interest in the enterprise or, where the enterprise is carried on by a body corporate, in that body corporate.

(3) Where a series of transactions includes a transaction falling within subsection (2)(b), any transaction occurring after the occurrence of that transaction is to be disregarded for the purposes of subsection (1).

(4) Where the period within which a series of transactions occurs exceeds two years, the transactions that may be treated as mentioned in subsection (1) are any of those transactions that occur within a period of two years.

(5) Sections 26(2) to (4) and 127(1), (2) and (4) to (6) shall apply for the purposes of this section to determine –

(a) whether an enterprise is brought under the control of a person or group of persons; and

(b) whether a transaction is one to which subsection (2) applies;

as they apply for the purposes of section 26 to determine whether enterprises are brought under common control.

(6) In determining for the purposes of this section the time at which any transaction occurs, no account shall be taken of any option or other conditional right until the option is exercised or the condition is satisfied.

30 Relevant customer benefits

(1) For the purposes of this Part a benefit is a relevant customer benefit if –

(a) it is a benefit to relevant customers in the form of –

(i) lower prices, higher quality or greater choice of goods or services in any market in the United Kingdom (whether or not the market or markets in which the substantial lessening of competition concerned has, or may have, occurred or (as the case may be) may occur); or

(ii) greater innovation in relation to such goods or services; and

(b) the decision-making authority believes –

(i) in the case of a reference or possible reference under section 22 or 45(2), as mentioned in subsection (2); and

(ii) in the case of a reference or possible reference under section 33 or 45(4), as mentioned in subsection (3).

(2) The belief, in the case of a reference or possible reference under section 22 or section 45(2), is that –

(a) the benefit has accrued as a result of the creation of the relevant merger situation concerned or may be expected to accrue within a reasonable period as a result of the creation of that situation; and

(b) the benefit was, or is, unlikely to accrue without the creation of that situation or a similar lessening of competition.

(3) The belief, in the case of a reference or possible reference under section 33 or 45(4), is that –

(a) the benefit may be expected to accrue within a reasonable period as a result of the creation of the relevant merger situation concerned; and

(b) the benefit is unlikely to accrue without the creation of that situation or a similar lessening of competition.

(4) In subsection (1) 'relevant customers' means –

(a) customers of any person carrying on an enterprise which, in the creation of the relevant merger situation concerned, has ceased to be, or (as the case may be) will cease to be, a distinct enterprise;

(b) customers of such customers; and

(c) any other customers in a chain of customers beginning with the customers mentioned in paragraph (a);

and in this subsection 'customers' includes future customers.

31 Information powers in relation to completed mergers

(1) The OFT may by notice to any of the persons carrying on the enterprises which have or may have ceased to be distinct enterprises request him to provide the OFT with such information as the OFT may require for the purpose of deciding whether to make a reference under section 22.

(2) The notice shall state –

(a) the information required;

(b) the period within which the information is to be provided; and

(c) the possible consequences of not providing the information within the stated period and in the authorised or required manner.

32 Supplementary provision for purposes of sections 25 and 31

(1) The Secretary of State may make regulations for the purposes of sections 25 and 31.

(2) The regulations may, in particular –

(a) provide for the manner in which any information requested by the OFT under section 31 is authorised or required to be provided, and the time at which such information is to be treated as provided (including the time at which it is to be treated as provided to the satisfaction of the OFT for the purposes of section 25(3));

(b) provide for the persons carrying on the enterprises which have or may have ceased to be distinct enterprises to be informed, in circumstances in which section 25(3) applies –

(i) of the fact that the OFT is satisfied as to the provision of the information requested by it or (as the case may be) of the OFT's decision to cancel the extension; and

(ii) of the time at which the OFT is to be treated as so satisfied or (as the case may be) of the time at which the cancellation is to be treated as having effect;

(c) provide for the persons carrying on the enterprises which have or may have ceased to be distinct enterprises to be informed, in circumstances in which section 25(5) applies –

(i) of the OFT's decision to cancel the extension; and

(ii) of the time at which the cancellation is to be treated as having effect;

(d) provide for the time at which any notice under section 25(4), (5)(b), (6) or (8) is to be treated as received;

(e) provide that a person is, or is not, to be treated, in such circumstances as may be specified in the regulations, as acting on behalf of a person carrying on an enterprise which has or may have ceased to be a distinct enterprise.

(3) A notice under section 25(2) –

(a) shall be given within 5 days of the end of the period within which the information is to be provided and which is stated in the notice under section 31; and

(b) shall inform the person to whom it is addressed of –

(i) the OFT's opinion as mentioned in section 25(2); and

(ii) the OFT's intention to extend the period for considering whether to make a reference.

(4) In determining for the purposes of section 25(1) or (5)(b) or subsection (3)(a) above any period which is expressed in the enactment concerned as a period of days or number of days no account shall be taken of –

(a) Saturday, Sunday, Good Friday and Christmas Day; and

(b) any day which is a bank holiday in England and Wales.

Duty to make references: anticipated mergers

33 Duty to make references in relation to anticipated mergers

(1) The OFT shall, subject to subsections (2) and (3), make a reference to the Commission if the OFT believes that it is or may be the case that –

(a) arrangements are in progress or in contemplation which, if carried into effect, will result in the creation of a relevant merger situation; and

(b) the creation of that situation may be expected to result in a substantial lessening of competition within any market or markets in the United Kingdom for goods or services.

(2) The OFT may decide not to make a reference under this section if it believes that –

(a) the market concerned is not, or the markets concerned are not, of sufficient importance to justify the making of a reference to the Commission;

(b) the arrangements concerned are not sufficiently far advanced, or are not sufficiently likely to proceed, to justify the making of a reference to the Commission; or

(c) any relevant customer benefits in relation to the creation of the relevant merger situation concerned outweigh the substantial lessening of competition concerned and any adverse effects of the substantial lessening of competition concerned.

(3) No reference shall be made under this section if –

(a) the making of the reference is prevented by section 69(1), 74(1) or 96(3) or paragraph 4 of Schedule 7;

(b) the OFT is considering whether to accept undertakings under section 73 instead of making such a reference;

(c) the arrangements concerned are being, or have been, dealt with in connection with a reference made under section 22;

(d) a notice under section 42(2) is in force in relation to the matter or the matter to which such a notice relates has been finally determined under Chapter 2 otherwise than in circumstances in which a notice is then given to the OFT under section 56(1); or

(e) the European Commission is considering a request made, in relation to the matter concerned, by the United Kingdom (whether alone or with others) under article 22(3) of the European Merger Regulations, is proceeding with the matter in pursuance of such a request or has dealt with the matter in pursuance of such a request.

(4) A reference under this section shall, in particular, specify –

(a) the enactment under which it is made; and

(b) the date on which it is made.

34 Supplementary provision in relation to anticipated mergers

(1) The Secretary of State may by order make such provision as he considers appropriate about the operation of sections 27 and 29 in relation to –

(a) references under this Part which relate to arrangements which are in progress or in contemplation; or

(b) notices under section 42(2), 59(2) or 67(2) which relate to such arrangements.

(2) An order under subsection (1) may, in particular –

(a) provide for sections 27(5) to (8) and 29 to apply with modifications in relation to such references or notices or in relation to particular descriptions of such references or notices;

(b) enable particular descriptions of events, arrangements or transactions which have already occurred –

(i)   to be taken into account for the purposes of deciding whether to make such references or such references of a particular description or whether to give such notices or such notices of a particular description;

(ii) to be dealt with under such references or such references of a particular description or under such notices or such notices of a particular description.

Determination of references

35 Questions to be decided in relation to completed mergers

(1) Subject to subsections (6) and (7) and section 127(3), the Commission shall, on a reference under section 22, decide the following questions –

(a) whether a relevant merger situation has been created; and

(b) if so, whether the creation of that situation has resulted, or may be expected to result, in a substantial lessening of competition within any market or markets in the United Kingdom for goods or services.

(2) For the purposes of this Part there is an anti-competitive outcome if –

(a) a relevant merger situation has been created and the creation of that situation has resulted, or may be expected to result, in a substantial lessening of competition within any market or markets in the United Kingdom for goods or services; or

(b) arrangements are in progress or in contemplation which, if carried into effect, will result in the creation of a relevant merger situation and the creation of that situation may be expected to result in a substantial lessening of competition within any market or markets in the United Kingdom for goods or services.

(3) The Commission shall, if it has decided on a reference under section 22 that there is an anti-competitive outcome (within the meaning given by subsection (2)(a)), decide the following additional questions –

(a) whether action should be taken by it under section 41(2) for the purpose of remedying, mitigating or preventing the substantial lessening of competition concerned or any adverse effect which has resulted from, or may be expected to result from, the substantial lessening of competition;

(b) whether it should recommend the taking of action by others for the purpose of remedying, mitigating or preventing the substantial lessening of competition concerned or any adverse effect which has resulted from, or may be expected to result from, the substantial lessening of competition; and

(c) in either case, if action should be taken, what action should be taken and what is to be remedied, mitigated or prevented.

(4) In deciding the questions mentioned in subsection (3) the Commission shall, in particular, have regard to the need to achieve as comprehensive a solution as is reasonable and practicable to the substantial lessening of competition and any adverse effects resulting from it.

(5) In deciding the questions mentioned in subsection (3) the Commission may, in particular, have regard to the effect of any action on any relevant customer benefits in relation to the creation of the relevant merger situation concerned.

(6) In relation to the question whether a relevant merger situation has been created, a reference under section 22 may be framed so as to require the Commission to exclude from consideration –

    (a) subsection (1) of section 23;

    (b) subsection (2) of that section; or

    (c) one of those subsections if the Commission finds that the other is satisfied.

(7) In relation to the question whether any such result as is mentioned in section 23(2)(b) has arisen, a reference under section 22 may be framed so as to require the Commission to confine its investigation to the supply of goods or services in a part of the United Kingdom specified in the reference.

36 Questions to be decided in relation to anticipated mergers

(1) Subject to subsections (5) and (6) and section 127(3), the Commission shall, on a reference under section 33, decide the following questions –

    (a) whether arrangements are in progress or in contemplation which, if carried into effect, will result in the creation of a relevant merger situation; and

    (b) if so, whether the creation of that situation may be expected to result in a substantial lessening of competition within any market or markets in the United Kingdom for goods or services.

(2) The Commission shall, if it has decided on a reference under section 33 that there is an anti-competitive outcome (within the meaning given by section 35(2)(b)), decide the following additional questions –

    (a) whether action should be taken by it under section 41(2) for the purpose of remedying, mitigating or preventing the substantial lessening of competition concerned or any adverse effect which may be expected to result from the substantial lessening of competition;

    (b) whether it should recommend the taking of action by others for the purpose of remedying, mitigating or preventing the substantial lessening of competition concerned or any adverse effect which may be expected to result from the substantial lessening of competition; and

    (c) in either case, if action should be taken, what action should be taken and what is to be remedied, mitigated or prevented.

(3) In deciding the questions mentioned in subsection (2) the Commission shall, in particular, have regard to the need to achieve as comprehensive a solution as is reasonable and practicable to the substantial lessening of competition and any adverse effects resulting from it.

(4) In deciding the questions mentioned in subsection (2) the Commission may, in particular, have regard to the effect of any action on any relevant customer benefits in relation to the creation of the relevant merger situation concerned.

(5) In relation to the question whether a relevant merger situation will be created, a reference under section 33 may be framed so as to require the Commission to exclude from consideration –

    (a) subsection (1) of section 23;

    (b) subsection (2) of that section; or

    (c) one of those subsections if the Commission finds that the other is satisfied.

(6) In relation to the question whether any such result as is mentioned in section 23(2)(b) will arise, a reference under section 33 may be framed so as to require the Commission to confine its investigation to the supply of goods or services in a part of the United Kingdom specified in the reference.

37 Cancellation and variation of references under section 22 or 33

(1) The Commission shall cancel a reference under section 33 if it considers that the proposal to make arrangements of the kind mentioned in the reference has been abandoned.

(2) The Commission may, if it considers that doing so is justified by the facts (including events occurring on or after the making of the reference concerned), treat a reference made under section 22 or 33 as if it had been made under section 33 or (as the case may be) 22; and, in such cases, references in this Part to references under those sections shall, so far as may be necessary, be construed accordingly.

(3) Where, by virtue of subsection (2), the Commission treats a reference made under section 22 or 33 as if it had been made under section 33 or (as the case may be) 22, sections 77 to 81 shall, in particular, apply as if the reference had been made under section 33 or (as the case may be) 22 instead of under section 22 or 33.

(4) Subsection (5) applies in relation to any undertaking accepted under section 80, or any order made under section 81, which is in force immediately before the Commission, by virtue of subsection (2), treats a reference made under section 22 or 33 as if it had been made under section 33 or (as the case may be) 22.

(5) The undertaking or order shall, so far as applicable, continue in force as if –

   (a) in the case of an undertaking or order which relates to a reference made under section 22, accepted or made in relation to a reference made under section 33; and

   (b) in the case of an undertaking or order which relates to a reference made under section 33, accepted or made in relation to a reference made under section 22;

   and the undertaking or order concerned may be varied, superseded, released or revoked accordingly.

(6) The OFT may at any time vary a reference under section 22 or 33.

(7) The OFT shall consult the Commission before varying any such reference.

(8) Subsection (7) shall not apply if the Commission has requested the variation concerned.

(9) No variation by the OFT under this section shall be capable of altering the period permitted by section 39 within which the report of the Commission under section 38 is to be prepared and published.

38 Investigations and reports on references under section 22 or 33

(1) The Commission shall prepare and publish a report on a reference under section 22 or 33 within the period permitted by section 39.

(2) The report shall, in particular, contain –

   (a) the decisions of the Commission on the questions which it is required to answer by virtue of section 35 or (as the case may be) 36;

   (b) its reasons for its decisions; and

   (c) such information as the Commission considers appropriate for facilitating a proper understanding of those questions and of its reasons for its decisions.

(3) The Commission shall carry out such investigations as it considers appropriate for the purposes of preparing a report under this section.

(4) The Commission shall, at the same time as a report prepared under this section is published, give it to the OFT.

39 Time-limits for investigations and reports

(1) The Commission shall prepare and publish its report under section 38 within the period of 24 weeks beginning with the date of the reference concerned.

(2) Where article 9(6) of the European Merger Regulations applies in relation to the reference under section 22 or 33, the Commission shall prepare and publish its report under section 38 –

   (a) within the period of 24 weeks beginning with the date of the reference; or

(b) if it is a shorter period, within such period as is necessary to ensure compliance with that article.

(3) The Commission may extend, by no more than 8 weeks, the period within which a report under section 38 is to be prepared and published if it considers that there are special reasons why the report cannot be prepared and published within that period.

(4) The Commission may extend the period within which a report under section 38 is to be prepared and published if it considers that a relevant person has failed (whether with or without a reasonable excuse) to comply with any requirement of a notice under section 109.

(5) In subsection (4) 'relevant person' means –

(a) any person carrying on any of the enterprises concerned;

(b) any person who (whether alone or as a member of a group) owns or has control of any such person; or

(c) any officer, employee or agent of any person mentioned in paragraph (a) or (b).

(6) For the purposes of subsection (5) a person or group of persons able, directly or indirectly, to control or materially to influence the policy of a body of persons corporate or unincorporate, but without having a controlling interest in that body of persons, may be treated as having control of it.

(7) An extension under subsection (3) or (4) shall come into force when published under section 107.

(8) An extension under subsection (4) shall continue in force until –

(a) the person concerned provides the information or documents to the satisfaction of the Commission or (as the case may be) appears as a witness in accordance with the requirements of the Commission; or

(b) the Commission publishes its decision to cancel the extension.

(9) References in this Part to the date of a reference shall be construed as references to the date specified in the reference as the date on which it is made.

(10) This section is subject to section 40.

40 Section 39: supplementary

(1) No extension is possible under subsection (3) or (4) of section 39 where the period within which the report is to be prepared and published is determined by virtue of subsection (2)(b) of that section.

(2) Where the period within which the report is to be prepared and published is determined by virtue of subsection (2)(a) of section 39, no extension is possible under subsection (3) or (4) of that section which extends that period beyond such period as is necessary to ensure compliance with article 9(6) of the European Merger Regulations.

(3) A period extended under subsection (3) of section 39 may also be extended under subsection (4) of that section and a period extended under subsection (4) of that section may also be extended under subsection (3) of that section.

(4) No more than one extension is possible under section 39(3).

(5) Where a period within which a report under section 38 is to be prepared and published is extended or further extended under section 39(3) or (4), the period as extended or (as the case may be) further extended shall, subject to subsections (6) and (7), be calculated by taking the period being extended and adding to it the period of the extension (whether or not those periods overlap in time).

(6) subsection (7) applies where –

(a) the period within which the report under section 38 is to be prepared and published is further extended;

(b) the further extension and at least one previous extension is made under section 39(4); and

(c) the same days or fractions of days are included in or comprise the further extension and are included in or comprise at least one such previous extension.

(7) In calculating the period of the further extension, any days or fractions of days of the kind mentioned in subsection (6)(c) shall be disregarded.

(8) The Secretary of State may by order amend section 39 so as to alter any one or more of the following periods –

    (a) the period of 24 weeks mentioned in subsection (1) of that section or any period for the time being mentioned in that subsection in substitution for that period;

    (b) the period of 24 weeks mentioned in subsection (2)(a) of that section or any period for the time being mentioned in that subsection in substitution for that period;

    (c) the period of 8 weeks mentioned in subsection (3) of that section or any period for the time being mentioned in that subsection in substitution for that period.

(9) No alteration shall be made by virtue of subsection (8) which results in the period for the time being mentioned in subsection (1) or (2)(a) of section 39 exceeding 24 weeks or the period for the time being mentioned in subsection (3) of that section exceeding 8 weeks.

(10) An order under subsection (8) shall not affect any period of time within which the Commission is under a duty to prepare and publish its report under section 38 in relation to a reference under section 22 or 33 if the Commission is already under that duty in relation to that reference when the order is made.

(11) Before making an order under subsection (8) the Secretary of State shall consult the Commission and such other persons as he considers appropriate.

(12) The Secretary of State may make regulations for the purposes of section 39(8).

(13) The regulations may, in particular –

    (a) provide for the time at which information or documents are to be treated as provided (including the time at which they are to be treated as provided to the satisfaction of the Commission for the purposes of section 39(8));

    (b) provide for the time at which a person is to be treated as appearing as a witness (including the time at which he is to be treated as appearing as a witness in accordance with the requirements of the Commission for the purposes of section 39(8));

    (c) provide for the persons carrying on the enterprises which have or may have ceased to be, or may cease to be, distinct enterprises to be informed, in circumstances in which section 39(8) applies, of the fact that –

        (i) the Commission is satisfied as to the provision of the information or documents required by it; or

        (ii) the person concerned has appeared as a witness in accordance with the requirements of the Commission;

    (d) provide for the persons carrying on the enterprises which have or may have ceased to be, or may cease to be, distinct enterprises to be informed, in circumstances in which section 39(8) applies, of the time at which the Commission is to be treated as satisfied as mentioned in paragraph (c)(i) above or the person concerned is to be treated as having appeared as mentioned in paragraph (c)(ii) above.

41 Duty to remedy effects of completed or anticipated mergers

(1) Subsection (2) applies where a report of the Commission has been prepared and published under section 38 within the period permitted by section 39 and contains the decision that there is an anti-competitive outcome.

(2) The Commission shall take such action under section 82 or 84 as it considers to be reasonable and practicable –

    (a) to remedy, mitigate or prevent the substantial lessening of competition concerned; and

    (b) to remedy, mitigate or prevent any adverse effects which have resulted from, or may be expected to result from, the substantial lessening of competition.

(3) The decision of the Commission under subsection (2) shall be consistent with its decisions as included in its report by virtue of section 35(3) or (as the case may be) 36(2)
unless there has been a material change of circumstances since the preparation of the
report or the Commission otherwise has a special reason for deciding differently.

(4) In making a decision under subsection (2), the Commission shall, in particular, have
regard to the need to achieve as comprehensive a solution as is reasonable and practicable to the substantial lessening of competition and any adverse effects resulting
from it.

(5) In making a decision under subsection (2), the Commission may, in particular, have
regard to the effect of any action on any relevant customer benefits in relation to the
creation of the relevant merger situation concerned.

CHAPTER 2   PUBLIC INTEREST CASES

Power to make references

42 Intervention by Secretary of State in certain public interest cases

(1) Subsection (2) applies where –

(a) the Secretary of State has reasonable grounds for suspecting that it is or may be
the case that a relevant merger situation has been created or that arrangements
are in progress or in contemplation which, if carried into effect, will result in the
creation of a relevant merger situation;

(b) no reference under section 22 or 33 has been made in relation to the relevant
merger situation concerned;

(c) no decision has been made not to make such a reference (other than a decision
made by virtue of subsection (2)(b) of section 33 or a decision to accept undertakings under section 73 instead of making such a reference); and

(d) no reference is prevented from being made under section 22 or 33 by virtue of –

(i)   section 22(3)(a) or (e) or (as the case may be) 33(3)(a) or (e); or

(ii) Community law or anything done under or in accordance with it.

(2) The Secretary of State may give a notice to the OFT (in this Part 'an intervention
notice') if he believes that it is or may be the case that one or more than one public
interest consideration is relevant to a consideration of the relevant merger situation
concerned.

(3) For the purposes of this Part a public interest consideration is a consideration which,
at the time of the giving of the intervention notice concerned, is specified in section
58 or is not so specified but, in the opinion of the Secretary of State, ought to be so
specified.

(4) No more than one intervention notice shall be given under subsection (2) in relation
to the same relevant merger situation.

(5) For the purposes of deciding whether a relevant merger situation has been created or
whether arrangements are in progress or in contemplation which, if carried into
effect, will result in the creation of a relevant merger situation, sections 23 to 32 (read
together with section 34) shall apply for the purposes of this Chapter as they do for
the purposes of Chapter 1 but subject to subsection (6).

(6) In their application by virtue of subsection (5) sections 23 to 32 shall have effect as
if –

(a) for paragraph (a) of section 23(9) there were substituted –

'(a) in relation to the giving of an intervention notice, the time when the notice
is given;

(aa) in relation to the making of a report by the OFT under section 44, the time
of the making of the report;

    (ab) in the case of a reference which is treated as having been made under section 45(2) or (3) by virtue of section 49(1), such time as the Commission may determine; and';

  (b) the references to the OFT in sections 25(1) to (3), (6) and (8) and 31 included references to the Secretary of State;

  (c) the references to the OFT in section 25(4) and (5) were references to the Secretary of State;

  (d) the reference in section 25(4) to section 73 were a reference to paragraph 3 of Schedule 7;

  (e) after section 25(5) there were inserted –

> '(5A) The Secretary of State may by notice to the persons carrying on the enterprises which have or may have ceased to be distinct enterprises extend the four month period mentioned in section 24(1)(a) or (2)(b) if, by virtue of section 46(5) or paragraph 3(6) of Schedule 7, he decides to delay a decision as to whether to make a reference under section 45.
>
> (5B) An extension under subsection (5A) shall be for the period of the delay.';

  (f) in section 25(10)(b) after the word '(4)' there were inserted ', (5A)';

  (g) the reference in section 25(12) to one extension were a reference to one extension by the OFT and one extension by the Secretary of State;

  (h) the powers to extend time-limits under section 25 as applied by subsection (5) above, and the power to request information under section 31(1) as so applied, were not exercisable by the OFT or the Secretary of State before the giving of an intervention notice but the existing time-limits in relation to possible references under section 22 or 33 were applicable for the purposes of the giving of that notice;

  (i) the existing time-limits in relation to possible references under section 22 or 33 (except for extensions under section 25(4)) remained applicable on and after the giving of an intervention notice as if any extensions were made under section 25 as applied by subsection (5) above but subject to further alteration by the OFT or the Secretary of State under section 25 as so applied;

  (j) in subsection (1) of section 31 for the words 'section 22' there were substituted 'section 45(2) or (3)' and, in the application of that subsection to the OFT, for the word 'deciding' there were substituted 'enabling the Secretary of State to decide';

  (k) in the case of the giving of intervention notices, the references in sections 23 to 32 to the making of a reference or a reference were, so far as necessary, references to the giving of an intervention notice or an intervention notice; and

  (l) the references to the OFT in section 32(2)(a) to (c) and (3) were construed in accordance with the above modifications.

(7) Where the Secretary of State has given an intervention notice mentioning a public interest consideration which, at that time, is not finalised, he shall, as soon as practicable, take such action as is within his power to ensure that it is finalised.

(8) For the purposes of this Part a public interest consideration is finalised if –

  (a) it is specified in section 58 otherwise than by virtue of an order under subsection (3) of that section; or

  (b) it is specified in that section by virtue of an order under subsection (3) of that section and the order providing for it to be so specified has been laid before, and approved by, Parliament in accordance with subsection (7) of section 124 and within the period mentioned in that subsection.

43 Intervention notices under section 42

(1) An intervention notice shall state –

  (a) the relevant merger situation concerned;

(b) the public interest consideration or considerations which are, or may be, relevant to a consideration of the relevant merger situation concerned; and

(c) where any public interest consideration concerned is not finalised, the proposed timetable for finalising it.

(2) Where the Secretary of State believes that it is or may be the case that two or more public interest considerations are relevant to a consideration of the relevant merger situation concerned, he may decide not to mention in the intervention notice such of those considerations as he considers appropriate.

(3) An intervention notice shall come into force when it is given and shall cease to be in force when the matter to which it relates is finally determined under this Chapter.

(4) For the purposes of this Part, a matter to which an intervention notice relates is finally determined under this Chapter if –

(a) the time within which the OFT is to report to the Secretary of State under section 44 has expired and no such report has been made;

(b) the Secretary of State decides to accept an undertaking or group of undertakings under paragraph 3 of Schedule 7 instead of making a reference under section 45;

(c) the Secretary of State otherwise decides not to make a reference under that section;

(d) the Commission cancels such a reference under section 48(1) or 53(1);

(e) the time within which the Commission is to prepare a report under section 50 and give it to the Secretary of State has expired and no such report has been prepared and given to the Secretary of State;

(f) the time within which the Secretary of State is to make and publish a decision under section 54(2) has expired and no such decision has been made and published;

(g) the Secretary of State decides under section 54(2) to make no finding at all in the matter;

(h) the Secretary of State otherwise decides under section 54(2) not to make an adverse public interest finding;

(i) the Secretary of State decides under section 54(2) to make an adverse public interest finding but decides neither to accept an undertaking under paragraph 9 of Schedule 7 nor to make an order under paragraph 11 of that Schedule; or

(j) the Secretary of State decides under section 54(2) to make an adverse public interest finding and accepts an undertaking under paragraph 9 of Schedule 7 or makes an order under paragraph 11 of that Schedule.

(5) For the purposes of this Part the time when a matter to which an intervention notice relates is finally determined under this Chapter is –

(a) in a case falling within subsection (4)(a), (e) or (f), the expiry of the time concerned;

(b) in a case falling within subsection (4)(b), the acceptance of the undertaking or group of undertakings concerned;

(c) in a case falling within subsection (4)(c), (d), (g) or (h), the making of the decision concerned;

(d) in a case falling within subsection (4)(i), the making of the decision neither to accept an undertaking under paragraph 9 of Schedule 7 nor to make an order under paragraph 11 of that Schedule; and

(e) in a case falling within subsection (4)(j), the acceptance of the undertaking concerned or (as the case may be) the making of the order concerned.

44 Investigation and report by OFT

(1) Subsection (2) applies where the Secretary of State has given an intervention notice in relation to a relevant merger situation.

(2) The OFT shall, within such period as the Secretary of State may require, give a report to the Secretary of State in relation to the case.

(3) The report shall contain –

    (a) advice from the OFT on the considerations relevant to the making of a reference under section 22 or 33 which are also relevant to the Secretary of State's decision as to whether to make a reference under section 45; and

    (b) a summary of any representations about the case which have been received by the OFT and which relate to any public interest consideration mentioned in the intervention notice concerned and which is or may be relevant to the Secretary of State's decision as to whether to make a reference under section 45.

(4) The report shall, in particular, include decisions as to whether the OFT believes that it is, or may be, the case that –

    (a) a relevant merger situation has been created or arrangements are in progress or in contemplation which, if carried into effect, will result in the creation of a relevant merger situation;

    (b) the creation of that situation has resulted, or may be expected to result, in a substantial lessening of competition within any market or markets in the United Kingdom for goods or services;

    (c) the market or markets concerned would not be of sufficient importance to justify the making of a reference to the Commission under section 22 or 33;

    (d) in the case of arrangements which are in progress or in contemplation, the arrangements are not sufficiently far advanced, or not sufficiently likely to proceed, to justify the making of such a reference;

    (e) any relevant customer benefits in relation to the creation of the relevant merger situation concerned outweigh the substantial lessening of competition and any adverse effects of the substantial lessening of competition; or

    (f) it would be appropriate to deal with the matter (disregarding any public interest considerations mentioned in the intervention notice concerned) by way of undertakings under paragraph 3 of Schedule 7.

(5) If the OFT believes that it is or may be the case that it would be appropriate to deal with the matter (disregarding any public interest considerations mentioned in the intervention notice concerned) by way of undertakings under paragraph 3 of Schedule 7, the report shall contain descriptions of the undertakings which the OFT believes are, or may be, appropriate.

(6) The report may, in particular, include advice and recommendations on any public interest consideration mentioned in the intervention notice concerned and which is or may be relevant to the Secretary of State's decision as to whether to make a reference under section 45.

(7) The OFT shall carry out such investigations as it considers appropriate for the purposes of producing a report under this section.

45 Power of Secretary of State to refer matter to Commission

(1) Subsections (2) to (5) apply where the Secretary of State –

    (a) has given an intervention notice in relation to a relevant merger situation; and

    (b) has received a report of the OFT under section 44 in relation to the matter.

(2) The Secretary of State may make a reference to the Commission if he believes that it is or may be the case that –

    (a) a relevant merger situation has been created;

    (b) the creation of that situation has resulted, or may be expected to result, in a substantial lessening of competition within any market or markets in the United Kingdom for goods or services;

    (c) one or more than one public interest consideration mentioned in the intervention notice is relevant to a consideration of the relevant merger situation concerned; and

(d)   taking account only of the substantial lessening of competition and the relevant public interest consideration or considerations concerned, the creation of that situation operates or may be expected to operate against the public interest.

(3)   The Secretary of State may make a reference to the Commission if he believes that it is or may be the case that –

(a)   a relevant merger situation has been created;

(b)   the creation of that situation has not resulted, and may be expected not to result, in a substantial lessening of competition within any market or markets in the United Kingdom for goods or services;

(c)   one or more than one public interest consideration mentioned in the intervention notice is relevant to a consideration of the relevant merger situation concerned; and

(d)   taking account only of the relevant public interest consideration or considerations concerned, the creation of that situation operates or may be expected to operate against the public interest.

(4)   The Secretary of State may make a reference to the Commission if he believes that it is or may be the case that –

(a)   arrangements are in progress or in contemplation which, if carried into effect, will result in the creation of a relevant merger situation;

(b)   the creation of that situation may be expected to result in a substantial lessening of competition within any market or markets in the United Kingdom for goods or services;

(c)   one or more than one public interest consideration mentioned in the intervention notice is relevant to a consideration of the relevant merger situation concerned; and

(d)   taking account only of the substantial lessening of competition and the relevant public interest consideration or considerations concerned, the creation of the relevant merger situation may be expected to operate against the public interest.

(5)   The Secretary of State may make a reference to the Commission if he believes that it is or may be the case that –

(a)   arrangements are in progress or in contemplation which, if carried into effect, will result in the creation of a relevant merger situation;

(b)   the creation of that situation may be expected not to result in a substantial lessening of competition within any market or markets in the United Kingdom for goods or services;

(c)   one or more than one public interest consideration mentioned in the intervention notice is relevant to a consideration of the relevant merger situation concerned; and

(d)   taking account only of the relevant public interest consideration or considerations concerned, the creation of the relevant merger situation may be expected to operate against the public interest.

(6)   For the purposes of this Chapter any anti-competitive outcome shall be treated as being adverse to the public interest unless it is justified by one or more than one public interest consideration which is relevant.

(7)   This section is subject to section 46.

46 References under section 45: supplementary

(1)   No reference shall be made under section 45 if –

(a)   the making of the reference is prevented by section 69(1), 74(1) or 96(3) or paragraph 4 of Schedule 7; or

(b)   the European Commission is considering a request made, in relation to the matter concerned, by the United Kingdom (whether alone or with others) under article 22(3) of the European Merger Regulations, is proceeding with the matter in pursuance of such a request or has dealt with the matter in pursuance of such a request.

(2) The Secretary of State, in deciding whether to make a reference under section 45, shall accept the decisions of the OFT included in its report by virtue of subsection (4) of section 44 and any descriptions of undertakings as mentioned in subsection (5) of that section.

(3) Where the decision to make a reference under section 45 is made at any time on or after the end of the period of 24 weeks beginning with the giving of the intervention notice concerned, the Secretary of State shall, in deciding whether to make such a reference, disregard any public interest consideration which is mentioned in the intervention notice but which has not been finalised before the end of that period.

(4) Subject to subsection (5), where the decision to make a reference under section 45(2) or (4) is made at any time before the end of the period of 24 weeks beginning with the giving of the intervention notice concerned, the Secretary of State shall, in deciding whether to make such a reference, disregard any public interest consideration which is mentioned in the intervention notice but which has not been finalised if its effect would be to prevent, or to help to prevent, an anti-competitive outcome from being adverse to the public interest.

(5) The Secretary of State may, if he believes that there is a realistic prospect of the public interest consideration mentioned in subsection (4) being finalised within the period of 24 weeks beginning with the giving of the intervention notice concerned, delay deciding whether to make the reference concerned until the public interest consideration is finalised or, if earlier, the period expires.

(6) A reference under section 45 shall, in particular, specify –

   (a) the subsection of that section under which it is made;
   (b) the date on which it is made; and
   (c) the public interest consideration or considerations mentioned in the intervention notice concerned which the Secretary of State is not under a duty to disregard by virtue of subsection (3) above and which he believes are or may be relevant to a consideration of the relevant merger situation concerned.

Reports on references

47 Questions to be decided on references under section 45

(1) The Commission shall, on a reference under section 45(2) or (3), decide whether a relevant merger situation has been created.

(2) If the Commission decides that such a situation has been created, it shall, on a reference under section 45(2), decide the following additional questions –

   (a) whether the creation of that situation has resulted, or may be expected to result, in a substantial lessening of competition within any market or markets in the United Kingdom for goods or services; and
   (b) whether, taking account only of any substantial lessening of competition and the admissible public interest consideration or considerations concerned, the creation of that situation operates or may be expected to operate against the public interest.

(3) If the Commission decides that a relevant merger situation has been created, it shall, on a reference under section 45(3), decide whether, taking account only of the admissible public interest consideration or considerations concerned, the creation of that situation operates or may be expected to operate against the public interest.

(4) The Commission shall, on a reference under section 45(4) or (5), decide whether arrangements are in progress or in contemplation which, if carried into effect, will result in the creation of a relevant merger situation.

(5) If the Commission decides that such arrangements are in progress or in contemplation, it shall, on a reference under section 45(4), decide the following additional questions –

    (a) whether the creation of that situation may be expected to result in a substantial lessening of competition within any market or markets in the United Kingdom for goods or services; and

    (b) whether, taking account only of any substantial lessening of competition and the admissible public interest consideration or considerations concerned, the creation of that situation may be expected to operate against the public interest.

(6) If the Commission decides that arrangements are in progress or in contemplation which, if carried into effect, will result in the creation of a relevant merger situation, it shall, on a reference under section 45(5), decide whether, taking account only of the admissible public interest consideration or considerations concerned, the creation of that situation may be expected to operate against the public interest.

(7) The Commission shall, if it has decided on a reference under section 45 that the creation of a relevant merger situation operates or may be expected to operate against the public interest, decide the following additional questions –

    (a) whether action should be taken by the Secretary of State under section 55 for the purpose of remedying, mitigating or preventing any of the effects adverse to the public interest which have resulted from, or may be expected to result from, the creation of the relevant merger situation;

    (b) whether the Commission should recommend the taking of other action by the Secretary of State or action by persons other than itself and the Secretary of State for the purpose of remedying, mitigating or preventing any of the effects adverse to the public interest which have resulted from, or may be expected to result from, the creation of the relevant merger situation; and

    (c) in either case, if action should be taken, what action should be taken and what is to be remedied, mitigated or prevented.

(8) Where the Commission has decided by virtue of subsection (2)(a) or (5)(a) that there is or will be a substantial lessening of competition within any market or markets in the United Kingdom for goods or services, it shall also decide separately the following questions (on the assumption that it is proceeding as mentioned in section 56(6)) –

    (a) whether action should be taken by it under section 41 for the purpose of remedying, mitigating or preventing the substantial lessening of competition concerned or any adverse effect which has resulted from, or may be expected to result from, the substantial lessening of competition;

    (b) whether the Commission should recommend the taking of action by other persons for the purpose of remedying, mitigating or preventing the substantial lessening of competition concerned or any adverse effect which has resulted from, or may be expected to result from, the substantial lessening of competition; and

    (c) in either case, if action should be taken, what action should be taken and what is to be remedied, mitigated or prevented.

(9) In deciding the questions mentioned in subsections (7) and (8) the Commission shall, in particular, have regard to the need to achieve as comprehensive a solution as is reasonable and practicable to –

    (a) the adverse effects to the public interest; or

    (b) (as the case may be) the substantial lessening of competition and any adverse effects resulting from it.

(10) In deciding the questions mentioned in subsections (7) and (8) in a case where it has decided by virtue of subsection (2)(a) or (5)(a) that there is or will be a substantial lessening of competition, the Commission may, in particular, have regard to the effect of any action on any relevant customer benefits in relation to the creation of the relevant merger situation concerned.

(11) In this section 'admissible public interest consideration' means any public interest consideration which is specified in the reference under section 45 and which the Commission is not under a duty to disregard.

48 Cases where references or certain questions need not be decided

(1) The Commission shall cancel a reference under section 45(4) or (5) if it considers that the proposal to make arrangements of the kind mentioned in that reference has been abandoned.

(2) In relation to the question whether a relevant merger situation has been created or the question whether a relevant merger situation will be created, a reference under section 45 may be framed so as to require the Commission to exclude from consideration –

  (a) subsection (1) of section 23;
  (b) subsection (2) of that section; or
  (c) one of those subsections if the Commission finds that the other is satisfied.

(3) In relation to the question whether any such result as is mentioned in section 23(2)(b) has arisen or the question whether any such result will arise, a reference under section 45 may be framed so as to require the Commission to confine its investigation to the supply of goods or services in a part of the United Kingdom specified in the reference.

49 Variation of references under section 45

(1) The Commission may, if it considers that doing so is justified by the facts (including events occurring on or after the making of the reference concerned), treat –

  (a) a reference made under subsection (2) or (3) of section 45 as if it had been made under subsection (4) or (as the case may be) (5) of that section; or
  (b) a reference made under subsection (4) or (5) of section 45 as if it had been made under subsection (2) or (as the case may be) (3) of that section;

and, in such cases, references in this Part to references under those enactments shall, so far as may be necessary, be construed accordingly.

(2) Where, by virtue of subsection (1), the Commission treats a reference made under subsection (2) or (3) of section 45 as if it had been made under subsection (4) or (as the case may be) (5) of that section, paragraphs 1, 2, 7 and 8 of Schedule 7 shall, in particular, apply as if the reference had been made under subsection (4) or (as the case may be) (5) of that section instead of under subsection (2) or (3) of that section.

(3) Where, by virtue of subsection (1), the Commission treats a reference made under subsection (4) or (5) of section 45 as if it had been made under subsection (2) or (as the case may be) (3) of that section, paragraphs 1, 2, 7 and 8 of Schedule 7 shall, in particular, apply as if the reference had been made under subsection (2) or (as the case may be) (3) of that section instead of under subsection (4) or (5) of that section.

(4) Subsection (5) applies in relation to any undertaking accepted under paragraph 1 of Schedule 7, or any order made under paragraph 2 of that Schedule, which is in force immediately before the Commission, by virtue of subsection (1), treats a reference as mentioned in subsection (1).

(5) The undertaking or order shall, so far as applicable, continue in force as if –

  (a) in the case of an undertaking or order which relates to a reference under subsection (2) or (3) of section 45, accepted or made in relation to a reference made under subsection (4) or (as the case may be) (5) of that section; and
  (b) in the case of an undertaking or order which relates to a reference made under subsection (4) or (5) of that section, accepted or made in relation to a reference made under subsection (2) or (as the case may be) (3) of that section;

and the undertaking or order concerned may be varied, superseded, released or revoked accordingly.

(6)   The Secretary of State may at any time vary a reference under section 45.

(7)   The Secretary of State shall consult the Commission before varying any such reference.

(8)   Subsection (7) shall not apply if the Commission has requested the variation concerned.

(9)   No variation by the Secretary of State under this section shall be capable of altering the public interest consideration or considerations specified in the reference or the period permitted by section 51 within which the report of the Commission under section 50 is to be prepared and given to the Secretary of State.

50 Investigations and reports on references under section 45

(1)   The Commission shall prepare a report on a reference under section 45 and give it to the Secretary of State within the period permitted by section 51.

(2)   The report shall, in particular, contain –

   (a)   the decisions of the Commission on the questions which it is required to answer by virtue of section 47;

   (b)   its reasons for its decisions; and

   (c)   such information as the Commission considers appropriate for facilitating a proper understanding of those questions and of its reasons for its decisions.

(3)   The Commission shall carry out such investigations as it considers appropriate for the purpose of producing a report under this section.

51 Time-limits for investigations and reports by Commission

(1)   The Commission shall prepare its report under section 50 and give it to the Secretary of State under that section within the period of 24 weeks beginning with the date of the reference concerned.

(2)   Where article 9(6) of the European Merger Regulations applies in relation to the reference under section 45, the Commission shall prepare its report under section 50 and give it to the Secretary of State –

   (a)   within the period of 24 weeks beginning with the date of the reference; or

   (b)   if it is a shorter period, within such period as is necessary to ensure compliance with that article.

(3)   The Commission may extend, by no more than 8 weeks, the period within which a report under section 50 is to be prepared and given to the Secretary of State if it considers that there are special reasons why the report cannot be prepared and given to the Secretary of State within that period.

(4)   The Commission may extend the period within which a report under section 50 is to be prepared and given to the Secretary of State if it considers that a relevant person has failed (whether with or without a reasonable excuse) to comply with any requirement of a notice under section 109.

(5)   In subsection (4) 'relevant person' means –

   (a)   any person carrying on any of the enterprises concerned;

   (b)   any person who (whether alone or as a member of a group) owns or has control of any such person; or

   (c)   any officer, employee or agent of any person mentioned in paragraph (a) or (b).

(6)   For the purposes of subsection (5) a person or group of persons able, directly or indirectly, to control or materially to influence the policy of a body of persons corporate or unincorporate, but without having a controlling interest in that body of persons, may be treated as having control of it.

(7)   An extension under subsection (3) or (4) shall come into force when published under section 107.

(8)   An extension under subsection (4) shall continue in force until –

   (a)   the person concerned provides the information or documents to the satisfaction of the Commission or (as the case may be) appears as a witness in accordance with the requirements of the Commission; or

(b) the Commission publishes its decision to cancel the extension.

(9) This section is subject to sections 52 and 53.

52 Section 51: supplementary

(1) No extension is possible under subsection (3) or (4) of section 51 where the period within which the report is to be prepared and given to the Secretary of State is determined by virtue of subsection (2)(b) of that section.

(2) Where the period within which the report is to be prepared and given to the Secretary of State is determined by virtue of subsection (2)(a) of section 51, no extension is possible under subsection (3) or (4) of that section which extends that period beyond such period as is necessary to ensure compliance with article 9(6) of the European Merger Regulations.

(3) A period extended under subsection (3) of section 51 may also be extended under subsection (4) of that section and a period extended under subsection (4) of that section may also be extended under subsection (3) of that section.

(4) No more than one extension is possible under section 51(3).

(5) Where a period within which a report under section 50 is to be prepared and given to the Secretary of State is extended or further extended under section 51(3) or (4), the period as extended or (as the case may be) further extended shall, subject to subsections (6) and (7), be calculated by taking the period being extended and adding to it the period of the extension (whether or not those periods overlap in time).

(6) Subsection (7) applies where –

(a) the period within which the report under section 50 is to be prepared and given to the Secretary of State is further extended;

(b) the further extension and at least one previous extension is made under section 51(4); and

(c) the same days or fractions of days are included in or comprise the further extension and are included in or comprise at least one such previous extension.

(7) In calculating the period of the further extension, any days or fractions of days of the kind mentioned in subsection (6)(c) shall be disregarded.

(8) The Secretary of State may by order amend section 51 so as to alter any one or more of the following periods –

(a) the period of 24 weeks mentioned in subsection (1) of that section or any period for the time being mentioned in that subsection in substitution for that period;

(b) the period of 24 weeks mentioned in subsection (2)(a) of that section or any period for the time being mentioned in that subsection in substitution for that period;

(c) the period of 8 weeks mentioned in subsection (3) of that section or any period for the time being mentioned in that subsection in substitution for that period.

(9) No alteration shall be made by virtue of subsection (8) which results in the period for the time being mentioned in subsection (1) or (2)(a) of section 51 exceeding 24 weeks or the period for the time being mentioned in subsection (3) of that section exceeding 8 weeks.

(10) An order under subsection (8) shall not affect any period of time within which the Commission is under a duty to prepare and give to the Secretary of State its report under section 50 in relation to a reference under section 45 if the Commission is already under that duty in relation to that reference when the order is made.

(11) Before making an order under subsection (8) the Secretary of State shall consult the Commission and such other persons as he considers appropriate.

(12) The Secretary of State may make regulations for the purposes of section 51(8).

(13) The regulations may, in particular –

    (a) provide for the time at which information or documents are to be treated as pro-vided (including the time at which they are to be treated as provided to the sat-isfaction of the Commission for the purposes of section 51(8));

    (b) provide for the time at which a person is to be treated as appearing as a witness (including the time at which he is to be treated as appearing as a witness in accordance with the requirements of the Commission for the purposes of section 51(8));

    (c) provide for the persons carrying on the enterprises which have or may have ceased to be, or may cease to be, distinct enterprises to be informed, in circum-stances in which section 51(8) applies, of the fact that –

        (i) the Commission is satisfied as to the provision of the information or documents required by it; or

        (ii) the person concerned has appeared as a witness in accordance with the requirements of the Commission;

    (d) provide for the persons carrying on the enterprises which have or may have ceased to be, or may cease to be, distinct enterprises to be informed, in circum-stances in which section 51(8) applies, of the time at which the Commission is to be treated as satisfied as mentioned in paragraph (c)(i) above or the person concerned is to be treated as having appeared as mentioned in paragraph (c)(ii) above.

53 Restrictions on action where public interest considerations not finalised

(1) The Commission shall cancel a reference under section 45 if –

    (a) the intervention notice concerned mentions a public interest consideration which was not finalised on the giving of that notice or public interest considerations which, at that time, were not finalised;

    (b) no other public interest consideration is mentioned in the notice;

    (c) at least 24 weeks has elapsed since the giving of the notice; and

    (d) the public interest consideration mentioned in the notice has not been finalised within that period of 24 weeks or (as the case may be) none of the public inter-est considerations mentioned in the notice has been finalised within that period of 24 weeks.

(2) Where a reference to the Commission under section 45 specifies a public interest consideration which has not been finalised before the making of the reference, the Commission shall not give its report to the Secretary of State under section 50 in relation to that reference unless –

    (a) the period of 24 weeks beginning with the giving of the intervention notice concerned has expired;

    (b) the public interest consideration concerned has been finalised; or

    (c) the report must be given to the Secretary of State to ensure compliance with article 9(6) of the European Merger Regulations.

(3) The Commission shall, in reporting on any of the questions mentioned in section 47(2)(b), (3), (5)(b), (6) and (7), disregard any public interest consideration which has not been finalised before the giving of the report.

(4) The Commission shall, in reporting on any of the questions mentioned in section 47(2)(b), (3), (5)(b), (6) and (7), disregard any public interest consideration which was not finalised on the giving of the intervention notice concerned and has not been finalised within the period of 24 weeks beginning with the giving of the notice concerned.

(5) Subsections (1) to (4) are without prejudice to the power of the Commission to carry out investigations in relation to any public interest consideration to which it might be able to have regard in its report.

Decisions of the Secretary of State

54 Decision of Secretary of State in public interest cases

(1) Subsection (2) applies where the Secretary of State has received a report of the Commission under section 50 in relation to a relevant merger situation.

(2) The Secretary of State shall decide whether to make an adverse public interest finding in relation to the relevant merger situation and whether to make no finding at all in the matter.

(3) For the purposes of this Part the Secretary of State makes an adverse public interest finding in relation to a relevant merger situation if, in relation to that situation, he decides –

   (a) in connection with a reference to the Commission under subsection (2) of section 45, that it is the case as mentioned in paragraphs (a) to (d) of that subsection or subsection (3) of that section;

   (b) in connection with a reference to the Commission under subsection (3) of that section, that it is the case as mentioned in paragraphs (a) to (d) of that subsection;

   (c) in connection with a reference to the Commission under subsection (4) of that section, that it is the case as mentioned in paragraphs (a) to (d) of that subsection or subsection (5) of that section; and

   (d) in connection with a reference to the Commission under subsection (5) of that section, that it is the case as mentioned in paragraphs (a) to (d) of that subsection.

(4) The Secretary of State may make no finding at all in the matter only if he decides that there is no public interest consideration which is relevant to a consideration of the relevant merger situation concerned.

(5) The Secretary of State shall make and publish his decision under subsection (2) within the period of 30 days beginning with the receipt of the report of the Commission under section 50.

(6) In making a decision under subsections (2) to (4), the Secretary of State shall disregard any public interest consideration not specified in the reference under section 45 and any public interest consideration disregarded by the Commission for the purposes of its report.

(7) In deciding whether to make an adverse public interest finding under subsection (2), the Secretary of State shall accept –

   (a) in connection with a reference to the Commission under section 45(2) or (4), the decision of the report of the Commission under section 50 as to whether there is an anti-competitive outcome; and

   (b) in connection with a reference to the Commission under section 45(3) or (5) –

      (i) the decision of the report of the Commission under section 50 as to whether a relevant merger situation has been created or (as the case may be) arrangements are in progress or in contemplation which, if carried into effect, will result in the creation of a relevant merger situation; and

      (ii) the decision of the report of the OFT under section 44 as to the absence of a substantial lessening of competition.

(8) In determining for the purposes of subsection (5) the period of 30 days no account shall be taken of –

   (a) Saturday, Sunday, Good Friday and Christmas Day; and

   (b) any day which is a bank holiday in England and Wales.

55 Enforcement action by Secretary of State

(1) Subsection (2) applies where the Secretary of State has decided under subsection (2) of section 54 within the period required by subsection (5) of that section to make

an adverse public interest finding in relation to a relevant merger situation and has published his decision within the period so required.

(2) The Secretary of State may take such action under paragraph 9 or 11 of Schedule 7 as he considers to be reasonable and practicable to remedy, mitigate or prevent any of the effects adverse to the public interest which have resulted from, or may be expected to result from, the creation of the relevant merger situation concerned.

(3) In making a decision under subsection (2) the Secretary of State shall, in particular, have regard to the report of the Commission under section 50.

(4) In making a decision under subsection (2) in any case of a substantial lessening of competition, the Secretary of State may, in particular, have regard to the effect of any action on any relevant customer benefits in relation to the creation of the relevant merger situation concerned.

Other

56 Competition cases where intervention on public interest grounds ceases

(1) Where the Secretary of State decides not to make a reference under section 45 on the ground that no public interest consideration to which he is able to have regard is relevant to a consideration of the relevant merger situation concerned, he shall by notice require the OFT to deal with the matter otherwise than under this Chapter.

(2) Where a notice is given to the OFT in the circumstances mentioned in subsection (1), the OFT shall decide whether to make a reference under section 22 or 33; and any time-limits in relation to the Secretary of State's decision whether to make a reference under section 45 (including any remaining powers of extension) shall apply in relation to the decision of the OFT whether to make a reference under section 22 or 33.

(3) Where the Commission cancels under section 53(1) a reference under section 45 and the report of the OFT under section 44 contains the decision that it is or may be the case that there is an anti-competitive outcome in relation to the relevant merger situation concerned, the Commission shall proceed under this Part as if a reference under section 22 or (as the case may be) 33 had been made to it by the OFT.

(4) In proceeding by virtue of subsection (3) to prepare and publish a report under section 38, the Commission shall proceed as if –

(a) the reference under section 22 or 33 had been made at the same time as the reference under section 45;

(b) the timetable for preparing and giving its report under section 50 (including any remaining powers of extension and as extended by an additional period of 20 days) were the timetable for preparing and publishing its report under section 38; and

(c) in relation to the question whether a relevant merger situation has been created or the question whether arrangements are in progress or in contemplation which, if carried into effect, will result in the creation of a relevant merger situation, the Commission were confined to the questions on the subject to be investigated by it under section 47.

(5) In determining the period of 20 days mentioned in subsection (4) no account shall be taken of –

(a) Saturday, Sunday, Good Friday and Christmas Day; and

(b) any day which is a bank holiday in England and Wales.

(6) Where the Secretary of State decides under section 54(2) to make no finding at all in the matter in connection with a reference under section 45(2) or (4), the Commission shall proceed under this Part as if a reference under section 22 or (as the case may be) 33 had been made to it instead of a reference under section 45 and as if its report to

the Secretary of State under section 50 had been prepared and published by it under section 38 within the period permitted by section 39.

(7) In relation to proceedings by virtue of subsection (6), the reference in section 41(3) to decisions of the Commission as included in its report by virtue of section 35(3) or 36(2) shall be construed as a reference to decisions which were included in the report of the Commission by virtue of section 47(8).

(8) Where the Commission becomes under a duty to proceed as mentioned in subsection (3) or (6), references in this Part to references under sections 22 and 33 shall, so far as may be necessary, be construed accordingly; and, in particular, sections 77 to 81 shall apply as if a reference has been made to the Commission by the OFT under section 22 or (as the case may be) 33.

57 Duties of OFT and Commission to inform Secretary of State

(1) The OFT shall, in considering whether to make a reference under section 22 or 33, bring to the attention of the Secretary of State any case which it believes raises any consideration specified in section 58 unless it believes that the Secretary of State would consider any such consideration immaterial in the context of the particular case.

(2) The OFT and the Commission shall bring to the attention of the Secretary of State any representations about exercising his powers under section 58(3) which have been made to the OFT or (as the case may be) the Commission.

58 Specified considerations

(1) The interests of national security are specified in this section.

(2) In subsection (1) 'national security' includes public security; and in this subsection 'public security' has the same meaning as in article 21(3) of the European Merger Regulations.

(3) The Secretary of State may by order modify this section for the purpose of specifying in this section a new consideration or removing or amending any consideration which is for the time being specified in this section.

(4) An order under this section may, in particular –

    (a) provide for a consideration to be specified in this section for a particular purpose or purposes or for all purposes;

    (b) apply in relation to cases under consideration by the OFT, the Commission or the Secretary of State before the making of the order as well as cases under consideration on or after the making of the order.

CHAPTER 3   OTHER SPECIAL CASES

Special public interest cases

59 Intervention by Secretary of State in special public interest cases

(1) Subsection (2) applies where the Secretary of State has reasonable grounds for suspecting that it is or may be the case that a special merger situation has been created or arrangements are in progress or in contemplation which, if carried into effect, will result in the creation of a special merger situation.

(2) The Secretary of State may give a notice to the OFT (in this Part 'a special intervention notice') if he believes that it is or may be the case that one or more than one consideration specified in section 58 is relevant to a consideration of the special merger situation concerned.

(3) For the purposes of this Part a special merger situation has been created if –

    (a) no relevant merger situation has been created because of section 23(1)(b) and (2)(b); but

(b)   a relevant merger situation would have been created if those enactments were disregarded;

and the conditions mentioned in subsection (4) are satisfied.

(4)   The conditions mentioned in this subsection are that, immediately before the enterprises concerned ceased to be distinct –

(a)   at least one of the enterprises concerned was carried on in the United Kingdom or by or under the control of a body corporate incorporated in the United Kingdom; and

(b)   a person carrying on one or more of the enterprises concerned was a relevant government contractor.

(5)   For the purposes of deciding whether a relevant merger situation has been created or whether arrangements are in progress or in contemplation which, if carried into effect, will result in the creation of a relevant merger situation, sections 23 to 32 (read together with section 34) shall apply for the purposes of this Chapter as they do for the purposes of Chapter 1 but subject to subsection (6).

(6)   In their application by virtue of subsection (5) sections 23 to 32 shall have effect as if –

(a)   for paragraph (a) of section 23(9) there were substituted –

'(a)   in relation to the giving of a special intervention notice, the time when the notice is given;

(aa)   in relation to the making of a report by the OFT under section 61, the time of the making of the report;

(ab)   in the case of a reference which is treated as having been made under section 62(2) by virtue of section 64(2), such time as the Commission may determine; and';

(b)   the references to the OFT in section 24(2)(a) and (b) included references to the Secretary of State;

(c)   the references to the OFT in sections 25(1) to (3), (6) and (8) and 31 included references to the Secretary of State;

(d)   the references to the OFT in section 25(4) and (5) were references to the Secretary of State;

(e)   the reference in section 25(4) to section 73 were a reference to paragraph 3 of Schedule 7;

(f)   the reference in section 25(12) to one extension were a reference to one extension by the OFT and one extension by the Secretary of State;

(g)   the powers to extend time-limits under section 25 as applied by subsection (5) above, and the power to request information under section 31(1) as so applied, were not exercisable by the OFT or the Secretary of State before the giving of a special intervention notice;

(h)   in subsection (1) of section 31 for the words 'section 22' there were substituted 'section 62(2)' and, in the application of that subsection to the OFT, for the word 'deciding' there were substituted 'enabling the Secretary of State to decide';

(i)   in the case of the giving of special intervention notices, the references in sections 23 to 32 to the making of a reference or a reference were, so far as necessary, references to the giving of a special intervention notice or a special intervention notice; and

(j)   the references to the OFT in section 32(2)(a) to (c) and (3) were construed in accordance with the above modifications.

(7)   No more than one special intervention notice shall be given under subsection (2) in relation to the same special merger situation.

(8)   In this section 'relevant government contractor' means –

(a)   a government contractor –

(i)   who has been notified by or on behalf of the Secretary of State of information, documents or other articles relating to defence and of a confidential nature which the government contractor or an employee of his may hold or receive in connection with being such a contractor; and

    (ii) whose notification has not been revoked by or on behalf of the Secretary of State; or

(b) a former government contractor who was so notified when he was a government contractor and whose notification has not been revoked by or on behalf of the Secretary of State.

(9) In this section –

    'defence' has the same meaning as in section 2 of the Official Secrets Act 1989 (c. 6); and

    'government contractor' has the same meaning as in the Act of 1989 and includes any sub-contractor of a government contractor, any sub-contractor of that sub-contractor and any other sub-contractor in a chain of sub-contractors which begins with the sub-contractor of the government contractor.

60 Special intervention notices under section 59

(1) A special intervention notice shall state –

    (a) the special merger situation concerned; and

    (b) the consideration specified in section 58 or considerations so specified which are, or may be, relevant to the special merger situation concerned.

(2) Where the Secretary of State believes that it is or may be the case that two or more considerations specified in section 58 are relevant to a consideration of the special merger situation concerned, he may decide not to mention in the special intervention notice such of those considerations as he considers appropriate.

(3) A special intervention notice shall come into force when it is given and shall cease to be in force when the matter to which it relates is finally determined under this Chapter.

(4) For the purposes of this Part, a matter to which a special intervention notice relates is finally determined under this Chapter if –

    (a) the time within which the OFT is to report to the Secretary of State under section 61 has expired and no such report has been made;

    (b) the Secretary of State decides to accept an undertaking or group of undertakings under paragraph 3 of Schedule 7 instead of making a reference under section 62;

    (c) the Secretary of State otherwise decides not to make a reference under that section;

    (d) the Commission cancels such a reference under section 64(1);

    (e) the time within which the Commission is to prepare a report under section 65 and give it to the Secretary of State has expired and no such report has been prepared and given to the Secretary of State;

    (f) the time within which the Secretary of State is to make and publish a decision under section 66(2) has expired and no such decision has been made and published;

    (g) the Secretary of State decides under subsection (2) of section 66 otherwise than as mentioned in subsection (5) of that section;

    (h) the Secretary of State decides under subsection (2) of section 66 as mentioned in subsection (5) of that section but decides neither to accept an undertaking under paragraph 9 of Schedule 7 nor to make an order under paragraph 11 of that Schedule; or

    (i) the Secretary of State decides under subsection (2) of section 66 as mentioned in subsection (5) of that section and accepts an undertaking under paragraph 9 of Schedule 7 or makes an order under paragraph 11 of that Schedule.

(5) For the purposes of this Part the time when a matter to which a special intervention notice relates is finally determined under this Chapter is –

    (a) in a case falling within subsection (4)(a), (e) or (f), the expiry of the time concerned;

(b) in a case falling within subsection (4)(b), the acceptance of the undertaking or group of undertakings concerned;

(c) in a case falling within subsection (4)(c), (d) or (g), the making of the decision concerned;

(d) in a case falling within subsection (4)(h), the making of the decision neither to accept an undertaking under paragraph 9 of Schedule 7 nor to make an order under paragraph 11 of that Schedule; and

(e) in a case falling within subsection (4)(i), the acceptance of the undertaking concerned or (as the case may be) the making of the order concerned.

61 Initial investigation and report by OFT

(1) Subsection (2) applies where the Secretary of State has given a special intervention notice in relation to a special merger situation.

(2) The OFT shall, within such period as the Secretary of State may require, give a report to the Secretary of State in relation to the case.

(3) The report shall contain –

(a) advice from the OFT on the considerations relevant to the making of a reference under section 22 or 33 which are also relevant to the Secretary of State's decision as to whether to make a reference under section 62; and

(b) a summary of any representations about the case which have been received by the OFT and which relate to any consideration mentioned in the special intervention notice concerned and which is or may be relevant to the Secretary of State's decision as to whether to make a reference under section 62.

(4) The report shall include a decision as to whether the OFT believes (disregarding section 59(4)(b)) that it is, or may be, the case that a special merger situation has been created or (as the case may be) arrangements are in progress or in contemplation which, if carried into effect, will result in the creation of a special merger situation.

(5) The report may, in particular, include advice and recommendations on any consideration mentioned in the special intervention notice concerned and which is or may be relevant to the Secretary of State's decision as to whether to make a reference under section 62.

(6) The OFT shall carry out such investigations as it considers appropriate for the purposes of producing a report under this section.

62 Power of Secretary of State to refer the matter

(1) Subsection (2) applies where the Secretary of State –

(a) has given a special intervention notice in relation to a special merger situation; and

(b) has received a report of the OFT under section 61 in relation to the matter.

(2) The Secretary of State may make a reference to the Commission if he believes that it is or may be the case that –

(a) a special merger situation has been created;

(b) one or more than one consideration mentioned in the special intervention notice is relevant to a consideration of the special merger situation concerned; and

(c) taking account only of the relevant consideration or considerations concerned, the creation of that situation operates or may be expected to operate against the public interest.

(3) The Secretary of State may make a reference to the Commission if he believes that it is or may be the case that –

(a) arrangements are in progress or in contemplation which, if carried into effect, will result in the creation of a special merger situation;

(b) one or more than one consideration mentioned in the special intervention notice is relevant to a consideration of the special merger situation concerned; and

(c)   taking account only of the relevant consideration or considerations concerned, the creation of that situation may be expected to operate against the public interest.

(4)   No reference shall be made under this section if the making of the reference is prevented by section 69(1) or paragraph 4 of Schedule 7.

(5)   The Secretary of State, in deciding whether to make a reference under this section, shall accept the decision of the OFT included in its report under section 61 by virtue of subsection (4) of that section.

(6)   A reference under this section shall, in particular, specify –

(a)   the subsection of this section under which it is made;

(b)   the date on which it is made; and

(c)   the consideration or considerations mentioned in the special intervention notice which the Secretary of State believes are, or may be, relevant to a consideration of the special merger situation concerned.

63 Questions to be decided on references under section 62

(1)   The Commission shall, on a reference under section 62(2), decide whether a special merger situation has been created.

(2)   The Commission shall, on a reference under section 62(3), decide whether arrangements are in progress or in contemplation which, if carried into effect, will result in the creation of a special merger situation.

(3)   If the Commission decides that a special merger situation has been created or that arrangements are in progress or in contemplation which, if carried into effect, will result in the creation of a special merger situation, it shall, on a reference under section 62, decide whether, taking account only of the consideration or considerations mentioned in the reference, the creation of that situation operates or may be expected to operate against the public interest.

(4)   The Commission shall, if it has decided on a reference under section 62 that the creation of a special merger situation operates or may be expected to operate against the public interest, decide the following additional questions –

(a)   whether action should be taken by the Secretary of State under section 66 for the purpose of remedying, mitigating or preventing any of the effects adverse to the public interest which have resulted from, or may be expected to result from, the creation of the special merger situation concerned;

(b)   whether the Commission should recommend the taking of other action by the Secretary of State or action by persons other than itself and the Secretary of State for the purpose of remedying, mitigating or preventing any of the effects adverse to the public interest which have resulted from, or may be expected to result from, the creation of the special merger situation concerned; and

(c)   in either case, if action should be taken, what action should be taken and what is to be remedied, mitigated or prevented.

64 Cancellation and variation of references under section 62

(1)   The Commission shall cancel a reference under section 62(3) if it considers that the proposal to make arrangements of the kind mentioned in that reference has been abandoned.

(2)   The Commission may, if it considers that doing so is justified by the facts (including events occurring on or after the making of the reference concerned), treat a reference made under subsection (2) or (3) of section 62 as if it had been made under subsection (3) or (as the case may be) (2) of that section; and, in such cases, references in this Part to references under those enactments shall, so far as may be necessary, be construed accordingly.

(3)   Where, by virtue of subsection (2), the Commission treats a reference made under subsection (2) or (3) of section 62 as if it had been made under subsection (3) or (as the case may be) (2) of that section, paragraphs 1, 2, 7 and 8 of Schedule 7 shall, in

particular, apply as if the reference had been made under subsection (3) or (as the case may be) (2) of that section instead of under subsection (2) or (3) of that section.

(4) Subsection (5) applies in relation to any undertaking accepted under paragraph 1 of Schedule 7, or any order made under paragraph 2 of that Schedule, which is in force immediately before the Commission, by virtue of subsection (2), treats a reference made under subsection (2) or (3) of section 62 as if it had been made under subsection (3) or (as the case may be) (2) of that section.

(5) The undertaking or order shall, so far as applicable, continue in force as if –

    (a) in the case of an undertaking or order which relates to a reference under subsection (2) of section 62, accepted or made in relation to a reference made under subsection (3) of that section; and

    (b) in the case of an undertaking or order which relates to a reference made under subsection (3) of that section, accepted or made in relation to a reference made under subsection (2) of that section;

and the undertaking or order concerned may be varied, superseded, released or revoked accordingly.

(6) The Secretary of State may at any time vary a reference under section 62.

(7) The Secretary of State shall consult the Commission before varying any such reference.

(8) Subsection (7) shall not apply if the Commission has requested the variation concerned.

(9) No variation by the Secretary of State under this section shall be capable of altering the consideration or considerations specified in the reference or the period permitted by virtue of section 65 within which the report of the Commission under that section is to be prepared and given to the Secretary of State.

65 Investigations and reports on references under section 62

(1) The Commission shall prepare a report on a reference under section 62 and give it to the Secretary of State within the period permitted by virtue of this section.

(2) The report shall, in particular, contain –

    (a) the decisions of the Commission on the questions which it is required to answer by virtue of section 63;

    (b) its reasons for its decisions; and

    (c) such information as the Commission considers appropriate for facilitating a proper understanding of those questions and of its reasons for its decisions.

(3) Sections 51 and 52 (but not section 53) shall apply for the purposes of a report under this section as they apply for the purposes of a report under section 50.

(4) The Commission shall carry out such investigations as it considers appropriate for the purpose of producing a report under this section.

66 Decision and enforcement action by Secretary of State

(1) Subsection (2) applies where the Secretary of State has received a report of the Commission under section 65 in relation to a special merger situation.

(2) The Secretary of State shall, in connection with a reference under section 62(2) or (3), decide the questions which the Commission is required to decide by virtue of section 63(1) to (3).

(3) The Secretary of State shall make and publish his decision under subsection (2) within the period of 30 days beginning with the receipt of the report of the Commission under section 65; and subsection (8) of section 54 shall apply for the purposes of this subsection as it applies for the purposes of subsection (5) of that section.

(4) In making his decisions under subsection (2), the Secretary of State shall accept the decisions of the report of the Commission under section 65 as to whether a special merger situation has been created or whether arrangements are in progress or in contemplation which, if carried into effect, will result in the creation of a special merger situation.

(5)   Subsection (6) applies where the Secretary of State has decided under subsection (2) that –

(a)   a special merger situation has been created or arrangements are in progress or in contemplation which, if carried into effect, will result in the creation of a special merger situation;

(b)   at least one consideration which is mentioned in the special intervention notice concerned is relevant to a consideration of the special merger situation concerned; and

(c)   taking account only of the relevant consideration or considerations concerned, the creation of that situation operates or may be expected to operate against the public interest;

and has so decided, and published his decision, within the period required by subsection (3).

(6)   The Secretary of State may take such action under paragraph 9 or 11 of Schedule 7 as he considers to be reasonable and practicable to remedy, mitigate or prevent any of the effects adverse to the public interest which have resulted from, or may be expected to result from, the creation of the special merger situation concerned.

(7)   In making a decision under subsection (6), the Secretary of State shall, in particular, have regard to the report of the Commission under section 65.

European mergers

67 Intervention to protect legitimate interests

(1)   Subsection (2) applies where –

(a)   the Secretary of State has reasonable grounds for suspecting that it is or may be the case that –

(i)   a relevant merger situation has been created or that arrangements are in progress or in contemplation which, if carried into effect, will result in the creation of a relevant merger situation; and

(ii)   a concentration with a Community dimension (within the meaning of the European Merger Regulations), or a part of such a concentration, has thereby arisen or will thereby arise;

(b)   a reference which would otherwise be possible under section 22 or 33 is prevented from being made under that section in relation to the relevant merger situation concerned by virtue of Community law or anything done under or in accordance with it; and

(c)   the Secretary of State is considering whether to take appropriate measures to protect legitimate interests as permitted by article 21(3) of the European Merger Regulations.

(2)   The Secretary of State may give a notice to the OFT (in this section 'a European intervention notice') if he believes that it is or may be the case that one or more than one public interest consideration is relevant to a consideration of the relevant merger situation concerned.

(3)   A European intervention notice shall state –

(a)   the relevant merger situation concerned;

(b)   the public interest consideration or considerations which are, or may be, relevant to a consideration of the relevant merger situation concerned; and

(c)   where any public interest consideration concerned is not finalised, the proposed timetable for finalising it.

(4)   Where the Secretary of State believes that it is or may be the case that two or more public interest considerations are relevant to a consideration of the relevant merger

situation concerned, he may decide not to mention in the intervention notice such of those considerations as he considers appropriate.

(5) No more than one European intervention notice shall be given under subsection (2) in relation to the same relevant merger situation.

(6) Where the Secretary of State has given a European intervention notice mentioning a public interest consideration which, at that time, is not finalised, he shall, as soon as practicable, take such action as is within his power to ensure that it is finalised.

(7) For the purposes of deciding whether a relevant merger situation has been created or whether arrangements are in progress or in contemplation which, if carried into effect, will result in the creation of a relevant merger situation, sections 23 to 32 (read together with section 34) shall apply for the purposes of this section as they do for the purposes of Chapter 1 but subject to subsection (8).

(8) In their application by virtue of subsection (7) sections 23 to 32 shall have effect as if –

(a) references in those sections to the decision-making authority were references to the Secretary of State;

(b) for paragraphs (a) and (b) of section 23(9) there were substituted ', in relation to the giving of a European intervention notice, the time when the notice is given';

(c) the references to the OFT in section 24(2)(a) and (b) included references to the Secretary of State;

(d) sections 25, 31 and 32 were omitted; and

(e) the references in sections 23 to 29 to the making of a reference or a reference were, so far as necessary, references to the giving of a European intervention notice or a European intervention notice.

(9) Section 42(3) shall, in its application to this section and section 68, have effect as if for the words 'intervention notice' there were substituted 'European intervention notice'.

68 Scheme for protecting legitimate interests

(1) The Secretary of State may by order provide for the taking of action, where a European intervention notice has been given, to remedy, mitigate or prevent effects adverse to the public interest which have resulted from, or may be expected to result from, the creation of a European relevant merger situation.

(2) In subsection (1) 'European relevant merger situation' means a relevant merger situation –

(a) which has been created or will be created if arrangements which are in progress or in contemplation are carried into effect;

(b) by virtue of which a concentration with a Community dimension (within the meaning of the European Merger Regulations), or a part of such a concentration, has arisen or will arise; and

(c) in relation to which a reference which would otherwise have been possible under section 22 or 33 was prevented from being made under that section by virtue of Community law or anything done under or in accordance with it.

(3) Provision made under subsection (1) shall include provision ensuring that considerations which are not public interest considerations mentioned in the European intervention notice concerned may not be taken into account in determining whether anything operates, or may be expected to operate, against the public interest.

(4) Provision made under subsection (1) shall include provision –

(a) applying with modifications sections 23 to 32 for the purposes of deciding for the purposes of this section whether a relevant merger situation has been created or whether arrangements are in progress or in contemplation which, if carried into effect, will result in the creation of a relevant merger situation;

(b) requiring the OFT to make a report to the Secretary of State before a reference is made;

> (c) enabling the Secretary of State to make a reference to the Commission;
> (d) requiring the Commission to investigate and report to the Secretary of State on such a reference;
> (e) enabling the taking of interim and final enforcement action.

(5) An order under this section may include provision (including provision for the creation of offences and penalties, the payment of fees and the delegation of functions) corresponding to any provision made in, or in connection with, this Part in relation to intervention notices or special intervention notices and the cases to which they relate.

(6) In this section 'European intervention notice' has the same meaning as in section 67.

Other

69 Newspaper mergers

(1) No reference shall, subject to subsection (2), be made under section 22, 33, 45 or 62 in relation to a transfer of a newspaper or of newspaper assets to which section 58(1) of the Fair Trading Act 1973 (c. 41) applies.

(2) Subsection (1) does not apply in a case falling within section 59(2) of the Act of 1973.

(3) In this section 'transfer of a newspaper or of newspaper assets' has the meaning given by section 57(2) of the Act of 1973.

70 Water mergers

(1) For sections 32 to 35 of the Water Industry Act 1991 (c. 56) (special provision for water merger references) there shall be substituted –

'32 Duty to refer merger of water or sewerage undertaking

Subject to section 33 below, it shall be the duty of the OFT to make a merger reference to the Competition Commission if the OFT believes that it is or may be the case –

> (a) that arrangements are in progress which, if carried into effect, will result in a merger of any two or more water enterprises; or
> (b) that such a merger has taken place otherwise than as a result of the carrying into effect of arrangements that have been the subject of a reference by virtue of paragraph (a) above.

33 Exclusion of small mergers from duty to make reference

(1) The OFT shall not make a merger reference under section 32 above in respect of any actual or prospective merger of two or more water enterprises if it appears to the OFT –

> (a) that the value of the turnover of the water enterprise being taken over does not exceed or, as the case may be, would not exceed £10 million; or
> (b) that the only water enterprises already belonging to the person making the take over are enterprises each of which has a turnover the value of which does not exceed or, as the case may be, would not exceed £10 million.

(2) For the purposes of subsection (1)(a) above, the value of the turnover of the water enterprise being taken over shall be determined by taking the total value of the turnover of the water enterprises ceasing to be distinct enterprises and deducting –

> (a) the turnover of any water enterprise continuing to be carried on under the same ownership and control; or
> (b) if there is no water enterprise continuing to be carried on under the same ownership and control, the turnover which, of all the turnovers concerned, is the turnover of the highest value.

(3) For the purposes of subsection (1)(b) above –

    (a) every water enterprise ceasing to be a distinct enterprise and whose turnover is to be deducted by virtue of subsection (2)(a) or (b) above shall be treated as a water enterprise belonging to the person making the take over; and

    (b) water enterprises shall be treated as separate enterprises so far as they are carried on by different companies holding appointments under Chapter 1 of this Part.

(4) For the purposes of this section the turnover of a water enterprise shall be determined in accordance with such provisions as may be specified in regulations made by the Secretary of State.

(5) Regulations under subsection (4) above may, in particular, make provision as to –

    (a) the amounts which are, or which are not, to be treated as comprising an enterprise's turnover; and

    (b) the date or dates by reference to which an enterprise's turnover is to be determined.

(6) Regulations under subsection (4) above may, in particular, make provision enabling the Secretary of State or the OFT to determine matters of a description specified in the regulations (including any of the matters mentioned in paragraphs (a) and (b) of subsection (5) above).

(7) The Secretary of State may by regulations amend subsection (1) above so as –

    (a) to alter the sum for the time being mentioned in paragraph (a) of that subsection or otherwise to modify the condition set out in that paragraph; or

    (b) to alter the sum for the time being mentioned in paragraph (b) of that subsection or otherwise to modify the condition set out in that paragraph.

(8) Regulations under subsection (7) above –

    (a) shall not make any modifications in relation to mergers on or before the coming into force of the regulations; and

    (b) may, in particular, include supplemental, consequential or transitional provision amending or repealing any provision of this section.

(9) References in this section to enterprises being carried on under the same ownership and control shall be construed in accordance with Part 3 of the 2002 Act.

34 Application of provisions of Enterprise Act 2002

The provisions of Schedule 4ZA to this Act shall have effect with respect to mergers of water enterprises.

35 Construction of merger provisions

(1) In this Chapter (including Schedule 4ZA) –

        "enterprise" has the same meaning as in Part 3 of the 2002 Act; and
        "water enterprise" means an enterprise carried on by a water undertaker.

(2) References in this Chapter (including Schedule 4ZA), in relation to any two or more enterprises, to the merger of those enterprises are references to those enterprises ceasing, within the meaning of Part 3 of the 2002 Act, to be distinct enterprises; and sections 27 and 29 of that Act and any provision made under section 34 of that Act (time at which enterprises cease to be distinct) shall have effect for the purposes of this Chapter (including Schedule 4ZA) as they have effect for the purposes of that Part.

(3) Nothing in sections 32 to 34 above (including Schedule 4ZA) shall prejudice any power of the OFT or the Secretary of State, in a case in which, or to any extent

to which, the OFT is not required to make a reference under section 32 above, to make a reference under Part 3 of the 2002 Act in respect of any actual or prospective merger of two or more water enterprises.

(4) Where two or more enterprises have merged or will merge as part of transactions or arrangements which also involve an actual or prospective merger of two or more water enterprises, Part 3 of the 2002 Act shall apply in relation to the actual or prospective merger of the enterprises concerned excluding the water enterprises; and references in that Part to the creation of a relevant merger situation shall be construed accordingly.

(5) Subject to subsections (3) and (4), Part 3 of the 2002 Act shall not apply in a case in which the OFT is required to make a reference under section 32 above except as applied by virtue of Schedule 4ZA.'

(2) Before Schedule 4A to the Act of 1991 there shall be inserted, as Schedule 4ZA, the Schedule set out in Schedule 6 to this Act.

CHAPTER 4   ENFORCEMENT

Powers exercisable before references under section 22 or 33

71 Initial undertakings: completed mergers

(1) Subsection (2) applies where the OFT is considering whether to make a reference under section 22.

(2) The OFT may, for the purpose of preventing pre-emptive action, accept from such of the parties concerned as it considers appropriate undertakings to take such action as it considers appropriate.

(3) No undertaking shall be accepted under subsection (2) unless the OFT has reasonable grounds for suspecting that it is or may be the case that a relevant merger situation has been created.

(4) An undertaking under this section –

(a) shall come into force when accepted;
(b) may be varied or superseded by another undertaking; and
(c) may be released by the OFT.

(5) An undertaking which –

(a) is in force under this section in relation to a possible reference or reference under section 22; and
(b) has not been adopted under section 80 or paragraph 1 of Schedule 7;

shall cease to be in force if an order under section 72 or 81 comes into force in relation to that reference or an order under paragraph 2 of that Schedule comes into force in relation to the matter.

(6) An undertaking under this section shall, if it has not previously ceased to be in force and if it has not been adopted under section 80 or paragraph 1 of Schedule 7, cease to be in force –

(a) where the OFT has decided to make the reference concerned under section 22, at the end of the period of 7 days beginning with the making of the reference;
(b) where the OFT has decided to accept an undertaking under section 73 instead of making that reference, on the acceptance of that undertaking;
(c) where an intervention notice is in force, at the end of the period of 7 days beginning with the giving of that notice; and
(d) where the OFT has otherwise decided not to make the reference concerned under section 22, on the making of that decision.

(7) The OFT shall, as soon as reasonably practicable, consider any representations received by it in relation to varying or releasing an undertaking under this section.

(8) In this section and section 72 'pre-emptive action' means action which might prejudice the reference concerned or impede the taking of any action under this Part which
may be justified by the Commission's decisions on the reference.

72 Initial enforcement orders: completed mergers

(1) Subsection (2) applies where the OFT is considering whether to make a reference
under section 22.
(2) The OFT may by order, for the purpose of preventing pre-emptive action –

   (a) prohibit or restrict the doing of things which the OFT considers would constitute
pre-emptive action;
   (b) impose on any person concerned obligations as to the carrying on of any activities
or the safeguarding of any assets;
   (c) provide for the carrying on of any activities or the safeguarding of any assets
either by the appointment of a person to conduct or supervise the conduct of any
activities (on such terms and with such powers as may be specified or described
in the order) or in any other manner;
   (d) do anything which may be done by virtue of paragraph 19 of Schedule 8.

(3) No order shall be made under subsection (2) unless the OFT has reasonable grounds
for suspecting that it is or may be the case that –

   (a) a relevant merger situation has been created; and
   (b) pre-emptive action is in progress or in contemplation.

(4) An order under this section –

   (a) shall come into force at such time as is determined by or under the order; and
   (b) may be varied or revoked by another order.

(5) An order which –

   (a) is in force under this section in relation to a possible reference or a reference
under section 22; and
   (b) has not been adopted under section 81 or paragraph 2 of Schedule 7;

   shall cease to be in force if an undertaking under section 71 or 80 comes into force in
relation to that reference or an undertaking under paragraph 1 of that Schedule comes
into force in relation to the matter.

(6) An order under this section shall, if it has not previously ceased to be in force and if it
is not adopted under section 81 or paragraph 2 of Schedule 7, cease to be in force –

   (a) where the OFT has decided to make the reference concerned under section 22,
at the end of the period of 7 days beginning with the making of the reference;
   (b) where the OFT has decided to accept an undertaking under section 73 instead of
making that reference, on the acceptance of that undertaking;
   (c) where an intervention notice is in force, at the end of the period of 7 days
beginning with the giving of that notice; and
   (d) where the OFT has otherwise decided not to make the reference concerned
under section 22, on the making of that decision.

(7) The OFT shall, as soon as reasonably practicable, consider any representations
received by it in relation to varying or revoking an order under this section.

73 Undertakings in lieu of references under section 22 or 33

(1) Subsection (2) applies if the OFT considers that it is under a duty to make a reference
under section 22 or 33 (disregarding the operation of section 22(3)(b) or (as the case
may be) 33(3)(b) but taking account of the power of the OFT under section 22(2) or
(as the case may be) 33(2) to decide not to make such a reference).
(2) The OFT may, instead of making such a reference and for the purpose of remedying, mitigating or preventing the substantial lessening of competition concerned or
any adverse effect which has or may have resulted from it or may be expected to

result from it, accept from such of the parties concerned as it considers appropriate undertakings to take such action as it considers appropriate.

(3) In proceeding under subsection (2), the OFT shall, in particular, have regard to the need to achieve as comprehensive a solution as is reasonable and practicable to the substantial lessening of competition and any adverse effects resulting from it.

(4) In proceeding under subsection (2), the OFT may, in particular, have regard to the effect of any action on any relevant customer benefits in relation to the creation of the relevant merger situation concerned.

(5) An undertaking under this section –

    (a) shall come into force when accepted;

    (b) may be varied or superseded by another undertaking; and

    (c) may be released by the OFT.

(6) An undertaking under this section which is in force in relation to a relevant merger situation shall cease to be in force if an order comes into force under section 75 or 76 in relation to that undertaking.

(7) The OFT shall, as soon as reasonably practicable, consider any representations received by it in relation to varying or releasing an undertaking under this section.

74 Effect of undertakings under section 73

(1) The relevant authority shall not make a reference under section 22, 33 or 45 in relation to the creation of a relevant merger situation if –

    (a) the OFT has accepted an undertaking or group of undertakings under section 73; and

    (b) the relevant merger situation is the situation by reference to which the undertaking or group of undertakings was accepted.

(2) Subsection (1) does not prevent the making of a reference if material facts about relevant arrangements or transactions, or relevant proposed arrangements or transactions, were not notified (whether in writing or otherwise) to the OFT or made public before any undertaking concerned was accepted.

(3) For the purposes of subsection (2) arrangements or transactions, or proposed arrangements or transactions, are relevant if they are the ones in consequence of which the enterprises concerned ceased or may have ceased, or may cease, to be distinct enterprises.

(4) In subsection (2) 'made public' means so publicised as to be generally known or readily ascertainable.

(5) In this section 'relevant authority' means –

    (a) in relation to a possible reference under section 22 or 33, the OFT; and

    (b) in relation to a possible reference under section 45, the Secretary of State.

75 Order-making power where undertakings under section 73 not fulfilled etc.

(1) Subsection (2) applies where the OFT considers that –

    (a) an undertaking accepted by it under section 73 has not been, is not being or will not be fulfilled; or

    (b) in relation to an undertaking accepted by it under that section, information which was false or misleading in a material respect was given to the OFT by the person giving the undertaking before the OFT decided to accept the undertaking.

(2) The OFT may, for any of the purposes mentioned in section 73(2), make an order under this section.

(3) Subsections (3) and (4) of section 73 shall apply for the purposes of subsection (2) above as they apply for the purposes of subsection (2) of that section.

(4) An order under this section may contain –

    (a) anything permitted by Schedule 8; and

(b) such supplementary, consequential or incidental provision as the OFT considers appropriate.

(5) An order under this section –

(a) shall come into force at such time as is determined by or under the order;

(b) may contain provision which is different from the provision contained in the undertaking concerned; and

(c) may be varied or revoked by another order.

(6) The OFT shall, as soon as reasonably practicable, consider any representations received by it in relation to varying or revoking an order under this section.

76 Supplementary interim order-making power

(1) Subsection (2) applies where –

(a) the OFT has the power to make an order under section 75 in relation to a particular undertaking and intends to make such an order; or

(b) the Commission has the power to make an order under section 83 in relation to a particular undertaking and intends to make such an order.

(2) The OFT or (as the case may be) the Commission may, for the purpose of preventing any action which might prejudice the making of that order, make an order under this section.

(3) No order shall be made under subsection (2) unless the OFT or (as the case may be) the Commission has reasonable grounds for suspecting that it is or may be the case that action which might prejudice the making of the order under section 75 or (as the case may be) 83 is in progress or in contemplation.

(4) An order under subsection (2) may –

(a) prohibit or restrict the doing of things which the OFT or (as the case may be) the Commission considers would prejudice the making of the order under section 75 or (as the case may be) 83;

(b) impose on any person concerned obligations as to the carrying on of any activities or the safeguarding of any assets;

(c) provide for the carrying on of any activities or the safeguarding of any assets either by the appointment of a person to conduct or supervise the conduct of any activities (on such terms and with such powers as may be specified or described in the order) or in any other manner;

(d) do anything which may be done by virtue of paragraph 19 of Schedule 8.

(5) An order under this section –

(a) shall come into force at such time as is determined by or under the order; and

(b) may be varied or revoked by another order.

(6) An order under this section shall, if it has not previously ceased to be in force, cease to be in force on –

(a) the coming into force of an order under section 75 or (as the case may be) 83 in relation to the undertaking concerned; or

(b) the making of the decision not to proceed with such an order.

(7) The OFT or (as the case may be) the Commission shall, as soon as reasonably practicable, consider any representations received by it in relation to varying or revoking an order under this section.

Interim restrictions and powers

77 Restrictions on certain dealings: completed mergers

(1) Subsections (2) and (3) apply where –

(a) a reference has been made under section 22 but not finally determined; and

(b) no undertakings under section 71 or 80 are in force in relation to the relevant merger situation concerned and no orders under section 72 or 81 are in force in relation to that situation.

(2) No relevant person shall, without the consent of the Commission –

    (a) complete any outstanding matters in connection with any arrangements which have resulted in the enterprises concerned ceasing to be distinct enterprises;

    (b) make any further arrangements in consequence of that result (other than arrangements which reverse that result); or

    (c) transfer the ownership or control of any enterprises to which the reference relates.

(3) No relevant person shall, without the consent of the Commission, assist in any of the activities mentioned in paragraphs (a) to (c) of subsection (2).

(4) The prohibitions in subsections (2) and (3) do not apply in relation to anything which the person concerned is required to do by virtue of any enactment.

(5) The consent of the Commission under subsection (2) or (3) –

    (a) may be general or special;

    (b) may be revoked by the Commission; and

    (c) shall be published in such manner as the Commission considers appropriate for the purpose of bringing it to the attention of any person entitled to the benefit of it.

(6) Paragraph (c) of subsection (5) shall not apply if the Commission considers that publication is not necessary for the purpose mentioned in that paragraph.

(7) Subsections (2) and (3) shall apply to a person's conduct outside the United Kingdom if (and only if) he is –

    (a) a United Kingdom national;

    (b) a body incorporated under the law of the United Kingdom or of any part of the United Kingdom; or

    (c) a person carrying on business in the United Kingdom.

(8) In this section 'relevant person' means –

    (a) any person who carries on any enterprise to which the reference relates or who has control of any such enterprise;

    (b) any subsidiary of any person falling within paragraph (a); or

    (c) any person associated with any person falling within paragraph (a) or any subsidiary of any person so associated.

78 Restrictions on certain share dealings: anticipated mergers

(1) Subsection (2) applies where –

    (a) a reference has been made under section 33; and

    (b) no undertakings under section 80 are in force in relation to the relevant merger situation concerned and no orders under section 81 are in force in relation to that situation.

(2) No relevant person shall, without the consent of the Commission, directly or indirectly acquire during the relevant period an interest in shares in a company if any enterprise to which the reference relates is carried on by or under the control of that company.

(3) The consent of the Commission under subsection (2) –

    (a) may be general or special;

    (b) may be revoked by the Commission; and

    (c) shall be published in such manner as the Commission considers appropriate for bringing it to the attention of any person entitled to the benefit of it.

(4) Paragraph (c) of subsection (3) shall not apply if the Commission considers that publication is not necessary for the purpose mentioned in that paragraph.

(5) Subsection (2) shall apply to a person's conduct outside the United Kingdom if (and only if) he is –

(a) a United Kingdom national;
(b) a body incorporated under the law of the United Kingdom or of any part of the United Kingdom; or
(c) a person carrying on business in the United Kingdom.

(6) In this section and section 79 –

'company' includes any body corporate;
'relevant period' means the period beginning with the making of the reference concerned and ending when the reference is finally determined;
'relevant person' means –

(a) any person who carries on any enterprise to which the reference relates or who has control of any such enterprise;
(b) any subsidiary of any person falling within paragraph (a); or
(c) any person associated with any person falling within paragraph (a) or any subsidiary of any person so associated; and

'share' means share in the capital of a company, and includes stock.

79 Sections 77 and 78: further interpretation provisions

(1) For the purposes of this Part a reference under section 22 or 33 is finally determined if –

(a) the reference is cancelled under section 37(1);
(b) the time within which the Commission is to prepare and publish a report under section 38 in relation to the reference has expired and no such report has been prepared and published;
(c) the report of the Commission under section 38 contains the decision that there is not an anti-competitive outcome;
(d) the report of the Commission under section 38 contains the decision that there is an anti-competitive outcome and the Commission has decided under section 41(2) neither to accept an undertaking under section 82 nor to make an order under section 84; or
(e) the report of the Commission under section 38 contains the decision that there is an anti-competitive outcome and the Commission has decided under section 41(2) to accept an undertaking under section 82 or to make an order under section 84.

(2) For the purposes of this Part the time when a reference under section 22 or 33 is finally determined is –

(a) in a case falling within subsection (1)(a), the making of the decision concerned;
(b) in a case falling within subsection (1)(b), the expiry of the time concerned;
(c) in a case falling within subsection (1)(c), the publication of the report;
(d) in a case falling within subsection (1)(d), the making of the decision under section 41(2); and
(e) in a case falling within subsection (1)(e), the acceptance of the undertaking concerned or (as the case may be) the making of the order concerned.

(3) For the purposes of section 78 and subject to subsection (4) below, the circumstances in which a person acquires an interest in shares include those where –

(a) he enters into a contract to acquire the shares (whether or not for cash);
(b) he is not the registered holder but acquires the right to exercise, or to control the exercise of, any right conferred by the holding of the shares; or
(c) he –

      (i)   acquires a right to call for delivery of the shares to himself or to his order or to acquire an interest in the shares; or

      (ii)   assumes an obligation to acquire such an interest.

(4) The circumstances in which a person acquires an interest in shares for the purposes of section 78 do not include those where he acquires an interest in pursuance of an obligation assumed before the publication by the OFT of the reference concerned.

(5) The circumstances in which a person acquires a right mentioned in subsection (3) –

    (a)   include those where he acquires a right, or assumes an obligation, whose exercise or fulfilment would give him that right; but

    (b)   do not include those where he is appointed as proxy to vote at a specified meeting of a company or of any class of its members or at any adjournment of the meeting or he is appointed by a corporation to act as its representative at any meeting of the company or of any class of its members.

(6) References to rights and obligations in subsections (3) to (5) include conditional rights and conditional obligations.

(7) References in sections 77 and 78 to a person carrying on or having control of any enterprise includes a group of persons carrying on or having control of an enterprise and any member of such a group.

(8) Sections 26(2) to (4) and 127(1), (2) and (4) to (6) shall apply for the purposes of sections 77 and 78 to determine whether any person or group of persons has control of any enterprise and whether persons are associated as they apply for the purposes of section 26 to determine whether enterprises are brought under common control.

(9) Sections 736 and 736A of the Companies Act 1985 (c. 6) shall apply for the purposes of sections 77 and 78 to determine whether a company is a subsidiary of an individual or of a group of persons as they apply to determine whether it is a subsidiary of a company; and references to a subsidiary in subsections (8) and (9) of section 736A as so applied shall be construed accordingly.

80 Interim undertakings

(1) Subsections (2) and (3) apply where a reference under section 22 or 33 has been made but is not finally determined.

(2) The Commission may, for the purpose of preventing pre-emptive action, accept from such of the parties concerned as it considers appropriate undertakings to take such action as it considers appropriate.

(3) The Commission may, for the purpose of preventing pre-emptive action, adopt an undertaking accepted by the OFT under section 71 if the undertaking is still in force when the Commission adopts it.

(4) An undertaking adopted under subsection (3) –

    (a)   shall continue in force, in accordance with its terms, when adopted;

    (b)   may be varied or superseded by an undertaking under this section; and

    (c)   may be released by the Commission.

(5) Any other undertaking under this section –

    (a)   shall come into force when accepted;

    (b)   may be varied or superseded by another undertaking; and

    (c)   may be released by the Commission.

(6) References in this Part to undertakings under this section shall, unless the context otherwise requires, include references to undertakings adopted under this section; and references to the acceptance or giving of undertakings under this section shall be construed accordingly.

(7) An undertaking which is in force under this section in relation to a reference under section 22 or 33 shall cease to be in force if an order under section 81 comes into force in relation to that reference.

(8) An undertaking under this section shall, if it has not previously ceased to be in force, cease to be in force when the reference under section 22 or 33 is finally determined.

(9) The Commission shall, as soon as reasonably practicable, consider any representations received by it in relation to varying or releasing an undertaking under this section.

(10) In this section and section 81 'pre-emptive action' means action which might prejudice the reference concerned or impede the taking of any action under this Part which may be justified by the Commission's decisions on the reference.

81 Interim orders

(1) Subsections (2) and (3) apply where a reference has been made under section 22 or 33 but is not finally determined.

(2) The Commission may by order, for the purpose of preventing pre-emptive action –

   (a) prohibit or restrict the doing of things which the Commission considers would constitute pre-emptive action;

   (b) impose on any person concerned obligations as to the carrying on of any activities or the safeguarding of any assets;

   (c) provide for the carrying on of any activities or the safeguarding of any assets either by the appointment of a person to conduct or supervise the conduct of any activities (on such terms and with such powers as may be specified or described in the order) or in any other manner;

   (d) do anything which may be done by virtue of paragraph 19 of Schedule 8.

(3) The Commission may, for the purpose of preventing pre-emptive action, adopt an order made by the OFT under section 72 if the order is still in force when the Commission adopts it.

(4) An order adopted under subsection (3) –

   (a) shall continue in force, in accordance with its terms, when adopted; and

   (b) may be varied or revoked by an order under this section.

(5) Any other order under this section –

   (a) shall come into force at such time as is determined by or under the order; and

   (b) may be varied or revoked by another order.

(6) References in this Part to orders under this section shall, unless the context otherwise requires, include references to orders adopted under this section; and references to the making of orders under this section shall be construed accordingly.

(7) An order which is in force under this section in relation to a reference under section 22 or 33 shall cease to be in force if an undertaking under section 80 comes into force in relation to that reference.

(8) An order under this section shall, if it has not previously ceased to be in force, cease to be in force when the reference under section 22 or 33 is finally determined.

(9) The Commission shall, as soon as reasonably practicable, consider any representations received by it in relation to varying or revoking an order under this section.

Final powers

82 Final undertakings

(1) The Commission may, in accordance with section 41, accept, from such persons as it considers appropriate, undertakings to take action specified or described in the undertakings.

(2) An undertaking under this section –

   (a) shall come into force when accepted;

(b) may be varied or superseded by another undertaking; and

(c) may be released by the Commission.

(3) An undertaking which is in force under this section in relation to a reference under section 22 or 33 shall cease to be in force if an order under section 76(1)(b) or 83 comes into force in relation to the subject-matter of the undertaking.

(4) No undertaking shall be accepted under this section in relation to a reference under section 22 or 33 if an order has been made under –

(a) section 76(1)(b) or 83 in relation to the subject-matter of the undertaking; or

(b) section 84 in relation to that reference.

(5) The Commission shall, as soon as reasonably practicable, consider any representations received by it in relation to varying or releasing an undertaking under this section.

83 Order-making power where final undertakings not fulfilled

(1) Subsection (2) applies where the Commission considers that –

(a) an undertaking accepted by it under section 82 has not been, is not being or will not be fulfilled; or

(b) in relation to an undertaking accepted by it under that section, information which was false or misleading in a material respect was given to the Commission or the OFT by the person giving the undertaking before the Commission decided to accept the undertaking.

(2) The Commission may, for any of the purposes mentioned in section 41(2), make an order under this section.

(3) Subsections (3) to (5) of section 41 shall apply for the purposes of subsection (2) above as they apply for the purposes of subsection (2) of that section.

(4) An order under this section may contain –

(a) anything permitted by Schedule 8; and

(b) such supplementary, consequential or incidental provision as the Commission considers appropriate.

(5) An order under this section –

(a) shall come into force at such time as is determined by or under the order;

(b) may contain provision which is different from the provision contained in the undertaking concerned; and

(c) may be varied or revoked by another order.

(6) No order shall be varied or revoked under this section unless the OFT advises that such a variation or revocation is appropriate by reason of a change of circumstances.

84 Final orders

(1) The Commission may, in accordance with section 41, make an order under this section.

(2) An order under this section may contain –

(a) anything permitted by Schedule 8; and

(b) such supplementary, consequential or incidental provision as the Commission considers appropriate.

(3) An order under this section –

(a) shall come into force at such time as is determined by or under the order; and

(b) may be varied or revoked by another order.

(4) No order shall be varied or revoked under this section unless the OFT advises that such a variation or revocation is appropriate by reason of a change of circumstances.

(5) No order shall be made under this section in relation to a reference under section 22 or 33 if an undertaking has been accepted under section 82 in relation to that reference.

Public interest and special public interest cases

85 Enforcement regime for public interest and special public interest cases

(1) Schedule 7 (which provides for the enforcement regime in public interest and special public interest cases) shall have effect.

(2) The OFT may advise the Secretary of State in relation to the taking by him of enforcement action under Schedule 7.

Undertakings and orders: general provisions

86 Enforcement orders: general provisions

(1) An enforcement order may extend to a person's conduct outside the United Kingdom if (and only if) he is –

    (a) a United Kingdom national;

    (b) a body incorporated under the law of the United Kingdom or of any part of the United Kingdom; or

    (c) a person carrying on business in the United Kingdom.

(2) Nothing in an enforcement order shall have effect so as to –

    (a) cancel or modify conditions in licences granted –

        (i) under a patent granted under the Patents Act 1977 (c. 37) or a European patent (UK) (within the meaning of the Act of 1977); or

        (ii) in respect of a design registered under the Registered Designs Act 1949 (c. 88);

        by the proprietor of the patent or design; or

    (b) require an entry to be made in the register of patents or the register of designs to the effect that licences under such a patent or such a design are to be available as of right.

(3) An enforcement order may prohibit the performance of an agreement already in existence when the order is made.

(4) Schedule 8 (which provides for the contents of certain enforcement orders) shall have effect.

(5) Part 1 of Schedule 9 (which enables certain enforcement orders to modify licence conditions etc. in regulated markets) shall have effect.

(6) In this Part 'enforcement order' means an order made under section 72, 75, 76, 81, 83 or 84 or under paragraph 2, 5, 6, 10 or 11 of Schedule 7.

87 Delegated power of directions

(1) An enforcement order may authorise the person making the order to give directions falling within subsection (2) to –

    (a) a person specified in the directions; or

    (b) the holder for the time being of an office so specified in any body of persons corporate or unincorporate.

(2) Directions fall within this subsection if they are directions –

    (a) to take such action as may be specified or described in the directions for the purpose of carrying out, or ensuring compliance with, the enforcement order concerned; or

    (b) to do, or refrain from doing, anything so specified or described which the person might be required by that order to do or refrain from doing.

(3) An enforcement order may authorise the person making the order to vary or revoke any directions so given.

(4) The court may by order require any person who has failed to comply with directions given by virtue of this section to comply with them, or otherwise remedy his failure, within such time as may be specified in the order.

(5) Where the directions related to anything done in the management or administration of a body of persons corporate or unincorporate, the court may by order require the body of persons concerned or any officer of it to comply with the directions, or otherwise remedy the failure to comply with them, within such time as may be specified in the order.

(6) An order under subsection (4) or (5) shall be made on the application of the person authorised by virtue of this section to give the directions concerned.

(7) An order under subsection (4) or (5) may provide for all the costs or expenses of, or incidental to, the application for the order to be met by any person in default or by any officers of a body of persons corporate or unincorporate who are responsible for its default.

(8) In this section 'the court' means –

(a) in relation to England and Wales or Northern Ireland, the High Court; and

(b) in relation to Scotland, the Court of Session.

88 Contents of certain enforcement orders

(1) This section applies in relation to any order under section 75, 83 or 84 or under paragraph 5, 10 or 11 of Schedule 7.

(2) The order or any explanatory material accompanying the order shall state –

(a) the actions that the persons or description of persons to whom the order is addressed must do or (as the case may be) refrain from doing;

(b) the date on which the order comes into force;

(c) the possible consequences of not complying with the order; and

(d) the section of this Part under which a review can be sought in relation to the order.

89 Subject-matter of undertakings

(1) The provision which may be contained in an enforcement undertaking is not limited to the provision which is permitted by Schedule 8.

(2) In this Part 'enforcement undertaking' means an undertaking under section 71, 73, 80 or 82 or under paragraph 1, 3 or 9 of Schedule 7.

90 Procedural requirements for certain undertakings and orders

Schedule 10 (which provides for the procedure for accepting certain enforcement undertakings and making certain enforcement orders and for their termination) shall have effect.

91 Register of undertakings and orders

(1) The OFT shall compile and maintain a register for the purposes of this Part.

(2) The register shall be kept in such form as the OFT considers appropriate.

(3) The OFT shall ensure that the following matters are entered in the register –

(a) the provisions of any enforcement undertaking accepted under this Part;

(b) the provisions of any enforcement order made under this Part;

(c) the details of any variation, release or revocation of such an undertaking or order; and

(d) the details of any consent given by the Commission under section 77(2) or (3) or 78(2) or by the Secretary of State under paragraph 7(2) or (3) or 8(2) of Schedule 7.

(4) The duty in subsection (3) does not extend to anything of which the OFT is unaware.

(5) The Commission and the Secretary of State shall inform the OFT of any matters which are to be included in the register by virtue of subsection (3) and which relate to enforcement undertakings accepted by them, enforcement orders made by them or consents given by them.

(6) The OFT shall ensure that the contents of the register are available to the public –

    (a) during (as a minimum) such hours as may be specified in an order made by the Secretary of State; and

    (b) subject to such reasonable fees (if any) as the OFT may determine.

(7) If requested by any person to do so and subject to such reasonable fees (if any) as the OFT may determine, the OFT shall supply the person concerned with a copy (certified to be true) of the register or of an extract from it.

Enforcement functions of OFT

92 Duty of OFT to monitor undertakings and orders

(1) The OFT shall keep under review –

    (a) the carrying out of any enforcement undertaking or any enforcement order; and

    (b) compliance with the prohibitions in sections 77(2) and (3) and 78(2) and in paragraphs 7(2) and (3) and 8(2) of Schedule 7.

(2) The OFT shall, in particular, from time to time consider –

    (a) whether an enforcement undertaking or enforcement order has been or is being complied with;

    (b) whether, by reason of any change of circumstances, an enforcement undertaking is no longer appropriate and –

        (i) one or more of the parties to it can be released from it; or

        (ii) it needs to be varied or to be superseded by a new enforcement undertaking; and

    (c) whether, by reason of any change of circumstances, an enforcement order is no longer appropriate and needs to be varied or revoked.

(3) The OFT shall give the Commission or (as the case may be) the Secretary of State such advice as it considers appropriate in relation to –

    (a) any possible variation or release by the Commission or (as the case may be) the Secretary of State of an enforcement undertaking accepted by it or (as the case may be) him;

    (b) any possible new enforcement undertaking to be accepted by the Commission or (as the case may be) the Secretary of State so as to supersede another enforcement undertaking given to the Commission or (as the case may be) the Secretary of State;

    (c) any possible variation or revocation by the Commission or (as the case may be) the Secretary of State of an enforcement order made by the Commission or (as the case may be) the Secretary of State;

    (d) any possible enforcement undertaking to be accepted by the Commission or (as the case may be) the Secretary of State instead of an enforcement order or any possible enforcement order to be made by the Commission or (as the case may be) the Secretary of State instead of an enforcement undertaking;

    (e) the enforcement by virtue of section 94(6) to (8) of any enforcement undertaking or enforcement order; or

    (f) the enforcement by virtue of section 95(4) and (5) of the prohibitions in sections 77(2) and (3) and 78(2) and in paragraphs 7(2) and (3) and 8(2) of Schedule 7.

(4) The OFT shall take such action as it considers appropriate in relation to –

    (a) any possible variation or release by it of an enforcement undertaking accepted by it;

    (b) any possible new enforcement undertaking to be accepted by it so as to supersede another enforcement undertaking given to it;

    (c) any possible variation or revocation by it of an enforcement order made by it;

    (d) any possible enforcement undertaking to be accepted by it instead of an enforcement order or any possible enforcement order to be made by it instead of an enforcement undertaking;

(e)   the enforcement by it by virtue of section 94(6) of any enforcement undertaking or enforcement order; or

(f)   the enforcement by it by virtue of section 95(4) and (5) of the prohibitions in sections 77(2) and (3) and 78(2) and in paragraphs 7(2) and (3) and 8(2) of Schedule 7.

(5)   The OFT shall keep under review the effectiveness of enforcement undertakings accepted under this Part and enforcement orders made under this Part.

(6)   The OFT shall, whenever requested to do so by the Secretary of State and otherwise from time to time, prepare a report of its findings under subsection (5).

(7)   The OFT shall –

(a)   give any report prepared by it under subsection (6) to the Commission;

(b)   give a copy of the report to the Secretary of State; and

(c)   publish the report.

93 Further role of OFT in relation to undertakings and orders

(1)   Subsections (2) and (3) apply where –

(a)   the Commission is considering whether to accept undertakings under section 80 or 82; or

(b)   the Secretary of State is considering whether to accept undertakings under paragraph 1, 3 or 9 of Schedule 7.

(2)   The Commission or (as the case may be) the Secretary of State (in this section 'the relevant authority') may require the OFT to consult with such persons as the relevant authority considers appropriate with a view to discovering whether they will offer undertakings which the relevant authority would be prepared to accept under section 80 or 82 or (as the case may be) paragraph 1, 3 or 9 of Schedule 7.

(3)   The relevant authority may require the OFT to report to the relevant authority on the outcome of the OFT's consultations within such period as the relevant authority may require.

(4)   A report under subsection (3) shall, in particular, contain advice from the OFT as to whether any undertakings offered should be accepted by the relevant authority under section 80 or 82 or (as the case may be) paragraph 1, 3 or 9 of Schedule 7.

(5)   The powers conferred on the relevant authority by subsections (1) to (4) are without prejudice to the power of the relevant authority to consult the persons concerned itself.

(6)   If asked by the relevant authority for advice in relation to the taking of enforcement action (whether or not by way of undertaking) in a particular case, the OFT shall give such advice as it considers appropriate.

Other

94 Rights to enforce undertakings and orders

(1)   This section applies to any enforcement undertaking or enforcement order.

(2)   Any person to whom such an undertaking or order relates shall have a duty to comply with it.

(3)   The duty shall be owed to any person who may be affected by a contravention of the undertaking or (as the case may be) order.

(4)   Any breach of the duty which causes such a person to sustain loss or damage shall be actionable by him.

(5)   In any proceedings brought under subsection (4) against a person to whom an enforcement undertaking or an enforcement order relates it shall be a defence for that person to show that he took all reasonable steps and exercised all due diligence to avoid contravening the undertaking or (as the case may be) order.

(6) Compliance with an enforcement undertaking or an enforcement order shall also be enforceable by civil proceedings brought by the OFT for an injunction or for interdict or for any other appropriate relief or remedy.

(7) Compliance with an undertaking under section 80 or 82, an order made by the Commission under section 76 or an order under section 81, 83 or 84, shall also be enforceable by civil proceedings brought by the Commission for an injunction or for interdict or for any other appropriate relief or remedy.

(8) Compliance with an undertaking under paragraph 1, 3 or 9 of Schedule 7, an order made by the Secretary of State under paragraph 2 of that Schedule or an order under paragraph 5, 6, 10 or 11 of that Schedule, shall also be enforceable by civil proceedings brought by the Secretary of State for an injunction or for interdict or for any other appropriate relief or remedy.

(9) Subsections (6) to (8) shall not prejudice any right that a person may have by virtue of subsection (4) to bring civil proceedings for contravention or apprehended contravention of an enforcement undertaking or an enforcement order.

95 Rights to enforce statutory restrictions

(1) The obligation to comply with section 77(2) or (3) or 78(2) or paragraph 7(2) or (3) or 8(2) of Schedule 7 shall be a duty owed to any person who may be affected by a contravention of the enactment concerned.

(2) Any breach of the duty which causes such a person to sustain loss or damage shall be actionable by him.

(3) In any proceedings brought under subsection (2) against a person who has an obligation to comply with section 77(2) or (3) or 78(2) or paragraph 7(2) or (3) or 8(2) of Schedule 7 it shall be a defence for that person to show that he took all reasonable steps and exercised all due diligence to avoid contravening the enactment concerned.

(4) Compliance with section 77(2) or (3) or 78(2) shall also be enforceable by civil proceedings brought by the OFT or the Commission for an injunction or for interdict or for any other appropriate relief or remedy.

(5) Compliance with paragraph 7(2) or (3) or 8(2) of Schedule 7 shall also be enforceable by civil proceedings brought by the OFT or the Secretary of State for an injunction or for interdict or for any other appropriate relief or remedy.

(6) Subsections (4) and (5) shall not prejudice any right that a person may have by virtue of subsection (2) to bring civil proceedings for contravention or apprehended contravention of section 77(2) or (3) or 78(2) or paragraph 7(2) or (3) or 8(2) of Schedule 7.

CHAPTER 5   SUPPLEMENTARY

Merger notices

96 Merger notices

(1) A person authorised to do so by regulations under section 101 may give notice to the OFT of proposed arrangements which might result in the creation of a relevant merger situation.

(2) Any such notice (in this Part a 'merger notice') –

(a) shall be in the prescribed form; and

(b) shall state that the existence of the proposal has been made public.

(3) No reference shall be made under section 22, 33 or 45 in relation to –

(a) arrangements of which notice is given under subsection (1) above or arrangements which do not differ from them in any material respect; or

(b) the creation of any relevant merger situation which is, or may be, created in consequence of carrying such arrangements into effect;

if the period for considering the merger notice has expired without a reference being made under that section in relation to those arrangements.

(4) Subsection (3) is subject to section 100.

(5) In this section and sections 99(5)(c) and 100(1)(c) 'prescribed' means prescribed by the OFT by notice having effect for the time being and published in the London, Edinburgh and Belfast Gazettes.

(6) In this Part 'notified arrangements' means arrangements of which notice is given under subsection (1) above or arrangements not differing from them in any material respect.

97 Period for considering merger notices

(1) The period for considering a merger notice is, subject as follows, the period of 20 days beginning with the first day after –

    (a) the notice has been received by the OFT; and

    (b) any fee payable by virtue of section 121 to the OFT in respect of the notice has been paid.

(2) Where no intervention notice is in force in relation to the matter concerned, the OFT may by notice to the person who gave the merger notice extend by a further 10 days the period for considering the merger notice.

(3) Where an intervention notice is in force in relation to the matter concerned and there has been no extension under subsection (2), the OFT may by notice to the person who gave the merger notice extend by a further 20 days the period for considering the merger notice.

(4) Where an intervention notice is in force in relation to the matter concerned and there has been an extension under subsection (2), the OFT may by notice to the person who gave the merger notice extend the period for considering the merger notice by a further number of days which, including any extension already made under subsection (2), does not exceed 20 days.

(5) The OFT may by notice to the person who gave the merger notice extend the period for considering a merger notice if the OFT considers that the person has failed to provide, within the period stated in a notice under section 99(2) and in the authorised or required manner, information requested of him in that notice.

(6) An extension under subsection (5) shall be for the period until the person concerned provides the information to the satisfaction of the OFT or, if earlier, the cancellation by the OFT of the extension.

(7) The OFT may by notice to the person who gave the merger notice extend the period for considering a merger notice if the OFT is seeking undertakings under section 73 or (as the case may be) the Secretary of State is seeking undertakings under paragraph 3 of Schedule 7.

(8) An extension under subsection (7) shall be for the period beginning with the receipt of the notice under that subsection and ending with the earliest of the following events –

    (a) the giving of the undertakings concerned;

    (b) the expiry of the period of 10 days beginning with the first day after the receipt by the OFT of a notice from the person from whom the undertakings are being sought stating that he does not intend to give the undertakings; or

    (c) the cancellation by the OFT of the extension.

(9) The Secretary of State may by notice to the person who gave the merger notice extend the period for considering a merger notice if, by virtue of paragraph 3(6) of Schedule 7, he decides to delay a decision as to whether to make a reference under section 45.

(10) An extension under subsection (9) shall be for the period of the delay.

(11) The OFT may by notice to the person who gave the merger notice extend the period for considering a merger notice if the European Commission is considering a request made, in relation to the matter concerned, by the United Kingdom (whether alone or

with others) under article 22(3) of the European Merger Regulations (but is not yet proceeding with the matter in pursuance of such a request).

(12) An extension under subsection (11) shall be for the period beginning with the receipt of the notice under that subsection and ending with the receipt of a notice under subsection (13).

(13) The OFT shall, in connection with any notice given by it under subsection (11), by notice inform the person who gave the merger notice of the completion by the European Commission of its consideration of the request of the United Kingdom.

98 Section 97: supplementary

(1) A notice under section 97(2), (3), (4), (5), (7), (9) or (11) shall be given, before the end of the period for considering the merger notice, to the person who gave the merger notice.

(2) A notice under section 97(5) –

   (a) shall also be given within 5 days of the end of the period within which the information is to be provided and which is stated in the notice under section 99(2); and

   (b) shall also inform the person who gave the merger notice of –

      (i) the OFT's opinion as mentioned in section 97(5); and

      (ii) the OFT's intention to extend the period for considering a merger notice.

(3) In determining for the purposes of section 97(1), (2), (3), (4) or (8)(b) or subsection (2)(a) above any period which is expressed in the enactment concerned as a period of days or number of days no account shall be taken of –

   (a) Saturday, Sunday, Good Friday and Christmas Day; and

   (b) any day which is a bank holiday in England and Wales.

(4) Any reference in this Part (apart from in section 97(1) and section 99(1)) to the period for considering a merger notice shall, if that period is extended by virtue of any one or more of subsections (2), (3), (4) (5), (7), (9) and (11) of section 97 in relation to a particular case, be construed in relation to that case as a reference to that period as so extended; but only one extension is possible under section 97(2), (3) or (4).

(5) Where the period for considering a merger notice is extended or further extended by virtue of section 97, the period as extended or (as the case may be) further extended shall, subject to subsections (6) and (7), be calculated by taking the period being extended and adding to it the period of the extension (whether or not those periods overlap in time).

(6) Subsection (7) applies where –

   (a) the period for considering a merger notice is further extended;

   (b) the further extension and at least one previous extension is made under one or more of subsections (5), (7), (9) and (11) of section 97; and

   (c) the same days or fractions of days are included in or comprise the further extension and are included in or comprise at least one such previous extension.

(7) In calculating the period of the further extension, any days or fractions of days of the kind mentioned in subsection (6)(c) shall be disregarded.

99 Certain functions of OFT and Secretary of State in relation to merger notices

(1) The OFT shall, so far as practicable and when the period for considering any merger notice begins, take such action as the OFT considers appropriate to bring –

   (a) the existence of the proposal;

   (b) the fact that the merger notice has been given; and

   (c) the date on which the period for considering the notice may expire;

   to the attention of those whom the OFT considers would be affected if the arrangements were carried into effect.

(2) The OFT may by notice to the person who gave the merger notice request him to provide the OFT with such information as the OFT or (as the case may be) the Secretary of State may require for the purpose of carrying out its or (as the case may be) his functions in relation to the merger notice.

(3) A notice under subsection (2) shall state –

(a) the information required;

(b) the period within which the information is to be provided; and

(c) the possible consequences of not providing the information within the stated period and in the authorised or required manner.

(4) A notice by the OFT under subsection (2) shall be given, before the end of the period for considering the merger notice, to the person who gave the merger notice.

(5) The OFT may, at any time before the end of the period for considering any merger notice, reject the notice if –

(a) the OFT suspects that any information given in respect of the notified arrangements (whether in the merger notice or otherwise) by the person who gave the notice or any connected person is in any material respect false or misleading;

(b) the OFT suspects that it is not proposed to carry the notified arrangements into effect;

(c) any prescribed information is not given in the merger notice or any information requested by notice under subsection (2) is not provided as required; or

(d) the OFT considers that the notified arrangements are, or if carried into effect would result in, a concentration with a Community dimension within the meaning of the European Merger Regulations.

(6) In this section and section 100 'connected person', in relation to the person who gave a merger notice, means –

(a) any person who, for the purposes of section 127, is associated with him; or

(b) any subsidiary of the person who gave the merger notice or of any person so associated with him.

100 Exceptions to protection given by merger notices

(1) Section 96(3) does not prevent any reference being made to the Commission if –

(a) before the end of the period for considering the merger notice, the OFT rejects the notice under section 99(5);

(b) before the end of that period, any of the enterprises to which the notified arrangements relate cease to be distinct from each other;

(c) any information (whether prescribed information or not) that –

(i) is, or ought to be, known to the person who gave the merger notice or any connected person; and

(ii) is material to the notified arrangements;

is not disclosed to the OFT by such time before the end of that period as may be specified in regulations under section 101;

(d) at any time after the merger notice is given but before the enterprises to which the notified arrangements relate cease to be distinct from each other, any of those enterprises ceases to be distinct from any enterprise other than an enterprise to which those arrangements relate;

(e) the six months beginning with the end of the period for considering the merger notice expires without the enterprises to which the notified arrangements relate ceasing to be distinct from each other;

(f) the merger notice is withdrawn; or

(g) any information given in respect of the notified arrangements (whether in the merger notice or otherwise) by the person who gave the notice or any connected person is in any material respect false or misleading.

(2) Subsection (3) applies where –

   (a) two or more transactions which have occurred, or, if any arrangements are carried into effect, will occur, may be treated for the purposes of a reference under section 22, 33 or 45 as having occurred simultaneously on a particular date; and

   (b) section 96(3) does not prevent such a reference in relation to the last of those transactions.

(3) Section 96(3) does not prevent such a reference in relation to any of those transactions which actually occurred less than six months before –

   (a) that date; or

   (b) the actual occurrence of another of those transactions in relation to which such a reference may be made (whether or not by virtue of this subsection).

(4) In determining for the purposes of subsections (2) and (3) the time at which any transaction actually occurred, no account shall be taken of any option or other conditional right until the option is exercised or the condition is satisfied.

(5) In this section references to the enterprises to which the notified arrangements relate are references to those enterprises that would have ceased to be distinct from one another if the arrangements mentioned in the merger notice concerned had been carried into effect at the time when the notice was given.

101 Merger notices: regulations

(1) The Secretary of State may make regulations for the purposes of sections 96 to 100.

(2) The regulations may, in particular –

   (a) provide for section 97(1), (2), (3) or (4) or section 100(1)(e) to apply as if any reference to a period of days or months were a reference to a period specified in the regulations for the purposes of the enactment concerned;

   (b) provide for the manner in which any merger notice is authorised or required to be rejected or withdrawn, and the time at which any merger notice is to be treated as received or rejected;

   (c) provide for the time at which any notice under section 97(7), (8)(b), (11) or (13) is to be treated as received;

   (d) provide for the manner in which any information requested by the OFT or any other material information is authorised or required to be provided or disclosed, and the time at which such information is to be treated as provided or disclosed (including the time at which it is to be treated as provided to the satisfaction of the OFT for the purposes of section 97(6));

   (e) provide for the person who gave the merger notice to be informed, in circumstances in which section 97(6) applies –

      (i) of the fact that the OFT is satisfied as to the provision of the information requested by the OFT or (as the case may be) of the OFT's decision to cancel the extension; and

      (ii) of the time at which the OFT is to be treated as so satisfied or (as the case may be) of the time at which the cancellation is to be treated as having effect;

   (f) provide for the person who gave the merger notice to be informed, in circumstances in which section 97(8) applies –

      (i) of any decision by the OFT to cancel the extension; and

      (ii) of the time at which such a cancellation is to be treated as having effect;

   (g) provide for the time at which any fee is to be treated as paid;

   (h) provide that a person is, or is not, to be treated, in such circumstances as may be specified in the regulations, as acting on behalf of a person authorised by regulations under this section to give a merger notice or a person who has given such a notice.

102 Power to modify sections 97 to 101

The Secretary of State may, for the purposes of determining the effect of giving a merger notice and the action which may be or is to be taken by any person in connection with such a notice, by order modify sections 97 to 101.

General duties in relation to references

103 Duty of expedition in relation to references

(1) In deciding whether to make a reference under section 22 or 33 the OFT shall have regard, with a view to the prevention or removal of uncertainty, to the need for making a decision as soon as reasonably practicable.

(2) In deciding whether to make a reference under section 45 or 62 the Secretary of State shall have regard, with a view to the prevention or removal of uncertainty, to the need for making a decision as soon as reasonably practicable.

104 Certain duties of relevant authorities to consult

(1) Subsection (2) applies where the relevant authority is proposing to make a relevant decision in a way which the relevant authority considers is likely to be adverse to the interests of a relevant party.

(2) The relevant authority shall, so far as practicable, consult that party about what is proposed before making that decision.

(3) In consulting the party concerned, the relevant authority shall, so far as practicable, give the reasons of the relevant authority for the proposed decision.

(4) In considering what is practicable for the purposes of this section the relevant authority shall, in particular, have regard to –

    (a) any restrictions imposed by any timetable for making the decision; and

    (b) any need to keep what is proposed, or the reasons for it, confidential.

(5) The duty under this section shall not apply in relation to the making of any decision so far as particular provision is made elsewhere by virtue of this Part for consultation before the making of that decision.

(6) In this section –

'the relevant authority' means the OFT, the Commission or the Secretary of State;

'relevant decision' means –

    (a) in the case of the OFT, any decision by the OFT –

        (i) as to whether to make a reference under section 22 or 33 or accept undertakings under section 73 instead of making such a reference; or

        (ii) to vary under section 37 such a reference;

    (b) in the case of the Commission, any decision on the questions mentioned in section 35(1) or (3), 36(1) or (2), 47 or 63; and

    (c) in the case of the Secretary of State, any decision by the Secretary of State –

        (i) as to whether to make a reference under section 45 or 62; or

        (ii) to vary under section 49 or (as the case may be) 64 such a reference; and

'relevant party' means any person who appears to the relevant authority to control enterprises which are the subject of the reference or possible reference concerned.

Information and publicity requirements

105 General information duties of OFT and Commission

(1) Where the OFT decides to investigate a matter so as to enable it to decide whether to make a reference under section 22 or 33, or so as to make a report under section 44 or 61, it shall, so far as practicable, take such action as it considers appropriate to bring information about the investigation to the attention of those whom it considers

might be affected by the creation of the relevant merger situation concerned or (as the case may be) the special merger situation concerned.

(2) Subsection (1) does not apply in relation to arrangements which might result in the creation of a relevant merger situation if a merger notice has been given in relation to those arrangements under section 96.

(3) The OFT shall give the Commission –

   (a) such information in its possession as the Commission may reasonably require to enable the Commission to carry out its functions under this Part; and

   (b) any other assistance which the Commission may reasonably require for the purpose of assisting it in carrying out its functions under this Part and which it is within the power of the OFT to give.

(4) The OFT shall give the Commission any information in its possession which has not been requested by the Commission but which, in the opinion of the OFT, would be appropriate to give to the Commission for the purpose of assisting it in carrying out its functions under this Part.

(5) The OFT and the Commission shall give the Secretary of State –

   (a) such information in their possession as the Secretary of State may by direction reasonably require to enable him to carry out his functions under this Part; and

   (b) any other assistance which the Secretary of State may by direction reasonably require for the purpose of assisting him in carrying out his functions under this Part and which it is within the power of the OFT or (as the case may be) the Commission to give.

(6) The OFT shall give the Secretary of State any information in its possession which has not been requested by the Secretary of State but which, in the opinion of the OFT, would be appropriate to give to the Secretary of State for the purpose of assisting him in carrying out his functions under this Part.

(7) The Commission shall have regard to any information given to it under subsection (3) or (4); and the Secretary of State shall have regard to any information given to him under subsection (5) or (6).

(8) Any direction given under subsection (5) –

   (a) shall be in writing; and

   (b) may be varied or revoked by a subsequent direction.

106 Advice and information about references under sections 22 and 33

(1) As soon as reasonably practicable after the passing of this Act, the OFT shall prepare and publish general advice and information about the making of references by it under section 22 or 33.

(2) The OFT may at any time publish revised, or new, advice or information.

(3) As soon as reasonably practicable after the passing of this Act, the Commission shall prepare and publish general advice and information about the consideration by it of references under section 22 or 33 and the way in which relevant customer benefits may affect the taking of enforcement action in relation to such references.

(4) The Commission may at any time publish revised, or new, advice or information.

(5) Advice and information published under this section shall be prepared with a view to –

   (a) explaining relevant provisions of this Part to persons who are likely to be affected by them; and

   (b) indicating how the OFT or (as the case may be) the Commission expects such provisions to operate.

(6) Advice (or information) published by virtue of subsection (1) or (3) may include advice (or information) about the factors which the OFT or (as the case may be) the Commission may take into account in considering whether, and if so how, to exercise a function conferred by this Part.

(7) Any advice or information published by the OFT or the Commission under this section shall be published in such manner as the OFT or (as the case may be) the Commission considers appropriate.

(8) In preparing any advice or information under this section, the OFT shall consult the Commission and such other persons as it considers appropriate.

(9) In preparing any advice or information under this section, the Commission shall consult the OFT and such other persons as it considers appropriate.

107 Further publicity requirements

(1) The OFT shall publish –

    (a) any reference made by it under section 22 or 33 or any decision made by it not to make such a reference (other than a decision made by virtue of subsection (2)(b) of section 33);

    (b) any variation made by it under section 37 of a reference under section 22 or 33;

    (c) such information as it considers appropriate about any decision made by it under section 57(1) to bring a case to the attention of the Secretary of State;

    (d) any enforcement undertaking accepted by it under section 71;

    (e) any enforcement order made by it under section 72 or 76 or paragraph 2 of Schedule 7;

    (f) any variation, release or revocation of such an undertaking or order;

    (g) any decision made by it as mentioned in section 76(6)(b); and

    (h) any decision made by it to dispense with the requirements of Schedule 10.

(2) The Commission shall publish –

    (a) any cancellation by it under section 37(1) of a reference under section 33;

    (b) any decision made by it under section 37(2) to treat a reference made under section 22 or 33 as if it had been made under section 32 or (as the case may be) 22;

    (c) any extension by it under section 39 of the period within which a report under section 38 is to be prepared and published;

    (d) any decision made by it to cancel an extension as mentioned in section 39(8)(b);

    (e) any decision made by it under section 41(2) neither to accept an undertaking under section 82 nor to make an order under section 84;

    (f) any decision made by it that there has been a material change of circumstances as mentioned in subsection (3) of section 41 or there is another special reason as mentioned in that subsection of that section;

    (g) any cancellation by it under section 48(1) or 53(1) of a reference under section 45 or any cancellation by it under section 64(1) of a reference under section 62;

    (h) any decision made by it under section 49(1) to treat –

        (i) a reference made under subsection (2) or (3) of section 45 as if it had been made under subsection (4) or (as the case may be) (5) of that section; or

        (ii) a reference made under subsection (4) or (5) of section 45 as if it had been made under subsection (2) or (as the case may be) (3) of that section;

    (i) any extension by it under section 51 of the period within which a report under section 50 is to be prepared and published;

    (j) any decision made by it under section 51(8)(b) to cancel such an extension;

    (k) any extension by it under section 51 as applied by section 65(3) of the period within which a report under section 65 is to be prepared and published;

    (l) any decision made by it under section 51(8)(b) as applied by section 65(3) to cancel such an extension;

    (m) any decision made by it under section 64(2) to treat a reference made under subsection (2) or (3) of section 62 as if it had been made under subsection (3) or (as the case may be) (2) of that section;

    (n) any decision made by it as mentioned in section 76(6)(b);

    (o) any enforcement order made by it under section 76 or 81;

(p) any enforcement undertaking accepted by it under section 80;
(q) any variation, release or revocation of such an order or undertaking; and
(r) any decision made by it to dispense with the requirements of Schedule 10.

(3) The Secretary of State shall publish –

(a) any intervention notice or special intervention notice given by him;
(b) any report of the OFT under section 44 or 61 which has been received by him;
(c) any reference made by him under section 45 or 62 or any decision made by him not to make such a reference;
(d) any variation made by him under section 49 of a reference under section 45 or under section 64 of a reference under section 62;
(e) any report of the Commission under section 50 or 65 which has been received by him;
(f) any decision made by him neither to accept an undertaking under paragraph 9 of Schedule 7 nor to make an order under paragraph 11 of that Schedule;
(g) any notice given by him under section 56(1);
(h) any enforcement undertaking accepted by him under paragraph 1 of Schedule 7;
(i) any variation or release of such an undertaking;
(j) any decision made by him as mentioned in paragraph 6(6)(b) of Schedule 7; and
(k) any decision made by him to dispense with the requirements of Schedule 10.

(4) Where any person is under a duty by virtue of subsection (1), (2) or (3) to publish the result of any action taken by that person or any decision made by that person, the person concerned shall, subject to subsections (5) and (6), also publish that person's reasons for the action concerned or (as the case may be) the decision concerned.

(5) Such reasons need not, if it is not reasonably practicable to do so, be published at the same time as the result of the action concerned or (as the case may be) as the decision concerned.

(6) Subsections (4) and (5) shall not apply in relation to any information published under subsection (1)(c).

(7) The Secretary of State shall publish his reasons for –

(a) any decision made by him under section 54(2) or 66(2); or
(b) any decision to make an order under section 58(3) or vary or revoke such an order.

(8) Such reasons may be published after –

(a) in the case of subsection (7)(a), the publication of the decision concerned; and
(b) in the case of subsection (7)(b), the making of the order or of the variation or revocation;

if it is not reasonably practicable to publish them at the same time as the publication of the decision or (as the case may be) the making of the order or variation or revocation.

(9) The Secretary of State shall publish –

(a) the report of the OFT under section 44 in relation to a matter no later than publication of his decision as to whether to make a reference under section 45 in relation to that matter; and
(b) the report of the Commission under section 50 in relation to a matter no later than publication of his decision under section 54(2) in relation to that matter.

(10) The Secretary of State shall publish –

(a) the report of the OFT under section 61 in relation to a matter no later than publication of his decision as to whether to make a reference under section 62 in relation to that matter; and
(b) the report of the Commission under section 65 in relation to a matter no later than publication of his decision under section 66(2) in relation to that matter.

(11) Where the Secretary of State has decided under section 55(2) or 66(6) to accept an undertaking under paragraph 9 of Schedule 7 or to make an order under paragraph 11 of that Schedule, he shall (after the acceptance of the undertaking or (as the case may be) the making of the order) lay details of his decision and his reasons for it, and the Commission's report under section 50 or (as the case may be) 65, before each House of Parliament.

108 Defamation

For the purposes of the law relating to defamation, absolute privilege attaches to any advice, guidance, notice or direction given, or decision or report made, by the OFT, the Commission or the Secretary of State in the exercise of any of their functions under this Part.

Investigation powers

109 Attendance of witnesses and production of documents etc.

(1) The Commission may, for the purpose of any investigation on a reference made to it under this Part, give notice to any person requiring him –

    (a) to attend at a time and place specified in the notice; and

    (b) to give evidence to the Commission or a person nominated by the Commission for the purpose.

(2) The Commission may, for the purpose of any investigation on a reference made to it under this Part, give notice to any person requiring him –

    (a) to produce any documents which –

        (i) are specified or described in the notice, or fall within a category of document which is specified or described in the notice; and

        (ii) are in that person's custody or under his control; and

    (b) to produce them at a time and place so specified and to a person so specified.

(3) The Commission may, for the purpose of any investigation on a reference made to it under this Part, give notice to any person who carries on any business requiring him –

    (a) to supply to the Commission such estimates, forecasts, returns or other information as may be specified or described in the notice; and

    (b) to supply it at a time and place, and in a form and manner, so specified and to a person so specified.

(4) A notice under this section shall include information about the possible consequences of not complying with the notice.

(5) The Commission or any person nominated by it for the purpose may, for the purpose of any investigation on a reference made to it under this Part, take evidence on oath, and for that purpose may administer oaths.

(6) The person to whom any document is produced in accordance with a notice under this section may, for the purpose of any investigation on a reference made to the Commission under this Part, copy the document so produced.

(7) No person shall be required under this section –

    (a) to give any evidence or produce any documents which he could not be compelled to give or produce in civil proceedings before the court; or

    (b) to supply any information which he could not be compelled to supply in evidence in such proceedings.

(8) No person shall be required, in compliance with a notice under this section, to go more than 10 miles from his place of residence unless his necessary travelling expenses are paid or offered to him.

(9) Any reference in this section to the production of a document includes a reference to the production of a legible and intelligible copy of information recorded otherwise than in legible form.

(10) In this section 'the court' means –

   (a)   in relation to England and Wales or Northern Ireland, the High Court; and
   (b)   in relation to Scotland, the Court of Session.

110 Enforcement of powers under section 109: general

(1) Where the Commission considers that a person has, without reasonable excuse, failed to comply with any requirement of a notice under section 109, it may impose a penalty in accordance with section 111.

(2) The Commission may proceed (whether at the same time or at different times) under subsection (1) and section 39(4) or (as the case may be) 51(4) (including that enactment as applied by section 65(3)) in relation to the same failure.

(3) Where the Commission considers that a person has intentionally obstructed or delayed another person in the exercise of his powers under section 109(6), it may impose a penalty in accordance with section 111.

(4) No penalty shall be imposed by virtue of subsection (1) or (3) if more than 4 weeks have passed since the publication of the report of the Commission on the reference concerned; but this subsection shall not apply in relation to any variation or substitution of the penalty which is permitted by virtue of this Part.

(5) A person, subject to subsection (6), commits an offence if he intentionally alters, suppresses or destroys any document which he has been required to produce by a notice under section 109.

(6) A person does not commit an offence under subsection (5) in relation to any act which constitutes a failure to comply with a notice under section 109 if the Commission has proceeded against that person under subsection (1) above in relation to that failure.

(7) A person who commits an offence under subsection (5) shall be liable –

   (a)   on summary conviction, to a fine not exceeding the statutory maximum;
   (b)   on conviction on indictment, to imprisonment for a term not exceeding two years or to a fine or to both.

(8) The Commission shall not proceed against a person under subsection (1) in relation to an act which constitutes an offence under subsection (5) if that person has been found guilty of that offence.

(9) In deciding whether and, if so, how to proceed under subsection (1) or (3) or section 39(4) or 51(4) (including that enactment as applied by section 65(3)), the Commission shall have regard to the statement of policy which was most recently published under section 116 at the time when the failure concerned or (as the case may be) the obstruction or delay concerned occurred.

(10) The reference in this section to the production of a document includes a reference to the production of a legible and intelligible copy of information recorded otherwise than in legible form; and the reference to suppressing a document includes a reference to destroying the means of reproducing information recorded otherwise than in legible form.

111 Penalties

(1)   A penalty imposed under section 110(1) or (3) shall be of such amount as the Commission considers appropriate.

(2)   The amount may, in the case of a penalty imposed under section 110(1), be a fixed amount, an amount calculated by reference to a daily rate or a combination of a fixed amount and an amount calculated by reference to a daily rate.

(3)   The amount shall, in the case of a penalty imposed under section 110(3), be a fixed amount.

(4) No penalty imposed under section 110(1) shall –

    (a) in the case of a fixed amount, exceed such amount as the Secretary of State may by order specify;

    (b) in the case of an amount calculated by reference to a daily rate, exceed such amount per day as the Secretary of State may so specify; and

    (c) in the case of a fixed amount and an amount calculated by reference to a daily rate, exceed such fixed amount and such amount per day as the Secretary of State may so specify.

(5) In imposing a penalty by reference to a daily rate –

    (a) no account shall be taken of any days before the service of the notice under section 112 on the person concerned; and

    (b) unless the Commission determines an earlier date (whether before or after the penalty is imposed), the amount payable shall cease to accumulate at the beginning of –

        (i) the day on which the requirement of the notice concerned under section 109 is satisfied or (as the case may be) the obstruction or delay is removed; or

        (ii) if earlier, the day on which the report of the Commission on the reference concerned is published (or, in the case of a report under section 50 or 65, given) or, if no such report is published (or given) within the period permitted for that purpose by this Part, the latest day on which the report may be published (or given) within the permitted period.

(6) No penalty imposed under section 110(3) shall exceed such amount as the Secretary of State may by order specify.

(7) An order under subsection (4) or (6) shall not specify –

    (a) in the case of a fixed amount, an amount exceeding £30,000;

    (b) in the case of an amount calculated by reference to a daily rate, an amount per day exceeding £15,000; and

    (c) in the case of a fixed amount and an amount calculated by reference to a daily rate, a fixed amount exceeding £30,000 and an amount per day exceeding £15,000.

(8) Before making an order under subsection (4) or (6) the Secretary of State shall consult the Commission and such other persons as he considers appropriate.

112 Penalties: main procedural requirements

(1) As soon as practicable after imposing a penalty under section 110(1) or (3), the Commission shall give notice of the penalty.

(2) The notice shall state –

    (a) that the Commission has imposed a penalty on the person concerned;

    (b) whether the penalty is of a fixed amount, of an amount calculated by reference to a daily rate or of both a fixed amount and an amount calculated by reference to a daily rate;

    (c) the amount or amounts concerned and, in the case of an amount calculated by reference to a daily rate, the day on which the amount first starts to accumulate and the day or days on which it might cease to accumulate;

    (d) the failure or (as the case may be) the obstruction or delay which the Commission considers gave it the power to impose the penalty;

    (e) any other facts which the Commission considers justify the imposition of a penalty and the amount or amounts of the penalty;

    (f) the manner in which, and place at which, the penalty is required to be paid to the Commission;

    (g) the date or dates, no earlier than the end of the relevant period beginning with the date of service of the notice on the person concerned, by which the penalty or (as the case may be) different portions of it are required to be paid;

(h) that the penalty or (as the case may be) different portions of it may be paid
      earlier than the date or dates by which it or they are required to be paid; and

(i) that the person concerned has the right to apply under subsection (3) below or
      to appeal under section 114 and the main details of those rights.

(3) The person against whom the penalty was imposed may, within 14 days of the date of
     service on him of a notice under subsection (1), apply to the Commission for it to
     specify a different date or (as the case may be) different dates by which the penalty or
     (as the case may be) different portions of it are to be paid.

(4) A notice under this section shall be given by –

(a) serving a copy of the notice on the person on whom the penalty was imposed; and

(b) publishing the notice.

(5) In this section 'relevant period' means the period of 28 days mentioned in subsection
     (3) of section 114 or, if another period is specified by the Secretary of State under that
     subsection, that period.

113 Payments and interest by instalments

(1) If the whole or any portion of a penalty is not paid by the date by which it is required
     to be paid, the unpaid balance from time to time shall carry interest at the rate for the
     time being specified in section 17 of the Judgments Act 1838 (c. 110).

(2) Where an application has been made under section 112(3), the penalty shall not
     be required to be paid until the application has been determined, withdrawn or
     otherwise dealt with.

(3) If a portion of a penalty has not been paid by the date required for it, the Commission may,
     where it considers it appropriate to do so, require so much of the penalty as has not
     already been paid (and is capable of being paid immediately) to be paid immediately.

(4) Any sums received by the Commission in or towards the payment of a penalty, or
     interest on a penalty, shall be paid into the Consolidated Fund.

114 Appeals in relation to penalties

(1) This section applies if a person on whom a penalty is imposed under section 110(1)
     or (3) is aggrieved by –

(a) the imposition or nature of the penalty;

(b) the amount or amounts of the penalty; or

(c) the date by which the penalty is required to be paid or (as the case may be) the
      different dates by which portions of the penalty are required to be paid.

(2) The person aggrieved may apply to the Competition Appeal Tribunal.

(3) If a copy of the notice under section 112(1) was served on the person on whom
     the penalty was imposed, the application to the Competition Appeal Tribunal shall,
     subject to subsection (4), be made within –

(a) the period of 28 days starting with the day on which the copy was served on the
      person concerned; or

(b) such other period as the Secretary of State may by order specify.

(4) If the application relates to a decision of the Commission on an application by the per-
     son on whom the penalty was imposed under section 112(3), the application to the
     Competition Appeal Tribunal shall be made within –

(a) the period of 28 days starting with the day on which the person concerned is
      notified of the decision; or

(b) such other period as the Secretary of State may by order specify.

(5) On an application under this section, the Competition Appeal Tribunal may –

(a) quash the penalty;

(b) substitute a penalty of a different nature or of such lesser amount or amounts as
      the Competition Appeal Tribunal considers appropriate; or

(c) in a case falling within subsection (1)(c), substitute for the date or dates imposed by the Commission an alternative date or dates;

if it considers it appropriate to do so.

(6) The Competition Appeal Tribunal shall not substitute a penalty of a different nature under subsection (5)(b) unless it considers that the person on whom the penalty is imposed will, or is likely to, pay less under the substituted penalty than he would have paid under the original penalty.

(7) Where an application has been made under this section –

(a) the penalty shall not be required to be paid until the application has been determined, withdrawn or otherwise dealt with; and

(b) the Commission may agree to reduce the amount or amounts of the penalty in settlement of the application.

(8) Where the Competition Appeal Tribunal substitutes a penalty of a different nature or of a lesser amount or amounts it may require the payment of interest on the substituted penalty at such rate or rates, and from such date or dates, as it considers appropriate.

(9) Where the Competition Appeal Tribunal specifies as a date by which the penalty, or a portion of the penalty, is to be paid a date before the determination of the application under this section it may require the payment of interest on the penalty, or portion, from that date at such rate as it considers appropriate.

(10) An appeal lies to the appropriate court –

(a) on a point of law arising from a decision of the Tribunal in proceedings under this section; or

(b) from a decision of the Tribunal in such proceedings as to the amount or amounts of a penalty.

(11) An appeal under subsection (10) –

(a) may be brought by a party to the proceedings before the Tribunal; and

(b) requires the permission of the Tribunal or the appropriate court.

(12) In this section 'the appropriate court' means the Court of Appeal or, in the case of Tribunal proceedings in Scotland, the Court of Session.

115 Recovery of penalties

Where a penalty imposed under section 110(1) or (3), or any portion of such a penalty, has not been paid by the date on which it is required to be paid and –

(a) no application relating to the penalty has been made under section 114 during the period within which such an application may be made, or

(b) any such application which has been made has been determined, withdrawn or otherwise dealt with,

the Commission may recover from the person on whom the penalty was imposed any of the penalty and any interest which has not been paid; and in England and Wales and Northern Ireland such penalty and interest may be recovered as a civil debt due to the Commission.

116 Statement of policy

(1) The Commission shall prepare and publish a statement of policy in relation to the enforcement of notices under section 109.

(2) The statement shall, in particular, include a statement about the considerations relevant to the determination of the nature and amount of any penalty imposed under section 110(1) or (3).

(3) The Commission may revise its statement of policy and, where it does so, it shall publish the revised statement.

(4) The Commission shall consult such persons as it considers appropriate when preparing or revising its statement of policy.

117 False or misleading information

(1) A person commits an offence if –

  (a) he supplies any information to the OFT, the Commission or the Secretary of State in connection with any of their functions under this Part;

  (b) the information is false or misleading in a material respect; and

  (c) he knows that it is false or misleading in a material respect or is reckless as to whether it is false or misleading in a material respect.

(2) A person commits an offence if he –

  (a) supplies any information to another person which he knows to be false or misleading in a material respect; or

  (b) recklessly supplies any information to another person which is false or misleading in a material respect;

knowing that the information is to be used for the purpose of supplying information to the OFT, the Commission or the Secretary of State in connection with any of their functions under this Part.

(3) A person who commits an offence under subsection (1) or (2) shall be liable –

  (a) on summary conviction, to a fine not exceeding the statutory maximum;

  (b) on conviction on indictment, to imprisonment for a term not exceeding two years or to a fine or to both.

Reports

118 Excisions from reports

(1) Subsection (2) applies where the Secretary of State is under a duty to publish –

  (a) a report of the OFT under section 44 or 61; or

  (b) a report of the Commission under section 50 or 65.

(2) The Secretary of State may exclude a matter from the report concerned if he considers that publication of the matter would be inappropriate.

(3) In deciding what is inappropriate for the purposes of subsection (2) the Secretary of State shall have regard to the considerations mentioned in section 244.

(4) The body which has prepared the report shall advise the Secretary of State as to the matters (if any) which it considers should be excluded by him under subsection (2).

(5) References in sections 38(4) and 107(11) to the giving or laying of a report of the Commission shall be construed as references to the giving or laying of the report as published.

119 Minority reports of Commission

(1) Subsection (2) applies where, on a reference to the Commission under this Part, a member of a group constituted in connection with the reference in pursuance of paragraph 15 of Schedule 7 to the Competition Act 1998 (c. 41), disagrees with any decisions contained in the report of the Commission under this Part as the decisions of the Commission.

(2) The report shall, if the member so wishes, include a statement of his disagreement and of his reasons for disagreeing.

Miscellaneous

120 Review of decisions under Part 3

(1) Any person aggrieved by a decision of the OFT, the Secretary of State or the Commission under this Part in connection with a reference or possible reference in

relation to a relevant merger situation or a special merger situation may apply to the Competition Appeal Tribunal for a review of that decision.

(2) For this purpose 'decision' –

(a) does not include a decision to impose a penalty under section 110(1) or (3); but

(b) includes a failure to take a decision permitted or required by this Part in connection with a reference or possible reference.

(3) Except in so far as a direction to the contrary is given by the Competition Appeal Tribunal, the effect of the decision is not suspended by reason of the making of the application.

(4) In determining such an application the Competition Appeal Tribunal shall apply the same principles as would be applied by a court on an application for judicial review.

(5) The Competition Appeal Tribunal may –

(a) dismiss the application or quash the whole or part of the decision to which it relates; and

(b) where it quashes the whole or part of that decision, refer the matter back to the original decision maker with a direction to reconsider and make a new decision in accordance with the ruling of the Competition Appeal Tribunal.

(6) An appeal lies on any point of law arising from a decision of the Competition Appeal Tribunal under this section to the appropriate court.

(7) An appeal under subsection (6) requires the permission of the Tribunal or the appropriate court.

(8) In this section –

'the appropriate court' means the Court of Appeal or, in the case of Tribunal proceedings in Scotland, the Court of Session; and

'Tribunal rules' has the meaning given by section 15(1).

121 Fees

(1) The Secretary of State may by order require the payment to him or the OFT of such fees as may be prescribed by the order in connection with the exercise by the Secretary of State, the OFT and the Commission of their functions under or by virtue of this Part, Part V of the Fair Trading Act 1973 (c. 41) and sections 32 to 34 of, and Schedule 4ZA to, the Water Industry Act 1991 (c. 56).

(2) An order under this section may, in particular, provide for fees to be payable –

(a) in respect of a merger notice;

(b) in respect of an application for the consent of the Secretary of State under section 58(1) of the Act of 1973 to the transfer of a newspaper or of newspaper assets; or

(c) on the occurrence of any event specified in the order.

(3) The events that may be specified in an order under this section by virtue of subsection (2)(c) include, in particular –

(a) the decision by the OFT in relation to a possible reference under section 22 or 33 that it is or may be the case that a relevant merger situation has been created or (as the case may be) that arrangements are in progress or in contemplation which, if carried into effect, will result in the creation of a relevant merger situation;

(b) the decision by the Secretary of State in relation to a possible reference under section 45 that it is or may be the case that a relevant merger situation has been created or (as the case may be) that arrangements are in progress or in contemplation which, if carried into effect, will result in the creation of a relevant merger situation;

(c) the decision by the Secretary of State in relation to a possible reference under section 62 that –

(i) it is or may be the case that a special merger situation has been created or (as the case may be) that arrangements are in progress or in contemplation which, if carried into effect, will result in the creation of a special merger situation; and

    (ii)   one or more than one consideration mentioned in the special intervention notice is relevant to a consideration of the special merger situation concerned; and

  (d) the decision by the OFT in relation to a possible reference under section 32 of the Act of 1991 that it is or may be the case that arrangements are in progress which, if carried into effect, will result in a merger of any two or more water enterprises or that such a merger has taken place otherwise than as a result of the carrying into effect of arrangements that have been the subject of a reference by virtue of paragraph (a) of that section.

(4) An order under this section may, in particular, contain provision –

  (a) for ascertaining the persons by whom fees are payable;

  (b) specifying whether any fee is payable to the Secretary of State or the OFT;

  (c) for the amount of any fee to be calculated by reference to matters which may include –

    (i)   in a case involving functions of the Secretary of State under sections 57 to 61 of the Act of 1973, the number of newspapers concerned, the number of separate editions (determined in accordance with the order) of each newspaper and the average circulation per day of publication (within the meaning of Part V of that Act) of each newspaper; and

    (ii) in any other case, the value of the turnover of the enterprises concerned;

  (d) as to the time when any fee is to be paid; and

  (e) for the repayment by the Secretary of State or the OFT of the whole or part of any fee in specified circumstances.

(5) For the purposes of subsection (4)(c)(ii) the turnover of an enterprise shall be determined in accordance with such provisions as may be specified in an order under this section.

(6) Provision made by virtue of subsection (5) may, in particular, include provision –

  (a) as to the amounts which are, or which are not, to be treated as comprising an enterprise's turnover;

  (b) as to the date or dates by reference to which an enterprise's turnover is to be determined;

  (c) restricting the turnover to be taken into consideration to turnover which has a connection of a particular description with the United Kingdom.

(7) An order under this section may, in particular, in connection with provisions of the kind mentioned in subsection (5) make provision enabling the Secretary of State or the OFT to determine matters of a description specified in the order (including any of the matters mentioned in paragraphs (a) to (c) of subsection (6)).

(8) In determining the amount of any fees to be prescribed by an order under this section, the Secretary of State may take into account all costs incurred by him and by the OFT in respect of the exercise by him, the OFT and the Commission of their respective functions under or by virtue of this Part, Part V of the Act of 1973 and sections 32 to 34 of, and Schedule 4ZA to, the Act of 1991.

(9) Fees paid to the Secretary of State or the OFT under this section shall be paid into the Consolidated Fund.

(10) In this section 'newspaper' has the same meaning as in Part V of the Act of 1973.

122 Primacy of Community law

(1) Advice and information published by virtue of section 106(1) or (3) shall include such advice and information about the effect of Community law, and anything done under or in accordance with it, on the provisions of this Part as the OFT or (as the case may be) the Commission considers appropriate.

(2) Advice and information published by the OFT by virtue of section 106(1) shall, in particular, include advice and information about the circumstances in which the duties of the OFT under sections 22 and 33 do not apply as a result of the European Merger Regulations or anything done under or in accordance with them.

(3) The duty or power to make a reference under section 22 or 45(2) or (3), and the power to give an intervention notice under section 42, shall apply in a case in which the relevant enterprises ceased to be distinct enterprises at a time or in circumstances not falling within section 24 if the condition mentioned in subsection (4) is satisfied.

(4) The condition mentioned in this subsection is that, because of the European Merger Regulations or anything done under or in accordance with them, the reference, or (as the case may be) the reference under section 22 to which the intervention notice relates, could not have been made earlier than 4 months before the date on which it is to be made.

(5) Where the duty or power to make a reference under section 22 or 45(2) or (3), or the power to give an intervention notice under section 42, applies as mentioned in subsection (3), references in this Part to the creation of a relevant merger situation shall be construed accordingly.

123 Power to alter share of supply test

(1) The Secretary of State may by order amend or replace the conditions which determine for the purposes of this Part whether a relevant merger situation has been created.

(2) The Secretary of State shall not exercise his power under subsection (1) –

    (a) to amend or replace the conditions mentioned in paragraphs (a) and (b) of subsection (1) of section 23;

    (b) to amend or replace the condition mentioned in paragraph (a) of subsection (2) of that section.

(3) In exercising his power under subsection (1) to amend or replace the condition mentioned in paragraph (b) of subsection (2) of section 23 or any condition which for the time being applies instead of it, the Secretary of State shall, in particular, have regard to the desirability of ensuring that any amended or new condition continues to operate by reference to the degree of commercial strength which results from the enterprises concerned having ceased to be distinct.

(4) Before making an order under this section the Secretary of State shall consult the OFT and the Commission.

(5) An order under this section may provide for the delegation of functions to the decision-making authority.

Other

124 Orders and regulations under Part 3

(1) Any power of the Secretary of State to make an order or regulations under this Part shall be exercisable by statutory instrument.

(2) Any power of the Secretary of State to make an order or regulations under this Part –

    (a) may be exercised so as to make different provision for different cases or different purposes; and

    (b) includes power to make such incidental, supplementary, consequential, transitory, transitional or saving provision as the Secretary of State considers appropriate.

(3) The power of the Secretary of State under section 34 or 123 (including that power as extended by subsection (2) above) may be exercised by modifying any enactment comprised in or made under this Act, or any other enactment.

(4) The power of the Secretary of State under section 40(8), 52(8) (including that enactment as applied by section 65(3)), 58(3), 68 or 102 as extended by subsection (2)

above may be exercised by modifying any enactment comprised in or made under this Act, or any other enactment.

(5) An order made by the Secretary of State under section 28 (including that enactment as applied by section 42(5), 59(5) and 67(7)), 40(8), 52(8) (including that enactment as applied by section 65(3)), 111(4) or (6), 114(3)(b) or (4)(b) or 121 or Schedule 7 shall be subject to annulment in pursuance of a resolution of either House of Parliament.

(6) No order shall be made by the Secretary of State under section 34, 68, 102, 123 or 128(6) unless a draft of it has been laid before, and approved by a resolution of, each House of Parliament.

(7) An order made by the Secretary of State under section 58(3) shall be laid before Parliament after being made and shall cease to have effect unless approved, within the period of 28 days beginning with the day on which it is made, by a resolution of each House of Parliament.

(8) In calculating the period of 28 days mentioned in subsection (7), no account shall be taken of any time during which Parliament is dissolved or prorogued or during which both Houses are adjourned for more than four days.

(9) If an order made by the Secretary of State ceases to have effect by virtue of subsection (7), any modification made by it of an enactment is repealed (and the previous enactment revived) but without prejudice to the validity of anything done in connection with that modification before the order ceased to have effect and without prejudice to the making of a new order.

(10) If, apart from this subsection, an order made by the Secretary of State under section 58(3) would be treated for the purposes of the standing orders of either House of Parliament as a hybrid instrument, it shall proceed in that House as if it were not such an instrument.

125 Offences by bodies corporate

(1) Where an offence under this Part committed by a body corporate is proved to have been committed with the consent or connivance of, or to be attributable to any neglect on the part of –

   (a) a director, manager, secretary or other similar officer of the body corporate, or
   (b) a person purporting to act in such a capacity,

   he as well as the body corporate commits the offence and shall be liable to be proceeded against and punished accordingly.

(2) Where the affairs of a body corporate are managed by its members, subsection (1) applies in relation to the acts and defaults of a member in connection with his functions of management as if he were a director of the body corporate.

(3) Where an offence under this Part is committed by a Scottish partnership and is proved to have been committed with the consent or connivance of a partner, or to be attributable to any neglect on the part of a partner, he as well as the partnership commits the offence and shall be liable to be proceeded against and punished accordingly.

(4) In subsection (3) 'partner' includes a person purporting to act as a partner.

126 Service of documents

(1) Any document required or authorised by virtue of this Part to be served on any person may be served –

   (a) by delivering it to him or by leaving it at his proper address or by sending it by post to him at that address;
   (b) if the person is a body corporate other than a limited liability partnership, by serving it in accordance with paragraph (a) on the secretary of the body;
   (c) if the person is a limited liability partnership, by serving it in accordance with paragraph (a) on a member of the partnership; or

(d) if the person is a partnership, by serving it in accordance with paragraph (a) on a partner or a person having the control or management of the partnership business.

(2) For the purposes of this section and section 7 of the Interpretation Act 1978 (c. 30) (service of documents by post) in its application to this section, the proper address of any person on whom a document is to be served shall be his last known address, except that –

(a) in the case of service on a body corporate (other than a limited liability partnership) or its secretary, it shall be the address of the registered or principal office of the body;

(b) in the case of service on a limited liability partnership or a member of the partnership, it shall be the address of the registered or principal office of the partnership;

(c) in the case of service on a partnership or a partner or a person having the control or management of a partnership business, it shall be the address of the principal office of the partnership.

(3) For the purposes of subsection (2) the principal office of a company constituted under the law of a country or territory outside the United Kingdom or of a partnership carrying on business outside the United Kingdom is its principal office within the United Kingdom.

(4) Subsection (5) applies if a person to be served under this Part with any document by another has specified to that other an address within the United Kingdom other than his proper address (as determined under subsection (2)) as the one at which he or someone on his behalf will accept documents of the same description as that document.

(5) In relation to that document, that address shall be treated as his proper address for the purposes of this section and section 7 of the Interpretation Act 1978 in its application to this section, instead of that determined under subsection (2).

(6) Any notice in writing or other document required or authorised by virtue of this Part to be served on any person may be served on that person by transmitting the text of the notice or other document to him by means of a telecommunication system (within the meaning of the Telecommunications Act 1984 (c. 12)) or by other means but while in electronic form provided the text is received by that person in legible form and is capable of being used for subsequent reference.

(7) This section does not apply to any document if rules of court make provision about its service.

(8) In this section references to serving include references to similar expressions (such as giving or sending).

127 Associated persons

(1) Associated persons, and any bodies corporate which they or any of them control, shall be treated as one person –

(a) for the purpose of deciding under section 26 whether any two enterprises have been brought under common ownership or common control; and

(b) for the purpose of determining what activities are carried on by way of business by any one person so far as that question arises in connection with paragraph 13(2) of Schedule 8.

(2) Subsection (1) shall not exclude from section 26 any case which would otherwise fall within that section.

(3) A reference under section 22, 33, 45 or 62 (whether or not made by virtue of this section) may be framed so as to exclude from consideration, either altogether or for a specified purpose or to a specified extent, any matter which, apart from this section, would not have been taken into account on that reference.

(4) For the purposes of this section –

    (a) any individual and that individual's spouse or partner and any relative, or spouse or partner of a relative, of that individual or of that individual's spouse or partner;

    (b) any person in his capacity as trustee of a settlement and the settlor or grantor and any person associated with the settlor or grantor;

    (c) persons carrying on business in partnership and the spouse or partner and relatives of any of them; or

    (d) two or more persons acting together to secure or exercise control of a body of persons corporate or unincorporate or to secure control of any enterprise or assets,

    shall be regarded as associated with one another.

(5) The reference in subsection (1) to bodies corporate which associated persons control shall be construed in accordance with section 26(3) and (4).

(6) In this section 'relative' means a brother, sister, uncle, aunt, nephew, niece, lineal ancestor or descendant (the stepchild of any person, or anyone adopted by a person, whether legally or otherwise, as his child being regarded as a relative or taken into account to trace a relationship in the same way as that person's child); and references to a spouse or partner shall include a former spouse or partner.

128 Supply of services and market for services etc.

(1) References in this Part to the supply of services shall be construed in accordance with this section; and references in this Part to a market for services and other related expressions shall be construed accordingly.

(2) The supply of services does not include the provision of services under a contract of service or of apprenticeship whether it is express or implied and (if it is express) whether it is oral or in writing.

(3) The supply of services includes –

    (a) performing for gain or reward any activity other than the supply of goods;

    (b) rendering services to order;

    (c) the provision of services by making them available to potential users.

(4) The supply of services includes making arrangements for the use of computer software or for granting access to data stored in any form which is not readily accessible.

(5) The supply of services includes making arrangements by means of a relevant agreement (within the meaning of section 189(2) of the Broadcasting Act 1990 (c. 42)) for sharing the use of telecommunications apparatus.

(6) The supply of services includes permitting or making arrangements to permit the use of land in such circumstances as the Secretary of State may by order specify.

129 Other interpretation provisions

(1) In this Part, unless the context otherwise requires –

    'action' includes omission; and references to the taking of action include references to refraining from action;

    'agreement' means any agreement or arrangement, in whatever way and whatever form it is made, and whether it is, or is intended to be, legally enforceable or not;

    'business' includes a professional practice and includes any other undertaking which is carried on for gain or reward or which is an undertaking in the course of which goods or services are supplied otherwise than free of charge;

    'change of circumstances' includes any discovery that information has been supplied which is false or misleading in a material respect;

'Community law' means –

(a) all the rights, powers, liabilities, obligations and restrictions from time to time created or arising by or under the Community Treaties; and

(b) all the remedies and procedures from time to time provided for by or under the Community Treaties;

'consumer' means any person who is –

(a) a person to whom goods are or are sought to be supplied (whether by way of sale or otherwise) in the course of a business carried on by the person supplying or seeking to supply them; or

(b) a person for whom services are or are sought to be supplied in the course of a business carried on by the person supplying or seeking to supply them;

and who does not receive or seek to receive the goods or services in the course of a business carried on by him;

'customer' includes a customer who is not a consumer;

'enactment' includes an Act of the Scottish Parliament, Northern Ireland legislation and an enactment comprised in subordinate legislation, and includes an enactment whenever passed or made;

'enterprise' means the activities, or part of the activities, of a business;

'the European Merger Regulations' means Council Regulation (EEC) No. 4064/89 of 21st December 1989 on the control of concentrations between undertakings as amended by Council Regulation (EC) No. 1310/97 of 30th June 1997;

'goods' includes buildings and other structures, and also includes ships, aircraft and hovercraft;

'modify' includes amend or repeal;

'notice' means notice in writing;

'price' includes any charge or fee (however described);

'subordinate legislation' has the same meaning as in the Interpretation Act 1978 (c. 30) and also includes an instrument made under an Act of the Scottish Parliament and an instrument made under Northern Ireland legislation;

'subsidiary' has the meaning given by section 736 of the Companies Act 1985 (c. 6);

'supply', in relation to the supply of goods, includes supply by way of sale, lease, hire or hire-purchase, and, in relation to buildings or other structures, includes the construction of them by a person for another person; and

'United Kingdom national' means an individual who is –

(a) a British citizen, a British overseas territories citizen, a British National (Overseas) or a British Overseas citizen;

(b) a person who under the British Nationality Act 1981 (c. 61) is a British subject; or

(c) a British protected person within the meaning of that Act.

(2) For the purposes of this Part any two bodies corporate are interconnected if –

(a) one of them is a body corporate of which the other is a subsidiary; or

(b) both of them are subsidiaries of one and the same body corporate;

and in this Part 'interconnected bodies corporate' shall be construed accordingly and 'group of interconnected bodies corporate' means a group consisting of two or more bodies corporate all of whom are interconnected with each other.

(3) References in this Part to a person carrying on business include references to a person carrying on business in partnership with one or more other persons.

(4) Any duty to publish which is imposed on a person by this Part shall, unless the context otherwise requires, be construed as a duty on that person to publish in

such manner as he considers appropriate for the purpose of bringing the matter concerned to the attention of those likely to be affected by it.

130 Index of defined expressions

In this Part, the expressions listed in the left-hand column have the meaning given by, or are to be interpreted in accordance with, the provisions listed in the right-hand column.

Expression	Provision of this Act
Action (and the taking of action)	Section 129(1)
Adverse public interest finding	Section 54(3)
Agreement	Section 129(1)
Anti-competitive outcome	Section 35(2)
Business (and carrying on business)	Section 129(1) and (3)
Change of circumstances	Section 129(1)
The Commission	Section 273
Community law	Section 129(1)
Consumer	Section 129(1)
Customer	Section 129(1)
Date of reference	Section 39(9)
The decision-making authority	Section 22(7)
Enactment	Section 129(1)
Enforcement order	Section 86(6)
Enforcement undertaking	Section 89(2)
Enterprise	Section 129(1)
Enterprises ceasing to be distinct	Section 26(1)
European Merger Regulations	Section 129(1)
Final determination of matter to which intervention notice relates	Section 43(4) and (5)
Final determination of matter to which special intervention notice relates	Section 60(4) and (5)
Final determination of reference under section 22 or 33	Section 79(1) and (2)
Goods	Section 129(1)
Interconnected bodies corporate (and a group of interconnected bodies corporate)	Section 129(2)
Intervention notice	Section 42(2)
Market for goods or services	Section 22(6)
Market in the United Kingdom	Section 22(6)
Merger notice	Section 96(2)
Modify	Section 129(1)
Notice	Section 129(1)
Notified arrangements	Section 96(6)
The OFT	Section 273
Orders under section 81	Section 81(6)
Orders under paragraph 2 of Schedule 7	Paragraph 2(7) of Schedule 7

Expression	Provision of this Act
The period for considering a merger notice	Sections 97 and 98
Price	Section 129(1)
Public interest consideration	Sections 42(3) and 67(9)
Public interest consideration being finalised	Section 42(8)
Publish	Section 129(4)
References under section 22, 33, 45 or 62	Sections 37(2), 49(1), 56(8) and 64(2)
Relevant customer benefit	Section 30
Relevant merger situation	Section 23 (as read with other enactments)
Reports of the Commission	Section 118(5)
Special intervention notice	Section 59(2)
Special merger situation	Section 59(3)
Subordinate legislation	Section 129(1)
Subsidiary	Section 129(1)
Supply (in relation to the supply of goods)	Section 129(1)
The supply of services (and a market for services etc.)	Section 128
The turnover in the United Kingdom of an enterprise	Section 28(2)
Undertakings under section 80	Section 80(6)
Undertakings under paragraph 1 of Schedule 7	Paragraph 1(7) of Schedule 7
United Kingdom national	Section 129(1)

PART 4   MARKET INVESTIGATIONS

CHAPTER 1   MARKET INVESTIGATION REFERENCES

Making of references

131 Power of OFT to make references

(1) The OFT may, subject to subsection (4), make a reference to the Commission if the OFT has reasonable grounds for suspecting that any feature, or combination of features, of a market in the United Kingdom for goods or services prevents, restricts or distorts competition in connection with the supply or acquisition of any goods or services in the United Kingdom or a part of the United Kingdom.

(2) For the purposes of this Part any reference to a feature of a market in the United Kingdom for goods or services shall be construed as a reference to –

(a) the structure of the market concerned or any aspect of that structure;

(b) any conduct (whether or not in the market concerned) of one or more than one person who supplies or acquires goods or services in the market concerned; or

(c) any conduct relating to the market concerned of customers of any person who supplies or acquires goods or services.

(3) In subsection (2) 'conduct' includes any failure to act (whether or not intentional) and any other unintentional conduct.

(4) No reference shall be made under this section if –

    (a) the making of the reference is prevented by section 156(1); or

    (b) a reference has been made under section 132 in relation to the same matter but has not been finally determined.

(5) References in this Part to a market investigation reference being finally determined shall be construed in accordance with section 183(3) to (6).

(6) In this Part –

    'market in the United Kingdom' includes –

        (a) so far as it operates in the United Kingdom or a part of the United Kingdom, any market which operates there and in another country or territory or in a part of another country or territory; and

        (b) any market which operates only in a part of the United Kingdom;

    'market investigation reference' means a reference under this section or section 132;

and references to a market for goods or services include references to a market for goods and services.

132 Ministerial power to make references

(1) Subsection (3) applies where, in relation to any goods or services, the appropriate Minister is not satisfied with a decision of the OFT not to make a reference under section 131.

(2) Subsection (3) also applies where, in relation to any goods or services, the appropriate Minister –

    (a) has brought to the attention of the OFT information which the appropriate Minister considers to be relevant to the question of whether the OFT should make a reference under section 131; but

    (b) is not satisfied that the OFT will decide, within such period as the appropriate Minister considers to be reasonable, whether to make such a reference.

(3) The appropriate Minister may, subject to subsection (4), make a reference to the Commission if he has reasonable grounds for suspecting that any feature, or combination of features, of a market in the United Kingdom for goods or services prevents, restricts or distorts competition in connection with the supply or acquisition of any goods or services in the United Kingdom or a part of the United Kingdom.

(4) No reference shall be made under this section if the making of the reference is prevented by section 156(1).

(5) In this Part 'the appropriate Minister' means –

    (a) the Secretary of State; or

    (b) the Secretary of State and one or more than one other Minister of the Crown acting jointly.

133 Contents of references

(1) A market investigation reference shall, in particular, specify –

    (a) the enactment under which it is made;

    (b) the date on which it is made; and

    (c) the description of goods or services to which the feature or combination of features concerned relates.

(2) A market investigation reference may be framed so as to require the Commission to confine its investigation into the effects of features of markets in the United Kingdom for goods or services of a description specified in the reference to the effects of features of such of those markets as exist in connection with –

    (a) a supply, of a description specified in the reference, of the goods or services concerned; or

(b) an acquisition, of a description specified in the reference, of the goods or services concerned.

(3) A description of the kind mentioned in subsection (2)(a) or (b) may, in particular, be by reference to –

(a) the place where the goods or services are supplied or acquired; or
(b) the persons by or to whom they are supplied or by or from whom they are acquired.

Determination of references

134 Questions to be decided on market investigation references

(1) The Commission shall, on a market investigation reference, decide whether any feature, or combination of features, of each relevant market prevents, restricts or distorts competition in connection with the supply or acquisition of any goods or services in the United Kingdom or a part of the United Kingdom.

(2) For the purposes of this Part, in relation to a market investigation reference, there is an adverse effect on competition if any feature, or combination of features, of a relevant market prevents, restricts or distorts competition in connection with the supply or acquisition of any goods or services in the United Kingdom or a part of the United Kingdom.

(3) In subsections (1) and (2) 'relevant market' means –

(a) in the case of subsection (2) so far as it applies in connection with a possible reference, a market in the United Kingdom –

(i) for goods or services of a description to be specified in the reference; and
(ii) which would not be excluded from investigation by virtue of section 133(2); and

(b) in any other case, a market in the United Kingdom –

(i) for goods or services of a description specified in the reference concerned; and
(ii) which is not excluded from investigation by virtue of section 133(2).

(4) The Commission shall, if it has decided on a market investigation reference that there is an adverse effect on competition, decide the following additional questions –

(a) whether action should be taken by it under section 138 for the purpose of remedying, mitigating or preventing the adverse effect on competition concerned or any detrimental effect on customers so far as it has resulted from, or may be expected to result from, the adverse effect on competition;

(b) whether it should recommend the taking of action by others for the purpose of remedying, mitigating or preventing the adverse effect on competition concerned or any detrimental effect on customers so far as it has resulted from, or may be expected to result from, the adverse effect on competition; and

(c) in either case, if action should be taken, what action should be taken and what is to be remedied, mitigated or prevented.

(5) For the purposes of this Part, in relation to a market investigation reference, there is a detrimental effect on customers if there is a detrimental effect on customers or future customers in the form of –

(a) higher prices, lower quality or less choice of goods or services in any market in the United Kingdom (whether or not the market to which the feature or features concerned relate); or

(b) less innovation in relation to such goods or services.

(6) In deciding the questions mentioned in subsection (4), the Commission shall, in particular, have regard to the need to achieve as comprehensive a solution as is reasonable and practicable to the adverse effect on competition and any detrimental effects on customers so far as resulting from the adverse effect on competition.

(7) In deciding the questions mentioned in subsection (4), the Commission may, in particular, have regard to the effect of any action on any relevant customer benefits of the feature or features of the market concerned.

(8) For the purposes of this Part a benefit is a relevant customer benefit of a feature or features of a market if –

    (a) it is a benefit to customers or future customers in the form of –

        (i) lower prices, higher quality or greater choice of goods or services in any market in the United Kingdom (whether or not the market to which the feature or features concerned relate); or

        (ii) greater innovation in relation to such goods or services; and

    (b) the Commission, the Secretary of State or (as the case may be) the OFT believes that –

        (i) the benefit has accrued as a result (whether wholly or partly) of the feature or features concerned or may be expected to accrue within a reasonable period as a result (whether wholly or partly) of that feature or those features; and

        (ii) the benefit was, or is, unlikely to accrue without the feature or features concerned.

135 Variation of market investigation references

(1) The OFT or (as the case may be) the appropriate Minister may at any time vary a market investigation reference made by it or (as the case may be) him.

(2) The OFT or (as the case may be) the appropriate Minister shall consult the Commission before varying any such reference.

(3) Subsection (2) shall not apply if the Commission has requested the variation concerned.

(4) No variation under this section shall be capable of altering the period permitted by section 137 within which the report of the Commission under section 136 is to be prepared and published or (as the case may be) the period permitted by section 144 within which the report of the Commission under section 142 is to be prepared and published or given.

136 Investigations and reports on market investigation references

(1) The Commission shall prepare and publish a report on a market investigation reference within the period permitted by section 137.

(2) The report shall, in particular, contain –

    (a) the decisions of the Commission on the questions which it is required to answer by virtue of section 134;

    (b) its reasons for its decisions; and

    (c) such information as the Commission considers appropriate for facilitating a proper understanding of those questions and of its reasons for its decisions.

(3) The Commission shall carry out such investigations as it considers appropriate for the purposes of preparing a report under this section.

(4) The Commission shall, at the same time as a report under this section is published –

    (a) in the case of a reference under section 131, give it to the OFT; and

    (b) in the case of a reference under section 132, give it to the appropriate Minister and give a copy of it to the OFT.

(5) Where a reference has been made by the OFT under section 131 or by the appropriate Minister under section 132 in circumstances in which a reference could have been made by a relevant sectoral regulator under section 131 as it has effect by virtue of a relevant sectoral enactment, the Commission shall, at the same time as the report under this section is published, give a copy of it to the relevant sectoral regulator concerned.

(6) Where a reference has been made by a relevant sectoral regulator under section 131 as it has effect by virtue of a relevant sectoral enactment, the Commission shall, at the same time as the report under this section is published, give a copy of it to the OFT.

(7) In this Part 'relevant sectoral enactment' means –

(a) in relation to the Director General of Telecommunications, section 50 of the Telecommunications Act 1984 (c. 12);

(b) in relation to the Gas and Electricity Markets Authority, section 36A of the Gas Act 1986 (c. 44) or (as the case may be) section 43 of the Electricity Act 1989 (c. 29);

(c) in relation to the Director General of Water Services, section 31 of the Water Industry Act 1991 (c. 56);

(d) in relation to the Director General of Electricity Supply for Northern Ireland, article 46 of the Electricity (Northern Ireland) Order 1992 (S.I. 1992/231 (N.I. 1));

(e) in relation to the Rail Regulator, section 67 of the Railways Act 1993 (c. 43);

(f) in relation to the Director General of Gas for Northern Ireland, article 23 of the Gas (Northern Ireland) Order 1996 (S.I. 1996/275 (N.I. 2)); and

(g) in relation to the Civil Aviation Authority, section 86 of the Transport Act 2000 (c. 38).

(8) In this Part 'relevant sectoral regulator' means the Director General of Telecommunications, the Gas and Electricity Markets Authority, the Director General of Water Services, the Director General of Electricity Supply for Northern Ireland, the Rail Regulator, the Director General of Gas for Northern Ireland or the Civil Aviation Authority.

(9) The Secretary of State may by order modify subsection (7) or (8).

137 Time-limits for market investigations and reports

(1) The Commission shall prepare and publish its report under section 136 within the period of two years beginning with the date of the market investigation reference concerned.

(2) Subsection (1) is subject to section 151(3) and (5).

(3) The Secretary of State may by order amend subsection (1) so as to alter the period of two years mentioned in that subsection or any period for the time being mentioned in that subsection in substitution for that period.

(4) No alteration shall be made by virtue of subsection (3) which results in the period for the time being mentioned in subsection (1) exceeding two years.

(5) An order under subsection (3) shall not affect any period of time within which the Commission is under a duty to prepare and publish its report under section 136 in relation to a market investigation reference if the Commission is already under that duty in relation to that reference when the order is made.

(6) Before making an order under subsection (3) the Secretary of State shall consult the Commission and such other persons as he considers appropriate.

(7) References in this Part to the date of a market investigation reference shall be construed as references to the date specified in the reference as the date on which it is made.

138 Duty to remedy adverse effects

(1) Subsection (2) applies where a report of the Commission has been prepared and published under section 136 within the period permitted by section 137 and contains the decision that there is one or more than one adverse effect on competition.

(2) The Commission shall, in relation to each adverse effect on competition, take such action under section 159 or 161 as it considers to be reasonable and practicable –

(a) to remedy, mitigate or prevent the adverse effect on competition concerned; and

(b) to remedy, mitigate or prevent any detrimental effects on customers so far as they have resulted from, or may be expected to result from, the adverse effect on competition.

(3) The decisions of the Commission under subsection (2) shall be consistent with its decisions as included in its report by virtue of section 134(4) unless there has been a material change of circumstances since the preparation of the report or the Commission otherwise has a special reason for deciding differently.

(4) In making a decision under subsection (2), the Commission shall, in particular, have regard to the need to achieve as comprehensive a solution as is reasonable and practicable to the adverse effect on competition concerned and any detrimental effects on customers so far as resulting from the adverse effect on competition.

(5) In making a decision under subsection (2), the Commission may, in particular, have regard to the effect of any action on any relevant customer benefits of the feature or features of the market concerned.

(6) The Commission shall take no action under subsection (2) to remedy, mitigate or prevent any detrimental effect on customers so far as it may be expected to result from the adverse effect on competition concerned if –

(a) no detrimental effect on customers has resulted from the adverse effect on competition; and

(b) the adverse effect on competition is not being remedied, mitigated or prevented.

CHAPTER 2   PUBLIC INTEREST CASES

Intervention notices

139 Public interest intervention by Secretary of State

(1) The Secretary of State may give a notice to the Commission if –

(a) a market investigation reference has been made to the Commission;

(b) no more than four months has passed since the date of the reference;

(c) the reference is not finally determined; and

(d) the Secretary of State believes that it is or may be the case that one or more than one public interest consideration is relevant to the case.

(2) The Secretary of State may give a notice to the OFT if –

(a) the OFT is considering whether to accept –

(i) an undertaking under section 154 instead of making a reference under section 131; or

(ii) an undertaking varying or superseding any such undertaking;

(b) the OFT has published a notice under section 155(1) or (4); and

(c) the Secretary of State believes that it is or may be the case that one or more than one public interest consideration is relevant to the case.

(3) In this Part 'intervention notice' means a notice under subsection (1) or (2).

(4) No more than one intervention notice shall be given under subsection (1) in relation to the same market investigation reference and no more than one intervention notice shall be given under subsection (2) in relation to the same proposed undertaking or in relation to proposed undertakings which do not differ from each other in any material respect.

(5) For the purposes of this Part a public interest consideration is a consideration which, at the time of the giving of the intervention notice concerned, is specified in section 153 or is not so specified but, in the opinion of the Secretary of State, ought to be so specified.

(6) Where the Secretary of State has given an intervention notice mentioning a public interest consideration which, at that time, is not finalised, he shall, as soon as practicable, take such action as is within his power to ensure that it is finalised.

(7) For the purposes of this Part a public interest consideration is finalised if –

    (a) it is specified in section 153 otherwise than by virtue of an order under subsection (3) of that section; or

    (b) it is specified in that section by virtue of an order under subsection (3) of that section and the order providing for it to be so specified has been laid before, and approved by, Parliament in accordance with subsection (6) of section 181 and within the period mentioned in that subsection.

Intervention notices under section 139(1)

140 Intervention notices under section 139(1)

(1) An intervention notice under section 139(1) shall state –

    (a) the market investigation reference concerned;

    (b) the date of the market investigation reference concerned;

    (c) the public interest consideration or considerations which are, or may be, relevant to the case; and

    (d) where any public interest consideration concerned is not finalised, the proposed timetable for finalising it.

(2) Where the Secretary of State believes that it is or may be the case that two or more public interest considerations are relevant to the case, he may decide not to mention in the intervention notice such of those considerations as he considers appropriate.

(3) The Secretary of State may at any time revoke an intervention notice which has been given under section 139(1) and which is in force.

(4) An intervention notice under section 139(1) shall come into force when it is given and shall cease to be in force when the matter to which it relates is finally determined under this Chapter.

(5) For the purposes of subsection (4) a matter to which an intervention notice under section 139(1) relates is finally determined under this Chapter if –

    (a) the period permitted by section 144 for the preparation of the report of the Commission under section 142 and for action to be taken in relation to it under section 143(1) or (3) has expired and no such report has been so prepared or no such action has been taken;

    (b) the Commission decides under section 145(1) to terminate its investigation;

    (c) the report of the Commission has been prepared under section 142 and published under section 143(1) within the period permitted by section 144;

    (d) the Secretary of State fails to make and publish a decision under subsection (2) of section 146 within the period required by subsection (3) of that section;

    (e) the Secretary of State decides under section 146(2) that no eligible public interest consideration is relevant;

    (f) the Secretary of State decides under section 147(2) neither to accept an undertaking under section 159 nor to make an order under section 161;

    (g) the Secretary of State accepts an undertaking under section 159 or makes an order under section 161; or

    (h) the Secretary of State decides to revoke the intervention notice concerned.

(6) For the purposes of subsections (4) and (5) the time when a matter to which an intervention notice under section 139(1) relates is finally determined under this Chapter is –

    (a) in a case falling within subsection (5)(a) or (d), the expiry of the period concerned;

    (b) in a case falling within subsection (5)(b), (e), (f) or (h), the making of the decision concerned;

    (c) in a case falling within subsection (5)(c), the publication of the report concerned; and

(d) in a case falling within subsection (5)(g), the acceptance of the undertaking concerned or (as the case may be) the making of the order concerned.

(7) In subsection (6)(d) the reference to the acceptance of the undertaking concerned or the making of the order concerned shall, in a case where the enforcement action under section 147(2) involves the acceptance of a group of undertakings, the making of a group of orders or the acceptance and making of a group of undertakings and orders, be treated as a reference to the acceptance or making of the last undertaking or order in the group; but undertakings or orders which vary, supersede or revoke earlier undertakings or orders shall be disregarded for the purposes of subsections (5)(g) and (6)(d).

141 Questions to be decided by Commission

(1) This section applies where an intervention notice under section 139(1) is in force in relation to a market investigation reference.

(2) The Commission shall decide whether any feature, or combination of features, of each relevant market (within the meaning given by section 134(3)) prevents, restricts or distorts competition in connection with the supply or acquisition of any goods or services in the United Kingdom or a part of the United Kingdom.

(3) The Commission shall, if it has decided that there is an adverse effect on competition, decide the following additional questions –

(a) whether action should be taken by the Secretary of State under section 147 for the purpose of remedying, mitigating or preventing the adverse effect on competition concerned or any detrimental effect on customers so far as it has resulted from, or may be expected to result from, the adverse effect on competition;

(b) whether the Commission should recommend the taking of other action by the Secretary of State or action by persons other than itself and the Secretary of State for the purpose of remedying, mitigating or preventing the adverse effect on competition concerned or any detrimental effect on customers so far as it has resulted from, or may be expected to result from, the adverse effect on competition; and

(c) in either case, if action should be taken, what action should be taken and what is to be remedied, mitigated or prevented.

(4) The Commission shall, if it has decided that there is an adverse effect on competition, also decide separately the following questions (on the assumption that it is proceeding as mentioned in section 148(1)) –

(a) whether action should be taken by it under section 138 for the purpose of remedying, mitigating or preventing the adverse effect on competition concerned or any detrimental effect on customers so far as it has resulted from, or may be expected to result from, the adverse effect on competition;

(b) whether the Commission should recommend the taking of action by other persons for the purpose of remedying, mitigating or preventing the adverse effect on competition concerned or any detrimental effect on customers so far as it has resulted from, or may be expected to result from, the adverse effect on competition; and

(c) in either case, if action should be taken, what action should be taken and what is to be remedied, mitigated or prevented.

(5) In deciding the questions mentioned in subsections (3) and (4), the Commission shall, in particular, have regard to the need to achieve as comprehensive a solution as is reasonable and practicable to the adverse effect on competition concerned and any detrimental effects on customers so far as resulting from the adverse effect on competition.

(6) In deciding the questions mentioned in subsections (3) and (4), the Commission may, in particular, have regard to the effect of any action on any relevant customer benefits of the feature or features of the market concerned.

142 Investigations and reports by Commission

(1) Where an intervention notice under section 139(1) is in force in relation to a market investigation reference, the Commission shall prepare a report on the reference and take action in relation to it under section 143(1) or (3) within the period permitted by section 144.

(2) The report shall, in particular, contain –

    (a) the decisions of the Commission on the questions which it is required to answer by virtue of section 141;

    (b) its reasons for its decisions; and

    (c) such information as the Commission considers appropriate for facilitating a proper understanding of those questions and of its reasons for its decisions.

(3) The Commission shall carry out such investigations as it considers appropriate for the purposes of preparing a report under this section.

143 Publication etc. of reports of Commission

(1) The Commission shall publish a report under section 142 if it contains –

    (a) the decision of the Commission that there is no adverse effect on competition; or

    (b) the decisions of the Commission that there is one or more than one adverse effect on competition but, on the question mentioned in section 141(4)(a) and in relation to each adverse effect on competition, that no action should be taken by it.

(2) The Commission shall, at the same time as the report is published under subsection (1) –

    (a) in the case of a reference under section 131, give it to the OFT; and

    (b) in the case of a reference under section 132, give it to the appropriate Minister and give a copy of it to the OFT.

(3) Where a report under section 142 contains the decisions of the Commission that there is one or more than one adverse effect on competition and, on the question mentioned in section 141(4)(a) and in relation to at least one such adverse effect, that action should be taken by it, the Commission shall give the report to the Secretary of State.

(4) The Secretary of State shall publish, no later than publication of his decision under section 146(2) in relation to the case, a report of the Commission given to him under subsection (3) and not required to be published by virtue of section 148(2).

(5) The Secretary of State shall, at the same time as a report of the Commission given to him under subsection (3) is published under subsection (4), give a copy of it –

    (a) in the case of a reference under section 131, to the OFT; and

    (b) in the case of a reference under section 132, to any other Minister of the Crown who made the reference and to the OFT.

(6) Where a reference has been made by the OFT under section 131 or by the appropriate Minister under section 132 in circumstances in which a reference could have been made by a relevant sectoral regulator under section 131 as it has effect by virtue of a relevant sectoral enactment, the relevant authority shall, at the same time as the report under section 142 is published under subsection (1) or (4), give a copy of it to the relevant sectoral regulator concerned.

(7) Where a reference has been made by a relevant sectoral regulator under section 131 as it has effect by virtue of a relevant sectoral enactment, the relevant authority shall, at the same time as the report under section 142 is published under subsection (1) or (4), give a copy of it to the OFT.

(8) In subsections (6) and (7) 'the relevant authority' means –

    (a) in the case of a report published under subsection (1), the Commission; and

    (b) in the case of a report published under subsection (4), the Secretary of State.

144 Time-limits for investigations and reports: Part 4

(1) The Commission shall, within the period of two years beginning with the date of the reference, prepare its report under section 142 and publish it under subsection (1) of section 143 or (as the case may be) give it to the Secretary of State under subsection (3) of that section.

(2) The Secretary of State may by order amend subsection (1) so as to alter the period of two years mentioned in that subsection or any period for the time being mentioned in that subsection in substitution for that period.

(3) No alteration shall be made by virtue of subsection (2) which results in the period for the time being mentioned in subsection (1) exceeding two years.

(4) An order under subsection (2) shall not affect any period of time within which, in relation to a market investigation reference, the Commission is under a duty to prepare its report under section 142 and take action in relation to it under section 143(1) or (3) if the Commission is already under that duty in relation to that reference when the order is made.

(5) Before making an order under subsection (2) the Secretary of State shall consult the Commission and such other persons as he considers appropriate.

145 Restrictions where public interest considerations not finalised: Part 4

(1) The Commission shall terminate its investigation under section 142 if –

    (a) the intervention notice concerned mentions a public interest consideration which was not finalised on the giving of that notice or public interest considerations which, at that time, were not finalised;

    (b) no other public interest consideration is mentioned in the notice;

    (c) at least 24 weeks has elapsed since the giving of the notice; and

    (d) the public interest consideration mentioned in the notice has not been finalised within that period of 24 weeks or (as the case may be) none of the public interest considerations mentioned in the notice has been finalised within that period of 24 weeks.

(2) Where the intervention notice concerned mentions a public interest consideration which is not finalised on the giving of the notice, the Commission shall not give its report under section 142 to the Secretary of State in accordance with section 143(3) unless the period of 24 weeks beginning with the giving of the intervention notice concerned has expired or the public interest consideration concerned has been finalised.

(3) The Commission shall, in reporting on any of the questions mentioned in section 141(3), disregard any public interest consideration which has not been finalised before the giving of the report.

(4) The Commission shall, in reporting on any of the questions mentioned in section 141(3), disregard any public interest consideration which was not finalised on the giving of the intervention notice concerned and has not been finalised within the period of 24 weeks beginning with the giving of the notice concerned.

(5) Subsections (1) to (4) are without prejudice to the power of the Commission to carry out investigations in relation to any public interest consideration to which it might be able to have regard in its report.

146 Decision of Secretary of State

(1) Subsection (2) applies where the Secretary of State has received a report of the Commission which –

    (a) has been prepared under section 142;

    (b) contains the decisions that there is one or more than one adverse effect on competition and, on the question mentioned in section 141(4)(a) and in relation to at least one such adverse effect, that action should be taken by it; and

    (c) has been given to the Secretary of State as required by section 143(3).

(2) The Secretary of State shall decide whether –

   (a) any eligible public interest consideration is relevant; or
   (b) any eligible public interest considerations are relevant;

   to any action which is mentioned in the report by virtue of section 141(4)(a) and (c) and which the Commission should take for the purpose of remedying, mitigating or preventing any adverse effect on competition concerned or any detrimental effect on customers so far as it has resulted or may be expected to result from any adverse effect on competition.

(3) The Secretary of State shall make and publish his decision under subsection (2) within the period of 90 days beginning with the receipt of the report of the Commission under section 142.

(4) In this section 'eligible public interest consideration' means a public interest consideration which –

   (a) was mentioned in the intervention notice concerned; and
   (b) was not disregarded by the Commission for the purposes of its report under section 142.

147 Remedial action by Secretary of State

(1) Subsection (2) applies where the Secretary of State –

   (a) has decided under subsection (2) of section 146 within the period required by subsection (3) of that section that an eligible public interest consideration is relevant as mentioned in subsection (2) of that section or eligible public interest considerations are so relevant; and
   (b) has published his decision within the period required by subsection (3) of that section.

(2) The Secretary of State may, in relation to any adverse effect on competition identified in the report concerned, take such action under section 159 or 161 as he considers to be –

   (a) reasonable and practicable –

      (i)   to remedy, mitigate or prevent the adverse effect on competition concerned; or
      (ii) to remedy, mitigate or prevent any detrimental effect on customers so far as it has resulted from, or may be expected to result from, the adverse effect on competition; and

   (b) appropriate in the light of the eligible public interest consideration concerned or (as the case may be) the eligible public interest considerations concerned.

(3) In making a decision under subsection (2), the Secretary of State shall, in particular, have regard to –

   (a) the need to achieve as comprehensive a solution as is reasonable and practicable to the adverse effect on competition concerned and any detrimental effects on customers so far as resulting from the adverse effect on competition; and
   (b) the report of the Commission under section 142.

(4) In having regard by virtue of subsection (3) to the report of the Commission under section 142, the Secretary of State shall not challenge the decision of the Commission contained in the report that there is one or more than one adverse effect on competition.

(5) In making a decision under subsection (2), the Secretary of State may, in particular, have regard to the effect of any action on any relevant customer benefits of the feature or features of the market concerned.

(6) The Secretary of State shall take no action under subsection (2) to remedy, mitigate or prevent any detrimental effect on customers so far as it may be expected to result from the adverse effect on competition concerned if –

   (a) no detrimental effect on customers has resulted from the adverse effect on competition; and
   (b) the adverse effect on competition is not being remedied, mitigated or prevented.

(7) In this section 'eligible public interest consideration' has the same meaning as in section 146.

148 Reversion of the matter to the Commission

(1) If –

  (a) the Secretary of State fails to make and publish his decision under subsection (2) of section 146 within the period required by subsection (3) of that section; or
  (b) the Secretary of State decides that no eligible public interest consideration is relevant as mentioned in subsection (2) of that section;

  the Commission shall proceed under section 138 as if the report had been prepared and published under section 136 within the period permitted by section 137.

(2) The Commission shall publish the report which has been prepared by it under section 142 (if still unpublished) as soon as it becomes able to proceed by virtue of subsection (1).

(3) The Commission shall, at the same time as its report is published under subsection (2), give a copy of it –

  (a) in the case of a reference under section 131, to the OFT; and
  (b) in the case of a reference under section 132, to any Minister of the Crown who made the reference (other than the Secretary of State) and to the OFT.

(4) Where a reference has been made by the OFT under section 131 or by the appropriate Minister under section 132 in circumstances in which a reference could have been made by a relevant sectoral regulator under section 131 as it has effect by virtue of a relevant sectoral enactment, the Commission shall, at the same time as its report is published under subsection (2), give a copy of it to the relevant sectoral regulator concerned.

(5) Where a reference has been made by a relevant sectoral regulator under section 131 as it has effect by virtue of a relevant sectoral enactment, the Commission shall, at the same time as its report is published under subsection (2), give a copy of it to the OFT.

(6) In relation to proceedings by virtue of subsection (1), the reference in section 138(3) to decisions of the Commission included in its report by virtue of section 134(4) shall be construed as a reference to decisions which were included in the report of the Commission by virtue of section 141(4).

(7) Where the Commission, in proceeding by virtue of subsection (1), intends to proceed in a way which is not consistent with its decisions as included in its report by virtue of section 141(4), it shall not so proceed without the consent of the Secretary of State.

(8) The Secretary of State shall not withhold his consent under subsection (7) unless he believes that the proposed alternative way of proceeding will operate against the public interest.

(9) For the purposes of subsection (8) a proposed alternative way of proceeding will operate against the public interest only if any eligible public interest consideration or considerations outweigh the considerations which have led the Commission to propose proceeding in that way.

(10) In deciding whether to withhold his consent under subsection (7), the Secretary of State shall accept the Commission's view of what, if the only relevant consideration were how to remedy, mitigate or prevent the adverse effect on competition concerned or any detrimental effect on customers so far as resulting from the adverse effect on competition, would be the most appropriate way to proceed.

(11) In this section 'eligible public interest consideration' has the same meaning as in section 146.

Intervention notices under section 139(2)

149 Intervention notices under section 139(2)

(1) An intervention notice under section 139(2) shall state –

    (a) the proposed undertaking which may be accepted by the OFT;

    (b) the notice under section 155(1) or (4);

    (c) the public interest consideration or considerations which are, or may be, relevant to the case; and

    (d) where any public interest consideration concerned is not finalised, the proposed timetable for finalising it.

(2) Where the Secretary of State believes that it is or may be the case that two or more public interest considerations are relevant to the case, he may decide not to mention in the intervention notice such of those considerations as he considers appropriate.

(3) The Secretary of State may at any time revoke an intervention notice which has been given under section 139(2) and which is in force.

(4) An intervention notice under section 139(2) shall come into force when it is given and shall cease to be in force on the occurrence of any of the events mentioned in subsection (5).

(5) The events are –

    (a) the acceptance by the OFT with the consent of the Secretary of State of an undertaking which is the same as the proposed undertaking mentioned in the intervention notice by virtue of subsection (1)(a) or which does not differ from it in any material respect;

    (b) the decision of the OFT to proceed neither with the proposed undertaking mentioned in the intervention notice by virtue of subsection (1)(a) nor a proposed undertaking which does not differ from it in any material respect; or

    (c) the decision of the Secretary of State to revoke the intervention notice concerned.

150 Power of veto of Secretary of State

(1) Where an intervention notice under section 139(2) is in force, the OFT shall not, without the consent of the Secretary of State, accept the proposed undertaking concerned or a proposed undertaking which does not differ from it in any material respect.

(2) The Secretary of State shall withhold his consent if he believes that it is or may be the case that the proposed undertaking will, if accepted, operate against the public interest.

(3) For the purposes of subsection (2) a proposed undertaking will, if accepted, operate against the public interest only if any public interest consideration which is mentioned in the intervention notice concerned and has been finalised, or any public interest considerations which are so mentioned and have been finalised, outweigh the considerations which have led the OFT to propose accepting the undertaking.

(4) In making his decision under subsection (2) the Secretary of State shall accept the OFT's view of what undertakings, if the only relevant consideration were how to remedy, mitigate or prevent the adverse effect on competition concerned or any detrimental effect on customers so far as resulting from the adverse effect on competition, would be most appropriate.

(5) Where a public interest consideration which is mentioned in the intervention notice concerned is not finalised on the giving of the notice, the Secretary of State shall not make his decision as to whether to give his consent under this section before –

    (a) the end of the period of 24 weeks beginning with the giving of the intervention notice; or

    (b) if earlier, the date on which the public interest consideration concerned has been finalised.

(6) Subject to subsections (2) to (5), the Secretary of State shall not withhold his consent under this section.

Other

151 Further interaction of intervention notices with general procedure

(1) Where an intervention notice under section 139(1) comes into force in relation to a market investigation reference, sections 134(1), (4), (6) and (7), 136(1) to (6), 137(1) to (6) and 138 shall cease to apply in relation to that reference.

(2) Where the Secretary of State revokes an intervention notice which has been given under section 139(1), the Commission shall instead proceed under sections 134 and 136 to 138.

(3) Where the Commission is proceeding by virtue of subsection (2), the period within which the Commission shall prepare and publish its report under section 136 shall be extended by an additional period of 20 days.

(4) Where the Commission terminates its investigation under section 145(1), the Commission shall proceed under sections 134 and 136 to 138.

(5) Where the Commission is proceeding by virtue of subsection (4), the period within which the Commission shall prepare and publish its report under section 136 shall be extended by an additional period of 20 days.

(6) In determining the period of 20 days mentioned in subsection (3) or (5) no account shall be taken of –

(a) Saturday, Sunday, Good Friday and Christmas Day; and
(b) any day which is a bank holiday in England and Wales.

152 Certain duties of OFT and Commission

(1) The OFT shall, in considering whether to make a reference under section 131, bring to the attention of the Secretary of State any case which it believes raises any consideration specified in section 153 unless it believes that the Secretary of State would consider any such consideration immaterial in the context of the particular case.

(2) The Commission shall, in investigating any reference made to it under section 131 or 132 within the previous four months, bring to the attention of the Secretary of State any case which it believes raises any consideration specified in section 153 unless it believes that the Secretary of State would consider any such consideration immaterial in the context of the particular case.

(3) The OFT and the Commission shall bring to the attention of the Secretary of State any representations about exercising his power under section 153(3) which have been made to the OFT or (as the case may be) the Commission.

153 Specified considerations: Part 4

(1) The interests of national security are specified in this section.

(2) In subsection (1) 'national security' includes public security; and in this subsection 'public security' has the same meaning as in article 21(3) of Council Regulation (EEC) No. 4064/89 of 21st December 1989 on the control of concentrations between undertakings as amended by Council Regulation (EC) No. 1310/97 of 30th June 1997.

(3) The Secretary of State may by order modify this section for the purpose of specifying in this section a new consideration or removing or amending any consideration which is for the time being specified in this section.

(4) An order under this section may apply in relation to cases under consideration by the OFT, by the Secretary of State, by the appropriate Minister (other than the Secretary of State acting alone) or by the Commission before the making of the order as well as cases under consideration on or after the making of the order.

CHAPTER 3 ENFORCEMENT

Undertakings and orders

154 Undertakings in lieu of market investigation references

(1) Subsection (2) applies if the OFT considers that it has the power to make a reference under section 131 and otherwise intends to make such a reference.

(2) The OFT may, instead of making such a reference and for the purpose of remedying, mitigating or preventing –

 (a) any adverse effect on competition concerned; or
 (b) any detrimental effect on customers so far as it has resulted from, or may be expected to result from, the adverse effect on competition;

 accept, from such persons as it considers appropriate, undertakings to take such action as it considers appropriate.

(3) In proceeding under subsection (2), the OFT shall, in particular, have regard to the need to achieve as comprehensive a solution as is reasonable and practicable to the adverse effect on competition concerned and any detrimental effects on customers so far as resulting from the adverse effect on competition.

(4) In proceeding under subsection (2), the OFT may, in particular, have regard to the effect of any action on any relevant customer benefits of the feature or features of the market concerned.

(5) The OFT shall take no action under subsection (2) to remedy, mitigate or prevent any detrimental effect on customers so far as it may be expected to result from the adverse effect on competition concerned if –

 (a) no detrimental effect on customers has resulted from the adverse effect on competition; and
 (b) the adverse effect on competition is not being remedied, mitigated or prevented.

(6) An undertaking under this section –

 (a) shall come into force when accepted;
 (b) may be varied or superseded by another undertaking; and
 (c) may be released by the OFT.

(7) The OFT shall, as soon as reasonably practicable, consider any representations received by it in relation to varying or releasing an undertaking under this section.

(8) This section is subject to sections 150 and 155.

155 Undertakings in lieu: procedural requirements

(1) Before accepting an undertaking under section 154 (other than an undertaking under that section which varies an undertaking under that section but not in any material respect), the OFT shall –

 (a) publish notice of the proposed undertaking; and
 (b) consider any representations made in accordance with the notice and not withdrawn.

(2) A notice under subsection (1) shall state –

 (a) that the OFT proposes to accept the undertaking;
 (b) the purpose and effect of the undertaking;
 (c) the situation that the undertaking is seeking to deal with;
 (d) any other facts which the OFT considers justify the acceptance of the undertaking;
 (e) a means of gaining access to an accurate version of the proposed undertaking at all reasonable times; and
 (f) the period (not less than 15 days starting with the date of publication of the notice) within which representations may be made in relation to the proposed undertaking.

(3) The matters to be included in a notice under subsection (1) by virtue of subsection (2) shall, in particular, include –

 (a) the terms of the reference under section 131 which the OFT considers that it has power to make and which it otherwise intends to make; and
 (b) the adverse effect on competition, and any detrimental effect on customers so far as resulting from the adverse effect on competition, which the OFT has identified.

(4) The OFT shall not accept the undertaking with modifications unless it –

 (a) publishes notice of the proposed modifications; and
 (b) considers any representations made in accordance with the notice and not withdrawn.

(5) A notice under subsection (4) shall state –

 (a) the proposed modifications;
 (b) the reasons for them; and
 (c) the period (not less than 7 days starting with the date of the publication of the notice under subsection (4)) within which representations may be made in relation to the proposed modifications.

(6) If, after publishing notice under subsection (1) or (4), the OFT decides –

 (a) not to accept the undertaking concerned; and
 (b) not to proceed by virtue of subsection (8) or (9);

 it shall publish notice of that decision.

(7) As soon as practicable after accepting an undertaking to which this section applies, the OFT shall –

 (a) serve a copy of the undertaking on any person by whom it is given; and
 (b) publish the undertaking.

(8) The requirements of subsection (4) (and those of subsection (1)) shall not apply if the OFT –

 (a) has already published notice under subsection (1) but not subsection (4) in relation to the proposed undertaking; and
 (b) considers that the modifications which are now being proposed are not material in any respect.

(9) The requirements of subsection (4) (and those of subsection (1)) shall not apply if the OFT –

 (a) has already published notice under subsections (1) and (4) in relation to the matter concerned; and
 (b) considers that the further modifications which are now being proposed do not differ in any material respect from the modifications in relation to which notice was last given under subsection (4).

(10) Paragraphs 6 to 8 (but not paragraph 9) of Schedule 10 (procedural requirements before terminating undertakings) shall apply in relation to the proposed release of undertakings under section 154 (other than in connection with accepting an undertaking under that section which varies or supersedes an undertaking under that section) as they apply in relation to the proposed release of undertakings under section 73.

156 Effect of undertakings under section 154

(1) No market investigation reference shall be made by the OFT or the appropriate Minister in relation to any feature, or combination of features, of a market in the United Kingdom for goods or services if –

 (a) the OFT has accepted an undertaking or group of undertakings under section 154 within the previous 12 months; and

(b) the goods or services to which the undertaking or group of undertakings relates are of the same description as the goods or services to which the feature, or combination of features, relates.

(2) Subsection (1) does not prevent the making of a market investigation reference if –

(a) the OFT considers that any undertaking concerned has been breached and has given notice of that fact to the person responsible for giving the undertaking; or

(b) the person responsible for giving any undertaking concerned supplied, in connection with the matter, information to the OFT which was false or misleading in a material respect.

157 Interim undertakings: Part 4

(1) Subsection (2) applies where –

(a) a market investigation reference has been made;

(b) a report has been published under section 136 within the period permitted by section 137 or (as the case may be) a report prepared under section 142 and given to the Secretary of State under section 143(3) within the period permitted by section 144 has been published; and

(c) the market investigation reference concerned is not finally determined.

(2) The relevant authority may, for the purpose of preventing pre-emptive action, accept, from such persons as the relevant authority considers appropriate, undertakings to take such action as the relevant authority considers appropriate.

(3) An undertaking under this section –

(a) shall come into force when accepted;

(b) may be varied or superseded by another undertaking; and

(c) may be released by the relevant authority.

(4) An undertaking under this section shall, if it has not previously ceased to be in force, cease to be in force when the market investigation reference is finally determined.

(5) The relevant authority shall, as soon as reasonably practicable, consider any representations received by the relevant authority in relation to varying or releasing an undertaking under this section.

(6) In this section and section 158 –

'pre-emptive action' means action which might impede the taking of any action under section 138(2) or (as the case may be) 147(2) in relation to the market investigation reference concerned; and

'the relevant authority' means –

(a) where an intervention notice is in force in relation to the market investigation reference, the Secretary of State;

(b) in any other case, the Commission.

158 Interim orders: Part 4

(1) Subsection (2) applies where –

(a) a market investigation reference has been made;

(b) a report has been published under section 136 within the period permitted by section 137 or (as the case may be) a report prepared under section 142 and given to the Secretary of State under section 143(3) within the period permitted by section 144 has been published; and

(c) the market investigation reference concerned is not finally determined.

(2) The relevant authority may by order, for the purpose of preventing pre-emptive action –

(a) prohibit or restrict the doing of things which the relevant authority considers would constitute pre-emptive action;

(b) impose on any person concerned obligations as to the carrying on of any
activities or the safeguarding of any assets;

(c) provide for the carrying on of any activities or the safeguarding of any assets
either by the appointment of a person to conduct or supervise the conduct of any
activities (on such terms and with such powers as may be specified or described
in the order) or in any other manner;

(d) do anything which may be done by virtue of paragraph 19 of Schedule 8.

(3) An order under this section –

(a) shall come into force at such time as is determined by or under the order; and

(b) may be varied or revoked by another order.

(4) An order under this section shall, if it has not previously ceased to be in force, cease
to be in force when the market investigation reference is finally determined.

(5) The relevant authority shall, as soon as reasonably practicable, consider any representations received by the relevant authority in relation to varying or revoking an
order under this section.

159 Final undertakings: Part 4

(1) The Commission may, in accordance with section 138, accept, from such persons as
it considers appropriate, undertakings to take action specified or described in the
undertakings.

(2) The Secretary of State may, in accordance with section 147, accept, from such persons
as he considers appropriate, undertakings to take action specified or described in the
undertakings.

(3) An undertaking under this section shall come into force when accepted.

(4) An undertaking under subsection (1) or (2) may be varied or superseded by another
undertaking under that subsection.

(5) An undertaking under subsection (1) may be released by the Commission and an
undertaking under subsection (2) may be released by the Secretary of State.

(6) The Commission or (as the case may be) the Secretary of State shall, as soon as reasonably practicable, consider any representations received by it or (as the case may
be) him in relation to varying or releasing an undertaking under this section.

160 Order-making power where final undertakings not fulfilled: Part 4

(1) Subsection (2) applies where the relevant authority considers that –

(a) an undertaking accepted by the relevant authority under section 159 has not
been, is not being or will not be fulfilled; or

(b) in relation to an undertaking accepted by the relevant authority under that section, information which was false or misleading in a material respect was given
to the relevant authority or the OFT by the person giving the undertaking before
the relevant authority decided to accept the undertaking.

(2) The relevant authority may, for any of the purposes mentioned in section 138(2) or
(as the case may be) 147(2), make an order under this section.

(3) Subsections (3) to (6) of section 138 or (as the case may be) 147 shall apply for the
purposes of subsection (2) above as they apply for the purposes of that section.

(4) An order under this section may contain –

(a) anything permitted by Schedule 8; and

(b) such supplementary, consequential or incidental provision as the relevant
authority considers appropriate.

(5) An order under this section –

(a) shall come into force at such time as is determined by or under the order;

(b) may contain provision which is different from the provision contained in the
undertaking concerned; and

(c) may be varied or revoked by another order.

(6) No order shall be varied or revoked under this section unless the OFT advises that such a variation or revocation is appropriate by reason of a change of circumstances.

(7) In this section 'the relevant authority' means –

    (a) in the case of an undertaking accepted under section 159 by the Commission, the Commission; and

    (b) in the case of an undertaking accepted under that section by the Secretary of State, the Secretary of State.

161 Final orders: Part 4

(1) The Commission may, in accordance with section 138, make an order under this section.

(2) The Secretary of State may, in accordance with section 147, make an order under this section.

(3) An order under this section may contain –

    (a) anything permitted by Schedule 8; and

    (b) such supplementary, consequential or incidental provision as the person making it considers appropriate.

(4) An order under this section –

    (a) shall come into force at such time as is determined by or under the order; and

    (b) may be varied or revoked by another order.

(5) No order shall be varied or revoked under this section unless the OFT advises that such a variation or revocation is appropriate by reason of a change of circumstances.

Enforcement functions of OFT

162 Duty of OFT to monitor undertakings and orders: Part 4

(1) The OFT shall keep under review the carrying out of any enforcement undertaking or any enforcement order.

(2) The OFT shall, in particular, from time to time consider –

    (a) whether an enforcement undertaking or enforcement order has been or is being complied with;

    (b) whether, by reason of any change of circumstances, an enforcement undertaking is no longer appropriate and –

        (i) one or more of the parties to it can be released from it; or

        (ii) it needs to be varied or to be superseded by a new enforcement undertaking; and

    (c) whether, by reason of any change of circumstances, an enforcement order is no longer appropriate and needs to be varied or revoked.

(3) The OFT shall give the Commission or (as the case may be) the Secretary of State such advice as it considers appropriate in relation to –

    (a) any possible variation or release by the Commission or (as the case may be) the Secretary of State of an enforcement undertaking accepted by it or (as the case may be) him;

    (b) any possible new enforcement undertaking to be accepted by the Commission or (as the case may be) the Secretary of State so as to supersede another enforcement undertaking given to the Commission or (as the case may be) the Secretary of State;

    (c) any possible variation or revocation by the Commission or (as the case may be) the Secretary of State of an enforcement order made by the Commission or (as the case may be) the Secretary of State;

(d) any possible enforcement undertaking to be accepted by the Commission or (as the case may be) the Secretary of State instead of an enforcement order or any possible enforcement order to be made by the Commission or (as the case may be) the Secretary of State instead of an enforcement undertaking; or

(e) the enforcement by virtue of section 167(6) to (8) of any enforcement undertaking or enforcement order.

(4) The OFT shall take such action as it considers appropriate in relation to –

(a) any possible variation or release by it of an undertaking accepted by it under section 154;

(b) any possible new undertaking to be accepted by it under section 154 so as to supersede another undertaking given to it under that section; or

(c) the enforcement by it by virtue of section 167(6) of any enforcement undertaking or enforcement order.

(5) The OFT shall keep under review the effectiveness of enforcement undertakings accepted under this Part and enforcement orders made under this Part.

(6) The OFT shall, whenever requested to do so by the Secretary of State and otherwise from time to time, prepare a report of its findings under subsection (5).

(7) The OFT shall –

(a) give any report prepared by it under subsection (6) to the Commission;

(b) give a copy of the report to the Secretary of State; and

(c) publish the report.

(8) In this Part –

'enforcement order' means an order made under section 158, 160 or 161; and

'enforcement undertaking' means an undertaking accepted under section 154, 157 or 159.

163 Further role of OFT in relation to undertakings and orders: Part 4

(1) Subsections (2) and (3) apply where the Commission or the Secretary of State (in this section 'the relevant authority') is considering whether to accept undertakings under section 157 or 159.

(2) The relevant authority may require the OFT to consult with such persons as the relevant authority considers appropriate with a view to discovering whether they will offer undertakings which the relevant authority would be prepared to accept under section 157 or (as the case may be) 159.

(3) The relevant authority may require the OFT to report to the relevant authority on the outcome of the OFT's consultations within such period as the relevant authority may require.

(4) A report under subsection (3) shall, in particular, contain advice from the OFT as to whether any undertakings offered should be accepted by the relevant authority under section 157 or (as the case may be) 159.

(5) The powers conferred on the relevant authority by subsections (1) to (4) are without prejudice to the power of the relevant authority to consult the persons concerned itself.

(6) If asked by the relevant authority for advice in relation to the taking of enforcement action (whether or not by way of undertakings) in a particular case, the OFT shall give such advice as it considers appropriate.

Supplementary

164 Enforcement undertakings and orders under this Part: general provisions

(1) The provision which may be contained in an enforcement undertaking is not limited to the provision which is permitted by Schedule 8.

(2) The following enactments in Part 3 shall apply in relation to enforcement orders under this Part as they apply in relation to enforcement orders under that Part –

    (a) section 86(1) to (5) (enforcement orders: general provisions); and

    (b) section 87 (power of directions conferred by enforcement order).

(3) An enforcement order under section 160 or 161 or any explanatory material accompanying the order shall state –

    (a) the actions that the persons or description of persons to whom the order is addressed must do or (as the case may be) refrain from doing;

    (b) the date on which the order comes into force;

    (c) the possible consequences of not complying with the order; and

    (d) the section of this Part under which a review can be sought in relation to the order.

165 Procedural requirements for certain undertakings and orders: Part 4

Schedule 10 (procedural requirements for certain undertakings and orders), other than paragraph 9 of that Schedule, shall apply in relation to undertakings under section 159 and orders under section 160 or 161 as it applies in relation to undertakings under section 82 and orders under section 83 or 84.

166 Register of undertakings and orders: Part 4

(1) The OFT shall compile and maintain a register for the purposes of this Part.

(2) The register shall be kept in such form as the OFT considers appropriate.

(3) The OFT shall ensure that the following matters are entered in the register –

    (a) the provisions of any enforcement undertaking accepted by virtue of this Part (whether by the OFT, the Commission, the Secretary of State or a relevant sectoral regulator);

    (b) the provisions of any enforcement order made by virtue of this Part (whether by the Commission, the Secretary of State or a relevant sectoral regulator); and

    (c) the details of any variation, release or revocation of such an undertaking or order.

(4) The duty in subsection (3) does not extend to anything of which the OFT is unaware.

(5) The Commission, the Secretary of State and any relevant sectoral regulator shall inform the OFT of any matters which are to be included in the register by virtue of subsection (3) and which relate to enforcement undertakings accepted by them or enforcement orders made by them.

(6) The OFT shall ensure that the contents of the register are available to the public –

    (a) during (as a minimum) such hours as may be specified in an order made by the Secretary of State; and

    (b) subject to such reasonable fees (if any) as the OFT may determine.

(7) If requested by any person to do so and subject to such reasonable fees (if any) as the OFT may determine, the OFT shall supply the person concerned with a copy (certified to be true) of the register or of an extract from it.

167 Rights to enforce undertakings and orders under this Part

(1) This section applies to any enforcement undertaking or enforcement order.

(2) Any person to whom such an undertaking or order relates shall have a duty to comply with it.

(3) The duty shall be owed to any person who may be affected by a contravention of the undertaking or (as the case may be) order.

(4) Any breach of the duty which causes such a person to sustain loss or damage shall be actionable by him.

(5) In any proceedings brought under subsection (4) against a person to whom an enforcement undertaking or enforcement order relates it shall be a defence for that

person to show that he took all reasonable steps and exercised all due diligence to avoid contravening the undertaking or (as the case may be) order.

(6) Compliance with an enforcement undertaking or an enforcement order shall also be enforceable by civil proceedings brought by the OFT for an injunction or for interdict or for any other appropriate relief or remedy.

(7) Compliance with an undertaking accepted under section 157 or 159, or an order under section 158, 160 or 161, shall also be enforceable by civil proceedings brought by the relevant authority for an injunction or for interdict or for any other appropriate relief or remedy.

(8) In subsection (7) 'the relevant authority' means –

   (a) in the case of an undertaking accepted by the Commission or an order made by the Commission, the Commission; and

   (b) in the case of an undertaking accepted by the Secretary of State or an order made by the Secretary of State, the Secretary of State.

(9) Subsections (6) to (8) shall not prejudice any right that a person may have by virtue of subsection (4) to bring civil proceedings for contravention or apprehended contravention of an enforcement undertaking or an enforcement order.

CHAPTER 4   SUPPLEMENTARY

Regulated markets

168 Regulated markets

(1) Subsection (2) applies where the Commission or the Secretary of State is considering for the purposes of this Part whether relevant action would be reasonable and practicable for the purpose of remedying, mitigating or preventing an adverse effect on competition or any detrimental effect on customers so far as resulting from such an effect.

(2) The Commission or (as the case may be) the Secretary of State shall, in deciding whether such action would be reasonable and practicable, have regard to the relevant statutory functions of the sectoral regulator concerned.

(3) In this section 'relevant action' means –

   (a) modifying the conditions of a licence granted under section 7 of the Telecommunications Act 1984 (c. 12);

   (b) modifying conditions in force under Part 4 of the Airports Act 1986 (c. 31) other than any conditions imposed or modified in pursuance of section 40(3) or (4) of that Act;

   (c) modifying the conditions of a licence granted under section 7 or 7A of the Gas Act 1986 (c. 44);

   (d) modifying the conditions of a licence granted under section 6 of the Electricity Act 1989 (c. 29);

   (e) modifying networking arrangements (within the meaning given by section 39(1) of the Broadcasting Act 1990 (c. 42));

   (f) modifying the conditions of a company's appointment under Chapter 1 of Part 2 of the Water Industry Act 1991 (c. 56);

   (g) modifying the conditions of a licence granted under article 10 of the Electricity (Northern Ireland) Order 1992 (S.I. 1992/231 (N.I. 1));

   (h) modifying the conditions of a licence granted under section 8 of the Railways Act 1993 (c. 43);

   (i) modifying an access agreement (within the meaning given by section 83(1) of the Act of 1993) or a franchise agreement (within the meaning given by section 23(3) of that Act);

(j) modifying conditions in force under Part 4 of the Airports (Northern Ireland) Order 1994 (S.I. 1994/426 (N.I. 1)) other than any conditions imposed or modified in pursuance of article 40(3) or (4) of that Order;

(k) modifying the conditions of a licence granted under article 8 of the Gas (Northern Ireland) Order 1996 (S.I. 1996/275 (N.I. 2));

(l) modifying the conditions of a licence granted under section 11 of the Postal Services Act 2000 (c. 26); or

(m) modifying the conditions of a licence granted under section 5 of the Transport Act 2000 (c. 38).

(4) In this section 'relevant statutory functions' means –

(a) in relation to any licence granted under section 7 of the Telecommunications Act 1984, the duties and obligations of the Director General of Telecommunications imposed on him by or in pursuance of any enactment or other provision mentioned in section 7(5)(a) of that Act;

(b) in relation to conditions in force under Part 4 of the Airports Act 1986 (c. 31) other than any conditions imposed or modified in pursuance of section 40(3) or (4) of that Act, the duties of the Civil Aviation Authority under section 39(2) and (3) of that Act;

(c) in relation to any licence granted under section 7 or 7A of the Gas Act 1986 (c. 44), the objectives and duties of the Gas and Electricity Markets Authority under section 4AA and 4AB(2) of that Act;

(d) in relation to any licence granted under section 6 of the Electricity Act 1989 (c. 29), the objectives and duties of the Gas and Electricity Markets Authority under section 3A and 3B(2) of that Act;

(e) in relation to any networking arrangements (within the meaning given by section 39(1) of the Broadcasting Act 1990 (c. 42)), the duties of the Independent Television Commission under section 2(2) of that Act;

(f) in relation to a company's appointment under Chapter 1 of Part 2 of the Water Industry Act 1991 (c. 56), the duties of the Director General of Water Services under section 2 of that Act;

(g) in relation to any licence granted under article 10 of the Electricity (Northern Ireland) Order 1992 (S.I. 1992/231 (N.I. 1)), the duty of the Director General of Electricity Supply for Northern Ireland under article 6 of that Order;

(h) in relation to any licence granted under section 8 of the Railways Act 1993 (c. 43) where none of the conditions of the licence relate to consumer protection, the duties of the Rail Regulator under section 4 of that Act;

(i) in relation to any licence granted under section 8 of the Act of 1993 where one or more than one condition of the licence relates to consumer protection, the duties of the Rail Regulator under section 4 of that Act and the duties of the Strategic Rail Authority under section 207 of the Transport Act 2000 (c. 38);

(j) in relation to any access agreement (within the meaning given by section 83(1) of the Act of 1993), the duties of the Rail Regulator under section 4 of the Act of 1993;

(k) in relation to any franchise agreement (within the meaning given by section 23(3) of the Act of 1993), the duties of the Strategic Rail Authority under section 207 of the Act of 2000;

(l) in relation to conditions in force under Part 4 of the Airports (Northern Ireland) Order 1994 (S.I. 1994/426 (N.I. 1)) other than any conditions imposed or modified in pursuance of article 40(3) or (4) of that Order, the duties of the Civil Aviation Authority under article 30(2) and (3) of that Order;

(m) in relation to any licence granted under article 8 of the Gas (Northern Ireland) Order 1996 (S.I. 1996/275 (N.I. 2)), the duties of the Director General of Gas for Northern Ireland under article 5 of that Order;

(n) in relation to any licence granted under section 11 of the Postal Services Act 2000 (c. 26), the duties of the Postal Services Commission under sections 3 and 5 of that Act; and

(o) in relation to any licence granted under section 5 of the Transport Act 2000, the duties of the Civil Aviation Authority under section 87 of that Act.

(5) In this section 'sectoral regulator' means –

(a) the Civil Aviation Authority;

(b) the Director General of Electricity Supply for Northern Ireland;

(c) the Director General of Gas for Northern Ireland;

(d) the Director General of Telecommunications;

(e) the Director General of Water Services;

(f) the Gas and Electricity Markets Authority;

(g) the Independent Television Commission;

(h) the Postal Services Commission;

(i) the Rail Regulator; or

(j) the Strategic Rail Authority.

(6) Subsection (7) applies where the Commission or the Secretary of State is considering for the purposes of this Part whether modifying the conditions of a licence granted under section 7 or 7A of the Gas Act 1986 (c. 44) or section 6 of the Electricity Act 1989 (c. 29) would be reasonable and practicable for the purpose of remedying, mitigating or preventing an adverse effect on competition or any detrimental effect on customers so far as resulting from such an effect.

(7) The Commission or (as the case may be) the Secretary of State may, in deciding whether modifying the conditions of such a licence would be reasonable and practicable, have regard to those matters to which the Gas and Electricity Markets Authority may have regard by virtue of section 4AA(4) of the Act of 1986 or (as the case may be) section 3A(4) of the Act of 1989.

(8) The Secretary of State may by order modify subsection (3), (4), (5), (6) or (7).

(9) Part 2 of Schedule 9 (which makes provision for functions under this Part to be exercisable by various sectoral regulators) shall have effect.

Consultation, information and publicity

169 Certain duties of relevant authorities to consult: Part 4

(1) Subsection (2) applies where the relevant authority is proposing to make a relevant decision in a way which the relevant authority considers is likely to have a substantial impact on the interests of any person.

(2) The relevant authority shall, so far as practicable, consult that person about what is proposed before making that decision.

(3) In consulting the person concerned, the relevant authority shall, so far as practicable, give the reasons of the relevant authority for the proposed decision.

(4) In considering what is practicable for the purposes of this section the relevant authority shall, in particular, have regard to –

(a) any restrictions imposed by any timetable for making the decision; and

(b) any need to keep what is proposed, or the reasons for it, confidential.

(5) The duty under this section shall not apply in relation to the making of any decision so far as particular provision is made elsewhere by virtue of this Part for consultation before the making of that decision.

(6) In this section –

'the relevant authority' means the OFT, the appropriate Minister or the Commission; and 'relevant decision' means –

(a) in the case of the OFT, any decision by the OFT –

  (i) as to whether to make a reference under section 131 or accept under-
       takings under section 154 instead of making such a reference; or
  (ii) to vary under section 135 such a reference;

(b) in the case of the appropriate Minister, any decision by the appropriate
     Minister –

  (i) as to whether to make a reference under section 132; or
  (ii) to vary under section 135 such a reference; and

(c) in the case of the Commission, any decision on the questions mentioned in
     section 134 or 141.

170 General information duties

(1) The OFT shall give the Commission –

(a) such information in its possession as the Commission may reasonably require to
     enable the Commission to carry out its functions under this Part; and

(b) any other assistance which the Commission may reasonably require for the pur-
     pose of assisting it in carrying out its functions under this Part and which it is
     within the power of the OFT to give.

(2) The OFT shall give the Commission any information in its possession which has not
     been requested by the Commission but which, in the opinion of the OFT, would be
     appropriate to give to the Commission for the purpose of assisting it in carrying out
     its functions under this Part.

(3) The OFT and the Commission shall give the Secretary of State or the appropriate
     Minister so far as he is not the Secretary of State acting alone –

(a) such information in their possession as the Secretary of State or (as the case may
     be) the appropriate Minister concerned may by direction reasonably require to
     enable him to carry out his functions under this Part; and

(b) any other assistance which the Secretary of State or (as the case may be) the
     appropriate Minister concerned may by direction reasonably require for the pur-
     pose of assisting him in carrying out his functions under this Part and which it
     is within the power of the OFT or (as the case may be) the Commission to give.

(4) The OFT shall give the Secretary of State or the appropriate Minister so far as he
     is not the Secretary of State acting alone any information in its possession which
     has not been requested by the Secretary of State or (as the case may be) the
     appropriate Minister concerned but which, in the opinion of the OFT, would be
     appropriate to give to the Secretary of State or (as the case may be) the appro-
     priate Minister concerned for the purpose of assisting him in carrying out his
     functions under this Part.

(5) The Commission shall have regard to any information given to it under subsection (1)
     or (2); and the Secretary of State or (as the case may be) the appropriate Minister con-
     cerned shall have regard to any information given to him under subsection (3) or (4).

(6) Any direction given under subsection (3) –

(a) shall be in writing; and
(b) may be varied or revoked by a subsequent direction.

171 Advice and information: Part 4

(1) As soon as reasonably practicable after the passing of this Act, the OFT shall prepare
     and publish general advice and information about the making of references by it
     under section 131.

(2) The OFT may at any time publish revised, or new, advice or information.

(3) As soon as reasonably practicable after the passing of this Act, the Commission shall prepare and publish general advice and information about the consideration by it of market investigation references and the way in which relevant customer benefits may affect the taking of enforcement action in relation to such references.

(4) The Commission may at any time publish revised, or new, advice or information.

(5) Advice and information published under this section shall be prepared with a view to –

   (a) explaining relevant provisions of this Part to persons who are likely to be affected by them; and
   (b) indicating how the OFT or (as the case may be) the Commission expects such provisions to operate.

(6) Advice and information published by virtue of subsection (1) or (3) shall include such advice and information about the effect of Community law, and anything done under or in accordance with it, on the provisions of this Part as the OFT or (as the case may be) the Commission considers appropriate.

(7) Advice (or information) published by virtue of subsection (1) or (3) may include advice (or information) about the factors which the OFT or (as the case may be) the Commission may take into account in considering whether, and if so how, to exercise a function conferred by this Part.

(8) Any advice or information published by the OFT or the Commission under this section shall be published in such manner as the OFT or (as the case may be) the Commission considers appropriate.

(9) In preparing any advice or information under this section, the OFT shall consult the Commission and such other persons as it considers appropriate.

(10) In preparing any advice or information under this section, the Commission shall consult the OFT and such other persons as it considers appropriate.

(11) In this section 'Community law' means –

   (a) all the rights, powers, liabilities, obligations and restrictions from time to time created or arising by or under the Community Treaties; and
   (b) all the remedies and procedures from time to time provided for by or under the Community Treaties.

172 Further publicity requirements: Part 4

(1) The OFT shall publish –

   (a) any reference made by it under section 131;
   (b) any variation made by it under section 135 of a reference under section 131;
   (c) any decision of a kind mentioned in section 149(5)(b); and
   (d) such information as it considers appropriate about any decision made by it under section 152(1) to bring a case to the attention of the Secretary of State.

(2) The Commission shall publish –

   (a) any decision made by it under section 138(2) neither to accept an undertaking under section 159 nor to make an order under section 161;
   (b) any decision made by it that there has been a material change of circumstances as mentioned in section 138(3) or there is another special reason as mentioned in that section;
   (c) any termination under section 145(1) of an investigation by it;
   (d) such information as it considers appropriate about any decision made by it under section 152(2) to bring a case to the attention of the Secretary of State;
   (e) any enforcement undertaking accepted by it under section 157;
   (f) any enforcement order made by it under section 158; and
   (g) any variation, release or revocation of such an undertaking or order.

(3) The Secretary of State shall publish –

   (a) any reference made by him under section 132;

    (b) any variation made by him under section 135 of a reference under section 132;

    (c) any intervention notice given by him;

    (d) any decision made by him to revoke such a notice;

    (e) any decision made by him under section 147(2) neither to accept an undertaking under section 159 nor to make an order under section 161;

    (f) any enforcement undertaking accepted by him under section 157;

    (g) any variation or release of such an undertaking; and

    (h) any direction given by him under section 170(3) in connection with the exercise by him of his functions under section 132(3).

(4) The appropriate Minister (other than the Secretary of State acting alone) shall publish –

    (a) any reference made by him under section 132;

    (b) any variation made by him under section 135 of a reference under section 132; and

    (c) any direction given by him under section 170(3) in connection with the exercise by him of his functions under section 132(3).

(5) Where any person is under an obligation by virtue of subsection (1), (2), (3) or (4) to publish the result of any action taken by that person or any decision made by that person, the person concerned shall, subject to subsections (6) and (7), also publish that person's reasons for the action concerned or (as the case may be) the decision concerned.

(6) Such reasons need not, if it is not reasonably practicable to do so, be published at the same time as the result of the action concerned or (as the case may be) as the decision concerned.

(7) Subsections (5) and (6) shall not apply in relation to any case falling within subsection (1)(d) or (2)(d).

(8) The Secretary of State shall publish his reasons for –

    (a) any decision made by him under section 146(2); or

    (b) any decision to make an order under section 153(3) or vary or revoke such an order.

(9) Such reasons may be published after –

    (a) in the case of subsection (8)(a), the publication of the decision concerned; and

    (b) in the case of subsection (8)(b), the making of the order or of the variation or revocation;

if it is not reasonably practicable to publish them at the same time as the publication of the decision or (as the case may be) the making of the order or variation or revocation.

(10) Where the Secretary of State has decided under section 147(2) to accept an undertaking under section 159 or to make an order under section 161, he shall (after the acceptance of the undertaking or (as the case may be) the making of the order) lay details of his decision and his reasons for it, and the Commission's report under section 142, before each House of Parliament.

173 Defamation: Part 4

For the purposes of the law relating to defamation, absolute privilege attaches to any advice, guidance, notice or direction given, or decision or report made, by the OFT, by the Secretary of State, by the appropriate Minister (other than the Secretary of State acting alone) or by the Commission in the exercise of any of their functions under this Part.

Investigation powers

174 Investigation powers of OFT

(1) The OFT may exercise any of the powers in subsections (3) to (5) for the purpose of assisting it in deciding whether to make a reference under section 131 or to accept undertakings under section 154 instead of making such a reference.

(2) The OFT shall not exercise any of the powers in subsections (3) to (5) for the purpose of assisting it as mentioned in subsection (1) unless it already believes that it has power to make such a reference.

(3) The OFT may give notice to any person requiring him –

    (a) to attend at a time and place specified in the notice; and

    (b) to give evidence to the OFT or a person nominated by the OFT for the purpose.

(4) The OFT may give notice to any person requiring him –

    (a) to produce any documents which –

        (i) are specified or described in the notice, or fall within a category of document which is specified or described in the notice; and

        (ii) are in that person's custody or under his control; and

    (b) to produce them at a time and place so specified and to a person so specified.

(5) The OFT may give notice to any person who carries on any business requiring him –

    (a) to supply to the OFT such estimates, forecasts, returns or other information as may be specified or described in the notice; and

    (b) to supply it at a time and place, and in a form and manner, so specified and to a person so specified.

(6) A notice under this section shall include information about the possible consequences of not complying with the notice.

(7) The person to whom any document is produced in accordance with a notice under this section may, for the purpose mentioned in subsection (1), copy the document so produced.

(8) No person shall be required under this section –

    (a) to give any evidence or produce any documents which he could not be compelled to give or produce in civil proceedings before the court; or

    (b) to supply any information which he could not be compelled to supply in evidence in such proceedings.

(9) No person shall be required, in compliance with a notice under this section, to go more than 10 miles from his place of residence unless his necessary travelling expenses are paid or offered to him.

(10) Any reference in this section to the production of a document includes a reference to the production of a legible and intelligible copy of information recorded otherwise than in legible form.

(11) In this section 'the court' means –

    (a) in relation to England and Wales or Northern Ireland, the High Court; and

    (b) in relation to Scotland, the Court of Session.

175 Enforcement of powers under section 174: offences

(1) A person commits an offence if he, intentionally and without reasonable excuse, fails to comply with any requirement of a notice under section 174.

(2) A person commits an offence if he intentionally and without reasonable excuse alters, suppresses or destroys any document which he has been required to produce by a notice under section 174.

(3) A person who commits an offence under subsection (1) or (2) shall be liable –

    (a) on summary conviction, to a fine not exceeding the statutory maximum;

(b) on conviction on indictment, to imprisonment for a term not exceeding two years or to a fine or to both.

(4) A person commits an offence if he intentionally obstructs or delays –

(a) the OFT in the exercise of its powers under section 174; or

(b) any person in the exercise of his powers under subsection (7) of that section.

(5) A person who commits an offence under subsection (4) shall be liable –

(a) on summary conviction, to a fine not exceeding the statutory maximum;

(b) on conviction on indictment, to a fine.

176 Investigation powers of the Commission

(1) The following sections in Part 3 shall apply, with the modifications mentioned in sub-sections (2) and (3) below, for the purposes of references under this Part as they apply for the purposes of references under that Part –

(a) section 109 (attendance of witnesses and production of documents etc.);

(b) section 110 (enforcement of powers under section 109: general);

(c) section 111 (penalties);

(d) section 112 (penalties: main procedural requirements);

(e) section 113 (payments and interest by instalments);

(f) section 114 (appeals in relation to penalties);

(g) section 115 (recovery of penalties); and

(h) section 116 (statement of policy).

(2) Section 110 shall, in its application by virtue of subsection (1) above, have effect as if –

(a) subsection (2) were omitted; and

(b) in subsection (9) the words from 'or section' to 'section 65(3))' were omitted.

(3) Section 111(5)(b)(ii) shall, in its application by virtue of subsection (1) above, have effect as if –

(a) for the words 'section 50 or 65, given' there were substituted 'section 142, published or given under section 143(1) or (3)'; and

(b) for the words '(or given)', in both places where they appear, there were substituted '(or published or given)'.

Reports

177 Excisions from reports: Part 4

(1) Subsection (2) applies where the Secretary of State is under a duty to publish a report of the Commission under section 142.

(2) The Secretary of State may exclude a matter from the report if he considers that publication of the matter would be inappropriate.

(3) In deciding what is inappropriate for the purposes of subsection (2) the Secretary of State shall have regard to the considerations mentioned in section 244.

(4) The Commission shall advise the Secretary of State as to the matters (if any) which it considers should be excluded by him under subsection (2).

(5) References in sections 136(4) to (6), 143(2) and (5) to (7), 148(3) to (5) and 172(10) to the giving or laying of a report of the Commission shall be construed as references to the giving or laying of the report as published.

178 Minority reports of Commission: Part 4

(1) Subsection (2) applies where, on a market investigation reference, a member of a group constituted in connection with the reference in pursuance of paragraph 15 of Schedule 7 to the Competition Act 1998 (c. 41), disagrees with any decisions contained in the report of the Commission under this Part as the decisions of the Commission.

(2)　The report shall, if the member so wishes, include a statement of his disagreement and of his reasons for disagreeing.

Other

179 Review of decisions under Part 4

(1)　Any person aggrieved by a decision of the OFT, the appropriate Minister, the Secretary of State or the Commission in connection with a reference or possible reference under this Part may apply to the Competition Appeal Tribunal for a review of that decision.

(2)　For this purpose 'decision' –

    (a)　does not include a decision to impose a penalty under section 110(1) or (3) as applied by section 176; but

    (b)　includes a failure to take a decision permitted or required by this Part in connection with a reference or possible reference.

(3)　Except in so far as a direction to the contrary is given by the Competition Appeal Tribunal, the effect of the decision is not suspended by reason of the making of the application.

(4)　In determining such an application the Competition Appeal Tribunal shall apply the same principles as would be applied by a court on an application for judicial review.

(5)　The Competition Appeal Tribunal may –

    (a)　dismiss the application or quash the whole or part of the decision to which it relates; and

    (b)　where it quashes the whole or part of that decision, refer the matter back to the original decision maker with a direction to reconsider and make a new decision in accordance with the ruling of the Competition Appeal Tribunal.

(6)　An appeal lies on any point of law arising from a decision of the Competition Appeal Tribunal under this section to the appropriate court.

(7)　An appeal under subsection (6) requires the permission of the Tribunal or the appropriate court.

(8)　In this section –

    'the appropriate court' means the Court of Appeal or, in the case of Tribunal proceedings in Scotland, the Court of Session; and

    'Tribunal rules' has the meaning given by section 15(1).

180 Offences

(1)　Sections 117 (false or misleading information) and 125 (offences by bodies corporate) shall apply, with the modifications mentioned in subsection (2) below, for the purposes of this Part as they apply for the purposes of Part 3.

(2)　Section 117 shall, in its application by virtue of subsection (1) above, have effect as if references to the Secretary of State included references to the appropriate Minister so far as he is not the Secretary of State acting alone.

181 Orders under Part 4

(1)　Any power of the Secretary of State to make an order under this Part shall be exercisable by statutory instrument.

(2)　Any power of the Secretary of State to make an order under this Part –

    (a)　may be exercised so as to make different provision for different cases or different purposes;

    (b)　includes power to make such incidental, supplementary, consequential, transitory, transitional or saving provision as the Secretary of State considers appropriate.

(3) The power of the Secretary of State under section 136(9), 137(3), 144(2), 153(3) or 168(8) as extended by subsection (2) above may be exercised by modifying any enactment comprised in or made under this Act, or any other enactment.

(4) An order made by the Secretary of State under section 137(3), 144(2), 158, 160 or 161, or under section 111(4) or (6) or 114(3)(b) or (4)(b) as applied by section 176, shall be subject to annulment in pursuance of a resolution of either House of Parliament.

(5) No order shall be made by the Secretary of State under section 136(9) or 168(8), or section 128(6) as applied by section 183(2), unless a draft of it has been laid before, and approved by a resolution of, each House of Parliament.

(6) An order made by the Secretary of State under section 153(3) shall be laid before Parliament after being made and shall cease to have effect unless approved, within the period of 28 days beginning with the day on which it is made, by a resolution of each House of Parliament.

(7) In calculating the period of 28 days mentioned in subsection (6), no account shall be taken of any time during which Parliament is dissolved or prorogued or during which both Houses are adjourned for more than four days.

(8) If an order made by the Secretary of State ceases to have effect by virtue of subsection (6), any modification made by it of an enactment is repealed (and the previous enactment revived) but without prejudice to the validity of anything done in connection with that modification before the order ceased to have effect and without prejudice to the making of a new order.

(9) If, apart from this subsection, an order made by the Secretary of State under section 153(3) would be treated for the purposes of the standing orders of either House of Parliament as a hybrid instrument, it shall proceed in that House as if it were not such an instrument.

(10) References in this section to an order made under this Part include references to an order made under section 111(4) or (6) or 114(3)(b) or (4)(b) as applied by section 176 and an order made under section 128(6) as applied by section 183(2).

182 Service of documents: Part 4

Section 126 shall apply for the purposes of this Part as it applies for the purposes of Part 3.

183 Interpretation: Part 4

(1) In this Part, unless the context otherwise requires –

'action' includes omission; and references to the taking of action include references to refraining from action;

'business' includes a professional practice and includes any other undertaking which is carried on for gain or reward or which is an undertaking in the course of which goods or services are supplied otherwise than free of charge;

'change of circumstances' includes any discovery that information has been supplied which is false or misleading in a material respect;

'consumer' means any person who is –

(a) a person to whom goods are or are sought to be supplied (whether by way of sale or otherwise) in the course of a business carried on by the person supplying or seeking to supply them; or

(b) a person for whom services are or are sought to be supplied in the course of a business carried on by the person supplying or seeking to supply them;

and who does not receive or seek to receive the goods or services in the course of a business carried on by him;

'customer' includes a customer who is not a consumer;

'enactment' includes an Act of the Scottish Parliament, Northern Ireland legislation and an enactment comprised in subordinate legislation, and includes an enactment whenever passed or made;

'goods' includes buildings and other structures, and also includes ships, aircraft and hovercraft;

'Minister of the Crown' means the holder of an office in Her Majesty's Government in the United Kingdom and includes the Treasury;

'modify' includes amend or repeal;

'notice' means notice in writing;

'subordinate legislation' has the same meaning as in the Interpretation Act 1978 (c. 30) and also includes an instrument made under an Act of the Scottish Parliament and an instrument made under Northern Ireland legislation; and

'supply', in relation to the supply of goods, includes supply by way of sale, lease, hire or hire-purchase, and, in relation to buildings or other structures, includes the construction of them by a person for another person.

(2) Sections 127(1)(b) and (4) to (6) and 128 shall apply for the purposes of this Part as they apply for the purposes of Part 3.

(3) For the purposes of this Part a market investigation reference is finally determined if –

(a) where no intervention notice under section 139(1) has been given in relation to it –

(i) the period permitted by section 137 for preparing and publishing a report under section 136 has expired and no such report has been prepared and published;

(ii) such a report has been prepared and published within the period permitted by section 137 and contains the decision that there is no adverse effect on competition;

(iii) the Commission has decided under section 138(2) neither to accept undertakings under section 159 nor to make an order under section 161; or

(iv) the Commission has accepted an undertaking under section 159 or made an order under section 161;

(b) where an intervention notice under section 139(1) has been given in relation to it –

(i) the period permitted by section 144 for the preparation of the report of the Commission under section 142 and for action to be taken in relation to it under section 143(1) or (3) has expired while the intervention notice is still in force and no such report has been so prepared or no such action has been taken;

(ii) the Commission has terminated under section 145(1) its investigation and the reference is finally determined under paragraph (a) above (disregarding the fact that the notice was given);

(iii) the report of the Commission has been prepared under section 142 and published under section 143(1) within the period permitted by section 144;

(iv) the intervention notice was revoked and the reference is finally determined under paragraph (a) above (disregarding the fact that the notice was given);

(v) the Secretary of State has failed to make and publish a decision under subsection (2) of section 146 within the period permitted by subsection (3) of that section and the reference is finally determined under paragraph (a) above (disregarding the fact that the notice was given);

(vi) the Secretary of State has decided under section 146(2) that no eligible public interest consideration is relevant and the reference is finally determined under paragraph (a) above (disregarding the fact that the notice was given);

    (vii)   the Secretary of State has decided under 146(2) that a public interest consideration is relevant but has decided under section 147(2) neither to accept an undertaking under section 159 nor to make an order under section 161; or

    (viii) the Secretary of State has decided under section 146(2) that a public interest consideration is relevant and has accepted an undertaking under section 159 or made an order under section 161.

(4) For the purposes of this Part the time when a market investigation reference is finally determined is –

    (a) in a case falling within subsection (3)(a)(i) or (b)(i), the expiry of the time concerned;

    (b) in a case falling within subsection (3)(a)(ii) or (b)(iii), the publication of the report;

    (c) in a case falling within subsection (3)(a)(iv) or (b)(viii), the acceptance of the undertaking concerned or (as the case may be) the making of the order concerned; and

    (d) in any other case, the making of the decision or last decision concerned or the taking of the action concerned.

(5) The references in subsection (4) to subsections (3)(a)(i), (ii) and (iv) include those enactments as applied by subsection (3)(b)(ii), (iv), (v) or (vi).

(6) In subsection (4)(c) the reference to the acceptance of the undertaking concerned or the making of the order concerned shall, in a case where the enforcement action concerned involves the acceptance of a group of undertakings, the making of a group of orders or the acceptance and making of a group of undertakings and orders, be treated as a reference to the acceptance or making of the last undertaking or order in the group; but undertakings or orders which vary, supersede or revoke earlier undertakings or orders shall be disregarded for the purposes of subsections (3)(a)(iv) and (b)(viii) and (4)(c).

(7) Any duty to publish which is imposed on a person by this Part shall, unless the context otherwise requires, be construed as a duty on that person to publish in such manner as that person considers appropriate for the purpose of bringing the matter concerned to the attention of those likely to be affected by it.

184 Index of defined expressions: Part 4

In this Part, the expressions listed in the left-hand column have the meaning given by, or are to be interpreted in accordance with, the provisions listed in the right-hand column.

Expression	Provision of this Act
Action (and the taking of action)	Section 183(1)
Adverse effect on competition	Section 134(2)
Appropriate Minister	Section 132(5)
Business	Section 183(1)
Change of circumstances	Section 183(1)
The Commission	Section 273
Consumer	Section 183(1)
Customer	Section 183(1)
Date of market investigation reference	Section 137(7)
Detrimental effect on customers	Section 134(5)
Enactment	Section 183(1)
Enforcement order	Section 162(8)

Expression	Provision of this Act
Enforcement undertaking	Section 162(8)
Feature of a market	Section 131(2)
Final determination of market investigation reference	Section 183(3) to (6)
Goods	Section 183(1)
Intervention notice	Section 139(3)
Market for goods or services	Section 131(6)
Market in the United Kingdom	Section 131(6)
Market investigation reference	Section 131(6)
Minister of the Crown	Section 183(1)
Modify	Section 183(1)
Notice	Section 183(1)
The OFT	Section 273
Public interest consideration	Section 139(5)
Public interest consideration being finalised	Section 139(7)
Publish	Section 183(7)
Relevant customer benefit	Section 134(8)
Relevant sectoral enactment	Section 136(7)
Relevant sectoral regulator	Section 136(8)
Reports of the Commission	Section 177(5)
Subordinate legislation	Section 183(1)
Supply (in relation to the supply of goods)	Section 183(1)
The supply of services (and a market for services etc.)	Section 183(2)

PART 5   THE COMPETITION COMMISSION

185 The Commission

Schedule 11 (which amends provisions relating to the constitution and powers of the Commission under Schedule 7 to the 1998 Act) has effect.

186 Annual report of Commission

After paragraph 12 of Schedule 7 to the 1998 Act (the Competition Commission) there is inserted –

> 'Annual reports
>
> 12A(1)   The Commission shall make to the Secretary of State a report for each financial year on its activities during the year.
>
> (2)   The annual report must be made before the end of August next following the financial year to which it relates.
>
> (3)   The Secretary of State shall lay a copy of the annual report before Parliament and arrange for the report to be published.'

187 Commission rules of procedure

(1) In section 45(7) of the 1998 Act (the Competition Commission) for the words 'Schedule 7 makes' there shall be substituted 'Schedules 7 and 7A make'.

(2) In paragraph 19 of Schedule 7 to that Act, after sub-paragraph (4), there shall be inserted –

'(5) This paragraph does not apply to groups for which rules must be made under paragraph 19A.'

(3) After paragraph 19 of that Schedule to that Act there shall be inserted –

'19A(1) The Chairman must make rules of procedure in relation to merger reference groups, market reference groups and special reference groups.

(2) Schedule 7A makes further provision about rules made under this paragraph but is not to be taken as restricting the Chairman's powers under this paragraph.

(3) The Chairman must publish rules made under this paragraph in such manner as he considers appropriate for the purpose of bringing them to the attention of those likely to be affected by them.

(4) The Chairman must consult the members of the Commission and such other persons as he considers appropriate before making rules under this paragraph.

(5) Rules under this paragraph may –

(a) make different provision for different cases or different purposes;

(b) be varied or revoked by subsequent rules made under this paragraph.

(6) Subject to rules made under this paragraph, each merger reference group, market reference group and special reference group may determine its own procedure.

(7) In determining how to proceed in accordance with rules made under this paragraph and in determining its procedure under sub-paragraph (6), a group must have regard to any guidance issued by the Chairman.

(8) Before issuing any guidance for the purposes of this paragraph the Chairman shall consult the members of the Commission and such other persons as he considers appropriate.

(9) In this paragraph and in Schedule 7A –

'market reference group' means any group constituted in connection with a reference under section 131 or 132 of the Enterprise Act 2002 (including that section as it has effect by virtue of another enactment);

'merger reference group' means any group constituted in connection with a reference under section 59 of the Fair Trading Act 1973 (c. 41), section 32 of the Water Industry Act 1991 (c. 56) or section 22, 33, 45 or 62 of the Enterprise Act 2002; and

'special reference group' means any group constituted in connection with a reference or (in the case of the Financial Services and Markets Act 2000 (c. 8)) an investigation under –

(a) section 11 of the Competition Act 1980 (c. 21);

(b) section 13 of the Telecommunications Act 1984 (c. 12);

(c) section 43 of the Airports Act 1986 (c. 31);

(d) section 24 or 41E of the Gas Act 1986 (c. 44);

(e) section 12 or 56C of the Electricity Act 1989 (c. 29);

(f) Schedule 4 to the Broadcasting Act 1990 (c. 42);

(g) section 12 or 14 of the Water Industry Act 1991 (c. 56);

(h) article 15 of the Electricity (Northern Ireland) Order 1992 (S.I. 1992/231 (N.I. 1));

         (i)   section 13 of, or Schedule 4A to, the Railways Act 1993 (c. 43);

         (j)   article 34 of the Airports (Northern Ireland) Order 1994 (S.I. 1994/426 (N.I. 1));

         (k) article 15 of the Gas (Northern Ireland) Order 1996 (S.I. 1996/275 (N.I. 2));

         (l)   section 15 of the Postal Services Act 2000 (c. 26);

         (m) section 162 or 306 of the Financial Services and Markets Act 2000 (c. 8); or

         (n)   section 12 of the Transport Act 2000 (c. 38).'

(4) After Schedule 7 to that Act there shall be inserted, as Schedule 7A, the Schedule set out in Schedule 12 to this Act.

PART 6   CARTEL OFFENCE

Cartel offence

188 Cartel offence

(1) An individual is guilty of an offence if he dishonestly agrees with one or more other persons to make or implement, or to cause to be made or implemented, arrangements of the following kind relating to at least two undertakings (A and B).

(2) The arrangements must be ones which, if operating as the parties to the agreement intend, would –

    (a) directly or indirectly fix a price for the supply by A in the United Kingdom (otherwise than to B) of a product or service,

    (b) limit or prevent supply by A in the United Kingdom of a product or service,

    (c) limit or prevent production by A in the United Kingdom of a product,

    (d) divide between A and B the supply in the United Kingdom of a product or service to a customer or customers,

    (e) divide between A and B customers for the supply in the United Kingdom of a product or service, or

    (f) be bid-rigging arrangements.

(3) Unless subsection (2)(d), (e) or (f) applies, the arrangements must also be ones which, if operating as the parties to the agreement intend, would –

    (a) directly or indirectly fix a price for the supply by B in the United Kingdom (otherwise than to A) of a product or service,

    (b) limit or prevent supply by B in the United Kingdom of a product or service, or

    (c) limit or prevent production by B in the United Kingdom of a product.

(4) In subsections (2)(a) to (d) and (3), references to supply or production are to supply or production in the appropriate circumstances (for which see section 189).

(5) 'Bid-rigging arrangements' are arrangements under which, in response to a request for bids for the supply of a product or service in the United Kingdom, or for the production of a product in the United Kingdom –

    (a) A but not B may make a bid, or

    (b) A and B may each make a bid but, in one case or both, only a bid arrived at in accordance with the arrangements.

(6) But arrangements are not bid-rigging arrangements if, under them, the person requesting bids would be informed of them at or before the time when a bid is made.

(7) 'Undertaking' has the same meaning as in Part 1 of the 1998 Act.

189 Cartel offence: supplementary

(1) For section 188(2)(a), the appropriate circumstances are that A's supply of the product or service would be at a level in the supply chain at which the product or service would at the same time be supplied by B in the United Kingdom.

(2) For section 188(2)(b), the appropriate circumstances are that A's supply of the product or service would be at a level in the supply chain –

   (a) at which the product or service would at the same time be supplied by B in the United Kingdom, or
   (b) at which supply by B in the United Kingdom of the product or service would be limited or prevented by the arrangements.

(3) For section 188(2)(c), the appropriate circumstances are that A's production of the product would be at a level in the production chain –

   (a) at which the product would at the same time be produced by B in the United Kingdom, or
   (b) at which production by B in the United Kingdom of the product would be limited or prevented by the arrangements.

(4) For section 188(2)(d), the appropriate circumstances are that A's supply of the product or service would be at the same level in the supply chain as B's.

(5) For section 188(3)(a), the appropriate circumstances are that B's supply of the product or service would be at a level in the supply chain at which the product or service would at the same time be supplied by A in the United Kingdom.

(6) For section 188(3)(b), the appropriate circumstances are that B's supply of the product or service would be at a level in the supply chain –

   (a) at which the product or service would at the same time be supplied by A in the United Kingdom, or
   (b) at which supply by A in the United Kingdom of the product or service would be limited or prevented by the arrangements.

(7) For section 188(3)(c), the appropriate circumstances are that B's production of the product would be at a level in the production chain –

   (a) at which the product would at the same time be produced by A in the United Kingdom, or
   (b) at which production by A in the United Kingdom of the product would be limited or prevented by the arrangements.

190 Cartel offence: penalty and prosecution

(1) A person guilty of an offence under section 188 is liable –

   (a) on conviction on indictment, to imprisonment for a term not exceeding five years or to a fine, or to both;
   (b) on summary conviction, to imprisonment for a term not exceeding six months or to a fine not exceeding the statutory maximum, or to both.

(2) In England and Wales and Northern Ireland, proceedings for an offence under section 188 may be instituted only –

   (a) by the Director of the Serious Fraud Office, or
   (b) by or with the consent of the OFT.

(3) No proceedings may be brought for an offence under section 188 in respect of an agreement outside the United Kingdom, unless it has been implemented in whole or in part in the United Kingdom.

(4) Where, for the purpose of the investigation or prosecution of offences under section 188, the OFT gives a person written notice under this subsection, no proceedings for an offence under section 188 that falls within a description specified in the notice may be brought against that person in England and Wales or Northern Ireland except in circumstances specified in the notice.

191 Extradition

The offences to which an Order in Council under section 2 of the Extradition Act 1870 (c. 52) (arrangements with foreign states) can apply include –

(a) an offence under section 188,
(b) conspiracy to commit such an offence, and
(c) attempt to commit such an offence.

Criminal investigations by OFT

192 Investigation of offences under section 188

(1) The OFT may conduct an investigation if there are reasonable grounds for suspecting that an offence under section 188 has been committed.

(2) The powers of the OFT under sections 193 and 194 are exercisable, but only for the purposes of an investigation under subsection (1), in any case where it appears to the OFT that there is good reason to exercise them for the purpose of investigating the affairs, or any aspect of the affairs, of any person ('the person under investigation').

193 Powers when conducting an investigation

(1) The OFT may by notice in writing require the person under investigation, or any other person who it has reason to believe has relevant information, to answer questions, or otherwise provide information, with respect to any matter relevant to the investigation at a specified place and either at a specified time or forthwith.

(2) The OFT may by notice in writing require the person under investigation, or any other person, to produce, at a specified place and either at a specified time or forthwith, specified documents, or documents of a specified description, which appear to the OFT to relate to any matter relevant to the investigation.

(3) If any such documents are produced, the OFT may –

(a) take copies or extracts from them;
(b) require the person producing them to provide an explanation of any of them.

(4) If any such documents are not produced, the OFT may require the person who was required to produce them to state, to the best of his knowledge and belief, where they are.

(5) A notice under subsection (1) or (2) must indicate –

(a) the subject matter and purpose of the investigation; and
(b) the nature of the offences created by section 201.

194 Power to enter premises under a warrant

(1) On an application made by the OFT to the High Court, or, in Scotland, by the procurator fiscal to the sheriff, in accordance with rules of court, a judge or the sheriff may issue a warrant if he is satisfied that there are reasonable grounds for believing –

(a) that there are on any premises documents which the OFT has power under section 193 to require to be produced for the purposes of an investigation; and
(b) that –

(i) a person has failed to comply with a requirement under that section to produce the documents;
(ii) it is not practicable to serve a notice under that section in relation to them; or
(iii) the service of such a notice in relation to them might seriously prejudice the investigation.

(2) A warrant under this section shall authorise a named officer of the OFT, and any other officers of the OFT whom the OFT has authorised in writing to accompany the named officer –

    (a) to enter the premises, using such force as is reasonably necessary for the purpose;

    (b) to search the premises and –

        (i)   take possession of any documents appearing to be of the relevant kind, or

        (ii) take, in relation to any documents appearing to be of the relevant kind, any other steps which may appear to be necessary for preserving them or preventing interference with them;

    (c) to require any person to provide an explanation of any document appearing to be of the relevant kind or to state, to the best of his knowledge and belief, where it may be found;

    (d) to require any information which is stored in any electronic form and is accessible from the premises and which the named officer considers relates to any matter relevant to the investigation, to be produced in a form –

        (i)   in which it can be taken away, and

        (ii) in which it is visible and legible or from which it can readily be produced in a visible and legible form.

(3) Documents are of the relevant kind if they are of a kind in respect of which the application under subsection (1) was granted.

(4) A warrant under this section may authorise persons specified in the warrant to accompany the named officer who is executing it.

(5) In Part 1 of Schedule 1 to the Criminal Justice and Police Act 2001 (c. 16) (powers of seizure to which section 50 of that Act applies), after paragraph 73 there is inserted –

'Enterprise Act 2002

73A. The power of seizure conferred by section 194(2) of the Enterprise Act 2002 (seizure of documents for the purposes of an investigation under section 192(1) of that Act).'

195 Exercise of powers by authorised person

(1) The OFT may authorise any competent person who is not an officer of the OFT to exercise on its behalf all or any of the powers conferred by section 193 or 194.

(2) No such authority may be granted except for the purpose of investigating the affairs, or any aspect of the affairs, of a person specified in the authority.

(3) No person is bound to comply with any requirement imposed by a person exercising powers by virtue of any authority granted under this section unless he has, if required to do so, produced evidence of his authority.

196 Privileged information etc.

(1) A person may not under section 193 or 194 be required to disclose any information or produce any document which he would be entitled to refuse to disclose or produce on grounds of legal professional privilege in proceedings in the High Court, except that a lawyer may be required to provide the name and address of his client.

(2) A person may not under section 193 or 194 be required to disclose any information or produce any document in respect of which he owes an obligation of confidence by virtue of carrying on any banking business unless –

    (a) the person to whom the obligation of confidence is owed consents to the disclosure or production; or

    (b) the OFT has authorised the making of the requirement.

(3) In the application of this section to Scotland, the reference in subsection (1) –

    (a) to proceedings in the High Court is to be read as a reference to legal proceedings generally; and

(b) to an entitlement on grounds of legal professional privilege is to be read as a reference to an entitlement by virtue of any rule of law whereby –

(i) communications between a professional legal adviser and his client, or

(ii) communications made in connection with or in contemplation of legal proceedings and for the purposes of those proceedings,

are in such proceedings protected from disclosure on the ground of confidentiality.

197 Restriction on use of statements in court

(1) A statement by a person in response to a requirement imposed by virtue of section 193 or 194 may only be used in evidence against him –

(a) on a prosecution for an offence under section 201(2); or

(b) on a prosecution for some other offence where in giving evidence he makes a statement inconsistent with it.

(2) However, the statement may not be used against that person by virtue of paragraph (b) of subsection (1) unless evidence relating to it is adduced, or a question relating to it is asked, by or on behalf of that person in the proceedings arising out of the prosecution.

198 Use of statements obtained under Competition Act 1998

In the 1998 Act, after section 30 there is inserted –

'30A Use of statements in prosecution

A statement made by a person in response to a requirement imposed by virtue of any of sections 26 to 28 may not be used in evidence against him on a prosecution for an offence under section 188 of the Enterprise Act 2002 unless, in the proceedings –

(a) in giving evidence, he makes a statement inconsistent with it, and

(b) evidence relating to it is adduced, or a question relating to it is asked, by him or on his behalf.'

199 Surveillance powers

(1) The Regulation of Investigatory Powers Act 2000 (c. 23) is amended as follows.

(2) In section 32 (authorisation of intrusive surveillance) –

(a) after subsection (3) there is inserted –

'(3A) In the case of an authorisation granted by the chairman of the OFT, the authorisation is necessary on grounds falling within subsection (3) only if it is necessary for the purpose of preventing or detecting an offence under section 188 of the Enterprise Act 2002 (cartel offence).';

(b) in subsection (6) after paragraph (m) there is inserted '; and

(n) the chairman of the OFT.'

(3) In section 33 (rules for grant of authorisations) after subsection (4) there is inserted –

'(4A) The chairman of the OFT shall not grant an authorisation for the carrying out of intrusive surveillance except on an application made by an officer of the OFT.'

(4) In subsection (5)(a) of that section, after 'officer' there is inserted 'or the chairman or an officer of the OFT'.

(5) In section 34 (grant of authorisation in the senior officer's absence) –

(a) in subsection (1)(a), after 'or by' there is inserted 'an officer of the OFT or';

(b) in subsection (2)(a), after 'may be,' there is inserted 'as chairman of the OFT or';

(c) in subsection (4), after paragraph (l) there is inserted –

'(m) a person is entitled to act for the chairman of the OFT if he is an officer of the OFT designated by it for the purposes of this paragraph as a person entitled so to act in an urgent case.'

(6) In section 35 (notification of authorisations for intrusive surveillance) –

(a) in subsections (1) and (10), for 'or customs' there is substituted ', customs or OFT';

(b) in subsection (10), after paragraph (b) there is inserted –

'(ba) the chairman of the OFT; or';

(c) in paragraph (c) of that subsection, at the end there is inserted 'or for a person falling within paragraph (ba).'

(7) In section 36 (approval required for authorisations to take effect) –

(a) in subsection (1), after paragraph (d) there is inserted '; or

(e) an officer of the OFT.';

(b) in subsection (6), after paragraph (g) there is inserted '; and

(h) where the authorisation was granted by the chairman of the OFT or a person entitled to act for him by virtue of section 34(4)(m), that chairman.'

(8) In section 37 (quashing of police and customs authorisations etc.) in subsection (1), after paragraph (d) there is inserted '; or

(e) an officer of the OFT.'

(9) In section 40 (information to be provided to Surveillance Commissioners) after paragraph (d) there is inserted ', and

(e) every officer of the OFT,'.

(10) In section 46 (restrictions on authorisations extending to Scotland), in subsection (3), after paragraph (d) there is inserted –

'(da) the OFT;'.

(11) In section 48 (interpretation of Part 2), in subsection (1), after the entry relating to 'directed' and 'intrusive' there is inserted –

'"OFT" means the Office of Fair Trading;'.

200 Authorisation of action in respect of property

(1) Part 3 of the Police Act 1997 (c. 50) (authorisation of action in respect of property) is amended as follows.

(2) In section 93 (authorisation to interfere with property etc.) –

(a) in subsection (1B), after 'customs officer' there is inserted 'or an officer of the Office of Fair Trading';

(b) after subsection (2A) there is inserted –

'(2AA) Where the authorising officer is the chairman of the Office of Fair Trading, the only purpose falling within subsection (2)(a) is the purpose of preventing or detecting an offence under section 188 of the Enterprise Act 2002.';

(c) in subsection (3), after paragraph (d) there is inserted ', or

(e) if the authorising officer is within subsection (5)(i), by an officer of the Office of Fair Trading.';

(d) in subsection (5), after paragraph (h) there is inserted '; or

(i) the chairman of the Office of Fair Trading.'

(3) In section 94 (authorisation given in absence of authorising officer) in subsection (2), after paragraph (f) there is inserted –

'(g) where the authorising officer is within paragraph (i) of that subsection, by an officer of the Office of Fair Trading designated by it for the purposes of this section.'

201 Offences

(1) Any person who without reasonable excuse fails to comply with a requirement imposed on him under section 193 or 194 is guilty of an offence and liable on summary conviction to imprisonment for a term not exceeding six months or to a fine not exceeding level 5 on the standard scale or to both.

(2) A person who, in purported compliance with a requirement under section 193 or 194 –

  (a) makes a statement which he knows to be false or misleading in a material particular; or

  (b) recklessly makes a statement which is false or misleading in a material particular,

  is guilty of an offence.

(3) A person guilty of an offence under subsection (2) is liable –

  (a) on conviction on indictment, to imprisonment for a term not exceeding two years or to a fine or to both; and

  (b) on summary conviction, to imprisonment for a term not exceeding six months or to a fine not exceeding the statutory maximum, or to both.

(4) Where any person –

  (a) knows or suspects that an investigation by the Serious Fraud Office or the OFT into an offence under section 188 is being or is likely to be carried out; and

  (b) falsifies, conceals, destroys or otherwise disposes of, or causes or permits the falsification, concealment, destruction or disposal of documents which he knows or suspects are or would be relevant to such an investigation,

  he is guilty of an offence unless he proves that he had no intention of concealing the facts disclosed by the documents from the persons carrying out such an investigation.

(5) A person guilty of an offence under subsection (4) is liable –

  (a) on conviction on indictment, to imprisonment for a term not exceeding 5 years or to a fine or to both; and

  (b) on summary conviction, to imprisonment for a term not exceeding six months or to a fine not exceeding the statutory maximum, or to both.

(6) A person who intentionally obstructs a person in the exercise of his powers under a warrant issued under section 194 is guilty of an offence and liable –

  (a) on conviction on indictment, to imprisonment for a term not exceeding 2 years or to a fine or to both; and

  (b) on summary conviction, to a fine not exceeding the statutory maximum.

202 Interpretation of sections 192 to 201

In sections 192 to 201 –

  'documents' includes information recorded in any form and, in relation to information recorded otherwise than in a form in which it is visible and legible, references to its production include references to producing it in a form in which it is visible and legible or from which it can readily be produced in a visible and legible form;

  'person under investigation' has the meaning given in section 192(2).

PART 7   MISCELLANEOUS COMPETITION PROVISIONS

Powers of entry under 1998 Act

203 Powers of entry

(1) The 1998 Act is amended as follows.

(2) In section 28 (power to enter premises under a warrant), after subsection (3) there is inserted –

'(3A) A warrant under this section may authorise persons specified in the warrant to accompany the named officer who is executing it.'

(3) In section 62 (power to enter premises: Commission investigations), after subsection (5) there is inserted –

'(5A) A warrant under this section may authorise persons specified in the warrant to accompany the named officer who is executing it.'

(4) In section 63 (power to enter premises: Director's special investigations), after subsection (5) there is inserted –

'(5A) A warrant under this section may authorise persons specified in the warrant to accompany the named authorised officer who is executing it.'

Directors disqualification

204 Disqualification

(1) The Company Directors Disqualification Act 1986 (c. 46) is amended as follows.
(2) The following sections are inserted after section 9 (matters for determining unfitness in certain cases) –

'Disqualification for competition infringements

9A Competition disqualification order

(1) The court must make a disqualification order against a person if the following two conditions are satisfied in relation to him.
(2) The first condition is that an undertaking which is a company of which he is a director commits a breach of competition law.
(3) The second condition is that the court considers that his conduct as a director makes him unfit to be concerned in the management of a company.
(4) An undertaking commits a breach of competition law if it engages in conduct which infringes any of the following –

   (a) the Chapter 1 prohibition (within the meaning of the Competition Act 1998) (prohibition on agreements, etc. preventing, restricting or distorting competition);
   (b) the Chapter 2 prohibition (within the meaning of that Act) (prohibition on abuse of a dominant position);
   (c) Article 81 of the Treaty establishing the European Community (prohibition on agreements, etc. preventing, restricting or distorting competition);
   (d) Article 82 of that Treaty (prohibition on abuse of a dominant position).

(5) For the purpose of deciding under subsection (3) whether a person is unfit to be concerned in the management of a company the court –

   (a) must have regard to whether subsection (6) applies to him;
   (b) may have regard to his conduct as a director of a company in connection with any other breach of competition law;
   (c) must not have regard to the matters mentioned in Schedule 1.

(6) This subsection applies to a person if as a director of the company –

   (a) his conduct contributed to the breach of competition law mentioned in subsection (2);
   (b) his conduct did not contribute to the breach but he had reasonable grounds to suspect that the conduct of the undertaking constituted the breach and he took no steps to prevent it;
   (c) he did not know but ought to have known that the conduct of the undertaking constituted the breach.

(7) For the purposes of subsection (6)(a) it is immaterial whether the person knew that the conduct of the undertaking constituted the breach.

(8) For the purposes of subsection (4)(a) or (c) references to the conduct of an undertaking are references to its conduct taken with the conduct of one or more other undertakings.

(9) The maximum period of disqualification under this section is 15 years.

(10) An application under this section for a disqualification order may be made by the OFT or by a specified regulator.

(11) Section 60 of the Competition Act 1998 (c. 41) (consistent treatment of questions arising under United Kingdom and Community law) applies in relation to any question arising by virtue of subsection (4)(a) or (b) above as it applies in relation to any question arising under Part 1 of that Act.

9B Competition undertakings

(1) This section applies if –

    (a)   the OFT or a specified regulator thinks that in relation to any person an undertaking which is a company of which he is a director has committed or is committing a breach of competition law,

    (b)   the OFT or the specified regulator thinks that the conduct of the person as a director makes him unfit to be concerned in the management of a company, and

    (c)   the person offers to give the OFT or the specified regulator (as the case may be) a disqualification undertaking.

(2) The OFT or the specified regulator (as the case may be) may accept a disqualification undertaking from the person instead of applying for or proceeding with an application for a disqualification order.

(3) A disqualification undertaking is an undertaking by a person that for the period specified in the undertaking he will not –

    (a)   be a director of a company;

    (b)   act as receiver of a company's property;

    (c)   in any way, whether directly or indirectly, be concerned or take part in the promotion, formation or management of a company;

    (d)   act as an insolvency practitioner.

(4) But a disqualification undertaking may provide that a prohibition falling within subsection (3)(a) to (c) does not apply if the person obtains the leave of the court.

(5) The maximum period which may be specified in a disqualification undertaking is 15 years.

(6) If a disqualification undertaking is accepted from a person who is already subject to a disqualification undertaking under this Act or to a disqualification order the periods specified in those undertakings or the undertaking and the order (as the case may be) run concurrently.

(7) Subsections (4) to (8) of section 9A apply for the purposes of this section as they apply for the purposes of that section but in the application of subsection (5) of that section the reference to the court must be construed as a reference to the OFT or a specified regulator (as the case may be).

9C Competition investigations

(1) If the OFT or a specified regulator has reasonable grounds for suspecting that a breach of competition law has occurred it or he (as the case may be) may carry out an investigation for the purpose of deciding whether to make an application under section 9A for a disqualification order.

(2) For the purposes of such an investigation sections 26 to 30 of the Competition Act 1998 (c. 41) apply to the OFT and the specified regulators as they apply to the OFT for the purposes of an investigation under section 25 of that Act.

(3) Subsection (4) applies if as a result of an investigation under this section the OFT or a specified regulator proposes to apply under section 9A for a disqualification order.

(4) Before making the application the OFT or regulator (as the case may be) must –

(a) give notice to the person likely to be affected by the application, and

(b) give that person an opportunity to make representations.

9D Co-ordination

(1) The Secretary of State may make regulations for the purpose of co-ordinating the performance of functions under sections 9A to 9C (relevant functions) which are exercisable concurrently by two or more persons.

(2) Section 54(5) to (7) of the Competition Act 1998 (c. 41) applies to regulations made under this section as it applies to regulations made under that section and for that purpose in that section –

(a) references to Part 1 functions must be read as references to relevant functions;

(b) references to a regulator must be read as references to a specified regulator;

(c) a competent person also includes any of the specified regulators.

(3) The power to make regulations under this section must be exercised by statutory instrument subject to annulment in pursuance of a resolution of either House of Parliament.

(4) Such a statutory instrument may –

(a) contain such incidental, supplemental, consequential and transitional provision as the Secretary of State thinks appropriate;

(b) make different provision for different cases.

9E Interpretation

(1) This section applies for the purposes of sections 9A to 9D.

(2) Each of the following is a specified regulator for the purposes of a breach of competition law in relation to a matter in respect of which he or it has a function –

(a) the Director General of Telecommunications;

(b) the Gas and Electricity Markets Authority;

(c) the Director General of Water Services;

(d) the Rail Regulator;

(e) the Civil Aviation Authority.

(3) The court is the High Court or (in Scotland) the Court of Session.

(4) Conduct includes omission.

(5) Director includes shadow director.'

(3) In section 1(1) (general provision about disqualification orders) for 'section 6' substitute 'sections 6 and 9A'.

(4) In section 8A (variation etc of disqualification undertaking) after subsection (2) there is inserted the following subsection –

'(2A) Subsection (2) does not apply to an application in the case of an undertaking given under section 9B, and in such a case on the hearing of the application whichever of the OFT or a specified regulator (within the meaning of section 9E) accepted the undertaking –

(a) must appear and call the attention of the court to any matters which appear to it or him (as the case may be) to be relevant;

(b) may give evidence or call witnesses.'

(5) In section 8A for subsection (3) there is substituted –

'(3) In this section "the court" –

(a) in the case of an undertaking given under section 9B means the High Court or (in Scotland) the Court of Session;

(b)   in any other case has the same meaning as in section 7(2) or 8 (as the case may be).'

(6) In section 16(3) for 'the Secretary of State or the official receiver or the liquidator' substitute 'a person falling within subsection (4)'.

(7) In section 16 after subsection (3) there is inserted the following subsection –

'(4) The following fall within this subsection –

(a)   the Secretary of State;
(b)   the official receiver;
(c)   the OFT;
(d)   the liquidator;
(e)   a specified regulator (within the meaning of section 9E).'

(8) In section 17 (applications for leave under an order or undertaking) after subsection (3) there is inserted the following subsection –

'(3A) Where a person is subject to a disqualification undertaking accepted at any time under section 9B any application for leave for the purposes of section 9B(4) must be made to the High Court or (in Scotland) the Court of Session.'

(9) In section 17(4) for 'or 1A(1)(a)' substitute '1A(1)(a) or 9B(4)'.

(10) In section 17 after subsection (5) there are inserted the following subsections –

'(6)   Subsection (5) does not apply to an application for leave for the purposes of section 1(1)(a) if the application for the disqualification order was made under section 9A.

(7)   In such a case and in the case of an application for leave for the purposes of section 9B(4) on the hearing of the application whichever of the OFT or a specified regulator (within the meaning of section 9E) applied for the order or accepted the undertaking (as the case may be) –

(a)   must appear and draw the attention of the court to any matters which appear to it or him (as the case may be) to be relevant;
(b)   may give evidence or call witnesses.'

(11) In section 18 (register of disqualification orders and undertakings) for subsection (2A) substitute –

'(2A) The Secretary of State must include in the register such particulars as he considers appropriate of –

(a)   disqualification undertakings accepted by him under section 7 or 8;
(b)   disqualification undertakings accepted by the OFT or a specified regulator under section 9B;
(c)   cases in which leave has been granted as mentioned in subsection (1)(d).'

Miscellaneous

205 Super-complaints to regulators other than OFT

(1)   The Secretary of State may by order provide that section 11 is to apply to complaints made to a specified regulator in relation to a market of a specified description' as it applies to complaints made to the OFT, with such modifications as may be specified.

(2)   An order under this section –

(a)   shall be made by statutory instrument, and
(b)   shall be subject to annulment in pursuance of a resolution of either House of Parliament.

(3)   In this section –

'regulator' has the meaning given in section 54(1) of the 1998 Act; and
'specified' means specified in the order.

206 Power to modify Schedule 8

(1) The Secretary of State may by order made by statutory instrument modify Schedule 8.

(2) An order under this section may make –

(a) different provision for different cases or different purposes;

(b) such incidental, supplementary, consequential, transitory, transitional or saving provision as the Secretary of State considers appropriate.

(3) An order under this section may, in particular, modify that Schedule in its application by virtue of Part 3 of this Act, in its application by virtue of Part 4 of this Act, in its application by virtue of any other enactment (whether by virtue of Part 4 of this Act as applied by that enactment or otherwise) or in its application by virtue of every enactment that applies it.

(4) An order under this section as extended by subsection (2) may modify any enactment comprised in or made under this Act, or any other enactment.

(5) No order shall be made under this section unless a draft of it has been laid before, and approved by a resolution of, each House of Parliament.

(6) No modification of Schedule 8 in its application by virtue of Part 3 of this Act shall be made by an order under this section if the modification relates to a relevant merger situation or (as the case may be) a special merger situation which has been created before the coming into force of the order.

(7) No modification shall be made by an order under this section of Schedule 8 in its application in relation to references made under section 22, 33, 45 or 62 before the coming into force of the order.

(8) No modification shall be made by an order under this section of Schedule 8 in its application in relation to references made under section 131 or 132 before the coming into force of the order (including references made under section 131 as applied by another enactment).

(9) Before making an order under this section, the Secretary of State shall consult the OFT and the Commission.

(10) Expressions used in this section which are also used in Part 3 of this Act have the same meaning in this section as in that Part.

207 Repeal of Schedule 4 to the 1998 Act

Section 3(1)(d) of and Schedule 4 to the 1998 Act (which provide for the exclusion from the Chapter 1 prohibition in cases involving designated professional rules) shall cease to have effect.

208 Repeal of Part 6 of Fair Trading Act 1973

Sections 78 to 80 of the 1973 Act (references to Commission other than monopoly and merger references) shall cease to have effect.

209 Reform of Community competition law

(1) The Secretary of State may by regulations make such modifications of the 1998 Act as he considers appropriate for the purpose of eliminating or reducing any differences between –

(a) the domestic provisions of the 1998 Act, and

(b) European Community competition law,

which result (or would otherwise result) from a relevant Community instrument made after the passing of this Act.

(2) In subsection (1) –

'the domestic provisions of the 1998 Act' means the provisions of the 1998 Act so far as they do not implement or give effect to a relevant Community instrument;

'European Community competition law' includes any Act or subordinate legislation so far as it implements or gives effect to a relevant Community instrument;

'relevant Community instrument' means a regulation or directive under Article 83 of the Treaty establishing the European Community.

(3) The Secretary of State may by regulations repeal or otherwise modify any provision of an Act (other than the 1998 Act) which excludes any matter from the Chapter I prohibition or the Chapter II prohibition (within the meaning of Part 1 of the 1998 Act).

(4) The power under subsection (3) may not be exercised –

(a) before the power under subsection (1) has been exercised; or

(b) so as to extend the scope of any exclusion that is not being removed by the regulations.

(5) Regulations under this section may –

(a) confer power to make subordinate legislation;

(b) make such consequential, supplementary, incidental, transitory, transitional or saving provision as the Secretary of State considers appropriate (including provision modifying any Act or subordinate legislation); and

(c) make different provision for different cases or circumstances.

(6) The power to make regulations under this section is exercisable by statutory instrument.

(7) No regulations may be made under this section unless a draft of them has been laid before and approved by a resolution of each House of Parliament.

(8) Paragraph 1(1)(c) of Schedule 2 to the European Communities Act 1972 (c. 68) (restriction on powers to legislate) shall not apply to regulations which implement or give effect to a relevant Community instrument made after the passing of this Act.

[. . .]

PART 9   INFORMATION

Restrictions on disclosure

237 General restriction

(1) This section applies to specified information which relates to –

(a) the affairs of an individual;

(b) any business of an undertaking.

(2) Such information must not be disclosed –

(a) during the lifetime of the individual, or

(b) while the undertaking continues in existence,

unless the disclosure is permitted under this Part.

(3) But subsection (2) does not prevent the disclosure of any information if the information has on an earlier occasion been disclosed to the public in circumstances which do not contravene –

(a) that subsection;

(b) any other enactment or rule of law prohibiting or restricting the disclosure of the information.

(4) Nothing in this Part authorises a disclosure of information which contravenes the Data Protection Act 1998 (c. 29).

(5) Nothing in this Part affects the Competition Appeal Tribunal.

(6) This Part (except section 244) does not affect any power or duty to disclose information which exists apart from this Part.

238 Information

(1) Information is specified information if it comes to a public authority in connection with the exercise of any function it has under or by virtue of –

    (a) Part 1, 3, 4, 6, 7 or 8;

    (b) an enactment specified in Schedule 14;

    (c) such subordinate legislation as the Secretary of State may by order specify for the purposes of this subsection.

(2) It is immaterial whether information comes to a public authority before or after the passing of this Act.

(3) Public authority (except in the expression 'overseas public authority') must be construed in accordance with section 6 of the Human Rights Act 1998 (c. 42).

(4) In subsection (1) the reference to an enactment includes a reference to an enactment contained in –

    (a) an Act of the Scottish Parliament;

    (b) Northern Ireland legislation;

    (c) subordinate legislation.

(5) The Secretary of State may by order amend Schedule 14.

(6) The power to make an order under subsection (5) includes power to add, vary or remove a reference to any provision of –

    (a) an Act of the Scottish Parliament;

    (b) Northern Ireland legislation.

(7) An order under this section must be made by statutory instrument subject to annulment in pursuance of a resolution of either House of Parliament.

(8) This section applies for the purposes of this Part.

Permitted disclosure

239 Consent

(1) This Part does not prohibit the disclosure by a public authority of information held by it to any other person if it obtains each required consent.

(2) If the information was obtained by the authority from a person who had the information lawfully and the authority knows the identity of that person the consent of that person is required.

(3) If the information relates to the affairs of an individual the consent of the individual is required.

(4) If the information relates to the business of an undertaking the consent of the person for the time being carrying on the business is required.

(5) For the purposes of subsection (4) consent may be given –

    (a) in the case of a company by a director, secretary or other officer of the company;

    (b) in the case of a partnership by a partner;

    (c) in the case of an unincorporated body or association by a person concerned in the management or control of the body or association.

240 Community obligations

This Part does not prohibit the disclosure of information held by a public authority to another person if the disclosure is required for the purpose of a Community obligation.

241 Statutory functions

(1) A public authority which holds information to which section 237 applies may disclose that information for the purpose of facilitating the exercise by the authority of any function it has under or by virtue of this Act or any other enactment.

(2) If information is disclosed under subsection (1) so that it is not made available to the public it must not be further disclosed by a person to whom it is so disclosed other than with the agreement of the public authority for the purpose mentioned in that subsection.

(3) A public authority which holds information to which section 237 applies may disclose that information to any other person for the purpose of facilitating the exercise by that person of any function he has under or by virtue of –

(a) this Act;

(b) an enactment specified in Schedule 15;

(c) such subordinate legislation as the Secretary of State may by order specify for the purposes of this subsection.

(4) Information disclosed under subsection (3) must not be used by the person to whom it is disclosed for any purpose other than a purpose relating to a function mentioned in that subsection.

(5) In subsection (1) the reference to an enactment includes a reference to an enactment contained in –

(a) an Act of the Scottish Parliament;

(b) Northern Ireland legislation;

(c) subordinate legislation.

(6) The Secretary of State may by order amend Schedule 15.

(7) The power to make an order under subsection (6) includes power to add, vary or remove a reference to any provision of –

(a) an Act of the Scottish Parliament;

(b) Northern Ireland legislation.

(8) An order under this section must be made by statutory instrument subject to annulment in pursuance of a resolution of either House of Parliament.

242 Criminal proceedings

(1) A public authority which holds information to which section 237 applies may disclose that information to any person –

(a) in connection with the investigation of any criminal offence in any part of the United Kingdom;

(b) for the purposes of any criminal proceedings there;

(c) for the purpose of any decision whether to start or bring to an end such an investigation or proceedings.

(2) Information disclosed under this section must not be used by the person to whom it is disclosed for any purpose other than that for which it is disclosed.

(3) A public authority must not make a disclosure under this section unless it is satisfied that the making of the disclosure is proportionate to what is sought to be achieved by it.

243 Overseas disclosures

(1) A public authority which holds information to which section 237 applies (the discloser) may disclose that information to an overseas public authority for the purpose mentioned in subsection (2).

(2) The purpose is facilitating the exercise by the overseas public authority of any function which it has relating to –

(a) carrying out investigations in connection with the enforcement of any relevant legislation by means of civil proceedings;

(b) bringing civil proceedings for the enforcement of such legislation or the conduct of such proceedings;

(c) the investigation of crime;

(d) bringing criminal proceedings or the conduct of such proceedings;

(e) deciding whether to start or bring to an end such investigations or proceedings.

(3) But subsection (1) does not apply to any of the following –

(a) information which is held by a person who is designated by virtue of section 213(4) as a designated enforcer for the purposes of Part 8;

(b) information which comes to a public authority in connection with an investigation under Part 4, 5 or 6 of the 1973 Act or under section 11 of the Competition Act 1980 (c. 21);

(c) competition information within the meaning of section 351 of the Financial Services and Markets Act 2000 (c. 8);

(d) information which comes to a public authority in connection with an investigation under Part 3 or 4 or section 174 of this Act.

(4) The Secretary of State may direct that a disclosure permitted by this section must not be made if he thinks that in connection with any matter in respect of which the disclosure could be made it is more appropriate –

(a) if any investigation is to be carried out, that it is carried out by an authority in the United Kingdom or in another specified country or territory;

(b) if any proceedings are to be brought, that they are brought in a court in the United Kingdom or in another specified country or territory.

(5) The Secretary of State must take such steps as he thinks are appropriate to bring a direction under subsection (4) to the attention of persons likely to be affected by it.

(6) In deciding whether to disclose information under this section a public authority must have regard in particular to the following considerations –

(a) whether the matter in respect of which the disclosure is sought is sufficiently serious to justify making the disclosure;

(b) whether the law of the country or territory to whose authority the disclosure would be made provides appropriate protection against self-incrimination in criminal proceedings;

(c) whether the law of that country or territory provides appropriate protection in relation to the storage and disclosure of personal data;

(d) whether there are arrangements in place for the provision of mutual assistance as between the United Kingdom and that country or territory in relation to the disclosure of information of the kind to which section 237 applies.

(7) Protection is appropriate if it provides protection in relation to the matter in question which corresponds to that so provided in any part of the United Kingdom.

(8) The Secretary of State may by order –

(a) modify the list of considerations in subsection (6);

(b) add to those considerations;

(c) remove any of those considerations.

(9) An order under subsection (8) must be made by statutory instrument subject to annulment in pursuance of a resolution of either House of Parliament.

(10) Information disclosed under this section –

(a) may be disclosed subject to the condition that it must not be further disclosed without the agreement of the discloser, and

(b) must not otherwise be used by the overseas public authority to which it is disclosed for any purpose other than that for which it is first disclosed.

(11) An overseas public authority is a person or body in any country or territory outside the United Kingdom which appears to the discloser to exercise functions of a public nature in relation to any of the matters mentioned in paragraphs (a) to (e) of subsection (2).

(12) Relevant legislation is –

(a) this Act, any enactment specified in Schedule 14 and such subordinate legislation as is specified by order for the purposes of section 238(1);

(b) any enactment or subordinate legislation specified in an order under section 211(2);

(c) any enactment or subordinate legislation specified in an order under section 212(3);

(d) legislation in any country or territory outside the United Kingdom which appears to the discloser to make provision corresponding to this Act or to any such enactment or subordinate legislation.

244 Specified information: considerations relevant to disclosure

(1) A public authority must have regard to the following considerations before disclosing any specified information (within the meaning of section 238(1)).

(2) The first consideration is the need to exclude from disclosure (so far as practicable) any information whose disclosure the authority thinks is contrary to the public interest.

(3) The second consideration is the need to exclude from disclosure (so far as practicable) –

(a) commercial information whose disclosure the authority thinks might significantly harm the legitimate business interests of the undertaking to which it relates, or

(b) information relating to the private affairs of an individual whose disclosure the authority thinks might significantly harm the individual's interests.

(4) The third consideration is the extent to which the disclosure of the information mentioned in subsection (3)(a) or (b) is necessary for the purpose for which the authority is permitted to make the disclosure.

Offences

245 Offences

(1) A person commits an offence if he discloses information to which section 237 applies in contravention of section 237(2).

(2) A person commits an offence if he discloses information in contravention of a direction given under section 243(4).

(3) A person commits an offence if he uses information disclosed to him under this Part for a purpose which is not permitted under this Part.

(4) A person who commits an offence under this section is liable –

(a) on summary conviction to imprisonment for a term not exceeding three months or to a fine not exceeding the statutory maximum or to both;

(b) on conviction on indictment to imprisonment for a term not exceeding two years or to a fine or to both.

General

246 Subordinate legislation

In this Part 'subordinate legislation' has the same meaning as in section 21(1) of the Interpretation Act 1978 (c. 30) and includes an instrument made under –

(a) an Act of the Scottish Parliament;

(b) Northern Ireland legislation.

247 Repeals

The following enactments (which make provision as to the disclosure of certain information) shall cease to have effect –

(a) section 28(5) and (5A) of the Trade Descriptions Act 1968 (c. 29);

(b) sections 30(3) and 133 of the 1973 Act;

(c) paragraph 12 of the Schedule to the Prices Act 1974 (c. 24);

(d) section 174 of the Consumer Credit Act 1974 (c. 39);

(e) section 10 of the Estate Agents Act 1979 (c. 38);

(f) section 19(1) to (3), (4)(c), (d) and (f) and (5) and (6) of the Competition Act 1980 (c. 21);

(g) section 38 of the Consumer Protection Act 1987 (c. 43);

(h) paragraph 7 of the Schedule to the Property Misdescriptions Act 1991 (c. 29);

(i) paragraph 5 of Schedule 2 to the Timeshare Act 1992 (c. 35);

(j) sections 55 and 56 of and Schedule 11 to the Competition Act 1998 (c. 41);

(k) section 351(1) to (3) and (7) of and Schedule 19 to the Financial Services and Markets Act 2000 (c. 8).

[. . .]

PART 11   SUPPLEMENTARY

273 Interpretation

In this Act –

'the 1973 Act' means the Fair Trading Act 1973 (c. 41);

'the 1998 Act' means the Competition Act 1998 (c. 41);

'the Commission' means the Competition Commission;

'the Director' means the Director General of Fair Trading; and

'the OFT' means the Office of Fair Trading.

274 Provision of financial assistance for consumer purposes

The Secretary of State may give financial assistance to any person for the purpose of assisting –

(a) activities which the Secretary of State considers are of benefit to consumers; or

(b) the provision of –

(i) advice or information about consumer matters;

(ii) educational materials relating to consumer matters; or

(iii) advice or information to the Secretary of State in connection with the formulation of policy in respect of consumer matters.

275 Financial provision

There shall be paid out of money provided by Parliament –

(a) any expenditure incurred by the OFT, the Secretary of State, any other Minister of the Crown or a government department by virtue of this Act; and

(b) any increase attributable to this Act in the sums payable out of money so provided by virtue of any other Act.

276 Transitional or transitory provision and savings

(1) Schedule 24 (which makes transitional and transitory provisions and savings) has effect.

(2) The Secretary of State may by order made by statutory instrument make such transitional or transitory provisions and savings as he considers appropriate in connection with the coming into force of any provision of this Act.

(3) An order under subsection (2) may modify any Act or subordinate legislation.

(4) Schedule 24 does not restrict the power under subsection (2) to make other transitional or transitory provisions and savings.

277 Power to make consequential amendments etc.

(1) The Secretary of State may by order make such supplementary, incidental or consequential provision as he thinks appropriate –

    (a) for the general purposes, or any particular purpose, of this Act; or

    (b) in consequence of any provision made by or under this Act or for giving full effect to it.

(2) An order under this section may –

    (a) modify any Act or subordinate legislation (including this Act);

    (b) make incidental, supplementary, consequential, transitional, transitory or saving provision.

(3) The power to make an order under this section is exercisable by statutory instrument subject to annulment in pursuance of a resolution of either House of Parliament.

(4) The power conferred by this section is not restricted by any other provision of this Act.

278 Minor and consequential amendments and repeals

(1) Schedule 25 (which contains minor and consequential amendments) has effect.

(2) Schedule 26 (which contains repeals and revocations) has effect.

279 Commencement

The preceding provisions of this Act shall come into force on such day as the Secretary of State may by order made by statutory instrument appoint; and different days may be appointed for different purposes.

280 Extent

(1) Sections 256 to 265, 267, 269 and 272 extend only to England and Wales.

(2) Sections 204, 248 to 255 and 270 extend only to England and Wales and Scotland (but subsection (3) of section 415A as inserted by section 270 extends only to England and Wales).

(3) Any other modifications by this Act of an enactment have the same extent as the enactment being modified.

(4) Otherwise, this Act extends to England and Wales, Scotland and Northern Ireland.

281 Short title

This Act may be cited as the Enterprise Act 2002.

SCHEDULES

SCHEDULE 1   THE OFFICE OF FAIR TRADING
Section 1

Membership

1 (1) The OFT shall consist of a chairman and no fewer than four other members, appointed by the Secretary of State.

 (2) The Secretary of State shall consult the chairman before appointing any other member.

Terms of appointment, remuneration, pensions etc.

2 (1) Subject to this Schedule, the chairman and other members shall hold and vacate office in accordance with the terms of their respective appointments.

 (2) The terms of appointment of the chairman and other members shall be determined by the Secretary of State.

3 (1) An appointment of a person to hold office as chairman or other member shall be for a term not exceeding five years.

 (2) A person holding office as chairman or other member –

 (a) may resign that office by giving notice in writing to the Secretary of State; and

 (b) may be removed from office by the Secretary of State on the ground of incapacity or misbehaviour.

 (3) A previous appointment as chairman or other member does not affect a person's eligibility for appointment to either office.

4 (1) The OFT shall pay to the chairman and other members such remuneration, and such travelling and other allowances, as may be determined by the Secretary of State.

 (2) The OFT shall, if required to do so by the Secretary of State –

 (a) pay such pension, allowances or gratuities as may be determined by the Secretary of State to or in respect of a person who holds or has held office as chairman or other member; or

 (b) make such payments as may be so determined towards provision for the payment of a pension, allowances or gratuities to or in respect of such a person.

 (3) If, where any person ceases to hold office as chairman or other member, the Secretary of State determines that there are special circumstances which make it right that he should receive compensation, the OFT shall pay to him such amount by way of compensation as the Secretary of State may determine.

Staff

5 (1) The Secretary of State shall, after consulting the chairman, appoint a person (who may, subject to sub-paragraph (2), also be a member of the OFT) to act as chief executive of the OFT on such terms and conditions as the Secretary of State may think appropriate.

 (2) A person appointed as chief executive after the end of the transitional period may not at the same time be chairman.

 (3) In sub-paragraph (2) 'the transitional period' means the period of two years beginning with the day on which this paragraph comes into force.

6   The OFT may, with the approval of the Minister for the Civil Service as to numbers and terms and conditions of service, appoint such other staff as it may determine.

Membership of committees or sub-committees of OFT

7   The members of a committee or sub-committee of the OFT may include persons who are not members of the OFT (and a sub-committee may include persons who are not members of the committee which established it).

Proceedings etc.

8   (1) The OFT may regulate its own procedure (including quorum).
      (2) The OFT shall consult the Secretary of State before making or revising its rules and procedures for dealing with conflicts of interest.
      (3) The OFT shall from time to time publish a summary of its rules and procedures for dealing with conflicts of interest.
9   The validity of anything done by the OFT is not affected by a vacancy among its members or by a defect in the appointment of a member.
10   (1) The application of the seal of the OFT shall be authenticated by the signature of –

      (a) any member; or
      (b) some other person who has been authorised for that purpose by the OFT, whether generally or specially.

      (2) Sub-paragraph (1) does not apply in relation to any document which is, or is to be, signed in accordance with the law of Scotland.
11   A document purporting to be duly executed under the seal of the OFT, or signed on its behalf, shall be received in evidence and, unless the contrary is proved, be taken to be so executed or signed.

Performance of functions

12   (1) Anything authorised or required to be done by the OFT (including exercising the power under this paragraph) may be done by –

      (a) any member or employee of the OFT who is authorised for that purpose by the OFT, whether generally or specially;
      (b) any committee of the OFT which has been so authorised.

      (2) Sub-paragraph (1)(b) does not apply to a committee whose members include any person who is not a member or employee of the OFT.

Supplementary powers

13   The OFT has power to do anything which is calculated to facilitate, or is conducive or incidental to, the performance of its functions.

Parliamentary Commissioner Act 1967 (c. 13)

14   In Schedule 2 to the Parliamentary Commissioner Act 1967 (departments and authorities subject to investigation), there is inserted at the appropriate place –

           'Office of Fair Trading.'

House of Commons Disqualification Act 1975 (c. 24)

15   In Part 2 of Schedule 1 to the House of Commons Disqualification Act 1975 (bodies of which all members are disqualified), there is inserted at the appropriate place –

'The Office of Fair Trading.'

Northern Ireland Assembly Disqualification Act 1975 (c. 25)

16   In Part 2 of Schedule 1 to the Northern Ireland Assembly Disqualification Act 1975 (bodies of which all members are disqualified), there is inserted at the appropriate place –

'The Office of Fair Trading.'

SCHEDULE 2   THE COMPETITION APPEAL TRIBUNAL   Section 12

Appointment, etc. of President and chairmen

1   (1)   A person is not eligible for appointment as President unless –

    (a)   he has a 10 year general qualification;

    (b)   he is an advocate or solicitor in Scotland of at least 10 years' standing; or

    (c)   he is a member of the Bar of Northern Ireland or solicitor of the Supreme Court of Northern Ireland of at least 10 years' standing;

and he appears to the Lord Chancellor to have appropriate experience and knowledge of competition law and practice.

    (2)   A person is not eligible for appointment as a chairman unless –

    (a)   he has a 7 year general qualification;

    (b)   he is an advocate or solicitor in Scotland of at least 7 years' standing; or

    (c)   he is a member of the Bar of Northern Ireland or solicitor of the Supreme Court of Northern Ireland of at least 7 years' standing;

and he appears to the Lord Chancellor to have appropriate experience and knowledge (either of competition law and practice or any other relevant law and practice).

    (3)   Before appointing an advocate or solicitor in Scotland under this paragraph, the Lord Chancellor must consult the Lord President of the Court of Session.

    (4)   In this paragraph 'general qualification' has the same meaning as in section 71 of the Courts and Legal Services Act 1990 (c. 41).

2   (1)   The members appointed as President or as chairmen shall hold and vacate office in accordance with their terms of appointment, subject to the following provisions.

    (2)   A person may not be a chairman for more than 8 years (but this does not prevent a temporary re-appointment for the purpose of continuing to act as a member of the Tribunal as constituted for the purposes of any proceedings instituted before the end of his term of office).

    (3)   The President and the chairmen may resign their offices by notice in writing to the Lord Chancellor.

    (4)   The Lord Chancellor may remove a person from office as President or chairman on the ground of incapacity or misbehaviour.

3   If the President is absent or otherwise unable to act the Lord Chancellor may appoint as acting President any person qualified for appointment as a chairman.

Appointment, etc. of ordinary members

4 (1) Ordinary members shall hold and vacate office in accordance with their terms of appointment, subject to the following provisions.

(2) A person may not be an ordinary member for more than 8 years (but this does not prevent a temporary re-appointment for the purpose of continuing to act as a member of the Tribunal as constituted for the purposes of any proceedings instituted before the end of his term of office).

(3) An ordinary member may resign his office by notice in writing to the Secretary of State.

(4) The Secretary of State may remove a person from office as an ordinary member on the ground of incapacity or misbehaviour.

Remuneration etc. for members

5 (1) The Competition Service shall pay to the President, the chairmen and the ordinary members such remuneration (whether by way of salaries or fees), and such allowances, as the Secretary of State may determine.

(2) The Competition Service shall, if required to do so by the Secretary of State –

(a) pay such pension, allowances or gratuities as may be determined by the Secretary of State to or in respect of a person who holds or has held office as President, a chairman or an ordinary member; or

(b) make such payments as may be so determined towards provision for the payment of a pension, allowance or gratuities to or in respect of such a person.

Compensation for loss of office

6   If, where any person ceases to hold office as President, a chairman or ordinary member, the Secretary of State determines that there are special circumstances which make it right that he should receive compensation, the Competition Service shall pay to him such amount by way of compensation as the Secretary of State may determine.

Staff, accommodation and property

7   Any staff, office accommodation or equipment required for the Tribunal shall be provided by the Competition Service.

Miscellaneous

8   The President must arrange such training for members of the Tribunal as he considers appropriate.

9   In this Schedule 'chairman' and 'ordinary member' mean respectively a member of the panel of chairmen, or a member of the panel of ordinary members, appointed under section 12.

10   In Part 2 of Schedule 1 to the House of Commons Disqualification Act 1975 (bodies of which all members are disqualified), there is inserted at the appropriate place –

'The Competition Appeal Tribunal.'

11   In Part 2 of Schedule 1 to the Northern Ireland Assembly Disqualification Act 1975 (bodies of which all members are disqualified), there is inserted at the appropriate place –

'The Competition Appeal Tribunal.'

SCHEDULE 3   THE COMPETITION SERVICE   Section 13

PART 1   CONSTITUTION ETC.

Membership of the Service

1   (1) The Service shall consist of –

      (a)   the President of the Competition Appeal Tribunal;

      (b)   the Registrar of the Competition Appeal Tribunal; and

      (c)   one or more appointed members.

  (2) An appointed member shall be appointed by the Secretary of State after consulting the President.

Chairman of Service

2   (1) Subject to sub-paragraph (2), the members shall choose one of their number to be chairman of the Service.

  (2) The Secretary of State shall designate one of the members to be the first chairman of the Service for such period as the Secretary of State may determine.

Appointed members

3   An appointed member shall hold and vacate office in accordance with the terms of his appointment (and is eligible for re-appointment).

Allowances, etc. for members

4   (1) The Service shall pay –

      (a)   such travelling and other allowances to its members, and

      (b)   such remuneration to any appointed member,

as may be determined by the Secretary of State.

  (2) The Service shall, if required to do so by the Secretary of State –

      (a)   pay such pension, allowances or gratuities as may be determined by the Secretary of State to or in respect of a person who holds or has held office as an appointed member; or

      (b)   make such payments as may be so determined towards provision for the payment of a pension, allowances or gratuities to or in respect of such a person.

5   If, where any person ceases to hold office as an appointed member, the Secretary of State determines that there are special circumstances which make it right that he should receive compensation, the Service shall pay to him such amount by way of compensation as the Secretary of State may determine.

Staff

6   (1) The Service may, with the approval of the Secretary of State as to numbers and terms and conditions of service, appoint such staff as it may determine.

  (2) The persons to whom section 1 of the Superannuation Act 1972 (c. 11) (persons to or in respect of whom benefits may be provided by schemes under that section) applies shall include the staff of the Service.

(3) The Service shall pay to the Minister for the Civil Service, at such times as he may direct, such sums as he may determine in respect of any increase attributable to sub-paragraph (2) in the sums payable out of money provided by Parliament under the Superannuation Act 1972.

Procedure

7   (1) The Service may regulate its own procedure (including quorum).

(2) The validity of anything done by the Service is not affected by a vacancy among its members or by a defect in the appointment of a member.

8   (1) The application of the seal of the Service shall be authenticated by the signature of –

(a) any member; or

(b) some other person who has been authorised for that purpose by the Service, whether generally or specially.

(2) Sub-paragraph (1) does not apply in relation to any document which is, or is to be, signed in accordance with the law of Scotland.

9   A document purporting to be duly executed under the seal of the Service, or signed on its behalf, shall be received in evidence and, unless the contrary is proved, be taken to be so executed or signed.

The Service's powers

10   The Service has power to do anything which is calculated to facilitate, or is conducive or incidental to, the performance of its functions.

Accounts

11 (1) The Service shall keep proper accounts and proper records in relation to its accounts.

(2) In performing that duty the Service shall, in addition to accounts and records relating to its own activities (including the services provided to the Tribunal), keep separate accounts and separate records in relation to the activities of the Tribunal.

12 (1) The Service shall –

(a) prepare a statement of accounts in respect of each of its financial years; and

(b) prepare a statement of accounts for the Tribunal for each of its financial years.

(2) The Service must send copies of the accounts required by sub-paragraph (1) to the Secretary of State and to the Comptroller and Auditor General before the end of August following the financial year to which they relate.

(3) Those accounts must comply with any directions given by the Secretary of State with the approval of the Treasury as to –

(a) the information to be contained in them;

(b) the manner in which that information is to be presented; and

(c) the methods and principles according to which they are to be prepared.

(4) The Comptroller and Auditor General shall –

(a) examine, certify and report on each statement of accounts received by him; and

(b) lay copies of each statement before Parliament.

(5) In this paragraph 'financial year' means the period of 12 months ending with 31st March.

PART 2   TRANSFERS OF PROPERTY ETC. BETWEEN THE COMMISSION AND THE SERVICE

13 (1) The Secretary of State may make one or more schemes for the transfer to the Service of defined property, rights and liabilities of the Commission (including rights and liabilities relating to contracts of employment).

(2) A scheme may define the property, rights and liabilities to be transferred by specifying or describing them or by referring to all (or all except anything specified or described) of the property, rights and liabilities comprised in a specified part of the undertaking of the transferor.

(3) The property, rights and liabilities which may be transferred include any that would otherwise be incapable of being transferred or assigned.

(4) A scheme may include supplementary, incidental, transitional and consequential provision.

14 (1) On the day appointed by a scheme under paragraph 13, the property, rights and liabilities which are the subject of the scheme shall, by virtue of this sub-paragraph, be transferred in accordance with the provisions of the scheme.

(2) If, after that day, the Commission and the Service so agree in writing, the scheme shall for all purposes be deemed to have come into force on that day with such modification as may be agreed.

(3) An agreement under sub-paragraph (2) may, in connection with giving effect to modifications to the scheme, include supplemental, incidental, transitional and consequential provision.

15   The transfer by paragraph 14(1) of the rights and liabilities relating to an individual's contract of employment does not break the continuity of his employment and, accordingly –

(a) he is not to be regarded for the purposes of Part 11 of the Employment Rights Act 1996 as having been dismissed by virtue of the transfer; and

(b) his period of employment with the transferor counts as a period of employment with the transferee for the purposes of that Act.

16 (1) Anything done by or in relation to the transferor for the purposes of or in connection with anything transferred by paragraph 14(1) which is in effect immediately before it is transferred shall be treated as if done by or in relation to the transferee.

(2) There may be continued by or in relation to the transferee anything (including legal proceedings) relating to anything so transferred which is in the process of being done by or in relation to the transferor immediately before it is transferred.

(3) A reference to the transferor in any document relating to anything so transferred shall be taken (so far as necessary for the purposes of or in consequence of the transfer) as a reference to the transferee.

(4) A transfer under paragraph 14(1) does not affect the validity of anything done by or in relation to the transferor before the transfer takes effect.

PART 3   MISCELLANEOUS

17   In Part 2 of Schedule 1 to the House of Commons Disqualification Act 1975 (bodies of which all members are disqualified), there is inserted at the appropriate place –

'The Competition Service.'

18   In Part 2 of Schedule 1 to the Northern Ireland Assembly Disqualification Act 1975 (bodies of which all members are disqualified), there is inserted at the appropriate place –

'The Competition Service.'

SCHEDULE 4   TRIBUNAL: PROCEDURE   Sections 14 and 15

PART 1   GENERAL

Decisions of the Tribunal

1   (1)   A decision of the Tribunal in any proceedings before it must –

    (a)   state the reasons for the decision and whether it was unanimous or taken by a majority;

    (b)   be recorded in a document signed and dated by the chairman of the Tribunal dealing with the proceedings.

  (2)   In preparing that document the Tribunal shall have regard to the need for excluding, so far as practicable –

    (a)   information the disclosure of which would in its opinion be contrary to the public interest;

    (b)   commercial information the disclosure of which would or might, in its opinion, significantly harm the legitimate business interests of the undertaking to which it relates;

    (c)   information relating to the private affairs of an individual the disclosure of which would, or might, in its opinion, significantly harm his interests.

  (3)   But the Tribunal shall also have regard to the extent to which any disclosure mentioned in sub-paragraph (2) is necessary for the purpose of explaining the reasons for the decision.

  (4)   The President shall make such arrangements for the publication of the decisions of the Tribunal as he considers appropriate.

Enforcement of decisions in Great Britain

2   If a decision of the Tribunal is registered in England and Wales in accordance with rules of court or any practice direction –

    (a)   payment of damages which are awarded by the decision;

    (b)   costs or expenses awarded by the decision; and

    (c)   any direction given as a result of the decision,

may be enforced by the High Court as if the damages, costs or expenses were an amount due in pursuance of a judgment or order of the High Court, or as if the direction were an order of the High Court.

3   If a decision of the Tribunal awards damages, costs or expenses, or results in any direction being given, the decision may be recorded for execution in the Books of Council and Session and shall be enforceable accordingly.

4   Subject to rules of court or any practice direction, a decision of the Tribunal may be registered or recorded for execution –

    (a)   for the purpose of enforcing a direction given as a result of the decision, by the Registrar of the Tribunal or a person who was a party to the proceedings;

    (b)   for the purpose of enforcing a decision to award damages, costs or expenses (other than a decision to which paragraph (c) applies), by the person to whom the sum concerned was awarded; and

    (c)   for the purpose of enforcing a decision to award damages which is the subject of an order under section 47B(6) of the 1998 Act, by the specified body concerned.

Enforcement of decisions in Northern Ireland

5 (1) A decision of the Tribunal may be enforced in Northern Ireland with the leave of the High Court in Northern Ireland –

(a) in the case of a direction given as a result of the decision, by the Registrar of the Tribunal or a person who was a party to the proceedings;

(b) for the purpose of enforcing a decision to award damages, costs or expenses (other than a decision to which paragraph (c) applies), by the person to whom the sum concerned was awarded; and

(c) for the purpose of enforcing a decision to award damages which is the subject of an order under section 47B(6) of the 1998 Act, by the specified body concerned.

(2) For the purpose of enforcing in Northern Ireland a decision to award damages, costs or expenses –

(a) payment may be enforced as if the damages, costs or expenses were an amount due in pursuance of a judgment or order of the High Court in Northern Ireland; and

(b) a sum equal to the amount of damages, costs or expenses shall be deemed to be payable under a money judgment within the meaning of Article 2(2) of the Judgments Enforcement (Northern Ireland) Order 1981 (S.I. 1981/226 (N.I. 6)) (and the provisions of that Order apply accordingly).

(3) For the purpose of enforcing in Northern Ireland a direction given as a result of a decision of the Tribunal, the direction may be enforced as if it were an order of the High Court in Northern Ireland.

Miscellaneous

6 A decision of the Tribunal in proceedings under section 47B of the 1998 Act which –

(a) awards damages to an individual in respect of a claim made or continued on his behalf (but is not the subject of an order under section 47B(6)); or

(b) awards costs or expenses to an individual in respect of proceedings in respect of a claim made under section 47A of that Act prior to its being continued on his behalf in the proceedings under section 47B,

may only be enforced by the individual concerned with the permission of the High Court or Court of Session.

7 An award of costs or expenses against a specified body in proceedings under section 47B of the 1998 Act may not be enforced against any individual on whose behalf a claim was made or continued in those proceedings.

8 In this Part of this Schedule any reference to damages includes a reference to any sum of money (other than costs or expenses) which may be awarded in respect of a claim made under section 47A of the 1998 Act or included in proceedings under section 47B of that Act.

PART 2   TRIBUNAL RULES

General

9 In this Schedule 'the Tribunal', in relation to any proceedings before it, means the Tribunal as constituted (in accordance with section 14) for the purposes of those proceedings.

10 Tribunal rules may make different provision for different kinds of proceedings.

Institution of proceedings

11 (1) Tribunal rules may make provision as to the period within which and the manner in which proceedings are to be brought.

    (2) That provision may, in particular –

        (a) provide for time limits for making claims to which section 47A of the 1998 Act applies in proceedings under section 47A or 47B;

        (b) provide for the Tribunal to extend the period in which any particular proceedings may be brought; and

        (c) provide for the form, contents, amendment and acknowledgement of the documents by which proceedings are to be instituted.

12   Tribunal rules may provide for the Tribunal to reject any proceedings (other than proceedings under section 47A or 47B of the 1998 Act) if it considers that –

        (a) the person instituting them does not have a sufficient interest in the decision with respect to which the proceedings are brought; or

        (b) the document by which he institutes them discloses no valid grounds for bringing them.

13   Tribunal rules may provide for the Tribunal –

        (a) to reject the whole of any proceedings under section 47B of the 1998 Act if it considers that the person bringing the proceedings is not entitled to do so or that the proceedings do not satisfy the requirements of section 47B(1);

        (b) to reject any claim which is included in proceedings under section 47B if it considers that –

            (i) the claim is not a consumer claim (within the meaning of section 47B(2)) which may be included in such proceedings; or

            (ii) the individual concerned has not consented to its being made or continued on his behalf in such proceedings; or

        (c) to reject any claim made under section 47A of the 1998 Act or included in proceedings under section 47B of that Act if it considers that there are no reasonable grounds for making it.

14   Tribunal rules may provide for the Tribunal to reject any proceedings if it is satisfied that the person instituting the proceedings has habitually and persistently and without any reasonable ground –

        (a) instituted vexatious proceedings (whether against the same person or against different persons); or

        (b) made vexatious applications in any proceedings.

15   Tribunal rules must ensure that no proceedings are rejected without giving the parties the opportunity to be heard.

Pre-hearing reviews and preliminary matters

16 (1) Tribunal rules may make provision for the carrying out by the Tribunal of a preliminary consideration of proceedings (a 'pre-hearing review').

    (2) That provision may include –

        (a) provision enabling such powers to be exercised on a pre-hearing review as may be specified in the rules;

        (b) provision for security and supplemental provision relating to security.

    (3) For the purposes of sub-paragraph (2)(b) –

        (a) 'provision for security' means provision authorising the Tribunal, in specified circumstances, to order a party to the proceedings, if he wishes to continue to participate in them, to pay a deposit not exceeding such sum as may be specified or calculated in a specified manner; and

(b) 'supplemental provision', in relation to security, means provision as to –

    (i) the manner in which the amount of a deposit is to be determined;

    (ii) the consequences of non-payment of a deposit;

    (iii) the circumstances in which the deposit, or any part of it, may be refunded to the person who paid it or paid to another party to the proceedings.

Conduct of the hearing

17 (1) Tribunal rules may make provision –

(a) as to the manner in which proceedings are to be conducted, including provision for any hearing to be held in private if the Tribunal considers it appropriate because it is considering information of a kind mentioned in paragraph 1(2);

(b) as to the persons entitled to appear on behalf of the parties;

(c) for requiring persons to attend to give evidence and produce documents, and for authorising the administration of oaths to witnesses;

(d) as to the evidence which may be required or admitted and the extent to which it should be oral or written;

(e) allowing the Tribunal to fix time limits with respect to any aspect of proceedings and to extend any time limit (before or after its expiry);

(f) enabling the Tribunal, on the application of any party or on its own initiative, to order –

    (i) the disclosure between, or the production by, the parties of documents or classes of documents; or

    (ii) such recovery or inspection of documents as might be ordered by a sheriff;

(g) for the appointment of experts for the purposes of proceedings;

(h) for the award of costs or expenses, including allowances payable to persons in connection with attendance before the Tribunal;

(i) for taxing or otherwise settling any costs or expenses awarded by the Tribunal or for the enforcement of any order awarding costs or expenses.

(2) Rules under sub-paragraph (1)(h) may provide, in relation to a claim made under section 47A of the 1998 Act which is continued on behalf of an individual in proceedings under section 47B of that Act, for costs or expenses to be awarded to or against that individual in respect of proceedings on that claim which took place before it was included in the proceedings under section 47B of that Act.

(3) Otherwise Tribunal rules may not provide for costs or expenses to be awarded to or against an individual on whose behalf a claim is made or continued in proceedings under section 47B of the 1998 Act.

(4) Tribunal rules may make provision enabling the Tribunal to refer any matter arising in any proceedings (other than proceedings under section 47A or 47B of the 1998 Act) back to the authority that made the decision to which the proceedings relate, if it appears that the matter has not been adequately investigated.

(5) A person who without reasonable excuse fails to comply with –

(a) any requirement imposed by virtue of sub-paragraph (1)(c); or

(b) any requirement with respect to the disclosure, production, recovery or inspection of documents which is imposed by virtue of sub-paragraph (1)(f),

is guilty of an offence and liable on summary conviction to a fine not exceeding level 3 on the standard scale.

Quorum

18   (1)   Tribunal rules may make provision as to the consequences of a member of the Tribunal being unable to continue after part of any proceedings have been heard.

(2)   The rules may allow the Tribunal to consist of the remaining members for the rest of the proceedings.

(3)   The rules may enable the President, if it is the chairman of the Tribunal who is unable to continue –

(a)   to appoint either of the remaining members to chair the Tribunal; and

(b)   if that person is not a member of the panel of chairmen, to appoint himself or some other suitably qualified person to attend the proceedings and advise the remaining members on any questions of law arising.

(4)   For the purpose of sub-paragraph (3) a person is 'suitably qualified' if he is, or is qualified for appointment as, a member of the panel of chairmen.

Interest

19   (1)   Tribunal rules may make provision allowing the Tribunal to order that interest is payable on any sum awarded by the Tribunal or on any fees ordered to be paid under paragraph 20.

(2)   That provision may include provision –

(a)   as to the circumstances in which such an order may be made;

(b)   as to the manner in which, and the periods in respect of which, interest is to be calculated and paid.

Fees

20   (1)   Tribunal rules may provide –

(a)   for fees to be chargeable in respect of specified costs of proceedings; and

(b)   for the amount of such costs to be determined by the Tribunal.

(2)   Any sums received in respect of such fees shall be paid into the Consolidated Fund.

Withdrawal of proceedings

21   (1)   Tribunal rules may make provision –

(a)   preventing a party who has instituted proceedings from withdrawing them without the permission of the Tribunal or, in specified circumstances, the President or the Registrar;

(b)   for the Tribunal to grant permission to withdraw proceedings on such conditions as it considers appropriate;

(c)   enabling the Tribunal to publish any decision which it would have made in any proceedings, had the proceedings not been withdrawn;

(d)   as to the effect of withdrawal of proceedings; and

(e)   as to the procedure to be followed if parties to proceedings agree to settle.

(2)   Tribunal rules may make, in relation to a claim included in proceedings under section 47B of the 1998 Act, any provision which may be made under sub-paragraph (1) in relation to the whole proceedings.

Interim orders

22   (1)   Tribunal rules may provide for the Tribunal to make an order, on an interim basis –

(a)   suspending the effect of any decision which is the subject matter of proceedings before it;

(b)   in the case of an appeal under section 46 or 47 of the 1998 Act, varying the conditions or obligations attached to an exemption;

(c)   granting any remedy which the Tribunal would have had power to grant in its final decision.

(2)   Tribunal rules may also make provision giving the Tribunal powers similar to those given to the OFT by section 35 of the 1998 Act.

Miscellaneous

23   (1)   Tribunal rules may make provision enabling the Tribunal to decide where to sit for the purposes of, or of any part of, any proceedings before it.

(2)   Tribunal rules may make provision enabling the Tribunal to decide that any proceedings before it are to be treated, for purposes connected with –

(a)   any appeal from a decision of the Tribunal made in those proceedings; and

(b)   any other matter connected with those proceedings,

as proceedings in England and Wales, Scotland or Northern Ireland (regardless of the decision made for the purposes of sub-paragraph (1)).

(3)   For the purposes of sub-paragraph (2), Tribunal rules may provide for each claim made or continued on behalf of an individual in proceedings under section 47B of the 1998 Act to be treated as separate proceedings.

24   Tribunal rules may make provision –

(a)   for a person who is not a party to be joined in any proceedings;

(b)   for hearing a person who is not a party where, in any proceedings, it is proposed to make an order or give a direction in relation to that person;

(c)   for proceedings to be consolidated on such terms as the Tribunal thinks appropriate in such circumstances as may be specified.

25   Tribunal rules may make provision for the Tribunal to transfer a claim made in proceedings under section 47A of the 1998 Act to –

(a)   the High Court or a county court in England and Wales or Northern Ireland; or

(b)   the Court of Session or a sheriff court in Scotland.

26   Tribunal rules may make provision in connection with the transfer of any proceedings from a court mentioned in paragraph 25 to the Tribunal under section 16.

SCHEDULE 5   PROCEEDINGS UNDER PART 1 OF THE 1998 ACT
Section 21

1   Part 1 of the 1998 Act is amended as follows.

2   In section 46 (appealable decisions) –

(a)   in subsections (1) and (2), for 'the Competition Commission' there is substituted 'the Tribunal';

(b)   in subsection (3) (in the full-out words), after 'other decision' there is inserted 'under this Part';

(c)   subsection (3)(h) shall cease to have effect.

3   Section 48 (appeal tribunals) shall cease to have effect.

4   For section 49 there is substituted –

'49 Further appeals

(1)   An appeal lies to the appropriate court –

(a)   from a decision of the Tribunal as to the amount of a penalty under section 36;

(b) from a decision of the Tribunal as to the award of damages or other sum in respect of a claim made in proceedings under section 47A or included in proceedings under section 47B (other than a decision on costs or expenses) or as to the amount of any such damages or other sum; and

(c) on a point of law arising from any other decision of the Tribunal on an appeal under section 46 or 47.

(2) An appeal under this section –

(a) may be brought by a party to the proceedings before the Tribunal or by a person who has a sufficient interest in the matter; and

(b) requires the permission of the Tribunal or the appropriate court.

(3) In this section "the appropriate court" means the Court of Appeal or, in the case of an appeal from Tribunal proceedings in Scotland, the Court of Session.'

5   In section 58(1) (findings of fact by director) –

(a) in paragraph (a), after 'appeal' there is inserted 'under section 46 or 47'; and

(b) in paragraph (b), for 'an appeal tribunal' there is substituted 'the Tribunal'.

6   In section 59(1) (interpretation of Part 1) –

(a) the definition of 'appeal tribunal' shall cease to have effect;

(b) after the definition of 'the Treaty' there is inserted –

> '"the Tribunal" means the Competition Appeal Tribunal;
> "Tribunal rules" means rules under section 15 of the Enterprise Act 2002.'

7   (1) Schedule 7 (the Competition Commission) is amended as follows.

(2) In paragraph 1 (interpretation) –

(a) the definitions of 'appeal panel member' and 'the President' shall cease to have effect; and

(b) in the definition of 'general functions', paragraph (a) and the word 'or' after it shall cease to have effect.

(3) In paragraph 2 (membership), sub-paragraphs (1)(a), (3)(a) and (4) shall cease to have effect.

(4) Paragraph 4 (the President) shall cease to have effect.

(5) In paragraph 5 (the Council) –

(a) sub-paragraph (2)(b), and

(b) in sub-paragraph (3), the words 'and paragraph 5 of Schedule 8',

shall cease to have effect.

(6) Part 3 (appeals) shall cease to have effect.

8   (1) Schedule 8 (appeals) is amended as follows.

(2) Paragraph 1 shall cease to have effect.

(3) In paragraph 2 (general procedure for appeals under Part 1) –

(a) in sub-paragraph (1), for the words from 'Competition' to 'Commission' (in the second place it appears) there is substituted 'Tribunal under section 46 or 47 must be made by sending a notice of appeal to it';

(b) in sub-paragraph (3), for 'tribunal' there is substituted 'Tribunal'; and

(c) after sub-paragraph (3) there is inserted –

> '(4) In this paragraph references to the Tribunal are to the Tribunal as constituted (in accordance with section 14 of the Enterprise Act 2002) for the purposes of the proceedings in question.
>
> (5) Nothing in this paragraph restricts the power under section 15 of the Enterprise Act 2002 (Tribunal rules) to make provision as to the manner of instituting proceedings before the Tribunal.'

(4) In paragraph 3, for 'tribunal' (in each place) there is substituted 'Tribunal'.

(5) Paragraphs 4 to 14 shall cease to have effect.

SCHEDULE 6   SCHEDULE TO BE INSERTED IN THE WATER INDUSTRY ACT 1991

Section 70

'SCHEDULE 4ZA   APPLICATION OF PROVISIONS OF ENTERPRISE ACT 2002 TO MERGERS OF WATER ENTERPRISES

Section 34

1   Part 3 of the 2002 Act (and any other provisions of that Act so far as relating to that Part) shall apply, with such prescribed modifications as the Secretary of State considers to be necessary or expedient, in relation to water mergers and merger references under section 32 of this Act as it applies in relation to relevant merger situations and references under Part 3 of that Act.

2   The modifications made by virtue of paragraph 1 above shall include modifications to give effect to paragraphs 3 to 6 below.

3   (1) The first questions to be decided by the Competition Commission on a merger reference under section 32(a) of this Act shall be –

  (a) whether arrangements are in progress which, if carried into effect, will result in a water merger; and

  (b) if so, whether that merger may be expected to prejudice the ability of the Director, in carrying out his functions by virtue of this Act, to make comparisons between different water enterprises.

  (2) The first questions to be decided by the Competition Commission on a merger reference under section 32(b) of this Act shall be –

  (a) whether a water merger has taken place; and

  (b) if so, whether that merger has prejudiced, or may be expected to prejudice, the ability of the Director, in carrying out his functions by virtue of this Act, to make comparisons between different water enterprises.

  (3) Any decision of the Competition Commission on a merger reference under section 32(a) of this Act that arrangements are in progress which, if carried into effect, will result in a water merger shall be treated as a decision that no arrangements are in progress which, if carried into effect, will result in a water merger if the decision is not that of at least two-thirds of the members of the group constituted in connection with the reference in pursuance of paragraph 15 of Schedule 7 to the Competition Act 1998 (c. 41).

  (4) Any decision of the Competition Commission on a merger reference under section 32(a) of this Act that a water merger may be expected to prejudice the ability of the Director, in carrying out his functions by virtue of this Act, to make comparisons between different water enterprises shall be treated as a decision that the water merger may be expected not to prejudice that ability of the Director if the decision is not that of at least two-thirds of the members of the group constituted in connection with the reference in pursuance of paragraph 15 of Schedule 7 to the Competition Act 1998.

  (5) Any decision of the Competition Commission on a merger reference under section 32(b) of this Act that a water merger has taken place shall be treated as a decision that no water merger has taken place if the decision is not that of at least two-thirds of the members of the group constituted in connection with the reference in pursuance of paragraph 15 of Schedule 7 to the Competition Act 1998.

(6)   Any decision of the Competition Commission on a merger reference under section 32(b) of this Act that a water merger has prejudiced, or may be expected to prejudice, the ability of the Director, in carrying out his functions by virtue of this Act, to make comparisons between different water enterprises shall be treated as a decision that the water merger has not prejudiced, or may be expected not to prejudice, that ability of the Director if the decision is not that of at least two-thirds of the members of the group constituted in connection with the reference in pursuance of paragraph 15 of Schedule 7 to the Competition Act 1998.

4   (1)   In deciding, on a merger reference under section 32(a) of this Act whether to take action for the purpose of remedying, mitigating or preventing the prejudice to the Director or any adverse effect which may be expected to result from the prejudice to the Director and, if so, what action should be taken, the Competition Commission may, in particular, have regard to the effect of any such action on any relevant customer benefits in relation to the merger concerned provided that –

(a)   a consideration of those benefits would not prevent a solution to the prejudice concerned; or

(b)   the benefits which may be expected to accrue are substantially more important than the prejudice concerned.

(2)   In deciding, on a merger reference under section 32(b) of this Act whether to take action for the purpose of remedying, mitigating or preventing the prejudice to the Director or any adverse effect which has resulted from, or may be expected to result from, the prejudice to the Director and, if so, what action should be taken, the Competition Commission may, in particular, have regard to the effect of any such action on any relevant customer benefits in relation to the merger concerned provided that –

(a)   a consideration of those benefits would not prevent a solution to the prejudice concerned; or

(b)   the benefits which have accrued, or may be expected to accrue, are substantially more important than the prejudice concerned.

(3)   This paragraph is without prejudice to the power of the Secretary of State to provide in regulations made under paragraph 1 above for other matters to which the Competition Commission may or must have regard in deciding the questions as mentioned in sub-paragraph (1) or (2) above (including matters which are to take priority over the effect of action on relevant customer benefits).

5   (1)   No enforcement action shall be taken on a merger reference under section 32(b) of this Act in respect of an actual merger unless the reference was made within the period of four months beginning with whichever is the later of –

(a)   the day on which the merger took place; and

(b)   the day on which the material facts about the transactions which resulted in the merger first came to the attention of the OFT or were made public (within the meaning given by section 24(3) of the 2002 Act).

(2)   This paragraph is without prejudice to the power of the Secretary of State to provide in regulations made under paragraph 1 above for extensions of the four month period; and, if any such provision is made in such regulations, the provision which is to be made in regulations under paragraph 1 above by virtue of sub-paragraph (1) above or paragraph 6 below may be adjusted accordingly.

6   If, on a merger reference under section 32(b) of this Act, the Competition Commission are satisfied that the reference was not made within the period of four months mentioned in paragraph 5 above, its report on the reference shall state that fact.

7   (1)   For the purposes of this Schedule a benefit is a relevant customer benefit if –

(a)   it is a benefit to relevant customers in the form of –

(i)   lower prices, higher quality or greater choice of goods or services in any market in the United Kingdom; or

(ii)   greater innovation in relation to such goods or services; and

(b)   the Competition Commission believes –

(i)   in the case of a merger reference under section 32(a) of this Act, as mentioned in sub-paragraph (2) below; and

(ii)   in the case of a merger reference under section 32(b) of this Act, as mentioned in sub-paragraph (3) below.

(2)   The belief, in the case of a merger reference under section 32(a) of this Act, is that –

(a)   the benefit may be expected to accrue within a reasonable period as a result of the merger concerned; and

(b)   the benefit is unlikely to accrue without the merger concerned or a similar prejudice to the Director.

(3)   The belief, in the case of a merger reference under section 32(b) of this Act is that –

(a)   the benefit has accrued as a result of the merger concerned or may be expected to accrue within a reasonable period as a result of the merger concerned; and

(b)   the benefit was, or is, unlikely to accrue without the merger concerned or a similar prejudice to the Director.

(4)   In sub-paragraph (1) above "relevant customers" means –

(a)   customers of any person carrying on an enterprise which, in the merger concerned, has ceased to be, or (as the case may be) will cease to be, a distinct enterprise;

(b)   customers of such customers; and

(c)   any other customers in a chain of customers beginning with the customers mentioned in paragraph (a);

and in this sub-paragraph "customers" includes future customers.

8   In this Schedule –

"customers", "goods", "market in the United Kingdom", "services" and "relevant merger situation" have the same meanings as in Part 3 of the 2002 Act; and

"water merger" means a merger of any two or more water enterprises.'

SCHEDULE 7   ENFORCEMENT REGIME FOR PUBLIC INTEREST AND SPECIAL PUBLIC INTEREST CASES
Section 85

Pre-emptive undertakings and orders

1   (1)   Sub-paragraph (2) applies where an intervention notice or special intervention notice is in force.

(2) The Secretary of State may, for the purpose of preventing pre-emptive action, accept from such of the parties concerned as he considers appropriate undertakings to take such action as he considers appropriate.

(3) Sub-paragraph (4) applies where an intervention notice is in force.

(4) The Secretary of State may, for the purpose of preventing pre-emptive action, adopt an undertaking accepted by the OFT under section 71 if the undertaking is still in force when the Secretary of State adopts it.

(5) An undertaking adopted under sub-paragraph (4) –

    (a)   shall continue in force, in accordance with its terms, when adopted;

    (b)   may be varied or superseded by an undertaking under this paragraph; and

    (c)   may be released by the Secretary of State.

(6) Any other undertaking under this paragraph –

    (a)   shall come into force when accepted;

    (b)   may be varied or superseded by another undertaking; and

    (c)   may be released by the Secretary of State.

(7) References in this Part to undertakings under this paragraph shall, unless the context otherwise requires, include references to undertakings adopted under this paragraph; and references to the acceptance or giving of undertakings under this paragraph shall be construed accordingly.

(8) An undertaking which is in force under this paragraph in relation to a reference or possible reference under section 45 or (as the case may be) 62 shall cease to be in force if an order under paragraph 2 or an undertaking under paragraph 3 comes into force in relation to that reference.

(9) An undertaking under this paragraph shall, if it has not previously ceased to be in force, cease to be in force when the intervention notice concerned or (as the case may be) special intervention notice concerned ceases to be in force.

(10) No undertaking shall be accepted by the Secretary of State under this paragraph before the making of a reference under section 45 or (as the case may be) 62 unless the undertaking relates to a relevant merger situation which has been, or may have been, created or (as the case may be) a special merger situation which has been, or may have been, created.

(11) The Secretary of State shall, as soon as reasonably practicable, consider any representations received by him in relation to varying or releasing an undertaking under this paragraph.

(12) In this paragraph and paragraph 2 'pre-emptive action' means action which might prejudice the reference or possible reference concerned under section 45 or (as the case may be) 62 or impede the taking of any action under this Part which may be justified by the Secretary of State's decisions on the reference.

2   (1)   Sub-paragraph (2) applies where an intervention notice or special intervention notice is in force.

    (2)   The Secretary of State or the OFT may by order, for the purpose of preventing pre-emptive action –

        (a)   prohibit or restrict the doing of things which the Secretary of State or (as the case may be) the OFT considers would constitute pre-emptive action;

        (b)   impose on any person concerned obligations as to the carrying on of any activities or the safeguarding of any assets;

        (c)   provide for the carrying on of any activities or the safeguarding of any assets either by the appointment of a person to conduct or supervise the conduct of any activities (on such terms and with such powers as may be specified or described in the order) or in any other manner;

        (d)   do anything which may be done by virtue of paragraph 19 of Schedule 8.

    (3)   Sub-paragraph (4) applies where an intervention notice is in force.

(4) The Secretary of State or the OFT may, for the purpose of preventing pre-emptive action, adopt an order made by the OFT under section 72 if the order is still in force when the Secretary of State or (as the case may be) the OFT adopts it.

(5) An order adopted under sub-paragraph (4) –

    (a)   shall continue in force, in accordance with its terms, when adopted; and

    (b)   may be varied or revoked by an order under this paragraph.

(6) Any other order under this paragraph –

    (a)   shall come into force at such time as is determined by or under the order; and

    (b)   may be varied or revoked by another order.

(7) References in this Part to orders under this paragraph shall, unless the context otherwise requires, include references to orders adopted under this paragraph; and references to the making of orders under this paragraph shall be construed accordingly.

(8) An order which is in force under this paragraph in relation to a reference or possible reference under section 45 or (as the case may be) 62 shall cease to be in force if an undertaking under paragraph 1 or 3 comes into force in relation to that reference.

(9) An order under this paragraph shall, if it has not previously ceased to be in force, cease to be in force when the intervention notice concerned or (as the case may be) special intervention notice concerned ceases to be in force.

(10) No order shall be made by the Secretary of State or the OFT under this paragraph before the making of a reference under section 45 or (as the case may be) 62 unless the order relates to a relevant merger situation which has been, or may have been, created or (as the case may be) a special merger situation which has been, or may have been, created.

(11) The Secretary of State or (as the case may be) the OFT shall, as soon as reasonably practicable, consider any representations received by that person in relation to varying or revoking an order under this paragraph.

Undertakings in lieu of reference under section 45 or 62

3   (1)   Sub-paragraph (2) applies if the Secretary of State has power to make a reference to the Commission under section 45 or 62 and otherwise intends to make such a reference.

    (2)   The Secretary of State may, instead of making such a reference and for the purpose of remedying, mitigating or preventing any of the effects adverse to the public interest which have or may have resulted, or which may be expected to result, from the creation of the relevant merger situation concerned or (as the case may be) the special merger situation concerned, accept from such of the parties concerned as he considers appropriate undertakings to take such action as he considers appropriate.

    (3)   In proceeding under sub-paragraph (2), the Secretary of State shall, in particular –

        (a)   accept the decisions of the OFT included in its report under section 44 so far as they relate to the matters mentioned in subsections (4) and (5) of that section; or

        (b)   (as the case may be) accept the decisions of the OFT included in its report under section 61 so far as they relate to the matters mentioned in subsections (3)(a) and (4) of that section.

    (4)   In proceeding under sub-paragraph (2) in relation to an anti-competitive outcome, the Secretary of State may, in particular, have regard to the effect of any action on any relevant customer benefits in relation to the creation of the relevant merger situation concerned.

(5) No undertaking shall be accepted by the Secretary of State under this paragraph in connection with a possible reference under section 45 if a public interest consideration mentioned in the intervention notice concerned has not been finalised and the period of 24 weeks beginning with the giving of that notice has not expired.

(6) The Secretary of State may delay making a decision as to whether to accept any such undertaking (and any related decision as to whether to make a reference under section 45) if he considers that there is a realistic prospect of the public interest consideration being finalised within the period of 24 weeks beginning with the giving of the intervention notice concerned.

(7) A delay under sub-paragraph (6) shall not extend beyond –

    (a)   the time when the public interest consideration is finalised; or

    (b)   if earlier, the expiry of the period of 24 weeks mentioned in that sub-paragraph.

(8) An undertaking under this paragraph –

    (a)   shall come into force when accepted;

    (b)   may be varied or superseded by another undertaking; or

    (c)   may be released by the Secretary of State.

(9) An undertaking under this paragraph which is in force in relation to a relevant merger situation or (as the case may be) a special merger situation shall cease to be in force if an order comes into force under paragraph 5 or 6 in relation to that undertaking.

(10) The Secretary of State shall, as soon as reasonably practicable, consider any representations received by him in relation to varying or releasing an undertaking under this section.

4   (1)   The relevant authority shall not make a reference under section 22, 33 or 45 in relation to the creation of a relevant merger situation or (as the case may be) a reference under section 62 in relation to the creation of a special merger situation if –

    (a)   the Secretary of State has accepted an undertaking or group of undertakings under paragraph 3; and

    (b)   the relevant merger situation or (as the case may be) the special merger situation is the situation by reference to which the undertaking or group of undertakings was accepted.

    (2)   In sub-paragraph (1) 'the relevant authority' means –

    (a)   in relation to a possible reference under section 22 or 33, the OFT; and

    (b)   in relation to a possible reference under section 45 or 62, the Secretary of State.

    (3)   Sub-paragraph (1) does not prevent the making of a reference if material facts about relevant arrangements or transactions, or relevant proposed arrangements or transactions, were not notified (whether in writing or otherwise) to the Secretary of State or the OFT or made public before any undertaking concerned was accepted.

    (4)   For the purposes of sub-paragraph (3) arrangements or transactions, or proposed arrangements or transactions, are relevant if they are the ones in consequence of which the enterprises concerned ceased or may have ceased, or may cease, to be distinct enterprises.

    (5)   In sub-paragraph (3) 'made public' means so publicised as to be generally known or readily ascertainable.

5   (1)   Sub-paragraph (2) applies where the Secretary of State considers that –

    (a)   an undertaking accepted by him under paragraph 3 has not been, is not being or will not be fulfilled; or

    (b)   in relation to an undertaking accepted by him under that paragraph, information which was false or misleading in a material respect was given to him or the OFT by the person giving the undertaking before he decided to accept the undertaking.

(2)   The Secretary of State may, for any of the purposes mentioned in paragraph 3(2), make an order under this paragraph.

(3)   Sub-paragraphs (3) and (4) of paragraph 3 shall apply for the purposes of sub-paragraph (2) above as they apply for the purposes of sub-paragraph (2) of that paragraph.

(4)   An order under this paragraph may contain –

    (a)   anything permitted by Schedule 8; and
    (b)   such supplementary, consequential or incidental provision as the Secretary of State considers appropriate.

(5)   An order under this paragraph

    (a)   shall come into force at such time as is determined by or under the order; and
    (b)   may contain provision which is different from the provision contained in the undertaking concerned.

(6)   No order shall be varied or revoked under this paragraph unless the OFT advises that such a variation or revocation is appropriate by reason of a change of circumstances.

6   (1)   Sub-paragraph (2) applies where –

    (a)   the Secretary of State has the power to make an order under paragraph 5 in relation to a particular undertaking and intends to make such an order; or
    (b)   the Secretary of State has the power to make an order under paragraph 10 in relation to a particular undertaking and intends to make such an order.

(2)   The Secretary of State may, for the purpose of preventing any action which might prejudice the making of that order, make an order under this paragraph.

(3)   No order shall be made under sub-paragraph (2) unless the Secretary of State has reasonable grounds for suspecting that it is or may be the case that action which might prejudice the making of the order under paragraph 5 or (as the case may be) 10 is in progress or in contemplation.

(4)   An order under sub-paragraph (2) may –

    (a)   prohibit or restrict the doing of things which the Secretary of State considers would prejudice the making of the order under paragraph 5 or 10;
    (b)   impose on any person concerned obligations as to the carrying on of any activities or the safeguarding of any assets;
    (c)   provide for the carrying on of any activities or the safeguarding of any assets either by the appointment of a person to conduct or supervise the conduct of any activities (on such terms and with such powers as may be specified or described in the order) or in any other manner;
    (d)   do anything which may be done by virtue of paragraph 19 of Schedule 8.

(5)   An order under this paragraph shall come into force at such time as is determined by or under the order.

(6)   An order under this paragraph shall, if it has not previously ceased to be in force, cease to be in force on –

    (a)   the coming into force of an order under paragraph 5 or (as the case may be) 10 in relation to the undertaking concerned; or
    (b)   the making of the decision not to proceed with such an order.

(7)   The Secretary of State shall, as soon as reasonably practicable, consider any representations received by him in relation to varying or revoking an order under this paragraph.

Statutory restrictions following reference under section 45 or 62

7   (1) Sub-paragraphs (2) and (3) apply where –

      (a) a reference has been made under section 45(2) or (3) or 62(2) but not finally determined; and

      (b) no undertakings under paragraph 1 are in force in relation to the relevant merger situation concerned or (as the case may be) the special merger situation concerned and no orders under paragraph 2 are in force in relation to that situation.

    (2) No relevant person shall, without the consent of the Secretary of State –

      (a) complete any outstanding matters in connection with any arrangements which have resulted in the enterprises concerned ceasing to be distinct enterprises;

      (b) make any further arrangements in consequence of that result (other than arrangements which reverse that result); or

      (c) transfer the ownership or control of any enterprises to which the reference relates.

    (3) No relevant person shall, without the consent of the Secretary of State, assist in any of the activities mentioned in paragraphs (a) to (c) of sub-paragraph (2).

    (4) The prohibitions in sub-paragraphs (2) and (3) do not apply in relation to anything which the person concerned is required to do by virtue of any enactment.

    (5) The consent of the Secretary of State under sub-paragraph (2) or (3) –

      (a) may be general or specific;

      (b) may be revoked by the Secretary of State; and

      (c) shall be published in such manner as the Secretary of State considers appropriate for bringing it to the attention of any person entitled to the benefit of it.

    (6) Paragraph (c) of sub-paragraph (5) shall not apply if the Secretary of State considers that publication is not necessary for the purpose mentioned in that paragraph.

    (7) Sub-paragraphs (2) and (3) shall apply to a person's conduct outside the United Kingdom if (and only if) he is –

      (a) a United Kingdom national;

      (b) a body incorporated under the law of the United Kingdom or of any part of the United Kingdom; or

      (c) a person carrying on business in the United Kingdom.

    (8) For the purpose of this paragraph a reference under section 45(2) or (3) is finally determined if –

      (a) the time within which the Commission is to prepare a report under section 50 in relation to the reference and give it to the Secretary of State has expired and no such report has been so prepared and given;

      (b) the Commission decides to cancel the reference under section 53(1);

      (c) the time within which the Secretary of State is to make and publish a decision under section 54(2) has expired and no such decision has been made and published;

      (d) the Secretary of State decides under section 54(2) to make no finding at all in the matter;

      (e) the Secretary of State otherwise decides under section 54(2) not to make an adverse public interest finding;

      (f) the Secretary of State decides under section 54(2) to make an adverse public interest finding but decides neither to accept an undertaking under paragraph 9 of this Schedule nor to make an order under paragraph 11 of this Schedule; or

(g) the Secretary of State decides under section 54(2) to make an adverse public interest finding and accepts an undertaking under paragraph 9 of this Schedule or makes an order under paragraph 11 of this Schedule.

(9) For the purpose of this paragraph a reference under section 62(2) is finally determined if –

(a) the time within which the Commission is to prepare a report under section 65 in relation to the reference and give it to the Secretary of State has expired and no such report has been so prepared and given;

(b) the time within which the Secretary of State is to make and publish a decision under section 66(2) has expired and no such decision has been made and published;

(c) the Secretary of State decides under subsection (2) of section 66 otherwise than as mentioned in subsection (5) of that section;

(d) the Secretary of State decides under subsection (2) of section 66 as mentioned in subsection (5) of that section but decides neither to accept an undertaking under paragraph 9 of this Schedule nor to make an order under paragraph 11 of this Schedule; or

(e) the Secretary of State decides under subsection (2) of section 66 as mentioned in subsection (5) of that section and accepts an undertaking under paragraph 9 of this Schedule or makes an order under paragraph 11 of this Schedule.

(10) For the purposes of this paragraph the time when a reference under section 45(2) or (3) or (as the case may be) 62(2) is finally determined is –

(a) in a case falling within sub-paragraph (8)(a) or (c) or (as the case may be) (9)(a) or (b), the expiry of the time concerned;

(b) in a case falling within sub-paragraph (8)(b), (d) or (e) or (as the case may be) (9)(c), the making of the decision concerned;

(c) in a case falling within sub-paragraph (8)(f) or (as the case may be) (9)(d), the making of the decision neither to accept an undertaking under paragraph 9 of this Schedule nor to make an order under paragraph 11 of this Schedule; and

(d) in a case falling within sub-paragraph (8)(g) or (as the case may be) (9)(e), the acceptance of the undertaking concerned or (as the case may be) the making of the order concerned.

(11) In this paragraph 'relevant person' means –

(a) any person who carries on any enterprise to which the reference relates or who has control of any such enterprise;

(b) any subsidiary of any person falling within paragraph (a); or

(c) any person associated with any person falling within paragraph (a) or any subsidiary of any person so associated.

8   (1) Sub-paragraph (2) applies where –

(a) a reference has been made under section 45(4) or (5) or 62(3); and

(b) no undertakings under paragraph 1 are in force in relation to the relevant merger situation concerned or (as the case may be) special merger situation concerned and no orders under paragraph 2 are in force in relation to that situation.

(2) No relevant person shall, without the consent of the Secretary of State, directly or indirectly acquire during the relevant period an interest in shares in a company if any enterprise to which the reference relates is carried on by or under the control of that company.

(3) The consent of the Secretary of State under sub-paragraph (2) –

(a) may be general or specific;

    (b)   may be revoked by the Secretary of State; and

    (c)   shall be published in such manner as the Secretary of State considers appropriate for bringing it to the attention of any person entitled to the benefit of it.

(4) Paragraph (c) of sub-paragraph (3) shall not apply if the Secretary of State considers that publication is not necessary for the purpose mentioned in that paragraph.

(5) Sub-paragraph (2) shall apply to a person's conduct outside the United Kingdom if (and only if) he is –

    (a)   a United Kingdom national;

    (b)   a body incorporated under the law of the United Kingdom or of any part of the United Kingdom; or

    (c)   a person carrying on business in the United Kingdom.

(6) In this paragraph –

      'company' includes any body corporate;

      'relevant period' means the period beginning with the publication of the decision of the Secretary of State to make the reference concerned and ending when the reference is finally determined;

      'relevant person' means –

    (a)   any person who carries on any enterprise to which the reference relates or who has control of any such enterprise;

    (b)   any subsidiary of any person falling within paragraph (a); or

    (c)   any person associated with any person falling within paragraph (a) or any subsidiary of any person so associated; and

      'share' means share in the capital of a company, and includes stock.

(7) For the purposes of the definition of 'relevant period' in sub-paragraph (6), a reference under section 45(4) or (5) is finally determined if –

    (a)   the Commission cancels the reference under section 48(1) or 53(1);

    (b)   the time within which the Commission is to prepare a report under section 50 in relation to the reference and give it to the Secretary of State has expired and no such report has been so prepared and given;

    (c)   the time within which the Secretary of State is to make and publish a decision under section 54(2) has expired and no such decision has been made and published;

    (d)   the Secretary of State decides under section 54(2) to make no finding at all in the matter;

    (e)   the Secretary of State otherwise decides under section 54(2) not to make an adverse public interest finding;

    (f)   the Secretary of State decides under section 54(2) to make an adverse public interest finding but decides neither to accept an undertaking under paragraph 9 of this Schedule nor to make an order under paragraph 11 of this Schedule; or

    (g)   the Secretary of State decides under section 54(2) to make an adverse public interest finding and accepts an undertaking under paragraph 9 of this Schedule or makes an order under paragraph 11 of this Schedule.

(8) For the purposes of the definition of 'relevant period' in sub-paragraph (6), a reference under section 62(3) is finally determined if –

    (a)   the Commission cancels the reference under section 64(1);

    (b)   the time within which the Commission is to prepare a report under section 65 in relation to the reference and give it to the Secretary of State has expired and no such report has been so prepared and given;

    (c)   the time within which the Secretary of State is to make and publish a decision under section 66(2) has expired and no such decision has been made and published;

(d) the Secretary of State decides under subsection (2) of section 66 otherwise than as mentioned in subsection (5) of that section;

(e) the Secretary of State decides under subsection (2) of section 66 as mentioned in subsection (5) of that section but decides neither to accept an undertaking under paragraph 9 of this Schedule nor to make an order under paragraph 11 of this Schedule; or

(f) the Secretary of State decides under subsection (2) of section 66 as mentioned in subsection (5) of that section and accepts an undertaking under paragraph 9 of this Schedule or makes an order under paragraph 11 of this Schedule.

(9) For the purposes of the definition of 'relevant period' in sub-paragraph (6) above, the time when a reference under section 45(4) or (5) or (as the case may be) 62(3) is finally determined is –

(a) in a case falling within sub-paragraph (7)(a), (d) or (e) or (as the case may be) (8)(a) or (d), the making of the decision concerned;

(b) in a case falling within sub-paragraph (7)(b) or (c) or (as the case may be) (8)(b) or (c), the expiry of the time concerned;

(c) in a case falling within sub-paragraph (7)(f) or (as the case may be) (8)(e), the making of the decision neither to accept an undertaking under paragraph 9 of this Schedule nor to make an order under paragraph 11 of this Schedule; and

(d) in a case falling within sub-paragraph (7)(g) or (as the case may be) (8)(f), the acceptance of the undertaking concerned or (as the case may be) the making of the order concerned.

(10) Section 79 shall apply for the purposes of paragraph 7 and this paragraph in relation to a reference under section 45 or 62 as it applies for the purposes of sections 77 and 78 in relation to a reference under section 22 or 33.

(11) In its application by virtue of sub-paragraph (10) section 79 shall have effect as if –

(a) subsections (1) and (2) were omitted; and

(b) for the reference in subsection (4) to the OFT there were substituted a reference to the Secretary of State.

Final undertakings and orders

9 (1) The Secretary of State may, in accordance with section 55 or (as the case may be) 66(5) to (7), accept, from such persons as he considers appropriate, undertakings to take action specified or described in the undertakings.

(2) An undertaking under this paragraph –

(a) shall come into force when accepted;

(b) may be varied or superseded by another undertaking; and

(c) may be released by the Secretary of State.

(3) An undertaking which is in force under this paragraph in relation to a reference under section 45 or 62 shall cease to be in force if an order under paragraph 6(1)(b) or 10 comes into force in relation to the subject-matter of the undertaking.

(4) No undertaking shall be accepted under this paragraph in relation to a reference under section 45 or 62 if an order has been made under –

(a) paragraph 6(1)(b) or 10 in relation to the subject-matter of the undertaking; or

(b) paragraph 11 in relation to that reference.

(5) The Secretary of State shall, as soon as reasonably practicable, consider any representations received by him in relation to varying or releasing an undertaking under this section.

10 (1) Sub-paragraph (2) applies where the Secretary of State considers that –

    (a) an undertaking accepted by him under paragraph 9 has not been, is not being or will not be fulfilled; or

    (b) in relation to an undertaking accepted by him under that paragraph, information which was false or misleading in a material respect was given to him or the OFT by the person giving the undertaking before he decided to accept the undertaking.

(2) The Secretary of State may, for any purpose mentioned in section 55(2) or (as the case may be) 66(6), make an order under this paragraph.

(3) Subsections (3) and (4) of section 55 or (as the case may be) subsection (7) of section 66 shall apply for the purposes of sub-paragraph (2) above as they or it applies for the purposes of section 55(2) or (as the case may be) 66(6).

(4) An order under this paragraph may contain –

    (a) anything permitted by Schedule 8; and

    (b) such supplementary, consequential or incidental provision as the Secretary of State considers appropriate.

(5) An order under this paragraph –

    (a) shall come into force at such time as is determined by or under the order; and

    (b) may contain provision which is different from the provision contained in the undertaking concerned.

(6) No order shall be varied or revoked under this paragraph unless the OFT advises that such a variation or revocation is appropriate by reason of a change of circumstances.

11 (1) The Secretary of State may, in accordance with section 55 or (as the case may be) 66(5) to (7), make an order under this paragraph.

(2) An order under this paragraph may contain –

    (a) anything permitted by Schedule 8; and

    (b) such supplementary, consequential or incidental provision as the Secretary of State considers appropriate.

(3) An order under this paragraph shall come into force at such time as is determined by or under the order.

(4) No order shall be made under this paragraph in relation to a reference under section 45 or (as the case may be) 62 if an undertaking has been accepted under paragraph 9 in relation to that reference.

(5) No order shall be varied or revoked under this paragraph unless the OFT advises that such a variation or revocation is appropriate by reason of a change of circumstances.

SCHEDULE 8   PROVISION THAT MAY BE CONTAINED IN CERTAIN ENFORCEMENT ORDERS   Section 86(4)

Introductory

1   This Schedule applies in relation to such orders, and to such extent, as is provided by this Part and Part 4 and any other enactment; and references in this Schedule to an order shall be construed accordingly.

General restrictions on conduct

2   (1)   An order may –

   (a)   prohibit the making or performance of an agreement;

   (b)   require any party to an agreement to terminate the agreement.

   (2)   An order made by virtue of sub-paragraph (1) shall not –

   (a)   prohibit the making or performance of; or

   (b)   require any person to terminate,

   an agreement so far as, if made, the agreement would relate, or (as the case may be) so far as the agreement relates, to the terms and conditions of employment of any workers or to the physical conditions in which any workers are required to work.

3   (1)   An order may prohibit the withholding from any person of –

   (a)   any goods or services;

   (b)   any orders for any such goods or services.

   (2)   References in sub-paragraph (1) to withholding include references to –

   (a)   agreeing or threatening to withhold; and

   (b)   procuring others to withhold or to agree or threaten to withhold.

4   An order may prohibit requiring as a condition of the supply of goods or services to any person –

   (a)   the buying of any goods;

   (b)   the making of any payment in respect of services other than the goods or services supplied;

   (c)   the doing of any other such matter or the refraining from doing anything mentioned in paragraph (a) or (b) or any other such matter.

5   An order may prohibit –

   (a)   discrimination between persons in the prices charged for goods or services;

   (b)   anything which the relevant authority considers to be such discrimination;

   (c)   procuring others to do anything which is such discrimination or which the relevant authority considers to be such discrimination.

6   An order may prohibit –

   (a)   giving, or agreeing to give in other ways, any preference in respect of the supply of goods or services or in respect of the giving of orders for goods or services;

   (b)   giving, or agreeing to give in other ways, anything which the relevant authority considers to be a preference in respect of the supply of goods or services or in respect of the giving of orders for goods or services;

   (c)   procuring others to do anything mentioned in paragraph (a) or (b).

7   An order may prohibit –

   (a)   charging, for goods or services supplied, prices differing from those in any published list or notification;

   (b)   doing anything which the relevant authority considers to be charging such prices.

8   (1)   An order may regulate the prices to be charged for any goods or services.

   (2)   No order shall be made by virtue of sub-paragraph (1) unless the relevant report in relation to the matter concerned identifies the prices charged for the goods or services as requiring remedial action.

   (3)   In this paragraph 'the relevant report' means the report of the Commission which is required by the enactment concerned before an order can be made under this Schedule.

9   An order may prohibit the exercise of any right to vote exercisable by virtue of the holding of any shares, stock or securities.

General obligations to be performed

10 (1) An order may require a person to supply goods or services or to do anything which the relevant authority considers appropriate to facilitate the provision of goods or services.

(2) An order may require a person who is supplying, or is to supply, goods or services to supply such goods or services to a particular standard or in a particular manner or to do anything which the relevant authority considers appropriate to facilitate the provision of such goods or services to that standard or in that manner.

11 An order may require any activities to be carried on separately from any other activities.

Acquisitions and divisions

12 (1) An order may prohibit or restrict –

(a) the acquisition by any person of the whole or part of the undertaking or assets of another person's business;

(b) the doing of anything which will or may result in two or more bodies corporate becoming interconnected bodies corporate.

(2) An order may require that if –

(a) an acquisition of the kind mentioned in sub-paragraph (1)(a) is made; or

(b) anything is done which results in two or more bodies corporate becoming interconnected bodies corporate;

the persons concerned or any of them shall observe any prohibitions or restrictions imposed by or under the order.

(3) This paragraph shall also apply to any result consisting in two or more enterprises ceasing to be distinct enterprises (other than any result consisting in two or more bodies corporate becoming interconnected bodies corporate).

13 (1) An order may provide for –

(a) the division of any business (whether by the sale of any part of the undertaking or assets or otherwise);

(b) the division of any group of interconnected bodies corporate.

(2) For the purposes of sub-paragraph (1)(a) all the activities carried on by way of business by any one person or by any two or more interconnected bodies corporate may be treated as a single business.

(3) An order made by virtue of this paragraph may contain such provision as the relevant authority considers appropriate to effect or take account of the division, including, in particular, provision as to –

(a) the transfer or creation of property, rights, liabilities or obligations;

(b) the number of persons to whom the property, rights, liabilities or obligations are to be transferred or in whom they are to be vested;

(c) the time within which the property, rights, liabilities or obligations are to be transferred or vested;

(d) the adjustment of contracts (whether by discharge or reduction of any liability or obligation or otherwise);

(e) the creation, allotment, surrender or cancellation of any shares, stock or securities;

(f) the formation or winding up of any company or other body of persons corporate or unincorporate;

(g) the amendment of the memorandum and articles or other instruments regulating any such company or other body of persons;

(h) the extent to which, and the circumstances in which, provisions of the order affecting a company or other body of persons corporate or unincorporate in its share capital, constitution or other matters may be altered by the company or other body of persons concerned;

(i) the registration of the order under any enactment by a company or other body of persons corporate or unincorporate which is affected by it as mentioned in paragraph (h);

(j) the continuation, with any necessary change of parties, of any legal proceedings;

(k) the approval by the relevant authority or another person of anything required by virtue of the order to be done or of any person to whom anything is to be transferred, or in whom anything is to be vested, by virtue of the order; or

(l) the appointment of trustees or other persons to do anything on behalf of another person which is required of that person by virtue of the order or to monitor the doing by that person of any such thing.

14   The references in paragraph 13 to the division of a business as mentioned in subparagraph (1)(a) of that paragraph shall, in the case of an order under section 75, 83, 84, 160 or 161, or an order under paragraph 5, 10 or 11 of Schedule 7, be construed as including references to the separation, by the sale of any part of any undertaking or assets concerned or other means, of enterprises which are under common control (within the meaning of section 26) otherwise than by reason of their being enterprises of interconnected bodies corporate.

Supply and publication of information

15 (1) An order may require a person supplying goods or services to publish a list of prices or otherwise notify prices.

(2) An order made by virtue of this paragraph may also require or prohibit the publication or other notification of further information.

16   An order may prohibit any person from notifying (whether by publication or otherwise) to persons supplying goods or services prices recommended or suggested as appropriate to be charged by those persons for those goods or services.

17 (1) An order may require a person supplying goods or services to publish –

(a) accounting information in relation to the supply of the goods or services;

(b) information in relation to the quantities of goods or services supplied;

(c) information in relation to the geographical areas in which they are supplied.

(2) In sub-paragraph (1) 'accounting information', in relation to a supply of goods or services, means information as to –

(a) the costs of the supply, including fixed costs and overheads;

(b) the manner in which fixed costs and overheads are calculated and apportioned for accounting purposes of the supplier; and

(c) the income attributable to the supply.

18   An order made by virtue of paragraph 15 or 17 may provide for the manner in which information is to be published or otherwise notified.

19   An order may –

(a) require any person to supply information to the relevant authority;

(b) where the OFT is not the relevant authority, require any person to supply information to the OFT;

(c) provide for the publication, by the person who has received information by virtue of paragraph (a) or (b), of that information.

National security

20 (1) An order may make such provision as the person making the order considers to be appropriate in the interests of national security (within the meaning of section 58(1)).

(2) Such provision may, in particular, include provision requiring a person to do, or not to do, particular things.

Supplementary

21 (1) An order, as well as making provision in relation to all cases to which it may extend, may make provision in relation to –

(a) those cases subject to specified exceptions; or

(b) any particular case or class of case.

(2) An order may, in relation to the cases in relation to which it applies, make the full provision which may be made by it or any less provision (whether by way of exception or otherwise).

(3) An order may make provision for matters to be determined under the order.

(4) An order may –

(a) make different provision for different cases or classes of case or different purposes;

(b) make such transitional, transitory or saving provision as the person making it considers appropriate.

22 (1) An order which may prohibit the doing of anything (or the refraining from doing anything) may in particular by virtue of paragraph 21(2) prohibit the doing of that thing (or the refraining from doing of it) except to such extent and in such circumstances as may be provided by or under the order.

(2) Any such order may, in particular, prohibit the doing of that thing (or the refraining from doing of it) –

(a) without the agreement of the relevant authority or another person; or

(b) by or in relation to a person who has not been approved by the relevant authority or another person.

Interpretation

23 References in this Schedule to the notification of prices or other information are not limited to the notification in writing of prices or other information.

24 In this Schedule 'the relevant authority' means –

(a) in the case of an order to be made by the OFT, the OFT;

(b) in the case of an order to be made by the Commission, the Commission; and

(c) in the case of an order to be made by the Secretary of State, the Secretary of State.

SCHEDULE 9 CERTAIN AMENDMENTS OF SECTORAL ENACTMENTS

Sections 86(5), 164(2) and 168(9)

PART 1 POWER OF ENFORCEMENT ORDERS TO AMEND LICENCE CONDITIONS ETC.

Telecommunications Act 1984 (c. 12)

1 (1) Section 95 of the Telecommunications Act 1984 (modification of licence conditions by order) shall be amended as follows.

(2) For subsections (1) and (2) there shall be substituted –

'(1) Where the Office of Fair Trading, the Commission or (as the case may be) the Secretary of State (in this section "the relevant authority") makes a relevant order, the order may also provide for the revocation or modification of licences granted under section 7 above to such extent as may appear to the relevant authority to be requisite or expedient for the purpose of giving effect to, or taking account of, any provision made by the order.

(2) In subsection (1) above, "relevant order" means –

(a) an order under section 75, 83 or 84 of, or paragraph 5, 10 or 11 of Schedule 7 to, the Enterprise Act 2002 where –

(i) one or more than one of the enterprises which have, or may have, ceased to be distinct enterprises was engaged in the carrying on of a commercial activity connected with telecommunications; or

(ii) one or more than one of the enterprises which will or may cease to be distinct enterprises is engaged in the carrying on of a commercial activity connected with telecommunications; or

(b) an order under section 160 or 161 of that Act where the feature, or combination of features, of the market in the United Kingdom for goods or services which prevents, restricts or distorts competition relates to commercial activities connected with telecommunications.'

(3) For subsection (3) there shall be substituted –

'(3) Expressions used in subsection (2) above and in Part 3 or (as the case may be) Part 4 of the Enterprise Act 2002 have the same meanings in that subsection as in that Part.'

Airports Act 1986 (c. 31)

2 (1) Section 54 of the Airports Act 1986 (modification of certain conditions in force under Part 4 of that Act) shall be amended as follows.

(2) For subsection (1) there shall be substituted –

'(1) Where the Office of Fair Trading, the Competition Commission or (as the case may be) the Secretary of State (in this section "the relevant authority") makes a relevant order, the order may also provide for the revocation or modification of any relevant conditions to such extent as may appear to the relevant authority to be requisite or expedient for the purpose of giving effect to, or taking account of, any provision made by the order.

(1A) In subsection (1) "relevant order" means –

(a) an order under section 75, 83 or 84 of, or paragraph 5, 10 or 11 of Schedule 7 to, the Enterprise Act 2002 where –

(i) one or more than one of the enterprises which have, or may have, ceased to be distinct enterprises was carried on by an airport operator; or

    (ii) one or more than one of the enterprises which will or may cease to be distinct enterprises is carried on by an airport operator; or

  (b) an order under section 160 or 161 of that Act where the feature, or combination of features, of the market in the United Kingdom for goods or services which prevents, restricts or distorts competition relates to the carrying on of any operational activities relating to one or more than one airport.'

 (3) Subsection (3) shall cease to have effect.

 (4) For subsection (4) there shall be substituted –

  '(4) Expressions used in subsection (1A) and in Part 3 or (as the case may be) Part 4 of the Enterprise Act 2002 have the same meanings in that subsection as in that Part.'

3   In paragraph 13 of Schedule 1 to that Act –

  (a) for 'section 54(3)(b)' there shall be substituted 'section 54(1A)';

  (b) for 'the reference' there shall be substituted 'references'; and

  (c) for 'a reference' there shall be substituted 'references'.

Gas Act 1986 (c. 44)

4 (1) Section 27 of the Gas Act 1986 (modification of licence conditions by order) shall be amended as follows.

 (2) For subsection (1) there shall be substituted –

  '(1) Where the Office of Fair Trading, the Competition Commission or (as the case may be) the Secretary of State (in this section "the relevant authority") makes a relevant order, the order may also provide for the modification of –

  (a) the conditions of a particular licence; or

  (b) the standard conditions of licences under section 7 above, licences under subsection (1) of section 7A above or licences under subsection (2) of that section,

  to such extent as may appear to the relevant authority to be requisite or expedient for the purpose of giving effect to, or taking account of, any provision made by the order.

 (1ZA) In subsection (1) above "relevant order" means –

  (a) an order under section 75, 83 or 84 of, or paragraph 5, 10 or 11 of Schedule 7 to, the Enterprise Act 2002 where –

   (i) one or more than one of the enterprises which have, or may have, ceased to be distinct enterprises was engaged in the carrying on of activities authorised or regulated by a licence; or

   (ii) one or more than one of the enterprises which will or may cease to be distinct enterprises is engaged in the carrying on of activities authorised or regulated by a licence; or

  (b) an order under section 160 or 161 of that Act where the feature, or combination of features, of the market in the United Kingdom for goods or services which prevents, restricts or distorts competition relates to –

   (i) activities authorised or regulated by a licence; or

   (ii) the storage of gas on terms which have been determined by the holder of a licence under section 7 above, or could have been determined by the holder if he had thought fit or had been required to determine them by or under a condition of the licence.'

(3)   In subsection (2) –

   (a)   for the words 'Secretary of State' there shall be substituted 'relevant authority';
   (b)   for the words 'section, he' there shall be substituted 'section, the relevant authority'; and
   (c)   for the words 'as he considers' there shall be substituted 'as the relevant authority considers'.

(4)   Subsections (3) and (4) shall cease to have effect.

(5)   In subsection (5) –

   (a)   for the words 'Secretary of State' there shall be substituted 'relevant authority'; and
   (b)   for the words 'he', in both places where they appear, there shall be substituted 'the relevant authority'.

(6)   For subsection (6) there shall be substituted –

   '(6)   Expressions used in subsection (1ZA) above and in Part 3 or (as the case may be) Part 4 of the Enterprise Act 2002 have the same meanings in that subsection as in that Part.'

Electricity Act 1989 (c. 29)

5   (1)   Section 15 of the Electricity Act 1989 (modification of licence conditions by order) shall be amended as follows.

(2)   For subsections (1) and (2) there shall be substituted –

   '(1)   Where the Office of Fair Trading, the Competition Commission or (as the case may be) the Secretary of State (in this section "the relevant authority") makes a relevant order, the order may also provide for the modification of the conditions of a particular licence, or the standard conditions of licences of any type mentioned in section 6(1), to such extent as may appear to the relevant authority to be requisite or expedient for the purpose of giving effect to, or taking account of, any provision made by the order.

   (2)   In subsection (1) above "relevant order" means –

      (a)   an order under section 75, 83 or 84 of, or paragraph 5, 10 or 11 of Schedule 7 to, the Enterprise Act 2002 where –

         (i)   one or more than one of the enterprises which have, or may have, ceased to be distinct enterprises was engaged in the carrying on of activities authorised or regulated by a licence; or
         (ii)   one or more than one of the enterprises which will or may cease to be distinct enterprises is engaged in the carrying on of activities authorised or regulated by a licence; or

      (b)   an order under section 160 or 161 of that Act where the feature, or combination of features, of the market in the United Kingdom for goods or services which prevents, restricts or distorts competition relates to the generation, transmission, distribution or supply of electricity.'

(3)   For subsection (2B) there shall be substituted –

   '(2B)   Where the relevant authority modifies under subsection (1) the standard conditions of licences of any type, the relevant authority –

      (a)   shall also make (as nearly as may be) the same modifications of those conditions for the purposes of their incorporation in licences of that type granted after that time; and
      (b)   may, after consultation with the Authority, make such incidental or consequential modifications as the relevant authority considers

necessary or expedient of any conditions of any licence of that type granted before that time.'

(4) In subsection (2C) –

    (a)   for the words 'Secretary of State' there shall be substituted 'relevant authority'; and

    (b)   for the words 'he', in both places where they appear, there shall be substituted 'the relevant authority'.

(5) For subsection (3) there shall be substituted –

    '(3)   Expressions used in subsection (2) above and in Part 3 or (as the case may be) Part 4 of the Enterprise Act 2002 have the same meanings in that subsection as in that Part.'

Broadcasting Act 1990 (c. 42)

6   For section 193 of the Broadcasting Act 1990 (modification of networking arrangements in consequence of reports under competition legislation) there shall be substituted –

'193 Modification of networking arrangements in consequence of competition legislation

(1) Where the Office of Fair Trading, the Competition Commission or (as the case may be) the Secretary of State (in this section "the relevant authority") makes a relevant order, the order may also provide for the modification of any networking arrangements to such extent as may appear to the relevant authority to be requisite or expedient for the purpose of giving effect to, or taking account of, any provision made by the order.

(2) In subsection (1) "relevant order" means –

    (a)   an order under section 75, 83 or 84 of, or paragraph 5, 10 or 11 of Schedule 7 to, the Enterprise Act 2002 where –

        (i)   one or more than one of the enterprises which have, or may have, ceased to be distinct enterprises was engaged in the provision of programmes for broadcasting in regional Channel 3 services; or

        (ii)   one or more than one of the enterprises which will or may cease to be distinct enterprises is engaged in the provision of such programmes; or

    (b)   an order under section 160 or 161 of that Act where the feature, or combination of features, of the market in the United Kingdom for goods or services which prevents, restricts or distorts competition relates to the provision of programmes for broadcasting in regional Channel 3 services.

(3) Expressions used in subsection (2) and in Part 3 or (as the case may be) Part 4 of the Enterprise Act 2002 have the same meanings in that subsection as in that Part.

(4) In this section –

        "networking arrangements" means any such arrangements as are mentioned in section 39(1) above; and

        "regional Channel 3 service" has the meaning given by section 14(6) above.'

Water Industry Act 1991 (c. 56)

7   (1)   Section 17 of the Water Industry Act 1991 (modification of conditions of appointment by order) shall be amended as follows.

(2) For subsections (1) and (2) there shall be substituted –

'(1) Where the OFT, the Competition Commission or (as the case may be) the Secretary of State (in this section "the relevant authority") makes a relevant order, the order may, subject to subsection (3), also provide for the modification of the conditions of a company's appointment under this Chapter to such extent as may appear to the relevant authority to be requisite or expedient for the purpose of giving effect to, or taking account of, any provision made by the order.

(2) In subsection (1) above "relevant order" means –

(a) an order under section 75, 83 or 84 of, or paragraph 5, 10 or 11 of Schedule 7 to, the 2002 Act where –

(i) one or more than one of the enterprises which have, or may have, ceased to be distinct enterprises was carried on by a relevant undertaker; or

(ii) one or more than one of the enterprises which will or may cease to be distinct enterprises is carried on by a relevant undertaker; or

(b) an order under section 160 or 161 of the 2002 Act where the feature, or combination of features, of the market in the United Kingdom for goods or services which prevents, restricts or distorts competition is –

(i) the structure or an aspect of the structure of a market for the supply of goods or services by a relevant undertaker; or

(ii) the conduct of a relevant undertaker or of customers of a relevant undertaker.'

(3) For subsection (4) there shall be substituted –

'(4) Expressions used in subsection (2) above and in Part 3 or (as the case may be) Part 4 of the 2002 Act have the same meanings in that subsection as in that Part.'

8   In section 36(1) of that Act (interpretation of Part 2 of that Act) –

(a) the definition of 'the 1973 Act', and the word 'and' at the end of the definition, shall cease to have effect; and

(b) at the end of the subsection there shall be inserted –

'"the 2002 Act" means the Enterprise Act 2002;'.

Electricity (Northern Ireland) Order 1992 (S.I. 1992/231 (N.I. 1))

9   For article 18 of the Electricity (Northern Ireland) Order 1992 (modification of licence conditions by order) there shall be substituted –

'18 Modification by order under other statutory provisions

(1) Where the Office of Fair Trading, the Competition Commission or (as the case may be) the Secretary of State (in this Article "the relevant authority") makes a relevant order, the order may also provide for the modification of the conditions of a licence to such extent as may appear to the relevant authority to be requisite or expedient for the purpose of giving effect to, or taking account of, any provision made by the order.

(2) In paragraph (1) "relevant order" means –

(a) an order under section 75, 83 or 84 of, or paragraph 5, 10 or 11 of Schedule 7 to, the Enterprise Act 2002 where –

(i) one or more than one of the enterprises which have, or may have, ceased to be distinct enterprises was engaged in the carrying on of activities authorised or regulated by a licence; or

(ii) one or more than one of the enterprises which will or may cease to be distinct enterprises is engaged in the carrying on of activities authorised or regulated by a licence; or

(b)   an order under section 160 or 161 of that Act where the feature, or combination of features, of the market in the United Kingdom for goods or services which prevents, restricts or distorts competition relates to the generation, transmission or supply of electricity.

(3)   In paragraph (2) expressions which are also used in Part 3 or, as the case may be, Part 4 of the Enterprise Act 2002 have the same meanings as in that Part of that Act.'

Railways Act 1993 (c. 43)

10   (1)   Section 16 of the Railways Act 1993 (modification of licence conditions by order) shall be amended as follows.

(2)   For subsections (1) and (2) there shall be substituted –

'(1)   Where the OFT, the Competition Commission or (as the case may be) the Secretary of State (in this section "the relevant authority") makes a relevant order, the order may also provide for the modification of the conditions of a licence to such extent as may appear to the relevant authority to be requisite or expedient for the purpose of giving effect to, or taking account of, any provision made by the order.

(2)   In subsection (1) above "relevant order" means –

(a)   an order under section 75, 83 or 84 of, or paragraph 5, 10 or 11 of Schedule 7 to, the Enterprise Act 2002 where –

(i)   one or more than one of the enterprises which have, or may have, ceased to be distinct enterprises was engaged in the supply of services relating to railways; or

(ii)   one or more than one of the enterprises which will or may cease to be distinct enterprises is engaged in the supply of services relating to railways; or

(b)   an order under section 160 or 161 of that Act where the feature, or combination of features, of the market in the United Kingdom for goods or services which prevents, restricts or distorts competition relates to the supply of services relating to railways.'

(3)   In subsection (3) for the words 'Secretary of State' there shall be substituted "relevant authority".

(4)   For subsection (5) there shall be substituted –

'(5)   Expressions used in subsection (2) above and in Part 3 or (as the case may be) Part 4 of the Enterprise Act 2002 have the same meanings in that subsection as in that Part; and in subsection (2) above "services relating to railways" has the same meaning as in section 67(2A) of this Act.'

Airports (Northern Ireland) Order 1994 (S.I. 1994/426 (N.I. 1))

11   (1)   Article 45 of the Airports (Northern Ireland) Order 1994 (modification of certain conditions in force under Part 4 of that Order) shall be amended as follows.

(2)   For paragraph (1) there shall be substituted –

'(1)   Where the Office of Fair Trading, the Competition Commission or (as the case may be) the Secretary of State (in this Article "the relevant authority") makes a relevant order, the order may also provide for the revocation or modification of any relevant conditions to such extent as may appear to the relevant authority to be requisite or expedient for the purpose of giving effect to, or taking account of, any provision made by the order.

(1A) In paragraph (1) "relevant order" means –

    (a)   an order under section 75, 83 or 84 of, or paragraph 5, 10 or 11 of Schedule 7 to, the Enterprise Act 2002 where –

        (i)   one or more than one of the enterprises which have, or may have, ceased to be distinct enterprises was carried on by an airport operator; or

        (ii) one or more than one of the enterprises which will or may cease to be distinct enterprises is carried on by an airport operator; or

    (b)   an order under section 160 or 161 of that Act where the feature, or combination of features, of the market in the United Kingdom for goods or services which prevents, restricts or distorts competition relates to the carrying on of any operational activities relating to one or more than one airport.'

(3) Paragraph (3) shall cease to have effect.

(4) For paragraph (4) there shall be substituted –

    '(4) Expressions used in paragraph (1A) and in Part 3 or (as the case may be) Part 4 of the Enterprise Act 2002 have the same meanings in that paragraph as in that Part.'

12   In paragraph 13 of Schedule 6 to that Order –

    (a)   for 'Article 45(3)(b)' there shall be substituted 'Article 45(1A)';

    (b)   for 'the reference' there shall be substituted 'references'; and

    (c)   for 'a reference' there shall be substituted 'references'.

Gas (Northern Ireland) Order 1996 (S.I. 1996/275 (N.I. 2))

13 (1) Article 18 of the Gas (Northern Ireland) Order 1996 (modification of licence conditions by order) shall be amended as follows.

    (2) For paragraph (1) there shall be substituted –

    '(1) Where the Office of Fair Trading, the Competition Commission or (as the case may be) the Secretary of State (in this Article "the relevant authority") makes a relevant order, the order may also provide for the modification of –

        (a)   the conditions of a particular licence; or

        (b)   the standard conditions of licences under sub-paragraph (a), (b) or (c) of Article 8(1),

to such extent as may appear to the relevant authority to be requisite or expedient for the purpose of giving effect to, or taking account of, any provision made by the order.

    (1A) In paragraph (1) "relevant order" means –

        (a)   an order under section 75, 83 or 84 of, or paragraph 5, 10 or 11 of Schedule 7 to, the Enterprise Act 2002 where –

            (i)   one or more than one of the enterprises which have, or may have, ceased to be distinct enterprises was engaged in the carrying on of activities authorised or regulated by a licence; or

            (ii) one or more than one of the enterprises which will or may cease to be distinct enterprises is engaged in the carrying on of activities authorised or regulated by a licence; or

     (b)   an order under section 160 or 161 of that Act where the feature, or combination of features, of the market in the United Kingdom for goods or services which prevents, restricts or distorts competition relates to activities authorised or regulated by a licence.'

(3) In paragraph (2) –

    (a)   for the words 'Secretary of State modifies under paragraph (1)(ii)' there shall be substituted 'relevant authority modifies under paragraph (1)(b)'; and

    (b)   for the word 'he', in both places where it appears, there shall be substituted 'the relevant authority'.

(4) Paragraph (3) shall cease to have effect.

(5) In paragraph (4) –

    (a)   for the words 'Secretary of State' there shall be substituted 'relevant authority'; and

    (b)   for the word 'he', in both places where it appears, there shall be substituted 'the relevant authority'.

(6) For paragraph (5) there shall be substituted –

    '(5) Expressions used in paragraph (1A) above and in Part 3 or (as the case may be) Part 4 of the Enterprise Act 2002 have the same meanings in that paragraph as in that Part.'

Postal Services Act 2000 (c. 26)

14 (1) Section 21 of the Postal Services Act 2000 (modification of licence conditions by order) shall be amended as follows.

    (2) For subsections (1) to (4) there shall be substituted –

    '(1) Where the Office of Fair Trading, the Competition Commission or (as the case may be) the Secretary of State (in this section "the relevant authority") makes a relevant order, the order may also provide for the modification of the conditions of a licence to such extent as may appear to the relevant authority to be requisite or expedient for the purpose of giving effect to, or taking account of, any provision made by the order.

    (2) In subsection (1) above "relevant order" means –

      (a)   an order under section 75, 83 or 84 of, or paragraph 5, 10 or 11 of Schedule 7 to, the Enterprise Act 2002 where –

        (i)   one or more than one of the enterprises which have, or may have, ceased to be distinct enterprises was engaged in the provision of postal services; or

        (ii) one or more than one of the enterprises which will or may cease to be distinct enterprises is engaged in the provision of postal services; or

      (b)   an order under section 160 or 161 of that Act where the feature, or combination of features, of the market in the United Kingdom for goods or services which prevents, restricts or distorts competition relates to the provision of postal services.'

    (3) In subsection (5) for the words 'Secretary of State' there shall be substituted 'relevant authority'.

    (4) For subsection (6) there shall be substituted –

    '(6) Expressions used in subsection (2) above and in Part 3 or (as the case may be) Part 4 of the Enterprise Act 2002 have the same meanings in that subsection as in that Part.'

Transport Act 2000 (c. 38)

15 (1) Section 19 of the Transport Act 2000 (modification of licence conditions by order) shall be amended as follows.

(2) For subsections (1) to (4) there shall be substituted –

'(1) Where the Office of Fair Trading, the Competition Commission or (as the case may be) the Secretary of State (in this section "the relevant authority") makes a relevant order, the order may also provide for the modification of the conditions of a licence to such extent as may appear to the relevant authority to be requisite or expedient for the purpose of giving effect to, or taking account of, any provision made by the order.

(2) In subsection (1) above "relevant order" means –

(a) an order under section 75, 83 or 84 of, or paragraph 5, 10 or 11 of Schedule 7 to, the 2002 Act where –

(i) one or more than one of the enterprises which have, or may have, ceased to be distinct enterprises was engaged in the provision of air traffic services; or

(ii) one or more than one of the enterprises which will or may cease to be distinct enterprises is engaged in the provision of air traffic services; or

(b) an order under section 160 or 161 of that Act where the feature, or combination of features, of the market in the United Kingdom for goods or services which prevents, restricts or distorts competition relates to the provision of air traffic services.'

(3) In subsection (5) for the words 'Secretary of State' there shall be substituted 'relevant authority'.

(4) For subsection (6) there shall be substituted –

'(6) Expressions used in subsection (2) above and in Part 3 or (as the case may be) Part 4 of the 2002 Act have the same meanings in that subsection as in that Part.'

(5) In subsection (7) for the words '1973 Act is the Fair Trading Act 1973' there shall be substituted '2002 Act is the Enterprise Act 2002'.

PART 2   APPLICATION OF PART 4 OF THIS ACT TO SECTORAL REGULATORS

Telecommunications Act 1984 (c. 12)

16 (1) Section 50 of the Telecommunications Act 1984 (application of monopoly provisions etc. to the Director General of Telecommunications) shall be amended as follows.

(2) For subsection (2) (monopoly functions to be exercisable concurrently by the Director General of Telecommunications) there shall be substituted –

'(2) The functions to which subsection (2A) below applies shall be concurrent functions of the Director and the Office of Fair Trading.

(2A) This subsection applies to the functions of the Office of Fair Trading under Part 4 of the Enterprise Act 2002 (other than sections 166 and 171) so far as relating to commercial activities connected with telecommunications.

(2B) So far as necessary for the purposes of, or in connection with, subsections (2) and (2A) above, references in Part 4 of the Act of 2002 to the Office of Fair Trading (including references in provisions of that Act applied by that

Part) shall be construed as including references to the Director (except in sections 166 and 171 of that Act and in any other provision of that Act where the context otherwise requires).'

(3) For subsection (4) there shall be substituted –

'(4) Before the Office of Fair Trading or the Director first exercises in relation to any matter functions which are exercisable concurrently by virtue of subsection (2) above, that person shall consult the other.

(4A) Neither the Office of Fair Trading nor the Director shall exercise in relation to any matter functions which are exercisable concurrently by virtue of subsection (2) above if functions which are so exercisable have been exercised in relation to that matter by the other.'

(4) In subsection (6) –

(a) for the words 'subsection (2)' there shall be substituted 'subsection (2A)';
(b) the words from 'or paragraph' to 'Act 1994' shall cease to have effect; and
(c) for the words 'Part IV or section 86 or 88 of the 1973 Act' there shall be substituted 'Part 4 of the Enterprise Act 2002'.

(5) For subsection (6A) there shall be substituted –

'(6A) Section 117 of the Enterprise Act 2002 (offences of supplying false or misleading information) as applied by section 180 of that Act shall have effect so far as relating to functions exercisable by the Director by virtue of subsection (2) above as if the references in section 117(1)(a) and (2) to the Office of Fair Trading included references to the Director.'

(6) Subsection (7) shall cease to have effect.

Gas Act 1986 (c. 44)

17 (1) Section 36A of the Gas Act 1986 (application of monopoly provisions etc. to the Gas and Electricity Markets Authority) shall be amended as follows.

(2) For subsection (2) (monopoly functions to be exercisable concurrently by the Gas and Electricity Markets Authority) there shall be substituted –

'(2) The functions to which subsection (2A) below applies shall be concurrent functions of the Authority and the Office of Fair Trading.

(2A) This subsection applies to the functions of the Office of Fair Trading under Part 4 of the Enterprise Act 2002 (other than sections 166 and 171) so far as relating to commercial activities connected with the carrying on of activities to which this subsection applies.

(2B) So far as necessary for the purposes of, or in connection with, subsections (2) and (2A) above, references in Part 4 of the Act of 2002 to the Office of Fair Trading (including references in provisions of that Act applied by that Part) shall be construed as including references to the Authority (except in sections 166 and 171 of that Act and in any other provision of that Act where the context otherwise requires).'

(3) In subsection (4) for the word '(2)' there shall be substituted '(2A)'.

(4) For subsection (5) there shall be substituted –

'(5) Before the Office of Fair Trading or the Authority first exercises in relation to any matter functions which are exercisable concurrently by virtue of subsection (2) above, it shall consult the other.

(5A) Neither the Office of Fair Trading nor the Authority shall exercise in relation to any matter functions which are exercisable concurrently by virtue of subsection (2) above if functions which are so exercisable have been exercised in relation to that matter by the other.'

(5)   In subsection (7) for the words 'Part IV or section 86 or 88 of the 1973 Act' there shall be substituted 'Part 4 of the Enterprise Act 2002'.

(6)   For subsection (8) there shall be substituted –

'(8)   Section 117 of the Enterprise Act 2002 (offences of supplying false or misleading information) as applied by section 180 of that Act shall have effect so far as relating to functions exercisable by the Authority by virtue of subsection (2) above as if the references in section 117(1)(a) and (2) to the Office of Fair Trading included references to the Authority.'

(7)   Subsection (9) shall cease to have effect.

(8)   In subsection (10) for the words 'mentioned in subsection (2) or (3) above' there shall be substituted 'exercisable by the Authority by virtue of subsection (2) or (3) above'.

Electricity Act 1989 (c. 29)

18   (1)   Section 43 of the Electricity Act 1989 (application of monopoly provisions etc. to the Gas and Electricity Markets Authority) shall be amended as follows.

(2)   For subsection (2) (monopoly functions to be exercisable concurrently by the Gas and Electricity Markets Authority) there shall be substituted –

'(2)   The functions to which subsection (2A) below applies shall be concurrent functions of the Authority and the Office of Fair Trading.

(2A)   This subsection applies to the functions of the Office of Fair Trading under Part 4 of the Enterprise Act 2002 (other than sections 166 and 171) so far as relating to commercial activities connected with the generation, transmission or supply of electricity.

(2B)   So far as necessary for the purposes of, or in connection with, subsections (2) and (2A) above, references in Part 4 of the Act of 2002 to the Office of Fair Trading (including references in provisions of that Act applied by that Part) shall be construed as including references to the Authority (except in sections 166 and 171 of that Act and in any other provision of that Act where the context otherwise requires).'

(3)   For subsection (4) there shall be substituted –

'(4)   Before the Office of Fair Trading or the Authority first exercises in relation to any matter functions which are exercisable concurrently by virtue of subsection (2) above, it shall consult the other.

(4A)   Neither the Office of Fair Trading nor the Authority shall exercise in relation to any matter functions which are exercisable concurrently by virtue of subsection (2) above if functions which are so exercisable have been exercised in relation to that matter by the other.'

(4)   In subsection (6) –

(a)   for the word '(2)' there shall be substituted '(2A)';

(b)   the words from 'or paragraph' to 'Act 1994' shall cease to have effect; and

(c)   for the words 'Part IV or section 86 or 88 of the 1973 Act' there shall be substituted 'Part 4 of the Enterprise Act 2002'.

(5)   For subsection (6A) there shall be substituted –

'(6A)   Section 117 of the Enterprise Act 2002 (offences of supplying false or misleading information) as applied by section 180 of that Act shall have effect so far as relating to functions exercisable by the Authority by virtue of subsection (2) above as if the references in section 117(1)(a) and (2) to the Office of Fair Trading included references to the Authority.'

(6)   Subsection (7) shall cease to have effect.

Water Industry Act 1991 (c. 56)

19 (1) Section 31 of the Water Industry Act 1991 (application of monopoly provisions etc. to the Director General of Water Services) shall be amended as follows.

(2) For subsection (2) (monopoly functions to be exercisable concurrently by the Director General of Water Services) there shall be substituted –

'(2) The functions to which subsection (2A) below applies shall be concurrent functions of the Director and the OFT.

(2A) This subsection applies to the functions of the OFT under Part 4 of the 2002 Act (other than sections 166 and 171) so far as relating to commercial activities connected with the supply of water or the provision of sewerage services.'

(3) For subsection (4) there shall be substituted –

'(4) So far as necessary for the purposes of, or in connection with, subsections (2) and (2A) above, references in Part 4 of the 2002 Act to the OFT (including references in provisions of that Act applied by that Part) shall be construed as including references to the Director (except in sections 166 and 171 of that Act and in any other provision of that Act where the context otherwise requires).'

(4) For subsections (5) and (6) there shall be substituted –

'(5) Before the OFT or the Director first exercises in relation to any matter functions which are exercisable concurrently by virtue of subsection (2) above, that person shall consult the other.

(6) Neither the OFT nor the Director shall exercise in relation to any matter functions which are exercisable concurrently by virtue of subsection (2) above if functions which are so exercisable have been exercised in relation to that matter by the other.'

(5) In subsection (8) –

(a) the words from 'or paragraph' to 'Act 1994' shall cease to have effect; and

(b) for the words 'Part IV or section 86 or 88 of the 1973 Act' there shall be substituted 'Part 4 of the 2002 Act'.

(6) For subsection (8A) there shall be substituted –

'(8A) Section 117 of the 2002 Act (offences of supplying false or misleading information) as applied by section 180 of that Act shall have effect so far as relating to functions exercisable by the Director by virtue of subsection (2) above as if the references in section 117(1)(a) and (2) to the OFT included references to the Director.'

(7) Subsection (9) shall cease to have effect.

Electricity (Northern Ireland) Order 1992 (S.I. 1992/231 (N.I. 1))

20 (1) Article 46 of the Electricity (Northern Ireland) Order 1992 (application of monopoly provisions etc. to the Director General of Electricity Supply for Northern Ireland) shall be amended as follows.

(2) For paragraph (2) (monopoly functions to be exercisable concurrently by the Director) there shall be substituted –

'(2) The functions to which paragraph (2A) applies shall be concurrent functions of the Director and the Office of Fair Trading.

(2A) This paragraph applies to the functions of the Office of Fair Trading under Part 4 of the Enterprise Act 2002 (other than sections 166 and 171) so far as relating to commercial activities connected with the generation, transmission or supply of electricity.

(2B) So far as necessary for the purposes of, or in connection with, paragraphs (2) and (2A), references in Part 4 of the Act of 2002 to the Office of Fair Trading (including references in provisions of that Act applied by that Part) shall be construed as including references to the Director (except in sections 166 and 171 of that Act and in any other provision of that Act where the context otherwise requires).'

(3) For paragraph (4) there shall be substituted –

    '(4) Before the Office of Fair Trading or the Director first exercises in relation to any matter functions which are exercisable concurrently by virtue of paragraph (2), it or he shall consult the other.

    (4A) Neither the Office of Fair Trading nor the Director shall exercise in relation to any matter functions which are exercisable concurrently by virtue of paragraph (2) if functions which are so exercisable have been exercised in relation to that matter by the other.'

(4) In paragraph (6) –

    (a) for the words 'paragraph (2)' there shall be substituted 'paragraph (2A)';

    (b) the words from 'or paragraph' to 'Act 1994' shall cease to have effect; and

    (c) for the words 'Part IV or section 86 or 88 of the 1973 Act' there shall be substituted 'Part 4 of the Enterprise Act 2002'.

(5) For paragraph (6A) there shall be substituted –

    '(6A) Section 117 of the Enterprise Act 2002 (offences of supplying false or misleading information) as applied by section 180 of that Act shall have effect so far as relating to functions exercisable by the Director by virtue of paragraph (2) as if the references in section 117(1)(a) and (2) to the Office of Fair Trading included references to the Director.'

(6) Paragraph (7) shall cease to have effect.

Railways Act 1993 (c. 43)

21 (1) Section 67 of the Railways Act 1993 (application of monopoly provisions etc. to the Rail Regulator) shall be amended as follows.

    (2) For subsection (2) (monopoly functions to be exercisable concurrently by the Rail Regulator) there shall be substituted –

        '(2) The functions to which subsection (2A) below applies shall be concurrent functions of the Regulator and the OFT.

        (2A) This subsection applies to the functions of the OFT under Part 4 of the Enterprise Act 2002 (other than sections 166 and 171) so far as relating to the supply of services relating to railways.

        (2B) So far as necessary for the purposes of, or in connection with, subsections (2) and (2A) above, references in Part 4 of the Act of 2002 to the OFT (including references in provisions of that Act applied by that Part) shall be construed as including references to the Regulator (except in sections 166 and 171 of that Act and in any other provision of that Act where the context otherwise requires).'

    (3) In subsection (3ZA) for the words 'subsection (3)' there shall be substituted 'subsections (2A) and (3)'.

    (4) For subsection (4) there shall be substituted –

        '(4) Before the OFT or the Regulator first exercises in relation to any matter functions which are exercisable concurrently by virtue of subsection (2) above, that person shall consult the other.

        (4A) Neither the OFT nor the Regulator shall exercise in relation to any matter functions which are exercisable concurrently by virtue of subsection (2) above if functions which are so exercisable have been exercised in relation to that matter by the other.'

(5) In subsection (7) –

    (a) for the words 'on a monopoly reference' there shall be substituted 'under section 136 or 142 of the Enterprise Act 2002';

    (b) the words from 'was made' to 'that it' shall cease to have effect; and

    (c) for the word 'him' there shall be substituted 'the Regulator'.

(6) In subsection (8) –

    (a) for the word '(2)' there shall be substituted '(2A)';

    (b) the words from 'or paragraph' to 'Act 1994' shall cease to have effect; and

    (c) for the words 'Part IV or section 86 or 88 of the 1973 Act' there shall be substituted 'Part 4 of the Enterprise Act 2002'.

(7) For subsection (9) there shall be substituted –

    '(9) Section 117 of the Enterprise Act 2002 (offences of supplying false or misleading information) as applied by section 180 of that Act shall have effect so far as relating to functions exercisable by the Regulator by virtue of subsection (2) above as if the references in section 117(1)(a) and (2) to the OFT included references to the Regulator.'

(8) Subsection (10) shall cease to have effect.

Gas (Northern Ireland) Order 1996 (S.I. 1996/275 (N.I. 2))

22 (1) Article 23 of the Gas (Northern Ireland) Order 1996 (application of monopoly provisions etc. to the Director General of Gas for Northern Ireland) shall be amended as follows.

   (2) For paragraph (2) (monopoly functions to be exercisable concurrently by the Director) there shall be substituted –

    '(2) The functions to which paragraph (2A) applies shall be concurrent functions of the Director and the Office of Fair Trading.

    (2A) This paragraph applies to the functions of the Office of Fair Trading under Part 4 of the Enterprise Act 2002 (other than sections 166 and 171) so far as relating to commercial activities connected with the conveyance, storage or supply of gas.

    (2B) So far as necessary for the purposes of, or in connection with, paragraphs (2) and (2A), references in Part 4 of the Act of 2002 to the Office of Fair Trading (including references in provisions of that Act applied by that Part) shall be construed as including references to the Director (except in sections 166 and 171 of that Act and in any other provision of that Act where the context otherwise requires).'

   (3) For paragraph (4) there shall be substituted –

    '(4) Before the Office of Fair Trading or the Director first exercises in relation to any matter functions which are exercisable concurrently by virtue of paragraph (2), it or he shall consult the other.

    (4A) Neither the Office of Fair Trading nor the Director shall exercise in relation to any matter functions which are exercisable concurrently by virtue of paragraph (2) if functions which are so exercisable have been exercised in relation to that matter by the other.'

   (4) In paragraph (6) for the words 'Part IV or section 86 or 88 of the 1973 Act' there shall be substituted 'Part 4 of the Enterprise Act 2002'.

   (5) For paragraph (7) there shall be substituted –

    '(7) Section 117 of the Enterprise Act 2002 (offences of supplying false or misleading information) as applied by section 180 of that Act shall have effect so far as relating to functions exercisable by the Director by virtue of paragraph (2) as if the references in section 117(1)(a) and (2) to the Office of Fair Trading included references to the Director.'

(6) Paragraph (8) shall cease to have effect.

(7) In paragraph (9) for the words 'mentioned in paragraph (2) or (3)' there shall be substituted 'exercisable by the Director by virtue of paragraph (2) or (3)'.

Transport Act 2000 (c. 38)

23 (1) Section 85 of the Transport Act 2000 (interpretation of Chapter V) shall be amended as follows.

(2) In subsection (1) for paragraph (a) there shall be substituted –

'(a) the 2002 Act is the Enterprise Act 2002;'.

(3) In subsection (3) –

(a) the words 'the 1973 Act or' shall cease to have effect; and

(b) for the words 'Act concerned' there shall be substituted '1998 Act'.

24 (1) Section 86 of that Act (functions exercisable by the CAA and the Director) shall be amended as follows.

(2) For subsection (2) there shall be substituted –

'(2) This subsection applies to the OFT's functions under Part 4 of the 2002 Act (other than sections 166 and 171) so far as they relate to the supply of air traffic services.'

(3) In subsection (4)(a) for the words from the beginning to 'Act' there shall be substituted 'Part 4 of the 2002 Act (except for sections 166 and 171 but including provisions of that Act applied by that Part)'.

(4) In subsection (7)(a) for the words from the beginning to 'Act' there shall be substituted 'Part 4 of the 2002 Act'.

25 In section 87 of that Act (CAA's 1973 Act functions) for the word '1973', wherever it appears, there shall be substituted '2002'.

26 In section 89 of that Act (carrying out functions) for the word '1973', wherever it appears, there shall be substituted '2002'.

SCHEDULE 10   PROCEDURAL REQUIREMENTS FOR CERTAIN ENFORCEMENT UNDERTAKINGS AND ORDERS   Section 90

Requirements for accepting undertakings and making orders

1   Paragraph 2 applies in relation to –

(a) any undertaking under section 73 or 82 or paragraph 3 or 9 of Schedule 7 (other than an undertaking under the enactment concerned which varies an undertaking under that enactment but not in any material respect); and

(b) any order under section 75, 83 or 84 or paragraph 5, 10 or 11 of Schedule 7 (other than an order under the enactment concerned which is a revoking order of the kind dealt with by paragraphs 6 to 8 below).

2 (1) Before accepting an undertaking to which this paragraph applies or making an order to which this paragraph applies, the OFT, the Commission or (as the case may be) the Secretary of State (in this Schedule 'the relevant authority') shall –

(a) give notice of the proposed undertaking or (as the case may be) order; and

374   Appendix: Enterprise Act 2002

    (b)   consider any representations made in accordance with the notice and not withdrawn.

(2) A notice under sub-paragraph (1) shall state –

    (a)   that the relevant authority proposes to accept the undertaking or (as the case may be) make the order;

    (b)   the purpose and effect of the undertaking or (as the case may be) order;

    (c)   the situation that the undertaking or (as the case may be) order is seeking to deal with;

    (d)   any other facts which the relevant authority considers justify the acceptance of the undertaking or (as the case may be) the making of the order;

    (e)   a means of gaining access to an accurate version of the proposed undertaking or (as the case may be) order at all reasonable times; and

    (f)   the period (not less than 15 days starting with the date of publication of the notice in the case of an undertaking and not less than 30 days starting with that date in the case of an order) within which representations may be made in relation to the proposed undertaking or (as the case may be) order.

(3) A notice under sub-paragraph (1) shall be given by –

    (a)   in the case of a proposed order, serving on any person identified in the order as a person on whom a copy of the order should be served a copy of the notice and a copy of the proposed order; and

    (b)   in every case, publishing the notice.

(4) The relevant authority shall not accept the undertaking with modifications or (as the case may be) make the order with modifications unless the relevant authority –

    (a)   gives notice of the proposed modifications; and

    (b)   considers any representations made in accordance with the notice and not withdrawn.

(5) A notice under sub-paragraph (4) shall state –

    (a)   the proposed modifications;

    (b)   the reasons for them; and

    (c)   the period (not less than 7 days starting with the date of the publication of the notice under sub-paragraph (4)) within which representations may be made in relation to the proposed modifications.

(6) A notice under sub-paragraph (4) shall be given by –

    (a)   in the case of a proposed order, serving a copy of the notice on any person identified in the order as a person on whom a copy of the order should be served; and

    (b)   in every case, publishing the notice.

3   (1) If, after giving notice under paragraph 2(1) or (4), the relevant authority decides –

    (a)   not to accept the undertaking concerned or (as the case may be) make the order concerned; and

    (b)   not to proceed by virtue of paragraph 5;

the relevant authority shall give notice of that decision.

(2) A notice under sub-paragraph (1) shall be given by –

    (a)   in the case of a proposed order, serving a copy of the notice on any person identified in the order as a person on whom a copy of the order should be served; and

    (b)   in every case, publishing the notice.

4   As soon as practicable after accepting an undertaking to which paragraph 2 applies or (as the case may be) making an order to which that paragraph applies,

the relevant authority shall (except in the case of an order which is a statutory instrument) –

    (a)   serve a copy of the undertaking on any person by whom it is given or (as the case may be) serve a copy of the order on any person identified in the order as a person on whom a copy of the order should be served; and

    (b)   publish the undertaking or (as the case may be) the order.

5   (1)   The requirements of paragraph 2(4) (and those of paragraph 2(1)) shall not apply if the relevant authority –

    (a)   has already given notice under paragraph 2(1) but not paragraph 2(4) in relation to the proposed undertaking or order; and

    (b)   considers that the modifications which are now being proposed are not material in any respect.

    (2)   The requirements of paragraph 2(4) (and those of paragraph 2(1)) shall not apply if the relevant authority –

    (a)   has already given notice under paragraphs 2(1) and (4) in relation to the matter concerned; and

    (b)   considers that the further modifications which are now being proposed do not differ in any material respect from the modifications in relation to which notice was last given under paragraph 2(4).

Termination of undertakings and orders

6   Paragraph 7 applies where the relevant authority is proposing to –

    (a)   release any undertaking under section 73 or 82 or paragraph 3 or 9 of Schedule 7 (other than in connection with accepting an undertaking under the enactment concerned which varies or supersedes an undertaking under that enactment); or

    (b)   revoke any order under section 75, 83 or 84 or paragraph 5, 10 or 11 of Schedule 7 (other than in connection with making an order under the enactment concerned which varies or supersedes an order under that enactment).

7   (1)   Before releasing an undertaking to which this paragraph applies or (as the case may be) revoking an order to which this paragraph applies, the relevant authority shall –

    (a)   give notice of the proposed release or (as the case may be) revocation; and

    (b)   consider any representations made in accordance with the notice and not withdrawn.

    (2)   A notice under sub-paragraph (1) shall state –

    (a)   the fact that a release or (as the case may be) revocation is proposed;

    (b)   the reasons for it; and

    (c)   the period (not less than 15 days starting with the date of publication of the notice in the case of an undertaking and not less than 30 days starting with that date in the case of an order) within which representations may be made in relation to the proposed release or (as the case may be) revocation.

    (3)   If after giving notice under sub-paragraph (1) the relevant authority decides not to proceed with the release or (as the case may be) the revocation, the relevant authority shall give notice of that decision.

    (4)   A notice under sub-paragraph (1) or (3) shall be given by –

    (a)   serving a copy of the notice on the person who gave the undertaking which is being released or (as the case may be) on any person identified in the order being revoked as a person on whom a copy of the order should be served; and

(b)   publishing the notice.

8   As soon as practicable after releasing the undertaking or making the revoking order, the relevant authority shall (except in the case of an order which is a statutory instrument) –

(a)   serve a copy of the release of the undertaking on the person who gave the undertaking or (as the case may be) serve a copy of the revoking order on any person identified in the order being revoked as a person on whom a copy of that order should be served; and

(b)   publish the release or (as the case may be) the revoking order.

Power to dispense with the requirements of the Schedule

9   The relevant authority may dispense with any or all of the requirements of this Schedule if the relevant authority considers that the relevant authority has special reasons for doing so.

SCHEDULE 11   THE COMPETITION COMMISSION   Section 185

1   Schedule 7 to the 1998 Act is amended as follows.

2   In paragraph 1 (interpretation), after the definition of 'newspaper merger reference' there is inserted –

'"newspaper panel member" means a member of the panel maintained under paragraph 22;'.

3   In paragraph 2 (appointment of members) –

(a)   in sub-paragraph (1)(c), for the words from the beginning to 'from' there is substituted 'the members of';

(b)   in sub-paragraph (1), after paragraph (d) there is inserted –

'(e)   one or more members appointed by the Secretary of State to serve on the Council.';

(c)   after sub-paragraph (1) there is inserted –

'(1A) A person may not be, at the same time, a member of the Commission and a member of the Tribunal.';

(d)   in sub-paragraph (2), for '(a)' there is substituted '(aa)'; and

(e)   in sub-paragraph (3), before paragraph (b) there is inserted –

'(aa) a newspaper panel member;'.

4   In paragraph 5 (the Council) –

(a)   in sub-paragraph (1), the word 'management' shall cease to have effect;

(b)   in sub-paragraph (2)(a), after 'Chairman' there is inserted 'and any deputy chairmen of the Commission';

(c)   in sub-paragraph (2), before paragraph (c) there is inserted –

'(bb) the member or members appointed under paragraph 2(1)(e);'; and

(d)   after sub-paragraph (3) there is inserted –

'(3A) Without prejudice to the question whether any other functions of the Commission are to be so discharged, the functions of the Commission under sections 106, 116, and 171 of the Enterprise Act 2002 (and under section 116 as applied for the purposes of references under Part 4 of that Act by section 176 of that Act) are to be discharged by the Council.'

5   In paragraph 6 (terms of appointment) –

(a)   in sub-paragraph (2), for 'five years at a time' there is substituted 'eight years (but this does not prevent a re-appointment for the purpose only of continuing to act as a member of a group selected under paragraph 15 before the end of his term of office)'; and

(b)   sub-paragraph (5) shall cease to have effect.

6   Paragraph 7(4) (approval of Treasury) shall cease to have effect.

7   Before paragraph 8 there is inserted –

'7A   The Commission may publish advice and information in relation to any matter connected with the exercise of its functions.'

8   In paragraph 9 (staff) –

(a)   sub-paragraph (2), and in sub-paragraph (3) the words 'and the President', shall cease to have effect;

(b)   in sub-paragraph (4), for paragraphs (a) and (b) there is substituted 'the Secretary of State as to numbers and terms and conditions of service'.

9   Paragraph 10 (procedure) shall cease to have effect.

10   (1)   Paragraph 15 (discharge of certain functions by groups) is amended as follows.

(2)   In sub-paragraph (1), after 'sub-paragraph (7)' there is inserted 'or (8)'.

(3)   For sub-paragraph (5) (members of newspaper panel) there is substituted –

'(5)   The Chairman must select one or more newspaper panel members to be members of the group dealing with functions relating to a newspaper merger reference and, if he selects at least three such members, the group may consist entirely of those members.'

(4)   In sub-paragraph (7) (Chairman's role in setting aside merger references), paragraph (b) (and the word 'or' before it) shall cease to have effect.

(5)   After sub-paragraph (7) there is inserted –

'(8)   The Chairman may exercise the power conferred by section 37(1), 48(1) or 64(1) of the Enterprise Act 2002 while a group is being constituted to perform a relevant general function of the Commission or, when it has been so constituted, before it has held its first meeting.'

11   (1)   Paragraph 20 (requirement for two-thirds majority on reports) is amended as follows.

(2)   In sub-paragraph (1), for 'sub-paragraph (2)' there is substituted 'sub-paragraphs (2) to (9)'.

(3)   For sub-paragraph (2) there is substituted –

'(2)   For the purposes of Part 3 of the Enterprise Act 2002 (mergers) any decision of a group under section 35(1) or 36(1) of that Act (questions to be decided on non-public interest merger references) that there is an anti-competitive outcome is to be treated as a decision under that section that there is not an anti-competitive outcome if the decision is not that of at least two-thirds of the members of the group.

(3)   For the purposes of Part 3 of the Act of 2002, if the decision is not that of at least two-thirds of the members of the group –

(a)   any decision of a group under section 47 of that Act (questions to be decided on public interest merger references) that a relevant merger situation has been created is to be treated as a decision under that section that no such situation has been created;

(b)   any decision of a group under section 47 of that Act that the creation of a relevant merger situation has resulted, or may be expected to result, in a substantial lessening of competition within any market or markets in the United Kingdom for goods or services is to be treated as a decision under that section that the creation of that situation has not resulted, or may be expected not to result, in such a substantial lessening of competition;

(c)   any decision of a group under section 47 of that Act that arrangements are in progress or in contemplation which, if carried into effect, will result in the creation of a relevant merger situation is to be treated as a decision under that section that no such arrangements are in progress or in contemplation; and

(d)   any decision of a group under section 47 of that Act that the creation of such a situation as is mentioned in paragraph (c) may be expected to result in a substantial lessening of competition within any market or markets in the United Kingdom for goods or services is to be treated as a decision under that section that the creation of that situation may be expected not to result in such a substantial lessening of competition.

(4)   For the purposes of Part 3 of the Act of 2002, if the decision is not that of at least two-thirds of the members of the group –

(a)   any decision of a group under section 63 of that Act (questions to be decided on special public interest merger references) that a special merger situation has been created is to be treated as a decision under that section that no such situation has been created; and

(b)   any decision of a group under section 63 of that Act that arrangements are in progress or in contemplation which, if carried into effect, will result in the creation of a special merger situation is to be treated as a decision under that section that no such arrangements are in progress or in contemplation.

(5)   For the purposes of Part 4 of the Act of 2002 (market investigations), if the decision is not that of at least two-thirds of the members of the group, any decision of a group under section 134 or 141 (questions to be decided on market investigation references) that a feature, or combination of features, of a relevant market prevents, restricts or distorts competition in connection with the supply or acquisition of any goods or services in the United Kingdom or a part of the United Kingdom is to be treated as a decision that the feature or (as the case may be) combination of features does not prevent, restrict or distort such competition.

(6)   Accordingly, for the purposes of Part 4 of the Act of 2002, a group is to be treated as having decided under section 134 or 141 that there is no adverse effect on competition if –

(a)   one or more than one decision of the group is to be treated as mentioned in sub-paragraph (5); and

(b)   there is no other relevant decision of the group.

(7)   In sub-paragraph (6) "relevant decision" means a decision which is not to be treated as mentioned in sub-paragraph (5) and which is that a feature, or combination of features, of a relevant market prevents, restricts or distorts competition in connection with the supply or acquisition of any goods or services in the United Kingdom or a part of the United Kingdom.

(8)   Expressions used in sub-paragraphs (2) to (7) shall be construed in accordance with Part 3 or (as the case may be) 4 of the Act of 2002.

(9)   Sub-paragraph (1) is also subject to specific provision made by or under other enactments about decisions which are not decisions of at least two-thirds of the members of a group.'

12   In paragraph 22 (panel of persons to act in newspaper merger references), for the words from the beginning to 'suitable' there is substituted 'There are to be members of the Commission appointed by the Secretary of State to form a panel of persons available'.

SCHEDULE 12   COMPETITION COMMISSION:
CERTAIN PROCEDURAL RULES   Section 187

'SCHEDULE 7A   THE COMPETITION COMMISSION: PROCEDURAL RULES FOR MERGERS AND MARKET REFERENCES ETC.

1   In this Schedule –

"market investigation" means an investigation carried out by a market reference group in connection with a reference under section 131 or 132 of the Enterprise Act 2002 (including that section as it has effect by virtue of another enactment);

"market reference group" has the meaning given by paragraph 19A(9) of Schedule 7 to this Act;

"merger investigation" means an investigation carried out by a merger reference group in connection with a reference under section 59 of the Fair Trading Act 1973 (c. 41), section 32 of the Water Industry Act 1991 (c. 56) or section 22, 33, 45 or 62 of the Act of 2002;

"merger reference group" has the meaning given by paragraph 19A(9) of Schedule 7 to this Act;

"relevant group" means a market reference group, merger reference group or special reference group;

"special investigation" means an investigation carried out by a special reference group –

(a)   in connection with a reference under a provision mentioned in any of paragraphs (a) to (l) and (n) of the definition of "special reference group" in paragraph 19A(9) of Schedule 7 to this Act; or

(b)   under a provision mentioned in paragraph (m) of that definition; and

"special reference group" has the meaning given by paragraph 19A(9) of Schedule 7 to this Act.

2   Rules may make provision –

(a)   for particular stages of a merger investigation, a market investigation or a special investigation to be dealt with in accordance with a timetable and for the revision of that timetable;

(b)   as to the documents and information which must be given to a relevant group in connection with a merger investigation, a market investigation or a special investigation;

(c)   as to the documents or information which a relevant group must give to other persons in connection with such an investigation.

3   Rules made by virtue of paragraph 2(a) and (b) may, in particular, enable or require a relevant group to disregard documents or information given after a particular date.

4   Rules made by virtue of paragraph 2(c) may, in particular, make provision for the notification or publication of, and for consultation about, provisional findings of a relevant group.

5   Rules may make provision as to the quorum of relevant groups.

6   Rules may make provision –

(a) as to the extent (if any) to which persons interested or claiming to be interested in a matter under consideration which is specified or described in the rules are allowed –

(i)   to be (either by themselves or by their representatives) present before a relevant group or heard by that group;

(ii) to cross-examine witnesses; or

(iii) otherwise to take part;

(b) as to the extent (if any) to which sittings of a relevant group are to be held in public; and

(c) generally in connection with any matters permitted by rules made under paragraph (a) or (b) (including, in particular, provision for a record of any hearings).

7   Rules may make provision for –

(a) the notification or publication of information in relation to merger investigations, market investigations or special investigations;

(b) consultation about such investigations.'

SCHEDULE 13   LISTED DIRECTIVES   Section 210

PART 1   DIRECTIVES

1   Council Directive 84/450/EEC of 10 September 1984 relating to the approximation of the laws, regulations and administrative provisions of the Member States concerning misleading advertising.

2   Council Directive 85/577/EEC of 20 December 1985 to protect the consumer in respect of contracts negotiated away from business premises.

3   Council Directive 87/102/EEC of 22 December 1986 for the approximation of the laws, regulations and administrative provisions of the Member States concerning consumer credit as last amended by Directive 98/7/EC.

4   Council Directive 90/314/EEC of 13 June 1990 on package travel, package holidays and package tours.

5   Council Directive 93/13/EEC of 5 April 1993 on unfair terms in consumer contracts.

6   Directive 94/47/EC of the European Parliament and of the Council of 26 October 1994 on the protection of purchasers in respect of certain aspects of contracts relating to the purchase of the right to use immovable properties on a timeshare basis.

7   Directive 97/7/EC of the European Parliament and of the Council of 20 May 1997 on the protection of consumers in respect of distance contracts.

8   Directive 1999/44/EC of the European Parliament and of the Council of 25 May 1999 on certain aspects of the sale of consumer goods and associated guarantees.

9   Directive 2000/31/EC of the European Parliament and of the Council of 8 June 2000 on certain legal aspects of information society services, in particular electronic commerce, in the Internal Market ('Directive on electronic commerce').

PART 2   PROVISIONS OF DIRECTIVES

10   Articles 10 to 21 of Council Directive 89/552/EEC of 3 October 1989 on the co-
        ordination of certain provisions laid down by law, regulation or administrative
        action in Member States concerning the pursuit of television broadcasting
        activities as amended by Directive 97/36/EC.

11   Articles 86 to 99 of the Directive 2001/83/EC of the European Parliament and of
        the Council of 6 November 2001 on the Community code relating to medicinal
        products for human use.

SCHEDULE 14   SPECIFIED FUNCTIONS   Sections 238 and 243

Parts 2, 3, 4, 5, 6, 7, 8 and 11 of the Fair Trading Act 1973 (c. 41).

Trade Descriptions Act 1968 (c. 29).

Prices Act 1974 (c. 24).

Consumer Credit Act 1974 (c. 39).

Estate Agents Act 1979 (c. 38).

Competition Act 1980 (c. 21).

Consumer Protection Act 1987 (c. 43).

Property Misdescriptions Act 1991 (c. 29).

Timeshare Act 1992 (c. 35).

Competition Act 1998 (c. 41).

Chapter 3 of Part 10 and Chapter 2 of Part 18 of the Financial Services and Markets Act
2000 (c. 8).

An order made under section 95 of that Act.

SCHEDULE 15   ENACTMENTS CONFERRING
FUNCTIONS   Section 241

Gun Barrel Proof Act 1868 (cap 113).

Gun Barrel Proof Act 1950 (cap 3).

Trade Descriptions Act 1968.

Unsolicited Goods and Services Act 1971 (c. 30).

Fair Trading Act 1973.

Hallmarking Act 1973 (c. 43).

Prices Act 1974.

Consumer Credit Act 1974.

Gun Barrel Proof Act 1978 (c. 9).

Estate Agents Act 1979.

Competition Act 1980.

National Audit Act 1983 (c. 44).

Telecommunications Act 1984 (c. 12).

Companies Act 1985 (c. 6).

Weights and Measures Act 1985 (c. 72).

Airports Act 1986 (c. 31).

Gas Act 1986 (c. 44).

Financial Services Act 1986 (c. 60).

Consumer Protection Act 1987 (c. 43).

Copyright, Designs and Patents Act 1988 (c. 48).

Water Act 1989 (c. 15).

Electricity Act 1989 (c. 29).

Courts and Legal Services Act 1990 (c. 41).

Broadcasting Act 1990 (c. 42).

Property Misdescriptions Act 1991 (c. 29).

Water Industry Act 1991 (c. 56).

Water Resources Act 1991 (c. 57).

Statutory Water Companies Act 1991 (c. 58).

Land Drainage Act 1991 (c. 59).

Timeshare Act 1992 (c. 35).

Railways Act 1993 (c. 43).

Coal Industry Act 1994 (c. 21).

Trade Marks Act 1994 (c. 26).

Gas Act 1995 (c. 45).

Broadcasting Act 1996 (c. 55).

Competition Act 1998 (c. 41).

Financial Services and Markets Act 2000 (c. 8).

Government Resources and Accounts Act 2000 (c. 20).

Postal Services Act 2000 (c. 26).

Utilities Act 2000 (c. 27).

Part 1 of the Transport Act 2000 (c. 38).

[. . .]

SCHEDULE 24   TRANSITIONAL AND TRANSITORY PROVISIONS AND SAVINGS
Section 276

Operation of references to OFT before commencement of section 2(3)

1   (1)   This paragraph applies to any provision contained in this Act, or made by virtue of this Act, which contains a reference to the OFT but comes into force before the time at which section 2(3) comes into force.

   (2)   Until that time any reference to the OFT is to be taken as a reference to the Director.

Pensions etc. of former Directors

2   In the case of any such person who has held the office of the Director as may be determined by the Secretary of State with the approval of the Minister for the Civil Service –

   (a)   such pension, allowance or gratuity shall be paid to or in respect of him on his retirement or death, or

(b)   such contributions or payments shall be paid towards provision for such a pension, allowance or gratuity,

as may be so determined.

First financial year of the OFT

3   (1)   If the period beginning with the day on which the OFT is established and ending with the next 31st March is six months or more, the first financial year of the OFT is that period.

    (2)   Otherwise the first financial year of the OFT is the period beginning with the day on which it is established and ending with 31st March in the following year.

First annual plan of the OFT

4   (1)   The OFT's first annual plan (as required by section 3(1)) shall be published within the period of three months beginning with the day on which it is established.

    (2)   Subject to sub-paragraph (3), that annual plan shall relate to the period beginning with the date of publication and ending with the next 31st March.

    (3)   If the period mentioned in sub-paragraph (2) is three months or less, that annual plan shall relate to the period beginning with the date of publication and ending with the 31st March in the following year.

Last annual report of the Director General of Fair Trading

5   (1)   After the abolition of the office of the Director, any duty of his to make an annual report, in relation to any calendar year for which such a report has not been made, shall be performed by the OFT.

    (2)   The period between the abolition of that office and the end of the preceding calendar year (if less than 12 months) shall be treated as the calendar year for which the last annual report is required.

    (3)   If that period is nine months or more, the OFT shall make the last annual report as soon as practicable after the end of that period.

    (4)   Otherwise the OFT shall make the last annual report no later than the making of its first report under section 4(1).

    (5)   In this paragraph 'annual report' means a report required by section 125(1) of the 1973 Act.

Effect of transfers under section 2

6   (1)   In this paragraph –

        'commencement' means the commencement of section 2(1);
        'transferred' means transferred by section 2(1).

    (2)   Anything which –

       (a)   has been done by or in relation to the Director for the purposes of or in connection with anything transferred; and

       (b)   is in effect immediately before commencement,

    shall be treated as if done by or in relation to the OFT.

    (3)   Anything (including legal proceedings) which –

       (a)   relates to anything transferred; and

(b)   is in the process of being done by or in relation to the Director immediately before it is transferred,

may be continued by or in relation to the OFT.

(4)   Nothing in section 2 or this paragraph affects the validity of anything done by or in relation to the Director before commencement.

First President and Registrar of the Competition Appeal Tribunal

7   The person who is President of the Competition Commission Appeal Tribunals (under paragraph 4 of Schedule 7 to the 1998 Act) immediately before the commencement of section 12 is on that date to become the President of the Competition Appeal Tribunal as if duly appointed under that section, on the same terms.

8   The person who is Registrar of Appeal Tribunals (under paragraph 5 of Schedule 8 to the 1998 Act) immediately before the commencement of section 12 is on that date to become the Registrar of the Competition Appeal Tribunal as if duly appointed under that section, on the same terms.

9   Any person who is a member of the Competition Commission appeal panel (but not a member of the panel of chairmen) immediately before the commencement of section 12 is on that date to become a member of the Competition Appeal Tribunal, on such terms and for such a period as the Secretary of State may determine.

10   Any member of the Competition Commission appeal panel who is, immediately before the commencement of section 12, a member of the panel of chairmen under paragraph 26 of Schedule 7 to the 1998 Act is on that date to become a chairman of the Competition Appeal Tribunal, on such terms and for such a period as the Lord Chancellor may determine.

11   Nothing in paragraph 7, 8, 9 or 10 applies to any person who, before the commencement of section 12, gives notice to the Secretary of State stating that he does not wish that paragraph to apply to him.

Tribunal rules

12   (1)   Any rules made under section 48 of the 1998 Act which are in force immediately before the commencement of section 15 above shall be treated after that commencement as having been made under section 15.

(2)   The Secretary of State may treat any consultation carried out with the President of the Competition Commission Appeal Tribunals (before the appointment of the President of the Competition Appeal Tribunal) as being as effective for the purposes of section 15(1) as if it had been carried out with the President of the Competition Appeal Tribunal.

Merger references

13   (1)   Subject to paragraphs 15 to 18, the old law shall continue to apply where –

(a)   two or more enterprises have ceased to be distinct enterprises (within the meaning of Part 5 of the 1973 Act); and

(b)   the cessation has occurred before the appointed day.

(2)   Subject to sub-paragraphs (3), (4) and (5) and paragraphs 15 to 18, the old law shall continue to apply in relation to any relevant arrangements which were in progress or in contemplation before the appointed day and are in progress or in contemplation on that day and (if events so require) the actual results of those arrangements where, before the appointed day –

   (a)   a merger notice was given, and not rejected under section 75B(7) of the
         1973 Act or withdrawn, in relation to the arrangements;
   (b)   no merger notice was so given but, in relation to the arrangements –
         (i)   a reference was made under section 75 of the 1973 Act;
         (ii)   undertakings were accepted under section 75G of that Act; or
         (iii) a decision was made by the Secretary of State neither to make a
                reference under section 75 of that Act nor to accept undertakings
                under section 75G of that Act; or
   (c)   a merger notice was so given, was rejected under section 75B(7) of the
         1973 Act or withdrawn, paragraph (a) does not apply in relation to a dif-
         ferent merger notice given in relation to the arrangements and, in relation
         to the arrangements, paragraph (b)(i), (ii) or (iii) applies.

(3) Subject to sub-paragraph (8), the new law shall, in a case of the kind mentioned
    in sub-paragraph (2)(a), apply in relation to any relevant arrangements and (if
    events so require) the actual results of those arrangements if, on or after the
    appointed day, a merger notice is rejected under section 75B(7) of the 1973 Act
    or withdrawn in relation to the arrangements.

(4) Subject to sub-paragraph (8), the new law shall, in a case of the kind mentioned
    in sub-paragraph (2)(a), apply in relation to any relevant arrangements and (if
    events so require) the actual results of those arrangements if –
   (a)   the making of a reference under section 64 or 75 of the 1973 Act in relation
         to those arrangements and (if events so require) the actual results of those
         arrangements was, immediately before the appointed day and by virtue of
         section 75C(1)(c), (e) or (g) of that Act, not prevented;
   (b)   the period for considering the merger notice has expired (whether before,
         on or after the appointed day); and
   (c)   no reference has been made under section 64 or 75 of the 1973 Act and no
         undertakings have been accepted under section 75G of that Act.

(5) Subject to sub-paragraph (8), the new law shall, in a case of the kind mentioned
    in sub-paragraph (2)(a), apply in relation to any relevant arrangements and (if
    events so require) the actual results of those arrangements if –
   (a)   the making of a reference under section 64 or 75 of the 1973 Act in relation
         to those arrangements and (if events so require) the actual results of those
         arrangements becomes, on or after the appointed day and by virtue of
         section 75C(1)(b), (c), (d), (e) or (g) of that Act, not prevented;
   (b)   the period for considering the merger notice has expired (whether before,
         on or after the appointed day); and
   (c)   no reference has been made under section 64 or 75 of the 1973 Act and no
         undertakings have been accepted under section 75G of that Act.

(6) Subject to sub-paragraph (8), the new law shall apply in relation to relevant
    arrangements and (if events so require) the actual results of those arrangements
    if –
   (a)   the arrangements were in progress or in contemplation before the
         appointed day and are in progress or in contemplation on that day;
   (b)   before the appointed day and in relation to the arrangements –
         (i)   no reference was made under section 75 of the 1973 Act;
         (ii)   no undertakings were accepted under section 75G of that Act; and
         (iii) a decision neither to make a reference under section 75 of that Act
                nor to accept undertakings under section 75G of that Act was not
                made by the Secretary of State; and
   (c)   no merger notice was given to the Director or the OFT before that day in
         relation to the arrangements.

(7) Subject to sub-paragraph (8), the new law shall, in a case of the kind mentioned in sub-paragraph (2)(c) (excluding the words from 'and' to the end), apply in relation to any relevant arrangements and (if events so require) the actual results of those arrangements if, in relation to the arrangements, sub-paragraph (2)(b)(i), (ii) and (iii) do not apply.

(8) Subject to paragraphs 15 to 18, the old law shall continue to apply in relation to concentrations with a Community dimension (within the meaning of the European Merger Regulations) notified before the appointed day to the European Commission under article 4 of those Regulations.

(9) In this paragraph references to relevant arrangements which are in progress or in contemplation on the appointed day include references to the actual results of those arrangements if the arrangements were in progress or in contemplation immediately before the appointed day and have, at the beginning of the appointed day, resulted in two or more enterprises ceasing to be distinct enterprises (within the meaning of Part 5 of the 1973 Act).

(10) In this paragraph –

'the European Merger Regulations' has the meaning given by section 129(1);

'merger notice' means a notice under section 75A(1) of the 1973 Act;

'the new law' means Part 3 of this Act and any related provision of law (including, in particular, any modification made under section 276(2) to that Part or any such provision);

'the old law' means sections 64 to 75K of the 1973 Act and any related provision of law (including, in particular, any modification made under section 276(2) to those sections or any such provision); and

'relevant arrangements' means arrangements which might result in two or more enterprises ceasing to be distinct enterprises (within the meaning of Part 5 of the 1973 Act).

Monopoly references

14 (1) Subject to paragraphs 15 to 18, the old law shall continue to apply in relation to any monopoly reference made before the appointed day under section 50 or 51 of the 1973 Act.

(2) No person has to comply on or after the appointed day with a requirement imposed before that day under section 44 of the 1973 Act.

(3) In this paragraph –

'monopoly reference' has the meaning given by section 5(3) of the 1973 Act; and

'the old law' means Part 4 of the 1973 Act and any related provision of law (including, in particular, any modification made under section 276(2) to that Part or any such provision).

Enforcement undertakings and orders

15 (1) Section 94(1) to (6) shall apply in relation to any undertaking –

(a) accepted (whether before, on or after the appointed day) by a Minister of the Crown –

(i)   in pursuance of a proposal under section 56A of the 1973 Act; or

(ii) under section 56F, 75G or 88 of that Act; and

(b) of a description specified in an order made by the Secretary of State under this paragraph;

as it applies in relation to enforcement undertakings under Part 3.

(2) Section 94(1) to (6) shall apply in relation to any order made by a Minister of the Crown under section 56, 73, 74, 75K or 89 of the 1973 Act (whether before, on or after the appointed day) and of a description specified in an order made by the Secretary of State under this paragraph as it applies in relation to enforcement orders under Part 3.

(3) Compliance with –

    (a)   an undertaking accepted by a Minister of the Crown under section 88 of the 1973 Act (whether before, on or after the appointed day) and of a description specified in an order made by the Secretary of State under this paragraph; or

    (b)   an order made by a Minister of the Crown under section 56, 73, 74 or 89 of the 1973 Act (whether before, on or after the appointed day) and of a description specified in an order made by the Secretary of State under this paragraph;

shall also be enforceable by civil proceedings brought by the Commission for an injunction or for interdict or for any other appropriate relief or remedy.

(4) Sub-paragraph (3) and section 94(6) as applied by virtue of sub-paragraph (1) or (2) shall not prejudice any right that a person may have by virtue of section 94(4) as so applied to bring civil proceedings for contravention or apprehended contravention of an undertaking or order.

(5) Sections 93 and 93A of the 1973 Act shall accordingly cease to apply in relation to undertakings and orders to which sub-paragraphs (1) to (3) above apply.

16 (1) Sub-paragraph (2) applies to any undertaking –

    (a)   accepted (whether before, on or after the appointed day) by a Minister of the Crown –

        (i)   in pursuance of a proposal under section 56A of the 1973 Act; or
        (ii)   under section 56F, 75G or 88 of that Act; and

    (b)   of a description specified in an order made by the Secretary of State under this paragraph.

(2) An undertaking to which this sub-paragraph applies may be –

    (a)   superseded by a new undertaking accepted by the relevant authority under this paragraph;

    (b)   varied by an undertaking accepted by the relevant authority under this paragraph; or

    (c)   released by the relevant authority.

(3) Subject to sub-paragraph (4) and any provision made under section 276(2), the power of the relevant authority under this paragraph to supersede, vary or release an undertaking is exercisable in the same circumstances, and on the same terms and conditions, as the power of the Minister concerned to supersede, vary or release the undertaking would be exercisable under the 1973 Act.

(4) The duty under section 75J(b) of the 1973 Act to give advice shall be a duty of the OFT to consider what action (if any) it should take.

(5) Where the relevant authority has the power by virtue of this paragraph to supersede, vary or release an undertaking accepted by a Minister of the Crown –

    (a)   in pursuance of a proposal under section 56A of the 1973 Act; or
    (b)   under section 56F, 75G or 88 of that Act;

the Minister concerned shall accordingly cease to have the power under that Act to supersede, vary or release the undertaking.

(6) In this paragraph 'the relevant authority' means –

    (a)   in the case of an undertaking accepted in pursuance of a proposal under section 56A of the 1973 Act or an undertaking under section 56F or 75G of that Act, the OFT; and

(b)   in the case of an undertaking accepted under section 88 of that Act, the Commission.

17 (1) Any order made by a Minister of the Crown under section 56, 73, 74 or 89 of the 1973 Act (whether before, on or after the appointed day) and of a description specified in an order made by the Secretary of State under this paragraph may be varied or revoked by an order made by the Commission under this paragraph.

(2) Any order made by a Minister of the Crown under section 75K of the 1973 Act (whether before, on or after the appointed day) and of a description specified in an order made by the Secretary of State under this paragraph may be varied or revoked by an order made by the OFT under this paragraph.

(3) Subject to sub-paragraph (4) and any provision made under section 276(2), the power of the Commission to make an order under sub-paragraph (1), and the power of the OFT to make an order under sub-paragraph (2), is exercisable in the same circumstances, and on the same terms and conditions, as the power of the Minister concerned to make a corresponding varying or revoking order under the 1973 Act would be exercisable.

(4) The power of the Commission to make an order under sub-paragraph (1), and the power of the OFT to make an order under sub-paragraph (2), shall not be exercisable by statutory instrument and shall not be subject to the requirements of section 134(1) of the 1973 Act.

(5) Where the Commission or the OFT has the power by virtue of this paragraph to vary or revoke an order made by a Minister of the Crown under section 56, 73, 74, 75K or 89 of the 1973 Act, the Minister concerned shall accordingly cease to have the power to do so under that Act.

18 (1) Section 94(1) to (6) shall apply in relation to undertakings accepted under paragraph 16 and orders made under paragraph 17 as it applies in relation to enforcement undertakings and enforcement orders under Part 3.

(2) Compliance with an undertaking accepted by the Commission under paragraph 16 or an order made by it under paragraph 17 shall also be enforceable by civil proceedings brought by the Commission for an injunction or for interdict or for any other appropriate relief or remedy.

(3) Sub-paragraph (2) and section 94(6) as applied by virtue of sub-paragraph (1) shall not prejudice any right that a person may have by virtue of section 94(4) as so applied to bring civil proceedings for contravention or apprehended contravention of an undertaking or order.

Paragraphs 13 to 18: supplementary provision

19 (1) In paragraphs 13 to 18 'the appointed day' means such day as the Secretary of State may by order made by statutory instrument appoint; and different days may be appointed for different purposes.

(2) An order made by the Secretary of State under paragraph 15, 16 or 17 –

(a)   may make different provision for different purposes; and

(b)   shall be made by statutory instrument which shall be subject to annulment in pursuance of a resolution of either House of Parliament.

Designation orders under Schedule 4 to the 1998 Act

20 (1) Subject to sub-paragraph (2), the repeals made by section 207 do not affect –

(a)   the operation of Schedule 4 to the 1998 Act in relation to any application for designation of a professional rule which is made before the commencement date;

(b) the operation of section 3(1)(d) of and Schedule 4 to the 1998 Act in re-
     lation to any designation effected by an order made before the commence-
     ment date or on an application mentioned in paragraph (a).

(2) No designation order (whenever made) shall have any effect in relation to any
     period of time after the end of the transitional period.

(3) Subject to sub-paragraph (2) a designation order may be made after the end of
     the transitional period on an application mentioned in sub-paragraph (1)(a).

(4) For the purposes of this paragraph –

    'commencement date' means the day on which section 207 comes into
        force;
    'designation' means designation under paragraph 2 of Schedule 4 to the
        1998 Act; and
    'the transitional period' means the period of three months beginning with
        the commencement date.

Proceedings under Part 3 of the 1973 Act

21   The repeal of section 133(3) of the 1973 Act does not affect any right to disclose
        information for the purposes of any proceedings before the Restrictive Practices
        Court to which paragraph 42 of Schedule 13 to the 1998 Act applies.

Supplementary

22   Any provision made by any of paragraphs 1 to 21 shall not apply if, and to the
        extent that, an order under section 276(2) makes alternative provision or pro-
        vides for it not to apply.

SCHEDULE 25   MINOR AND CONSEQUENTIAL
AMENDMENTS   Section 278

Registered Designs Act 1949 (c. 88)

1   (1) The Registered Designs Act 1949 is amended as follows.

     (2) In section 11A(1) (powers exercisable in consequence of report of Competition
          Commission), paragraphs (a) and (b) shall cease to have effect.

     (3) After section 11A there is inserted –

'11AB Powers exercisable following merger and market investigations

(1) Subsection (2) below applies where –

    (a) section 41(2), 55(2), 66(6), 75(2), 83(2), 138(2), 147(2) or 160(2) of, or
         paragraph 5(2) or 10(2) of Schedule 7 to, the Enterprise Act 2002 (powers
         to take remedial action following merger or market investigations) applies;

    (b) the Competition Commission or (as the case may be) the Secretary of State
         considers that it would be appropriate to make an application under this
         section for the purpose of remedying, mitigating or preventing a matter
         which cannot be dealt with under the enactment concerned; and

    (c) the matter concerned involves conditions in licences granted in respect of
         a registered design by its proprietor restricting the use of the design by the
         licensee or the right of the proprietor to grant other licences.

(2) The Competition Commission or (as the case may be) the Secretary of State may
     apply to the registrar to take action under this section.

(3) Before making an application the Competition Commission or (as the case may be) the Secretary of State shall publish, in such manner as it or he thinks appropriate, a notice describing the nature of the proposed application and shall consider any representations which may be made within 30 days of such publication by persons whose interests appear to it or him to be affected.

(4) The registrar may, if it appears to him on an application under this section that the application is made in accordance with this section, by order cancel or modify any condition concerned of the kind mentioned in subsection (1)(c) above.

(5) An appeal lies from any order of the registrar under this section.

(6) References in this section to the Competition Commission shall, in cases where section 75(2) of the Enterprise Act 2002 applies, be read as references to the Office of Fair Trading.

(7) References in section 35, 36, 47, 63, 134 or 141 of the Enterprise Act 2002 (questions to be decided by the Competition Commission in its reports) to taking action under section 41(2), 55, 66, 138 or 147 shall include references to taking action under subsection (2) above.

(8) An order made by virtue of this section in consequence of action under subsection (2) above where an enactment mentioned in subsection (1)(a) above applies shall be treated, for the purposes of sections 91(3), 92(1)(a), 162(1) and 166(3) of the Enterprise Act 2002 (duties to register and keep under review enforcement orders etc.), as if it were made under the relevant power in Part 3 or (as the case may be) 4 of that Act to make an enforcement order (within the meaning of the Part concerned).'

Agricultural Marketing Act 1958 (c. 47)

2   (1) The Agricultural Marketing Act 1958 is amended as follows.

(2) In section 19A (action following report by Commission) –

(a)   for subsection (1) there is substituted –

'(1) Subsection (2) applies in any of the following cases.

(1A) The first case is where section 138(2) of the Enterprise Act 2002 (duty to remedy adverse effects following market investigation reference) applies and whatever is to be remedied, mitigated or prevented relates to any provision of a scheme or any act or omission of a board administering a scheme.

(1B) The second case is where section 147(2) of the Enterprise Act 2002 (power to remedy adverse effects in public interest cases) applies and whatever is to be remedied, mitigated or prevented relates to any provision of a scheme or any act or omission of a board administering a scheme.

(1C) The third case is where –

(a)   a report of the Competition Commission under section 11 of the Competition Act 1980 (c. 21) (references of public bodies etc.), as laid before Parliament, contains conclusions to the effect that –

(i)   certain matters indicated in the report operate against the public interest, and

(ii)   those matters consist of or include any provision of a scheme or any act or omission of a board administering a scheme, and

(b)   none of the conclusions is to be disregarded by virtue of section 11C(3) of that Act (requirement for two-thirds majority).';

(b)   in subsection (2) –

(i)   the words from the beginning of the subsection to 'this section' shall cease to have effect;

(ii)   for the words from 'those conclusions' to the end of the subsection there is substituted 'a report of a committee of investigation had contained the conclusion that the provision of the scheme in question, or the act or omission in question, is contrary to the interests of consumers of the regulated product';

(c)   after subsection (2) there is inserted –

'(3)   An order made by virtue of this section in a case mentioned in subsection (1A) or (1B) shall be treated, for the purposes of sections 162(1) and 166(3) of the Enterprise Act 2002 (duties to register and keep under review enforcement orders etc.), as if it were made under the relevant power in Part 4 of that Act to make an enforcement order (within the meaning of that Part).'

(3)   For the purposes of the Scotland Act 1998 (c. 46) the amendments made by subparagraph (2) shall be taken to be pre-commencement enactments within the meaning of that Act.

(4)   In section 47(2) (restrictions on disclosing certain information obtained under Act), in paragraph (aa) of the proviso –

(a)   for 'the Director General of Fair Trading or any of the staff appointed by that Director General' there is substituted 'the Office of Fair Trading';

(b)   for 'the Director General to perform any functions of theirs or his' there is substituted 'the Office of Fair Trading to perform any functions of theirs or its';

(c)   at the end there is inserted 'or the Enterprise Act 2002'.

Public Records Act 1958 (c. 51)

3   (1)   The Public Records Act 1958 is amended as follows.

(2)   In Part 2 of the Table at the end of paragraph 3 of Schedule 1 (definition of public records) –

(a)   the entry relating to the Office of the Director General of Fair Trading shall cease to have effect;

(b)   the following entries are inserted at the appropriate places –

'Competition Service'
'Office of Fair Trading.'

Superannuation Act 1972 (c. 11)

4   (1)   The Superannuation Act 1972 is amended as follows.

(2)   In Schedule 1 (kinds of employment in relation to which pension schemes may be made), in the list of 'Other Bodies', there is inserted at the appropriate place –

'The Competition Service.'

Fair Trading Act 1973 (c. 41)

5   (1)   The 1973 Act is amended as follows.

(2)   In section 5 (principal functions of Commission), in subsection (2) –

(a)   for 'the Director' there is substituted 'the Office of Fair Trading';

(b)   for 'his' (in each place) there is substituted 'its'.

(3) Sections 34 to 42 (additional functions of Director for protection of consumers) shall cease to have effect.

(4) In section 93B (false or misleading information) –

    (a)   in subsection (1) –

        (i)   for 'the Director' there is substituted 'the Office of Fair Trading';

        (ii) for 'Parts IV, V, VI' there is substituted 'Part 5';

        (iii) the words 'or under the Competition Act 1980' shall cease to have effect;

    (b)   after subsection (4) there is inserted –

        '(5) This section shall not have effect in relation to the furnishing of information to the Commission in connection with its functions under any provision of the Enterprise Act 2002 as applied by virtue of section 13B of the Telecommunications Act 1984 or section 44B of the Airports Act 1986.'

Consumer Credit Act 1974 (c. 39)

6   (1) The Consumer Credit Act 1974 is amended as follows.

    (2) In section 1 (general functions of Director) –

       (a)   in subsection (1) –

          (i)   for 'the Director General of Fair Trading ("the Director")' there is substituted 'the Office of Fair Trading ("the OFT")';

          (ii) for 'him' there is substituted 'it';

          (iii) for 'himself' there is substituted 'itself';

       (b)   in subsection (2) –

          (i)   for 'Director' there is substituted 'OFT';

          (ii) for 'him' there is substituted 'it';

       (c)   in the sidenote, for 'Director' there is substituted 'OFT';

    and in the heading before that section, for 'DIRECTOR GENERAL OF FAIR TRADING' there is substituted 'OFFICE OF FAIR TRADING'.

    (3) In section 2 (powers of Secretary of State) –

       (a)   for 'Director' (in each place) there is substituted 'OFT';

       (b)   in subsections (1)(b) and (2), for 'his' there is substituted 'its';

       (c)   in subsection (4), for 'him' there is substituted 'it'.

    (4) In section 4 (dissemination of information and advice) –

       (a)   for 'Director' there is substituted 'OFT';

       (b)   for 'he', 'him' and 'his' there is substituted 'it', 'it' and 'its' respectively.

    (5) In section 6 (form etc. of applications) –

       (a)   for 'Director' (in each place) there is substituted 'OFT';

       (b)   in subsection (3), for 'him' there is substituted 'it'.

    (6) In section 7 (penalty for false information), for 'Director' (in each place) there is substituted 'OFT'.

    (7) In section 22 (standard and group licences) –

       (a)   for 'Director' (in each place) there is substituted 'OFT';

       (b)   in subsection (1)(b), for 'his' and 'he' there is substituted 'its' and 'it' respectively;

       (c)   in subsection (5), for 'him' there is substituted 'it'.

    (8) In section 25 (licensee to be a fit person) –

       (a)   for 'Director' (in each place) there is substituted 'OFT';

       (b)   in subsection (2), for 'him' there is substituted 'it'.

(9) In section 27 (determination of applications) –

    (a)   for 'Director' (in each place) there is substituted 'OFT';

    (b)   in subsection (1) –

        (i)   for 'he' (in both places) there is substituted 'it';

        (ii)   in paragraph (a), for 'his' there is substituted 'its';

    (c)   in subsection (2), for 'him' (in both places) there is substituted 'it'.

(10) In section 28 (exclusion from a group licence) –

    (a)   for 'Director' (in both places) there is substituted 'OFT';

    (b)   for 'he' there is substituted 'it';

    (c)   in paragraph (a), for 'his' there is substituted 'its'.

(11) In section 29 (renewal) –

    (a)   for 'Director' (in each place) there is substituted 'OFT';

    (b)   in subsection (2), for 'his' there is substituted 'its'.

(12) In section 30 (variation by request) –

    (a)   for 'Director' and 'he' (in each place) there is substituted 'OFT' and 'it' respectively;

    (b)   in subsection (4)(a), for 'his' there is substituted 'its'.

(13) In section 31 (compulsory variation) –

    (a)   for 'Director' (in each place) there is substituted 'OFT';

    (b)   in subsection (1), for 'he' (in both places) there is substituted 'it';

    (c)   in subsection (2)(a), for 'his' there is substituted 'its';

    (d)   in subsection (3), for 'he', 'his' and 'him' there is substituted respectively 'it', 'its' and 'it' respectively;

    (e)   in subsection (4)(a), for 'his' there is substituted 'its'.

(14) In section 32 (suspension and revocation) –

    (a)   for 'Director' (in each place) there is substituted 'OFT';

    (b)   in subsection (1), for 'he' (in both places) there is substituted 'it';

    (c)   in subsection (2)(a), for 'his' there is substituted 'its';

    (d)   in subsection (3), for 'he', 'his' and 'him' there is substituted 'it', 'its' and 'it' respectively;

    (e)   in subsection (4)(a), for 'his' there is substituted 'its';

    (f)   in subsection (5), for 'he' there is substituted 'it';

    (g)   in subsection (8), for 'him' there is substituted 'it'.

(15) In section 33 (application to end suspension) –

    (a)   for 'Director' and 'he' (in each place) there is substituted 'OFT' and 'it' respectively;

    (b)   in subsection (2)(a), for 'his' there is substituted 'its'.

(16) In section 34 (representations to Director) –

    (a)   for 'Director' (in each place) there is substituted 'OFT';

    (b)   in subsections (2) and (3), for 'his' there is substituted 'its'.

(17) In section 35 (the register) –

    (a)   for 'Director' (in each place) there is substituted 'OFT';

    (b)   in subsections (1) and (4), for 'he' there is substituted 'it';

    (c)   in subsection (1)(c), for 'him' there is substituted 'it'.

(18) In section 36 (duty to notify changes) –

    (a)   for 'Director' (in each place) there is substituted 'OFT';

    (b)   in subsection (6), for 'him' there is substituted 'it'.

(19) In section 39 (offences against Part 3), for 'Director' there is substituted 'OFT'.

(20) In section 40 (enforcement of agreements made by unlicensed trader) –

    (a)   for 'Director' (in each place) there is substituted 'OFT';

    (b)   in subsection (3) –

        (i)   for 'he' (in both places) there is substituted 'it';

        (ii) in paragraph (a), for 'his' there is substituted 'its';

    (c)   in subsection (5), for 'he' there is substituted 'it'.

(21) In section 41 (appeals to Secretary of State under Part 3), in subsection (1), for 'Director' there is substituted 'OFT'.

(22) In section 49 (prohibition of canvassing debtor-creditor agreements off trade premises), for 'Director' (in each place) there is substituted 'OFT'.

(23) In section 60 (form and content of agreements), in subsections (3) and (4), for 'Director' (in each place) and 'he' (in each place) there is substituted 'OFT' and 'it' respectively.

(24) In section 64 (duty to give notice of cancellation rights), for 'Director' (in each place) there is substituted 'OFT'.

(25) In section 74 (exclusion of certain agreements from Part 5) –

    (a)   for 'Director' (in each place) there is substituted 'OFT';

    (b)   in subsection (3A), for 'he' there is substituted 'it'.

(26) In section 101 (right to terminate hire agreement), in subsection (8), for 'Director' (in each place) and 'he' there is substituted 'OFT' and 'it' respectively.

(27) In section 113 (Act not to be evaded by use of security), in subsection (2), for 'Director' there is substituted 'OFT'.

(28) In section 148 (agreement for services of unlicensed trader) –

    (a)   for 'Director' (in each place) there is substituted 'OFT';

    (b)   in subsection (3) –

        (i)   for 'he' (in both places) there is substituted 'it';

        (ii) in paragraph (a), for 'his' there is substituted 'its';

    (c)   in subsection (5), for 'he' there is substituted 'it'.

(29) In section 149 (regulated agreements made on introductions by unlicensed credit-broker) –

    (a)   for 'Director' (in each place) there is substituted 'OFT';

    (b)   in subsection (3) –

        (i)   for 'he' (in both places) there is substituted 'it';

        (ii) in paragraph (a), for 'his' there is substituted 'its';

    (c)   in subsection (5), for 'he' there is substituted 'it'.

(30) In section 159 (correction of wrong information), for 'Director' there is substituted 'OFT'.

(31) In section 160 (alternative procedure for business consumers) –

    (a)   for 'Director' (in each place) there is substituted 'OFT';

    (b)   in subsection (1), for 'he' there is substituted 'it'.

(32) In section 161 (enforcement authorities) –

    (a)   for 'Director' (in each place) there is substituted 'OFT';

    (b)   subsection (2) (requirement to notify Director of intended prosecution) is omitted;

    (c)   in subsection (3), for 'he' and 'him' there is substituted 'it'.

(33) In section 162 (powers of entry and inspection), in subsection (5), for 'Director' there is substituted 'OFT'.

(34) In section 166 (notification of convictions and judgments to Director), for 'Director' (in each place), 'Director's' and 'his' there is substituted 'OFT', 'OFT's' and 'its' respectively.

(35) In section 170 (no further sanctions for breach of Act), for 'his', 'Director' and 'him' there is substituted 'its', 'OFT' and 'it' respectively.

(36) In section 173 (contracting-out forbidden), in subsection (3), for 'Director' there is substituted 'OFT'.

(37) In section 183 (determinations etc. by Director), for 'Director' (in both places) and 'him' there is substituted 'OFT' and 'it' respectively.

(38) In section 189 (general interpretation provisions) –

    (a)   in subsection (1) –

        (i)   the definition of 'Director' shall cease to have effect;

        (ii)   in the definition of 'general notice', for 'Director' and 'him' there is substituted 'OFT' and 'it' respectively;

        (iii)   after the definition of 'notice of cancellation' there is inserted –
            ''OFT' means the Office of Fair Trading;';

        (iv)   in the definition of 'register', for 'Director' there is substituted 'OFT';

    (b)   in subsection (5), for 'Director' (in both places) there is substituted 'OFT'.

(39) In section 191 (special provisions as to Northern Ireland) –

    (a)   for 'Director' (in both places) there is substituted 'OFT';

    (b)   in subsection (1), for 'his' and 'him' there is substituted 'the OFT's' and 'the OFT' respectively.

(40) In Schedule 1 (prosecution and punishment of offences), in the entry relating to section 7, for 'Director' there is substituted 'OFT'.

Restrictive Practices Court Act 1976 (c. 33)

7   (1) The Restrictive Practices Court Act 1976 is amended as follows.

    (2) In section 9 (procedure), in subsection (2)(d), for 'the Director General of Fair Trading' there is substituted 'the Office of Fair Trading'.

Patents Act 1977 (c. 37)

8   (1) The Patents Act 1977 is amended as follows.

    (2) After section 50 there is inserted –

'50A Powers exercisable following merger and market investigations

    (1)   Subsection (2) below applies where –

        (a)   section 41(2), 55(2), 66(6), 75(2), 83(2), 138(2), 147(2) or 160(2) of, or paragraph 5(2) or 10(2) of Schedule 7 to, the Enterprise Act 2002 (powers to take remedial action following merger or market investigations) applies;

        (b)   the Competition Commission or (as the case may be) the Secretary of State considers that it would be appropriate to make an application under this section for the purpose of remedying, mitigating or preventing a matter which cannot be dealt with under the enactment concerned; and

        (c)   the matter concerned involves –

            (i)   conditions in licences granted under a patent by its proprietor restricting the use of the invention by the licensee or the right of the proprietor to grant other licences; or

            (ii)   a refusal by the proprietor of a patent to grant licences on reasonable terms.

(2)   The Competition Commission or (as the case may be) the Secretary of State may apply to the comptroller to take action under this section.

(3)   Before making an application the Competition Commission or (as the case may be) the Secretary of State shall publish, in such manner as it or he thinks appropriate, a notice describing the nature of the proposed application and shall consider any representations which may be made within 30 days of such publication by persons whose interests appear to it or him to be affected.

(4)   The comptroller may, if it appears to him on an application under this section that the application is made in accordance with this section, by order cancel or modify any condition concerned of the kind mentioned in subsection (1)(c)(i) above or may, instead or in addition, make an entry in the register to the effect that licences under the patent are to be available as of right.

(5)   References in this section to the Competition Commission shall, in cases where section 75(2) of the Enterprise Act 2002 applies, be read as references to the Office of Fair Trading.

(6)   References in section 35, 36, 47, 63, 134 or 141 of the Enterprise Act 2002 (questions to be decided by the Competition Commission in its reports) to taking action under section 41(2), 55, 66, 138 or 147 shall include references to taking action under subsection (2) above.

(7)   Action taken by virtue of subsection (4) above in consequence of an application under subsection (2) above where an enactment mentioned in subsection (1)(a) above applies shall be treated, for the purposes of sections 91(3), 92(1)(a), 162(1) and 166(3) of the Enterprise Act 2002 (duties to register and keep under review enforcement orders etc.), as if it were the making of an enforcement order (within the meaning of the Part concerned) under the relevant power in Part 3 or (as the case may be) 4 of that Act.'

(3)   In section 51(1) (powers exercisable in consequence of report of Competition Commission), paragraphs (a) and (b) shall cease to have effect.

(4)   In section 53(2) (statements in certain reports of the Competition Commission to be prima facie evidence of the matters stated) after '1980' there is inserted 'or published under Part 3 or 4 of the Enterprise Act 2002'.

Estate Agents Act 1979 (c. 38)

9   (1)   The Estate Agents Act 1979 is amended as follows.

(2)   In section 3 (orders prohibiting unfit persons from doing estate agency work) –

(a)   in subsection (1), for 'the Director General of Fair Trading (in this Act referred to as "the Director")' there is substituted 'the Office of Fair Trading (in this Act referred to as 'the OFT')';

(b)   for 'Director' (in each place) there is substituted 'OFT';

(c)   in subsection (2), for 'he' there is substituted 'it';

(d)   in subsections (4) and (5), for 'he' (in each place) and 'him' there is substituted 'it';

and in the cross-heading before that section, for 'Director General of Fair Trading' there is substituted 'Office of Fair Trading'.

(3)   In section 4 (warning orders) –

(a)   for 'Director' (in each place) there is substituted 'OFT';

(b)   in subsection (1), for 'he' there is substituted 'it'.

(4)   In section 5 (supplementary provisions as to orders under sections 3 and 4), for 'Director' (in each place) there is substituted 'OFT'.

(5) In section 6 (revocation and variation of orders under sections 3 and 4) –

    (a)   for 'Director' (in each place) there is substituted 'OFT';

    (b)   in subsection (1), for 'him' there is substituted 'it';

    (c)   in subsections (3) to (5), for 'he' (in each place) there is substituted 'it';

    (d)   in subsection (3), for 'his' there is substituted 'its'.

(6) In section 7 (appeals), in subsection (1), for 'Director' (in both places) there is substituted 'OFT'.

(7) In section 8 (register of orders etc.) –

    (a)   for 'Director' (in each place) there is substituted 'OFT';

    (b)   in subsection (1), for 'him' and 'his' there is substituted 'it' and 'its' respectively;

    (c)   in subsection (3), for 'his' there is substituted 'its';

    (d)   in subsection (4), for 'he' there is substituted 'it';

    (e)   in subsection (5), for 'him' there is substituted 'it'.

(8) In section 9 (information for the Director) –

    (a)   for 'Director' (in each place) there is substituted 'OFT';

    (b)   in subsection (1), for 'him' (in each place) and 'his' there is substituted 'it' and 'its' respectively.

(9) In –

    (a)   section 11 (powers of entry and inspection),

    (b)   section 13 (clients' money held on trust or as agent), and

    (c)   section 15 (interest on clients' money),

for 'Director' there is substituted 'OFT'.

(10) In section 17 (exemptions from section 16) –

    (a)   for 'Director' (in each place) there is substituted 'OFT';

    (b)   in subsection (1), for 'he' and 'him' there is substituted 'it';

    (c)   in subsection (5), for 'he' and 'his' (in both places) there is substituted 'it' and 'its' respectively.

(11) In –

    (a)   section 19 (regulation of pre-contract deposits outside Scotland),

    (b)   section 20 (regulation of pre-contract deposits in Scotland), and

    (c)   section 21 (transactions in which an estate agent has a personal interest),

for 'Director' there is substituted 'OFT'.

(12) In section 25 (general duties of Director) –

    (a)   for 'Director' (in each place) there is substituted 'OFT';

    (b)   in subsection (1), for 'himself' there is substituted 'itself';

    (c)   in subsections (2) and (3), for 'him' there is substituted 'it';

    (d)   in subsection (3), for 'he' there is substituted 'it'.

(13) In section 26 (enforcement authorities) –

    (a)   for 'Director' (in each place) there is substituted 'OFT';

    (b)   subsection (2) (requirement to notify Director of intended prosecution) is omitted;

    (c)   in subsection (4), for 'him' and 'he' there is substituted 'it'.

(14) In –

    (a)   section 29 (service of notices etc.), and

    (b)   section 30 (orders and regulations),

for 'Director' (in each place) there is substituted 'OFT'.

(15) In section 33 (general interpretation provisions) –

    (a)   the definition of 'Director' shall cease to have effect;

> (b)   in the definition of 'general notice', for 'Director' and 'him' there is substi-
> tuted 'OFT' and 'it' respectively;
>
> (c)   after the definition of 'general notice' there is inserted –
>
> '"OFT" means the Office of Fair Trading;'.

(16) In Schedule 2 (procedure etc.) –

> (a)   for 'Director' and 'Director's' (in each place) there is substituted 'OFT' and
> 'OFT's';
>
> (b)   in paragraph 1, for 'his' and 'he' there is substituted 'its' and 'it' respectively;
>
> (c)   in paragraphs 3 and 5, for 'he' there is substituted 'it';
>
> (d)   in paragraph 6, for 'his' (in both places) and 'he' (in both places) there is
> substituted 'its' and 'it' respectively;
>
> (e)   in paragraph 7, for 'his' and 'he' there is substituted 'its' and 'it' respectively;
>
> (f)   in paragraph 8, for 'his', 'he' (in both places) and 'him' there is substituted
> 'its', 'it' and 'it' respectively;
>
> (g)   in paragraph 9(1), for 'his' (in both places) there is substituted 'its';
>
> (h)   in paragraph 10(2), for 'he' there is substituted 'it'.

Competition Act 1980 (c. 21)

10   (1)   The Competition Act 1980 is amended as follows.

(2)   In section 11 (references of public bodies and certain other persons to the
Commission) –

> (a)   in subsection (1) –
>
> > (i)   at the end of paragraph (a) there is inserted 'or';
> >
> > (ii)   paragraph (c) and the word 'or' before it shall cease to have effect;
> >
> > (iii) for 'paragraph (a), (b) or (c)' there is substituted 'paragraph (a) or (b)';
>
> (b)   subsections (2), (9) and (9A) shall cease to have effect.

(3)   After section 11 there is inserted –

'11A References under section 11: time-limits

> (1)   Every reference under section 11 above shall specify a period (not longer
> than six months beginning with the date of the reference) within which a
> report on the reference is to be made.
>
> (2)   A report of the Commission on a reference under section 11 above shall not
> have effect (and no action shall be taken in relation to it under section 12
> below) unless the report is made before the end of the period specified in
> the reference or such further period (if any) as may be allowed by the
> Secretary of State under subsection (3) below.
>
> (3)   The Secretary of State may, if he has received representations on the subject
> from the Commission and is satisfied that there are special reasons why the
> report cannot be made within the period specified in the reference, extend
> that period by no more than three months.
>
> (4)   No more than one extension is possible under subsection (3) above in rela-
> tion to the same reference.
>
> (5)   The Secretary of State shall publish any extension made by him under sub-
> section (3) above in such manner as he considers most suitable for bring-
> ing it to the attention of persons who in his opinion would be affected by
> it or be likely to have an interest in it.

11B References under section 11: powers of investigation and penalties

> (1)   The following sections of Part 3 of the Enterprise Act 2002 shall apply, with
> the modifications mentioned in subsections (2) and (3) below, for the pur-

poses of references under section 11 above as they apply for the purposes of references under that Part –

(a) section 109 (attendance of witnesses and production of documents etc.);

(b) section 110 (enforcement of powers under section 109: general);

(c) section 111 (penalties);

(d) section 112 (penalties: main procedural requirements);

(e) section 113 (payments and interest by instalments);

(f) section 114 (appeals in relation to penalties);

(g) section 115 (recovery of penalties); and

(h) section 116 (statement of policy).

(2) Section 110 shall, in its application by virtue of subsection (1) above, have effect as if –

(a) subsection (2) were omitted;

(b) in subsection (4), for the word "publication" there were substituted "laying before both Houses of Parliament"; and

(c) in subsection (9) the words from "or section" to "section 65(3))" were omitted.

(3) Section 111(5)(b)(ii) shall, in its application by virtue of subsection (1) above, have effect as if –

(a) for the words "published (or, in the case of a report under section 50 or 65, given)" there were substituted "made";

(b) for the words "published (or given)", in both places where they appear, there were substituted "made"; and

(c) the words "by this Part" were omitted.

11C References under section 11: further supplementary provisions

(1) Section 117 of the Enterprise Act 2002 (false or misleading information) shall apply in relation to functions under this Act as it applies in relation to functions under Part 3 of that Act but as if, in subsections (1)(a) and (2), the words "the OFT," were omitted.

(2) Section 125 of the Enterprise Act 2002 (offences by bodies corporate) shall apply for the purposes of this Act as it applies for the purposes of Part 3 of that Act.

(3) For the purposes of section 12 below, a conclusion contained in a report of the Commission is to be disregarded if the conclusion is not that of at least two-thirds of the members of the group constituted in connection with the reference concerned in pursuance of paragraph 15 of Schedule 7 to the Competition Act 1998.

11D Interim orders

(1) Subsection (2) below applies where, in the circumstances specified in subsection (1) of section 12 below, the Secretary of State has under consideration the making of an order under subsection (5) of that section.

(2) The Secretary of State may by order, for the purpose of preventing pre-emptive action –

(a) prohibit or restrict the doing of things which the Secretary of State considers would constitute pre-emptive action;

(b) impose on any person concerned obligations as to the carrying on of any activities or the safeguarding of any assets;

(c) provide for the carrying on of any activities or the safeguarding of any assets either by the appointment of a person to conduct or supervise the conduct of any activities (on such terms and with such powers as may be specified or described in the order) or in any other manner;

(d)   do anything which may be done by virtue of paragraph 19 of Schedule 8 to the Enterprise Act 2002 (information powers).

(3)   An order under this section shall come into force at such time as is determined by or under the order.

(4)   An order under this section shall, if it has not previously ceased to be in force, cease to be in force on the making of the order under section 12(5) below or (as the case may be) on the making of the decision not to make such an order.

(5)   The Secretary of State shall publish any decision made by him not to make an order under section 12(5) below in such manner as he considers most suitable for bringing it to the attention of persons who in his opinion would be affected by it or be likely to have an interest in it.

(6)   The Secretary of State shall, as soon as reasonably practicable, consider any representations received by him in relation to varying or revoking an order under this section.

(7)   The following provisions of Part 3 of the Enterprise Act 2002 shall apply in relation to orders under this section as they apply in relation to orders under paragraph 2 of Schedule 7 to that Act –

(a)   section 86(2) and (3) (enforcement orders: general provisions);
(b)   section 87 (delegated power of directions); and
(c)   section 94(1) to (5), (8) and (9) (rights to enforce orders).

(8)   In this section "pre-emptive action" means action which might impede the making of an order under section 12(5) below.'

(4) In section 12 (orders following report under section 11) –

(a)   in subsection (5) for the words from 'by order' to the end there is substituted 'make an order under this subsection';
(b)   after subsection (5) there is inserted –

'(5A) An order under subsection (5) above may contain anything permitted by Schedule 8 to the Enterprise Act 2002, except paragraphs 8, 13 and 14 of that Schedule.

(5B) An order under subsection (5) above shall come into force at such time as is determined by or under the order.';

(c)   for subsection (6) there is substituted –

'(6)   The following provisions of Part 3 of the Enterprise Act 2002 shall apply in relation to orders under subsection (5) above as they apply in relation to orders under paragraph 11 of Schedule 7 to that Act –

(a)   section 86(2) and (3) (enforcement orders: general provisions);
(b)   section 87 (delegated power of directions);
(c)   section 88 (contents of certain enforcement orders);
(d)   section 94(1) to (5), (8) and (9) (rights to enforce orders); and
(e)   Schedule 10 (procedural requirements for orders).

(7)   The Secretary of State shall publish any decision made by him to dispense with the requirements of Schedule 10 to the Enterprise Act 2002 as applied by subsection (6) above; and shall do so in such manner as he considers most suitable for bringing the decision to the attention of persons who in his opinion would be affected by it or be likely to have an interest in it.'

(5) In section 16 (general provision as to reports) –

(a)   subsection (1) shall cease to have effect;

(b) in subsection (2) the words 'or of the Director' shall cease to have effect.

(6) In section 17 (laying before Parliament and publication of reports) –

(a) in subsections (1), (3) and (4), the words 'or 13(5)' shall cease to have effect;

(b) in subsection (4), for the words 'against the public interest' there is substituted 'inappropriate';

(c) for subsection (5) there is substituted –

'(5) In deciding what is inappropriate for the purposes of subsection (4) the Secretary of State shall have regard to the considerations mentioned in section 244 of the Enterprise Act 2002.'

(7) Sections 18 (information and advice about operation of Act), 21 (monopoly references by Secretary of State alone) and 24 (modification of provisions about performance of Commission's functions) shall cease to have effect.

(8) In section 31 (orders and regulations) –

(a) in subsection (1) the words 'or regulations' shall cease to have effect;

(b) in subsection (3) –

(i) the words 'regulations under this Act or' shall cease to have effect;

(ii) after '11(4)' there is inserted ', 11D';

(iii) after 'above' there is inserted ', or section 111(4) or (6) or 114(3)(b) or (4)(b) of the Enterprise Act 2002 as applied by section 11B(1)(c) or (f) above,';

(c) subsection (4) shall cease to have effect;

(d) after subsection (4) there is inserted –

'(5) Any power of the Secretary of State to make an order under this Act –

(a) may be exercised so as to make different provision for different cases or different purposes; and

(b) includes power to make such incidental, supplementary, consequential, transitory, transitional or saving provision as the Secretary of State considers appropriate.'

(9) In section 33 (interpretation), for subsection (2) there is substituted –

'(2) Unless the context otherwise requires, in this Act 'Minister' includes a government department and the following expressions shall have the same meanings as they have in Part 3 of the Enterprise Act 2002 –

"business"
"the Commission"
"enactment"
"goods"
"services"
"supply (in relation to the supply of goods)"
"the supply of services".'

(10) For the purposes of the Scotland Act 1998 (c. 46) the amendments made by this paragraph shall be taken to be pre-commencement enactments within the meaning of that Act.

Civil Aviation Act 1982 (c. 16)

11 (1) The Civil Aviation Act 1982 is amended as follows.

(2) In section 4 (general objectives), in subsections (3) and (4), for 'the Director General of Fair Trading' there is substituted 'the Office of Fair Trading'.

Agricultural Marketing (Northern Ireland) Order 1982 (S.I. 1982/1080 (N.I. 12))

12 (1) The Agricultural Marketing (Northern Ireland) Order 1982 is amended as follows.

(2) For article 23 (action following report by Commission) there is substituted –

'23 **Action following report by Competition Commission**

(1) Paragraph (5) applies in any of the following cases.

(2) The first case is where section 138(2) of the Enterprise Act 2002 (duty to remedy adverse effects following market investigation reference) applies and whatever is to be remedied, mitigated or prevented relates to any provision of a scheme or any act or omission of a board administering a scheme.

(3) The second case is where section 147(2) of the Enterprise Act 2002 (power to remedy adverse effects in public interest cases) applies and whatever is to be remedied, mitigated or prevented relates to any provision of a scheme or any act or omission of a board administering a scheme.

(4) The third case is where –

(a) a report of the Competition Commission under section 11 of the Competition Act 1980 (c. 21) (references of public bodies etc.), as laid before Parliament, contains conclusions to the effect that –

(i) certain matters indicated in the report operate against the public interest, and

(ii) those matters consist of or include any provision of a scheme or any act or omission of a board administering a scheme, and

(b) none of the conclusions is to be disregarded by virtue of section 11C(3) of that Act (requirement for two-thirds majority).

(5) The Department shall have the like power to make orders under Article 22 as if a report of a committee of investigation had contained the conclusion that the provision of the scheme in question, or the act or omission in question, is contrary to the interests of consumers of the regulated product.

(6) An order made by virtue of this Article in a case falling within paragraph (2) or (3) shall be treated, for the purposes of sections 162(1) and 166(3) of the Enterprise Act 2002 (duties to register and keep under review enforcement orders etc.), as if it were made under the relevant power in Part 4 of that Act to make an enforcement order (within the meaning of that Part).'

(3) In article 42 (action following report by Commission) –

(a) for paragraph (1) there is substituted –

'(1) Paragraph (1D) applies in any of the following cases.

(1A) The first case is where section 138(2) of the Enterprise Act 2002 (duty to remedy adverse effects following market investigation reference) applies and whatever is to be remedied, mitigated or prevented relates to any provision of a scheme or any act or omission of a board administering a scheme.

(1B) The second case is where section 147(2) of the Enterprise Act 2002 (power to remedy adverse effects in public interest cases) applies and whatever is to be remedied, mitigated or prevented relates to any provision of a scheme or any act or omission of a board administering a scheme.

(1C) The third case is where –

(a) a report of the Competition Commission under section 11 of the Competition Act 1980 (c. 21) (references of public bodies etc.), as laid before Parliament, contains conclusions to the effect that –

    (i)   certain matters indicated in the report operate against the public interest, and

    (ii)   those matters consist of or include any provision of a scheme or any act or omission of a board administering a scheme, and

(b)   none of the conclusions is to be disregarded by virtue of section 11C(3) of that Act (requirement for two-thirds majority).

(1D) The Department, if it thinks fit so to do –

    (a)   may by order make such amendments in the scheme as it considers necessary or expedient for the purpose of rectifying the matter;

    (b)   may by order revoke the scheme;

    (c)   in the event of the matter being one which it is within the power of the board to rectify, may by order direct the board to take such steps to rectify the matter as may be specified in the order, and thereupon it shall be the duty of the board forthwith to comply with the order.';

(b)   in paragraph (2) for 'paragraph (1)' there is substituted 'paragraph (1D)';

(c)   in paragraph (3) for 'paragraph (1)(b)(iii)' there is substituted 'paragraph (1D)(c)';

(d)   in paragraph (5) –

    (i)   for 'paragraph (1)(i) or (iii)' there is substituted 'paragraph (1D)(a) or (c)';

    (ii)   for 'paragraph (1)(ii)' there is substituted 'paragraph (1D)(b)';

(e)   after paragraph (5) there is inserted –

'(5A) Any order made under this Article in a case falling within paragraph (1A) or (1B) shall be treated, for the purposes of sections 162(1) and 166(3) of the Enterprise Act 2002 (duties to register and keep under review enforcement orders etc.), as if it were made under the relevant power in Part 4 of that Act to make an enforcement order (within the meaning of that Part).'

Telecommunications Act 1984 (c. 12)

13   (1)   The Telecommunications Act 1984 is amended as follows.

    (2)   In section 3 (general duties of Secretary of State and Director), in subsection (3C), for 'the Director General of Fair Trading' there is substituted 'the Office of Fair Trading'.

    (3)   In section 13 (licence modification references to Commission), subsections (9) and (9A) shall cease to have effect.

    (4)   After section 13 there is inserted –

'13A References under section 13: time limits

    (1)   Every reference under section 13 above shall specify a period (not longer than six months beginning with the date of the reference) within which a report on the reference is to be made.

    (2)   A report of the Commission on a reference under section 13 above shall not have effect (and no action shall be taken in relation to it under section 15 below) unless the report is made before the end of the period specified in the reference or such further period (if any) as may be allowed by the Director under subsection (3) below.

(3)   The Director may, if he has received representations on the subject from the Commission and is satisfied that there are special reasons why the report cannot be made within the period specified in the reference, extend that period by no more than six months.

(4)   No more than one extension is possible under subsection (3) above in relation to the same reference.

(5)   The Director shall, in the case of an extension made by him under subsection (3) above –

(a)   publish that extension in such manner as he considers appropriate for the purpose of bringing it to the attention of persons likely to be affected by it; and

(b)   in the case of a licence granted to a particular person, send to that person a copy of what has been published by him under paragraph (a) above.

13B References under section 13: powers of investigation

(1)   The following sections of Part 3 of the Enterprise Act 2002 shall apply, with the modifications mentioned in subsections (2) and (3) below, for the purposes of references under section 13 above as they apply for the purposes of references under that Part –

(a)   section 109 (attendance of witnesses and production of documents etc.);

(b)   section 110 (enforcement of powers under section 109: general);

(c)   section 111 (penalties);

(d)   section 112 (penalties: main procedural requirements);

(e)   section 113 (payments and interest by instalments);

(f)   section 114 (appeals in relation to penalties);

(g)   section 115 (recovery of penalties); and

(h)   section 116 (statement of policy).

(2)   Section 110 shall, in its application by virtue of subsection (1) above, have effect as if –

(a)   subsection (2) were omitted; and

(b)   in subsection (9) the words from "or section" to "section 65(3))" were omitted.

(3)   Section 111(5)(b)(ii) shall, in its application by virtue of subsection (1) above, have effect as if –

(a)   for the words "published (or, in the case of a report under section 50 or 65, given)" there were substituted "made";

(b)   for the words "published (or given)", in both places where they appear, there were substituted "made"; and

(c)   the words "by this Part" were omitted.

(4)   Provisions of Part 3 of the Enterprise Act 2002 which have effect for the purposes of sections 109 to 116 of that Act (including, in particular, provisions relating to offences and the making of orders) shall, for the purposes of the application of those sections by virtue of subsection (1) above, have effect in relation to those sections as applied by virtue of that subsection.

(5)   Accordingly, corresponding provisions of this Act shall not have effect in relation to those sections as applied by virtue of that subsection.'

(5)   In section 14 (reports on licence modification references) –

(a)   after subsection (1) there is inserted –

'(1A) For the purposes of section 15 below, a conclusion contained in a report of the Commission is to be disregarded if the conclusion is not that of at least two-thirds of the members of the group constituted in connection with the reference concerned in pursuance of paragraph 15 of Schedule 7 to the Competition Act 1998.

(1B) If a member of a group so constituted disagrees with any conclusions contained in a report made on a reference under section 13 above as the conclusions of the Commission, the report shall, if the member so wishes, include a statement of his disagreement and of his reasons for disagreeing.';

(b)   for subsection (3) there is substituted –

'(3)   For the purposes of the law relating to defamation, absolute privilege attaches to any report made by the Commission on a reference under section 13 above.

(3A) In making any report on a reference under section 13 above the Commission must have regard to the following considerations before disclosing any information.

(3B) The first consideration is the need to exclude from disclosure (so far as practicable) any information whose disclosure the Commission thinks is contrary to the public interest.

(3C) The second consideration is the need to exclude from disclosure (so far as practicable) –

(a)   commercial information whose disclosure the Commission thinks might significantly harm the legitimate business interests of the undertaking to which it relates, or

(b)   information relating to the private affairs of an individual whose disclosure the Commission thinks might significantly harm the individual's interests.

(3D) The third consideration is the extent to which the disclosure of the information mentioned in subsection (3C)(a) or (b) is necessary for the purposes of the report.'

(6)   In section 47 (general functions), in subsection (4) –

(a)   for 'the Director General of Fair Trading' there is substituted 'the Office of Fair Trading';

(b)   for 'that Director' there is substituted 'the Office of Fair Trading'.

(7)   In section 48 (publication of information and advice), after subsection (3) there is inserted –

'(3A) The Office of Fair Trading shall consult the Director before publishing under section 6 of the Enterprise Act 2002 any information or advice which may be published by the Director under this section.'

(8)   In section 50 (functions under 1973 and 1980 Acts) –

(a)   subsection (1) shall cease to have effect;

(b)   in subsection (3) –

(i)   for 'the Director General of Fair Trading' there is substituted 'the Office of Fair Trading';

(ii)   for 'that Director' there is substituted 'the Office of Fair Trading';

(c)   in subsection (3A), for 'the Director General of Fair Trading' there is substituted 'the Office of Fair Trading';

(d)   in subsection (6), for 'the Director General of Fair Trading' there is substituted 'the Office of Fair Trading'.

(9)   In section 101 (general restrictions on disclosure of information) –

(a)   in subsection (2)(b), for 'the Director General of Fair Trading' there is substituted 'the Office of Fair Trading';

(b)   in subsection (3), after paragraph (o) there is inserted –

'(p) the Enterprise Act 2002';

(c)   in subsection (6) –
   (i)   for 'the Director General of Fair Trading' there is substituted 'the Office of Fair Trading';
   (ii)   for 'sections 55 and 56 of that Act (disclosure)' there is substituted 'Part 9 of the Enterprise Act 2002 (Information)'.

(10) In section 103 (time limits for summary proceedings) –
   (a)   that section shall be renumbered as subsection (1) of that section;
   (b)   after that subsection there is inserted –

'(2) Subsection (1) above shall not apply for the purposes of an offence under any provision of the Enterprise Act 2002 as applied by virtue of section 13B above.'

Airports Act 1986 (c. 31)

14   (1)   The Airports Act 1986 is amended as follows.
   (2)   In section 44 (supplementary provisions relating to references to Commission), subsections (3) and (3A) shall cease to have effect.
   (3)   After section 44 there is inserted –

'44A References under section 43: time limits

   (1)   Every reference under section 43 shall specify a period (not longer than six months beginning with the date of the reference) within which a report on the reference is to be made.
   (2) A report of the Commission on a reference under section 43 shall not have effect (and no action shall be taken in relation to it under section 46) unless the report is made before the end of the period specified in the reference or such further period (if any) as may be allowed by the CAA under subsection (3).
   (3)   The CAA may, if it has received representations on the subject from the Commission and is satisfied that there are special reasons why the report cannot be made within the period specified in the reference, extend that period by no more than six months.
   (4)   No more than one extension is possible under subsection (3) in relation to the same reference.
   (5)   The CAA shall, in the case of an extension made by it under subsection (3) –

      (a)   publish that extension in such manner as it considers appropriate for the purpose of bringing it to the attention of persons likely to be affected by it; and
      (b)   send a copy of what has been published by it under paragraph (a) to the airport operator concerned and the Secretary of State.

44B References under section 43: powers of investigation

   (1)   The following sections of Part 3 of the Enterprise Act 2002 shall apply, with the modifications mentioned in subsections (2) and (3), for the purposes of references under section 43 as they apply for the purposes of references under that Part –
      (a)   section 109 (attendance of witnesses and production of documents etc.);
      (b)   section 110 (enforcement of powers under section 109: general);
      (c)   section 111 (penalties);

(d)   section 112 (penalties: main procedural requirements);

(e)   section 113 (payments and interest by instalments);

(f)   section 114 (appeals in relation to penalties);

(g)   section 115 (recovery of penalties); and

(h)   section 116 (statement of policy).

(2)   Section 110 shall, in its application by virtue of subsection (1), have effect as if –

(a)   subsection (2) were omitted; and

(b)   in subsection (9) the words from 'or section' to 'section 65(3))' were omitted.

(3)   Section 111(5)(b)(ii) shall, in its application by virtue of subsection (1), have effect as if –

(a)   for the words "published (or, in the case of a report under section 50 or 65, given)" there were substituted "made";

(b)   for the words "published (or given)", in both places where they appear, there were substituted "made"; and

(c)   the words "by this Part" were omitted.

(4)   Provisions of Part 3 of the Enterprise Act 2002 which have effect for the purposes of sections 109 to 116 of that Act (including, in particular, provisions relating to offences and the making of orders) shall, for the purposes of the application of those sections by virtue of subsection (1), have effect in relation to those sections as applied by virtue of that subsection.

(5)   Accordingly, corresponding provisions of this Act shall not have effect in relation to those sections as applied by virtue of that subsection.'

(4) In section 45 (reports on references) –

(a)   after subsection (2) there is inserted –

'(2A) For the purposes of section 46(2), a conclusion contained in a report of the Commission is to be disregarded if the conclusion is not that of at least two-thirds of the members of the group constituted in connection with the reference concerned in pursuance of paragraph 15 of Schedule 7 to the Competition Act 1998.

(2B) If a member of a group so constituted disagrees with any conclusions contained in a report made on a reference under section 43 as the conclusions of the Commission, the report shall, if the member so wishes, include a statement of his disagreement and of his reasons for disagreeing.';

(b)   for subsection (4) there is substituted –

'(4)   For the purposes of the law relating to defamation, absolute privilege attaches to any report made by the Commission on a reference under section 43.

(4A) In making any report on a reference under section 43 the Commission must have regard to the following considerations before disclosing any information.

(4B) The first consideration is the need to exclude from disclosure (so far as practicable) any information whose disclosure the Commission thinks is contrary to the public interest.

(4C) The second consideration is the need to exclude from disclosure (so far as practicable) –

(a)   commercial information whose disclosure the Commission thinks might significantly harm the legitimate business interests of the undertaking to which it relates, or

        (b)   information relating to the private affairs of an individual whose disclosure the Commission thinks might significantly harm the individual's interests.

      (4D) The third consideration is the extent to which the disclosure of the information mentioned in subsection (4C)(a) or (b) is necessary for the purposes of the report.'

(5) In section 56 (co-ordination of exercise of functions by CAA and Director General of Fair Trading) –

    (a) in paragraph (a) –

        (i) for 'the Director General of Fair Trading of functions under the 1973 Act' there is substituted 'the Office of Fair Trading of functions under the Enterprise Act 2002';

       (ii) for 'the Director' there is substituted 'the Office of Fair Trading';

    (b) in paragraph (b), for 'the Director' there is substituted 'the Office of Fair Trading'.

(6) In section 74 (restriction on disclosure of information) –

    (a) in subsection (2), for 'the Director General of Fair Trading' there is substituted 'the Office of Fair Trading';

    (b) in subsection (3), at the end there is inserted –

    '(r) the Enterprise Act 2002'.

Gas Act 1986 (c. 44)

15 (1) The Gas Act 1986 is amended as follows.

    (2) In section 4B (exceptions from sections 4AA to 4A), in subsection (3), for 'the Director General of Fair Trading' there is substituted 'the Office of Fair Trading'.

    (3) In section 24 (licence modification references to Commission) –

       (a) subsections (7) and (7A) shall cease to have effect;

       (b) in subsection (8), after 'sections' there is inserted '24A,'.

    (4) After section 24 there is inserted –

'24A References under section 24: time limits

    (1) Every reference under section 24 above shall specify a period (not longer than six months beginning with the date of the reference) within which a report on the reference is to be made.

    (2) A report of the Competition Commission on a reference under section 24 above shall not have effect (and no action shall be taken in relation to it under section 26 below) unless the report is made before the end of the period specified in the reference or such further period (if any) as may be allowed by the Authority under subsection (3) below.

    (3) The Authority may, if it has received representations on the subject from the Competition Commission and is satisfied that there are special reasons why the report cannot be made within the period specified in the reference, extend that period by no more than six months.

    (4) No more than one extension is possible under subsection (3) above in relation to the same reference.

    (5) The Authority shall, in the case of an extension made by it under subsection (3) above –

       (a) publish that extension in such manner as it considers appropriate for the purpose of bringing it to the attention of persons likely to be affected by it; and

(b)   send a copy of what has been published by it under paragraph (a) above to the holder of the licence or, as the case may be, the relevant licence holders.

24B References under section 24: powers of investigation

(1)   The following sections of Part 3 of the Enterprise Act 2002 shall apply, with the modifications mentioned in subsections (2) and (3) below, for the purposes of references under section 24 above as they apply for the purposes of references under that Part –

(a)   section 109 (attendance of witnesses and production of documents etc.);
(b)   section 110 (enforcement of powers under section 109: general);
(c)   section 111 (penalties);
(d)   section 112 (penalties: main procedural requirements);
(e)   section 113 (payments and interest by instalments);
(f)   section 114 (appeals in relation to penalties);
(g)   section 115 (recovery of penalties); and
(h)   section 116 (statement of policy).

(2)   Section 110 shall, in its application by virtue of subsection (1) above, have effect as if –

(a)   subsection (2) were omitted; and
(b)   in subsection (9) the words from "or section" to "section 65(3))" were omitted.

(3)   Section 111(5)(b)(ii) shall, in its application by virtue of subsection (1) above, have effect as if –

(a)   for the words "published (or, in the case of a report under section 50 or 65, given)" there were substituted "made";
(b)   for the words "published (or given)", in both places where they appear, there were substituted "made"; and
(c)   the words "by this Part" were omitted.

(4)   Provisions of Part 3 of the Enterprise Act 2002 which have effect for the purposes of sections 109 to 116 of that Act (including, in particular, provisions relating to offences and the making of orders) shall, for the purposes of the application of those sections by virtue of subsection (1) above, have effect in relation to those sections as applied by virtue of that subsection.

(5)   Accordingly, corresponding provisions of this Act shall not have effect in relation to those sections as applied by virtue of that subsection.'

(5)   In section 25 (reports on licence modification references) –

(a)   after subsection (1) there is inserted –

'(1A) For the purposes of sections 26 and 26A below, a conclusion contained in a report of the Competition Commission is to be disregarded if the conclusion is not that of at least two-thirds of the members of the group constituted in connection with the reference concerned in pursuance of paragraph 15 of Schedule 7 to the Competition Act 1998.

(1B) If a member of a group so constituted disagrees with any conclusions contained in a report made on a reference under section 24 above as the conclusions of the Competition Commission, the report shall, if the member so wishes, include a statement of his disagreement and of his reasons for disagreeing.';

(b)   for subsection (3) there is substituted –

'(3)   For the purposes of the law relating to defamation, absolute privilege attaches to any report made by the Competition Commission on a reference under section 24 above.

(3A)   In making any report on a reference under section 24 above the Competition Commission must have regard to the following considerations before disclosing any information.

(3B)   The first consideration is the need to exclude from disclosure (so far as practicable) any information whose disclosure the Competition Commission thinks is contrary to the public interest.

(3C)   The second consideration is the need to exclude from disclosure (so far as practicable) –

(a)   commercial information whose disclosure the Competition Commission thinks might significantly harm the legitimate business interests of the undertaking to which it relates, or

(b)   information relating to the private affairs of an individual whose disclosure the Competition Commission thinks might significantly harm the individual's interests.

(3D)   The third consideration is the extent to which the disclosure of the information mentioned in subsection (3C)(a) or (b) above is necessary for the purposes of the report.'

(6)   In section 26A (Commission's power to veto modifications following report) –

(a)   after subsection (11) there is inserted –

'(11A)   For the purposes of the law relating to defamation, absolute privilege attaches to any notice under subsection (4)(a), (6) or (8).

(11B)   In giving any notice under subsection (4)(a) or (6), or publishing any notice under subsection (8), the Commission must have regard to the following considerations before disclosing any information.

(11C)   The first consideration is the need to exclude from disclosure (so far as practicable) any information whose disclosure the Commission thinks is contrary to the public interest.

(11D)   The second consideration is the need to exclude from disclosure (so far as practicable) –

(a)   commercial information whose disclosure the Commission thinks might significantly harm the legitimate business interests of the undertaking to which it relates, or

(b)   information relating to the private affairs of an individual whose disclosure the Commission thinks might significantly harm the individual's interests.

(11E)   The third consideration is the extent to which the disclosure of the information mentioned in subsection (11D)(a) or (b) is necessary for the purposes of the notice.

(11F)   The following sections of Part 3 of the Enterprise Act 2002 shall apply, with the modifications mentioned in subsections (11G) and (11H), for the purposes of any investigation by the Commission for the purposes of the exercise of its functions under this section, as they apply for the purposes of any investigation on references under that Part –

(a)   section 109 (attendance of witnesses and production of documents etc.);

(b)   section 110 (enforcement of powers under section 109: general);

    (c)   section 111 (penalties);
    (d)   section 112 (penalties: main procedural requirements);
    (e)   section 113 (payments and interest by instalments);
    (f)   section 114 (appeals in relation to penalties);
    (g)   section 115 (recovery of penalties); and
    (h)   section 116 (statement of policy).

(11G) Section 110 shall, in its application by virtue of subsection (11F), have effect as if –

    (a)   subsection (2) were omitted;
    (b)   in subsection (4), for the words "the publication of the report of the Commission on the reference concerned" there were substituted "the publication by the Commission of a notice under section 26A(8) of the Gas Act 1986 in connection with the reference concerned or, if no direction has been given by the Commission under section 26A(1) of that Act in connection with the reference concerned and within the period permitted for that purpose, the latest day on which it was possible to give such a direction within the permitted period"; and
    (c)   in subsection (9) the words from "or section" to "section 65(3))" were omitted.

(11H) Section 111(5)(b) shall, in its application by virtue of subsection (11F), have effect as if for sub-paragraph (ii) there were substituted –

    "(ii) if earlier, the day on which a notice is published by the Commission under section 26A(8) of the Gas Act 1986 in connection with the reference concerned or, if no direction is given by the Commission under section 26A(1) of that Act in connection with the reference concerned and within the period permitted for that purpose, the latest day on which such a direction may be given within the permitted period.".

(11I) Provisions of Part 3 of the Enterprise Act 2002 which have effect for the purposes of sections 109 to 116 of that Act (including, in particular, provisions relating to offences and the making of orders) shall, for the purposes of the application of those sections by virtue of subsection (11F) above, have effect in relation to those sections as applied by virtue of that subsection.

(11J) Accordingly, corresponding provisions of this Act shall not have effect in relation to those sections as applied by virtue of that subsection.';

  (b)   subsections (12) and (13) shall cease to have effect.

(7) In section 33 (power of Council to investigate other matters), in subsection (4), for 'the Director General of Fair Trading' there is substituted 'the Office of Fair Trading'.

(8) In section 34 (general functions), in subsection (4) –

    (a)   for 'the Director General of Fair Trading' there is substituted 'the Office of Fair Trading'; and
    (b)   for 'that Director' there is substituted 'the Office of Fair Trading'.

(9) In section 35 (publication of information and advice), after subsection (3) there is inserted –

    '(3A) The Office of Fair Trading shall consult the Authority before publishing under section 6 of the Enterprise Act 2002 any information or advice which may be published by the Authority under this section.'

(10) In section 36A (functions with respect to competition) –

(a)   subsection (1) shall cease to have effect;

(b)   in subsection (3), for 'the Director General of Fair Trading, the functions of that Director' there is substituted 'the Office of Fair Trading, the functions of the Office of Fair Trading';

(c)   in subsection (3A), for 'the Director General of Fair Trading' there is substituted 'the Office of Fair Trading';

(d)   in subsection (7), for 'the Director General of Fair Trading' there is substituted 'the Office of Fair Trading'.

(11) In section 41E (references to Commission about activities which are not licensable), subsections (7) and (8) shall cease to have effect.

(12) After section 41E there is inserted –

'41E References under section 41E: time limits

(1)   Every reference under section 41E above shall specify a period (not longer than six months beginning with the date of the reference) within which a report on the reference is to be made.

(2)   A report of the Competition Commission on a reference under section 41E above shall not have effect (in particular for the purposes of section 41D(5) above) unless the report is made before the end of the period specified in the reference or such further period (if any) as may be allowed by the Authority under subsection (3) below.

(3)   The Authority may, if it has received representations on the subject from the Competition Commission and is satisfied that there are special reasons why the report cannot be made within the period specified in the reference, extend that period by no more than six months.

(4)   No more than one extension is possible under subsection (3) above in relation to the same reference.

(5)   The Authority shall publish an extension under subsection (3) above in such manner as it considers appropriate for the purpose of bringing it to the attention of persons likely to be affected by it.

41EB References under section 41E: application of Enterprise Act 2002

(1)   The following sections of Part 3 of the Enterprise Act 2002 shall apply, with the modifications mentioned in subsections (2) and (3) below, for the purposes of references under section 41E above as they apply for the purposes of references under that Part –

(a)   section 109 (attendance of witnesses and production of documents etc.);

(b)   section 110 (enforcement of powers under section 109: general);

(c)   section 111 (penalties);

(d)   section 112 (penalties: main procedural requirements);

(e)   section 113 (payments and interest by instalments);

(f)   section 114 (appeals in relation to penalties);

(g)   section 115 (recovery of penalties); and

(h)   section 116 (statement of policy).

(2)   Section 110 shall, in its application by virtue of subsection (1) above, have effect as if –

(a)   subsection (2) were omitted; and

(b)   in subsection (9) the words from "or section" to "section 65(3))" were omitted.

(3)   Section 111(5)(b)(ii) shall, in its application by virtue of subsection (1) above, have effect as if –

(a)   for the words "published (or, in the case of a report under section 50 or 65, given)" there were substituted "made";

(b)   for the words "published (or given)", in both places where they appear, there were substituted "made"; and

(c)   the words "by this Part" were omitted.

(4)   Section 117 of the Enterprise Act 2002 (false or misleading information) shall apply in relation to functions of the Competition Commission in connection with references under section 41E above as it applies in relation to its functions under Part 3 of that Act but as if, in subsections (1)(a) and (2), the words "the OFT," and "or the Secretary of State" were omitted.

(5)   Provisions of Part 3 of the Enterprise Act 2002 which have effect for the purposes of sections 109 to 117 of that Act (including, in particular, provisions relating to offences and the making of orders) shall, for the purposes of the application of those sections by virtue of subsection (1) or (4) above, have effect in relation to those sections as applied by virtue of those subsections.

(6)   Accordingly, corresponding provisions of this Act shall not have effect in relation to those sections as applied by virtue of those subsections.'

(13) In section 41F (reports on references under section 41E) –

(a)   after subsection (3) there is inserted –

'(3A) For the purposes of section 41D(5), a conclusion contained in a report of the Competition Commission is to be disregarded if the conclusion is not that of at least two-thirds of the members of the group constituted in connection with the reference concerned in pursuance of paragraph 15 of Schedule 7 to the Competition Act 1998.

(3B) If a member of a group so constituted disagrees with any conclusions contained in a report made on a reference under section 41E as the conclusions of the Competition Commission, the report shall, if the member so wishes, include a statement of his disagreement and of his reasons for disagreeing.';

(b)   for subsection (4) there is substituted –

'(4) For the purposes of the law relating to defamation, absolute privilege attaches to any report made by the Competition Commission on a reference under section 41E.

(4A) In making any report on a reference under section 41E the Competition Commission must have regard to the following considerations before disclosing any information.

(4B) The first consideration is the need to exclude from disclosure (so far as practicable) any information whose disclosure the Competition Commission thinks is contrary to the public interest.

(4C) The second consideration is the need to exclude from disclosure (so far as practicable) –

(a)   commercial information whose disclosure the Competition Commission thinks might significantly harm the legitimate business interests of the undertaking to which it relates, or

(b)   information relating to the private affairs of an individual whose disclosure the Competition Commission thinks might significantly harm the individual's interests.

(4D) The third consideration is the extent to which the disclosure of the information mentioned in subsection (4C)(a) or (b) is necessary for the purposes of the report.'

(14) In section 62 (exclusion of certain agreements from Restrictive Trade Practices Act 1976), for 'the Director General of Fair Trading' (in both places) there is substituted 'the Office of Fair Trading'.

Consumer Protection Act 1987 (c. 43)

16   (1)   The Consumer Protection Act 1987 is amended as follows.

      (2)   In section 25 (codes of practice), in subsection (1), for 'the Director General of Fair Trading' there is substituted 'the Office of Fair Trading'.

      (3)   In section 26 (power to make regulations), in subsection (1), for the 'Director General of Fair Trading' there is substituted 'the Office of Fair Trading'.

Consumer Protection (Northern Ireland) Order 1987 (S.I. 1987/2049 (N.I. 20))

17   (1)   The Consumer Protection (Northern Ireland) Order 1987 is amended as follows.

      (2)   In Article 18 (codes of practice), in paragraph (1), for 'the Director General of Fair Trading' there is substituted 'the Office of Fair Trading'.

      (3)   In Article 19 (power to make regulations), in paragraph (1), for the 'Director General of Fair Trading' there is substituted 'the Office of Fair Trading'.

Copyright, Designs and Patents Act 1988 (c. 48)

18   (1)   The Copyright, Designs and Patents Act 1988 is amended as follows.

      (2)   In section 144 (powers exercisable in consequence of report of Commission) for subsections (1) and (2) there is substituted –

          '(1)   Subsection (1A) applies where whatever needs to be remedied, mitigated or prevented by the Secretary of State, the Office of Fair Trading or (as the case may be) the Competition Commission under section 12(5) of the Competition Act 1980 or section 41(2), 55(2), 66(6), 75(2), 83(2), 138(2), 147(2) or 160(2) of, or paragraph 5(2) or 10(2) of Schedule 7 to, the Enterprise Act 2002 (powers to take remedial action following references to the Commission in connection with public bodies and certain other persons, mergers or market investigations) consists of or includes –

               (a)   conditions in licences granted by the owner of copyright in a work restricting the use of the work by the licensee or the right of the copyright owner to grant other licences; or

               (b)   a refusal of a copyright owner to grant licences on reasonable terms.

          (1A)   The powers conferred by Schedule 8 to the Enterprise Act 2002 include power to cancel or modify those conditions and, instead or in addition, to provide that licences in respect of the copyright shall be available as of right.

          (2)   The references to anything permitted by Schedule 8 to the Enterprise Act 2002 in section 12(5A) of the Competition Act 1980 and in sections 75(4)(a), 83(4)(a), 84(2)(a), 89(1), 160(4)(a), 161(3)(a) and 164(1) of, and paragraphs 5, 10 and 11 of Schedule 7 to, the Act of 2002 shall be construed accordingly.'

      (3)   In section 144(3) –

          (a)   for 'A Minister' there is substituted 'The Secretary of State, the Office of Fair Trading or (as the case may be) the Competition Commission';

          (b)   after 'he' there is inserted 'or it'.

      (4)   In section 238 (powers exercisable for protection of the public interest), for subsections (1) and (2) there is substituted –

          '(1)   Subsection (1A) applies where whatever needs to be remedied, mitigated or prevented by the Secretary of State, the Competition Commission or (as the case may be) the Office of Fair Trading under section 12(5) of the Competition Act 1980 or section 41(2), 55(2), 66(6), 75(2), 83(2), 138(2), 147(2) or 160(2) of, or paragraph 5(2) or 10(2) of Schedule 7 to, the Enterprise Act 2002 (powers to take remedial action following references to the Commission in connection with public bodies and certain other persons, mergers or market investigations etc.) consists of or includes –

(a) conditions in licences granted by a design right owner restricting the use of the design by the licensee or the right of the design right owner to grant other licences, or

(b) a refusal of a design right owner to grant licences on reasonable terms.

(1A) The powers conferred by Schedule 8 to the Enterprise Act 2002 include power to cancel or modify those conditions and, instead or in addition, to provide that licences in respect of the design right shall be available as of right.

(2) The references to anything permitted by Schedule 8 to the Enterprise Act 2002 in section 12(5A) of the Competition Act 1980 and in sections 75(4)(a), 83(4)(a), 84(2)(a), 89(1), 160(4)(a), 161(3)(a) and 164(1) of, and paragraphs 5, 10 and 11 of Schedule 7 to, the Act of 2002 shall be construed accordingly.'

(5) In Schedule 2A, in paragraph 17 (powers exercisable in consequence of competition report) –

(a) for sub-paragraphs (1) and (2) there is substituted –

'(1) Sub-paragraph (1A) applies where whatever needs to be remedied, mitigated or prevented by the Secretary of State, the Competition Commission or (as the case may be) the Office of Fair Trading under section 12(5) of the Competition Act 1980 or section 41(2), 55(2), 66(6), 75(2), 83(2), 138(2), 147(2) or 160(2) of, or paragraph 5(2) or 10(2) of Schedule 7 to, the Enterprise Act 2002 (powers to take remedial action following references to the Commission in connection with public bodies and certain other persons, mergers or market investigations etc.) consists of or includes –

(a) conditions in licences granted by the owner of a performer's property rights restricting the use to which a recording may be put by the licensee or the right of the owner to grant other licenses, or

(b) a refusal of an owner of a performer's property rights to grant licences on reasonable terms.

(1A) The powers conferred by Schedule 8 to the Enterprise Act 2002 include power to cancel or modify those conditions and, instead or in addition, to provide that licences in respect of the performer's property rights shall be available as of right.

(2) The references to anything permitted by Schedule 8 to the Enterprise Act 2002 in section 12(5A) of the Competition Act 1980 and in sections 75(4)(a), 83(4)(a), 84(2)(a), 89(1), 160(4)(a), 161(3)(a) and 164(1) of, and paragraphs 5, 10 and 11 of Schedule 7 to, the Act of 2002 shall be construed accordingly.';

(b) in sub-paragraph (3) –

(i) for 'A Minister' there is substituted 'The Secretary of State, the Competition Commission or (as the case may be) the Office of Fair Trading';

(ii) after 'he' there is inserted 'or it'.

Water Act 1989 (c. 15)

19   (1)   The Water Act 1989 is amended as follows.

    (2)   In section 174 (general restrictions on disclosure of information) –

        (a)   in subsection (2)(d), for sub-paragraph (ii) there is substituted –

            '(ii)   the Office of Fair Trading;'

        (b)   in subsection (3), after paragraph (lm) there is inserted –

            '(ln) the Enterprise Act 2002;'.

Electricity Act 1989 (c. 29)

20   (1)   The Electricity Act 1989 is amended as follows.

    (2)   In section 3D (exceptions from sections 3A to 3C), in subsection (4), for 'the Director General of Fair Trading' there is substituted 'the Office of Fair Trading'.

    (3)   In section 12 (licence modification references to Commission) –

        (a)   in subsection (6A), after 'sections' there is inserted '12A, ';

        (b)   subsections (8) and (8A) shall cease to have effect.

    (4)   After section 12 there is inserted –

'12A References under section 12: time limits

    (1)   Every reference under section 12 above shall specify a period (not longer than six months beginning with the date of the reference) within which a report on the reference is to be made.

    (2)   A report of the Competition Commission on a reference under section 12 above shall not have effect (and no action shall be taken in relation to it under section 14 below) unless the report is made before the end of the period specified in the reference or such further period (if any) as may be allowed by the Authority under subsection (3) below.

    (3)   The Authority may, if it has received representations on the subject from the Competition Commission and is satisfied that there are special reasons why the report cannot be made within the period specified in the reference, extend that period by no more than six months.

    (4)   No more than one extension is possible under subsection (3) above in relation to the same reference.

    (5)   The Authority shall, in the case of an extension made by it under subsection (3) above –

        (a)   publish that extension in such manner as it considers appropriate for the purpose of bringing it to the attention of persons likely to be affected by it; and

        (b)   send a copy of what has been published by it under paragraph (a) above to the holder of the licence or, as the case may be, the relevant licence holders.

12B References under section 12: powers of investigation

    (1)   The following sections of Part 3 of the Enterprise Act 2002 shall apply, with the modifications mentioned in subsections (2) and (3) below, for the purposes of references under section 12 above as they apply for the purposes of references under that Part –

        (a)   section 109 (attendance of witnesses and production of documents etc.);

        (b)   section 110 (enforcement of powers under section 109: general);

        (c)   section 111 (penalties);

    (d)   section 112 (penalties: main procedural requirements);

    (e)   section 113 (payments and interest by instalments);

    (f)   section 114 (appeals in relation to penalties);

    (g)   section 115 (recovery of penalties); and

    (h)   section 116 (statement of policy).

(2)   Section 110 shall, in its application by virtue of subsection (1) above, have effect as if –

    (a)   subsection (2) were omitted; and

    (b)   in subsection (9) the words from "or section" to "section 65(3))" were omitted.

(3)   Section 111(5)(b)(ii) shall, in its application by virtue of subsection (1) above, have effect as if –

    (a)   for the words "published (or, in the case of a report under section 50 or 65, given)" there were substituted "made";

    (b)   for the words "published (or given)", in both places where they appear, there were substituted "made"; and

    (c)   the words "by this Part" were omitted.

(4)   Provisions of Part 3 of the Enterprise Act 2002 which have effect for the purposes of sections 109 to 116 of that Act (including, in particular, provisions relating to offences and the making of orders) shall, for the purposes of the application of those sections by virtue of subsection (1) above, have effect in relation to those sections as applied by virtue of that subsection.

(5)   Accordingly, corresponding provisions of this Act shall not have effect in relation to those sections as applied by virtue of that subsection.'

(5) In section 13 (reports on licence modification references) –

    (a)   after subsection (1) there is inserted –

       '(1A) For the purposes of sections 14 and 14A below, a conclusion contained in a report of the Competition Commission is to be disregarded if the conclusion is not that of at least two-thirds of the members of the group constituted in connection with the reference concerned in pursuance of paragraph 15 of Schedule 7 to the Competition Act 1998.

       (1B) If a member of a group so constituted disagrees with any conclusions contained in a report made on a reference under section 12 above as the conclusions of the Competition Commission, the report shall, if the member so wishes, include a statement of his disagreement and of his reasons for disagreeing.';

    (b)   for subsection (3) there is substituted –

       '(3)   For the purposes of the law relating to defamation, absolute privilege attaches to any report made by the Competition Commission on a reference under section 12 above.

       (3A) In making any report on a reference under section 12 above the Competition Commission must have regard to the following considerations before disclosing any information.

       (3B) The first consideration is the need to exclude from disclosure (so far as practicable) any information whose disclosure the Competition Commission thinks is contrary to the public interest.

       (3C) The second consideration is the need to exclude from disclosure (so far as practicable) –

          (a)   commercial information whose disclosure the Competition Commission thinks might significantly harm the legitimate business interests of the undertaking to which it relates, or

(b) information relating to the private affairs of an individual whose disclosure the Competition Commission thinks might significantly harm the individual's interests.

(3D) The third consideration is the extent to which the disclosure of the information mentioned in subsection (3C)(a) or (b) above is necessary for the purposes of the report.'

(6) In section 14A (Commission's power to veto modifications following report) –

(a) after subsection (11) there is inserted –

'(11A) For the purposes of the law relating to defamation, absolute privilege attaches to any notice under subsection (4)(a), (6) or (8).

(11B) In giving any notice under subsection (4)(a) or (6), or publishing any notice under subsection (8), the Commission must have regard to the following considerations before disclosing any information.

(11C) The first consideration is the need to exclude from disclosure (so far as practicable) any information whose disclosure the Commission thinks is contrary to the public interest.

(11D) The second consideration is the need to exclude from disclosure (so far as practicable) –

(a) commercial information whose disclosure the Commission thinks might significantly harm the legitimate business interests of the undertaking to which it relates, or

(b) information relating to the private affairs of an individual whose disclosure the Commission thinks might significantly harm the individual's interests.

(11E) The third consideration is the extent to which the disclosure of the information mentioned in subsection (11D)(a) or (b) is necessary for the purposes of the notice.

(11F) The following sections of Part 3 of the Enterprise Act 2002 shall apply, with the modifications mentioned in subsections (11G) and (11H), for the purposes of any investigation by the Commission for the purposes of the exercise of its functions under this section, as they apply for the purposes of any investigation on references under that Part –

(a) section 109 (attendance of witnesses and production of documents etc.);

(b) section 110 (enforcement of powers under section 109: general);

(c) section 111 (penalties);

(d) section 112 (penalties: main procedural requirements);

(e) section 113 (payments and interest by instalments);

(f) section 114 (appeals in relation to penalties);

(g) section 115 (recovery of penalties); and

(h) section 116 (statement of policy).

(11G) Section 110 shall, in its application by virtue of subsection (11F), have effect as if –

(a) subsection (2) were omitted;

(b) in subsection (4), for the words "the publication of the report of the Commission on the reference concerned" there were substituted "the publication by the Commission of a notice under section 14A(8) of the Electricity Act 1989 in connection with the reference concerned or, if no direction has been given by the Commission under section 14A(1) of that Act in connection with the reference concerned and within the period permitted for that purpose, the latest day on which it was possible to give such a direction within the permitted period;" and

(c) in subsection (9) the words from "or section" to "section 65(3))" were omitted.

(11H) Section 111(5)(b) shall, in its application by virtue of subsection (11F), have effect as if for sub-paragraph (ii) there were substituted –

"(ii) if earlier, the day on which a notice is published by the Commission under section 14A(8) of the Electricity Act 1989 in connection with the reference concerned or, if no direction is given by the Commission under section 14A(1) of that Act in connection with the reference concerned and within the period permitted for that purpose, the latest day on which such a direction may be given within the permitted period."

(11I) Provisions of Part 3 of the Enterprise Act 2002 which have effect for the purposes of sections 109 to 116 of that Act (including, in particular, provisions relating to offences and the making of orders) shall, for the purposes of the application of those sections by virtue of subsection (11F) above, have effect in relation to those sections as applied by virtue of that subsection.

(11J) Accordingly, corresponding provisions of this Act shall not have effect in relation to those sections as applied by virtue of that subsection.';

(b) subsections (12) and (13) shall cease to have effect.

(7) In section 43 (functions with respect to competition) –

(a) subsection (1) shall cease to have effect;

(b) in subsection (3), for 'the Director General of Fair Trading, the functions of that Director' there is substituted 'the Office of Fair Trading, the functions of the Office of Fair Trading';

(c) in subsection (3A), for 'the Director General of Fair Trading' there is substituted 'the Office of Fair Trading';

(d) in subsection (6), for 'the Director General of Fair Trading' there is substituted 'the Office of Fair Trading'.

(8) In section 46A (power of Council to investigate other matters), in subsection (2), for 'the Director General of Fair Trading' there is substituted 'the Office of Fair Trading'.

(9) In section 47 (general functions), in subsection (3) –

(a) for 'the Director General of Fair Trading' there is substituted 'the Office of Fair Trading';

(b) for 'that Director' there is substituted 'the Office of Fair Trading'.

(10) In section 48 (publication of information and advice), in subsection (3), –

(a) for 'The Director General of Fair Trading' there is substituted 'The Office of Fair Trading';

(b) for 'section 124 of the 1973 Act' there is substituted 'section 6 of the Enterprise Act 2002'.

(11) In section 56C (references to Commission about activities which are not licensable), subsections (7) and (8) shall cease to have effect.

(12) After section 56C there is inserted –

'56CA References under section 56C: time limits

(1) Every reference under section 56C above shall specify a period (not longer than six months beginning with the date of the reference) within which a report on the reference is to be made.

(2) A report of the Competition Commission on a reference under section 56C above shall not have effect (in particular for the purposes of section 56B(5) above) unless the report is made before the end of the period specified in the reference or such further period (if any) as may be allowed by the Authority under subsection (3) below.

(3) The Authority may, if it has received representations on the subject from the Competition Commission and is satisfied that there are special reasons why the report cannot be made within the period specified in the reference, extend that period by no more than six months.

(4) No more than one extension is possible under subsection (3) above in relation to the same reference.

(5) The Authority shall publish an extension under subsection (3) above in such manner as it considers appropriate for the purpose of bringing it to the attention of persons likely to be affected by it.

56CB References under section 56C: application of Enterprise Act 2002

(1) The following sections of Part 3 of the Enterprise Act 2002 shall apply, with the modifications mentioned in subsections (2) and (3) below, for the purposes of references under section 56C above as they apply for the purposes of references under that Part –

(a) section 109 (attendance of witnesses and production of documents etc.);

(b) section 110 (enforcement of powers under section 109: general);

(c) section 111 (penalties);

(d) section 112 (penalties: main procedural requirements);

(e) section 113 (payments and interest by instalments);

(f) section 114 (appeals in relation to penalties);

(g) section 115 (recovery of penalties); and

(h) section 116 (statement of policy).

(2) Section 110 shall, in its application by virtue of subsection (1) above, have effect as if –

(a) subsection (2) were omitted; and

(b) in subsection (9) the words from "or section" to "section 65(3))" were omitted.

(3) Section 111(5)(b)(ii) shall, in its application by virtue of subsection (1) above, have effect as if –

(a) for the words "published (or, in the case of a report under section 50 or 65, given)" there were substituted "made";

(b) for the words "published (or given)", in both places where they appear, there were substituted "made"; and

(c) the words "by this Part" were omitted.

(4) Section 117 of the Enterprise Act 2002 (false or misleading information) shall apply in relation to functions of the Competition Commission in connection with references under section 56C above as it applies in relation to its functions under Part 3 of that Act but as if, in subsections (1)(a) and (2), the words 'the OFT,' and 'or the Secretary of State' were omitted.

(5) Provisions of Part 3 of the Enterprise Act 2002 which have effect for the purposes of sections 109 to 117 of that Act (including, in particular, provisions relating to offences and the making of orders) shall, for the pur-

poses of the application of those sections by virtue of subsection (1) or (4) above, have effect in relation to those sections as applied by virtue of those subsections.

(6)   Accordingly, corresponding provisions of this Act shall not have effect in relation to those sections as applied by virtue of those subsections.'

(13) In section 56D (reports on references under section 56C) –

(a)   after subsection (3) there is inserted –

'(3A) For the purposes of section 56B(5), a conclusion contained in a report of the Competition Commission is to be disregarded if the conclusion is not that of at least two-thirds of the members of the group constituted in connection with the reference concerned in pursuance of paragraph 15 of Schedule 7 to the Competition Act 1998.

(3B) If a member of a group so constituted disagrees with any conclusions contained in a report made on a reference under section 56C as the conclusions of the Competition Commission, the report shall, if the member so wishes, include a statement of his disagreement and of his reasons for disagreeing.';

(b)   for subsection (4) there is substituted –

'(4)   For the purposes of the law relating to defamation, absolute privilege attaches to any report made by the Competition Commission on a reference under section 56C.

(4A) In making any report on a reference under section 56C the Competition Commission must have regard to the following considerations before disclosing any information.

(4B) The first consideration is the need to exclude from disclosure (so far as practicable) any information whose disclosure the Competition Commission thinks is contrary to the public interest.

(4C) The second consideration is the need to exclude from disclosure (so far as practicable) –

(a)   commercial information whose disclosure the Competition Commission thinks might significantly harm the legitimate business interests of the undertaking to which it relates, or

(b)   information relating to the private affairs of an individual whose disclosure the Competition Commission thinks might significantly harm the individual's interests.

(4D) The third consideration is the extent to which the disclosure of the information mentioned in subsection (4C)(a) or (b) is necessary for the purposes of the report.'

Companies Act 1989 (c. 40)

21   (1)   The Companies Act 1989 is amended as follows.

(2)   In section 47 (restrictive practices), in subsection (3)(c), for 'Director General of Fair Trading' there is substituted 'the Office of Fair Trading'.

(3)   In section 87 (exceptions from restrictions on disclosure), in subsection (4), for the entry relating to the Director General of Fair Trading there is substituted –

'The Office of Fair Trading.'

(4)   In Schedule 14 (supervisory and qualifying bodies: restrictive practices) –

(a)   in paragraph 1 –

(i)   in sub-paragraph (1), for 'the Director General of Fair Trading (in this Schedule referred to as "the Director")' there is substituted 'the Office of Fair Trading (in this Schedule referred to as "the OFT")' and for 'Director' there is substituted 'OFT';

(ii) in sub-paragraph (2), for 'Director' and 'his' there is substituted 'OFT' and 'its' respectively;

(b) in paragraph 3 –

(i) for 'Director' (in each place) there is substituted 'OFT';

(ii) in sub-paragraph (1), for 'he' (in both places) and 'his' (in both places) there is substituted 'it' and 'its' respectively;

(iii) in sub-paragraph (3), for 'his' there is substituted 'its';

(iv) in sub-paragraph (4), for 'he' (in both places) and 'his' there is substituted 'it' and 'its' respectively;

and in the cross-heading before that paragraph, for 'Director General of Fair Trading' there is substituted 'Office of Fair Trading';

(c) in paragraph 4 –

(i) for 'Director' (in each place) there is substituted 'OFT';

(ii) in sub-paragraph (1), for 'his' there is substituted 'its';

(iii) in sub-paragraph (2), for 'him' there is substituted 'it';

(iv) sub-paragraph (5) shall cease to have effect;

and in the cross-heading before that paragraph, for 'Director' there is substituted 'OFT';

(d) after paragraph 4 there is inserted –

'Enforcement

4A (1) The court may, on an application by the OFT, enquire into whether any person ("the defaulter") has refused or otherwise failed, without reasonable excuse, to comply with a notice under paragraph 4.

(2) An application under sub-paragraph (1) shall include details of the possible failure which the OFT considers has occurred.

(3) In enquiring into a case under sub-paragraph (1), the court shall hear any witness who may be produced against or on behalf of the defaulter and any statement which may be offered in defence.

(4) Sub-paragraphs (5) and (6) apply where the court is satisfied, after hearing any witnesses and statements as mentioned in sub-paragraph (3), that the defaulter has refused or otherwise failed, without reasonable excuse, to comply with the notice under paragraph 4.

(5) The court may punish the defaulter as it would have been able to punish him had he been guilty of contempt of court.

(6) Where the defaulter is a body corporate, the court may punish any director or officer of the defaulter as it would have been able to punish that director or officer had the director or officer been guilty of contempt of court.

(7) In this section "the court" –

(a) in relation to England and Wales, means the High Court, and

(b) in relation to Scotland, means the Court of Session.

4B (1) A person commits an offence if he intentionally alters, suppresses or destroys a document which he has been required to produce by a notice under paragraph 4.

(2) A person who commits an offence under sub-paragraph (1) shall
be liable –

(a) on summary conviction, to a fine not exceeding the statutory
maximum;

(b) on conviction on indictment, to imprisonment for a term not
exceeding two years or to a fine or to both.';

(e) in paragraph 5, for 'Director', 'he' (in both places), 'him' and 'his' there is
substituted 'OFT', 'it', 'it' and 'its' respectively, and, in the cross-heading
before paragraph 5, for 'Director's' there is substituted 'OFT's';

(f) in paragraphs 6 and 7, for 'Director' (in each place) there is substituted
'OFT';

(g) paragraph 8 (exemption from monopoly provisions) shall cease to have
effect.

Companies (Northern Ireland) Order 1989 (S.I. 1990/593 (N.I. 5))

22 (1) The Companies (Northern Ireland) Order 1989 is amended as follows.

(2) In Article 49 (restrictive practices), in paragraph (3)(c), for 'Director General of
Fair Trading' there is substituted 'the Office of Fair Trading'.

(3) In Schedule 14 (supervisory and qualifying bodies: restrictive practices) –

(a) in paragraph 1 –

(i) in sub-paragraph (1), for 'the Director General of Fair Trading (in this
Schedule referred to as "the Director")' there is substituted 'the Office
of Fair Trading (in this Schedule referred to as "the OFT")' and for
'Director' there is substituted 'OFT';

(ii) in sub-paragraph (2), for 'Director' and 'his' there is substituted 'OFT'
and 'its' respectively;

(b) in paragraph 3 –

(i) for 'Director' (in each place) there is substituted 'OFT';

(ii) in sub-paragraph (1), for 'he' (in both places) and 'his' (in both
places) there is substituted 'it' and 'its' respectively;

(iii) in sub-paragraph (3), for 'his' there is substituted 'its';

(iv) in sub-paragraph (4), for 'he' (in both places) and 'his' there is
substituted 'it' and 'its' respectively;

and in the cross-heading before that paragraph, for 'Director General of Fair
Trading' there is substituted 'Office of Fair Trading';

(c) in paragraph 4 –

(i) for 'Director' (in each place) there is substituted 'OFT';

(ii) in sub-paragraph (1), for 'his' there is substituted 'its';

(iii) in sub-paragraph (2), for 'him' there is substituted 'it';

and in the cross-heading before that paragraph, for 'Director' there is
substituted 'OFT';

(d) in paragraph 5, for 'Director', 'he' (in both places), 'him' and 'his' there is
substituted 'OFT', 'it', 'it' and 'its' respectively, and, in the cross-heading
before paragraph 5, for 'Director's' there is substituted 'OFT's';

(e) in paragraphs 6 and 7, for 'Director' (in each place) there is substituted
'OFT'.

Courts and Legal Services Act 1990 (c. 41)

23 (1) The Courts and Legal Services Act 1990 is amended as follows.

(2) In section 45 (advisory and supervisory functions of Director General of Fair Trading) –

(a) for 'Director' (in each place) there is substituted 'OFT';

(b) in subsection (3), for 'he' (in both places) and 'his' there is substituted 'it' and 'its' respectively;

(c) in subsection (5), for 'he' and 'his' there is substituted 'it' and 'its' respectively;

(d) in subsection (6), for 'Director's' there is substituted 'OFT's';

(e) in subsection (7), for 'him' (in both places) there is substituted 'it';

(f) in subsection (8), for 'Director's' there is substituted 'its';

(g) in the sidenote, for 'Director General of Fair Trading' there is substituted 'Office of Fair Trading'.

(3) In section 46 (investigatory powers of Director) –

(a) in subsection (1), for 'Director' and 'him' (in each place) there is substituted 'OFT' and 'it' respectively;

(b) in the sidenote, for 'Director' there is substituted 'OFT';

(c) subsection (3) shall cease to have effect.

(4) After section 46 there is inserted –

'46A Enforcement of notices under section 46

(1) The High Court may, on an application by the OFT, enquire into whether any person ("the defaulter") has refused or otherwise failed, without reasonable excuse, to comply with a notice under section 46(1).

(2) An application under subsection (1) shall include details of the possible failure which the OFT considers has occurred.

(3) In enquiring into a case under subsection (1), the High Court shall hear any witness who may be produced against or on behalf of the defaulter and any statement which may be offered in defence.

(4) Subsections (5) and (6) apply where the High Court is satisfied, after hearing any witnesses and statements as mentioned in subsection (3), that the defaulter has refused or otherwise failed, without reasonable excuse, to comply with the notice under section 46(1).

(5) The High Court may punish the defaulter as it would have been able to punish him had he been guilty of contempt of court.

(6) Where the defaulter is a body corporate, the High Court may punish any director or officer of the defaulter as it would have been able to punish that director or officer had the director or officer been guilty of contempt of court.

46B Altering, etc. documents required to be produced under section 46

(1) A person commits an offence if he intentionally alters, suppresses or destroys a document which he has been required to produce by a notice under section 46(1).

(2) A person who commits an offence under subsection (1) shall be liable –

(a) on summary conviction, to a fine not exceeding the statutory maximum;

(b) on conviction on indictment, to imprisonment for a term not exceeding two years or to a fine or to both.'

(5) In section 50 (exceptions from restrictions on disclosure), in subsection (2)(m) –

(a) for 'Director to discharge any of his' there is substituted 'OFT to discharge any of its';

    (b)   after sub-paragraph (ix) there is inserted –

        '(x)   the Enterprise Act 2002;'.

(6) In section 69 (exemption from liability for damages etc.), in subsection (2) –

    (a)   for 'Director' there is substituted 'OFT';

    (b)   after 'him' there is inserted 'or it'.

(7) In section 105 (tying-in arrangements: supplemental provisions), in subsection (10), for 'Director' there is substituted 'OFT'.

(8) In section 107 (tying-in: enforcement) –

    (a)   for 'Director' (in each place) there is substituted 'OFT';

    (b)   in subsection (5), for 'him' and 'he' there is substituted 'it'.

(9) In section 119(1) (interpretation) –

    (a)   the definition of 'the Director' shall cease to have effect; and

    (b)   after the definition of 'officer' there is inserted –

    '"the OFT" means the Office of Fair Trading;'.

(10) In Schedule 4 (authorised bodies) –

    (a)   for 'Director' (in each place) there is substituted 'OFT';

    (b)   in paragraph 3 –

        (i)   in sub-paragraph (2), for 'he' there is substituted 'it';

        (ii)   in sub-paragraph (3), for 'his' and 'he' (in both places) there is substituted 'its' and 'it' respectively;

        (iii)   in sub-paragraph (4), for 'him' there is substituted 'it';

        (iv)   in sub-paragraph (5), for 'the Director's' there is substituted 'its';

    and in the cross-heading before that paragraph, for 'Director General of Fair Trading' there is substituted 'Office of Fair Trading';

    (c)   in paragraph 12 –

        (i)   in sub-paragraph (3), for 'he' there is substituted 'it';

        (ii)   in sub-paragraph (4), for 'his' and 'he' (in both places) there is substituted 'its' and 'it' respectively;

        (iii)   in sub-paragraph (5), for 'him' there is substituted 'it';

        (iv)   in sub-paragraph (6), for 'the Director's' there is substituted 'its';

    and in the cross-heading before that paragraph, for 'Director General of Fair Trading' there is substituted 'Office of Fair Trading';

    (d)   in paragraph 20 –

        (i)   in sub-paragraph (2), for 'he' there is substituted 'it';

        (ii)   in sub-paragraph (3), for 'his' and 'he' (in both places) there is substituted 'its' and 'it' respectively;

        (iii)   in sub-paragraph (4), for 'him' there is substituted 'it';

        (iv)   in sub-paragraph (5), for 'the Director's' there is substituted 'its';

    and in the cross-heading before that paragraph, for 'Director General of Fair Trading' there is substituted 'Office of Fair Trading';

    (e)   in paragraph 28 –

        (i)   in sub-paragraph (2), for 'he' there is substituted 'it';

        (ii)   in sub-paragraph (3), for 'his' and 'he' (in both places) there is substituted 'its' and 'it' respectively;

        (iii)   in sub-paragraph (4), for 'him' there is substituted 'it';

        (iv)   in sub-paragraph (5), for 'the Director's' there is substituted 'its';

    and in the cross-heading before that paragraph, for 'Director General of Fair Trading' there is substituted 'Office of Fair Trading'.

Broadcasting Act 1990 (c. 42)

24 (1) The Broadcasting Act 1990 is amended as follows.

(2) In section 2 (regulation by Commission of provision of television services), in subsection (3) –

(a) for 'the Director General of Fair Trading' there is substituted 'the Office of Fair Trading';

(b) for 'any of his or their' there is substituted 'any of their'.

(3) In section 39 (networking arrangements between holders of regional Channel 3 licences) –

(a) in subsection (2), for 'the Director General of Fair Trading' there is substituted 'the Office of Fair Trading';

(b) in subsection (3) –

(i) for 'the Director General of Fair Trading' there is substituted 'the Office of Fair Trading';

(ii) for 'he' there is substituted 'it';

(c) in subsection (12) –

(i) for 'the Director General of Fair Trading' there is substituted 'the Office of Fair Trading';

(ii) for 'him' there is substituted 'it'.

(4) In section 85 (licensing functions of Authority), in subsection (4) –

(a) for 'the Director General of Fair Trading' there is substituted 'the Office of Fair Trading';

(b) for 'any of his or their' there is substituted 'any of their'.

(5) In section 186 (duty of BBC to include independent productions in their television services) –

(a) in subsection (3) –

(i) for 'The Director General of Fair Trading ("the Director")' there is substituted 'The Office of Fair Trading ("the OFT")';

(ii) for 'his' there is substituted 'its';

(b) in subsection (4) –

(i) for 'the Director' there is substituted 'the OFT';

(ii) for 'his' (in each place) there is substituted 'its';

(iii) for 'him' there is substituted 'it';

(c) in subsection (5), for 'Director' (in both places) there is substituted 'OFT';

(d) in subsection (6) –

(i) for 'Director' (in each place) there is substituted 'OFT';

(ii) for 'him' there is substituted 'it';

(iii) for 'he' (in each place) there is substituted 'it';

(e) in subsections (7) and (8), for 'the Director' there is substituted 'the OFT'.

(6) In section 187 (information to be furnished by BBC for purposes of reports under section 186) –

(a) in subsection (1) –

(i) for 'Director' there is substituted 'Office of Fair Trading';

(ii) for 'him' (in both places) there is substituted 'it';

(iii) for 'he' there is substituted 'it';

(b) subsection (3) shall cease to have effect.

(7) In section 194A (relevant agreements) –

(a) for 'Director' (in each place) there is substituted 'OFT';

(b)   in subsection (7)(a) –

   (i)   for 'he' there is substituted 'it';
   (ii)   for 'his' there is substituted 'its';

(c)   in subsection (8), for 'he' (in both places) there is substituted 'it';
(d)   in subsection (9) –

   (i)   the definition of 'Director' shall cease to have effect; and
   (ii)   after the definition of 'Chapter III powers' there is inserted –

     '"OFT" means the Office of Fair Trading;'.

(8)   In section 197 (restriction on disclosure of information) –

(a)   in subsection (2)(a)(ii) –

   (i)   for 'the Director General of Fair Trading' there is substituted 'the Office of Fair Trading';
   (ii)   after 'the Competition Act 1998' there is inserted ', the Enterprise Act 2002';

(b)   in subsection (2)(c), after 'the Competition Act 1998' there is inserted ', the Enterprise Act 2002'.

(9)   In Schedule 4 (references with respect to networking arrangements) –

(a)   in paragraph 1 –

   (i)   for 'the Director General of Fair Trading ("the Director")' there is substituted 'the Office of Fair Trading ("the OFT")';
   (ii)   for 'Director' (in each place), 'he' (in each place), 'his' (in each place) and 'Director's' there is substituted 'OFT', 'it', 'its' and 'OFT's' respectively;

   and in the cross-heading before that paragraph, for 'Director' there is substituted 'OFT';

(b)   in paragraph 2, in sub-paragraph (3), for 'Director' there is substituted 'OFT';

(c)   in paragraph 3, for 'Director's' (in both places) and 'Director' there is substituted 'OFT's' and 'OFT' respectively, and, in the cross-heading before that paragraph, for 'Director's' there is substituted 'OFT's';

(d)   in paragraph 4 –

   (i)   for 'Director's' (in both places), 'Director', 'him' and 'he' there is substituted 'OFT's', 'OFT', 'it' and 'it' respectively;
   (ii)   sub-paragraphs (7) and (7A) shall cease to have effect;

(e)   after paragraph 4 there is inserted –

'Further provision about references under paragraph 4

4A (1)   The following sections of Part 3 of the Enterprise Act 2002 shall apply, with the modifications mentioned in sub-paragraphs (2) and (3), for the purposes of references under paragraph 4 as they apply for the purposes of references under that Part –

   (a)   section 109 (attendance of witnesses and production of documents etc.);
   (b)   section 110 (enforcement of powers under section 109: general);
   (c)   section 111 (penalties);
   (d)   section 112 (penalties: main procedural requirements);
   (e)   section 113 (payments and interest by instalments);
   (f)   section 114 (appeals in relation to penalties);

(g)   section 115 (recovery of penalties); and

(h)   section 116 (statement of policy).

(2)   Section 110 shall, in its application by virtue of sub-paragraph (1), have effect as if –

(a)   subsection (2) were omitted; and

(b)   in subsection (9) the words from "or section" to "section 65(3))" were omitted.

(3)   Section 111(5)(b)(ii) shall, in its application by virtue of sub-paragraph (1), have effect as if –

(a)   for the words "published (or, in the case of a report under section 50 or 65, given)" there were substituted "made";

(b)   for the words "published (or given)", in both places where they appear, there were substituted "made"; and

(c)   the words "by this Part" were omitted.

(4)   Provisions of Part 3 of the Enterprise Act 2002 which have effect for the purposes of sections 109 to 116 of that Act (including, in particular, provisions relating to offences and the making of orders) shall, for the purposes of the application of those sections by virtue of sub-paragraph (1), have effect in relation to those sections as applied by virtue of that sub-paragraph.

(5)   Accordingly, corresponding provisions of this Act shall not have effect in relation to those sections as applied by virtue of that sub-paragraph.';

(f)   in paragraph 5 –

(i)   for 'Director' (in each place) there is substituted 'OFT';

(ii)   sub-paragraph (5) shall cease to have effect;

(iii)   after sub-paragraph (5) there is inserted –

'(5A) For the purposes of paragraph 6, a conclusion contained in a report of the Competition Commission is to be disregarded if the conclusion is not that of at least two-thirds of the members of the group constituted in connection with the reference concerned in pursuance of paragraph 15 of Schedule 7 to the Competition Act 1998.

(5B) If a member of a group so constituted disagrees with any conclusions contained in a report made on a reference under paragraph 4 as the conclusions of the Competition Commission, the report shall, if the member so wishes, include a statement of his disagreement and of his reasons for disagreeing.

(5C) For the purposes of the law relating to defamation, absolute privilege attaches to any report made by the Competition Commission on a reference under paragraph 4.

(5D) In making any report on a reference under paragraph 4 the Competition Commission must have regard to the following considerations before disclosing any information.

(5E) The first consideration is the need to exclude from disclosure (so far as practicable) any information whose disclosure the Competition Commission thinks is contrary to the public interest.

(5F) The second consideration is the need to exclude from disclosure (so far as practicable) –

(a)   commercial information whose disclosure the Competition Commission thinks might significantly harm the legitimate business interests of the undertaking to which it relates, or

(b) information relating to the private affairs of an individual whose disclosure the Competition Commission thinks might significantly harm the individual's interests.

(5G) The third consideration is the extent to which the disclosure of the information mentioned in sub-paragraph (5F)(a) or (b) is necessary for the purposes of the report.';

(g) in paragraph 6, for 'Director' (in each place) there is substituted 'OFT';

(h) in paragraph 7, for 'Director' (in each place), 'he' (in each place) and 'him' there is substituted 'OFT', 'it' and 'it' respectively, and, in the cross-heading before that paragraph, for '*Director*' there is substituted '*OFT*';

(i) in paragraph 8 –

(i) for 'Director' (in each place) there is substituted 'OFT';

(ii) in sub-paragraph (1)(b), for 'him' there is substituted 'the OFT' and for 'he' there is substituted 'it';

(iii) sub-paragraphs (3) and (4) shall cease to have effect;

(j) after paragraph 8 there is inserted –

'*Enforcement*

8A (1) The court may, on an application by the OFT, enquire into whether any person ("the defaulter") has refused or otherwise failed, without reasonable excuse, to comply with a notice under paragraph 8(1).

(2) An application under sub-paragraph (1) shall include details of the possible failure which the OFT considers has occurred.

(3) In enquiring into a case under sub-paragraph (1), the court shall hear any witness who may be produced against or on behalf of the defaulter and any statement which may be offered in defence.

(4) Sub-paragraphs (5) and (6) apply where the court is satisfied, after hearing any witnesses and statements as mentioned in sub-paragraph (3), that the defaulter has refused or otherwise failed, without reasonable excuse, to comply with the notice under paragraph 8(1).

(5) The court may punish the defaulter as it would have been able to punish him had he been guilty of contempt of court.

(6) Where the defaulter is a body corporate, the court may punish any director or officer of the defaulter as it would have been able to punish that director or officer had the director or officer been guilty of contempt of court.

(7) In this section "the court" –

(a) in relation to England and Wales or Northern Ireland, means the High Court, and

(b) in relation to Scotland, means the Court of Session.

8B (1) A person commits an offence if he intentionally alters, suppresses or destroys a document which he has been required to produce by a notice under paragraph 8(1).

(2) A person who commits an offence under sub-paragraph (1) shall be liable –

(a) on summary conviction, to a fine not exceeding the statutory maximum;

(b)   on conviction on indictment, to imprisonment for a term not exceeding two years or to a fine or to both.

False or misleading information

8C (1)   A person commits an offence if –

(a)   he supplies any information to the OFT or the Competition Commission in connection with any of their functions under this Schedule;

(b)   the information is false or misleading in a material respect; and

(c)   he knows that it is false or misleading in a material respect or is reckless as to whether it is false or misleading in a material respect.

(2)   A person commits an offence if he –

(a)   supplies any information to another person which he knows to be false or misleading in a material respect; or

(b)   recklessly supplies any information to another person which is false or misleading in a material respect;

knowing that the information is to be used for the purpose of supplying information to the OFT or the Competition Commission in connection with any of their functions under this Schedule.

(3)   A person who commits an offence under sub-paragraph (1) or (2) shall be liable –

(a)   on summary conviction, to a fine not exceeding the statutory maximum;

(b)   on conviction on indictment, to imprisonment for a term not exceeding two years or to a fine or to both.

(4)   This paragraph shall not have effect in relation to the supplying of information to the Competition Commission in connection with its functions under any provision of the Enterprise Act 2002 as applied by virtue of paragraph 4A.';

(k)   in paragraph 9, for 'Director' and 'his' (in each place) there is substituted 'OFT' and 'its' respectively, and, in the cross-heading before that paragraph, for 'Director' there is substituted 'OFT';

(l)   in paragraph 10 –

(i)   the definition of 'the Director' shall cease to have effect;

(ii)   after the definition of 'the ITC' there is inserted –

'"the OFT" means the Office of Fair Trading.'

Water Industry Act 1991 (c. 56)

25   (1)   The Water Industry Act 1991 is amended as follows.

(2)   In section 2 (general duties with respect to water industry), in subsection (6B), for 'the Director General of Fair Trading' there is substituted 'the Office of Fair Trading (in this Act referred to as "the OFT")'.

(3)   In section 12(5) (determinations under conditions of appointment) for 'the 1973 Act' there is substituted 'the Enterprise Act 2002'.

(4)   In section 14 (conditions of appointment: modification references to Commission), subsections (7) and (7A) shall cease to have effect.

(5)   After section 14 there is inserted –

'14A References under section 14: time limits

(1)   Every reference under section 14 above shall specify a period (not longer than six months beginning with the date of the reference) within which a report on the reference is to be made.

(2)   A report of the Competition Commission on a reference under section 14 above shall not have effect (and no action shall be taken in relation to it under section 16 below) unless the report is made before the end of the period specified in the reference or such further period (if any) as may be allowed by the Director under subsection (3) below.

(3)   The Director may, if he has received representations on the subject from the Competition Commission and is satisfied that there are special reasons why the report cannot be made within the period specified in the reference, extend that period by no more than six months.

(4)   No more than one extension is possible under subsection (3) above in relation to the same reference.

(5)   The Director shall, in the case of an extension made by him under subsection (3) above –

(a)   publish that extension in such manner as he considers appropriate for the purpose of bringing it to the attention of persons likely to be affected by it; and

(b)   send a copy of what has been published by him under paragraph (a) above to the company whose appointment is mentioned in the reference.

14B References under section 14: powers of investigation

(1)   The following sections of Part 3 of the Enterprise Act 2002 shall apply, with the modifications mentioned in subsections (2) and (3) below, for the purposes of references under section 14 above as they apply for the purposes of references under that Part –

(a)   section 109 (attendance of witnesses and production of documents etc.);

(b)   section 110 (enforcement of powers under section 109: general);

(c)   section 111 (penalties);

(d)   section 112 (penalties: main procedural requirements);

(e)   section 113 (payments and interest by instalments);

(f)   section 114 (appeals in relation to penalties);

(g)   section 115 (recovery of penalties); and

(h)   section 116 (statement of policy).

(2)   Section 110 shall, in its application by virtue of subsection (1) above, have effect as if –

(a)   subsection (2) were omitted; and

(b)   in subsection (9) the words from "or section" to "section 65(3))" were omitted.

(3)   Section 111(5)(b)(ii) shall, in its application by virtue of subsection (1) above, have effect as if –

(a)   for the words "published (or, in the case of a report under section 50 or 65, given)" there were substituted "made";

(b)   for the words "published (or given)", in both places where they appear, there were substituted "made"; and

(c)   the words "by this Part" were omitted.

(4)   Provisions of Part 3 of the Enterprise Act 2002 which have effect for the purposes of sections 109 to 116 of that Act (including, in particular,

provisions relating to offences and the making of orders) shall, for the purposes of the application of those sections by virtue of subsection (1) above, have effect in relation to those sections as applied by virtue of that subsection.

(5)   Accordingly, corresponding provisions of this Act shall not have effect in relation to those sections as applied by virtue of that subsection.'

(6)   In section 15 (reports on modification references) –

(a)   after subsection (1) there is inserted –

'(1A) For the purposes of section 16 below, a conclusion contained in a report of the Competition Commission is to be disregarded if the conclusion is not that of at least two-thirds of the members of the group constituted in connection with the reference concerned in pursuance of paragraph 15 of Schedule 7 to the Competition Act 1998.

(1B) If a member of a group so constituted disagrees with any conclusions contained in a report made on a reference under section 14 above as the conclusions of the Competition Commission, the report shall, if the member so wishes, include a statement of his disagreement and of his reasons for disagreeing.';

(b)   for subsection (3) there is substituted –

'(3)   For the purposes of the law relating to defamation, absolute privilege attaches to any report made by the Competition Commission on a reference under section 14 above.

(3A) In making any report on a reference under section 14 above the Competition Commission must have regard to the following considerations before disclosing any information.

(3B) The first consideration is the need to exclude from disclosure (so far as practicable) any information whose disclosure the Competition Commission thinks is contrary to the public interest.

(3C) The second consideration is the need to exclude from disclosure (so far as practicable) –

(a)   commercial information whose disclosure the Competition Commission thinks might significantly harm the legitimate business interests of the undertaking to which it relates, or

(b)   information relating to the private affairs of an individual whose disclosure the Competition Commission thinks might significantly harm the individual's interests.

(3D) The third consideration is the extent to which the disclosure of the information mentioned in subsection (3C)(a) or (b) above is necessary for the purposes of the report.'

(7)   In section 27 (general duty of Director to keep matters under review), in subsection (4) –

(a)   for 'the Director General of Fair Trading' there is substituted 'the OFT';

(b)   for 'that Director' there is substituted 'the OFT'.

(8)   In section 31 (functions of Director with respect to competition) –

(a)   subsection (1) shall cease to have effect;

(b)   in subsection (3), for 'the Director General of Fair Trading, the functions of that Director' there is substituted 'the OFT, the functions of the OFT';

(c)   in subsection (4A), for 'the Director General of Fair Trading' there is substituted 'the OFT';

(d)   in subsection (8), for 'the Director General of Fair Trading' there is substituted 'the OFT'.

(9) In section 201 (publication of certain information and advice), at the end there is inserted –

'(4)   The OFT shall consult the Director before publishing under section 6 of the Enterprise Act 2002 any information or advice which may be published by the Director under subsection (2) of this section.'

(10) In section 206 (restriction on disclosure of information), in subsection (9A) –

(a)   for 'the Director General of Fair Trading' there is substituted 'the OFT';

(b)   for 'sections 55 and 56 of that Act (disclosure)' there is substituted 'Part 9 of the Enterprise Act 2002 (Information)'.

(11) In section 219 (general interpretation), in subsection (1), after the definition of 'notice' there is inserted –

'"the OFT" means the Office of Fair Trading;'.

(12) In Part 1 of Schedule 15 (disclosure of information) –

(a)   in Part 1, for the entry relating to the Director General of Fair Trading there is substituted –
'The OFT.';

(b)   in Part 2, after the entry relating to Part I of the Transport Act 2000, there is inserted –
'The Enterprise Act 2002.'

Water Resources Act 1991 (c. 57)

26   (1)   The Water Resources Act 1991 is amended as follows.

(2)   In Schedule 24 (disclosure of information) –

(a)   in Part 1, for the entry relating to the Director General of Fair Trading there is substituted –
'The Office of Fair Trading.';

(b)   in Part 2, after the entry relating to Part I of the Transport Act 2000, there is inserted –
'The Enterprise Act 2002.'

Tribunals and Inquiries Act 1992 (c. 53)

27   (1)   The Tribunals and Inquiries Act 1992 is amended as follows.

(2)   In section 11 (appeals from certain tribunals), in subsection (6), for 'the Director General of Fair Trading' there is substituted 'the Office of Fair Trading'.

(3)   In section 14 (restricted application of Act in relation to certain tribunals), in subsection (1)(b), for 'the Director General of Fair Trading' there is substituted 'the Office of Fair Trading'.

(4)   In Part 1 of Schedule 1 (tribunals under direct supervision of council), in column 2 –

(a)   for paragraph 9A there is substituted –

'9A.   The Competition Appeal Tribunal established under section 12 of the Enterprise Act 2002.';

(b)   for paragraph 17 there is substituted –

'17.   The Office of Fair Trading in respect of its functions under the Consumer Credit Act 1974 and the Estate Agents Act 1979, and any member of its staff authorised to exercise those functions.'

Electricity (Northern Ireland) Order 1992 (S.I. 1992/231 (N.I. 1))

28 (1) The Electricity (Northern Ireland) Order 1992 is amended as follows.
    (2) In Article 15 (licence modification references to Commission) paragraphs (8) and (8A) shall cease to have effect.
    (3) After Article 15 there is inserted –

'15A References under Article 15: time limits

(1) Every reference under Article 15 shall specify a period (not longer than six months beginning with the date of the reference) within which a report on the reference is to be made.

(2) A report of the Competition Commission on a reference under Article 15 shall not have effect (and no action shall be taken in relation to it under Article 17) unless the report is made before the end of the period specified in the reference or such further period (if any) as may be allowed by the Director under paragraph (3).

(3) The Director may, if he has received representations on the subject from the Competition Commission and is satisfied that there are special reasons why the report cannot be made within the period specified in the reference, extend that period by no more than six months.

(4) No more than one extension is possible under paragraph (3) in relation to the same reference.

(5) The Director shall, in the case of an extension made by him under paragraph (3) –

   (a) publish that extension in such manner as he considers appropriate for the purpose of bringing it to the attention of persons likely to be affected by it; and

   (b) send a copy of what has been published by him under sub-paragraph (a) to the licence holder.

15B References under Article 15: powers of investigation

(1) The following sections of Part 3 of the Enterprise Act 2002 shall apply, with the modifications mentioned in paragraphs (2) and (3), for the purposes of references under Article 15 as they apply for the purposes of references under that Part –

   (a) section 109 (attendance of witnesses and production of documents etc.);

   (b) section 110 (enforcement of powers under section 109: general);

   (c) section 111 (penalties);

   (d) section 112 (penalties: main procedural requirements);

   (e) section 113 (payments and interest by instalments);

   (f) section 114 (appeals in relation to penalties);

   (g) section 115 (recovery of penalties); and

   (h) section 116 (statement of policy).

(2) Section 110 shall, in its application by virtue of paragraph (1), have effect as if –

   (a) subsection (2) were omitted; and

   (b) in subsection (9) the words from "or section" to "section 65(3))" were omitted.

(3) Section 111(5)(b)(ii) shall, in its application by virtue of paragraph (1), have effect as if –

   (a) for the words "published (or, in the case of a report under section 50 or 65, given)" there were substituted "made";

(b) for the words "published (or given)", in both places where they appear, there were substituted "made"; and

(c) the words "by this Part" were omitted.

(4) Provisions of Part 3 of the Enterprise Act 2002 which have effect for the purposes of sections 109 to 116 of that Act (including, in particular, provisions relating to offences and the making of orders) shall, for the purposes of the application of those sections by virtue of paragraph (1), have effect in relation to those sections as applied by virtue of that paragraph.

(5) Accordingly, corresponding provisions of this Order shall not have effect in relation to those sections as applied by virtue of that paragraph.'

(4) In Article 16 (reports on licence modification references) –

(a) after paragraph (1) there is inserted –

'(1A) For the purposes of Article 17, a conclusion contained in a report of the Competition Commission is to be disregarded if the conclusion is not that of at least two-thirds of the members of the group constituted in connection with the reference concerned in pursuance of paragraph 15 of Schedule 7 to the Competition Act 1998.

(1B) If a member of a group so constituted disagrees with any conclusions contained in a report made on a reference under Article 15 as the conclusions of the Competition Commission, the report shall, if the member so wishes, include a statement of his disagreement and of his reasons for disagreeing.';

(b) for paragraph (3) there is substituted –

'(3) For the purposes of the law relating to defamation, absolute privilege attaches to any report made by the Competition Commission on a reference under Article 15.

(3A) In making any report on a reference under Article 15 the Competition Commission must have regard to the following considerations before disclosing any information.

(3B) The first consideration is the need to exclude from disclosure (so far as practicable) any information whose disclosure the Competition Commission thinks is contrary to the public interest.

(3C) The second consideration is the need to exclude from disclosure (so far as practicable) –

(a) commercial information whose disclosure the Competition Commission thinks might significantly harm the legitimate business interests of the undertaking to which it relates, or

(b) information relating to the private affairs of an individual whose disclosure the Competition Commission thinks might significantly harm the individual's interests.

(3D) The third consideration is the extent to which the disclosure of the information mentioned in paragraph (3C)(a) or (b) is necessary for the purposes of the report.'

(5) In Article 46 (functions with respect to competition) –

(a) paragraph (1) shall cease to have effect;

(b) in paragraph (3), for 'the Director General of Fair Trading, the functions of that Director' there is substituted 'the Office of Fair Trading, the functions of the Office of Fair Trading';

(c) in paragraph (3A), for 'the Director General of Fair Trading' there is substituted 'the Office of Fair Trading';

(d) in paragraph (6), for 'the Director General of Fair Trading' there is substituted 'the Office of Fair Trading'.

(6)   In Article 50 (general functions), in paragraph (3) –

    (a)   for 'the Director General of Fair Trading' there is substituted 'the Office of Fair Trading';

    (b)   for 'that Director' there is substituted 'the Office of Fair Trading'.

(7)   In Article 51 (publication of information and advice), in paragraph (3) –

    (a)   for 'The Director General of Fair Trading' there is substituted 'The Office of Fair Trading';

    (b)   for 'section 124 of the 1973 Act' there is substituted 'section 6 of the Enterprise Act 2002'.

Osteopaths Act 1993 (c. 21)

29   (1)   The Osteopaths Act 1993 is amended as follows.

    (2)   In section 33(2) (competition and anti-competitive practices) –

        (a)   for the words from the beginning to 'orders)' there is substituted 'Schedule 8 to the Enterprise Act 2002 (provision that may be contained in enforcement orders)';

        (b)   for 'a competition' there is substituted 'an enforcement'.

    (3)   After section 33(2) there is inserted –

        '(2A) The references to anything permitted by Schedule 8 to the Enterprise Act 2002 in sections 160(4)(a), 161(3)(a) and 164(1) of that Act shall be construed accordingly.'

    (4)   In section 33(3), for 'A competition' there is substituted 'An enforcement'.

    (5)   For section 33(4) there is substituted –

        '(4)   In this section 'an enforcement order' means an order under –

            (a)   section 160 of the Enterprise Act 2002 (orders following failure to fulfil final undertakings); or

            (b)   section 161 of that Act (final orders following market investigation reports).'

    (6)   For section 33(5) there is substituted –

        '(5)   For the purposes of an enforcement order section 86(3) of the Enterprise Act 2002 as applied by section 164(2)(a) of that Act (power to apply orders to existing agreements) shall have effect in relation to a regulatory provision as it has effect in relation to an agreement.'

Railways Act 1993 (c. 43)

30   (1)   The Railways Act 1993 is amended as follows.

    (2)   In section 4 (general duties of the Secretary of State and the Regulator) –

        (a)   in subsection (2)(a), the words from 'in cases where' to 'market' shall cease to have effect;

        (b)   in subsection (7B), for 'the Director General of Fair Trading' there is substituted 'the Office of Fair Trading';

        (c)   subsection (8) shall cease to have effect.

    (3)   In section 13 (licence modification references to Commission) –

        (a)   in subsection (1A), after 'section' in the first place where it appears there is inserted ', section 13A below';

        (b)   subsections (8) and (8A) shall cease to have effect.

    (4)   After section 13 there is inserted –

'13A References under section 13: time limits

(1) Every reference under section 13 above shall specify a period (not longer than six months beginning with the date of the reference) within which a report on the reference is to be made.

(2) A report of the Competition Commission on a reference under section 13 above shall not have effect (and no action shall be taken in relation to it under section 15 below) unless the report is made before the end of the period specified in the reference or such further period (if any) as may be allowed by the appropriate authority under subsection (3) below.

(3) The appropriate authority may, if it has received representations on the subject from the Competition Commission and is satisfied that there are special reasons why the report cannot be made within the period specified in the reference, extend that period by no more than six months.

(4) No more than one extension is possible under subsection (3) above in relation to the same reference.

(5) The appropriate authority shall, in the case of an extension made by it under subsection (3) above –

(a) publish that extension in such manner as it considers appropriate for the purpose of bringing it to the attention of persons likely to be affected by it; and

(b) send a copy of what has been published by it under paragraph (a) above to the holder of the licence.

13B References under section 13: application of Enterprise Act 2002

(1) The following sections of Part 3 of the Enterprise Act 2002 shall apply, with the modifications mentioned in subsections (2) and (3) below, for the purposes of references under section 13 above as they apply for the purposes of references under that Part –

(a) section 109 (attendance of witnesses and production of documents etc.);

(b) section 110 (enforcement of powers under section 109: general);

(c) section 111 (penalties);

(d) section 112 (penalties: main procedural requirements);

(e) section 113 (payments and interest by instalments);

(f) section 114 (appeals in relation to penalties);

(g) section 115 (recovery of penalties); and

(h) section 116 (statement of policy).

(2) Section 110 shall, in its application by virtue of subsection (1) above, have effect as if –

(a) subsection (2) were omitted; and

(b) in subsection (9) the words from "or section" to "section 65(3))" were omitted.

(3) Section 111(5)(b)(ii) shall, in its application by virtue of subsection (1) above, have effect as if –

(a) for the words "published (or, in the case of a report under section 50 or 65, given)" there were substituted "made";

(b) for the words "published (or given)", in both places where they appear, there were substituted "made"; and

(c) the words "by this Part" were omitted.

(4) Section 117 of the Enterprise Act 2002 (false or misleading information) shall apply in relation to functions of the Competition Commission in connection with references under section 13 as it applies in relation to its

functions under Part 3 of that Act but as if, in subsections (1)(a) and (2), the words "the OFT," and "or the Secretary of State" were omitted.

(5)   Provisions of Part 3 of the Enterprise Act 2002 which have effect for the purposes of sections 109 to 117 of that Act (including, in particular, provisions relating to offences and the making of orders), shall, for the purposes of the application of those sections by virtue of subsection (1) or (4) above, have effect in relation to those sections as applied by those subsections.

(6)   Accordingly, corresponding provisions of this Act shall not have effect in relation to those sections as applied by virtue of those subsections.'

(5)   In section 14 (reports on licence modification references) –

(a)   after subsection (1) there is inserted –

'(1A) For the purposes of sections 15 to 15B below, a conclusion contained in a report of the Competition Commission is to be disregarded if the conclusion is not that of at least two-thirds of the members of the group constituted in connection with the reference concerned in pursuance of paragraph 15 of Schedule 7 to the Competition Act 1998.

(1B) If a member of a group so constituted disagrees with any conclusions contained in a report made on a reference under section 13 above as the conclusions of the Competition Commission, the report shall, if the member so wishes, include a statement of his disagreement and of his reasons for disagreeing.';

(b)   for subsection (3) there is substituted –

'(3)   For the purposes of the law relating to defamation, absolute privilege attaches to any report made by the Competition Commission on a reference under section 13 above.

(3A) In making any report on a reference under section 13 above the Competition Commission must have regard to the following considerations before disclosing any information.

(3B) The first consideration is the need to exclude from disclosure (so far as practicable) any information whose disclosure the Competition Commission thinks is contrary to the public interest.

(3C) The second consideration is the need to exclude from disclosure (so far as practicable) –

(a)   commercial information whose disclosure the Competition Commission thinks might significantly harm the legitimate business interests of the undertaking to which it relates, or

(b)   information relating to the private affairs of an individual whose disclosure the Competition Commission thinks might significantly harm the individual's interests.

(3D) The third consideration is the extent to which the disclosure of the information mentioned in subsection (3C)(a) or (b) above is necessary for the purposes of the report.'

(6)   In section 15C (provisions supplementary to Commission's power to veto modifications following report), for subsections (1) and (2) there is substituted –

'(1)   For the purposes of the law relating to defamation, absolute privilege attaches to any notice under section 15A(4) or 15B(3) above.

(2)   In giving any notice under section 15A(4) or 15B(3) above, the Competition Commission must have regard to the following considerations before disclosing any information.

(2A) The first consideration is the need to exclude from disclosure (so far as practicable) any information whose disclosure the Competition Commission thinks is contrary to the public interest.

(2B) The second consideration is the need to exclude from disclosure (so far as practicable) –

    (a)   commercial information whose disclosure the Competition Commission thinks might significantly harm the legitimate business interests of the undertaking to which it relates, or

    (b)   information relating to the private affairs of an individual whose disclosure the Competition Commission thinks might significantly harm the individual's interests.

(2C) The third consideration is the extent to which the disclosure of the information mentioned in subsection (2B)(a) or (b) above is necessary for the purposes of the notice.

(2D) The following sections of Part 3 of the Enterprise Act 2002 shall apply, with the modifications mentioned in subsections (2E) and (2F) below, for the purposes of any investigation by the Competition Commission for the purposes of the exercise of its functions under section 15A or 15B above, as they apply for the purposes of any investigation on references under that Part –

    (a)   section 109 (attendance of witnesses and production of documents etc.);

    (b)   section 110 (enforcement of powers under section 109: general);

    (c)   section 111 (penalties);

    (d)   section 112 (penalties: main procedural requirements);

    (e)   section 113 (payments and interest by instalments);

    (f)   section 114 (appeals in relation to penalties);

    (g)   section 115 (recovery of penalties); and

    (h)   section 116 (statement of policy).

(2E) Section 110 shall, in its application by virtue of subsection (2D) above, have effect as if –

    (a)   subsection (2) were omitted;

    (b)   in subsection (4), for the words "the publication of the report of the Commission on the reference concerned" there were substituted "the sending of a copy to the Regulator under section 15B(5) of the Railways Act 1993 of the modifications made by the Commission in connection with the reference concerned or, if no direction has been given by the Commission under section 15A(1) of that Act in connection with the reference concerned and within the period permitted for that purpose, the latest day on which it was possible to give such a direction within the permitted period"; and

    (c)   in subsection (9) the words from "or section" to "section 65(3))" were omitted.

(2F) Section 111(5)(b) shall, in its application by virtue of subsection (2D) above, have effect as if for sub-paragraph (ii) there were substituted –

"(ii) if earlier, the day on which a copy of the modifications made by the Commission in connection with the reference concerned is sent to the Regulator under section 15B(5) of the Railways Act 1993 or, if no direction is given by the Commission under section 15A(1) of that Act in connection with the reference concerned and within the period permitted for that purpose, the latest day on which such a direction may be given within the permitted period.".

(2G) Section 117 of the Enterprise Act 2002 (false or misleading information) shall apply in relation to functions of the Competition
Commission in connection with the exercise of its functions under
section 15A and 15B above as it applies in relation to its functions
under Part 3 of that Act but as if, in subsections (1)(a) and (2), the
words "the OFT," and "or the Secretary of State" were omitted.

(2H) Provisions of Part 3 of the Enterprise Act 2002 which have effect for
the purposes of sections 109 to 117 of that Act (including, in particular, provisions relating to offences and the making of orders)
shall, for the purposes of the application of those sections by virtue of
subsection (2D) or (2G) above, have effect in relation to those sections as applied by virtue of those subsections.

(2I) Accordingly, corresponding provisions of this Act shall not have effect
in relation to those sections as applied by virtue of those subsections.'

(7) In section 22 (amendment of access agreements), in subsection (6A), for 'the
Director General of Fair Trading' there is substituted 'the Office of Fair Trading'.

(8) In section 66 (amendments of the Fair Trading Act 1973) –

(a)   for subsection (3) there is substituted –

'(3) For the purposes of Part 3 of the Enterprise Act 2002 (merger references), where a person enters into a franchise agreement as a fran-
chisee, there shall be taken to be brought under his control an
enterprise engaged in the supply of the railway services to which the
agreement relates.';

(b)   for subsection (6) there is substituted –

'(6) Expressions used in subsection (3) above and in Part 3 of the
Enterprise Act 2002 have the same meaning in that subsection as they
have in that Part.'

(9) In section 67 (respective functions of the Regulator and the Director General of
Fair Trading, and functions of the Competition Commission) –

(a)   subsection (1) shall cease to have effect;
(b)   in subsections (3), (3A) and (8), for 'the Director' (in each place) there is
substituted 'the OFT';
(c)   in the sidenote, for 'the Director General of Fair Trading' there is substituted 'OFT'.

(10) In section 69 (general functions), in subsection (3), for 'the Director' (in both
places) there is substituted 'the OFT'.

(11) In section 71 (publication of information and advice), in subsection (3) –

(a)   for 'The Director' there is substituted 'The OFT';
(b)   for 'section 124 of the 1973 Act' there is substituted 'section 6 of the
Enterprise Act 2002'.

(12) In section 74(7) (annual and other reports of the Regulator), for 'Section 125(1)
of the 1973 Act (annual and other reports)' there is substituted 'Paragraph
12A(1) of Schedule 7 to the Competition Act 1998 (annual reports of the
Competition Commission)'.

(13) In section 83(1) –

(a)   the definition of 'the Director' shall cease to have effect; and
(b)   after the definition of 'notice period' there is inserted –
'"the OFT" means the Office of Fair Trading;'.

(14) In section 145 (general restrictions on disclosure of information) –

(a)   in subsection (2)(b), for paragraph (ii) there is substituted –
'(ii) the Office of Fair Trading;';

(b) in subsection (3), after paragraph (qr) there is inserted –
'(qs) the Enterprise Act 2002;'

(c) in subsection (6A) –

(i) for 'the Director of Fair Trading' there is substituted 'the Office of Fair Trading';

(ii) for 'sections 55 and 56 of that Act (disclosure)' there is substituted 'Part 9 of the Enterprise Act 2002 (Information)'.

(15) In Schedule 4A (review of access charges by Regulator) –

(a) for paragraph 10 there is substituted –

'References under paragraph 9: time limits

10 (1) Every reference under paragraph 9 above shall specify a period (not longer than six months beginning with the date of the reference) within which a report on the reference is to be made.

(2) A report of the Competition Commission on a reference under paragraph 9 above shall not have effect (and no action shall be taken in relation to it under paragraph 12 below) unless the report is made before the end of the period specified in the reference or such further period (if any) as may be allowed by the Regulator under sub-paragraph (3) below.

(3) The Regulator may, if he has received representations on the subject from the Competition Commission and is satisfied that there are special reasons why the report cannot be made within the period specified in the reference, extend that period by no more than six months.

(4) No more than one extension is possible under sub-paragraph (3) above in relation to the same reference.

(5) The Regulator shall, in the case of an extension made by him under sub-paragraph (3) above –

(a) publish that extension in such manner as he considers appropriate for the purpose of bringing it to the attention of persons likely to be affected by it; and

(b) send a copy of what has been published by him under paragraph (a) above to the persons on whom a copy of the review notice was served.

References under paragraph 9: application of Enterprise Act 2002

10A (1) The following sections of Part 3 of the Enterprise Act 2002 shall apply, with the modifications mentioned in sub-paragraphs (2) and (3) below, for the purposes of references under paragraph 9 above as they apply for the purposes of references under that Part –

(a) section 109 (attendance of witnesses and production of documents etc.);

(b) section 110 (enforcement of powers under section 109: general);

(c) section 111 (penalties);

(d) section 112 (penalties: main procedural requirements);

(e) section 113 (payments and interest by instalments);

(f)   section 114 (appeals in relation to penalties);
(g)   section 115 (recovery of penalties); and
(h)   section 116 (statement of policy).

(2) Section 110 shall, in its application by virtue of sub-paragraph (1) above, have effect as if –

(a)   subsection (2) were omitted; and
(b)   in subsection (9) the words from "or section" to "section 65(3))" were omitted.

(3) Section 111(5)(b)(ii) shall, in its application by virtue of sub-paragraph (1) above, have effect as if –

(a)   for the words "published (or, in the case of a report under section 50 or 65, given)" there were substituted "made";
(b)   for the words "published (or given)", in both places where they appear, there were substituted "made"; and
(c)   the words "by this Part" were omitted.

(4) Section 117 of the Enterprise Act 2002 (false or misleading information) shall apply in relation to functions of the Competition Commission in connection with references under paragraph 9 above as it applies in relation to its functions under Part 3 of that Act but as if, in subsections (1)(a) and (2), the words "the OFT," and 'or the Secretary of State' were omitted.

(5) Provisions of Part 3 of the Enterprise Act 2002 which have effect for the purposes of sections 109 to 117 of that Act (including, in particular, provisions relating to offences and the making of orders) shall, for the purposes of the application of those sections by virtue of sub-paragraph (1) or (4) above, have effect in relation to those sections as applied by virtue of those sub-paragraphs.

(6) Accordingly, corresponding provisions of this Act shall not have effect in relation to those sections as applied by virtue of those sub-paragraphs.';

(b) in paragraph 11 –

(i)   after sub-paragraph (4) there is inserted –

'(4A) For the purposes of paragraphs 12 to 14 below, a conclusion contained in a report of the Competition Commission is to be disregarded if the conclusion is not that of at least two-thirds of the members of the group constituted in connection with the reference concerned in pursuance of paragraph 15 of Schedule 7 to the Competition Act 1998.

(4B) If a member of a group so constituted disagrees with any conclusions contained in a report made on a reference under paragraph 9 above as the conclusions of the Competition Commission, the report shall, if the member so wishes, include a statement of his disagreement and of his reasons for disagreeing.';

(ii) for sub-paragraph (5) there is substituted –

'(5) For the purposes of the law relating to defamation, absolute privilege attaches to any report made by the Competition Commission on a reference under paragraph 9 above.

(5A) In making any report on a reference under paragraph 9 above the Competition Commission must have regard to the following considerations before disclosing any information.

(5B) The first consideration is the need to exclude from disclosure (so far as practicable) any information whose disclosure the Competition Commission thinks is contrary to the public interest.

(5C) The second consideration is the need to exclude from disclosure (so far as practicable) –

    (a)   commercial information whose disclosure the Competition Commission thinks might significantly harm the legitimate business interests of the undertaking to which it relates, or

    (b)   information relating to the private affairs of an individual whose disclosure the Competition Commission thinks might significantly harm the individual's interests.

(5D) The third consideration is the extent to which the disclosure of the information mentioned in sub-paragraph (5C)(a) or (b) above is necessary for the purposes of the report.';

(c)   in paragraph 15, for sub-paragraphs (1) and (2) there is substituted –

'(1)   For the purposes of the law relating to defamation, absolute privilege attaches to any notice under paragraph 13(4) or 14(3) above.

(2)   In giving any notice under paragraph 13(4) or 14(3) above, the Competition Commission must have regard to the following considerations before disclosing any information.

(2A) The first consideration is the need to exclude from disclosure (so far as practicable) any information whose disclosure the Competition Commission thinks is contrary to the public interest.

(2B) The second consideration is the need to exclude from disclosure (so far as practicable) –

    (a)   commercial information whose disclosure the Competition Commission thinks might significantly harm the legitimate business interests of the undertaking to which it relates, or

    (b)   information relating to the private affairs of an individual whose disclosure the Competition Commission thinks might significantly harm the individual's interests.

(2C) The third consideration is the extent to which the disclosure of the information mentioned in sub-paragraph (2B)(a) or (b) above is necessary for the purposes of the notice.

(2D) The following sections of Part 3 of the Enterprise Act 2002 shall apply, with the modifications mentioned in sub-paragraphs (2E) and (2F) below, in relation to any investigation by the Competition Commission for the purposes of the exercise of its functions under paragraph 13 or 14 above, as they apply for the purposes of any investigation on references under that Part –

    (a)   section 109 (attendance of witnesses and production of documents etc.);

    (b)   section 110 (enforcement of powers under section 109: general);

    (c)   section 111 (penalties);

    (d)   section 112 (penalties: main procedural requirements);

    (e)   section 113 (payments and interest by instalments);

    (f)   section 114 (appeals in relation to penalties);

    (g)   section 115 (recovery of penalties); and

    (h)   section 116 (statement of policy).

(2E) Section 110 shall, in its application by virtue of sub-paragraph (2D) above, have effect as if –

    (a)   subsection (2) were omitted;

    (b)   in subsection (4), for the words "the publication of the report of the Commission on the reference concerned" there were substituted "the sending of a copy to the Regulator under paragraph 14 of Schedule

4A to the Railways Act 1993 of the relevant changes made by the Commission in connection with the reference concerned or, if no direction has been given by the Commission under paragraph 13(1) of that Schedule to that Act in connection with the reference concerned and within the period permitted for that purpose, the latest day on which it was possible to give such a direction within the permitted period"; and

(c)   in subsection (9) the words from "or section" to "section 65(3))" were omitted.

(2F) Section 111(5)(b) shall, in its application by virtue of sub-paragraph (2D) above, have effect as if for sub-paragraph (ii) there were substituted –

"(ii)   if earlier, the day on which a copy of the relevant changes made by the Commission in connection with the reference concerned is sent to the Regulator under paragraph 14 of Schedule 4A to the Railways Act 1993 or, if no direction is given by the Commission under paragraph 13(1) of that Schedule to that Act in connection with the reference concerned and within the period permitted for that purpose, the latest day on which such a direction may be given within the permitted period.".

(2G) Section 117 of the Enterprise Act 2002 (false or misleading information) shall apply in relation to functions of the Competition Commission in connection with the exercise of its functions under paragraph 13 or 14 above as it applies in relation to its functions under Part 3 of that Act but as if, in subsections (1)(a) and (2), the words "the OFT," and "or the Secretary of State" were omitted.

(2H) Provisions of Part 3 of the Enterprise Act 2002 which have effect for the purposes of sections 109 to 117 of that Act (including, in particular, provisions relating to offences and the making of orders) shall, for the purposes of the application of those sections by virtue of sub-paragraph (2D) or (2G) above, have effect in relation to those sections as applied by virtue of those sub-paragraphs.

(2I) Accordingly, corresponding provisions of this Act shall not have effect in relation to those sections as applied by virtue of those sub-paragraphs.'

Chiropractors Act 1994 (c. 17)

31 (1) The Chiropractors Act 1994 is amended as follows.
    (2) In section 33(2) (competition and anti-competitive practices) –
        (a)   for the words from the beginning to 'orders)' there is substituted 'Schedule 8 to the Enterprise Act 2002 (provision that may be contained in enforcement orders)';
        (b)   for 'a competition' there is substituted 'an enforcement'.
    (3) After section 33(2) there is inserted –
        '(2A) The references to anything permitted by Schedule 8 to the Enterprise Act 2002 in sections 160(4)(a), 161(3)(a) and 164(1) of that Act shall be construed accordingly.'
    (4) In section 33(3), for 'A competition' there is substituted 'An enforcement'.
    (5) For section 33(4) there is substituted –
        '(4)   In this section "an enforcement order" means an order under –
            (a)   section 160 of the Enterprise Act 2002 (orders following failure to fulfil final undertakings); or
            (b)   section 161 of that Act (final orders following market investigation reports).'

(6) For section 33(5) there is substituted –

'(5) For the purposes of an enforcement order section 86(3) of the Enterprise Act 2002 as applied by section 164(2)(a) of that Act (power to apply orders to existing agreements) shall have effect in relation to a regulatory provision as it has effect in relation to an agreement.'

Coal Industry Act 1994 (c. 21)

32 (1) The Coal Industry Act 1994 is amended as follows.

(2) In section 59 (information to be kept confidential by the Authority) –

(a) in subsection (3)(e)(v), for 'the Director General of Fair Trading' there is substituted 'the Office of Fair Trading';

(b) in subsection (4), after paragraph (n) there is inserted –

'(o) the Enterprise Act 2002.'

Airports (Northern Ireland) Order 1994 (S.I. 1994/426 (N.I. 1))

33 (1) The Airports (Northern Ireland) Order 1994 is amended as follows.

(2) In Article 35 (supplementary provisions relating to references to the Commission), paragraphs (3) and (3A) shall cease to have effect.

(3) After Article 35 there is inserted –

'35A References under Article 34: time limits

(1) Every reference under Article 34 shall specify a period (not longer than six months beginning with the date of the reference) within which a report on the reference is to be made.

(2) A report of the Commission on a reference under Article 34 shall not have effect (and no action shall be taken in relation to it under Article 37) unless the report is made before the end of the period specified in the reference or such further period (if any) as may be allowed by the CAA under paragraph (3).

(3) The CAA may, if it has received representations on the subject from the Commission and is satisfied that there are special reasons why the report cannot be made within the period specified in the reference, extend that period by no more than six months.

(4) No more than one extension is possible under paragraph (3) in relation to the same reference.

(5) The CAA shall, in the case of an extension made by it under paragraph (3) –

(a) publish that extension in such manner as it considers appropriate for the purpose of bringing it to the attention of persons likely to be affected by it; and

(b) send a copy of what has been published by it under sub-paragraph (a) to the airport operator concerned and the Department.

35B References under Article 34: powers of investigation

(1) The following sections of Part 3 of the Enterprise Act 2002 shall apply, with the modifications mentioned in paragraphs (2) and (3), for the purposes of references under Article 34 as they apply for the purposes of references under that Part –

(a) section 109 (attendance of witnesses and production of documents etc.);

(b) section 110 (enforcement of powers under section 109: general);

      (c)   section 111 (penalties);

      (d)   section 112 (penalties: main procedural requirements);

      (e)   section 113 (payments and interest by instalments);

      (f)   section 114 (appeals in relation to penalties);

      (g)   section 115 (recovery of penalties); and

      (h)   section 116 (statement of policy).

(2)   Section 110 shall, in its application by virtue of paragraph (1), have effect as if –

      (a)   subsection (2) were omitted; and

      (b)   in subsection (9) the words from "or section" to "section 65(3))" were omitted.

(3)   Section 111(5)(b)(ii) shall, in its application by virtue of paragraph (1), have effect as if –

      (a)   for the words "published (or, in the case of a report under section 50 or 65, given)" there were substituted "made";

      (b)   for the words "published (or given)", in both places where they appear, there were substituted "made"; and

      (c)   the words "by this Part" were omitted.

(4)   Provisions of Part 3 of the Enterprise Act 2002 which have effect for the purposes of sections 109 to 116 of that Act (including, in particular, provisions relating to offences and the making of orders) shall, for the purposes of the application of those sections by virtue of paragraph (1), have effect in relation to those sections as applied by virtue of that paragraph.

(5)   Accordingly, corresponding provisions of this Order shall not have effect in relation to those sections as applied by virtue of that paragraph.'

(4) In Article 36 (reports on references) –

    (a)   after paragraph (2) there is inserted –

        '(2A) For the purposes of Article 37(2), a conclusion contained in a report of the Commission is to be disregarded if the conclusion is not that of at least two-thirds of the members of the group constituted in connection with the reference concerned in pursuance of paragraph 15 of Schedule 7 to the Competition Act 1998.

        (2B) If a member of a group so constituted disagrees with any conclusions contained in a report made on a reference under Article 34 as the conclusions of the Commission, the report shall, if the member so wishes, include a statement of his disagreement and of his reasons for disagreeing.';

    (b)   for paragraph (4) there is substituted –

        '(4) For the purposes of the law relating to defamation, absolute privilege attaches to any report made by the Commission on a reference under Article 34.

        (4A) In making any report on a reference under Article 34 the Commission must have regard to the following considerations before disclosing any information.

        (4B) The first consideration is the need to exclude from disclosure (so far as practicable) any information whose disclosure the Commission thinks is contrary to the public interest.

        (4C) The second consideration is the need to exclude from disclosure (so far as practicable) –

            (a)   commercial information whose disclosure the Commission thinks might significantly harm the legitimate business interests of the undertaking to which it relates, or

      (b)   information relating to the private affairs of an individual whose disclosure the Commission thinks might significantly harm the individual's interests.

    (4D) The third consideration is the extent to which the disclosure of the information mentioned in paragraph (4C)(a) or (b) is necessary for the purposes of the report.'

(5) In Article 47 (co-ordination of exercise of functions by CAA and Director General of Fair Trading) –

   (a) in paragraph (a) –

      (i) for 'the Director General of Fair Trading of functions under the 1973 Act or the 1980 Act' there is substituted 'the Office of Fair Trading of functions under the Enterprise Act 2002';

     (ii) for 'the Director' there is substituted 'the Office of Fair Trading';

   (b) in paragraph (b), for 'the Director' there is substituted 'the Office of Fair Trading'.

(6) In Article 49 (restriction on disclosure of information) –

   (a) in paragraph (2), for 'the Director General of Fair Trading' there is substituted 'the Office of Fair Trading';

   (b) in paragraph (3), at the end there is inserted –

     '(t) the Enterprise Act 2002'.

Broadcasting Act 1996 (c. 55)

34 (1) The Broadcasting Act 1996 is amended as follows.

    (2) In section 142 (standards for transmission hit), in subsection (6), for paragraph (f) there is substituted –

     '(f) the Office of Fair Trading,'.

Channel Tunnel Rail Link Act 1996 (c. 61)

35 (1) The Channel Tunnel Rail Link Act 1996 is amended as follows.

    (2) In section 21 (duties as to exercise of regulatory functions), in subsection (7)(b) –

   (a) for 'the Director General of Fair Trading' there is substituted 'the Office of Fair Trading';

   (b) for 'he' there is substituted 'it'.

    (3) In section 22 (restriction of functions in relation to competition etc.) –

   (a) subsection (1) shall cease to have effect;

   (b) in subsection (3), for 'the Director General of Fair Trading' there is substituted 'the Office of Fair Trading';

   (c) in subsection (4) –

      (i) for 'the Director General of Fair Trading' there is substituted 'the Office of Fair Trading';

     (ii) for 'the Director' there is substituted 'the Office of Fair Trading'.

Gas (Northern Ireland) Order 1996 (S.I. 1996/275 (N.I. 2))

36 (1) The Gas (Northern Ireland) Order 1996 is amended as follows.
    (2) In Article 15 (licence modification references to Commission) –
        (a) paragraphs (9) and (9A) shall cease to have effect;
        (b) in paragraph (10), after 'Articles' there is inserted '15A,'.
    (3) After Article 15 there is inserted –

'15A References under Article 15: time limits

    (1) Every reference under Article 15 shall specify a period (not longer than six
         months beginning with the date of the reference) within which a report on
         the reference is to be made.
    (2) A report of the Competition Commission on a reference under Article 15
         shall not have effect (and no action shall be taken in relation to it under
         Article 17) unless the report is made before the end of the period specified
         in the reference or such further period (if any) as may be allowed by the
         Director under paragraph (3).
    (3) The Director may, if he has received representations on the subject from the
         Competition Commission and is satisfied that there are special reasons why
         the report cannot be made within the period specified in the reference,
         extend that period by no more than six months.
    (4) No more than one extension is possible under paragraph (3) in relation to
         the same reference.
    (5) The Director shall, in the case of an extension made by him under
         paragraph (3) –
        (a) publish that extension in such manner as he considers appropriate for
             the purpose of bringing it to the attention of persons likely to be
             affected by it; and
        (b) send a copy of what has been published by him under sub-paragraph
             (a) to the holder of the licence or, as the case may be, the relevant
             licence holders.

15B References under Article 15: powers of investigation

    (1) The following sections of Part 3 of the Enterprise Act 2002 shall apply, with
         the modifications mentioned in paragraphs (2) and (3), for the purposes of
         references under Article 15 as they apply for the purposes of references
         under that Part –
        (a) section 109 (attendance of witnesses and production of documents etc.);
        (b) section 110 (enforcement of powers under section 109: general);
        (c) section 111 (penalties);
        (d) section 112 (penalties: main procedural requirements);
        (e) section 113 (payments and interest by instalments);
        (f) section 114 (appeals in relation to penalties);
        (g) section 115 (recovery of penalties); and
        (h) section 116 (statement of policy).
    (2) Section 110 shall, in its application by virtue of paragraph (1), have effect
         as if –
        (a) subsection (2) were omitted; and
        (b) in subsection (9) the words from "or section" to "section 65(3))"
             were omitted.
    (3) Section 111(5)(b)(ii) shall, in its application by virtue of paragraph (1),
         have effect as if –
        (a) for the words "published (or, in the case of a report under section 50
             or 65, given)" there were substituted "made";

     (b) for the words "published (or given)", in both places where they appear, there were substituted "made"; and

     (c) the words "by this Part" were omitted.

(4) Provisions of Part 3 of the Enterprise Act 2002 which have effect for the purposes of sections 109 to 116 of that Act (including, in particular, provisions relating to offences and the making of orders) shall, for the purposes of the application of those sections by virtue of paragraph (1), have effect in relation to those sections as applied by virtue of that paragraph.

(5) Accordingly, corresponding provisions of this Order shall not have effect in relation to those sections as applied by virtue of that paragraph.'

(4) In Article 16 (reports on licence modification references) –

    (a) after paragraph (1) there is inserted –

      '(1A) For the purposes of Article 17, a conclusion contained in a report of the Competition Commission is to be disregarded if the conclusion is not that of at least two-thirds of the members of the group constituted in connection with the reference concerned in pursuance of paragraph 15 of Schedule 7 to the Competition Act 1998.

      (1B) If a member of a group so constituted disagrees with any conclusions contained in a report made on a reference under Article 15 as the conclusions of the Competition Commission, the report shall, if the member so wishes, include a statement of his disagreement and of his reasons for disagreeing.';

    (b) for paragraph (3) there is substituted –

      '(3) For the purposes of the law relating to defamation, absolute privilege attaches to any report made by the Competition Commission on a reference under Article 15.

      (3A) In making any report on a reference under Article 15 the Competition Commission must have regard to the following considerations before disclosing any information.

      (3B) The first consideration is the need to exclude from disclosure (so far as practicable) any information whose disclosure the Competition Commission thinks is contrary to the public interest.

      (3C) The second consideration is the need to exclude from disclosure (so far as practicable) –

        (a) commercial information whose disclosure the Competition Commission thinks might significantly harm the legitimate business interests of the undertaking to which it relates, or

        (b) information relating to the private affairs of an individual whose disclosure the Competition Commission thinks might significantly harm the individual's interests.

      (3D) The third consideration is the extent to which the disclosure of the information mentioned in paragraph (3C)(a) or (b) is necessary for the purposes of the report.'

(5) In Article 23 (functions with respect to competition) –

    (a) paragraph (1) shall cease to have effect;

    (b) in paragraph (3), for 'the Director General of Fair Trading, the functions of that Director' there is substituted 'the Office of Fair Trading, the functions of the Office of Fair Trading';

    (c) in paragraph (3A), for 'the Director General of Fair Trading' there is substituted 'the Office of Fair Trading';

    (d) in paragraph (6), for 'the Director General of Fair Trading' there is substituted 'the Office of Fair Trading'.

(6) In Article 27 (general functions), in paragraph (3) –

    (a) for 'the Director General of Fair Trading' there is substituted 'the Office of Fair Trading'; and

    (b) for 'that Director' there is substituted 'the Office of Fair Trading'.

(7) In Article 28 (publication of information and advice), for paragraph (3) there is substituted –

    '(3A) The Office of Fair Trading shall consult the Director before publishing under section 6 of the Enterprise Act 2002 any information or advice which may be published by the Director under this Article.'

(8) In Article 41(2) (exclusion of certain agreements from Restrictive Trade Practices Act 1976), for 'the Director General of Fair Trading' there is substituted 'the Office of Fair Trading'.

Data Protection Act 1998 (c. 29)

37 (1) The Data Protection Act 1998 is amended as follows.

    (2) In section 31 (regulatory activity), in subsection (5)(a), for 'the Director General of Fair Trading' there is substituted 'the Office of Fair Trading'.

Competition Act 1998 (c. 41)

38 (1) The 1998 Act is amended as follows.

    (2) In section 3(4)(b) (excluded agreements), for 'the Fair Trading Act 1973' there is substituted 'the Enterprise Act 2002'.

    (3) In section 4 (individual exemptions), for 'Director' (in each place), 'him' and 'he' there is substituted 'OFT', 'it' and 'it' respectively.

    (4) In section 5 (cancellation etc. of individual exemptions), for 'Director' (in each place), 'he' (in each place) and 'his' (in both places) there is substituted 'OFT', 'it' and 'its' respectively.

    (5) In section 6 (block exemptions) –

        (a) for 'Director' (in each place) there is substituted 'OFT';

        (b) in subsection (6)(c), for 'he' there is substituted 'it'.

    (6) In section 7 (block exemptions: opposition), for 'Director' (in each place), and 'his' (in both places) there is substituted 'OFT' and 'its' respectively.

    (7) In section 8 (block exemptions: procedure) –

        (a) for 'Director' (in each place) there is substituted 'OFT';

        (b) in subsection (1), for 'his', 'he' and 'him' there is substituted 'its', 'it' and 'it' respectively;

        (c) in subsection (3), for 'he' there is substituted 'it'.

    (8) In section 10 (parallel agreements) –

        (a) for 'Director' (in each place) there is substituted 'OFT';

        (b) in subsection (8), for 'his', 'him' and 'he' there is substituted 'its', 'it' and 'it' respectively.

    (9) In section 12 (requests for Director to examine agreements), for 'Director' (in each place) there is substituted 'OFT'.

    (10) In section 13 (notification for guidance), for 'Director' (in each place), 'him', 'his' (in both places) and 'he' there is substituted 'OFT', 'the OFT', 'its' and 'it' respectively.

    (11) In section 14 (notification for a decision), for 'Director' (in each place) and 'him' there is substituted 'OFT' and 'the OFT' respectively.

    (12) In section 15 (effect of guidance), for 'Director' (in each place), 'he' (in each place), 'his' (in each place) and 'him' (in each place) there is substituted 'OFT', 'it', 'its' and 'it' respectively.

(13) In section 16 (effect of a decision that the Chapter 1 prohibition has not been infringed), for 'Director' (in each place), 'he' (in each place), 'his' (in each place) and 'him' there is substituted 'OFT', 'it', 'its' and 'it' respectively.

(14) In section 20 (requests for Director to consider conduct), for 'Director' (in each place) there is substituted 'OFT'.

(15) In section 21 (notification for guidance), for 'Director' (in both places), 'him' and 'his' there is substituted 'OFT', 'the OFT' and 'its' respectively.

(16) In section 22 (notification for a decision), for 'Director' (in both places) and 'him' there is substituted 'OFT' and 'the OFT' respectively.

(17) In section 23 (effect of guidance), for 'Director' (in each place), 'he' (in each place), 'his' (in each place) and 'him' (in both places) there is substituted 'OFT', 'it', 'its' and 'it' respectively.

(18) In section 24 (effect of a decision that the Chapter 2 prohibition has not been infringed), for 'Director' (in each place), 'he' (in each place), 'his' (in each place) and 'him' there is substituted 'OFT', 'it', 'its' and 'it' respectively.

(19) In section 25 (Director's power to investigate), for 'Director's' and 'Director' there is substituted 'OFT's' and 'OFT' respectively.

(20) In section 26 (powers when conducting investigations) –

    (a)   in subsection (1), for 'Director', 'him' (in both places) and 'he' there is substituted 'OFT', 'it' and 'it' respectively;

    (b)   in subsection (5), for 'Director' there is substituted 'OFT'.

(21) In section 27 (power to enter premises without a warrant) –

    (a)   for 'Director' (in each place) there is substituted 'OFT';

    (b)   in subsection (3), for 'he' (in both places) there is substituted 'it'.

(22) In section 28 (power to enter premises under a warrant) –

    (a)   in subsection (1), for 'Director' (in both places) there is substituted 'OFT';

    (b)   in subsection (2) –

        (i)   for 'Director' there is substituted 'OFT';

        (ii)   for 'his officers whom he' there is substituted 'the OFT's officers whom the OFT'.

(23) In section 31 (decisions following an investigation), for 'Director' (in both places) there is substituted 'OFT'.

(24) In section 32 (directions in relation to agreements) –

    (a)   in subsection (1), for 'Director' and 'he' (in each place) there is substituted 'OFT' and 'it' respectively;

    (b)   in subsection (2), for 'Director's', 'his' and 'him' there is substituted 'OFT's', 'its' and 'it' respectively.

(25) In section 33 (directions in relation to conduct) –

    (a)   in subsection (1), for 'Director' and 'he' (in each place) there is substituted 'OFT' and 'it' respectively;

    (b)   in subsection (2), for 'Director's', 'his' and 'him' there is substituted 'OFT's', 'its' and 'it' respectively.

(26) In section 34 (enforcement of directions), for 'Director' there is substituted 'OFT'.

(27) In section 35 (interim measures), for 'Director' (in each place), 'his' (in both places), 'him' and 'he' (in each place) there is substituted 'OFT', 'its', 'it' and 'it' respectively.

(28) In section 36 (penalty for infringing Chapter 1 or Chapter 2 prohibition) –

    (a)   for 'Director' (in each place) there is substituted 'OFT';

    (b)   in subsections (1) and (2), for 'him' there is substituted 'the OFT';

    (c)   in subsection (3), for 'he' there is substituted 'the OFT'.

(29) In section 37 (recovery of penalties), for 'Director' and 'him' there is substituted 'OFT' and 'the OFT' respectively.

(30) In section 38 (the appropriate level of a penalty), for 'Director' (in each place), 'he' (in each place) and 'his' there is substituted 'OFT', 'it' and 'its' respectively.

(31) In section 39 (limited immunity for small agreements), for 'Director' (in each place), 'he' (in both places) and 'his' (in both places) there is substituted 'OFT', 'it' and 'its' respectively.

(32) In section 40 (limited immunity in relation to the Chapter 2 prohibition) –

    (a)   for 'Director' (in each place) there is substituted 'OFT';

    (b)   in subsection (4), for 'he' (in both places) and 'his' there is substituted 'it' and 'its' respectively;

    (c)   in subsection (5), for 'his' there is substituted 'its'.

(33) In section 41 (agreements notified to the Commission), for 'Director' there is substituted 'OFT'.

(34) In section 44 (false or misleading information), for 'Director' (in each place) and 'his' there is substituted 'OFT' and 'its' respectively.

(35) In section 45 (the Competition Commission), after subsection (7) there is inserted –

    '(8)   The Secretary of State may by order make such modifications in Part 2 of Schedule 7 and in Schedule 7A (performance of the Competition Commission's general functions) as he considers appropriate for improving the performance by the Competition Commission of its functions.'

(36) In section 46 (appealable decisions), for 'Director' (in each place) there is substituted 'OFT'.

(37) In section 50 (vertical agreements and land agreements), for 'Director' there is substituted 'OFT'.

(38) In section 51 –

    (a)   in subsection (1), for 'Director' and 'he' there is substituted 'OFT' and 'it' respectively;

    (b)   in subsection (2), for 'Director's' there is substituted 'OFT's';

    (c)   in subsection (3), for 'Director' and 'he' (in both places) there is substituted 'OFT' and 'it' respectively;

    (d)   in subsections (5) to (9), for 'Director' (in each place) there is substituted 'OFT';

    (e)   in subsection (10), for 'Director' and 'his' there is substituted 'OFT' and 'its';

and in the cross-heading before that section, for '*Director's*' there is substituted '*OFT's*'.

(39) In section 52 (advice and information) –

    (a)   in subsections (2) and (3), for 'Director' there is substituted 'OFT';

    (b)   in subsection (4), for 'Director' and 'him' there is substituted 'OFT' and 'it' respectively;

    (c)   in subsection (5), for 'Director' and 'he' there is substituted 'OFT' and 'it' respectively;

    (d)   in subsection (6), for 'Director' and 'he' (in both places) there is substituted 'OFT' and 'it' respectively;

    (e)   in subsection (8), for 'Director' there is substituted 'OFT'.

(40) In section 53 (fees), for 'Director' (in each place) and 'him' there is substituted 'OFT' and 'it' respectively.

(41) In section 54 (regulators) –

    (a)   in subsection (1), for the words from 'any person' to the end of the subsection there is substituted ' –

        (a)   the Director General of Telecommunications;

        (b)   the Gas and Electricity Markets Authority;

        (c)   the Director General of Electricity Supply for Northern Ireland;

      (d)   the Director General of Water Services;

      (e)   the Rail Regulator;

      (f)   the Director General of Gas for Northern Ireland; and

      (g)   the Civil Aviation Authority.';

  (b)   for 'Director' (in each place) there is substituted 'OFT'.

(42) In section 57 (defamation), for 'Director' and 'his' there is substituted 'OFT' and 'its' respectively.

(43) In section 58 (findings of fact by Director) –

  (a)   for 'Director' (in each place) there is substituted 'OFT';

  (b)   for 'a Director's' (in both places) there is substituted 'an OFT's';

and in the cross-heading before that section, for '*Director*' there is substituted '*OFT*'.

(44) In section 59 (interpretation of Part 1) –

  (a)   in subsection (1), the definition of 'the Director' shall cease to have effect and after the definition of 'officer' there is inserted –

       '"the OFT" means the Office of Fair Trading;';

  (b)   in subsection (4), for 'Director' and 'he' there is substituted 'OFT' and 'it' respectively.

(45) In section 60 (principles to be applied in determining questions), for 'Director' (in both places) there is substituted 'OFT'.

(46) In section 61 (introduction) –

  (a)   in subsection (1) –

     (i)   in the definition of 'authorised officer', for 'Director' there is substituted 'OFT';

     (ii)   the definition of 'the Director' shall cease to have effect;

     (iii)   after the definition of 'Commission investigation' there is inserted –

       '"the OFT" means the Office of Fair Trading;';

     (iv)   for '"Director's investigation" means an investigation conducted by the Director' there is substituted '"OFT's investigation" means an investigation conducted by the OFT';

     (v)   for '"Director's special investigation" means a Director's' there is substituted '"OFT's special investigation" means an OFT's';

     (vi)   in the definition of 'premises', for 'a Director's' there is substituted 'an OFT's';

  (b)   in subsection (2) –

     (i)   for 'a Director's' there is substituted 'an OFT's';

     (ii)   for 'Director' there is substituted 'OFT';

  (c)   in subsection (3), for 'Director' there is substituted 'OFT'.

(47) In section 62 (power to enter premises: Commission investigation) –

  (a)   in subsection (1), for 'Director' there is substituted 'OFT', and

  (b)   in subsection (5) –

     (i)   in paragraph (a), for 'Director' there is substituted 'OFT';

     (ii)   in paragraph (b), for 'his officers whom he' there is substituted 'the OFT's officers whom the OFT'.

(48) In section 63 (power to enter premises: Director's special investigations) –

  (a)   in subsection (1), for 'Director, that a Director's' there is substituted 'OFT, that an OFT's';

  (b)   in subsections (2) to (4), for 'A Director's' and 'Director' there is substituted 'An OFT's' and 'OFT' respectively;

  (c)   in subsection (5), for 'Director' there is substituted 'OFT';

  (d)   in the sidenote, for 'Director's' there is substituted 'OFT's'.

(49) In section 71 (regulations, orders and rules), in subsection (4), after paragraph (c) there is inserted –

'(ca) section 45(8),'.

(50) In Schedule 1 (exclusions: mergers and concentrations) –

    (a)   in paragraph 1 –

        (i)   in sub-paragraph (1), for the words from 'Part V' to '1973 Act')' there is substituted 'Part 3 of the Enterprise Act 2002 ("the 2002 Act")';

        (ii)   in sub-paragraph (4), for 'Section 65 of the 1973 Act' there is substituted 'Section 26 of the 2002 Act';

    (b)   in paragraph 2 –

        (i)   in sub-paragraph (1)(a), for 'Part V of the 1973 Act' there is substituted 'Part 3 of the 2002 Act';

        (ii)   in sub-paragraph (2), for 'Section 65 of the 1973 Act' there is substituted 'Section 26 of the 2002 Act';

    (c)   in paragraph 4 –

        (i)   for 'Director' (in each place) there is substituted 'OFT';

        (ii)   in sub-paragraph (2), for 'he' (in both places) and 'him' there is substituted 'it' and 'the OFT' respectively;

        (iii)   in sub-paragraph (5), for 'he' (in both places) there is substituted 'it';

    (d)   in paragraph 5, for paragraphs (a) to (d) there is substituted –

        '(a)   the OFT or (as the case may be) the Secretary of State has published its or his decision not to make a reference to the Competition Commission under section 22, 33, 45 or 62 of the 2002 Act in connection with the agreement;

        (b)   the OFT or (as the case may be) the Secretary of State has made a reference to the Competition Commission under section 22, 33, 45 or 62 of the 2002 Act in connection with the agreement and the Commission has found that the agreement has given rise to, or would if carried out give rise to, a relevant merger situation or (as the case may be) a special merger situation;

        (c)   the agreement does not fall within paragraph (a) or (b) but has given rise to, or would if carried out give rise to, enterprises to which it relates being regarded under section 26 of the 2002 Act as ceasing to be distinct enterprises (otherwise than as the result of subsection (3) or (4)(b) of that section); or

        (d)   the OFT has made a reference to the Competition Commission under section 32 of the Water Industry Act 1991 in connection with the agreement and the Commission has found that the agreement has given rise to, or would if carried out give rise to, a merger of any two or more water enterprises of the kind to which that section applies.'

(51) In Schedule 3 (general exclusions) –

    (a)   in paragraph 2 –

        (i)   for 'Director' (in each place) there is substituted 'OFT';

        (ii)   in sub-paragraph (4), for 'he' (in both places) and 'him' there is substituted 'it' and 'the OFT' respectively;

        (iii)   in sub-paragraph (7), for 'if he' and 'he is' there is substituted 'if it' and 'the OFT is' respectively;

    (b)   in paragraph 9 –

        (i)   for 'Director' (in each place) there is substituted 'OFT';

        (ii)   in sub-paragraph (4), for 'he' (in both places) and 'him' there is substituted 'it' and 'the OFT' respectively;

        (iii)   in sub-paragraph (7), for 'he' (in both places) there is substituted 'it'.

(52) In Schedule 5 (notification under Chapter 1: procedure) –

    (a)   for 'Director' (in each place) there is substituted 'OFT';

    (b)   in paragraph 3, for 'he' (in the first place) and 'his' there is substituted 'it' and 'its' respectively;

    (c)   in paragraph 5(2) –

        (i)   for 'he thinks' there is substituted 'it thinks';

        (ii) for 'bringing it' there is substituted 'bringing the application';

        (iii) for 'he is' there is substituted 'the OFT is';

        (iv) the words 'for him' shall cease to have effect;

    (d)   in paragraph 5(3), for 'him' there is substituted 'it';

    (e)   in paragraph 6, for 'he' and 'his' (in both places) there is substituted 'it' and 'its' respectively.

(53) In Schedule 6 (notification under Chapter 2: procedure) –

    (a)   for 'Director' (in each place) there is substituted 'OFT';

    (b)   in paragraph 3(1) and (2), for 'he' there is substituted 'it';

    (c)   in paragraph 5(2) –

        (i)   for 'he thinks' there is substituted 'it thinks';

        (ii) for 'bringing it' there is substituted 'bringing the application';

        (iii) for 'he is' there is substituted 'the OFT is';

        (iv) the words 'for him' shall cease to have effect;

    (d)   in paragraph 5(3), for 'him' there is substituted 'it';

    (e)   in paragraph 6, for 'he' and 'his' (in both places) there is substituted 'it' and 'its' respectively.

(54) In Schedule 8 (appeals) –

    (a)   for 'Director' (in each place) there is substituted 'OFT';

    (b)   in paragraph 2(2)(c), for 'Director's exercise of his' there is substituted 'OFT's exercise of its';

    (c)   in paragraph 3(2)(d) and (e), for 'himself' there is substituted 'itself'.

(55) In Schedule 9 (Director's rules), for 'Director' (in each place), 'he' (in each place), 'Director's' (in each place) and 'him' there is substituted 'OFT', 'it', 'OFT's' and 'it' respectively.

Greater London Authority Act 1999 (c. 29)

39   (1) The Greater London Authority Act 1999 is amended as follows.

     (2) In section 235 (restrictions on disclosure of information) –

        (a)   in subsection (2)(c), for sub-paragraph (ii) there is substituted –
           '(ii) the Office of Fair Trading,';

        (b)   in subsection (3), after paragraph (rr) there is inserted –
           '(rs) the Enterprise Act 2002;'.

Financial Services and Markets Act 2000 (c. 8)

40   (1) The Financial Services and Markets Act 2000 is amended as follows.

     (2) In section 159(1) (interpretation of Chapter 3 of Part 10), for the definition of 'Director' there is substituted –
        '"OFT" means the Office of Fair Trading;'.

     (3) In section 160 (reports by Director General of Fair Trading) –

        (a)   for 'Director' (in each place), 'he' (in each place) and 'him' there is substituted 'OFT', 'the OFT' and 'it' respectively;

(b)   in the sidenote, for 'Director General of Fair Trading' there is substituted 'OFT'.

(4) In section 161 (power of Director to request information), for 'Director' (in each place) and 'him' (in each place) there is substituted 'OFT' and 'it' respectively.

(5) In section 162 (consideration by Competition Commission), for 'Director' (in both places) and 'he' there is substituted 'OFT' and 'the OFT' respectively.

(6) In section 194 (general grounds on which power of intervention is exercisable), in subsection (3), for 'the Director General of Fair Trading' there is substituted 'the Office of Fair Trading'.

(7) In section 203 (power to prohibit the carrying on of Consumer Credit Act business) –

(a)   in subsection (1) –

(i)   for 'the Director General of Fair Trading ("the Director")' there is substituted 'the Office of Fair Trading ("the OFT")';

(ii)   for 'he' there is substituted 'it';

(b)   in subsection (2), for 'Director' and 'he' there is substituted 'OFT' and 'it' respectively;

(c)   in subsections (6) and (7), for 'Director' there is substituted 'OFT';

and in the cross-heading before that section, for 'Director General of Fair Trading' there is substituted 'Office of Fair Trading'.

(8) In section 204 (power to restrict the carrying on of Consumer Credit Act business), for 'Director' (in each place) and 'him' there is substituted 'OFT' and 'it' respectively.

(9) In section 295 (notification), for 'Director' there is substituted 'OFT'.

(10) In section 303 (initial report by Director) –

(a)   in subsection (1), for 'Director' there is substituted 'OFT';

(b)   in subsection (2), for 'Director', 'him' and 'his' there is substituted 'OFT', 'the OFT' and 'its' respectively;

(c)   in subsection (3), for 'Director' and 'him' (in both places) there is substituted 'OFT' and 'it' respectively;

(d)   in subsection (4), for 'Director's', 'he' and 'his' there is substituted 'OFT's', 'it' and 'its' respectively;

(e)   in subsection (5), for 'Director' and 'he' there is substituted 'OFT' and 'the OFT' respectively;

(f)   in the sidenote, for 'Director' there is substituted 'OFT';

and in the cross-heading before that section, for 'Director General of Fair Trading' there is substituted 'Office of Fair Trading'.

(11) In section 304 –

(a)   for 'Director' (in each place) and 'he' (in each place) there is substituted 'OFT' and 'the OFT' respectively;

(b)   in subsection (5)(b), for 'him' there is substituted 'the OFT'.

(12) In section 305 (investigations by Director), for 'Director' (in each place) and 'him' (in each place) there is substituted 'OFT' and 'it' respectively.

(13) In section 306 (consideration by Competition Commission), for 'Director's', 'Director' (in each place) and 'him' (in each place) there is substituted 'OFT's', 'OFT' and 'the OFT' respectively.

(14) In –

(a)   section 307 (recognition orders: role of the Treasury), and

(b)   section 310 (procedure on exercise of certain powers by the Treasury),

for 'Director' there is substituted 'OFT'.

(15) In section 313(1) (interpretation of Part 18), for the definition of 'Director' there is substituted –

'"OFT" means the Office of Fair Trading;'.

(16) In section 399 (misleading the Director General of Fair Trading) –

    (a)   for 'the Director General of Fair Trading' there is substituted 'the Office of Fair Trading';

    (b)   in the sidenote, for 'the Director General of Fair Trading' there is substituted 'the OFT'.

(17) In section 401 (proceedings for offences), in subsection (4), for 'the Director General of Fair Trading' there is substituted 'the Office of Fair Trading'.

(18) In section 427(3)(a) (transitional provisions), for 'the Director General of Fair Trading' there is substituted 'the Office of Fair Trading'.

(19) In Schedule 3 (EEA passport rights) –

    (a)   in paragraph 15(3), for 'the Director General of Fair Trading' and 'him' there is substituted 'the Office of Fair Trading' and 'it' respectively;

    (b)   in paragraph 23(2), for 'the Director of Fair Trading' there is substituted 'the Office of Fair Trading'.

(20) In Schedule 14 (role of Competition Commission) –

    (a)   in paragraph 2(a), for 'Director' and 'it' there is substituted 'OFT' and 'the Commission' respectively;

    (b)   after paragraph 2 there is inserted –

'Investigations under section 162: application of Enterprise Act 2002

2A (1)   The following sections of Part 3 of the Enterprise Act 2002 shall apply, with the modifications mentioned in sub-paragraphs (2) and (3), for the purposes of any investigation by the Commission under section 162 of this Act as they apply for the purposes of references under that Part –

    (a)   section 109 (attendance of witnesses and production of documents etc.);

    (b)   section 110 (enforcement of powers under section 109: general);

    (c)   section 111 (penalties);

    (d)   section 112 (penalties: main procedural requirements);

    (e)   section 113 (payments and interest by instalments);

    (f)   section 114 (appeals in relation to penalties);

    (g)   section 115 (recovery of penalties); and

    (h)   section 116 (statement of policy).

(2)   Section 110 shall, in its application by virtue of sub-paragraph (1), have effect as if –

    (a)   subsection (2) were omitted; and

    (b)   in subsection (9) the words from "or section" to "section 65(3))" were omitted.

(3)   Section 111(5)(b) shall, in its application by virtue of sub-paragraph (1), have effect as if for sub-paragraph (ii) there were substituted –

    "(ii) if earlier, the day on which the report of the Commission on the investigation concerned is made or, if the Commission decides not to make a report, the day on which the Commission makes the statement required by section 162(3) of the Financial Services and Markets Act 2000."

(4)   Section 117 of the Enterprise Act 2002 (false or misleading information) shall apply in relation to functions of the Commission in connection with an investigation under section 162 of this Act as it applies in relation to its functions under Part 3 of that Act but as if, in subsections (1)(a) and (2), the words "the OFT," and "or the Secretary of State" were omitted.

(5)   Provisions of Part 3 of the Enterprise Act 2002 which have effect for the purposes of sections 109 to 117 of that Act (including, in particular, provisions relating to offences and the making of orders) shall, for the purposes of the application of those sections by virtue of sub-paragraph (1) or (4) above, have effect in relation to those sections as applied by virtue of those sub-paragraphs.

(6)   Accordingly, corresponding provisions of this Act shall not have effect in relation to those sections as applied by virtue of those sub-paragraphs.

Section 162: modification of Schedule 7 to the Competition Act 1998

2B   For the purposes of its application in relation to the function of the Commission of deciding in accordance with section 162(2) of this Act not to make a report, paragraph 15(7) of Schedule 7 to the Competition Act 1998 (power of the Chairman to act on his own while a group is being constituted) has effect as if, after paragraph (a), there were inserted '; or

(aa)   in the case of an investigation under section 162 of the Financial Services and Markets Act 2000, decide not to make a report in accordance with subsection (2) of that section (decision not to make a report where no useful purpose would be served).'

Reports under section 162: further provision

2C   (1)   For the purposes of section 163 of this Act, a conclusion contained in a report of the Commission is to be disregarded if the conclusion is not that of at least two-thirds of the members of the group constituted in connection with the investigation concerned in pursuance of paragraph 15 of Schedule 7 to the Competition Act 1998.

(2)   If a member of a group so constituted disagrees with any conclusions contained in a report made under section 162 of this Act as the conclusions of the Commission, the report shall, if the member so wishes, include a statement of his disagreement and of his reasons for disagreeing.

(3)   For the purposes of the law relating to defamation, absolute privilege attaches to any report made by the Commission under section 162.';

(c)   paragraph 3 (applied provisions) shall cease to have effect.

(21) In Schedule 16 (prohibitions and restrictions imposed by Director General of Fair Trading) –

(a)   in the heading, for 'DIRECTOR GENERAL OF FAIR TRADING' there is substituted 'OFFICE OF FAIR TRADING';

(b) for 'Director' (in each place), 'his' (in each place), 'he' (in both places) and 'him' (in both places) there is substituted 'OFT', 'its', 'the OFT' and 'the OFT' respectively.

Terrorism Act 2000 (c. 11)

41 (1) The Terrorism Act 2000 is amended as follows.
    (2) In Schedule 3A (regulated sector and supervisory authorities), in paragraph 4(1), for paragraph (d) there is substituted –
         '(d) the Office of Fair Trading;'.

Postal Services Act 2000 (c. 26)

42 (1) The Postal Services Act 2000 is amended as follows.
    (2) After section 15 (licence modification references to Commission) there is inserted –

'15A References under section 15: time limits

(1) Every reference under section 15 shall specify a period (not longer than six months beginning with the date of the reference) within which a report on the reference is to be made.

(2) A report of the Competition Commission on a reference under section 15 shall not have effect (and no action shall be taken in relation to it under section 17) unless the report is made before the end of the period specified in the reference or such further period (if any) as may be allowed by the Commission under subsection (3).

(3) The Commission may, if it has received representations on the subject from the Competition Commission and is satisfied that there are special reasons why the report cannot be made within the period specified in the reference, extend that period by no more than six months.

(4) No more than one extension is possible under subsection (3) in relation to the same reference.

(5) The Commission shall, in the case of an extension made by it under subsection (3) –

(a) publish that extension in such manner as it considers appropriate for the purpose of bringing it to the attention of persons likely to be affected by it; and

(b) send a copy of what has been published by it under paragraph (a) to the licence holder and the Secretary of State.

15B References under section 15: application of Enterprise Act 2002

(1) The following sections of Part 3 of the Enterprise Act 2002 shall apply, with the modifications mentioned in subsections (2) and (3), for the purposes of references under section 15 as they apply for the purposes of references under that Part –

(a) section 109 (attendance of witnesses and production of documents etc.);

(b) section 110 (enforcement of powers under section 109: general);

(c) section 111 (penalties);

(d) section 112 (penalties: main procedural requirements);

(e) section 113 (payments and interest by instalments);

(f) section 114 (appeals in relation to penalties);

(g) section 115 (recovery of penalties); and

(h) section 116 (statement of policy).

(2)   Section 110 shall, in its application by virtue of subsection (1), have effect as if –

    (a)   subsection (2) were omitted; and

    (b)   in subsection (9) the words from "or section" to "section 65(3))" were omitted.

(3)   Section 111(5)(b)(ii) shall, in its application by virtue of subsection (1), have effect as if –

    (a)   for the words "published (or, in the case of a report under section 50 or 65, given)" there were substituted "made";

    (b)   for the words "published (or given)", in both places where they appear, there were substituted "made"; and

    (c)   the words "by this Part" were omitted.

(4)   Section 117 of the Enterprise Act 2002 (false or misleading information) shall apply in relation to functions of the Competition Commission in connection with references under section 15 as it applies in relation to its functions under Part 3 of that Act but as if, in subsections (1)(a) and (2), the words "the OFT," and "or the Secretary of State" were omitted.

(5)   Provisions of Part 3 of the Enterprise Act 2002 which have effect for the purposes of sections 109 to 117 of that Act (including, in particular, provisions relating to offences and the making of orders) shall, for the purposes of the application of those sections by virtue of subsection (1) or (4), have effect in relation to those sections as applied by virtue of those subsections.

(6)   Accordingly, corresponding provisions of this Act shall not have effect in relation to those sections as applied by virtue of those subsections.'

(3)   After section 16 (reports on licence modification references), there is inserted –

'16A Reports on references under section 15: further provision

(1)   For the purposes of sections 17 and 18, a conclusion contained in a report of the Competition Commission is to be disregarded if the conclusion is not that of at least two-thirds of the members of the group constituted in connection with the reference concerned in pursuance of paragraph 15 of Schedule 7 to the Competition Act 1998.

(2)   If a member of a group so constituted disagrees with any conclusions contained in a report made on a reference under section 15 as the conclusions of the Competition Commission, the report shall, if the member so wishes, include a statement of his disagreement and of his reasons for disagreeing.

(3)   For the purposes of the law relating to defamation, absolute privilege attaches to any report made by the Competition Commission on a reference under section 15.

(4)   In making any report on a reference under section 15 the Competition Commission must have regard to the following considerations before disclosing any information.

(5)   The first consideration is the need to exclude from disclosure (so far as practicable) any information whose disclosure the Competition Commission thinks is contrary to the public interest

(6)   The second consideration is the need to exclude from disclosure (so far as practicable) –

    (a)   commercial information whose disclosure the Competition Commission thinks might significantly harm the legitimate business interests of the undertaking to which it relates, or

    (b)   information relating to the private affairs of an individual whose disclosure the Competition Commission thinks might significantly harm the individual's interests.

(7)   The third consideration is the extent to which the disclosure of the information mentioned in subsection (6)(a) or (b) is necessary for the purposes
of the report.'

(4) After section 19 (procedural requirements in relation to modification) there is
inserted –

'19A Sections 18 and 19: further provision

(1)   For the purposes of the law relating to defamation, absolute privilege
attaches to any notice under section 19(6) or (8).

(2)   In giving any notice under section 19(6) or (8), the Competition
Commission must have regard to the following considerations before disclosing any information.

(3)   The first consideration is the need to exclude from disclosure (so far as
practicable) any information whose disclosure the Competition Commission thinks is contrary to the public interest.

(4)   The second consideration is the need to exclude from disclosure (so far as
practicable) –

(a)   commercial information whose disclosure the Competition Commission thinks might significantly harm the legitimate business
interests of the undertaking to which it relates, or

(b)   information relating to the private affairs of an individual whose disclosure the Competition Commission thinks might significantly harm
the individual's interests.

(5)   The third consideration is the extent to which the disclosure of the information mentioned in subsection (4)(a) or (b) is necessary for the purposes
of the notice.

(6)   The following sections of Part 3 of the Enterprise Act 2002 shall
apply, with the modifications mentioned in subsections (7) and (8), in
relation to any investigation by the Competition Commission for the
purposes of the exercise of its functions under section 18 as they
apply for the purposes of any investigation on references under that
Part –

(a)   section 109 (attendance of witnesses and production of documents
etc.);

(b)   section 110 (enforcement of powers under section 109: general);

(c)   section 111 (penalties);

(d)   section 112 (penalties: main procedural requirements);

(e)   section 113 (payments and interest by instalments);

(f)   section 114 (appeals in relation to penalties);

(g)   section 115 (recovery of penalties); and

(h)   section 116 (statement of policy).

(7)   Section 110 shall, in its application by virtue of subsection (6), have effect
as if –

(a)   subsection (2) were omitted;

(b)   in subsection (4), for the words from "the publication" to "reference
concerned" there were substituted "the sending of a copy to the
Secretary of State under section 19(11) of the Postal Services Act
2000 of the modifications made by the Competition Commission in
connection with the reference concerned or, if no direction has been
given by the Competition Commission under section 18(2) of that
Act in connection with the reference concerned and within the period
permitted for that purpose, the latest day on which it was possible to
give such a direction within the permitted period"; and

(c)   in subsection (9) the words from "or section" to "section 65(3))" were omitted.

(8)   Section 111(5)(b) shall, in its application by virtue of subsection (6), have effect as if for sub-paragraph (ii) there were substituted –

"(ii)   if earlier, the day on which a copy of the modifications made by the Competition Commission in connection with the reference concerned is sent to the Secretary of State under section 19(11) of the Postal Services Act 2000 or, if no direction is given by the Competition Commission under section 18(2) of that Act in connection with the reference concerned and within the period permitted for that purpose, the latest day on which such a direction may be given within the permitted period."

(9)   Section 117 of the Enterprise Act 2002 (false or misleading information) shall apply in relation to functions of the Competition Commission in connection with the exercise of its functions under section 18 as it applies in relation to its functions under Part 3 of that Act but as if, in subsections (1)(a) and (2), the words "the OFT," and "or the Secretary of State" were omitted.

(10)   Provisions of Part 3 of the Enterprise Act 2002 which have effect for the purposes of sections 109 to 117 of that Act (including, in particular, provisions relating to offences and the making of orders) shall, for the purposes of the application of those sections by virtue of subsection (6) or (9), have effect in relation to those sections as applied by virtue of those subsections.

(11)   Accordingly, corresponding provisions of this Act shall not have effect in relation to those sections as applied by virtue of those subsections.'

(5)   Section 20 (application of competition legislation to references, etc.) shall cease to have effect.

(6)   In section 57 (power of the Council to investigate other matters), in subsection (2), for paragraph (c) there is substituted –

'(c)   the Office of Fair Trading,'.

(7)   In Schedule 7 (disclosure of information), in paragraph 3 –

(a)   in sub-paragraph (2), for paragraph (d) there is substituted –
'(d)   the Office of Fair Trading,';

(b)   in sub-paragraph (3), after paragraph (gg) there is inserted –
'(gh) the Enterprise Act 2002,'.

Utilities Act 2000 (c. 27)

43   (1)   The Utilities Act 2000 is amended as follows.

(2)   In section 5(9) (annual and other reports of the Authority), for 'Section 125(1) of the Fair Trading Act 1973 (annual and other reports)' there is substituted 'Paragraph 12A(1) of Schedule 7 to the Competition Act 1998 (annual reports of the Competition Commission)'.

(3)   In section 105 (general restrictions on disclosure of information) –

(a)   in subsection (5), for paragraph (c) there is substituted –
'(c)   the Office of Fair Trading;';

(b)   in subsection (6), after paragraph (r) there is inserted –
'(s)   the Enterprise Act 2002';

(c)   in subsection (11) –

(i)   for 'the Director General of Fair Trading' there is substituted 'the Office of Fair Trading';

(ii)   for 'sections 55 and 56 of that Act (disclosure)' there is substituted 'Part 9 of the Enterprise Act 2002 (Information)'.

Transport Act 2000 (c. 38)

44 (1) The Transport Act 2000 is amended as follows.

(2) In section 12 (licence modification references to Commission), subsections (9), (10) and (11) shall cease to have effect.

(3) After section 12 there is inserted –

'12A References under section 12: time limits

(1) Every reference under section 12 shall specify a period (not longer than six months beginning with the date of the reference) within which a report on the reference is to be made.

(2) A report of the Competition Commission on a reference under section 12 shall not have effect (and no action shall be taken in relation to it under section 14) unless the report is made before the end of the period specified in the reference or such further period (if any) as may be allowed by the CAA under subsection (3).

(3) The CAA may, if it has received representations on the subject from the Competition Commission and is satisfied that there are special reasons why the report cannot be made within the period specified in the reference, extend that period by no more than six months.

(4) No more than one extension is possible under subsection (3) in relation to the same reference.

(5) The CAA shall, in the case of an extension made by it under subsection (3) –

(a) publish that extension in such manner as it considers appropriate for the purpose of bringing it to the attention of persons likely to be affected by it; and

(b) send a copy of what has been published by it under paragraph (a) to the licence holder and the Secretary of State.

12B References under section 12: application of Enterprise Act 2002

(1) The following sections of Part 3 of the Enterprise Act 2002 shall apply, with the modifications mentioned in subsections (2) and (3), for the purposes of references under section 12 as they apply for the purposes of references under that Part –

(a) section 109 (attendance of witnesses and production of documents etc.);

(b) section 110 (enforcement of powers under section 109: general);

(c) section 111 (penalties);

(d) section 112 (penalties: main procedural requirements);

(e) section 113 (payments and interest by instalments);

(f) section 114 (appeals in relation to penalties);

(g) section 115 (recovery of penalties); and

(h) section 116 (statement of policy).

(2) Section 110 shall, in its application by virtue of subsection (1), have effect as if –

(a) subsection (2) were omitted; and

(b) in subsection (9) the words from "or section" to "section 65(3))" were omitted.

(3) Section 111(5)(b)(ii) shall, in its application by virtue of subsection (1), have effect as if –

(a) for the words "published (or, in the case of a report under section 50 or 65, given)" there were substituted "made";

(b) for the words "published (or given)", in both places where they appear, there were substituted "made"; and

(c) the words "by this Part" were omitted.

(4)   Section 117 of the Enterprise Act 2002 (false or misleading information) shall apply in relation to functions of the Competition Commission in connection with references under section 12 as it applies in relation to its functions under Part 3 of that Act but as if, in subsections (1)(a) and (2), the words "the OFT," and "or the Secretary of State" were omitted.

(5)   Provisions of Part 3 of the Enterprise Act 2002 which have effect for the purposes of sections 109 to 117 of that Act (including, in particular, provisions relating to offences and the making of orders) shall, for the purposes of the application of those sections by virtue of subsection (1) or (4), have effect in relation to those sections as applied by virtue of those subsections.

(6)   Accordingly, corresponding provisions of this Act shall not have effect in relation to those sections as applied by virtue of those subsections.'

(4)   In section 13 (reports on licence modification references) –

(a)   after subsection (1) there is inserted –

'(1A) For the purposes of sections 14 to 17, a conclusion contained in a report of the Competition Commission is to be disregarded if the conclusion is not that of at least two-thirds of the members of the group constituted in connection with the reference concerned in pursuance of paragraph 15 of Schedule 7 to the Competition Act 1998.

(1B) If a member of a group so constituted disagrees with any conclusions contained in a report made on a reference under section 12 as the conclusions of the Competition Commission, the report shall, if the member so wishes, include a statement of his disagreement and of his reasons for disagreeing.';

(b)   for subsection (2) there is substituted –

'(2) For the purposes of the law relating to defamation, absolute privilege attaches to any report made by the Competition Commission on a reference under section 12.

(2A) In making any report on a reference under section 12 the Competition Commission must have regard to the following considerations before disclosing any information.

(2B) The first consideration is the need to exclude from disclosure (so far as practicable) any information whose disclosure the Competition Commission thinks is contrary to the public interest.

(2C) The second consideration is the need to exclude from disclosure (so far as practicable) –

(a)   commercial information whose disclosure the Competition Commission thinks might significantly harm the legitimate business interests of the undertaking to which it relates, or

(b)   information relating to the private affairs of an individual whose disclosure the Competition Commission thinks might significantly harm the individual's interests.

(2D) The third consideration is the extent to which the disclosure of the information mentioned in subsection (2C)(a) or (b) is necessary for the purposes of the report.'

(5)   For section 18 (provisions supplementary to exercise by Commission of functions under sections 15 and 16) there is substituted –

'18 Sections 15 and 16: general

(1)   For the purposes of the law relating to defamation, absolute privilege attaches to any notice under section 15(4) or 16(4) or (6).

(2)   In publishing or serving any notice under section 15(4) or 16(4) or (6), the Competition Commission must have regard to the following considerations before disclosing any information.

(3)   The first consideration is the need to exclude from disclosure (so far as practicable) any information whose disclosure the Competition Commission thinks is contrary to the public interest.

(4)   The second consideration is the need to exclude from disclosure (so far as practicable) –

   (a)   commercial information whose disclosure the Competition Commission thinks might significantly harm the legitimate business interests of the undertaking to which it relates, or

   (b)   information relating to the private affairs of an individual whose disclosure the Competition Commission thinks might significantly harm the individual's interests.

(5)   The third consideration is the extent to which the disclosure of the information mentioned in subsection (4)(a) or (b) is necessary for the purposes of the notice.

(6)   The following sections of Part 3 of the Enterprise Act 2002 shall apply, with the modifications mentioned in subsections (7) and (8), for the purposes of any investigation by the Competition Commission for the purposes of the exercise of its functions under section 15 or 16, as they apply for the purposes of any investigation on references under that Part –

   (a)   section 109 (attendance of witnesses and production of documents etc.);

   (b)   section 110 (enforcement of powers under section 109: general);

   (c)   section 111 (penalties);

   (d)   section 112 (penalties: main procedural requirements);

   (e)   section 113 (payments and interest by instalments);

   (f)   section 114 (appeals in relation to penalties);

   (g)   section 115 (recovery of penalties); and

   (h)   section 116 (statement of policy).

(7)   Section 110 shall, in its application by virtue of subsection (6), have effect as if –

   (a)   subsection (2) were omitted;

   (b)   in subsection (4), for the words "the publication of the report of the Commission on the reference concerned" there were substituted "the publication by the Commission of a notice under section 16(6) of the Transport Act 2000 in connection with the reference concerned or, if no direction has been given by the Commission under section 15(2) of that Act in connection with the reference concerned and within the period permitted for that purpose, the latest day on which it was possible to give such a direction within the permitted period"; and

   (c)   in subsection (9) the words from "or section" to "section 65(3))" were omitted.

(8)   Section 111(5)(b) shall, in its application by virtue of subsection (6), have effect as if for sub-paragraph (ii) there were substituted –

   "(ii)   if earlier, the day on which a notice is published by the Commission under section 16(6) of the Transport Act 2000 in connection with the reference concerned or, if no direction is given by the Commission under section 15(2) of that Act in connection with the reference concerned and within the period permitted for that purpose, the latest day on which such a direction may be given within the permitted period."

(9) Section 117 of the Enterprise Act 2002 (false or misleading information) shall apply in relation to functions of the Competition Commission in connection with the exercise of its functions under section 15 or 16 as it applies in relation to its functions under Part 3 of that Act but as if, in subsections (1)(a) and (2), the words "the OFT," and "or the Secretary of State" were omitted.

(10) Provisions of Part 3 of the Enterprise Act 2002 which have effect for the purposes of sections 109 to 117 of that Act (including, in particular, provisions relating to offences and the making of orders) shall, for the purposes of the application of those sections by virtue of subsection (6) or (9), have effect in relation to those sections as applied by virtue of those subsections.

(11) Accordingly, corresponding provisions of this Act shall not have effect in relation to those sections as applied by virtue of those subsections.'

(6) In section 85 (interpretation of Chapter 5), in subsection (1), for paragraph (c) there is substituted –

'(c)   the OFT is the Office of Fair Trading.'

(7) In section 86 (functions exercisable by CAA and the Director) –

    (a)   in subsections (1), (4) and (7), for 'the Director' there is substituted 'the OFT';

    (b)   in subsection (3), for 'the Director's' there is substituted 'the OFT's'.

(8) In section 89 (carrying out functions) –

    (a)   for 'the Director' (in each place) there is substituted 'the OFT';

    (b)   in subsection (2), for 'he or it' there is substituted 'it'.

(9) In section 90 (publication of information and advice) –

    (a)   in subsection (6), for 'The Director must consult the CAA before publishing under section 124 of the 1973 Act' there is substituted 'The Office of Fair Trading must consult the CAA before publishing under section 6 of the Enterprise Act 2002';

    (b)   subsection (8) shall cease to have effect.

(10) In section 91 (review and information) –

    (a)   in subsections (3) and (4), for 'the Director' (in each place) there is substituted 'the Office of Fair Trading';

    (b)   subsection (5) shall cease to have effect.

(11) In Schedule 9 (air traffic: information) –

    (a)   in paragraph 3 –

        (i)   in sub-paragraph (2), for paragraph (b) there is substituted –
           '(b)   the Office of Fair Trading;';

        (ii)   in sub-paragraph (3), after paragraph (r) there is inserted –
           '(ra) the Enterprise Act 2002;'

    (b)   in paragraph 5, in sub-paragraph (3), for 'Director General of Fair Trading' there is substituted 'the Office of Fair Trading'.

(12) In Schedule 10 (competition test for exercise of bus functions) –

    (a)   for 'Director' (in each place) there is substituted 'OFT';

    (b)   in paragraph 3(1), for 'the Director General of Fair Trading (in this Schedule referred to as "the Director") for him' there is substituted 'the Office of Fair Trading (in this Schedule referred to as "the OFT") for it';

    (c)   in paragraph 4, in sub-paragraph (3) –

        (i)   for 'he thinks' there is substituted 'it thinks';

        (ii)   for 'bringing it' there is substituted 'bringing the application';

    (iii) for 'he is' there is substituted 'the OFT is';

    (iv) the words 'for him' shall cease to have effect;

 (d) in paragraph 4 –

    (i) in sub-paragraph (4), for 'he' (in both places) there is substituted 'it';

    (ii) in sub-paragraph (5), for 'him' there is substituted 'it';

 (e) in paragraph 5, for 'he' there is substituted 'it';

 (f) in paragraph 6(1), for 'him' (in each place) and 'he' there is substituted 'it' and 'the OFT' respectively;

 (g) in paragraph 9, for 'he' there is substituted 'the OFT';

 (h) in paragraph 10, for 'he' and 'his' (in both places) there is substituted 'the OFT' and 'its' respectively;

 (i) in paragraph 11, for 'he' (in each place) and 'his' (in both places) there is substituted 'the OFT' and 'its' respectively;

 (j) in paragraph 12(1), for 'he' (in both places) there is substituted 'the OFT';

 (k) in paragraphs 13 to 15, for 'his' (in each place) there is substituted 'its';

 (l) in paragraph 16, for 'him' and 'his' there is substituted 'the OFT' and 'its' respectively.

SCHEDULE 26 REPEALS AND REVOCATIONS   Section 278

Reference	Extent of repeal or revocation
Registered Designs Act 1949 (c. 88)	In section 11A(1), paragraphs (a) and (b).
Agricultural Marketing Act 1958 (c. 47)	In section 19A(2), the words from the beginning of the subsection to 'this section'.
Public Records Act 1958 (c. 51)	In Schedule 1, in Part 2, the entry relating to the Office of the Director General of Fair Trading.
Parliamentary Commissioner Act 1967 (c. 13)	In Schedule 2, the entry relating to the Office of the Director General of Fair Trading.
Trade Descriptions Act 1968 (c. 29)	Section 28(5) and (5A).
Local Government Act 1972 (c. 70)	Section 81(1) and (2).

Fair Trading Act 1973 (c. 41)	Sections 1 to 3.
	In section 5 –
	  in subsection (1), paragraph (a) and the word 'or' at the end of it, and paragraph (c) and the word 'or' before it;
	  subsection (3).
	Sections 6 to 22.
	In section 30, subsection (3) and, in subsection (5), the words ', subsection (3)'.
	Sections 34 to 42.
	Sections 44 to 56G.
	Sections 63 to 76.
	In section 77 –
	  subsection (1)(b) and (c);
	  in subsection (2), paragraph (b) and the word 'or' before it;
	  subsection (3);

Reference	*Extent of repeal or revocation*
Fair Trading Act 1973 (c. 41) – cont.	in subsection (5), paragraph (b) and the word 'and' before it.
	Sections 78 to 81.
	In section 82 –
	in subsection (1), the words 'the Advisory Committee or', and, in paragraph (b), the words 'the Advisory Committee or of' and the words ', as the case may be,';
	in subsection (2), the words 'the Advisory Committee or of';
	subsection (3);
	in subsection (4), the words 'other than a monopoly reference limited to the facts'.
	In section 83 –
	in subsection (1), the words from 'any report of the Advisory Committee' to 'applies, or';
	in subsections (3) and (4), the words 'of the Advisory Committee or'.
	Section 84.
	Section 86.
	Sections 88 to 93A.
	In section 93B(1), the words 'or under the Competition Act 1980'.
	Sections 124 and 125.
	In section 129(4), the words 'or 46(2)'.
	Sections 130 and 131.
	In section 132(1), the words 'section 46,'.
	Section 133.
	In section 137(2), the definitions of 'the Advisory Committee' and 'the Director'.
	In section 138, the words 'Parts II and III,'.
	Schedules 1, 2 and 4 to 9.
	In Schedule 12, the entry relating to the Public Records Act 1958.
Prices Act 1974 (c. 24)	In the Schedule, paragraph 12.
Consumer Credit Act 1974 (c. 39)	Section 5.
	Section 161(2).
	Section 174.
	In section 189(1), the definition of 'Director'
	In Schedule 4, paragraph 28.
House of Commons Disqualification Act 1975 (c. 24)	In Schedule 1, in Part 3, the entry relating to the Director General of Fair Trading.
Northern Ireland Assembly Disqualification Act 1975 (c. 25)	In Schedule 1, in Part 3, the entry relating to the Director General of Fair Trading.
Patents Act 1977 (c. 37)	In section 51(1), paragraphs (a) and (b).
	In Schedule 5, paragraph 7.
Estate Agents Act 1979 (c. 38)	Section 9(5).
	Section 10.
	Section 26(2).
	In section 33(1), the definition of 'Director'.

Reference	Extent of repeal or revocation
Competition Act 1980 (c. 21)	In section 11, in subsection (1), paragraph (c) and the word 'or' before it, and subsections (2), (9) and (9A). Section 13. In section 16, subsection (1) and, in subsection (2), the words 'or of the Director'. In section 17, in subsections (1), (3) and (4), the words 'or 13(5)'. Section 18. In section 19, subsections (1) to (3), (4)(c), (d) and (f) and (5) and (6). Sections 20, 21 and 24. In section 31, in subsection (1), the words 'or regulations', in subsection (3), the words 'regulations under this Act or', and subsection (4).
Telecommunications Act 1984 (c. 12)	In section 13, subsections (9) and (9A). In section 50 – subsection (1); in subsection (6), the words from 'or paragraph' to 'Act 1994'; subsection (7). In Schedule 4, paragraphs 57, 60(2), 72 and 73.
Dentists Act 1984 (c. 24)	In Schedule 5, paragraph 6.
Companies Consolidation (Consequential Provisions) Act 1985 (c. 9)	In Schedule 2, the entry relating to section 92 of the Fair Trading Act 1973.
Administration of Justice Act 1985 (c. 61)	In section 60(6), the words 'in paragraph 10A of Schedule 4 to the Fair Trading Act 1973 and'.
Insolvency Act 1985 (c. 65)	In Schedule 8, paragraph 22.
Bankruptcy (Scotland) Act 1985 (c. 66)	In Schedule 3, paragraphs 1 to 3 and 8 to 8C.
Weights and Measures Act 1985 (c. 72)	In Schedule 12, paragraph 6.
Airports Act 1986 (c. 31)	In section 44, subsections (3) and (3A). In section 54, subsection (3). In Schedule 4, paragraphs 3, 4, 6 and 7.
Gas Act 1986 (c. 44)	In section 24, subsections (7) and (7A). In section 26A, subsections (12) and (13). Section 27(3) and (4). In section 36A, subsections (1) and (9). In section 41E, subsections (7) and (8). In Schedule 7, paragraphs 15, 19, 27 and 28.
Insolvency Act 1986 (c. 45)	In section 212 – in subsection (1)(b), the word ', administrator'; in subsection (2), in each place, the words 'or administrator'; in subsection (4), the words 'or administrator'. Section 230(1). In section 231, in each place, the word 'administrator,'. In section 232, the word 'administrator,'.

Reference	*Extent of repeal or revocation*
Insolvency Act 1986 (c. 45) – *cont.*	In section 240(1), the word 'and' before paragraph (c).
	In section 245(3), the word 'or' before paragraph (c).
	Section 275.
	Section 282(5).
	In section 292(1)(a), the words 'except at a time when a certificate for the summary administration of the bankrupt's estate is in force,'.
	In section 293(1), the words 'and no certificate for the summary administration of the bankrupt's estate has been issued,'.
	In section 294(1), paragraph (b) and the word 'and' before it.
	In section 297 –
	subsections (2) and (3);
	in subsection (4), the words 'but no certificate for the summary administration of the estate is issued'.
	Section 298(3).
	In section 300 –
	subsection (5);
	in subsections (6) and (7), the words 'or (5)'.
	In section 310(1), the words ', on the application of the trustee,'.
	Sections 361 and 362.
	Section 405.
	In section 427 –
	in subsection (1), the words 'England and Wales or';
	subsection (7).
	In Schedule 6, paragraphs 1 to 7.
	In Schedule 10 –
	the entry for section 12(2);
	the entry for section 15(8);
	the entry for section 18(5);
	the entry for section 21(3);
	the entry for section 22(6);
	the entry for section 23(3);
	the entry for section 24(7);
	the entry for section 27(6);
	in the entry for section 31, the word 'Undischarged';
	the entries for sections 361 and 362.
Consumer Protection Act 1987 (c. 43)	Section 38.
	In Schedule 4, paragraphs 2(2), 3, 4 and 7.
Consumer Protection (Northern Ireland) Order 1987 (S.I. 1987/2049 (N.I. 20))	In Schedule 3, paragraphs 2 and 4.
Income and Corporation Taxes Act 1988 (c. 1)	In Schedule 29, in paragraph 32, in the Table, the references relating to the Insolvency Act 1986.
Criminal Justice Act 1988 (c. 33)	Section 62(2)(a).
Copyright, Designs and Patents Act 1988 (c. 48)	In Schedule 7, paragraph 15.

Reference	Extent of repeal or revocation
Control of Misleading Advertisements Regulations 1988 (S.I. 1988/915)	Regulation 7(6)(a), (b), (d) and (e).
Water Act 1989 (c. 15)	In Schedule 25, paragraphs 45(3), 47, 57 and 59(2).
Electricity Act 1989 (c. 29)	In section 12, subsections (8) and (8A). In section 14A, subsections (12) and (13). In section 43 – subsection (1); in subsection (6), the words from 'or paragraph' to 'Act 1994'; subsection (7). In section 56C, subsections (7) and (8). In Schedule 16, paragraphs 16, 17(2), 24, 25 and 36.
Companies Act 1989 (c. 40)	Sections 146 to 150. Section 152. In Schedule 14, paragraphs 4(5) and 8. In Schedule 20, paragraphs 3 to 11, 14 to 16 and 19.
Courts and Legal Services Act 1990 (c. 41)	Section 46(3). In section 119(1), the definition of 'the Director'. In Schedule 18, paragraphs 4, 6, 22 and 23.
Broadcasting Act 1990 (c. 42)	Section 187(3). Section 192. In section 194A(9), the definition of 'Director'. In Schedule 4, in paragraph 4, sub-paragraphs (7) and (7A), in paragraph 5, sub-paragraph (5), in paragraph 8, sub-paragraphs (3) and (4) and, in paragraph 10, the definition of 'the Director'. In Schedule 20, paragraphs 20 and 28.
EEC Merger Control (Consequential Provisions) Regulations 1990 (S.I. 1990/1563)	Regulation 2.
Property Misdescriptions Act 1991 (c. 29)	In the Schedule, paragraphs 2 and 7.
Finance Act 1991 (c. 31)	In Schedule 2, paragraphs 21A and 22.
Water Industry Act 1991 (c. 56)	In section 14, subsections (7) and (7A). In section 31 – subsection (1); in subsection (8), the words from 'or paragraph' to 'Act 1994'; subsection (9). In section 36(1), the definition of 'the 1973 Act' and the word 'and' at the end of it.
Water Consolidation (Consequential Provisions) Act 1991 (c. 60)	In Schedule 1, paragraphs 24, 26, 33, 34 and 52.
Social Security (Consequential Provisions) Act 1992 (c. 6)	In Schedule 2, paragraph 73.
Timeshare Act 1992 (c. 35)	In Schedule 2, paragraphs 2(1) and 5.

Reference	*Extent of repeal or revocation*
Electricity (Northern Ireland) Order 1992 (S.I. 1992/231 (N.I. 1))	Article 15(8) and (8A). In Article 46, paragraph (1), in paragraph (6), the words from 'or paragraph' to 'Act 1994', and paragraph (7). In Schedule 12, paragraphs 9, 10, 14, 20, 21 and 31.
Finance Act 1993 (c. 34)	Section 36(1) to (3).
Railways Act 1993 (c. 43)	In section 4, in subsection (2)(a), the words from 'in cases where' to 'market', and subsection (8). Section 13(8) and (8A). Section 66(1) and (2). In section 67 – subsection (1); in subsection (7), the words from 'was made' to 'that it'; in subsection (8), the words from 'or paragraph' to 'Act 1994'; subsection (10). In section 83(1), the definition of 'the Director'. In Schedule 12, paragraphs 7, 8, 11, 12(2) and (3) and 26.
Finance Act 1994 (c. 9)	In Schedule 6, paragraph 13(1) and (2). In Schedule 7, paragraph 7(2).
Coal Industry Act 1994 (c. 21)	In Schedule 9, paragraphs 14, 15, 21 and 23.
Value Added Tax Act 1994 (c. 23)	In Schedule 14, paragraph 8.
Deregulation and Contracting Out Act 1994 (c. 40)	Section 7(1). Section 9. Schedule 2. In Schedule 4, paragraph 2. In Schedule 11, paragraphs 2(3) and (4) and 4(6).
Airports (Northern Ireland) Order 1994 (S.I. 1994/426)	Article 35(3) and (3A). In Article 45, paragraph (3). In Schedule 9, paragraphs 2, 4, 7 and 8.
Finance Act 1995 (c. 4)	In section 17, the words 'section 386(1) of the Insolvency Act 1986) (categories of preferential debts) and'.
Finance Act 1996 (c. 8)	In Schedule 5, paragraph 12(1) and (2).
Employment Rights Act 1996 (c. 18)	In sections 166(7)(a) and 183(3)(a), the words 'or an administration order.' Section 189(4).
Channel Tunnel Rail Link Act 1996 (c. 61)	Section 22(1).
Gas (Northern Ireland) Order 1996 (S.I. 1996/275 (N.I. 2))	Article 15(9) and (9A). Article 18(3). Article 23(1) and (8). In Schedule 6, the entries relating to sections 16 and 133 of the Fair Trading Act 1973, the entry relating to the Estate Agents Act 1979, the entry relating to the Competition Act 1980 and the entries relating to section 38 of the Consumer Protection Act 1987.

Reference	*Extent of repeal or revocation*
Deregulation (Fair Trading Act 1973)(Amendment)(Merger Reference Time Limits) Order 1996 (S.I. 1996/345)	The whole Order.
Finance Act 1997 (c. 16)	In Schedule 2, paragraph 6.
Justices of the Peace Act 1997 (c. 25)	Section 65.

Competition Act 1998 (c. 41)	In section 3(1), paragraph (d) and the word 'or' before it.
	Section 46(3)(h).
	Section 48.
	Sections 55 and 56.
	In section 59(1), the definitions of 'appeal tribunal' and 'the Director'.
	In section 61(1), the definition of 'the Director'.
	Sections 66 and 67.
	Schedule 4.
	In Schedule 5, in paragraph 5(2), the words 'for him'.
	In Schedule 6, in paragraph 5(2), the words 'for him'.
	In Schedule 7 –
	in paragraph 1, the definitions of 'appeal panel member' and 'President' and, in the definition of 'general functions', paragraph (a) and the word 'or' at the end of it;
	paragraph 2(1)(a), (3)(a) and (4);
	paragraph 4;
	in paragraph 5, in sub-paragraph (1), the word 'management', sub-paragraph (2)(b) and, in sub-paragraph (3), the words 'and paragraph 5 of Schedule 8';
	paragraph 6(5);
	paragraph 7(4);
	in paragraph 9, sub-paragraph (2) and in sub-paragraph (3), the words 'and the President'.
	paragraph 10;
	in paragraph 15(7), paragraph (b) and the word 'or' before it;
	paragraphs 23 to 27.
	In Schedule 8, paragraphs 1 and 4 to 14.
	In Schedule 10 –
	paragraph 1;
	paragraph 2(7) and (10);
	paragraph 3(6) and (9) to (11);
	paragraph 4(6) and (9);
	paragraph 5(7), (9), (10) and (13);
	paragraph 6(6) and (9);
	paragraph 7(6) and (9);
	paragraph 8(6) and (9) to (11);
	paragraph 9(5);
	paragraph 10(4);

Reference	*Extent of repeal or revocation*

Competition Act 1998 (c. 41) – *cont.*	paragraph 12(4) and (6);
	 paragraph 13(8);
	 paragraph 15(4);
	 paragraph 17(6).
	 Schedule 11.
	 In Schedule 12 –
	 paragraph 1(4) to (7) and (14);
	 paragraph 3;
	 paragraph 4(3), (4), (9), (10), (12) and (15)(a);
	 paragraph 10.

Competition Act 1998 (Competition Commission) Transitional, Consequential and Supplemental Provisions Order 1999 (S.I. 1999/ 506)	Article 22.
Financial Services and Markets Act 2000 (c. 8)	Section 351(1) to (3) and (7). In Schedule 14, paragraph 3. Schedule 19.
Finance Act 2000 (c. 17)	In Schedule 7, paragraphs 2 and 3.
Regulation of Investigatory Powers Act 2000 (c. 23)	In section 32(6), the word 'and' at the end of paragraph (l). In section 35(10), the word 'or' at the end of paragraph (b). In section 36 – in subsection (1), the word 'or' at the end of paragraph (c); in subsection (6), the word 'and' at the end of paragraph (f). In section 37(1), the word 'or' at the end of paragraph (c).
Postal Services Act 2000 (c. 26)	Section 20.
Utilities Act 2000 (c. 27)	Section 40(2), (4) and (5). In Schedule 6, paragraph 9.
Transport Act 2000 (c. 38)	Section 12(9), (10) and (11). In section 85(3), the words 'the 1973 Act or'. Section 90(8). Section 91(5). In Schedule 8, paragraphs 11 and 12. In Schedule 10, in paragraph 4(3), the words 'for him'.
Insolvency Act 2000 (c. 39)	Section 9. In Schedule 4, paragraph 13(3).
Competition Act 1998 (Transitional, Consequential and Supplemental Provisions) Order 2000 (S.I. 2000/311)	Article 9(5).
Finance Act 2001 (c. 9)	In Schedule 5, paragraphs 17(1) and (2) and 18.

Reference	Extent of repeal or revocation
Anti-terrorism, Crime and Security Act 2001 (c. 24)	In Schedule 4, paragraphs 5, 9, 10, 11, 17, 27, 30 and 33.
Stop Now Orders (E.C. Directive) Regulations 2001 (S.I. 2001/1422)	The whole Regulations.
EC Competition Law (Articles 84 and 85) Enforcement Regulations 2001 (S.I. 2001/2916)	Regulation 35(1) and (2).

INDEX